Classical Literature: An

Classical Literature: An Introduction provides a series of essays on all the major authors of Greek and Latin literature, as well as on a number of writers less often read. An introductory chapter provides information on important general topics, such as poetic metres, patronage and symposia. The literature is put in historical context, and the material is organized chronologically, but also by genre or author, as appropriate; each section or chapter has suggestions for further reading. The book ranges from Homer to the writers of the later Roman empire and includes a glossary, a chronology of literary and political events and useful maps showing the origins of ancient writers. The collection will be essential for students and others who want a structured and informative introduction to the literature of the classical world.

Neil Croally is Head of Classics at Dulwich College, and has been a Principal Examiner and reviser for Ancient History A-level. Previous publications include *Euripidean Polemic: The Trojan Women and the Function of Tragedy* (1994), and 'Tragedy's Teaching' in *The Blackwell's Companion to Greek Tragedy* (ed. Justina Gregory; 2005).

Roy Hyde was Head of Classics at University College School, Hampstead for twenty years, and has served as Chief Examiner for both Greek and Latin at A-level for many years. He has published *Latin Unseen Translations* (2002).

Downside School
Upper Sixth Form Classics Prize
Awarded to Matthew McRae

June 2012

To George, Dora and Jo
(NC)

In memory of my father
(RH)

Classical Literature

An Introduction

Edited by
Neil Croally and Roy Hyde

 Routledge
Taylor & Francis Group

LONDON AND NEW YORK

First published 2011
by Routledge
2 Park Square, Milton Park, Abingdon, Oxon OX14 4RN

Simultaneously published in the USA and Canada
by Routledge
711 Third Avenue, New York, NY 10017

Routledge is an imprint of the Taylor & Francis Group, an informa business

British Library Cataloguing in Publication Data
A catalogue record for this book is available from the British Library

Library of Congress Cataloging in Publication Data
A catalog record for this book has been requested

ISBN: 978-0-415-46812-1 (hbk)
ISBN: 978-0-415-46813-8 (pbk)
ISBN: 978-0-203-81850-3 (ebk)

Typeset in Garamond and Gill Sans
by Book Now Ltd, London

MIX
Paper from
responsible sources
FSC® C004839
www.fsc.org

Printed and bound in Great Britain by
CPI Antony Rowe, Chippenham, Wiltshire

Contents

Contributors

Judith Affleck taught for nine years at Eton College before becoming Head of Classics at Harrow School from 1996 to 2007. While there, she began to collaborate on the CUP series, *Translations from Greek Drama*, which now runs to ten volumes. She has taught regularly on the JACT Greek Summer School and produced a number of plays in both English and Greek. She is now Head of Classics at King Edward VI Grammar School, Stratford-upon-Avon, a move she made to help promote access to Classics in the state sector. She lectures regularly on a variety of topics, in particular Greek literature and early imperial Roman history.

Caroline Butler taught at Winchester College before becoming Head of Classics at St Paul's School. She is now Academic Deputy Head at Colfe's School. She has been Principal Examiner in Latin Literature for OCR and a syllabus developer for the Cambridge Pre-U Classics specification.

Neil Croally has been Head of Classics at Dulwich College since 1997. He has worked for OCR as an examiner in Ancient History, and is currently Chief Examiner of Pre-U Latin. His publications include *Euripidean Polemic: The Trojan Women and the Function of Tragedy* (1994) and 'Tragedy's Teaching' in Gregory (2005).

Terry Edwards has recently retired from teaching classical subjects. He has been an examiner for OCR Ancient History since the 1980s and Chief Examiner since 2001. He has also worked for OCR in various capacities for the Classics suite, writing material for both Ancient History A Level and Ancient History GCSE.

John Godwin is Head of Classics at Shrewsbury School. He has published a complete edition of all the poetry of Catullus and was the reviser of the Penguin Classics translation of Lucretius. More recent books include: *Lucretius* (2004) and *Reading Catullus* (2008).

Hilary Goy taught Classics for over 30 years and was lucky enough to enjoy the halcyon days before results were more important than education and knowledge had to be macerated to achieve them. She is is now enjoying retirement and supervising at Cambridge University.

Roy Hyde was for 20 years Head of Classics at University College School, Hampstead in London. He has been an examiner in Greek and Latin at all levels, and is currently the Chief Examiner of A-level Greek. He is the author of *Latin Unseen Translation* (1998).

Jonathan Katz studied Classics and Oriental Languages at Oxford. After two years teaching at Westminster School he became Head of the Indian Institute in the Bodleian Library, Oxford. Returning to London in 1987, he was Master of the Queen's Scholars and then Head of Classics at Westminster, where he also taught Philosophy and Modern Languages. He has been an examiner at both secondary and university levels. He is a musician and musicologist with interests in both Western and Indian music, and has been a Research Fellow at Wolfson College, Oxford, a Visiting Fellow at Princeton University and a Visiting Fellow at All Souls College, Oxford. His publications include translations from German and Italian as well as books and articles in Latin, Greek and classical Indian subjects.

Stephen Kern is a long-standing member of the Classics Department at the Perse School, Cambridge; he is the joint author (with Paul McKechnie) of an edition of the *Hellenic Oxyrhynchia* (1988); he has been an examiner with Oxford and Cambridge and with OCR, and currently contributes to intensive Greek teaching for beginners in the Classics Faculty, Cambridge University.

Robert Shorrock teaches Classics at Eton College, Windsor and is co-editor of the journal *Greece & Rome*. He holds a PhD from Cambridge University and has published widely on epic poetry and the classical tradition. His monograph, *The Myth of Paganism. Nonnus, Dionysus and the World of Late Antiquity*, will be published by Duckworth in 2011.

John Taylor has been Head of Classics at Tonbridge School since 1992. He is the author of several Greek and Latin textbooks.

Seb Wakely has taught Classics at Dulwich College since 1995.

David Woodhead is Head of Classics at University College School in Hampstead, London. He has worked as an A-level examiner in Latin, and was educated at Durham and Cambridge.

Editors' introduction

This book is designed for students and teachers studying or teaching A levels and their equivalents; we hope that the book may also be of some use to undergraduates. All the contributors have been or are practising teachers, while a large number of them either also work for examination boards in the UK or have had scholarly work published.

We have tried to include the majority of classical authors, including those who at the moment are not favoured as set texts by examination boards (critical fashions do change, after all). At the same time, we do not apologise for the fact that certain authors and genres have received lengthier treatment than others. Aware that many readers will want to use this book for perhaps only one or two chapters or even sections within chapters, we have tried to make each chapter as self-contained as possible: glossary items for each chapter are listed at the beginning of each chapter; suggestions for further reading can be found at the end of each section or chapter. Some information, however, which is commonly applied to more than one author or genre, and which cannot be explained in a sentence or so has been included in the first chapter ('Introductions'). Items that appear in 'Introductions' are referred to clearly in the main body of the text. At the end of the book there are also some maps and a chronology. Cross-references within the text are given in the form 'see 9f' where the number relates to the chapter and the letter to the section, as shown in the Contents list.

Further reading

In our suggestions for further reading, we have, for the most part, listed books and not included articles, though readers now have access to a great many articles in learned journals through the splendid JSTOR. Moreover, most of the books recommended themselves have fuller bibliographies. There already exist a number of very good introductions to parts of classical literature, and readers may want to consult some of those works as well. On classical literature generally, we suggest Ash and Sharrock (2002); Rutherford (2005). On Greek literature, see Easterling and Knox (1985); Said and Trédé (1999); Taplin (2000); on Latin literature, there is Braund (2002); Kenney and Clausen (1983); Conte (1994); Harrison (2005); Taplin (2001). Fantham (1996) is an interesting exploration of Roman literary culture from Cicero to Apuleius; Feeney (1998) concentrates of the importance of religion in Latin literature; Hinds (1998) deals with the important topic of intertextuality in Latin literature. There are a number of articles on various classical Latin authors in West and Woodman's two collections (1975 and 1979). One could also consult Howatson's *Oxford Companion to Classical Literature* (1997). Another excellent reference work is the *Oxford Classical Dictionary* (Hornblower and Spawforth, 2003), which is now also available online. There are good collections of articles on a wide variety of topics in the *Oxford Illustrated History of the Classical World* (Boardman *et al.*, 1986; also published in two separate volumes, one for the Greek world, the other for the Roman), in the *Cambridge Illustrated History of Ancient Greece* (Cartledge, 2002b) and the *Cambridge Illustrated History of the Roman World* (Woolf, 2003). There is an interesting collection of articles on a variety of subjects to do with the Greek world in Powell (1995). And for good and wide-ranging information on both Athens and Rome, see *The World of Athens* (Jones, 1984) and *The World of Rome* (Jones and Sidwell, 1997).

Texts and translations

The majority of classical texts are available in the *Oxford Classical Text* series.[1] There is also a growing collection of texts (with translation and commentary) in the *Aris & Phillips Classical Texts* series.[2] There are quite a few Greek texts online at The Little Sailing;[3] a large number of Latin texts are online at The Latin Library.[4] In our suggestions for further reading we have only mentioned a text when it is not available as an Oxford Classical Text. There are a large number of good texts with commentary in the Cambridge Greek and Latin Classics series.[5] As for translations, there are a large number of classical works in the Penguin Classics series,[6] and a smaller number in the World's Classics series.[7] Readers can also consult a Loeb,[8] many of which are available online at the Internet Classics Archive.[9]

Finally, we would both like to thank all our contributors, and our respective friends and families for putting up with us while we put this book together.

Neil Croally and Roy Hyde
London, 2010

Notes

1   http://fds.oup.com/www.oup.co.uk/pdf/catalogues/classics/oct2006.pdf
2   These can be searched for www.oxbowbooks.com.
3   www.mikrosapoplous.gr/en/
4   www.thelatinlibrary.com
5   http://uk.cambridge.org/classics
6   www.penguinclassics.com
7   www.worldsclassics.co.uk
8   The Loeb Classical Library: www.hup.harvard.edu/loeb/
9   http://classics.mit.edu/

Chapter 1

Introductions

Neil Croally and Roy Hyde

> Glossary items: *aulos, aulētris; dithyramb; elegiac couplet; epinikian; hexameter; iambic trimeter; monody; pentameter; polis; stichic metres; strophic metres.*

Classical authors tended to work within literary traditions; they also produced their work in a cultural context that retained many similar features, both over the wide geographical area covered by the Graeco-Roman world and also through the many centuries in which Graeco-Roman culture dominated the Mediterranean. For that reason, and because we wish to avoid repetition, we have included in this introductory chapter a number of the aforementioned features. They are arranged alphabetically, and reminders of their presence here in this opening chapter will be made in the following chapters.

Greek dialects

The English spoken today by a native of London may sound very different to that spoken by, for example, a New Yorker, an Australian or a Glaswegian, though each of them will – more or less, and perhaps with some effort – be able to make sense of what the other says. Ancient Greek, too, showed considerable regional variations, with the important difference for us (as readers, rather than speakers, of the language) that, while English for the most part follows a standard system of spelling, in Greek, variations were written as well as pronounced. Thus, where an Athenian would say (and write, if he could write) *theoi* when referring to 'the gods', a Spartan would say *sioi*; to a Spartan, *amera* was the day, *selana* the moon: an Athenian would have said *hēmera* and *selēnē*, and so on.

Scholars classify the dialects of Ancient Greek under five major headings: *Attic-Ionic*, spoken in Attica and those Aegean islands and parts of the coast that had been colonized by Ionian Greeks; *Doric*, in the Peloponnese and

Dorian colonies; *Aeolic*, in Thessaly, Boeotia, and some eastern settlements such as Lesbos; *Arcado-Cypriot*, in Arcadia in the Peloponnese and Cyprus; and *North-West Greek*, in the northern and   western parts of mainland Greece. (North-West Greek and Doric are sometimes treated as varieties of West Greek.) The dialect 'map' of Greece, then, is complicated by the mobility of the Greeks around the Mediterranean, and by their colonizing activities. As far as literature is concerned, it is further complicated by the tendency of particular dialects, or mixtures of them, to become associated with particular literary genres. Thus, the dialect of the *Iliad* and the *Odyssey*, which is essentially Ionic with some Aeolic and Arcado-Cypriot colouring, becomes the language of epic poetry: so that the epic poet Apollonius, who came from Rhodes and worked in Alexandria, several centuries after Homer, still writes his *Argonautica* in recognizably Homeric Greek; and, for that matter, more than a thousand years after Homer, the Christian Egyptian epic poet Nonnus could write about the pagan god Dionysus in Homeric Greek (see 12g). Literary tradition was stronger than regional boundaries: in Athens, the iambic sections of tragedies (the parts spoken by the actors) were conventionally written in Homerically influenced Attic, while those parts sung by the choruses were in the traditional Doric-influenced language used in choral lyric poetry (see 'Metre, music, genre' in this chapter).

Literary dialects, then, like the writers themselves, crossed regional boundaries, and outlasted whatever origins they had had in the speech of everyday life. The use of local dialects was also undermined by the spread of the *koinē* (from *koinē dialektos* – 'common speech'), which derived from the classical Attic Greek that most of us begin by learning, and spread through the near east, first as a result of the increase of Athenian influence from the fifth century BCE onwards, and later – and more widely – as a result of Philip of Macedon's adoption of Attic Greek as the language of the Macedonian court and the subsequent conquests of his son Alexander the Great. No doubt the ordinary Greek in Laconia or Boeotia continued to speak the dialect his fathers and grandfathers had spoken: but even when the eastern Mediterranean came under Roman control, the *koinē* remained its language of administration and of commerce, and eventually became the bureaucratic language of the Byzantine empire which survived until 1453 CE.

Further reading

Buck (1998; 2009); Horrocks (1997).

Literacy

The Mycenaeans were literate, but their cumbersome Linear B script seems to have been used only for limited administrative purposes, and there is no indication that it was used to write down 'literature', or that any significant proportion of the population could read or write. After the Mycenaeans, there is no sign of writing in Greece until the eighth century BCE, and at first it seems to have been used to indicate ownership of objects (e.g. names written on pots), and for religious purposes such as dedications or curses. The new Greek alphabet was derived from that of the Phoenicians, with the refinement that symbols were now used to indicate vowels, which was not the case for Phoenician (or for Linear B).

Books (probably papyrus rolls) existed in the sixth century BCE, if not before. Hesiod, around 700, may have used writing to preserve his poems (though this does not mean that he himself could write: his technique is essentially that of an oral poet), and the Homeric poems were probably written down about the same time. In the sixth century, Peisistratus, tyrant of Athens, had the *Iliad* and the *Odyssey* written down, in order to try to establish a definitive text. By about 500, book-rolls were being used for educational purposes, though – like writing materials – they continued to be expensive throughout antiquity, and few people owned many.

Early literature is in verse, as verse is easier to remember. The advent of writing was thus of vital importance to the development of prose as a means of recording and communicating ideas in the fifth century BCE, and in the wider and quicker dissemination of knowledge and theory. But memorization of texts remained central to Greek educational methods, because books continued to be relatively rare, expensive to produce, and difficult to read, as punctuation was largely unknown. Book-rolls were also hard to consult, so that authors frequently misquote each other through relying on memory. Oral performance continued to be central not only for verse, but also for prose texts, and literature was aurally received, rather than read on the page, by most people.

It has been estimated that the level of literacy never rose above 20–30 per cent in ancient Greece (Harris, 1989). But literacy does not only mean the ability to read books: perhaps few people were ever able to read long complex texts easily, and fewer still to write them. But far more were probably able to read simple notices or inscriptions, or to write their names, if little more. In Athens in the late fifth century, for example, public inscriptions of all kinds, including laws, proliferated, and this must have encouraged people to learn to read at least a little, if not to write.

There is no firm evidence for oral poetry at Rome: from the beginning, Latin literature – frequently translated or adapted from Greek – seems to have been written down. This does not necessarily mean that it was always read; throughout Rome's history most 'literature' was probably first aurally received, through the widespread practice of *recitationes*, readings of an author's work to an invited audience. Education, and consequently literacy, were prized by the wealthier classes, which does not, of course, provide evidence for the population at large, whose experience remains, as usual, mostly obscure. On the other hand, archaeological evidence, such as graffiti at

Pompeii, papyri from Egypt, and the writing-tablets from Vindolanda on Hadrian's Wall, testify to some degree of more widespread literacy, not least amongst soldiers. The extent of the later empire makes generalization impossible: levels of literacy were no doubt lower in rural areas than in cities, but Varro (first century CE) recommends that even an estate-owner's head shepherd (who would be a slave) should have some degree of literacy.

It is important to remember, in an age when the ability to read and write is frequently equated with intelligence and civilization, and when most of us get our information and pass it on in written form, that a non-literate society, or one in which literacy levels are low, is not necessarily a backward one. Non-literate societies manage to remember and to disseminate large amounts of complex information successfully. Writing and reading facilitate the spread and exchange of information and ideas, but do not necessarily improve their quality.

Further reading

Bowman and Woolf (1994); Harris (1989); Havelock (1982); Thomas (1992). On literacy and democracy in classical Athens, see now Missiou (2010).

Metre, music, genre

The metres of Greek and Latin poetry (unlike conventional English poetry) are based not on which syllable of a word is stressed, but on the length of syllables: thus, for example, diphthongs (two vowels pronounced as one, such as *ai* in Greek or *ae* in Latin) make a syllable long, whereas a syllable with a single vowel may be long (for example, *a* as in 'father') or short (*a* in 'fat') depending on how it is pronounced.

Metres come in two basic kinds: *stichic* metres are composed in recurring lines of the same type, such as the hexameters of Homer and Virgil, or the iambic trimeters of Attic tragedy; a variation on this is the elegiac couplet, consisting of one hexameter followed always by one pentameter. *Strophic* metres are composed in stanzas, in one of two basic forms: the typical monodic lyric poem (of, for example, many of the poems of Sappho, Alcaeus and Anacreon) is in stanzas all of the same form; choral lyric poetry (such as that of Alcman or the choral odes in Attic tragedy; and Pindar's odes, which may or may not have been chorally performed) are triadic, consisting of a pair of stanzas each in the same metrical form followed by a third in a related but not identical form.

Some common metrical feet (˘ = short; - = long)

The shortness or length of a syllable in Greek and Latin verse is a matter of how long it would take to pronounce the syllable. Classical metres were not based on stress, as those of English verse are. Long syllables could be either:

1   those that include a naturally long vowel, such as an omega in Greek, or a diphthong (two vowels put together to form one sound, such as – *ae* in Latin), or

2   those in which a vowel is followed by two consonants, whether those consonants are part of the same word as the preceding vowel or not. Below are listed some of the common units (or feet) of classical metres.

Anapaest   ˇ ˇ –
Dactyl   – ˇ ˇ
Iamb   ˇ –
Spondee   – –
Tribrach   ˇ ˇ ˇ
Trochee   – ˇ

Some common metrical schemes

Hexameter   The metre most famously of epic poetry, made up of six feet and dominated by the dactyl.

So variation is allowed in the first four feet, and in the last syllable. It is certainly not normal to have a spondee in the fifth foot (Virgil has such a fifth foot rarely, though it is more common in, for example, Catullus 64). Normally, the caesura – a natural break in the line – comes either after the first syllable of the third foot or after the first syllable of the fourth foot (normally the former).

Elegiac couplet   The first line of the couplet is as the hexameter above; the second is as follows:

Little variation is allowed here, though Alexandrian poetry is less rigidly tied to the scheme than Ovid.

Iambic trimeter	This metre is made of three metra, with each metron consisting of two feet. This is the metre of much of Greek tragedy; there seems to have been more variation in later tragedies.

1	2	3	4	5	6
˘ —	˘ —	˘ —	˘ —	˘ —	˘ —
— —	— —	— —	— —	— —	— —
˘ ˘ ˘	˘ ˘ ˘	˘ ˘ ˘	˘ ˘ ˘		
— ˘ ˘		— ˘ ˘			
˘ ˘ —					

The caesura is again after the first syllable of the third or fourth foot.

In Greece, poetry and music were originally intimately connected: almost all poetry had some kind of musical accompaniment, except the iambic sections of drama and obvious cases such as funerary epigram. But, with the increase in literacy and the tendency of poets to write rather than compose with music in mind (and the rise of the reader in addition to the listener), the importance of music declined. The Romans in general took over Greek metrical forms, except for the (probably) native Saturnian metre in which some early poetry was written but which rapidly disappeared under Greek influence, although the musical element was lacking: music was an important element in Greek education, as it was not at Rome; most educated Greeks had some musical competence, whereas upper-class Romans tended to look down on musicians. As far as we know, Horace's *Centennial Hymn* (*Carmen Saeculare*) was the only Latin poem which was intended to be sung. And the emperor Nero, for example, who liked to sing and play the lyre in public, was generally vilified, not because he was bad at it but because he did it at all.

The instruments most frequently played were various forms of the lyre, a stringed instrument somewhat like a small harp (and played like one, by plucking the strings), though its size and the number of strings varied. Lyric poems, both monodic and choral, were sung to lyre accompaniment, and sometimes to that of the *aulos* as well. This was not a flute, as the word is often wrongly translated, but more like an oboe; *auloi* were often played in pairs by the same player. This suggests that harmony might have been possible, but in fact it seems that for the most part instruments, and voices with instrumental accompaniment, played and sang in unison. Other instruments were known, but not much used in ordinary music-making: trumpets, for example, were usually used only in military contexts for giving signals, though the Romans used them at funerals, and percussion instruments of various kinds were used, often in a religious context. But music was not a static art. The organ, at first powered by water and later by air pressure, and recognizably the ancestor of the modern organ, was invented in Alexandria in the third century BCE, and became quite popular, especially with the unmusical Romans, who are said to have liked it because it made plenty of noise.

Fashions in music, of course, changed too. Towards the end of the fourth century BCE, for example, 'new music' became popular and controversial (it was criticized on moral as well as aesthetic grounds by conservatives, as innovations in the arts so often are). The basis of Greek music was the mode: modern western musical scales can begin on any note, and the intervals between notes in any scale are the same (depending on whether it is major or minor); the various Greek modes (*harmoniai*) each consisted of a different sequence of intervals, and generally a composition was played and sung wholly in the same mode (lyres presumably had to be tuned to a particular mode). One of the innovations of the new musicians appears to have been modulation between modes; harmonic experimentation may also have been involved – it is hard to imagine that Timotheus, for example, the great *virtuoso* of the new music, would have been satisfied with mere unison of voice and accompaniment. We do not have any of his music, but a substantial part of the text of one of his dithyrambs survives, and if the music matched the words (highly ornate: excessively so, in some opinions), he must have been doing some quite remarkable things.

No doubt, though, the ordinary individual with a basic musical education continued to play and sing much as his father and grandfather had. Conservatism also characterizes the Greek and (without the musical element) Roman attitude to metre, music and genre. That is, for most of antiquity, particular metres continued to be associated with particular literary genres, because the earliest examples of them used that metre. The metre of epic poetry, for example, was established as the hexameter by the precedent of Homer, and remained fixed. Though the Homeric bard sang, or chanted, to the accompaniment of the lyre, it is unlikely that Apollonius of Rhodes, for example, did so – and Roman epic poets certainly did not, though they retained the metre. In Greece, dialects too were associated with particular genres: the basically Ionic dialect used by Homer continued to be the dialect of epic, regardless of the poet's native dialect. Similarly, the dialect of triadic lyric song was traditionally (basically) Doric, and it clearly appeared natural enough to the audience at an Athenian tragedy that the actors spoke Attic while the Chorus, when it sang, sang in Doric.

Further reading

On ancient Greek music, see Hagel (2009); West (1994). On Greek metre, see West (1987); on Latin metre, see Raven (1965).

The Olympic and other games

The Olympic Games, held at Olympia in the north-west Peloponnese, like the three other major Greek games, the Pythian (at Delphi), the Nemean (at Nemea in the north-east Peloponnese, and the Isthmian (at Corinth) were a religious festival, not simply a sporting event. Like the modern Olympics, they took place every four years, and were of such importance that the Greeks dated events by them: 'so-and-so happened in the third year of the twentieth Olympiad'. The first Olympics are traditionally held to have taken place in 776 BCE, though another legend holds that this was just a revival, and that they were originally founded by Heracles. Of the other games, the Pythian and Isthmian were thought to have begun in 582 BCE, the Nemean in 573 BCE. The Pythian took place every four years, and the others every two years, such that ambitious athletes could compete in a major event every year, in the sequence Olympic, Nemean, Isthmian, Pythian, Nemean, Isthmian, Olympic, and so on. As well as these, there were numerous minor games in many different places.

Events in the various games included running, over various distances, including races in armour; the long jump; boxing; wrestling; the *pancration*, a kind of 'martial art' in which only biting and eye-gouging were forbidden; the pentathlon (running, long jump, wrestling, discus, and javelin); and chariot racing. In some games, in some events, there were also 'junior' competitions for boys or younger men. (Needless to say, in Ancient Greece, there were no competitions for women, though Spartan girls practised gymnastics and athletics.)

Prizes at the major festivals consisted only of garlands (of different kinds of leaves in different places – olive, at Olympia for instance), but the prestige was enormous, for the winner, for his family and for his city. Would-be competitors were by definition rich: only a wealthy man could afford the time needed for the intensive training put in by ancient, as much as by modern, athletes; they also employed trainers, like their modern counterparts, and skilled trainers were much in demand. To win at one of the major games was to achieve sporting stardom, something like winning one of the four major golf championships, today, or a grand-slam event in tennis. To win at all four, as did, for example, the boxer Diagoras of Rhodes, was to achieve superstar status.

Chariot racing differed from the other events in that the victor was the owner of the winning team of horses, rather than the charioteer, though occasionally an owner did drive his own chariot. In the case of chariot racing, then, the prestige accrued not from athletic prowess, but from conspicuous expenditure, 'not only for his own benefit but for that of his city', as Thucydides (6.16) makes the Athenian politician Alcibiades say: he had entered seven chariots in one Olympics, and come first, third, and fourth. Victors of all kinds celebrated their achievements lavishly with feasting, drinking, song and dance: the tragedian Euripides wrote a victory song for Alcibiades. Many such *epinikians* were written by Simonides, Bacchylides and Pindar – the most famous poets of their day.

The origins of the Greek games were essentially commemorative and religious (see the funeral games in the *Iliad*, or those at which Hesiod sang): Roman games, of which the most familiar will be gladiatorial contests and chariot racing, seem to have had similar beginnings, and the former reached Rome in the third century BCE from Campania, and perhaps originally Etruria, the shedding of the blood of combatants at funerals being probably an offering to the deceased (the word *munus*, plural *munera*, meaning 'gift' or 'offering', continued to be the word for a gladiatorial show). By the end of the republic, gladiatorial shows had become frequent and enormously popular, and although at first their commemorative function was not forgotten, became an important tool in the self-promotion of ambitious politicians. It became incumbent upon emperors too, therefore, to exhibit shows of increasing magnificence. Originally condemned criminals, some gladiators became popular heroes, to the extent that free men, in some cases of high social status, sometimes took up the career; even some emperors, no doubt with suitable safeguards, appeared in the arena. The adulation and favouritism extended to individual gladiators and gladiatorial teams not infrequently led to disturbances and even full-scale riots. The same was true of chariot racing, in which the competitors at Rome in time became organized into 'factions' (eventually Reds, Blues, Greens and Whites with the charioteers wearing the colours of their factions); successful charioteers, too, earned popular adulation.

Gladiatorial shows became less frequent in the later empire, partly perhaps because they wasted potential manpower and because they were expensive to put on. There had always been educated Romans who disapproved of these bloody spectacles; criticism increased as Christianity became more widespread, and eventually Constantine put an end to them in 325 CE. Chariot racing continued at Rome until the end of the western empire, and somewhat later at Byzantium it continued to be popular, enjoying the same fanatical support: in 532 CE the emperor Justinian was almost overthrown by the activities of the Hippodrome factions. Thereafter it seems to have suffered something of a decline, though the Hippodrome at Constantinople was still in use at the beginning of the thirteenth century.

Further reading

On sport in the ancient world, see Kyle (2007). On the Olympic Games, see Finley and Pleket (1976); Spivey (2005). On athletics in Athens, see Kyle (1987). On games and gladiators in Rome, see Futrell (1997); Kyle (1998); Wiedemann (1992).

Patrons and authors

Greek and Roman authors made no money from their books: they received no royalties, publishers' advances or payment from sale of books. If an author was not independently wealthy, he (she only in very rare cases) would, in order both to exist and to write, have to seek the support of a patron to offer some measure of financial security. In some cases, those who supported authors may have done so out of genuine regard for their work, and for literature in general; many more will have done so because of the return it brought them: not a financial one, but the prestige of sponsoring a successful writer and the prospect of achieving some kind of immortality through the association. Clearly the case of each individual author is different, and conditions varied widely during the millennium or more from Homer to the end of the western Roman empire, and this account is only intended to offer general guidelines for thinking about the nature of patronage in antiquity.

The earliest poets we know of, the bards of the Homeric tradition, were professional poets. Some, if we can believe what Homer tells us, were employed by kings and lords, to entertain them and no doubt sing their praises; others travelled around, making a living where they could. Their social status was equivocal: as effectively the equivalent of artisans, their status was low (though not as low as, for example, sculptors, since the latter worked with their hands); yet they possessed the power to elevate the status of those they served. Most early non-epic poetry, on the other hand, was produced by members of the upper classes, for their own entertainment and that of their peers, particularly in the context of the symposium (see later in this chapter). Here, any kind of payment would have been out of the question: this is a literature of equals. Yet some poets who emerge from this tradition took on also a social role: Alcman, for example, or Sappho. We do not know if the public poetry of such as Alcman received any specific recompense; if it did, it is perhaps more likely to have been in the tradition of gift-giving commonly practised amongst aristocrats. (Possessing the degree of education necessary to write poetry at all, and the leisure to take up the craft, implies considerable social status to begin with: Hesiod may have been a farmer, but he cannot have been a peasant.) Even Pindar, who has been seen as a professional poet, writing to commission, may well have been paid in kind rather than in cash. But by his time (early fifth century BCE), the tyrants (see 3a) – had emerged as patrons who recognized the prestige to be gained from supporting poetry and the other arts: the Peisistratids at Athens, for example, or Polycrates of Samos, to whose court went Anacreon and Ibycus – the latter from distant Sicily. The Sicilian tyrants themselves continued to vie with each other in the prestige stakes, but in the fifth century Athens became the literary centre of Greece: the frequent festivals and competitions for poetry and music attracted artists from all over the Greek world. Here the arts were practised in the name of democracy, but the paradigm was not far removed from the earlier aristocratic one: the glorification of the *polis* seems to have been the vision of Pericles, an aristocrat himself. The poets themselves competed ostensibly for prestige rather than for money; but success could no doubt bring financial rewards in its train. Euripides, for example, who was evidently wealthy enough to spend much of his time writing plays for no financial gain, at the end of his life went to live at the court of king Archelaus of Macedon, and was presumably well rewarded for doing so. The example of Socrates, too, though not a writer, shows how, in the Athens of this time, a man of relatively low social status could evidently manage to earn his keep without actually being employed, by virtue of having wealthy friends. Itinerant sophists too make their appearance in the later fifth century (see 6a and 6c). Not all of them wrote, but those who did earned the leisure to do so by the money they earned from teaching. Literature was becoming a profession.

In the fourth century, the Homer-loving Alexander of Macedon included literary men in his entourage and thereby ensured his reputation. But it was his general Ptolemaeus, on becoming Ptolemy I of Egypt (or perhaps his son Ptolemy II) who did most to advance the professionalizing of literature, in his determination to make Alexandria the cultural centre of the Greek world by establishing there the famous Library. Most of the major literary figures of the Hellenistic period were in some way associated with the Library, where scholarship for the first time became a salaried profession. Other Hellenistic kings followed suit, aware of the promotional power of the word.

The centres of culture that evolved in this period in the eastern Mediterranean continued to be such for centuries to come for the Greek-speaking world. The coming of Rome saw the end of the royal dynasties that had patronized the arts, but opened up new avenues of opportunity: professional literary men can be found practising as rhetoricians, teaching Greek and Roman alike, and Greek poets such as Archias (first century BCE) now wrote in praise of Roman aristocrats. There was also the possibility of employment as an imperial official, a position which Lucian held; some sophists continued to travel and teach or display their talents in public recitals, while others acted as valuable intermediaries between Greeks and Roman officialdom. In Rome itself, interaction between poet and patron must be seen within the wider context of the patron-client relationship which permeated Roman society at all levels, to the extent that even men of wealth and influence are to be found as clients to those of more distinguished lineage, especially if they came from outside the city of Rome itself. Thus the connections a writer made might be more important in getting his works publicized in Roman society than literary quality – although, to judge from what has survived, it was quality that ensured their survival in the end.

In fact, the first major Roman poet (according to Roman tradition) was both an outsider – a Greek – and a freed slave: Livius Andronicus, who also made a living teaching Greek. Ennius, in the early second century BCE, was an Italian but not a Roman, and rose to eminence through the assistance of aristocratic Romans. The important early Roman dramatists Terence and Plautus are said to have been respectively an ex-slave and an Umbrian: it was no doubt advantageous to such men that plays at Rome could be sold for performance, unlike at Athens, though Terence at least enjoyed aristocratic patronage too. Also unlike Athens, Rome's more rigid social structure could pose problems; another early dramatist, Naevius, is said to have been imprisoned for attacking important men on stage; whereas the satirist Lucilius, who came from a senatorial family and who was almost a contemporary of Terence, attacked with impunity whomever he liked.

In the later republic, the pattern of gaining influential friends continues. Most of the writers of whom we know were themselves from well-to-do backgrounds, for whom patronage meant getting to know the right people rather than receiving payment in cash or in kind. Catullus, for example, dedicates his book of poems to Cornelius Nepos, a north Italian like himself, and therefore a peer in social terms rather than a patron; if Catullus' Lesbia is really the aristocratic Clodia, he was clearly quite at home in aristocratic society, and his poetry shows him to have been no respecter of reputations. Nevertheless, Roman aristocrats were conscious of the prestige value of poetry; the Greek poet Archias wrote poems on the military achievements of Marius and Lucullus, and self-evidently cannot have been seen by such men as a social equal, although there was by now an established tradition of noble Romans receiving into their homes Greek intellectuals, as well as Italians.

The coming of the principate had the effect of setting one particular patron, the emperor, at the top of the social pyramid. Augustus, the first emperor, was highly sensitive to the power of image-making, through both the visual arts and literature. His relationship with Virgil is hard to fathom: the poet had reason to be grateful to Augustus for services rendered before he became emperor; thereafter he was probably financially secure, but, through his association with Augustus' associate Maecenas, the figure of the emperor must have loomed significantly large in the poet's thoughts as he worked on the *Aeneid*. If Virgil had doubts about the Augustan regime, he was subtle enough not to express them openly: Ovid, however, was clearly not (though we do not know exactly what his offence was), and suffered miserable exile as a result. The example of Ovid exemplifies the new status of patronage at Rome: there is now one supreme patron; if his approval is not openly sought, his displeasure must be at all costs avoided. The outstanding example of the effect of Augustan patronage is Horace, whose father was a freedman (though wealthy enough to send Horace to Rome to be educated). Through contact with Virgil, his poetry attracted the attention of Maecenas, who gave him a house and farm; if Horace felt kindly towards the Augustan regime, and said so, he can hardly be blamed.

After Augustus, individual rich men continued to patronize literature at Rome – though not enough to prevent Martial from complaining that there are no Maecenases any more – but the presence of the emperor cast a long shadow. An emperor interested in literature might be a blessing to a writer who attracted his attention – as Domitian was to Statius or, much later, Claudian to Honorius (at the beginning of the fifth century CE: perhaps the nearest thing to a court poet in Roman history); one who was *too* interested might prove a curse – as Nero was to Lucan.

Further reading

On literary patronage, see Gold (2009); for patronage in the Augustan Age in particular, see White (1993). On non-literary patronage, see Saller (2002); Wallace-Hadrill (1990).

Religion and mythology

There is something odd about the religion of the ancient Greeks and Romans, as I hope this story will show. A ritual called the *Bouphonia* (slaughter of an ox) occurred annually at Athens at a festival in honour of Zeus Polieus (Zeus the protector of the city). Every year selected oxen were led through the streets of the city until, at a preappointed time (perhaps after one of the oxen had touched some sacred objects on a bronze table), a priest killed the ox with the axe and then skinned it with a knife. He then fled. The axe and the knife were then put on trial, found guilty of murder and thrown into the sea. (Walter Burkert thought that this ritual was a 'comedy of innocence', in which humans displayed their ambivalence about killing animals.) Sacrifice – of domestic animals, to honour various deities, in private or public rituals – was common, indeed central, but we still do not know – and some doubt whether the ancients did – what sacrifice was all about.

So we may have to accept that we will never really understand Greek and Roman religion; we may also have to accept that the ancients themselves carried out their rituals in a state of some bafflement. But we can say that religion in both Greece and Rome was polytheistic; indeed, there is a bewildering number and variety of gods. Not only are there the 12 famous Olympians (see the table below); there are also the Titans who were overthrown by Zeus and his allies, the older chthonic deities (such as the furies), there are the muses, nymphs, deified heroes and, of course, in the Roman era, deified emperors. Different cities and different regions all had their own particular emphases when it came to religious practice. So, for example, for obvious reasons, one of Athens' biggest festivals – the Panathenaea – honoured its patron deity, Athene. Gods too have different functions and areas of concern, depending on where and the context in which they are being honoured. So, Zeus can be worshipped as god of the marketplace or as god of suppliants; Artemis can be the virgin goddess of the hunt, or the goddess who oversees childbirth.

Such variety of belief and practice goes hand in hand with the fact that, for the ancients, there was no one text that claimed to be the word of god. This lack of an equivalent to the Bible or the Qu'ran meant that there was no religious orthodoxy or doctrine that had to be guarded by an institution such

Table 1.1 The Olympian Gods (with some, though certainly not all, of the areas in which they had an interest)

Zeus/Jupiter	King of the gods; also god of the marketplace, money and supplication, etc.
Hera/Juno	Wife (and sister) of Zeus/Jupiter
Aphrodite/Venus	Goddess of desire; mother of Aeneas
Apollo	Son of Zeus/Jupiter; god of the sun, music and healing
Ares/Mars	God of war
Artemis/Diana	Virgin goddess of the hunt, and of childbirth
Athene/Minerva	Goddess of wisdom and cultivation
Dionysus (Bacchus)	God of wine, the mask, theatre, and the fig
Hades (Dis)	God of the underworld
Hephaestus/Vulcan	The blacksmith god who lives under Mount Etna; husband of Aphrodite/Venus
Hermes/Mercury	The messenger god
Poseidon/Neptune	The god of the sea; brother of Zeus/Jupiter

as the church. Ancient Greek and Roman society does not suffer from wars based on religion, until, that is, the advent of Christianity. Insofar as religion was institutionalized, those institutions were political. In Greece, it was the *polis* that determined religious practice and the calendar of festivals. In Rome, religion was also political, with some priesthoods being elected offices (note, for instance, Julius Caesar as chief priest or *pontifex maximus*).

Whether a Greek or Roman was worshipping publically – making offerings at the altars that were situated in front of the gods' temples or attending one of the many festivals organized by the city – or privately in the house, it is difficult for us to know to what extent the ancients had faith in anything like the Christian sense. Gods, we have to remember, were not necessarily good, but they were powerful. It looks, then, as though as most religious practice was intended to seek the favour of the gods or, at the very least, to avoid the gods' disfavour. The cultural elites of Greece and Rome may not have believed in the gods in any real sense, but a knowledge of religion and its practices pervades Greek and Roman literature. At the same time, throughout antiquity there was an interest in various philosophies as guides for living: the literature of the ancients is not only run through with references to and uses of religious language and practice, it is also influenced by such systems of thought as stoicism, Epicureanism and, later of course, Christianity.

As stated above, there was no one sacred text in Greek and Roman religion. However, there were a large number of stories, or myths, about gods and heroes. We do not know the origin or original versions of these stories, but it is through the literature of the Greeks and Romans that they have come down to us. Many of the stories do not have any specific religious content, but their survival and repetition would tend to suggest they say something about the human condition. The fact that a great deal of Greek and Roman poetry used mythological stories meant that authors were presenting their audience with something familiar; it also meant that they could demonstrate their art and creativity not so much by the invention as by the treatment of the story. That last point is one of the explanations of the great variety within classical mythology, of sometimes surprisingly different versions. But, however much variety there was in mythology, we must recognize that it was the basic material of much classical literature and, through Ovid's *Metamorphoses* especially, later European literature as well.

Further reading

For a good reference work, see Price and Kearns (2003). For Greek religion, see Bremmer (2004); Bruit Zaidman and Schmitt Pantel (1992); Burkert (1985); Easterling and Muir (1985); Ogden (2010); Parker (1996; 2005); Price (1999). For Roman religion, see Beard *et al.*, (1998); Dowden (1992); North (2000); Price (1984) (a lot here on the imperial cult). For an interesting work on the importance of religion in Latin literature, see Feeney (1998). For Greek mythology, there is some excellent work. See Buxton (1994; 2001; 2004); Edmunds (1989); Morford and Lenardon (2000); Vernant (1980; 1983); Woodard (2008).

Rhetoric and education

Training in rhetoric was, of course, only the last stage in education – the nearest ancient equivalent of a modern university education – and only available for the wealthy and privileged few. Basic education was provided by teachers specializing in three main areas: reading and writing; music and singing; and physical education. This again was the preserve of the better-off, at least until the Hellenistic period, when there is evidence that basic education was, in some places, made available for all free-born boys; the coming of democracy in Athens in the fifth century BCE may have acted as a stimulus to literacy. Schools of some kind are attested in the Greek world from the beginning of the fifth century. Throughout antiquity, girls might or might not receive some education, dependent on the inclinations of their parents.

In Greece, in the classical period, training in rhetoric was at first the domain of sophists, who came under fire from conservative thinkers on the grounds that persuasiveness is not necessarily truthfulness, and indeed may make wrong appear right. (See Aristophanes' *Clouds*, and frequent references in Plato, especially *Gorgias* and *Phaedrus*.) Isocrates, in the fourth century, attempted to make rhetoric more acceptable by insisting on the need for a rhetorical education to develop the orator's character as well as his eloquence. Political oratory became less important in the Hellenistic period, with Greece under the domination of greater powers, but by no means died out, and rhetoric never lost its important educational role.

Roman elementary education was essentially similar to Greek, though with less emphasis on physical education. Greek rhetoric and rhetorical theory were regarded with suspicion in early Rome but, by the second century BCE, upper-class Romans were learning Greek, and Greek teachers of rhetoric were active there. Rome's greatest orator, Cicero, was influenced by Greek theory, and himself wrote books on rhetorical theory, as well as serving as the prime example of how a man without political connections could, initially by virtue of his success as a forensic orator, rise to prominence through the practice of rhetoric. During the principate, political oratory again declined in importance, though Latin forensic oratory continued to be important. (See the frequent references in the letters of the younger Pliny to his forensic activities.) At the same time, Greek oratory enjoyed something of a revival, probably not least because the Greeks' Roman masters were interested in studying rhetoric. For some two centuries from the early first century CE, a new breed of sophist was active throughout the Roman empire, especially in the east (the second sophistic). Like their predecessors, these men taught rhetoric and gave displays of their own skill as orators; unlike them, they were often men of importance and wealth in their communities, and used their skills in representations to Roman officials, and sometimes even to the emperor himself. The study of rhetoric never died out: after the division of the Roman empire, Greek theory continued to be studied in the east, and later under the Byzantine empire; in the west, it survived to become part of the standard curriculum of the medieval universities.

The prevalence of rhetorical teaching in Greece and Rome means that almost all authors from the fifth century BCE onwards received some training in rhetoric. Consequently, rhetorical features can be found in almost all classical literature, even in the most unlikely places.

Further reading

Translations of the Greek works mentioned above are readily available, as is Aristotle's *Rhetorica*. There is a good deal of later Greek theoretical writing, but most of it is not translated, and is in any case technical and less than enthralling. In Latin, however, Quintilian's *Institutio Oratoria* (first century CE) contains much information on Greek theory, and is available in the Loeb Classical Library, as are Cicero's rhetorical works, Tacitus' *Dialogus de Oratoribus*, and the *Suasoriae* and *Controversiae* of the elder Seneca.

For introductions to classical rhetoric, see Gunderson (2009); Habinek (2005); Kennedy (1994). On Greek rhetoric, see Kennedy (1963); Russell (1983); Wardy (1998); Worthington (1994; 2007); Yunis (1996). For rhetoric in relation to poetics, see Walker (2000). On Roman rhetoric, see Kennedy (1972). On ancient education, see Jaeger (1945); Marrou (1956).

The sexes and sexuality

Throughout Greek history, the female sex was regarded as secondary to the male. This supposed inferiority was reinforced in the fourth century BCE by the authority of Aristotle, who believed he could show scientifically that the female body was a less perfect form of the male one. In saying this, Aristotle was perhaps doing little more than making respectable a distinction that had existed in practice, reinforced by custom and by law, from time immemorial.

As usual, our sources tell us most about what was the case in Athens, and amongst the more well-to-do classes of society (about the 'lower' classes we rarely have reliable information; as far as this particular issue is concerned, we can assume with reasonable certainty that the situation was much the same through-out Greece amongst the property-owning classes, though Spartan women enjoyed greater rights under the law). Here, a woman passed from being the 'property' of her father (or of a male kinsman, if her father died), to being that of her husband. Most marriages were arranged, and the woman's purpose was to bear children for the continuance of the family and for the good of the *polis*.

Arranged marriages, as can be seen in some societies today, can be perfectly happy ones, and the concept of romantic love between man and woman was certainly not absent from the Greek view of life, even in the fifth century, and comes to play a greater role in later literature, for example in the comedies of Menander and in the Greek novels. It was, however, accepted that for sexual pleasure, a man would probably have recourse to prostitutes or slave-girls and, since girls (and indeed older married women) led sheltered and segre-gated lives, opportunities for young men and women to meet would be rare.

In early Rome, the situation of women was perhaps not dissimilar. There is, though, evidence even from the early republic of women taking an interest in politics, although at no time were they (officially) permitted actual politi-cal involvement. Their primary role was seen as that of child-bearer and supervisor of the home, but the latter role also extended to the early education even of male children, unlike the customary Greek paradigm. They were also more visible in public: certainly by the Augustan period, women were to be seen at the theatre and at the games, and at dinner parties alongside their husbands. They also appear to have been able to own property. Already, towards the end of the republic, we find women of ability and independent spirit eliciting male disapproval (mingled with fascination) for their activi-ties: see for example Clodia in Cicero's *Pro Caelio*, and – if she is the same person – as Catullus' 'Lesbia', and especially Sempronia in Sallust's *War with Catiline* (25) – beautiful, educated, talented, and, if we are to believe Sallust, sexually predatory and unscrupulous. Under the empire, women of the ruling households, from Augustus' wife Livia onwards, could wield enormous power, and in some cases effectively governed the empire for periods of time.

It is conventional, and essentially not unreasonable, to see women through-out the ancient world as a subordinated class. On the other hand, recent work has begun to explore ways in which women, within the parameters of essen-tially male-constructed societies, were able to use these structures to their own advantage and to live satisfying lives of their own. We may not hear much from them, but their influence may be far greater than we can know.

In Greece, from puberty onwards, young men began to be assimilated into adult male society, for example through physical and military training and in the symposium, and it is in this context that we find a kind of institutionalized homosexuality. Typically, an older man (the *erastēs*: 'lover') would 'court' a younger one (the *erōmenos*: 'beloved'), with the aim of gaining sexual favours, but also with the assumption that he would initiate the younger man into the kind of behaviour required of a man of his particular social standing (evidence for this can be found in the poems of Theognis addressed to Cyrnus, which are by turns erotic and politically didactic). The resulting relationship between partners would thus be intimate, though the extent to which it would be physically consummated is not wholly clear. Scenes of homosexual activity are common in vase paintings, though here the passive participants may often be slaves. Sexual penetration was indicative of possession and superiority, and thus problematical between males who, regardless of age difference, were social equals. Where it did take place, it seems to have been regarded as a matter between partners, and not to be talked of or boasted about publicly. An acceptable alternative seems to have been 'intercrural' intercourse, where the *erastēs* ejaculated between the thighs of the *erōmenos*, so that the problem of superiority was side-stepped. Oral sex was regarded as degrading, and therefore unacceptable, as was passive homosexuality if practised later in life. The bond between male lovers was seen as a potent one (and as part of the bonding of the male social group): at Thebes, for example, the 300 strong elite hoplite squad, the 'Sacred Band' is said to have been constituted of 150 pairs of male lovers. This bonding seems to be traceable a long way back in history: the relationship between Achilles and Patroclus in the *Iliad* is not specifically stated to be a homosexual one (later Greeks were uncertain as to how it should be seen), but is certainly one stronger than simple friendship.

Roman society appears to have lacked this kind of institutionalized homosexuality, and the Roman attitude has been conventionally seen as one of disapproval. In fact, as in Greece, questions of dominance again arise: to penetrate a male slave was acceptable, but not a free-born man; in literature of all periods we find the passive homosexual, especially the male prostitute, as an object of disapproval. It may be the case that as Greek *mores* became known and assimilated at Rome, male homosexuality became more acceptable, but to practise it was still to invite vilification, as Julius Caesar and Nero, for example, were vilified for their bisexuality. Perhaps at some periods it was more acceptable, and prevalent, than at others – for example, in the time of Hadrian who, although of course married, was almost undoubtedly predominantly homosexual.

Scenes of female homosexuality are found in Greek vase paintings, perhaps as much for male titillation as anything else (women were proverbially regarded, by men, as lascivious creatures). Though opportunities for socializing outside the confines of the home were fewer, nevertheless women, like men, tended to associate mostly with their own sex, and no doubt homosexual relationships developed. It may be the case, in certain places and at certain periods, that such relationships were institutionalized, in the same way as was male homosexuality. In early Sparta, for example, the poems of Alcman strongly suggest that girls were brought up together in a context where sexual attraction was at least acceptable, if not actively encouraged. In many respects, Sparta worked differently from other Greek states; but in Lesbos, too, the little that survives of the work of the poet Sappho suggests that she, and no doubt others like her, was in some way responsible for the education of young girls, and their initiation into womanhood. Although the name of her homeland has given rise to the word 'lesbian', the extent of her intimacy with other women is controversial.

There is very little about female homosexuality in Roman sources, though some evidence of (male) interest from the Augustan period onwards; the 'butch' lesbian, with exaggerated masculine characteristics, appears occasionally as a figure of disapproval. Overall, however, our understanding of female sexuality in the ancient world is limited and fragile, as a result of the almost complete lack of female voices in the surviving sources, and of male stereotyping and male prurience.

Further reading

Much work has been done in this area in recent years. For the sources on sexuality, see Johnson and Ryan (2004); McClure (2002). Otherwise, see Brown (1990); Nussbaum (2002); Ormand (2008); Skinner (2004). For a collection of sources to do with women in the ancient world, see Lefkowitz and Fant (2005); for a collection of articles see Hawley and Levick (1995). For women in classical Athens, see Blundell (1998); Just (1989); Keuls (1985); in Rome, see D'Ambra (2006); Gardner (1987). On homosexuality, see Davidson (2008); Dover (1980).

Slavery

There is much to admire about the ancient world, indeed it could be argued that we still live in a world importantly determined by Greco-Roman culture. However, there is one especially large blot on the classical achievement, and that is the existence of slavery. We know that the ancients were aware of how disastrous it was to become a slave: in Homer's *Iliad* (6.463) the day one becomes a slave is seen as the day one loses half of one's self. For the Greeks, though, slavery was an accepted fact. In the fourth century – it is true – there was some discussion of whether slavery was conventional or natural (e.g. Aristotle *Politics* 1253b, 1255a), though very little criticism of the institution in principle (excepting perhaps Alcidamas, pupil of Gorgias: scholium at Aristotle *Rhetoric* 1373b). The Romans also accepted slavery as a fact, though with that remarkable pragmatism which was one feature of their not entirely consistent national character, the Romans seem to have freed more slaves, and were willing to accept the sons of ex-slaves as citizens (as, say, in the case of the poet Horace). In trying to understand the experience of slaves in the ancient world we confront an insuperable historiographical problem: we have little or no evidence from slaves themselves. Such evidence that we do have comes from what we might term the slave-owning class.

But who were these slaves? In both the Greek and Roman worlds there was something like a tabu against enslaving one's own people (though there were exceptions: the helots of Sparta were from the Greek city of Messene; in the Peloponnesian War the Athenians on a couple of occasions enslaved the whole population of a Greek city). The main source of slaves was war, though children born of slave mothers were also by definition slaves. Slaves in both Greek and Roman societies had no legal rights. However, it would be wrong therefore to assume that they were distinguishable from the free by the activities they performed. Slaves in fact performed just about every task also performed by a free person, with the exception of being members of political and legal institutions. Slaves at the bottom of the rung, those who worked in the mines or as galley slaves, very likely had a dismal experience and a short life-span. At the other end of the spectrum, there were highly educated slaves who worked as secretaries, administrators and the like, with rich owners, who if seen in the street would seem superior in dress, manners and even language to many of the free. The Old Oligarch (1.10ff.) makes just such a complaint about fifth-century Athens, and Tiro, the secretary of Cicero, who possibly invented a system of shorthand and wrote many learned dissertations, is an excellent example of a slave at the top end of the social spectrum. As to the numbers of slaves, we lack sufficient data to be sure. But the best modern estimates are as follows: in Attica in the classical period there were probably between 80,000 and 100,000 slaves, which is an extraordinary number given the likelihood that in the same period the citizen body of Athens did not exceed 50,000. In Rome, towards the end of the first century BCE, the number of slaves is likely to have been roughly 2,000,000 (with a free population in Italy of around 6,000,000). It is no surprise, then, that there was a persistent fear of slaves fleeing and, worse, revolting. The Spartans, in particular, are sometimes argued to have organized their whole society as a defence against any possible helot revolt: but the helots are *sui generis*. That slave rebellions in societies other than the Spartan were so uncommon is probably because slaves were not united by their activities (as said above) or by language or culture. The devastating rebellion of Spartacus in 73–71 BCE, sometimes called the Third Servile War, was the only slave rebellion which occurred in Italy and seriously threatened the republic (the other two servile wars – in 135–132 BCE and 104–100 BCE – both occurred in Sicily). Spartacus' rebellion stands then as a highly distinctive episode.

Much of Greek and Latin literature concerns itself with war, starting with the *Iliad*. It is not therefore surprising that slavery also features because, as we have seen, the defeated are nearly always enslaved. This threat and then this experience appears regularly in Greek tragedy. In new comedy we encounter the figure of the clever slave; it could be argued that this is part of the carnivalesque inversion to be expected of a (dramatic) festival. And, of course, slaves and slavery make an appearance from time to time in the great histories, in accounts of distinctive episodes (such as the murder of Pedanius Secundus by his slaves and the subsequent contrasting responses of senate and people; see Tacitus *Annals* 14.42–5), and occasionally in the works of the philosophers. It is a truism of economic history that the Greek and Roman economy and society were built on slave labour. Given what we know about the class or social status of most classical authors, the sobering thought is that the same would seem to be true of classical literature.

Further reading

Generally, see Finley, (1960; 1980; 1987); Garlan (1988); Garnsey (1996); McKeown (2007); de Ste. Croix (1981); Wiedemann (1987). On Greek slavery, see Fisher (1998). On Roman slavery, Bradley (1994); Brunt (1971); Fitzgerald (2000); Hopkins (1978). On the ancient economy more generally, see Finley (1973; 1981); Manning and Morris (2005).

The symposium

Symposion means 'drinking together'. Sharing food or drink is an act which brings together the participants in a demonstration of friendship or solidarity, and can be found in our earliest sources for Greek society. By the seventh century BCE at least the practice of Greek males drinking together after a meal (eating and drinking were kept separate) was well established, especially amongst the upper classes: elaborate rituals were devised, which differed in different places, and rules for the conduct of the symposiasts. The symposium typically took place in the *andron*, the men's room in the host's house, and – in most places – the participants reclined on couches. Proceedings would begin with offerings to the gods. A 'symposiarch' was elected, whose most important role was to decide the strength of wine to be drunk – the Greeks normally drank their wine mixed with water: everyone present would then drink wine of the same strength, and all were expected to drink the same number of cups. As at any meeting of friends or of business associates, no doubt a good deal of gossip and networking went on; since the symposiasts were of similar social class, and since men of similar views will gravitate towards each other, the symposium also frequently took on a political complexion. Symposiasts were expected to contribute to the communal entertainment; they might sing, to the accompaniment of the lyre (much lyric, elegiac and iambic poetry originated in the symposium), either their own compositions or those of others (some songs seem to have become symposium classics), or they might make speeches on some specified theme. Favourite topics for conversation or song seem to have been women, boys, political matters and – obviously enough – the pleasures of drinking. At more elaborate symposia, entertainment would be provided: musicians, acrobats, dancers, and so on. These entertainers were often female – the only women present at symposia, as citizen women did not attend – and most were slaves. Music, including accompaniment for singing, was often provided by *aulētrides* (plural of *aulētris*), slave girls who played the *aulos* (a wind instrument something like an oboe; see 'Metre, music, genre' earlier in this chapter). The word *aulētris* became a synonym for prostitute and cheap ones could be picked up on the streets. More skilled ones, and no doubt more attractive ones, were in demand for symposia; either way, their contribution might well be sexual as well as musical. Not all symposia ended in drunken debauchery, and many were no doubt relatively sober and serious affairs. But the traditional end to the symposium was the *kōmos*, in which the symposiasts went out into the streets in procession singing and shouting. Essentially this was as much an expression of group solidarity as the symposium itself but if the symposiasts were sufficiently drunk, might well degenerate into vandalism, fights with similar groups or assaults on passers-by. (But cf. Bowie (1997), who argues that there was some pressure on the host to ensure that his guests did not become too drunk.)

The two surviving literary *Symposia* from the classical period, by Plato and Xenophon, and both featuring Socrates, are of course idealized, but still contain many authentic features of real symposia.

Further reading

Bowie (1997); Lissarague (1990); Murray (1990). There is some interesting material on Theognis and the symposium in Figueira and Nagy (1985).

Texts and fragments

The Greek and Roman literature we have has reached us in one of two ways: either through manuscripts, or by way of what scholars call fragments.

In the ancient world, of course, everything was copied by hand. The works of the major Latin writers continued to be copied, in a continuous tradition, even after the fall of the Roman empire in the west (476 CE), through the dark ages and the middle ages, until the advent of printing in the late fifteenth century. Knowledge of Greek gradually declined in the west during the later Roman empire, but Greek remained the language of the eastern Roman empire which continued to exist until 1453 CE. (The eastern empire is sometimes called Byzantine, after Byzantium, the earlier name of Constantinople, which was established by the emperor Constantine in 330 CE to be the administrative centre of the east.) Ancient Greek texts were read, studied, and copied throughout the history of the Byzantine empire.

Towards the end of its existence, scholars, with their manuscripts, began to migrate to western Europe, bringing about the renewed interest in Greek literature of the renaissance.

Fragments come in two forms. One is in the shape of quotations in the texts of other authors, especially authors interested in literary criticism, grammar and language. Many brief quotations from the Greek lyric poets, for example, were preserved in this way, by scholars more interested in their linguistic content than their poetry. The other is in the form of pieces of papyrus preserved, by a quirk of the climate, in Egypt (and a very small number in other places, for example the works of the philosopher Philodemus, preserved in Herculaneum, probably in the villa in which he lived). These papyri are often brief, damaged and hard to read, but there have been some major discoveries: substantial parts of some of the comedies of Menander, several poems by the Greek lyric poet Bacchylides and a short but important fragment from the Roman elegiac poet Gallus.

Both manuscripts and fragments pose problems in interpretation. The continuous process of copying introduced many errors into manuscripts. Fragments preserved in other authors are obviously subject to similar errors; and they can be inaccurate, as a result of the habit of ancient authors of quoting from memory (looking up references in a papyrus roll, which was the usual form of book used in the ancient world, must have been difficult and time-consuming). Surviving papyri are often damaged, so that scholars have to try to reconstruct what was on missing parts. The practice of textual criticism – trying to establish what a classical writer *really* said – has gone on since ancient times, and goes on still.

Further reading

This is rather a technical area, but see Wilson and Reynolds (1974).

War

War was central to the experience of Greeks and Romans in the classical era. Moses Finley once said that most Greek city states were engaged in military operations most years (1983: 60). Nor was the Roman empire gained without enormous and persistent military effort. In the Greek city the norm was for the city's armies to be made up of citizens: indeed, to be a citizen one had to be prepared to fight in the army. In this context Rome, with its professional standing army, looks distinctive. But it was still supposed to be the case that citizenship was a necessary condition for serving in the army (the rule was bent in various ways from time to time).

Because war was so important to classical societies, it should be no surprise that it was also a common and important theme of classical literature. The very first poem of western literature – the *Iliad* – has war as its context and central theme. Many Greek tragedies are also concerned with the (catastrophic) effects of war. The Roman epics of Virgil and Lucan deal with mythical and historical wars respectively. The writing of history begins in Herodotus and Thucydides as an enterprise that justifies itself by referring to the impact of the wars that are their subject. In Thucydides, the Peloponnesian War is explicitly measured against the Trojan War as described in Homer. Why should war be such a frequent theme of classical literature? The paradoxical figure of Cassandra may have starkly asserted that all sane people think that war is stupid (Euripides *Trojan Women* 400), but war was also the place where men (and it is usually only men) sought fame and glory, and where cities competed for wealth and power. It is because war is an extreme event and a challenging experience, it is because in war character, mettle, values – both individual and collective – are tested and revealed, that the ancients used it so often as context or theme.

Further reading

There is much good work on warfare in the ancient world. For the sources, see Sage (1996); in general, and most substantially, see Sabin *et al.* (2007); also see Garlan (1975); Hanson (1989); Havelock (1972); Sidebottom (2004). For warfare in Greece, see Hanson (1991); Pritchett (1971–91): very detailed; Rich and Shipley (1993a); Van Wees (2004; 2009); Vernant, 'War' in (1980). For war and the Romans, see Campbell (2002); Harris (1979); Rich and Shipley (1993b).

Chapter 2

Homer

Judith Affleck

All dates in this chapter are BCE unless otherwise stated. Glossary items: *allegory; alliteration; epithets (stock); hexameter; kleos; moira (aisa); nostos; Panathenaea; rhapsode; timē; xenia.*

THE HOMERIC POEMS

Two of the longest, oldest and greatest poems in world literature are ascribed to the Greek poet known as Homer. By the fifth century these poems had become so firmly rooted in Greek culture that a young Athenian could claim to listen 'nearly every day' to recitations of Homer's *Iliad* and *Odyssey* and be able to repeat by heart all 27,800 lines (Xenophon, *Symposium* 3.5–6). The poems were regularly performed by *rhapsodes* (professional reciters of poetry, like Ion in Plato's dialogue of the same name), taught in schools and widely studied. When Plato depicts Socrates as banning the works of Homer, 'the educator of Greece', from his model state in *The Republic*, he uses the metaphor of a lover reluctantly putting aside the object of his love. The impact of the *Iliad* and the *Odyssey* on the ancient Greeks was unique.

How did these two poems come to hold this special place in Greek culture? The simple answer must be the quality and humanity of the poems, recognized by modern as well as ancient readers. When and how these poems originated, however, and who created them remains largely the subject of speculation.

The date of the Homeric poems

Ancient authors and commentators were interested in who Homer was and when he might have written. For example, Herodotus, writing in the second half of the fifth century, writes 'I think Homer and Hesiod came four hundred years before me – no more than that' (Hdt. 2.53). His near-contemporary

Thucydides, perhaps countering earlier claims that Homer lived much closer to the age of heroes, simply says he 'came much later than the time of the Trojan War' (Thuc. 1.3). In the ancient world, the traditional date for the end of the ten-year siege of Troy, central to both poems, was 1184, at the close of what is now known as the Mycenaean period. Today, the late eighth or early seventh century is broadly accepted as the likely period when the poems were composed, but, as we shall see, the poems did not come into existence in isolation and their birth was part of a long and complex process reaching back to an oral tradition, where poems were composed extempore and adapted or passed down by word of mouth. By the sixth century at least, a group of poems including the *Odyssey* and *Iliad* were attributed to Homer and came to be preserved in written form, but questions about date, authorship and the identity of Homer, if such a person ever existed, are very difficult to unravel and even harder to answer.

Who was Homer?

Some minor works were also attributed in the ancient world to Homer. Thucydides treats a line from one of these, the Homeric *Hymn to Apollo*, as autobiographical, 'He is a blind man and lives on rugged Chios' (Thuc. 3.104). When people began to speculate about Homer's identity, the temptation to identify the author with one of his own creations, the blind bard Demodocus in the *Odyssey*, may have proved strong. Chios, however, is not the only state that claimed Homer as her own and from early on six other cities disputed the claim made in the *Hymn to Apollo*. The debate about who Homer was, when, what and whether he (or even she) wrote continues. Not all scholars today agree that the *Iliad* and the *Odyssey* are by the same person, or that a single mind is responsible for either poem. (For convenience, though, most scholars still refer to Homer as the author of the *Iliad* and the *Odyssey*.) Most scholars would agree, though, that the *Odyssey* is composed after the *Iliad*, or at least with the *Iliad* in mind. Before Achilles returns to the battle after the death of Patroclus, he appears before the Trojans, terrifying them with his shouts and the fire that appears above his head (*Il.* 18.225–7). There seems to be a comic parody of this in the *Odyssey* when Odysseus, before his identity has been revealed, causes much mirth among the suitors because the light from the braziers reflects off his bald pate (*Od.* 18.351–5).

What other kind of answer could there be about the authorship or origins of poems as long and sophisticated as the *Iliad* and *Odyssey*? Composing a poem and writing it down may be entirely separate activities and the author of a poem need not be the one who first committed it to writing. Let us briefly review the history of Greek literacy before considering the role of the bard (see also 1b), the historical truth behind the poems, other creative influences and, finally, methods of composition.

Writing

Writing had an interrupted tradition in the ancient Greek-speaking world. Clay tablets from the age of Homer's heroes, the so-called Mycenaean age, which came to an end early in the twelfth century, were discovered in large quantities during the excavations of Knossos in Crete by Sir Arthur Evans and have since been found elsewhere. These Linear B tablets, deciphered in the early 1950s, are written in an early form of Greek. So far they have been found to record only lists, such as palace supplies, rather than literature and, with the collapse of the Mycenaean palace culture, the use of this script seems to have ended.

When Greek writing re-emerged, perhaps several hundred years later, at about the time the Homeric poems are thought to have been created, it used new symbols derived from Phoenician. The coincidence in timing may be part of a wider pattern of increased travel and contact with the near east. Certainly the Greeks were moving around the whole Mediterranean. One of the earliest examples of this new alphabet was found off the west coast of Italy on a late eighth-century cup, which shows familiarity with the Greek king Nestor and 'fair-crowned Aphrodite', goddess of Love, both of whom figure prominently in the Homeric poems. The person who wrote on the cup also uses the poetic metre of the *Iliad* and *Odyssey* – the hexameter – and possibly makes a playful comparison between the more modest clay cup and the great gold cup that Nestor brings out in *Iliad* 11. None of this helps us to know whether the author of the Homeric poems was literate, though it seems probable that some of those who first heard the poems were.

The one possible mention of writing in the Homeric poems themselves is inconclusive, but perhaps suggests that literacy was a strange concept yet to become widespread: in *Iliad* 6 there is a lull in the fighting around Troy while two heroes, Glaucus, a Trojan ally from Lycia, and the great Diomedes, discuss their ancestry. Glaucus tells the story of the heroic labours of his grandfather Bellerophon. Falsely accused of adultery by the queen of Argos, Bellerophon is sent to his death by her jealous husband who dispatches him to the king of Lycia bearing 'grievous signs, inscribed in a folded tablet, full of death' (*Il.* 6.168–9). The signs could be pictograms, but they may also reflect the perception that an illiterate person might have of writing.

In conclusion, we simply do not know when the poems were first written down or how long after their composition. The first specific references to a written text are from the tyranny of Peisistratus of Athens (560–27) whose library, presumably consisting of rolls of papyrus or leather, Xerxes is said to have removed to Persia when he sacked Athens in 480. Peisistratus or his son Hipparchus is credited with systematizing the text of Homer for performance by *rhapsodes* at Athens' great festival, the Panathenaea and, as we saw at the start of this chapter, most people in classical Athens experienced the Homeric poems aurally rather than by reading them. The divisions of each poem into 24 'books', one for each letter of the Greek alphabet, were probably made for practical reasons to do with reading and storing scrolls, if not in the time of Peisistratus, perhaps by Zenodotus, the first librarian of Alexandria in the third century.

The bard: status and skills

Long before the Homeric poems were created and even before the age of the heroes they celebrate there is material evidence that the singer/poet was honoured in parts of Greece: a little stone sculpture, which comes from the Cycladic island of Keros, dates from the third millennium and has images of a solo singer accompanying himself on a stringed instrument are familiar throughout the history of Greece.

The poems themselves provide evidence for the role of song and the poet. The opening words of each poem, seeking inspiration from the goddess or Muse, draw attention to the mystery of the poet's craft. In the *Iliad* there are moments when characters themselves reflect upon how their deeds will be sung in future (e.g. Helen in *Il.* 6.357–8). The central character, Achilles, seems to reject the prospect of such future fame (*kleos*) by withdrawing from the fighting 'where men win glory', but he passes some of his period of inactivity celebrating in song the 'famous deeds of men': his friends find him 'delighting his mind with a sweet-sounding lyre, beautifully crafted, with a silver bridge' when they come to try and persuade him to rejoin the fighting (*Il.* 9.186–9).

It is in the *Odyssey*, however, that we get our clearest picture of the bard. The blind singer Demodocus seems to be minstrel-in-residence at the magnificent palace of the Phaeacians on Scherie and, on Ithaca, Phemius is pressed into service by the suitors who have taken up residence in Odysseus' palace. Both the bards and their instruments are treated with the greatest respect by the poet, who takes care over details like the hanging of the lyre on its peg. The hero Odysseus leads the way in the respect he pays both bards: he sees that they are well fed and, in the midst of the carnage at the end of the poem, respects Phemius' plea for mercy, 'I am at your knees, Odysseus. Respect and pity me. There will be pain for you in the future if you kill a bard, who sings for gods and men. I taught myself, but it was a god who implanted in my mind every kind of path' (*Od.* 22.344–8). The wily Odysseus, like Achilles, is close to being a bard himself, as we shall see.

Though subservient, the bard commands great power. He may sing with authority of the affairs of the gods, as Demodocus does in his tale exposing the adulterous affair of Aphrodite and Ares. The song suits the broader themes and morality of the *Odyssey*, but is light-hearted in tone, verging on the irreverent. Other 'songs within songs' in the two poems concentrate on the deeds of men and command powerful emotional responses from listeners within the poems. Odysseus is twice reduced to tears when Demodocus sings of his exploits at Troy and Penelope breaks down when she hears Phemius sing of the *nostoi* (homecomings) of the Greeks who fought at Troy, thinking only of how her own husband has still not returned home. Although these characters weep at events which touch them personally, and Telemachus, when scolding his mother for requesting a change of song, says that 'an audience appreciates the latest tales best' (*Od*. 1.352), the power of the bard to stir is manifestly not restricted to those who have experienced recent suffering or want to hear of the latest events. To a modern reader the irony in Telemachus' rebuke is clear: countless readers over the centuries have been reduced to tears by remote events, like the wag of an old dog's tail (*Od*. 17. 291–327).

Telemachus implies that a bard should be up to date and ready to respond to requests. Demodocus shows precisely this skill and versatility, but he is also praised by Odysseus for a further quality: veracity. Odysseus admires the accuracy of Demodocus's account of the Trojan War, 'as if you were there or heard it from another' (*Od*. 8.491) and seeks to test him by requesting his own tale – the story of the wooden horse, 'If you tell the tale as it really was, I shall declare at once to all men how generous the god has been in his gift of divine song' (*Od*. 8.497–8).

When Odysseus takes his turn to entertain the company in Phaeacia with stories (*Od*. 9–12), there is no invocation to the Muse or mention of a lyre or song, but his words, despite the fantastical content (cannibals, nymphomaniacs and one-eyed monsters), appear true because they are a first-hand account, conveniently enough with no surviving human witnesses to most of his tale. Even when we *know* Odysseus is telling lies, as we do later in the poem, for example when he offers a false but plausible account of his past to Eumaeus, his words have a power that makes them seem true to the swineherd: 'it is like looking at a minstrel, who has learned enchanting words from the gods and sings them for mankind; when he sings, people long to listen and never stop' (*Od*. 17.518–20).

Reflections of a 'true' past?

The questions of veracity (being true) and verisimilitude (seeming to be true) are inevitably raised when thinking about Homer's poems. On a sensationalist level, 'Did the Trojan War really happen?', 'Is Homer's account based on a true story?' are questions to which we would like (but will not ever be able) to know the answers. Nevertheless, these questions are relevant to our understanding of the poetic tradition within which the poems were written. Is the poet, like Odysseus in the *Odyssey*, engaged in his own work of unverifiable fiction or, as in the case of Demodocus, has the story been accurately relayed through the generations so that it could be recognizable to one who was there?

Places and people

The *Iliad* and *Odyssey*, unlike *The Lord of the Rings*, for example, are not set in a fictional landscape. The locations were well-known in archaic and classical times and, if some failed to match the impressions of size and power created in the Homeric poems, fifth-century historians understood how such things might alter over time (Hdt. 1.5.4; Thuc. 1.10.1). The fact that some places mentioned in the *Catalogue of Ships* in *Iliad* 2 prospered as Mycenaean centres but had fallen into insignificance by the eighth century suggests that the poet of the *Iliad* used details passed down directly from earlier generations.

Characters in the poems were worshipped as cult figures in various cities in Greece, as Ajax was at Athens and Salamis; the locations of their tombs were – accurately or not – preserved in the collective memory. In the fourth century, Alexander the Great's campaign against Persia brought him to the Troad (the area around Troy) and he is said to have exchanged his own armour, which he dedicated in Athene's temple on the citadel of Ilium, for arms reputedly from the Trojan War (Arrian, *Anabasis* 1.11.7–8). Before laying a wreath at the tomb of Achilles, Alexander prayed that Priam's shade should not feel wrath (*mēnin*) with the descendants of Achilles' son. His use of *mēnin*, the first word of the *Iliad*, which establishes the heroic theme of the poem, is no accident. The vividness of this encounter, itself perhaps in part the product of Alexander's imagination, dimmed over time, and the physical world of Homer's heroes was largely lost to obscurity. It came as a shock, then, to western scholars in the nineteenth and twentieth centuries when, through the work of another devotee of Homer, the extent of correspondence between physical details in the poems and discoveries on and in the ground began to be revealed.

Walls and palaces

The excavations of Heinrich Schliemann at Troy, Mycenae and Tiryns in the 1870s and 1880s revolutionized visual perceptions of the Mycenaean world. Subsequent excavations and ongoing discoveries like the workers' huts at Tiryns or the wrecks of bronze age ships in the Dardanelles, the straits that link the Mediterranean with the Black Sea, continue to give impressive substance to the world of the Homeric poems. A few examples will have to suffice.

The walls of Troy, as tradition had it, were impregnable because they were built by the god Poseidon whom Zeus forced to work for Laomedon, king of Troy, for a year.

Poseidon describes his fortifications as 'wide and very fine' (*Il.* 21.447), but expresses anxiety that the fame of these walls might be eclipsed. He need not have worried! Schliemann was disappointed by the walls he found in his excavations at Troy, but shortly before his death his successor Dörpfeld unearthed an outer set of city walls, beautifully built and with a striking slant to them. A fine tower looked out over the plain. For a romantic, some of the details are almost too good to be true: when Patroclus leads Achilles' men into battle and pushes the Trojans back to their walls, Apollo stands on a 'well-built tower' and when Patroclus 'three times set his foot on the elbow of the high wall, three times Apollo pushed him off ' (*Il.* 16.700–4). It is not clear what a wall's 'elbow' (*angkōn*) is, except that it involves a bend, either a corner or an angle, not inconsistent with the slant of the walls that can be admired at the site today.

Palaces figure prominently in the *Odyssey*, both in the travels of Odysseus and his son Telemachus and in the action of the second half of the poem, much of which takes place in Odysseus' beleaguered palace. One of Schliemann's greatest triumphs was his excavation of Tiryns, a Mycenaean stronghold. If you visit the site today you make your way up through power-ful defences into a series of courts before entering the *megaron*, or 'great hall'. Schliemann found the walls decorated with alabaster inlaid with a paste of blue glass. 'Bronze walls ran round this way and that from the entrance through to the interior; they were topped by a cornice of dark-blue' (*Od.* 7.86–7) says Homer of the magnificent, unfortified palace of the Phaeacians. Odysseus has been told that he will find the queen sitting by the hearth, leaning against a pillar with her maids behind her (*Od.* 6.305–7) and Odysseus himself makes his petition sitting 'on the hearth in the ash by the fire' (*Od.* 7.153–4). A large circular central hearth with four columns support-ing a ceiling is now well-known to be typical of Mycenaean palaces, of which the best preserved is Nestor's palace at 'sandy Pylos' (excavated in 1939). The arrangement of storerooms, courtyards and *megaron* may help a modern reader to visualize scenes in the *Odyssey*, particularly the climactic acts of *Odyssey* 21 when Odysseus secures the palace and slaughters the suitors.

Arms and objects

Life at the time Homer is thought to have been composing had changed in two important respects from the age of heroes. The age of the palaces had passed and a technical revolution had taken place: Homer is the product not of a bronze age but an age of iron, as his likely contemporary Hesiod com-plains. Iron is certainly not unknown in the poem – a great weight of it is both the equipment and the prize in the discus hurling event of the funeral games for Patroclus – but most weapons of the *Iliad* are bronze, often with gold or silver studs, like the sword Menelaus uses in his duel with Paris: 'The son of Atreus, drawing his silver-studded sword, lifted it high and struck the helmet's peak. There it shattered into several pieces and fell from his hand' (*Il.* 3.361–3); the Mycenaean dagger is made of friable bronze inlaid with other metals, like the 'unyielding bronze, and tin, and valuable gold and silver' Hephaestus throws on the fire in readiness for making Achilles' great new shield; the god's work is marvellous in its complexity, including scenes of all human life: 'Fashioned in gold, four herdsmen walked with their oxen, followed by nine swift-footed dogs. But two terrible lions at the front of the herd had hold of a roaring bull . . . ' (*Il.* 18.474–5 and 577–9).

A gold-studded dagger found by Schliemann shows four men battling with three lions over their fallen companion whom the lions have killed. Two lions flee and the third has received a mortal wound. Amongst other Iliadic echoes, we see how the hunters are armed: two have mighty ox-hide shields fashioned like a figure of eight and two have 'tower shields' like that of Ajax, 'Ajax drew near carrying a shield like a tower, made of bronze and seven ox-hides' (*Il.* 7.219–20). The gold-studded dagger, which was found in one of the 'shaft' graves at Mycenae is thought to belong to the sixteenth century, four hundred years earlier than the Trojan War. Homer's descriptions of physical objects, like the cup of Nestor or the boar's tooth helmet Odysseus wears in *Iliad* 10, are largely the weapons of the heroic bronze age rather than of the poet's age of iron. Such details have been referred to as 'mere flotsam and jetsam' from the remote past, but they show impressive continuity, linking by means of a long and precise oral tradition the poet with the age he brings so vividly back to life for his audience.

Oriental influences

As well as some sort of unbroken oral tradition between the Mycenaean period through the so-called dark ages, the Homeric poems emerge from a period of increased contact with other cultures, particularly from Egypt and the near east.

Other tales had, of course, been created or adapted and passed down, long before the eighth century, notably the Mesopotamian epic poem, *Gilgamesh*, composed by the second millennium and copied onto tablets, some of which survive from the eighth century. Although written in a different language, elements in this poem are also found in Homer, for example the use of similes and epithets, extensive use of direct speech, scenes where the gods meet in council to discuss the affairs of men, and some complex narrative techniques, such as the story within a story. Occasional parallels are striking: in *Gilgamesh*, Ishtar, goddess of Love, complains to her father, Anu, in a tone which recalls the Greek goddess of love Aphrodite's plea for sympathy from her divine parent when wounded by Diomedes in *Iliad* 5.

Ishtar's wound was emotional rather than physical. This powerful female's sexual advances have been rejected by Gilgamesh, the hero of the poem. Variants of this generic story appear in *Genesis*, where Joseph pays dearly for disappointing Potiphar's wife. Perhaps they also lurk behind the hostility to the Trojans of Hera and Athene, whose beauty the young shepherd Paris slights. The story of Bellerophon in *Iliad* 6 offers a closer parallel. Greek travellers may have absorbed and exchanged tales like these, just as impressions of what constitutes a great battle may have been coloured by what they had seen or heard in other lands, like the much vaunted triumph of Rameses II in the battle of Qadesh (*c.* 1275), in which the Egyptian king fights from his chariot in heroic isolation. 'So fell the heads of the fleeing Trojans under Agamemnon, son of Atreus, and behind the strong-necked horses many empty chariots rattled back through the battle lines . . . ' (*Il.* 11.158–60). One of Odysseus' lying tales on his return to Ithaca involves an improbable meeting with the king of Egypt on the battlefield: 'I went up to his horses and took hold of the king's knees and kissed them. He spared me and showed me pity; setting me in his chariot he drove me home, while I wept' (*Od.* 14.278–80).

Conclusions: the oral tradition

Important research was done by an American called Milman Parry in the first half of the twentieth century. He created an archive of interviews with poets and recordings of orally composed poetry from the former Yugoslavia. Study of this material has helped our understanding of how oral poetry works – the way it evolves or is preserved as it is passed on from generation to generation. His interviews reveal the importance of precise memory (the ancient Greeks thought of Mnēmosynē, memory, as the mother of the muses); they also help us understand how a child immersed in the culture of oral poetry could absorb and learn to create for himself the rhythms, music and patterns of speech in storytelling that might make him a master of his craft, just as Bach or Duke Ellington assimilated and then used the baroque or jazz musical language with which each was surrounded. Like jazz riffs or baroque ornamentations, the comforting predictability of some patterns in oral poetry, like a regular metre, formulaic expressions, stock scenes (e.g. sacrifices or arming scenes), and repeated passages, are part of the learning process, but when deployed with skill serve to heighten the originality of a work. The analogy may also help us to remember that the Homeric poems emerged from a tradition in which both originality and repetition had a place, a tradition within which each performance was unique.

STORYTELLING

The processes which culminated in the creation of the Homeric poems leave an indelible mark on the texture of the poems. For an ancient Greek, what makes the *Iliad* and *Odyssey* 'poetry' rather than 'prose' is the fact that they follow a metrical scheme, which makes the words easier to commit to memory. Each line consists of six (Greek: *hex*) 'bars' (Greek: *metra*), a pattern that came to be associated with epic poetry in the classical world. Each 'bar' has two beats; the first (in bold in the line below) is always a full beat, the second may be either one full (long) or two half (short) beats. The lines tend to end with a regular cadence: '*long, short-short /long, long*' (the final beat of the line may also be short; on metre, see 1c). For example, the opening line of the *Odyssey* transliterated sounds like this:

> ***andr**-a moi-**enn**-e-pe, **Mous**-a,/ pol-**u**-trop-on **bos** mal-a **poll**-a*

This has practical implications for composition: some phrases will fit, others will not. Bards working within such constraints may rely upon or find useful for their craft 'stock' phrases, so Odysseus can be *dios* (godlike/noble), *polutlas* (much enduring) or *polumētis* (wily) depending on the rest of the line. On the whole, however, thinking in terms of expediency or ease of composition is a very limited way in which to reflect critically on the richness of the Homeric poems.

Repetition, lists, digressions

It has been estimated that about a fifth of the lines in the Homeric poems involve repetition, whether of individual words, short phrases or longer passages. Sometimes these repeated passages may rest a performer's memory or offer an audience relief, but there may be method behind the poet's choice: throughout the books of fighting in the *Iliad*, for example, one hears the thud of falling bodies in an alliterative refrain at the start of a line, *doupēsen de pesōn*, 'and he fell with a thud' (*Il.* 13.442 etc). Cumulatively the repetition is powerful rather than uninspired. Subtle differences may characterize the first and second delivery of a message, or a scene of sacrifice. Repetition may sometimes be formulaic, but it is always worth questioning why the poet repeats words, phrases or passages.

Perhaps the crudest form of composition is a list, like those clay tablets of ancient Mycenae, largely devoid of literary merit. Lists occur several times in Homer's poems, most extensively in the *Catalogue of Ships* (*Il.* 2.483–785) and the corresponding list of the Trojans and their allies (*Il.* 2.786–877). As suggested above, these seem to represent an ancient element in oral composition. A list of the names of 33 sea-nymphs occurs in book 18, but it is placed at one of the great emotional climaxes of the *Iliad*, the moment when the death of Patroclus is reported to Achilles. The depth and length of Achilles' cry when he first gives in to grief at the news of his beloved Patroclus' death is captured by the way each nymph hears and joins her cry to that of the hero's mother, the sea-nymph Thetis. The effect is mesmeric: poet and audience, as well as the characters within the poem, are given time to adjust to the crucial shift in events. The poet makes similar use of digressions, like the origins of Andromache's bridal veil that falls from her head when she understands that her husband Hector has been killed (*Il.* 22.470–2), or the occasion when Odysseus received the scar that identifies him beyond doubt (*Od.* 19.395–466).

Ancient and potentially crude poetic components can, then, be used in a sophisticated way. The poet's use of epithets (stock descriptions) provides another example. An author on an eighth-century pottery cup used the epithet 'fair-crowned' of Aphrodite in his hexameter line. Homer uses it too, but he has other epithets for the Greek goddess of Love: 'golden', 'divine', 'Cyprian', 'Cytherean'. The one he chooses at the moment when Aphrodite is wounded and in tears is 'laughter-loving'. This ironic touch is poignant in context. As we shall see, irony, whether used for humorous or tragic effect, or for something harder to pin down, is one of the poet's most developed techniques.

The emotional intensity of Achilles' immediate grief at Patroclus' death was communicated through a simple list. At other times the poet might use minutely observed details or a simile. The second half of the *Odyssey* is punctuated by a sequence of emotionally tense recognition scenes as the hero re-establishes himself in his own home. The varied nature of these revelations in itself shows the inventiveness of the poet: no two scenes are alike. The final recognition scene comes when Odysseus is united with his own father, Laertes, who has let himself go in grief at his son's absence. Odysseus seeks him out and follows his usual method of testing the loved one to see if he or she has remained loyal in his absence. Then suddenly, in a moment of heart-wrenching empathy, Odysseus' usual stream of lies dries up. 'His spirit was roused and, as he looked at his father, a sharp pang shot up through his nostrils' (*Od.* 24.318–9). With this tiny physical detail we sense what Odysseus feels; and afterwards we hear the patience and affection with which Odysseus enumerates for his father, as the test is turned on him, each fruit tree they planted together when Odysseus was a child: 'thirteen pear-trees, ten apple-trees, forty fig-trees, fifty rows of vines . . . ' (*Od.* 24.340–2). The poet takes his time, but his judicious use of detail contributes to the intensity of the poem.

Metaphor and simile

Homer uses imagery, in particular similes, to enliven or enrich his narrative. Before Odysseus reveals himself to his wife, Penelope, after an absence of 20 years, Odysseus spends part of an evening in her company disguised as a beggar. His words allow her to hope for her lost husband and the poet likens Penelope to the snows on a mountain which start to thaw under the warming east and west winds. Homer anticipates and reinforces the simile with a repeated metaphor: her flesh and cheeks literally 'melt', *tēketo* (*Od.* 19.204–09) as she listens to the lies of the man who sits beside her (man can mean 'husband' in Greek). We get a glimpse of how hard Penelope's long wait has been, of her emotional sensitivity, of the power of Odysseus' words and presence.

Later in the poem when Penelope and Odysseus finally embrace, the poet uses another simile to communicate Penelope's feelings: she is like a sailor who has escaped a shipwreck (*Od.* 23.233–9). The imagery forces us to recall the first half of the poem and the struggles of the man she loves; it is as surprising as the moment when Odysseus weeps like a woman being wrenched from the body of her dead husband into slavery (*Od.* 8.521–531). The verb used of Odysseus there as he dissolves into tears is *tēketo* – he melted. There is an implicit empathy between the two characters hinted at by this thematic imagery.

Similes are used in the Homeric poems with great versatility, to illuminate an intensely private moments or to deal with the challenge of, for example, describing a battle. Within the battle narrative of the *Iliad*, the focus shifts between minute detail and broad panoramic 'shot'. Opening the battle narrative at the start of *Iliad* 3, two great similes evoke the broad movements and sounds of battle: the noise of the advancing Trojans is likened to the cries of aggressive cranes, to be contrasted immediately with the deadly silence of the more disciplined Achaeans (Greeks). Confusion follows as the dust rises thickly under the feet of the advancing forces like a thick mist (*Il.* 3.2–7 and 10–14). Despite some charming incidental detail, the two similes presage the violence that will follow, later represented powerfully but enigmatically through the metaphor of a 'knot' of strife that can be neither broken or loosened (*Il.* 13.358–60).

Narrative technique

A full performance of either of Homer's poems might take between 13 and 18 hours, perhaps spread over a period of three days. The experience must have been intense and absorbing, especially in an age when forms of entertainment were largely restricted to the 'here and now'. The shaping of the two poems is often complex, but the poet helps the audience to follow his tale. A large percentage of each poem consists of extended direct speech, which gives scope for characterization and variety of pace within a performance, almost like a one-man play. A characteristic of epic is the clear way in which the beginnings and ends of speeches are marked off by the poet, 'X addressed him/her in reply, saying . . . '/'So s/he spoke . . . '. Digressions and other subordinate narrative elements are also sign-posted, usually by a method known as 'ring composition'. For example, after that intimate meeting between Penelope and the beggar Odysseus, the queen instructs an old family servant to wash Odysseus' feet. In doing so Eurycleia, who nursed Odysseus as a child, recognizes a scar which reveals his identity. While the audience wait breathless to see if Penelope will become aware of her husband's proximity we are taken on a 72-line digression explaining how Odysseus came by the scar. The digression opens with the words 'When he (Odysseus) went to Parnassus to see Autolycus and his sons' (*Od.* 19.394). It closes, 'When he went to Parnassus with the sons of Autolycus' (*Od.* 19.466). The close of the episode is clearly signalled to the listener.

The story of the Cyclops

To explore other aspects of Homer's narrative technique let us consider a specific episode: the story of the Cyclops, one of the best known parts of the *Odyssey*. The significance of the encounter between Odysseus and the Cyclops is flagged up long before we come to it. Zeus tells Athene that the reason why Odysseus has been kept so long from home is because he has angered Poseidon by blinding his son, Polyphemus (*Od.* 1.68–75). Then on Ithaca we briefly meet the father of Antiphus, one of the men killed and eaten by 'the savage Cyclops in his hollow cave' (*Od.* 2.19–20). In other words, the audience's expectations are aroused long before the storytelling begins, which leaves scope for dramatic irony: we know that Odysseus will blind the Cyclops, but not how or why. The story seems well established before the version we find in *Odyssey* 9, which might explain why a key detail like the fact that the Cyclops has only one eye is never made explicit.

The tale is told as part of a long first-person narrative that fills in events between the hero's departure from Troy and arrival at Calypso's island, where he languishes at the start of the poem. Odysseus himself is the narrator and is speaking to the Phaeacians. Before revealing his identity, Odysseus had already explained how he came to Phaeacia from Calypso's shores (*Od.* 7), closing the narrative circle of books 5–12. The extravagant use of detail immediately draws us into the story: the careful description of the island where most of Odysseus' men wait, the elaborate arrangements inside the cave for storing dairy produce, the nature of the stake that ultimately blinds the monster. Aspects of the story are made graphic by use of similes: smashing the men's heads on the ground like puppies, the process by which the stake is sharpened and the noise it makes as it enters the eye. Elements we might expect in a modern telling are absent: through similes we get a sense of the scale of the monster, but barely any physical details are given; the six men whom Odysseus loses and mourns are neither named or individualized. Told with the benefit of hindsight, the emphasis instead is on suspense, problem-solving and Odysseus' own brilliant role in the adventure: he initiates it by insisting on exploring the cave, and he engineers the more or less satisfactory outcome by blinding rather than killing the Cyclops; he masterminds their escape under the sheep; then, after making sure no other Cyclopes come to Polyphemus' aid through his 'No-man' ruse, he boasts to his victim using his true name and, not without further mishap, makes his escape.

Although it is only in the second half of the *Odyssey* that we become fully aware of how unreliable a narrator Odysseus can be, we are troubled less by whether or not any of this account is 'true' than by how we should respond to Odysseus' words and actions. The Phaeacians are so entranced by their guest that they increase their already generous gifts in recognition of his self-proclaimed fame and virtuosity, demonstrating at the same time their superior understanding of the laws of *xenia* (hospitality – see below), but as 'Homer's audience' do we feel wiser and more critical than Odysseus's Phaeacian listeners?

The poet engages his audience by creating moral complications. Clearly the Cyclops is the villain and Odysseus the hero, but details of the Cyclops' domestic arrangements and care for his flock, his affectionate words for his old ram and his wisdom after the event, soften the impression of man-eating monster. This may be comic or arouse pathos, depending on the performance and listener's sensitivities, but it adds depth to the lonely figure of the Cyclops. On the other hand, Odysseus is arguably at his least sympathetic when he insists on exploring the cave and meeting its resident 'in case he might give me guest-gifts' (*Od.* 9.229), or when he provokes the creature he has blinded, if only because he repeatedly endangers the lives of his own men.

Polyphemus is undeniably guilty of brutishly perverting *xenia* (the rules of hospitality safeguarded by Zeus) by eating rather than feeding Odysseus' men, offering the barbaric 'guest-gift' of being devoured last if Odysseus will give away his name and trapping his guests in his cave rather than sending them on their way; when they finally do contrive their escape, he provides an escort of ballistic missiles (*Od.* 9.252–542). Not for him the nicety in Menelaus' gracious parting words, 'hurrying a guest reluctant to go is just as bad as detaining one who wants to stay' (*Od.* 15.72–3). On the other hand, Odysseus and his men offer some provocation: like pirates, they help themselves to the produce of the flocks Polyphemus tends and we laugh less hard at each of Odysseus' clever tricks. These anxieties may be more problematic for a modern reader than for an ancient one, but they are difficult to edit out entirely. Part of Homer's skill as a storyteller is the way he draws his listener in to the action and its consequences, forcing us to engage with as well as to enjoy the tale.

GODS AND MORTALS

A defining feature of the poetic world of the two Homeric poems is that it is inhabited by gods as well as by men. These gods, though human in form, character and speech, are distinguished from man by their scale, immortality and powers. When Poseidon roars to rally the Trojans his cry is like the voice of nine or ten thousand men (*Il.* 14.148–51); when Athene smashes Ares' head with a rock and he falls to the ground his body covers seven *plethra* (*Il.* 21.407: a *plethron* is 10,000 square feet). Pressed by the Trojans, the Greeks labour to build a wall around their camp, which Apollo destroys with complete ease, like a child on a beach playing with a sandcastle (*Il.* 7.436–41 and 15.361–4). When gods appear to mortals, they generally do so disguised as mortals, as in the final battle of the *Odyssey* when Athene supports Odysseus looking like Mentor. Despite her mortal appearance, she retains her divine power: the goddess' cry makes the colour drain from the Ithacans' cheeks and the weapons drop from their hands (*Od.* 24.502–35).

An impression of the gods' power is given by the way they move. For mortals, travel is slow and perilous, as tales in the *Odyssey* constantly reinforce. Odysseus sails for 18 days after leaving Calypso's remote island and, after his raft is wrecked, he swims for a further two days before he sees land; even then he is challenged as to how he can reach the shore without destroying himself. By contrast, when the winged god Hermes visits Calypso's island he skims the waves like a sea-gull after a fish (*Od.* 5.50–54). Gods cover distances with consummate ease and pace, as when Iris drops through the waters to Thetis like a lead sinker (*Il.* 24.80–82) or through the air like snow or hail (*Il.* 15.170).

Gods and mortals do not eat the same food: Calypso serves Hermes nectar and ambrosia but when, shortly afterwards, Odysseus occupies the same chair, 'she placed beside him all kinds of food to eat and drink – the sort that mortal men eat' (*Od.* 5.196–7) There is a rare exception to this distinction in the *Iliad* when Athene, 'dripped nectar and lovely ambrosia into the breast of Achilles' (*Il.* 19.352–4) countering Achilles' stubborn refusal to eat until he has avenged Patroclus' death, but Achilles is a special case, as Hera argues elsewhere when she contrasts Achilles, the son of a goddess and her special protégé, with Hector, 'a mortal who suckled at a woman's breast' (*Il.* 24.58); Achilles is truly 'god-like' when, even before he has rejoined the fighting, his battle-cry from the Greek ditch terrifies 12 Trojans to their deaths as Athene's fire flashes round his temples (*Il.* 18.223–31). When gods eat or drink, it seems to be purely social or for pleasure, for mortals it is essential, as the shrewd commander Odysseus insists when he gives orders that the men *must* eat before battle 'so that we can fight the enemy harder and relentlessly' (*Il.* 19.231–2), or acknowledges, when he assumes the role of destitute beggar in Ithaca, 'it is impossible to hide an eager stomach, a deadly thing that brings man much trouble: people fit out fine-benched ships and sail over the barren sea bringing trouble to their enemies because of it' (*Od.* 17.286–9).

Ambrosia (which literally means 'non-mortal') has other qualities – Hera washes in it before her seduction of Zeus (*Il.* 14.170–1) and Thetis uses it to keep the body of Patroclus, Achilles' dead companion, from decay; she drips ambrosia and nectar through his nostrils to stop flies laying maggot-eggs in his decomposing flesh, the graphic fear Achilles expresses (*Il.* 19.38–9). Blood runs in mortal veins, and is spilt fatally, 'his liver slid out and his lap filled with the black blood that poured from it. Darkness hid his eyes as he lost his life' (*Il.* 20.470–2). But the gods have *ichōr*. When, as we saw earlier, the goddess Aphrodite is wounded in the hand by Diomedes, her mother Dione 'wiped away the *ichōr* from her hand with both of hers. The hand healed and the fierce pain was soothed' (*Il.* 5.416–7).

Most fundamentally, though, gods are immortal. Death is as impossible for gods as it is inevitable for mortals. We get glimpses of what this means for mortals in both poems. The ghost of Patroclus appears to Achilles 'exactly as he was, in size, lovely eyes and voice' (*Il.* 23.65–6). Patroclus laments that he and Achilles will never more in life 'sit away from our dear companions and lay our plans' (*Il.* 23.77–8) and requests a swift burial so that he can cross the river of the underworld into Hades' realm of the dead. As Achilles tries to touch him one last time, the ghost 'disappeared underground like smoke, twittering' (*Il.* 23.100–1). The same twittering sound is used three times in the opening lines of *Odyssey* 24 where the cries of the souls of the dead suitors being ushered to Hades are likened to the noises of bats in a cave. When Odysseus meets Achilles in the underworld, the ghost is only able to speak after it has drunk sacrificial blood; he then summarizes the emptiness of death in famous words, 'Do not speak lightly of death, glorious Odysseus. I would rather be a land-slave to an impoverished man who barely had the means to live than be king over all the lost dead' (*Od.* 11.488–93). Life after death exists in faint reflection, a suspended, insubstantial world lightened for Achilles only by the news Odysseus gives him of his living son. All this intensifies the brilliance of life.

The epithets most frequently used of the gods are *athanatos* and *ageraos* 'immortal' and 'ageless'. More literally, these mean 'free from death' and 'free from old-age'. Given what we have seen of the dead Achilles, this sounds alluring, but it is the offer Odysseus 'by far the best of mortal men in counsel and speech' (*Od.* 13.297–8) rejects when he leaves Calypso. Escaping the misery of death does not necessarily imply happiness for immortals: Calypso's wretched loneliness could be interminable and a divine mother's loss of her son in his prime, like the loss which Thetis with her divine knowledge anticipates throughout the *Iliad*, is a tragedy with no hope of closure. Zeus sums up the misery of parallel mortal and immortal worlds when Achilles' horses stand listless on the battlefield and weep warm tears for Patroclus, 'Unhappy pair, why did we give you to lord Peleus, a mortal, when you are free from age and death? Was it so that you might share the pain of wretched men? Nothing is more miserable than man, of all the creatures that breathe and creep on earth!' (*Il.* 17.443–6).

All-powerful Zeus?

Homer's gods are not entirely ageless or timeless in the more conventional sense: Zeus recalls when, like love-sick adolescents, he and Hera 'first lay together in love and used to creep into bed, evading their dear parents' notice' (*Il.* 14.295–6). As brother and sister, they have just one set of parents, Cronus and Rhea, and their father, as Zeus pointedly reminds Hera after an argument, sits 'enjoying neither the rays of Hyperion the Sun nor any breeze, enclosed by the depths of Tartarus' (*Il.* 8.479–81), ousted from power by Zeus himself. The full story of this usurpation of power through three generations (Ouranos-Cronus-Zeus) is told in Hesiod's *Theogony* (see 3b).

In the *Iliad* there are subtle reminders that the divine *status quo*, with Zeus as supreme ruler, is relatively recent and not necessarily stable. At the start of the poem we learn that the nymph Thetis has a favour to call in, as she once protected Zeus from a *coup d'état* led by his sister-wife, Hera, his brother, Poseidon, and daughter, Athene (*Il.* 1.396–406). By granting this favour Zeus agrees to give the Trojans supremacy during Achilles' absence from the battlefield and this leads to further friction with Hera and Poseidon in particular. Zeus has to assert his dominance over his younger brother, 'Since I am much stronger than him in might and older by birth; but his heart has the effrontery to claim equality with me, whom all others dread' (*Il.* 15.165–7). In response to this Poseidon reminds Zeus that they are brothers and equals in so far as each was allocated his own realm – Zeus the sky, Poseidon the sea, the third brother, Hades, the underworld, but that 'earth and great Olympus were common to all' (*Il.* 15.187–93). Nevertheless, Poseidon, like Hera, acknowledges Zeus's superior strength 'I would not like the rest of us to fight against Zeus, son of Cronus, since he is far stronger' (*Il.* 8.210–1) and is willing to obey him, provided Zeus keeps to the understanding that Troy will eventually fall.

The road to that fate, however, is a tortuous one. At the very beginning of the poem we are told that the will of Zeus is near completion (*Il.* 1.5). We can reasonably assume that this refers to the fall of Troy, a fate confirmed later when Odysseus recalls the interpretation by the seer Calchas of an omen sent by Zeus. But Zeus' will, and indeed the course of fate, is not always so clear. Apart from the fact that Zeus has to reprimand the other gods for not following his instructions on at least a couple of occasions (notably *Il.* 8.5ff. and 15.14ff.), he himself also has an unclear relationship with fate.

The will of Zeus, for instance, is not a clearly defined thing. We do not quite know whether it is equivalent to fate or not; what we do know, however, is that the other gods see Zeus' will as something that can be changed or adapted, especially if they appeal to fate (*aisa*). We also see that Zeus himself ponders different courses of action and gives his nod to various requests. However, when he balances his golden scales, placing two fates in the pans to see which side will fall, and holds the beam in the centre, he allows another force to do its work. This arrangement is not, though, always to Zeus' liking. When confronted by the imminent death of his son, Sarpedon, Zeus contemplates challenging what has been determined, until Hera's threat that 'none of the rest of us gods will approve', silences him and he is left to express his grief by raining drops of blood on the plain of Troy (*Il.* 16.433–61).

Beyond this, it must be noted that Zeus sometimes seems to act against himself and the fate that he (apparently) administers. So, while it is made clear that Zeus is in some way the guarantor of Troy's fall, he is led by Thetis' supplication (*Il.* 1.503 ff.) to initiate a series of actions that nearly brings about a Trojan victory. The Greeks, without Achilles, are thoroughly routed (with Zeus' help); they are saved first by the intervention of Patroclus and then by Achilles. Zeus, having earlier ordered the gods to avoid the battlefield, now urges them to get involved again, worried that Achilles might take Troy, contrary to what is fated (*Il.* 20.30).

Zeus' fallibility

Agamemnon, the most powerful mortal ruler, who is beset by rather more significant problems of leadership than Zeus, regrets his foolishness in slighting Achilles and argues that even Zeus has fallen victim to folly (*atē*): by an unfortunate miscalculation Zeus allowed Hera to persecute his most famous illegitimate son, the hero Heracles. Agamemnon tactfully implies that Zeus' authority was actually strengthened as a consequence: in a symbolic act Zeus literally flung Folly away to work her damage on men, to Agamemnon's cost (*Il*. 19.95–131)!

Nevertheless, a vestige of Zeus' fallibility remains as we see in the glorious scene where Hera exploits her husband's sexual susceptibility. Reinforcing her own charms with a girdle borrowed from Aphrodite 'highly decorated, wrought with every charm, incorporating love, desire and sweet talk, which robs even the wise of their sanity' (*Il*. 14.215–7), Hera distracts Zeus's attention from the critical struggle between Greeks and Trojans on which his eyes have been fixed. While, in accordance with Zeus' will, the Trojans sweep Hera's beloved Greeks back through their battered defences and the Greeks debate what to do next, the goddess takes matters into her own hands. Zeus awakes from Hera's arms to see his Trojan champion Hector spitting blood, but his reaction is surprisingly gracious. He gives reassurances for the future and merely reminds Hera of the special punishment reserved for her last time: 'you were hung on high, and from your feet I suspended two anvils, while round your hands I fastened an unbreakable chain of gold. You hung in the sky among the clouds and the gods throughout mighty Olympus were furious' (*Il*. 15.18–21); on this occasion there is no recourse to violence. Hera's spirit is not wholly broken, 'Though she smiled with her lips, her forehead over her black brows was not softened' (*Il*. 15.101–2), but her meddling, like Poseidon's complaints, seems now to represent no serious challenge to the authority of Zeus.

One of the arguments used by those who think the author of the *Iliad* may not be the same as that of the *Odyssey* is the difference in the representation of the gods within the two poems. In the *Odyssey*, Hera hardly features. The friction and occasional humour that her role as scheming wife inspires are gone and Zeus is less under attack. Otherwise, with the exception of various nymphs, the cast of divine characters is much the same in both poems: Zeus, Athene, Hermes and Poseidon all play prominent roles. Following a similar pattern to that in the *Iliad*, we learn near the start of the poem from the interpretation of a bird omen sent by Zeus, that Odysseus will return to his native Ithaca. The seer Halitherses predicts that Odysseus will 'suffer much, lose all his companions and reach home, wholly unrecognized, in the twentieth year' (*Od*. 2.174–5). The only god who opposes his homecoming is Poseidon, angry because Odysseus blinded his son Polyphemus the Cyclops. In the *Iliad*, as we have seen, Poseidon also opposes Zeus when he allows the Trojans success on the battlefield. A detailed comparison of Poseidon's role in the two poems may help us to explore differences between them, in particular their thematic and moral agendas.

Poseidon in the *Iliad* and *Odyssey*

Like many of the moments of divine interference in the *Iliad*, Poseidon's rallying of the Greeks, which begins when he emerges in his chariot from

the sea, clad in gold, and ends when he sinks back into his realm on Zeus'
command (*Il.* 13.17–15.219), is a poetic way of representing what might
anyway have happened. Hector has just led the Trojan assault on the Greek
wall and broken inside their fortifications: the Greeks need to rally if they
are to survive and surely the adrenaline must be pumping! This technique
is sometimes known as 'dual determination' – the action can be explained
in two different ways, as divinely motivated or as a natural human
response. When Poseidon approaches the two Ajaxes, in the form of the
seer Calchas, his words breathe spirit into them in much the same way that
Athene's presence as Mentes breathes spirit into Telemachus (*Od.* 1.320–3).
The human characters feel their spirits lift with the presence of the god,
just as later the Greeks experience an inexplicable sense of loss when
Poseidon departs. Using this dramatic technique the poet gives his audience a clearer understanding of the feelings of those involved in the action
than they have themselves. At the same time, in this instance the audience
are helped to follow the movement of the story: the appearance and later
disappearance of the god frames an episode – the rallying of the Greeks in
the face of the Trojans' advance. Poseidon's disappearance is an indicator
that this section is at an end and the final movement of Zeus's plan is now
in motion (*Il.* 15.59–71).

Although Poseidon, as god of the sea, has more of an allegorical role in the
Odyssey, a similar pattern of divine intervention applies to both poems.
Poseidon's anger becomes a framing device for the first half of the *Odyssey*,
from his first mention as the god who is filled with 'violent rage against god-
like Odysseus' (*Od.* 1.20; in Greek, Odysseus' very name comes to signify the
hatred Poseidon bears him: *odyssomai* = *I hate/am angry with*) to the prayers and
sacrifices offered to him by the fearful Phaeacian leaders who have deposited
Odysseus safe and sound on his island kingdom (*Od.* 13.185–7). The audience
recognize Poseidon both as an individual god motivated by anger and as a
representation of the cosmic forces that confront Odysseus and any man who
entrusts himself to the sea.

In the *Iliad*, Poseidon supports the Greeks but shows admirable personal
qualities in his willingness to moderate the excesses of other gods, taking on
the role of peace-maker. He stops Hera from letting the violence escalate once
Zeus allows the gods to join the fighting, 'Hera, don't let your anger exceed
your sense. There is no need for you to do so. I would not want god to be
driven against fellow god in strife' (*Il.* 20.133–5); he also tries to reason with
Apollo who supports the Trojans, but who shows his respect by refusing to
enter into conflict with his uncle 'over wretched mortals – who are like leaves'
(*Il.* 21.463–6). Poseidon plays a similar role in the section of the *Odyssey*
where the bard Demodocus is singing his song about the illicit love of Ares
and Aphrodite to the Phaeacians and Odysseus. Poseidon steps in, like a
senior statesman, to resolve the scandalous but amusing tension of the
trapped adulterers by gravely offering to pay Ares' fine (*Od.* 8.344–8).

When Poseidon intervenes later in the *Iliad*, he is again motivated in part by a sense of responsibility, but this time he acts on behalf of a mortal, the Trojan Aeneas. Aeneas is the first serious opponent to face Achilles when he rejoins the fighting after Patroclus' death. Inspired to fight by Apollo, he finds himself in a deadly situation (*Il.* 20.290–1). The poet could have chosen Aphrodite, Aeneas' divine mother, to save her son for his divine destiny (to rule whatever remained of Troy after its destruction), even if her earlier attempt had proved painfully unsuccessful and led to her being warned off the battlefield by Apollo (*Il.* 5.311–43). The Trojan-hating Poseidon is therefore a surprising agent in the ruthless context of war, 'Why does this man now suffer pointlessly for another man's grief when he is not to blame?' (*Il.* 20.297–8). The god's compassion foreshadows the closing movement of the poem when the hero learns to pity his enemy, king Priam. Poseidon's is not the only act or expression of pity to come from a god in the *Iliad*, but it contributes to an overall sense of humanity in the poem. The gods, not all of them good, are represented as individual moral agents in the *Iliad*.

The *Odyssey*, like the *Iliad*, also draws to a close with the hero pitying an old man (Odysseus' reunion with Laertes in *Odyssey* 24), but this is merely the prelude to the final resolution of the drama, when three generations of Odysseus' family stand ready to fight, as the gods bring to an abrupt end their feud with the suitors' families. Like the *Iliad*, it is a poem about revenge on an epic scale, yet, unlike the *Iliad*, compassion, as we shall see, is far from evident in this context. Instead, the poem focuses with unmistakable clarity on the universal consequences of transgression (*atasthalia*). Let us see how Poseidon fits into this pattern by first considering the punishment of the lesser Ajax, a minor episode recounted by Menelaus to Telemachus on his visit to Sparta.

Poseidon wrecked but then rescued Ajax, son of Oileus, who 'would have escaped death in spite of Athene's wrath had he not let fly an arrogant boast, showing great folly, by saying that he had escaped the mighty gulf of ocean against the gods' wishes' (*Od.* 4.502–4). For this blasphemy Poseidon split the rock he was clinging to and drowned him. This is a pattern of divine punishment central to Homeric and later Greek thought, an example of divine retribution for human arrogance or recklessness. There are examples of this in the *Iliad*, such as when the omniscient narrator suddenly springs us forward in time to the moment when, after the sack of Troy, Apollo, Poseidon and Zeus will demolish the defences the Achaeans built around their ships. 'It was built against the immortal gods' will' says the poet 'and did not stand firm for long' (*Il.* 12.8–9). In the *Odyssey*, however, this pattern of interaction between gods and men is more central.

In the first half of the *Odyssey*, Poseidon's desire for revenge takes two different forms: he wishes to punish Odysseus for his act of violence against his son the Cyclops, but also to teach the Phaeacians a lesson for providing

Odysseus and others with the means of getting home safely by ship. Let us consider these two cases in turn.

Poseidon, Odysseus and Polyphemus

Odysseus's crime against Poseidon is that he has blinded the sea-god's son; we may feel some sympathy for Polyphemus as he prays to his father for vengeance. Poseidon's anger seems justified and 'proportionality' is not something we generally associate with Greek gods, but the sea god's 'vengeance' seems unimpressive. Rather than drown him at once, as he did Ajax, he waits while Odysseus is subjected to a series of set-backs at sea, like the opening of the bag of winds, the destruction of his fleet in the harbour of the Laestrygonians, the long journey to the underworld and the devastating consequences of his men's decision to devour the cattle of the Sun. Not one of these is explicitly Poseidon's doing, and the most devastating punishment is visited by Zeus (*Od.* 12.415–7):

> In a single move Zeus thundered and struck the ship with his thunderbolt. The whole ship quivered, stricken by Zeus's thunderbolt and as she filled with sulphur, the men tumbled out.

We do not see the final effects of Poseidon's rage until after Odysseus' seven-year sojourn with Calypso when, chancing to see him bobbing on the waves, Poseidon wrecks his home-built raft and retorts, 'Roam the seas, then, after your long suffering, until you find yourself among a people favoured by Zeus. I don't expect you'll count your misfortunes trifling!' (*Od.* 5.377–9). These are hardly words to inspire terror and awe and Poseidon's powers seem emasculated. Later Poseidon confirms that he has accepted Odysseus' return to Ithaca out of deference to Zeus' will, manifested by his nod (*Od.* 13.131). Poseidon, like Zeus in the *Iliad* dropping tears of blood for his son, is constrained by some power, perhaps the collective will of the gods now securely united under Zeus. Poseidon's hatred is tamed, just as 'the father of gods and men' had confidently predicted to Athene: 'Poseidon will relax his anger. For he will not be able to struggle against the united will of the immortal gods on his own' (*Od.* 1.77–9).

Are other powers at work? The words Polyphemus uses in his prayer that Odysseus may never get home have the ring of 'fate' or prophecy about them: 'but if it is his destiny (*moira*) to see his loved ones and reach his well-built house and his native land, let his coming be wretched and late, let him lose all his companions, arrive on a foreign ship and find troubles in his home' (*Od.* 9.532–5) and as soon as Polyphemus hears the name 'Odysseus' he recalls the words of the prophet-Cyclops, Telemus 'that I would be spoiled of my sight at the hands of Odysseus' (*Od.* 9.512). This may have implications for how we view Odysseus' actions, but the authority behind the prophecy seems to be none other than Zeus himself, as is explicitly the case early in the poem when the seer Halitherses interprets the omen of the eagles sent by Zeus as a warning to the suitors.

Poseidon and the Phaeacians

Poseidon's second revenge in the Odyssey is less personal. He is not a father standing up for the injury done his son, but a primal power. As 'sea-god' he resents the safe-passage that Phaeacians offer their guests in their ships that steer by their own wits (*Od.* 8.556), reducing the hazardous element inherent in sea-faring. Nevertheless, the simple good-hearted warmth the Phaeacians, themselves descended from Poseidon, display to Odysseus makes their punishment seem harsh. They too are subject to a prophecy, known to Alcinous and his father, that a Phaeacian ship would be turned to stone in the harbour and the city ringed with mountains. This is to be a lesson, a warning to the Phaeacians of Poseidon's 'resentment at their offering safe passage to all' (*Od.* 13.173–4).

Poseidon seeks revenge out of anxiety for his dignity, which he expresses to his brother: 'Father Zeus, I will no longer go honoured among the immortal gods since these Phaeacian mortals will not pay me honour . . . '. Zeus responds diplomatically and authoritatively, 'Well, well, mighty earth-shaker, what a thing to say! The gods not honour you! It would be a grave matter if there were to be an attack on the honour of someone so senior and of outstanding character' (*Od.* 13.128–9 and 140–2). Poseidon then fulfils the first part of the prophecy 'with a smack of his hand' (*Od.* 13.164) and the crew is lost. Zeus suggests Poseidon be content with that; simultaneously, the Phaeacians pray for release from the second threat and, though not explicit, we are left with a sense of hope that part of the Phaeacians' punishment may have been evaded. If so, 'fate' has been modified and Poseidon's anger sensitively moderated by Zeus. Things have moved on from the lack of divine cooperation in the *Iliad*. Zeus comes across as a secure and established ruler, respectful to his team, but himself the embodiment of both fate and justice.

Divine punishment in the *Odyssey*

The poem opens with a divine invocation in which Odysseus' men are blamed for their own deaths because they angered the god of the Sun by devouring his cattle. The first glimpse we have of Zeus is of him pondering the fate of Aegisthus, who paid with his life for rejecting divine advice. Both these cases prefigure the climax of the poem, the slaughter of the suitors.

In the case of Aegisthus, who committed adultery and murder despite Zeus sending his messenger Hermes to warn him of the consequences, it is difficult to feel much sympathy or see any moral complexity. Odysseus' men, on the other hand, feel that they are making a direct choice between two deaths when they kill and eat the Sun's cattle. 'Any form of death is abhorrent to wretched mortals, but to die of starvation is the worst way to face the end' (*Od.* 12.341–2). Unable to see any alternative and perhaps to comprehend the crime inherent in eating these non-breeding cosmic cows (*Od.* 12.127–31), they disobey Odysseus' commands and, through loss of faith, forfeit their homecoming. This seems harsh, especially when we have already heard Halitherses' prophecy that Odysseus 'would suffer much, lose all his companions and reach home, wholly unrecognized, in the twentieth year' (*Od.* 2.174–5). Did his men really have the choice implicit in Tiresias' words, 'You may yet reach home, albeit after much suffering, if you are ready to control your own spirits and those of your companions' (*Od.* 11.104–5)?

The ruthless punishment of the suitors presents a similar dilemma, perhaps more acute for a modern reader but a challenge to any audience. While still disguised as a beggar, Odysseus takes Amphinomus with his 'good mind' aside (*Od.* 16.398) and warns him explicitly to keep away from the palace to avoid retribution. Although Amphinomus leaves the interview 'pained in heart, his head down, for his heart sensed trouble' the warning does not save him, 'for him too Athene had bound to defeat at Telemachus's hands and powerful spear' (*Od.* 18.153–6). This is not the only advice given to the suitors. They and their families are warned by a divine omen interpreted by the seer Halitherses to mend their ways before Telemachus sets out on his voyage, but the seer is ridiculed by Eurymachus (*Od.* 2.146–93), and, far from reforming, the suitors take advantage of Telemachus' absence by attempting to murder him on his return. A more surreal omen follows Telemachus' safe return: when Telemachus refuses to force his mother's hand, 'Pallas Athene roused in the suitors a laughter they could not control; she caused their wits to stray. The jaws they laughed with were not their own, spattered with blood and the meat they'd been eating. Their eyes brimmed with tears and the thoughts of their hearts were full of grief' (*Od.* 20.345–50). Theoclymenus, another seer and a suppliant welcomed by Telemachus, follows this up with a dire warning that the suitors seem unable to hear. Like Amphinomus' failure to heed Odysseus' warning, this mental block is psychologically convincing but proves fatal, as smokers know their habit kills but cannot or will not reform. It is precisely the problem that Zeus reflects on at the start of the poem – Aegisthus' blindness to what is good for him.

Divine and human understanding

Humans differ from gods in Homer's poems because their knowledge is restricted. They know they will die, but they do not know when (though Achilles is a partial exception to this), so Hector facing Achilles considers the remote but, to him, real possibility that he might defeat Achilles, 'If Zeus grants that I last through this and I take your life, I shall inflict no terrible disgrace' (*Il.* 22.256–7). Hope and fear are both products of this ignorance, so Andromache and her maids 'grieved for Hector in his own house, though he lived, for they declared that he would no more return again from war, escaping the might and hands of the Achaeans' (*Il.* 6.500–2), but 'had called to the lovely-haired maids in the house to set a great tripod over the fire so that there would be hot water for Hector when he came home from battle' (*Il.* 22.442–4). While her husband's corpse is trailing from Achilles' chariot she sits 'embroidering elaborate flowers into thick purple cloth' (*Il.* 22.441). Achilles experiences the same shock at news of Patroclus's death. It is part of Achilles' godlike nature that his mother Thetis 'would report back to him mighty Zeus' every thought', in particular that if he fights he will die before the sack of Troy, a burden of knowledge that informs his behaviour; 'but on this occasion his mother had not told him the terrible thing that had happened, that his best-loved companion by far was dead' (*Il.* 17.409–11). It is partly by contrast with the world of the gods and partly as omniscient narrator that Homer uses dramatic irony to point up so delicately the tragic nature of the limits of human understanding; another theme, like the rejection of prophetic advice, later by developed the tragedians of the fifth century.

Like Achilles, some of Odysseus' godlike qualities come from his unique understanding of the world around him and close relationship with the gods. The same could be said of the swineherd Eumaeus who also earns the heroic epithet *dios* (godlike/noble). Eumaeus is singled out in the *Odyssey*, as is Achilles (occasionally) and Patroclus (frequently) in the *Iliad*, to be addressed affectionately by the poet in the second person. 'And you, swineherd Eumaeus, addressed him in response' (*Od.* 14.165). Both Patroclus and Eumaeus are remarkable for their kindness, sensitivity and loyalty. Athene directs Odysseus to Eumaeus' hut to stage his reunion with Telemachus, 'His thoughts towards you are kind, he loves your son and your discreet Penelope' (*Od.* 13.405–6). Odysseus is welcomed with exemplary generosity but can't resist testing the limits with a calculating story 'to see if he would take off his cloak and give it to him' (*Od.* 14.460–1). As we have seen, Eumaeus enjoys Odysseus' stories, but expects no return for his hospitality from his guest (*Od.* 14.388–9): 'That is not the reason for my respect and friendship for you; that comes from fear of Zeus, god of guests, and pity for you.'

Homer's most powerful god in the *Odyssey*, Zeus, is the champion of the weakest, of suppliants, beggars and strangers. Contrasting starkly with the wilful and reprehensible ignorance of the suitors, Eumaeus' wisdom and intuitive respect for Zeus' compassionate and just divine order makes him an unlikely but memorable 'godlike/noble' hero. This is not so different from the *Iliad* which closes with an act of compassion as the 'godlike/noble' Achilles earns the heroic accolade paid to him by Zeus, 'he is not witless, sightless or godless, but will show a suppliant true and heartfelt mercy' (*Il.* 24.157–8).

The gods of both the *Iliad* and *Odyssey* are awe-inspiring figures: Apollo in the opening sequence of the Iliad presents a terrifying figure, 'The arrows clashed on the shoulders of the god as he moved in anger. He came like night'

(*Il*. 1.46–7). The thunderbolt hurled by aegis-bearing Zeus to close the *Odyssey* is a symbolic reminder of that power. Some of the time Homer's gods seem whimsical and cruel, as when Athene pretends to fight by Hector's side as Deiphobus or Apollo smacks Patroclus on the back, exposing him to his death blow, but they accept a concept of *moira/aisa* (fate) and ultimately behave as guardians of a compassionate moral code. Acknowledgement of their power is necessary but not sufficient to ensure human prosperity, so the women of Troy may offer Athene in her temple in the heart of their citadel a most precious robe and pray with fervour, unaware that her answer to their prayer is a curt and devastating nod of refusal. Our humanity is defined in Homer's poetry by reference to the things we lack: we are not immortal, age-less, free from physical concerns or omniscient; we have to face death, physi-cal suffering, loss, hope and fear, but we may become god-like in the struggle and, with a poet to celebrate it, immortal in the attempt.

HOMERIC VALUES

In *Iliad* 22 Hector makes the agonizing choice to stand and face Achilles in mortal combat but, as Achilles approaches, Hector begins to run for his life (*Il*. 22.158–61):

> Ahead, a brave man was in flight, but pursuing him was one far better, moving swiftly, since the two men were not competing for a sacrificial animal or for an ox-hide shield – the prizes for men in a foot-race – but for the soul of horse-taming Hector.

To a modern reader, the comparison between a man's life and a material object like a shield seems grimly ironic; even the evaluation of Achilles as 'far better' than Hector is an uncomfortable concept in our own self-consciously egalitarian age. Such evaluations are, however, commonplace in both poems and to some extent they are one of the means by which big questions are explored: what is a man's life – or his dead body – worth? How should one value a woman?

Female value

Let us start with the last question. Women play a driving role in both poems. In the *Odyssey*, the hero's longing to return to his wife keeps him going and is so strong that he ranks growing old with her above the 'immortality and agelessness' offered by the nymph Calypso. Early in the *Iliad*, we are reminded that this war is being fought for Helen. The old men of Troy watch her on the battlements and agree, 'Nothing for the Trojans and well-greaved Achaeans to resent, suffering long years of pain over a woman like this!' (*Il*. 3.156–7). No doubt is left over the course of the *Iliad* as to just how immense those agonies are, so is their remark flippant, a well-worn cliché, or are we to take seriously the idea that the lives and suffering of countless men and women are of less value than one woman's beauty? By contrast, when Achilles sets out the prizes for the wrestling competition in the funeral games for Patroclus, 'a woman highly skilled in handicrafts' is second prize after 'a great tripod to go over the fire'. The watching Greeks assess these prizes more precisely: the tripod is worth twelve oxen, the woman four (*Il.* 23.700–5).

What are the qualities for which women are valued? One of Penelope's suitors, the vile Antinous, lists the queen's strengths: 'her skill in fine handicrafts, her excellent wits and her wiles the like of which we've never heard, even from long ago, from the lovely haired Achaean women of old, like Tyro, Alcmene and garlanded Mycene . . . ' (*Od.* 2.117–20). Agamemnon, rejecting a father's 'countless ransom', compares the captive Chryseis to his own wife, 'she is in no way inferior to her, in figure, stature, wit or handicrafts' (*Il.* 1.114–5). Beauty, brains and skills might, then, constitute a list of objective female standards as judged by men, with surprisingly little emphasis on child-bearing capacity. Motherhood, then as now, conferred status; the love Hector so clearly feels for Andromache is in part for the mother of his son and Hecuba's unchallenged position as chief queen presumably rests partly on the 19 out of 50 sons she bore Priam, but greater emphasis is placed in the *Iliad* on Hecuba's advice and lifelong companionship, like the relationship between Alcinous and Arete or Odysseus and Penelope. One might sense a silent reproach in the childless nature of Helen's and Paris' liaison, but there is no sense of Helen's failure as a woman in only ever producing a single daughter.

Wealth and breeding are also relevant: another of Priam's wives, Laothoe, as well as being the mother of Lycaon and Polydrus, has status through her dowry (*Il.* 22.48–51). The daughter of a rich man, like Eetion's daughter Andromache, might be 'richly dowered', and have fetched 'a countless bride-price' from Hector, prince of Troy, but no woman's value is fixed: Hector imagines the day his wife may have to face the indignities of slavery, 'in Argos, weaving at another woman's loom and carrying water . . . ' (*Il.* 6.456–7).

Let us consider the case of one particular woman, Briseis, the source of so much anger and wounded pride in the *Iliad*. Is this because of who she is or what she represents? Like Helen, she is the focus of a male dispute and she is delicately sketched. Initially she is introduced as a simple matter of compensation, a girl for a girl: Briseis for Chryseis. Each is a *geras*, a gift of honour awarded to a man; they share an epithet, 'fair-cheeked'. Even their names are equivalent, names that simply mean 'daughter of . . . '. We eventually learn about Briseis' life before she is taken prisoner in *Iliad* 19 when, on the news of Patroclus' death, she recalls his acts of kindness. 'I saw the husband my father and lady mother gave me, lie in front of our city cut by sharp bronze. The three brothers my mother bore, whom I loved, all faced their day of death. But when swift Achilles killed my husband and sacked the city of god-like Mynes, you would not let me weep; you said you would make me godlike Achilles' wedded wife' (*Il.* 19.291–8). Even before this passage, Briseis has started to move from 'tripod status' to that of an active agent and honoured human being. In book 1, we learn that she is taken from Achilles' hut by Agamemnon 'against her will' (*Il.* 1.348). When attempts are made to soften Achilles' anger in *Iliad* 9 and the offer is made to give Briseis back – along with seven other choice women – Achilles bridles at the offer and tries to set his feelings in context (*Il.* 9.335–43):

> Of all the Achaeans it is my wife he has chosen, who pleased me well . . .
> Of all men graced with speech is it only the sons of Atreus who love their
> wives? Any good man with any sense loves and cares for his own woman,
> as I loved this woman from the heart, though I won her by my spear.

The question of whether or not Agamemnon has slept with Briseis matters; although in *Iliad* 9 he vows that he has not, he is forced to swear a formal oath to that effect in *Iliad* 19. Here then, we see an amalgamation of wartime values with those of peace: even allowing for rhetoric, Achilles reveres Briseis in language not dissimilar to the wise words of Odysseus, offering advice to Nausicaa as she approaches the threshold of marriage, 'There is nothing better or finer than when a man and a woman who share the same thoughts keep house; they cause their enemies great grief and their friends great joy, benefiting themselves from their reputation' (*Od.* 6.182–5). When Achilles sleeps with Briseis at the end of the poem, the act has more significance than that recommended by his mother – 'it is a good thing to make love to a woman' (*Il.* 24.130–1; 675–6) – it is a moment of harmony in the brief stretch of life that Achilles has before him and a whispered promise of future loss.

Male values

Although women are important in both poems, the great momentum of the *Iliad* is fired by Achilles' wild response to the loss of his male friend, Patroclus, leaving sentimental musings about Briseis in the shade. When Patroclus dies, Achilles' behaviour has all the excess of a bereaved lover. The intimacy between the two men is unique and there is no doubt that *this* man is valued by Achilles above any woman. Some of Patroclus' qualities are no different from those valued in women, his companionship and advice, his gentleness, perhaps his skills as cook and healer, but Achilles mourns above all for Patroclus' lost 'manliness', a word cognate with bravery. Patroclus' final and defining moments are as a reckless killing machine, embodying many of the warlike elements that make up the Homeric hero: 'Patroclus came out like Ares' (*Il.* 11.604).

Let us consider the qualities that define heroism and confer male status in the two poems. The best men are strong and brave, driven by a desire for glory (*kleos*) and concerned that they be treated with honour and respect (*timē*). This drive can make Homeric heroes seem profoundly egocentric, with little care for those who may be dependent on them. Achilles, in response to what he feels is Agamemnon's slight to his honour, seems content that the Greeks should suffer as a result of his absence from the battlefield. The advice given by a father to his son as he set off to fight at Troy, 'always to be the best and to surpass others' (*Il*. 6.208) underlines the competitive nature of these values. A hero may excel and win glory through his actions, his words or his wit. So when Hector challenges any Greek to a duel in *Iliad* 7, he imagines the fame victory in action would bring him (*Il*. 7.90): 'Someone perhaps from a future generation as he sails over the wine dark sea in his many-benched ship will say, "This mound marks a man long since dead, killed at the height of his powers by glorious Hector".'

Although advanced in years, his past actions celebrated mainly in his own words, Nestor received 'lovely-haired Hecamede' as a heroic prize or *geras* 'since he surpassed everyone in giving advice' (*Il*. 11.626–7). Odysseus, famed for his wits, is keen to hear how he has been immortalized by Demodocus for his part in the trick of the wooden horse, ironically offering the storyteller himself glory: 'If you tell the tale as it really was, I shall declare at once to all men how generous the god has been in his gift of divine song' (*Od*. 8.497–8). Fame, then as now, cuts both ways and Helen imagines her and Paris' eternal notoriety, 'Zeus has set down a grim fate for us, to be the subject of songs for future generations in years to come' (*Il*. 6.357–8).

As with women, physical beauty is a prized quality in a man, Achilles is not only the best fighter at Troy, he is also the most handsome. This factor is perhaps best illustrated by the counter-example of Thersites whose extreme ugliness, mercilessly detailed in *Iliad* 2, denotes an equally despicable character. Nonetheless, a man's appearance may be deceptive, like the rude Phaeacian Euryalus, of whom Odysseus says, 'You are a fine-looking man, not even a god could match you – but you are an idiot' (*Od*. 8.176–7); Odysseus is equally direct with the suitor Antinous 'Ah well, too much, then, to expect brains on top of beauty!' (*Od*. 17.454). Furthermore, it was no secret to the Greeks that physical beauty is subject to the ravages of time. Priam's last plea to Hector not to risk his life includes the lines (*Il*. 22.71–6):

> All looks well when a young man is slain in war and lies cut by the sharp bronze; though dead all there is to see is beautiful. But when the grey head and grey beard and genitals of an old man are disfigured by dogs, nothing is more pitiful for wretched mortals.

The loss of status that accompanies physical decline is nowhere better exemplified than in the pitiful picture that greets Odysseus when he finally sees his father: 'No gentle care is bestowed upon you, but you bear grievous old age and go foully unwashed and shamefully dressed' (*Od*. 24.249–50); but even Laertes' abject state does not fool his son and cannot conceal his princely qualities, 'but to look at you, there is nothing servile in your looks or build'

(*Od*. 24.252–3). When Athene works on Laertes' appearance, as she has for both Telemachus and Odysseus at key moments in the poem, even the shrewd Odysseus is amazed at the transformation (*Od*. 24.370–1) as Laertes regains heroic stature.

Physical and mental qualities combined with the desire for fame are not sufficient for heroic status. Birth and material wealth are of key importance. A bastard son has lower status than a true born one, as exemplified in the harmonious partnership of Ajax and his half brother Teucer (*Il*. 8.266–72):

> Teucer, pulling his curved bow taut, took his stand from under the shield of Telamonian Ajax. Ajax would cover him there with his shield, then the hero, peeping out, would shoot his arrow and hit someone in the crowd who would fall right there, his life lost. And like a child sheltering under his mother, he would move back again to Ajax who would conceal him with his gleaming shield.

Teucer's choice of weapon, the bow and arrows, is an indication that he, like Paris, is a lesser fighter than his brother, however deadly his aim. Agamemnon has higher status than Achilles because, as Nestor says, 'a sceptred king to whom Zeus has granted glory is never equalled in his share of honour' (*Il*. 1.280). Agamemnon's status, like Teucer's, is derived both from his parentage, Atreus' son, and also from the physical object, the sceptre, which he wields so incompetently for much of the *Iliad*.

Objects of value themselves confer value: by wearing Achilles' armour, Patroclus is elevated; by stripping it from him and wearing it himself, Hector's heroic status is greatly enhanced; putting on the gift of new, divinely made armour from his mother is part of Achilles' path to undying fame. Sometimes an object has intrinsic value because of its materials, like bronze cauldrons or the lump of pig-iron used as both discus and prize in the funeral games for Patroclus 'the winner will have a supply for five circling years . . . his shepherd or ploughman won't be going to town because he is short of iron; no, he will be supplied' (*Il*. 23.833–5). This raw value can be enhanced by craftsmanship and/or by pedigree. The pig-iron, for example, gains value from the fact that it belonged to Eetion before being pillaged by Achilles then offered as a prize in these games. Telemachus' path to fame is given a helping hand by Helen's portentous gift of a robe for his future bride. Odysseus' bow, like countless objects in Homer's poems, has its own *kleos*, its own life story, embracing friendship. When he strings the bow, Odysseus' proves his heroic superiority, though the poet wittily hints at a future rival, 'And indeed as he (Telemachus) drew it back for a fourth time using his power he would have strung it had Odysseus not shaken his head and checked his eagerness' (*Od*. 21.128–9).

That material objects have a correlation with status is an assumption running through both poems, sometimes made explicit. In the *Odyssey*, Odysseus' obsession with gifts he might get or has received may strike a modern reader as crude, but not the goddess Athene, 'I made all the Phaeacians befriend you. And now I have come here to weave a plan with you and hide all the things which the noble Phaeacians gave you as you left for home, following my plan and idea' (*Od.* 13.302–5). Telemachus is equally cautious with the gifts he received from Menelaus during his travels (*Od.* 17.75–81) and Odysseus smiles when he sees his like-minded wife, prompted by Athene who wishes Penelope to be 'esteemed more highly than before by both her husband and son', dangerously beguiling the suitors into giving her gifts (*Od.* 18.158–61 and 275–305).

In the *Iliad*, the conventional correlation between gifts and honour is challenged twice. The poem begins with an old man offering 'countless ransom' (*apoina*) for his daughter. In an unpopular and selfish move the offer of Apollo's priest Chryses is rejected by Agamemnon, who prefers his own private satisfaction to public approval. He is quickly proven to be in the wrong by Apollo's swift intervention. Later in the poem Agamemnon himself twice offers recompense (the word is also *apoina*) for insulting his best fighter, but Achilles shows an arrogance not unlike that of Agamemnon when he goes against the advice of friends and at first rejects the handsome proposal. Achilles' response, unlike that of Agamemnon, seems to represent a powerful challenge to the established order.

When presented with the argument, 'if you enter man-destroying battle without gifts, then even if you drive the fighting back, you will not be held in such honour' Achilles responds (*Il.* 9.604–5 and 607–10):

> Of that honour I have no need. What honour I have is, I think, through Zeus's dispensation, and it will stay with me by the beaked ships so long as the breath remains in my chest and my knees can lift me.

Taken together with his remarks in *Iliad* 1, Achilles rejects the honour that mortals can confer, for example by taking or bestowing gifts, in favour of a more abstract concept of honour conferred by the gods. His rejection of the conventional pattern of human transgression followed by forgiveness/compensation has fatal consequences. Zeus nevertheless continues to show a direct concern for Achilles' honour out of respect for Thetis and he sets in motion a plan that reconciles human and divine interests. Achilles' gracious acceptance of Priam's ransom for his son's body is dually determined – Thetis' intervention accords with Achilles' inclinations – and a balanced order, one in which honour is satisfied by the acceptance of gifts, prevails. Whether this effaces the questions provoked by Achilles' earlier actions is for the reader to decide.

Valuing the dead

Finally, let us consider the value of a corpse in the Homeric poems. When a hero falls in the *Iliad* the battle for his corpse begins. The fighting over

Patroclus lasts throughout *Iliad* 17. Why does it matter so much? In the case of Patroclus there are two phases in the fighting: the battle for Achilles' armour, which Hector wins, and the battle for the body which is a hard won victory for the Greeks. This two-stage conflict mirrors many earlier encounters in the poem. We have already discussed the seriousness of material gain in Homer's world and Hector wears his spoils proudly, though not for long, as Zeus intimates when he sees Hector arming himself, 'Ah, poor wretch, no thought of death is in your heart, though he is drawing near you' (*Il.* 17.201–2). The body once rescued is brought home to Achilles, protected from the natural process of decay by Thetis and ultimately honoured with games and sacrifices, including the sacrifice of twelve Trojan youths, four horses and two dogs (*Il.* 23.171–6). The urgency of this last honour is impressed upon Achilles and the reader by the chilling encounter with Patroclus' ghost who requests, 'Let the same vessel hold both our bones, the two-handled vessel of gold which your lady mother gave you' (*Il.* 23.90–1). In the last book of the *Odyssey* we hear that this request is honoured after Achilles' death and that the Greeks buried this within 'a magnificent great tomb, on a jutting headland overlooking the broad Hellespont, so that it might be visible from far out at sea both by men of today and by those in the future' (*Od.* 24.82–4). Here then, is one reason such importance is attached to having the mortal remains, the duty of the living to remember the dead.

But that is not all. Priam's actions are not motivated by a desire to build his son a tomb, but by some more basic human need. The value of the corpse to Priam, Hecuba and Andromache in particular is almost impossible to express in words, but that is what the poet tries to communicate. Although willing to return Hector's corpse, Achilles keeps the body out of Priam's sight until morning, fearful of the intensity of emotions it will provoke, empathizing with Priam's need to weep over his son's corpse, just as Achilles himself has wept and raged over Patroclus. 'The sands were drenched with tears, and the men's armour was drenched: such was the man, the rouser of panic, whom they longed to have back' (*Il.* 23.15–16). When the corpse is brought back, 'sweet and fresh as dew', Hector's wife and mother are able to touch the body of the man they have lost while giving vent to some of their confused emotions. Strangely, it is Helen who has the last word as she weeps for herself and the new tide of desolation she feels. The death of a loved one changes the identity of those who survive.

That is perhaps why a strange simile in the *Odyssey* works so well. When Odysseus is nearly home, he is entertained by the Phaeacians with poetry as well as more physical comforts. Each time the poet's song touches on the hero's own experiences Odysseus weeps (*Od.* 8.521–31):

This is what the famous minstrel sang. And Odysseus melted; the tears welled beneath his eyelids and soaked his cheeks. As a woman weeps, embracing her beloved husband who has fallen in front of his city and his people, fighting to protect his city and children from the pitiless day. As she watches him dying, as he takes his final breath, she wraps him in her arms and keens shrilly. Behind her they strike her back and shoulders with their spears and lead her off in captivity for her share of toil and misery. Her cheeks are wasted by her most pitiful grief. So Odysseus let the pitiful tears fall from beneath his brow.

Demodocus' song is about the sack of Troy, but Odysseus' tears are not for the victims, they are for himself, for a sense of his own identity, for the fact of being remembered, if only in song.

The Homeric poems have survived the test of time so well because of their wonderful accessibility, the universality of their themes and the countless insights into human nature they offer. Testament to this legacy is found not only in the fact that people still read the poems in their original language but in a recurrent blossoming of translations and works inspired by the poems. These maintain a dialogue with that remote past while renewing perspectives on contemporary life and society, in the past and today.

Further reading

There are very many books written about Homer. For work on both poems, see Fowler (2004); Griffin (1980); Jenkyns (1998); Morris and Powell (1997); Powell (2004); Rutherford (1996); Taplin (2000: chapter 1). On the *Iliad*, see Cairns (2002); Edwards (1987); Redfield (1975); Schein (1984); Scully (1990); Silk (1987). On the *Odyssey*, see Austin (1975); Goldhill (1991: chapter 1); Griffin (1987); Hall (2008); Jones (1992); Schein (1996); Segal (1995b).

Modern works inspired by Homer's Iliad or Odyssey

Armitage (2006); Atwood (2005); Joyce (1922); Logue (1981; 1991; 1994; 2003; 2005); Walcott (1990; 1993).

The translations of both poems by Robert Fagles, published in Penguin, are very good. The latest edition of the *Iliad* was published in 1991; of the *Odyssey* in 2006.

Chapter 3

From Homer to tragedy

All dates in this chapter are BCE unless otherwise stated. Glossary items: *aetiology; agōgē; aischrologia; Alcaic; aoidos; aulos; choliambic; chōra; dithyramb; elegiac couplet; encomium; epic cycle; epinikian; gnōmē; hexameter; hyporchēmata; iambic; Judgement of Paris; kleos; leschē; melos; monody; Muses; paean; partheneion; pentameter; polis; priamel; proem; Sapphic; strophic; syssitia; triadic; trochaic; xenia.*

ARCHAIC GREECE: THE RISE OF THE *POLIS*

Neil Croally

The period called Archaic Greece was preceded by the dark ages, which began with the collapse of the Mycenean civilization at the end of the thirteenth century and continued until the re-emergence of writing in the early eighth century: lack of writing is what makes the dark ages dark. So, although the Homeric epics were probably composed through the dark ages, they were first written down along with other Greek literature during the archaic period (roughly the eighth, seventh and sixth centuries). And the context in which they were written down was the new social, political and cultural organization known as the *polis*.

The essential ingredients of the *polis* are already in place in Homer. But the origin and location of the *polis* (1000 or 800; mainland Greece, modern Turkey or Sicily and Italy) is, for us, not so important. It is useful to know, however, the extent to which the development of the *polis* was coincidental with the establishment of religious sanctuaries, and of the four panhellenic sanctuaries in Olympia, Delphi, Isthmia and Nemea. It is important that the *polis* was the context in which there occurred the political, cultural, literary, philosophical and architectural innovation for which the archaic and classical Greeks are so rightly famous.

Polis – originally meaning fortification – comes to mean both 'city' and 'state', and sometimes the two terms are conflated as 'city-state'. This formula is not quite as helpful as it first might appear, for it neither helps us to understand the variety of *poleis* nor does it really explain on what particular bases *poleis* were organized. The *polis* – as city, state or city-state – tends to have a *chōra* attached. *Chōra* refers to the territory in which the *polis* was situated and over which it had control. In the classical period there may have been up to 1,000 *poleis*: some may have been very small, with citizen bodies of only 1,000, and with territories of only 25 km^2; other cities, notably Sparta and Athens, had very extensive territories and some cities, such as Corinth, Aegina and Athens, had very large populations.

Within those populations some – citizens – were politically defined and others – women, slaves and so on – had a legally defined status. Indeed, it is important to understand the extent to which the *polis* was identified with its citizen body. (The modern state, by contrast, can be seen as separate from its citizens.) That citizen body is most sharply defined as the city's fighters: war helps to define the *polis*, and also operates as one of the main ways that different cities interact with each other (the earliest example in the archaic period is the Lelantine War between Chalchis and Eretria). In the early part of the seventh century there also seems to have been what is sometimes called the hoplite revolution. This refers to the way that the city's political organization changed to grant full citizenship to the non-aristocratic, heavy-armed infantry (hoplites) who increasingly fought the city's wars. If the hoplite revolution – probably more gradual than the word 'revolution' implies – is associated with any one place and person, it is with the tyrant of Argos, Pheidon, whose new-model army defeated the Spartans at Hysiae in 669. Over the seventh and sixth centuries, the *polis* developed in a variety of ways and at different paces in different places. But a broad outline can still be seen. The *polis* at minimum had annually elected magistrates, a council (normally of elders) and an assembly of fighters. To regulate the relationship between these different parts of the constitution and, in particular, to limit the powers of the magistrates, we see written laws being developed, as in the case of Solon's reforms in Athens (*c.* 590s). In addition, over time the rights and responsibilities of the citizens become more strictly encoded.

One special political development in the seventh and sixth centuries was the emergence of tyrannies. Tyranny was not a new and specific constitutional arrangement, but it was a move away from aristocracy to a more inclusive political organization. Also, not every city – Sparta is the most famous example – experienced a tyranny, and tyrannies occurred at different times in different cities. The most famous tyrants in the seventh century were the aforementioned Pheidon in Argos, and Cypselus and Periander in Corinth; Cleisthenes of Sicyon may have ruled in the late seventh into the early sixth; prominent in the sixth century were Polycrates of Samos and Peisistratus and his sons in Athens. Typically, tyrants fronted previously excluded groups (such as hoplites) who were discontented at the imbalance between their military or economic importance and lack of political power. Tyrannies could boast that they boosted prosperity and trade, that they established important cults and festivals (such as the Great Dionysia, established or remodelled by Peisistratus in Athens), that they beautified their cities with public works (such as Polycrates' temple of Hera in Samos), and that they patronized the arts (note Peisistratus and tragedy). However, tyrannies rarely lasted more than two generations, and the tyrants themselves became the problem. By the end of the sixth century, in mainland Greece at least, the word *tyrannos*, which had originally just meant 'ruler', had become associated with the use of power that ignored the rule of law and other constitutional niceties. (Herodotus has some fantastic tales of tyrannical excess.) The assassination of the tyrant in Athens in 514 (actually the wrong man was killed) made the assassins, Aristogeiton and Harmodius, famous once democracy was established. However, the one *polis* not affected by tyranny was Sparta, and Sparta's political development was so peculiar (even to the other ancient Greeks) that it is worth examining.

In the eighth century, Sparta annexed the territory of Messenia in the western Peloponnese (the first Messenian War). This annexation had long-term consequences, as the Spartans chose to enslave the Messenians, who became known as helots. Arguably the very existence of these helots shaped Sparta's political development for the next two or three centuries. In the early part of the seventh century, the Messenians revolted (the second Messenian War). Although at around the same time the Spartans were defeated at the battle of Hysiae (669) by Pheidon of Argos, in the seventh and sixth centuries the Spartans built up a fearsome military reputation. In antiquity it was thought that the Spartans' military prowess was fostered by a set of reforms associated with a shadowy, possibly seventh-century figure called Lycurgus. It is more likely that the reforms were more gradual. Important manpower was supplied by the helots, and political stability (*eunomia*) by the citizen assembly, the *gerousia* (council of elders), the annually elected ephors and the unique dual kingship. But probably the most celebrated aspects of the reforms were the *agōgē* and the *syssitia*. The *agōgē* was the famous, public training of Spartan children, noted for its austerity and brutality, and designed to produce the sorts of warriors who could suppress helot revolt and win hoplite battles. The *syssitia* were the messes in which Spartan warriors were organized. To us, as it did to the ancient Greeks, Sparta looks like a very peculiar place indeed, but that does not mean that its distinctive warrior ethos and social homogeneity have not been admired.

By the end of the sixth century, Sparta had established itself as a regional power, partly through its development of the Peloponnesian League; it also had a settled and distinctive political system. By the same time, Athens had become a democracy. Thus, after three hundred years dominated by the development of the *polis*, and by the spreading through colonization of Greek civilization in Asia Minor and Sicily and Italy, the Greeks faced a century dominated by two conflicts, that between the Greeks – led by the Spartans and the Athenians – and the Persians, and then that between the two dominant Greek cities themselves.

Further reading

There are a number of good histories of archaic Greece and the *polis* now available. See, for instance, Buckley (1996); Hall (2006); Hansen (2006); Murray (1993); Osborne (2004; 2009); Snodgrass (1980). On tyrants, the classic remains Andrewes (1956). On Sparta, see Cartledge (2003); Forrest (1980); Jones (1967).

EARLY GREEK POETRY: HESIOD

Roy Hyde

As well as the *Iliad* and the *Odyssey*, the Greeks knew a good deal of other hexameter epic poetry on similarly legendary material. Much of it concerned events related to the Trojan War, and is usually known as the *epic cycle*, though there were also epics about the deeds of Heracles and the Theban legends. We know the names of some of the supposed authors, but only fragments (see 1k) survive, and summaries of some of the plots. Though apparently regarded as inferior to the *Iliad* and the *Odyssey*, they were probably important as a source for material that is not in Homer, such as the *Judgement of Paris* and the fall of Troy, as well as for other legends that became part of the staple diet of much later poetry, especially Attic tragedy. They probably date from the seventh and sixth centuries, but there is no reason why they cannot have incorporated much earlier material. Anyway, epic poetry continued: there was, for instance, the Heracles story by Panyassis of Halicarnassus (early fifth century). But no complete epic poem has survived after Homer until Apollonius of Rhodes wrote the *Argonautica* in the third century.

Two other poems wrongly attributed to Homer are, first, the *Margites*, a sort of parody of epic concerned with the misadventures of a village-idiot figure (the eponymous Margites), and, second, the *Batrachomyomachia*, which is probably Hellenistic (i.e. late fourth or third century). In pseudo-Homeric hexameters, this latter poem deals with a battle between frogs and mice, and seems to have been only one of a number of animal epics, which included ones concerning spiders, cranes and starlings.

More serious in subject matter, also in superficially Homeric style, but also not by Homer, are the *Homeric Hymns*. Thucydides believed that one of them at least – the *Hymn to Apollo* – was by Homer, but actually they seem to date variously from the seventh century to the fifth century. They appear to be preludes, designed for use in religious festivals to introduce or precede the recital of other, perhaps epic, material. Some are only a few lines long; four of them – to Demeter, Apollo, Hermes and Aphrodite – are much longer. The short ones are not particularly skilled compositions. The longer ones are variable in quality, and in some cases seem to combine contributions from more than one poet, but contain some passages of fine poetry as well as having considerable religious and antiquarian interest.

Hesiod

The first Greek poet about whom we know anything biographical at all is
Hesiod, who lived about 700. According to what he tells us, he lived in a
village called Ascra in Boeotia. His father, a merchant seafarer, had
migrated to there from Cyme, on the Aegean coast of what is now Turkey,
'to escape poverty'. Hesiod speaks disparagingly of Ascra (a place 'bad in
winter, nasty in summer, and good at no time'; *Works and Days* (*WD*)
639f.). Poverty, and how to avoid it, is a recurrent theme in his *Works and
Days*, and it is tempting to imagine him as a peasant farmer. Tempting, but
wrong: not least because he was obviously able to devote a good deal of
time to learning the craft of poetry – his technique owes a good deal to that
of the bards of the Homeric tradition, whom he must have at least listened
to a good deal, even if he was not actually taught by one – and then to
practising it. It was by reason of his poetry that he made the one (short)
journey by sea that he had undertaken before composing *Works and Days*:
to Chalcis in Euboea, to enter a competition held at the funeral games of
Archidamas, a nobleman killed in a sea-battle in the Lelantine War. He
won the competition, very likely with his *Theogony*, along with *Works and
Days* one of his two surviving works.

Works and Days is a poem of just over 800 lines. It begins with a dedication to Zeus, at the end of which Hesiod says he has some things to tell his
brother Perses (1–10). Man, he says, must work for his living, by the will of
Zeus, as exemplified in the myth of Prometheus and Pandora, and men must
observe justice, a warning that he addresses not only to Perses, but in lines
11–285 to the *basileis* (kings or, more likely in Hesiod, rulers; see below). If
Perses will work hard and be just, he will prosper, and he is given advice on
a variety of topics, such as how to conduct himself amongst other people,
the sort of wife to get and what to do on his farm and when (286–705).
There follows a list of miscellaneous 'do's and don'ts' (706–64), and a calendar of days which are favourable or unfavourable for doing various things
(765–828). The structure of the poem, as this summary suggests, is loose,
so that it has seemed to some to be little more than a compilation of miscellaneous advice stitched together, rather than a coherent whole. There are
certainly sections in which it is easy to feel that Hesiod has lost the plot:
lines 706–64, for example, read like a list of aphorisms or proverbs: don't
behave boorishly at feasts, don't make libations to Zeus unless you've had a
wash, don't urinate facing the sun, and so on. Sometimes it may appear that
Hesiod is simply putting in whatever comes to mind, and to an extent this
is probably the case, though closer reading suggests that there is a more
coherent train of thought.

There is also a thematic unity. The prelude (or *proem*) invokes the *Muses*, to
enable Hesiod to sing of Zeus, so that the poem as a whole may be seen as a
hymn to Zeus, and indeed a statement of how Hesiod views the world under
the authority of Zeus: the hard work that is the lot of mankind is ordained

by Zeus, and the Justice by which a man can attain prosperity, personified as the daughter of Zeus, is under his special protection. (The existence of Perses, the advice to whom is a development of this theme, is sometimes doubted; this may not matter.) The advice Hesiod offers on how to live one's life is, in the end, offered not just to him, but to mankind in general. None of us likes to be lectured; maybe Hesiod was subtle enough to see that we may take more notice of advice offered to someone else rather than more pointedly to ourselves.

Works and Days is often seen as the first didactic poem in Greek and Roman literature (didactic poetry – from the Greek *didaskō* meaning 'I teach' – is supposed to teach the reader). While it is true that the later didactic tradition owes much to Hesiod, it is more fruitful to read *Works and Days* in the context of what is called wisdom literature. Wisdom literature purports to pass on good advice, often to a (recalcitrant) son, sometimes, in a more respectful tone, to a ruler. (A good deal of it survives from the near east and Egypt, some of it earlier than Hesiod. An accessible example is the biblical *Book of Proverbs*, which was in fact not compiled in its present form until some centuries after Hesiod, and which claims to be the wisdom of Solomon as imparted to his son.) The debt of early Greek poetry to the near east is now generally acknowledged, and it may well be that Hesiod composes with a distant awareness of such literature. Rather than a son, Hesiod addresses a brother (which may be an argument in favour of Perses' existence: if Hesiod was going to invent, why not invent a son?), but he also addresses the *basileis*. The word *basileus* (plural *basileis*) is usually translatable as 'king', but in Hesiod it clearly refers to the local 'lords', or 'aristocrats' (not necessarily that grand), who, having in his opinion deprived him of a part of his inheritance in favour of the undeserving Perses, are nevertheless exhorted to observe justice.

Greek poetry must always be considered in the context of its performance. And we should see Hesiod not as a professional poet in the manner of the Homeric *aoidos* (singer) – notwithstanding his excursion to Chalcis – but as a farmer who happened to be a poet as well. It has been suggested that, given the hymnic nature of the poem, it was intended for performance at a religious festival. This may well be the case. But while much early Greek poetry was composed for, and even in, the symposium (see 1j), Hesiod seems an unlikely symposiast. However, in *Works and Days* (493–4), he warns Perses not to be tempted to hang around wasting time in the winter in the smithy and the *leschē*. A smithy would be a nice warm place to stand around and gossip in winter; the *leschē* was a room often attached to a smithy (the invention, presumably, of some enterprising smith who realized he could make a profit out of lingering gossips) where men of Hesiod's type met and talked and, probably, ate and drank – the natural environment of a wastrel like Perses. It would be a nice irony if Hesiod himself entertained his fellow farmers in the *leschē*.

The performance context of Hesiod's other surviving poem, the *Theogony*, can perhaps be identified, though not with complete certainty, as the funeral games of the Euboean *basileus* Amphidamas. (The *basileis* are treated with considerably more sympathy in the *Theogony*, and the lines about the healing power of song to the bereaved would be apt in the circumstances: 98–105.) The *Theogony* too is a hymn, this time to the Muses, the goddesses of music and song, who are described as meeting Hesiod himself as he pastured his sheep on Mount Helicon and inspiring him to his poetic vocation. Since the Muses themselves spend their time hymning Zeus and the other gods, it is also, in a sense, a hymn to all the gods.

Its theme is exactly that: the gods, their genesis (which is what *Theogony* means), their relationships and their doings. Some of it consists of little more than lists, such as the 41 daughters of Oceanus and Tethys in 12 lines (349–61) named in a virtuoso display of memory and metre – but, interspersed amongst the versified family trees are the stories of the power struggles of the generations of the gods, culminating in the victory of Zeus, the story of Prometheus and of Pandora, and the final battle of Zeus against the Titans. The *Theogony* is about the world of the gods where *Works and Days* is about the world of man, but they complement each other in their overall world-view: there is justice in the world, but there are afflictions too, which are part of the fabric of existence, and it is the lot of man to make his way by work and by doing right.

Like *Works and Days*, the *Theogony* may be read in the context of near-eastern literature. The biblical *Book of Genesis* is a loose parallel, with the creation of the world by God followed by genealogies, not of gods, but of the earliest generations of men. A closer match can be found in the Babylonian *Enuma Elish*, in which is related the creation of the world, the generations of the gods, and the struggles of Marduk to establish himself as ruler of the gods. Similar parallels could be cited from other eastern literature: again, the cultural base of the Boeotian farmer can be shown to be remarkably wide.

Hesiod composed recognizably in the tradition of oral poetry, though is not quite as close to Homer in dialect and use of formulae as superficially appears to be the case. Writing was in its infancy in Hesiod's day, and there can be little doubt that he composed orally. But someone wrote his poems down, and the most likely candidate is the poet himself, perhaps (as Martin West suggests) first the *Theogony*, in order to record as accurately as possible his prize-winning achievement, and later the *Works and Days*.

Though his reputation in the ancient world was high, partly because of his extreme antiquity and because of (fictitious) tales of his rivalry with Homer, Hesiod does not perhaps at first glance strike one as a great poet. But he rewards closer reading. We may not all be enthralled by lists of nymphs, or much interested that the eighth day of the month is the best for castrating bulls, but there is a grim majesty in his descriptions of the earth-born monsters that rise up to fight the gods, in the Children of Night and the awesome Styx, and the dread places under the earth, and an unexpected lightness of touch in his treatment of the songs of the Muses and their dancing-places. Tedious injunctions may be enlightened by memorable images: 'another time to sail is when you see that the leaves on the topmost branch of the fig-tree are as large as a crow's footprint' (WD 678ff.). And it is hard not to warm to the working man in the height of the Greek summer when 'goats are fattest and the wine sweetest, and women randiest and men feeblest' (WD 585ff.), who wants nothing more than to lie in the shade of a rock, feel a cooling breeze on his face and relax with a glass of wine. The farmer-bard has the imagination of a poet and the observation of a countryman.

Further reading

Hamilton (1989) is a detailed piece of formal literary criticism of Hesiod. Much valuable information is contained in West's two texts and commentaries, on *Theogony* (1966); on *Works and Days* (1978). For the eastern context of Hesiod's work, see West (1997). For translations in the Loeb series, see West (2003a; 2003b).

EARLY GREEK POETRY: ELEGY, IAMBUS AND LYRIC

Roy Hyde

This section will discuss not only lyric poetry, but also elegy and iambus. What these forms have in common, as opposed to epic poetry, is that they are, or at least appear to be, 'personal' poems: the poet, at first sight anyway, appears to be relating or reflecting on his or her own experience. This led to a once widely held belief that the age of Greek lyric poetry represented something like a development in human psychology: a 'discovery of the self'. This idea is now largely discredited: a more likely explanation is that personal poetry has survived from this period, but not from earlier. The songs that Achilles sang to entertain or console himself, if we only knew what they were, were surely as personal as the songs of Sappho. (All references to lyric poems are to the Oxford World Classics translation by West (1993).)

In any case, the poetic 'I' of the lyric poets (for the purposes of this discussion I include *iambic* and *elegiac* poets) is in itself controversial. When Sappho tells us *she* is in love, when Archilochus relates how *he* threw away his shield in battle and ran away, when Mimnermus laments the passing of youth, we tend to assume that they are speaking as *themselves*. There is no reason to think that this must be the case: poets are after all capable of invention. This is not to say that Greek lyric poets *never* write as themselves. But we can never be sure.

Apart from Pindar and the works attributed to Theognis (which are themselves a compilation, and not all by him), all the lyric poetry which we have has survived either in quotations by other authors or on pieces of papyrus discovered in Egypt which are often no more than scraps. Scholars who study lyric poetry thus spend a good deal of their time trying to reconstruct fragmentary poems; and it is an unfortunate fact that we have very, very few complete poems, and even when we think we have, we may well be wrong.

As I noted above, I have so far treated lyric poetry as including elegiac and iambic poetry, by contrast with poetry written in *hexameters*. But they are by no means the same thing. Elegiac poetry is, quite simply, poetry written in the elegiac metre: couplets, consisting of one hexameter followed by one *pentameter* (see 1c). The word 'elegy' has come to have funereal connotations, and in later Greece the metre was frequently used for epitaphs; in our period, however, almost anything could be written in elegiac metre, and its early use seems to have often been exhortatory in some way (see below, particularly on Tyrtaeus, Callinus and Archilochus). Its most frequent performance context seems to have been the symposium (see 1j). Elegiac poetry seems generally to have been sung, or perhaps chanted, to the accompaniment of the *aulos*, an oboe-like instrument (see 1c). Elegiac poetry is defined by its *form*, the elegiac metre. Iambic poetry, by contrast, is not *necessarily* written in the iambic metre (although it often is); it is defined, rather, by its *content*. It is the poetry of mockery, abuse and invective, and is often graphic and sexually explicit. It may have a cult origin: *aischrologia*, 'scurrility', was associated with certain religious rites, and is the aspect of them that grew into Athenian comedy and gave rise to the satyr plays which accompanied the tragic performances, both at festivals of the god Dionysus. In the *Homeric Hymn to Demeter*, which provides an *aetiology* for the cult of the Mysteries at Eleusis, a female servant called Iambe, by her jokes and teasing, manages to cheer up the goddess Demeter who is mourning the disappearance of her daughter. The performance context of iambic poetry is then probably religious in origin, but there is much that looks as if it probably belongs to the symposium. Unlike elegiac and lyric poetry proper, iambic poetry seems generally to have been chanted or spoken rather than sung; the actual iambic metre is closer than other metres to the ordinary rhythms of speech – it was the metre used later for speech and dialogue in Attic tragedy.

Lyric poetry proper, which *was* designed to be sung (it is sometimes called melic poetry, from *melos*, 'song') falls broadly into two categories. Monodic lyric is that intended for the solo voice, and is composed in short stanzas all of the same form. Most monodic lyric songs are themselves short and were sung to the accompaniment of the lyre (see 1c). Choral lyric was, as the name suggests, performed by choirs, to the accompaniment of the lyre and sometimes the *aulos* as well, and often, if not always, included dancing. It is almost always *triadic* in form: two stanzas of identical metrical form followed

by one in a different but related metre. The triads can continue almost
indefinitely: some poems in this form are enormously long (see especially
Stesichorus and Pindar). Generally speaking, monodic lyric is more private
in context, to be sung in the symposium or similar gatherings, whereas choral is more public, designed for processional or cult occasions. None of the
distinctions made here between the several forms discussed below, however,
is hard and fast: it is, for example, controversial whether Pindar's *epinikian*
odes, which look like choral lyric, were actually sung by a chorus or by the
solo voice; the issue is complicated by the fact that Pindar frequently refers
to himself in the first person. Did the performance of choral lyric involve
both the solo voice and choir? As for so much else connected with these
genres, we simply do not know.

The dates given for the authors in the following sections are approximate,
and sometimes controversial.

Archilochus (mid-seventh century)

The first poet apart from Homer and Hesiod who is more than a name is
Archilochus, from the island of Paros, though he migrated to Thasos. His
reputation in antiquity was high, and the reasonably extensive remains of his
poetry that survive support this judgement: he is also a poet entirely in control of his material, and was surely composing in a well-established tradition,
rather than experimenting with new forms.

Archilochus wrote lyric proper, though hardly anything survives, but it
was for his elegiac and iambic poetry that he was best known. He was famous
for the power of his invective (a judgement that does no justice to his poetic
range), and especially for that against one Lycambes, who is said to have
promised his daughter Neobule to Archilochus in marriage, then changed his
mind: in revenge, Archilochus seduced Neobule's sister, and his poetic
attacks on the family drove them all to suicide. This may be taken with a
pinch of salt. It has been suggested that Lycambes and his daughters were not
in fact real people, but that his poetry about them has some sort of cultic
context, and that they were stock figures somewhat like those in the Italian
Commedia dell'Arte.

This is an illustration of the problem of the poetic 'I': to what extent can
we say that a poet is writing 'in his own person', and can we therefore reasonably use his works to say anything meaningful about him? We can find some
safer ground with regard to Archilochus: a shrine to him on Paros testifies to
his aristocratic standing there. We can surely accept his statement that he was
a 'servant of Enyalius [god of war] and the *Muses*'; quite a number of the fragments of his poems have military connections, and a soldierly fondness for
drinking. The context of such poetry is likely to be the symposium, an appropriately aristocratic setting for Archilochus, and very much in keeping with
what we know of symposiastic poetry from elsewhere. One of his most famous

epigrams is more complex, especially if viewed alongside Tyrtaeus or Callinus: in battle, he says, he ran away and left his shield under a bush, 'but saved myself. What do I care for the shield? I'll get another just as good' (West: 5). Self-mockery? Deliberate subversion of the symposiastic and political context? Is he even referring to himself? There is no easy answer, but it is a beautifully crafted little piece.

Archilochus is not all war, wine and invective: most aspects of life are there, and if we had his whole output, no doubt his range would be even wider. The gods are there and the resignation we must adopt in the face of their will. There is consolation, for the loss of lives at sea, and a reminder that even grief will pass in time. There is sex: a seduction, sensual but not graphic; more explicit is someone otherwise unidentified with 'a cock like a corn-fed donkey from Priene' (West: 43). A gift for description appears in a reference to Thasos, 'like a donkey's back, crowned with wild woodland' (West: 21). There is moralizing, though not, seemingly, with a heavy hand, and there are fables: 'a fox knows many tricks, a hedgehog one good one' (West: 201).

Callinus (mid-seventh century)

Only 25 lines survive, 21 in one long fragment. Roughly contemporary with Archilochus, he lived in Ephesus. The 21-line fragment, in elegiacs, suggests a skilful and powerful exhortatory voice: how long, he asks, will the young men lie idle, while the land is full of war? We die anyway: better to die gloriously in war than unlamented at home; 'when a brave man dies, all the people miss him, and if he lives, he lives as a demi-god, for he seems a tower of strength in their eyes, and he does the deeds of many men, though he is only one' (West: 1).

Tyrtaeus (mid-seventh century)

Tyrtaeus came from Sparta, and his militaristic elegiacs were learned by young Spartan men and sung or chanted in the mess while on campaign (the martial equivalent of the domestic symposium). About 150 lines of Tyrtaeus' work survive, in fragments of some length. He appears to have written about Spartan history and politics as well, but what survives is almost entirely exhortatory and military. Tyrtaeus pulls no punches: war is a grim business, but it is what a man has to do. 'It is a fine thing for a good man to fall and die in the front line, fighting for his country' (West: 10): a fine thing, if only because the alternative is to be driven from his lands and go begging with his wife and children and aged parents. Fighting is the task of the young: it is shameful to see a greybeard breathing out his life on the battlefield, holding in his bloody guts with his hands; but (a curious, almost erotic, image, and not easily translatable) a young man 'splendid for men to look upon while he lives, and desirable to women, splendidly falls in the front line' (West: 10). An apparently early reference to fighting in the hoplite phalanx characteristic of classical Greek warfare exhorts a man to stand firm without flinching, shoulder to shoulder, 'making his own life his enemy, regarding the dark spirits of death as dear as the rays of the sun' (West: 11). Athletic prowess, good looks, rhetoric, wealth – all are worthless: only the man who has looked on the horror of war and endured is truly a man. He alone is honoured amongst the living, and revered after death: 'let every man aspire to this peak of courage, let him not rest from war' (West: 12).

Tyrtaeus seems to have written his exhortations to the Spartans at the time of the Messenian wars, the outcome of which was the subjection of the Messenians (as helots; see 3a) which both resulted in and enabled the militarization of Spartan society. It is not, perhaps, great poetry, but it captures the spirit of its time, and it encapsulates what Sparta came to embody, both in its own eyes and those of the rest of Greece.

Mimnermus (late seventh century)

A less martial exponent of elegiacs, at least as far as the extant fragments go, is Mimnermus of Colophon. In fact, one of his two 'books', the *Smyrneis*, was historical in theme and thus somewhat different from what we know of his work, and from the other elegiac poetry we have seen so far. If it was a continuous narrative, it is perhaps unlikely to have been symposiastic in context, and may be an early example of a more public kind of elegy (see below on Simonides). His other book, the *Nanno*, seems to have been a collection of love poems about or addressed to a woman, perhaps an *aulētris* (see 1h), with whom he was in love. He is thus a remote ancestor of the Roman love elegists, as one of them, Propertius, suggests (see 10e). The two most substantial surviving fragments have a predominantly wistful air, elegantly expressed: 'what is life, what pleasure is there, without Aphrodite the golden? Let me die when I no longer enjoy these things – secret love, sweet gifts, and sex' (West: 1); 'like the leaves that come in the season of spring of many flowers when swiftly they grow in the rays of the sun, like them we enjoy for a brief time the flowers of youth' (West: 2).

Solon (fl. 600)

A figure of whom we know much more is Solon. Archon at Athens in 594–3, his constitutional reforms were of major importance in the history of Athens. He wrote in the iambic and *trochaic* metres as well as the elegiacs that predominate in his reasonably substantial surviving works. His subject matter is for the most part political, sometimes in justification of his policies:

for to the people I gave as much privilege as is suitable, neither adding nor taking away, but to those who held power and were admirable for wealth, for them too I took care that they should not suffer unduly (West: 5).

It is hardly a theme for great poetry, and Solon is perhaps to be seen rather as a skilful versifier: the survival of so much of his work is attributable to his political rather than literary pre-eminence. The symposium is an eminently suitable context for political poetry, but some of Solon's poems seem to have been of considerable length, and one wonders how many elegiac couplets his fellow-symposiasts were prepared to listen to before the cup went round again. There is a story that he declaimed in the *agora* his poem urging the Athenians to occupy Salamis; if it is true, perhaps we should imagine a more public context for some of his other poetry. As well as, or included within, his political elegies, is some moralistic and aphoristic verse somewhat reminiscent of the 'wisdom' tradition of Hesiod's *Works and Days*.

Theognis (c. 600)

At first sight, Theognis seems the best represented of the early poets. Two books, one of 1,230 lines, the other of 158, all elegiacs, survive. Unfortunately the case is more complex than this: the Theognidean *corpus* is in fact a collection of elegiac pieces, some of them identical to poems elsewhere attributed to other authors, some presumably by the real Theognis, others by unidentified poets. Very likely there was a poet called Theognis who lived around 600 in Megara (controversy again: the Megara in Greece or Megara in Sicily?) but, in view of the above, attempts to reconstruct a coherent poetical *persona* are doomed to failure. The performance context is undoubtedly the symposium: indeed the poems may well have been brought together as a collection of classic symposiastic songs. The prevalent stance is oligarchic and aristocratic: regret for lost lands and lost privilege, exile, resentment of the *nouveaux riches*. There is a strong erotic strain: many of the poems are addressed to Cyrnus, the *erōmenos* of Theognis (see 1h), but the standard complaints of the *erastēs* are outweighed by advice on conduct and reflections on life addressed to him: the symposium as the theatre of coming-of-age and socialization into the world of the citizen.

Xenophanes (c. 570–after Persian Wars)

Deserving of a brief mention in the history of elegiac poetry is the itinerant philosopher-poet Xenophanes of Colophon, who wrote also in hexameters. One elegiac fragment at least is symposiastic (West: 1), for it describes the preparations for a symposium: noteworthy is the atmosphere of holiness and cleanliness, a corrective for the view of the symposium as merely an excuse for drunken revelry. Xenophanes was interested in religion: he criticizes the anthropomorphism of gods (Aethiopians have black gods, Thracians red-haired ones), and in another fragment advocates monotheism (see 6c). Such reflections belong to the history of philosophy (of which Aristotle considered Xenophanes one of the founding fathers); as far as literary history is concerned, we seem to see here another use of public elegy, with Xenophanes as a forerunner of the public displays of cleverness of the sophists, but in verse rather than prose.

Semonides (seventh century)

The surviving output of the poets discussed so far is predominantly elegiac, though that of Archilochus inclines towards the iambic in terms of content rather than form. In the case of Semonides, almost all that survives is iambic both in content and in metre. Most of the shorter fragments are moralizing in tone, or 'gnomic' (a *gnōmē* neatly encapsulates some truism, rather as a proverb does), but one longer piece (118 lines: West: 7) is devoted to the bane of men's lives: women. Women, Semonides says, are of a completely different nature from men, and the various species of them partake of the nature of whatever animal or natural phenomenon the god who made them had in mind when they were created. Some are descendants of a sow, some of a vixen or a bitch or an ape or a mare, some of the earth, some of the sea, etc: the sow-woman, of course, is a filthy slattern and keeps a filthy house, the bitch-woman has her nose in everything and barks at nothing, the sea-woman is all smiles one day and all storms the next, and so on. Only the bee-woman makes a good wife: she, of course, is industrious, thrifty, modest. Despite all this, each man defends his own wife in public, and men will even fight over women: they may be hard to live with, but they are impossible to live without. The poem is not without wit, though wit frequently spills over into bitterness. The context, of this and Semonides' other work, seems to be symposiastic; he is said to have led a colony from Samos to Amorgos, placing him firmly in the symposiastic class. Robin Osborne (2009: 215) aptly refers to 'Semonidean man, bitching with his male friends'.

Hipponax (late sixth century)

Even more caustic is Hipponax of Clazomenae (perhaps originally from Colophon). Fragments of poems in various metres survive, but he was particularly famous for those in a form of iambic known as *choliambic*. In his case, the distinction between the man and his poetic *persona* is reasonably clear. Hipponax is an aristocratic name: behind the scurrilous verse is an educated mind (one or more of his pieces seems to have been a parody of the *Odyssey*, or of part of it); there was a story that he was exiled – only wealthy men of some importance were exiled, not lowlifes of the type that his *persona* affects to be. Hipponax's (imaginary) world is one of poverty, criminality and sex, narrated, as far as we can tell, in his own person. Two characters, however, the sculptors Bupalus and Athenis, appear to have been real, and to have incurred Hipponax's wrath for making insulting statues of him. (As with Archilochus and Lycambes, Bupalus and Athenis are said to have been driven to suicide by Hipponax's attacks: we need not believe this either.) The performance context is unclear. Did Hipponax's fellow-symposiasts look forward to another episode in an ongoing sleazy soap-opera? Or are we to look for some cultic context? (See above on iambos and scurrility.) Several mentions of the *pharmakos*, the 'scapegoat' – a slave or poor person on whom the wrongs of a community were symbolically heaped, and who was then driven out of the community – may support this. Conceivably the invectives against Bupalus and Athenis, and their insults to Hipponax, may be seen against the background of some cultic context of the type from which Athenian comedy developed. But this is as far as we can go: again, unfortunately, this interesting and individual figure is shrouded in mystery.

Lyric poetry

Lyric poetry is actually nothing other than song, or poetry accompanied by a lyre; and people have, as far as we can tell, always sung songs. In Homer, people sing: Achilles sings, Calypso sings, we hear of choruses singing, the women of Troy sing lamentations over Hector, and so on. What songs they sang, we do not know: but we do know (a little) of the songs that Sappho or Alcaeus, for example, sang, because by the time they composed their songs, the Greeks had learned the skill of writing, so that their work could be preserved in a way that earlier songs could not.

Writing does not mean that lyric poets wrote down their songs as they composed them: some may have done, but we have no evidence one way or the other. What they *did* do was sing them, or compose them for other people, solo or in groups, to sing. In many cases, especially choral lyric, performance included dance as well. We do not know much about Greek music (see 1c), and have no examples from the early period, but it cannot be emphasized too strongly that all the poetry that this chapter discusses was written to form part of a performance that encompassed all or some of vocal and instrumental music, dance and spectacle. These are not poems written by poets sitting at their desks to commit their inner feelings to posterity, to be read and pondered over; they were created with specific occasions in mind, to be performed, not silently perused. The poetic immortality that became a commonplace of later Greek and Latin literature was perhaps not on the agenda of the authors discussed here, though there are indications in Theognis, for example, that the concept was coming into being, no doubt as the possibilities of writing as a means of preserving one's creation were being explored. The fact that some authors became classics, as their works were written down and disseminated in written form, must also have encouraged the belief that one's compositions might in some way outlive one's self. Interestingly enough, the establishment of a 'classical' pantheon of lyric poets, transmitted by way of written texts, may actually have encouraged 'repeat' performances of well-known pieces, and consequently discouraged the creation of new ones. It is certainly the case that the great age of Greek lyric poetry, which begins in the early seventh century, coincides with the early history of literacy, and peters out in the mid-fifth century, by which time writing had become (relatively) commonplace.

The nine poets discussed below – the lyric poets proper – were considered by Hellenistic scholars to be the nine greatest. The number of the 'Alexandrian Canon' is suspicious (there were nine *Muses*), though some added a tenth, the Boeotian female poet Corinna, whom scholars now generally consider to have lived in the Hellenistic period. But the quality of their surviving work (almost all fragments, until we get to Pindar) tends to support the Alexandrians' judgement.

Alcaeus (fl. 600)

Alcaeus was an aristocrat of Mytilene, on Lesbos. Like Archilochus, whom he somewhat resembles, he and his family were deeply involved in politics, which seems to have caused his exile, and he vigorously expresses his opposition to the various 'tyrants' from rival factions who ruled the city – 'Myrsilus is dead', he says cheerfully after the demise one of them, 'time for drinking and sex' (West: 332). His poetry seems to have been almost all monodic in form, much of it in the Alcaic stanzas which take their name from him, and most – perhaps all – of it is appropriate to the symposium (some of his compositions became symposium classics): aristocratic values, politics, warfare, drinking and love. 'Take away the metre', one ancient critic remarked, 'and you would find political rhetoric' – not, we might think, much of a recommendation, and, indeed, by no means a rounded assessment. It is hard not to read Solon as a political figure who happened to write poetry: Alcaeus is a poet who was deeply involved in politics. His reflections are shot through with mythological references (the Roman critic Quintilian regarded him as 'very similar to Homer'), and his imagery reveals a poet's imagination: 'I can make no sense of the warring of the winds. On one side the billows surge, and on the other, and we in the midst of them are borne along on our black ship' (West: 208), he writes, in a poem we might take at face value as a description of a storm at sea, but for the fact that the critic who quotes it states that it is about the turmoil caused by tyrants. The word translated here as 'warring' is *stasis*: a less loaded translation could be the position or disposition of the winds, and on one level the word carries this sense; but *stasis* is also the usual word for civil strife.

Alcaeus' hostility towards his enemies is implacable (he is said to have written that 'anger is the last thing to grow old'), and warfare is a dominant presence in his world, but he lacks, insofar as we can tell, the jingoistic militarism of Tyrtaeus: 'the great house is bright with bronze', he writes, in a fragment that is in a sense no more than a list of items of military equipment ready for use, but yet manages to *be* more; 'these (the arms) we cannot forget, the moment we set this enterprise in motion' (West: 140). We do not know what the enterprise was, but the tone of foreboding is unmistakable, and is thrown into sharp relief against the description of the gleaming weaponry. His world is a serious one, but has room for self-mockery – like Archilochus, he admitted to saving his skin by abandoning his arms – and for the pleasures of love and drinking: the harshness of winter can be kept at bay with a good fire, and with wine, 'the best medicine' (West: 335). He also wrote some hymns to gods, which show a light touch and some originality in treatment of myth. These too seem to be monodic in form: the context of Alcaeus' poetry, though often public in outlook, seems always to be the more restricted one of the symposium.

Although it is always a dangerous assumption, Alcaeus' *oeuvre* seems to present us with a poetic *persona* that is consistent within itself and consistent with what we know of the man and of his time and place. He was not the only poet working in Lesbos at the end of the seventh century; a fragment attributed to him introduces another: 'holy Sappho, sweetly smiling, your hair like violets, I'd like to tell you something, but modesty forbids' (West: 365, with Sappho at West: 137).

Sappho (fl. 600)

There is, in fact, no firm evidence that Sappho and Alcaeus knew each other. The second line of the fragment quoted above is probably not genuine, and the whole may not even be by Alcaeus. The same applies to Sappho's alleged reply (to the effect that, if what Alcaeus had to say for himself was anything like respectable, he would not be ashamed to come out and say it – West: 137); but, to tradition, the presence of two of the acknowledged masters of the lyric genre in the same small island at the same time was too good to miss. Although they must have lived at some time in reasonably close proximity, however, the turbulent politics of Lesbos leave no mark on the poetry of Sappho (except for one reference to exile, which she may have experienced, as her husband is said to have been a wealthy man and would thus necessarily have been politically engaged, and which can help to place Sappho in a similar social *stratum* to Alcaeus): Alcaeus' world is almost paradigmatic of the world of the aristocratic Greek male of the period; in Sappho's poetry we have a rare glimpse into the world of that otherwise almost silent species, the Greek woman.

That Sappho's voice is the only female one that has come down to us from this period (coupled with the extremely high quality of her verse which earned her the sobriquet of 'tenth Muse', and with the enigmatically fragmentary nature of the pieces that have survived) has made her a figure of endless fascination. As a woman she was, by definition, debarred from the symposium, and her world is a woman's world; a *priamel* specifically rejects the martial world of the male (and the symposium): 'some say that an army of cavalry is the finest thing on the dark earth, some an army of infantry or of ships, but I say it is whoever one loves' (West: 16). But many of her poems have the intimacy of a closed group not unlike the symposium, and it seems likely that she was in some way in charge of successive groups of girls and their education and socialization into adult society. This accords with the shifting patterns of affection we see in her work, and provides a counterpart to the socialization of young males in the symposium (see on Theognis above). We have seen that homoeroticism was a part of this process, and so it is with Sappho (hence the word 'lesbian'). It is natural to ask how far such affection went, and there is no easy answer; she has been seen as everything from a predatory virago to a Victorian schoolmistress figure, depending, as often as not, on the preoccupations of her interpreters. As usual with the lyric poets, given the fragmentary nature of their *oeuvres*, readers may take their choice. Similar considerations complicate the problem of the poetic 'I': is it always Sappho speaking? Even if it is, in what role does she speak?

Almost all of her surviving poetry is concerned with love and is monodic in form (in the Aeolic dialect, and frequently in the *sapphic* stanza named for her), and seems appropriate to small select gatherings, though she also wrote wedding songs and hymns which suggest a wider audience, and may be for choral performance (see below on Alcman). These contain much mythological material, but again with a particularly female slant: it is not the Trojan War that concerns Sappho, but the wedding of Hector and Andromache (West: 44). Sappho's mastery of her craft is consummate: nothing is wasted, images are conjured up in a few telling words; art conceals art, and defies translation. 'The stars around the fair moon hide their bright forms when she is at her full and fills the earth with light' (West: 34); 'love has shaken my heart, as the wind falls upon the oaks on the mountain' (West: 47). Only one poem (probably) survives complete (West: 1), and we seem to have most of a few others (West: 2, 16). These deserve to be read in full and not butchered by quotation.

Anacreon (c. 575–c. 490)

The poets we have discussed so far seem to have written mostly to please themselves or for the amusement or edification of their immediate communities: they were not professional poets. Anacreon of Teos, who must have been born when Sappho and Alcaeus were old, if they were still alive, was. He lived and worked at the court of Polycrates, tyrant of Samos *c.* 535–*c.* 522, subsequently at that of the Peisistratid tyrants of Athens, and may have then moved to Thessaly. He was regarded in ancient times as the archetypal poet of love and wine, and his poetry spawned a large body of imitations, the *Anacreonta*, from the Hellenistic period onwards. His poetry is largely small in scale, carefully crafted with no waste of words, light, elegant, witty and sometimes wistful. Written in the Ionic dialect, most of the surviving poems and fragments are in short stanzas, and monodic in form. He – or his poetic *persona* – is always in love, with boys or girls indiscriminately, not always successfully (West: 358 – a disdainful girl from (meaningfully) Lesbos), sometimes because he is too old (West: 395 is a poignant expression of the fear of death and the underworld whence 'one who goes down never returns'. Sometimes, though, age offers experience): in West: 417, in a lightly disguised double entendre, what a 'Thracian filly' needs is an experienced rider to tame her. Occasional fragments hint at the intrusion of the outside world – West: 419 is on a young man killed in battle; and there is some invective – the *nouveau riche* Artemon is satirized (West: 388) and a woman called Herotima is a 'public highway' (West: 346b). With love goes drinking but, belying Anacreon's later reputation as a drunkard, drinking should be done in moderation, without quarrelling and noise (West: 356b; Elegy 2), but to the accompaniment of good music (his own, presumably). Despite his courtly connections, Anacreon's poetry seems not to have any overtones of propaganda, and is essentially sympotic: he is, indeed, the sympotic poet par excellence.

Alcman (later seventh century)

The work of the poets discussed so far seems largely to have been composed for the solo voice and for essentially 'private' occasions, though that of Tyrtaeus in time assumed a more public status. For the first exponent of choral lyric, we have to step back in time to the later seventh century, and return to Sparta. In fact, Alcman was sometimes regarded as the inventor of love poetry, and some fragments survive which suggest that he may indeed have written monodic love poetry. But the most substantial pieces we have are unquestionably choral in context, in *strophic* form, and predominantly in Laconian dialect. The longest ones (W1 and 3), of which substantial fragments have been preserved on papyrus, are *partheneia*, to be sung by choirs of girls on some public occasion, apparently cultic, and also competitive. There are, as is usual in choral lyric, references to myth and local legend. How much space such material occupied in the complete poems is uncertain, but more seems to be devoted to praise of the members of the chorus themselves (both quotations are West: 1):

Agido, bright as the sun . . .

Hagesichora, whose hair shines like unalloyed gold, her complexion like silver.

As in Sappho, there is a homoerotic element: as Robin Osborne says, the relationship between the girls is 'both competitive and passionate' (Osborne, 2009: 171). The performance context too evokes that suggested for Sappho's poetry, though on a more explicitly public and civic level. Alcman's choral lyrics, like Tyrtaeus' elegiacs, became classics at Sparta; their emphasis on the appearance and accomplishments of the girls who sang them characterize Sparta as 'a society which takes seriously female fulfilment, and reckons to integrate women as much as men into the life of the city' (Osborne, 2009: 171). But Alcman is no dreary civic propagandist; his imagery is vivid, his powers of description rich:

> the mountain peaks and the glens sleep, the ridges and the stream-beds, and the tribes of creeping things that the dark earth nourishes, the mountain-dwelling creatures and the race of bees, the monsters in the depths of the dark salt sea; and the tribes of long-winged birds sleep (West: 89).

From some fragments of (presumably) non-choral works, we seem to hear Alcman's own voice. There is a cheerful reference to the soup he likes to eat in the winter ('he eats nothing fancy' – just ordinary things, like ordinary people (West: 17)), and, perhaps from a prelude to one of his choral songs: 'no longer, honey-sweet holy-voiced maidens, can my legs carry me. Damn! I wish I were a kingfisher, sea-dark holy bird, that flits across the foam of the sea with the halcyons, fearless at heart!' (West: 26). One tradition said that Alcman (the same was said of Tyrtaeus: see above) was not a native of Sparta. It is very likely false and testimony only to the fact the other Greeks found the liveliness, colour and humour of his poetry hard to reconcile with the later Sparta they knew.

Stesichorus (fl. c. 600–c. 550)

Stesichorus is the first major poet of the western Greek world. His native city is unknown, but he is said to have died either at Catana or Himera in Sicily, and references show him as active in this region. Superficially his poetry resembles that of Alcman, being *triadic* in form and in the Doric dialect associated with choral lyric (see 1a); and his name – or nickname? – appears to mean one who 'sets up' the chorus. But it has been argued that his poems were too long to have been performed chorally (one is known to have been at least 1,300 lines long, another to have been divided into two 'books'), and that they were designed for the solo voice, possibly with choral accompaniment. At the moment, this remains uncertain; in what survives, there is no indication of performance context, as there is in the case of Alcman. The fragments that can be placed with certainty are mythological in theme: on the story of Troy and the House of Atreus, on the Theban legends, on Heracles, for example. The narrative is leisurely – Stesichorus was considered 'Homeric', and his poems have been described as 'lyric epics' – with, apparently, a good deal of direct speech, and his language and imagery are rich. Sometimes his approach to traditional material seems to have been individual: he seems to have been responsible for the story that Helen never went to Troy, but spent the period of the Trojan War in Egypt, a version used by Euripides in his *Helen*. Again, the longest surviving fragment concerns the combat of Heracles and the three-bodied and three-headed monster Geryon. Geryon ought to be grotesque, but is in fact treated sympathetically: his mother appeals to him not to fight Heracles, but he says that if it is fate to die, he will die with honour; the image of one of his heads drooping on to his shoulder like a dying poppy is memorable. The resonances are Homeric, but their treatment, as seems to have been characteristic of Stesichorus, individual and original.

Ibycus (mid–later sixth century)

Probably a generation or so younger than Stesichorus, Ibycus too came from the west Greek world, from Rhegium in Southern Italy, but at some point, like Anacreon, lived at the court of Samos – an interesting indication of the cultural links between distant parts of the Greek world. The little of his poetry that survives is somewhat reminiscent of Stesichorus in dialect and form, but more elaborate in imagery and language (West: 286):

> In Spring, the Cydonian quinces, watered by the river-streams where the inviolate garden of the Nymphs is, bloom; and the vine-shoots growing in the shade of the branches. But for me at no season is love at rest . . .

Other fragments also deal with love, but there is some evidence that Ibycus also wrote longer poems closer to Stesichorus in manner and content: the longest one has an extended section on the Trojan War, but in the end turns into an *encomium* on Polycrates, somewhat in the manner of the major lyric poets of the next two generations, Simonides, Bacchylides and Pindar.

The poets discussed above wrote, for the most part, for their communities, for a circle of friends, or perhaps for themselves. Both Anacreon and Ibycus, however, were associated at some time with the courts of tyrants. To what extent they were dependent on the tyrants for patronage – in simple terms, were they paid employees? – we do not know (see 1e). The last three poets we discuss wrote much of their poetry for individuals, or for competitions, or communities other than their own. All three travelled extensively, and achieved great fame; they were professional poets in a way that Alcaeus, for

(Continued)

(Continued)

example, was not, in that poetry was what they spent their lives doing. It has tended to be assumed that when one of them wrote, for example, a poem celebrating someone's victory at the Olympic games, he would receive a fee for it. There is, in fact, no firm evidence for this, and the relationship between poet and patron at this time may be more complex. It is notable, for example, that Pindar can refer to his patrons as *xenoi*: the relationship between *xenos* ('guest-friend') and *xenos* was one of equals, not of superior and inferior, and was expressed partly in terms of gift-giving. This is not to deny that the poet would receive suitable recompense for his own gift – that of *kleos*, fame: but poets themselves were individuals of high social standing, and it is possible that what they received in return should be seen in terms of something more like reciprocal gift-giving or hospitality, rather than simple payment. (On this topic, which is the subject of scholarly debate at the moment, see Pelliccia in Budelmann, 2009: 240ff.)

Simonides (mid-sixth century–after 479)

Born on the island of Ceos, Simonides travelled widely for much of his long life, and wrote an enormous quantity of poetry, hardly any of which has survived complete. His 'patrons' can be found all over mainland Greece, and seem to have included the Peisitratid tyrants of Athens and Hieron of Syracuse. He was regarded (the tradition is not very explicit) as being fond of money: the extent to which this means that he charged fees for his poetry is uncertain (see the boxed text above). He wrote in most of the traditional lyric forms, from symposiastic to choral, in what was by now the standard Doricized lyric dialect, but was perhaps especially well-known for his *dithyrambs*, frequently winning prizes in the recently established competitions for this type of verse at Athens, elegiac poetry, and *epinikians*, a genre which he may have started (see below on Pindar) and certainly pioneered. It is hard to come to an estimate of Simonides' qualities as a poet from what has survived, but his range is evident even from this. He was famed for his command of pathos which is evident in, for example, his lament for the Spartan king Leonidas 'who has left a monument of his greatness, and undying fame' (West: 531), or the beautifully observed vignette of Danae, cast out to sea in a chest with her baby Perseus who sleeps peacefully in her arms, heedless of their plight (West: 543). On the other hand, probably symposiastic elegiac poems such as West 19 to 23 evoke the traditional themes of love and wine and growing old. His reputation for the evocation of pathos perhaps came about to an extent as a result of the large number of epigrams, many in the form of epitaphs, which were falsely attributed to him: he does seem to have become something of a 'national' poet in old age, after the Persian Wars, which probably accounts for these attributions, as does the talent for epigrammatic 'gnomic' utterances which is evident from a good number of quotations that have been preserved; a fine reputation 'is the last thing to go down into the earth' (West: 594); 'in a tight spot even what's hard seems attractive' (West: 590).

We do not know whether Simonides performed his works himself, but much of what we have is public rather than private in nature. This is especially true of the longest fragment, the recently discovered incomplete elegy on the battle of Plataea – an apparently unusual public use of the elegiac form. The poem opens with a section on the Trojan War. Simonides then invokes the *Muses* who had inspired Homer to immortalize the heroes of Troy to help him similarly to commemorate the deeds of the men who stood firm for Greece against the Persians. Little more remains except a damaged description of the Greeks marching out to Plataea. We do not know the occasion of the poem, or where it was performed; its elevation of his contemporaries to the level of the heroes of old implies also some kind of elevation of the poet himself; Simonides did not, of course, finally eclipse the fame of Homer, but it is perhaps fitting that the first Greek poet of historical times whose activities encompassed most of the Greek world should become, at least for a time, the national poet of Greece.

Bacchylides (c. 520–c. 450)

Bacchylides also came from Ceos, and is said to have been Simonides' nephew. Like him, he travelled widely, and composed in almost all the lyric forms, in the usual Doric dialect: poems to the gods, *partheneia*, processional hymns, love poetry, and *dithyrambs*. He was famous in antiquity, but most of his works were lost until significant papyrus discoveries, from the end of the nineteenth century onwards, provided us with most of his *epinikian* odes and some dithyrambs in reasonably complete form. Bacchylides was a contemporary (tradition said a rival) of Pindar, and moved in similar circles to him and Simonides, composing dithyrambs for Athens and epinikians for, amongst others, the Sicilian tyrants. Like Pindar and Simonides, we do not know to what extent he was involved in the performance of his own poetry. Dithyrambs were sung by choruses (though one of Bacchylides', on Theseus, has parts for a chorus-leader as Aegeus, and full chorus as citizens of Athens); the poet-composer trained the chorus, but there is no evidence that he necessarily took part. It used to be thought that epinikians, celebrations in song and dance composed for victorious competitors in the Olympic and similar games, were sung by the poet, partly because they frequently refer to themselves as 'I', but scholarly opinion now tends to think that they too were performed chorally. As for much else concerning lyric poetry, we simply do not know.

Bacchylides' reputation has suffered since ancient times from comparison with Pindar (see below); a Greek critic known as Longinus (not his real name) pointedly asked 'would you rather be Bacchylides than Pindar?', given that, smooth and faultless though his style may be, he never 'sets everything on fire' as Pindar can (*On the Sublime* 33). There is some truth in this. Both of the genres from which complete examples survive, epinikian and dithyramb, use mythological material extensively: compared with Pindar's allusive and complex use of myth, Bacchylides' narrative can seem pedestrian. It does, however, have the virtue of clarity – what is happening is never obscure – and, as Longinus implies, his use of language is elegant and seemingly effortless. But he is not dull; from the beginning of *Dithyramb* 12, on Theseus and the young Athenians on their way to Crete:

> The dark-prowed ship, bearing Theseus, steadfast in the din of battle, and twice seven fine young folk of the Ionians, clove through the Cretan Sea, for on its far-gleaming sail fell the breezes of the north wind, at the will of mighty Athene of the warlike *aegis*.

Or again, from the conclusion of *Epinikian* 31, to Hieron of Syracuse:

> Hieron, you have shown forth to mortals the finest flower of riches; and to one who has achieved greatly, it is not the gift of silence that finds him, but the truth of fine deeds shall be with you, and someone shall sing the gift of the honey-tongued nightingale of Ceos.

(The word translated here as 'gift', *charis*, has a complex of meanings including 'gift', 'favour', 'grace' and 'glory', all of which must be taken into account. The 'nightingale' is Bacchylides himself: see below on Pindar for the conventions of the epinikian.)

Bacchylides should not be under-rated: it is his misfortune to have been the contemporary of, and constantly to be compared with, one of the most extraordinary poets to have written in any language: Pindar.

Pindar (518–after 446)

Pindar was regarded in ancient times as the greatest of the lyric poets. Like many great figures, apocryphal stories attached themselves to him, so that it is hard to reconstruct any sort of biography. But he was born near Thebes which, despite his extensive travels, remained his home. His family was probably aristocratic: his attitudes throughout his life appear to have remained aristocratic and elitist, which has sometimes had an adverse effect on critical responses to his work, and his religious beliefs were conservative. One story which may be true relates that when Alexander the Great sacked Thebes, the only house left standing, on Alexander's orders, was that of Pindar; true or not, though, it is worth quoting for what it tells us both about Alexander and for its confirmation of Pindar's classic status – especially, perhaps, in the eyes of a king.

Seventeen books of Pindar's poetry were catalogued in the Library at Alexandria, including hymns, *paeans*, *dithyrambs*, processional hymns, *partheneia*, *hyporchēmata* and *encomia*. Only the four of books of his *epinikia* survive intact, but enough remains of his other works to indicate that (given the differing requirements of different genres) his poetical voice and technique were essentially consistent across the whole of his output. As a result of this accident of survival, though, it is through the epinikia alone that we can assess the truth of his ancient reputation.

The epinikian, an ode in celebration of a victory in one of the major athletic competitions, seems to have been pioneered, if not actually inaugurated, by Simonides, though the only surviving epinikia are those of Pindar and Bacchylides. It was *triadic* in form, composed in the standard Doric of choral lyric, and routinely contained praise of the victor's achievement along with appropriate mythological and moralizing content. Epinikia vary greatly in length, from a single triad (e.g. Pindar's *Olympian* 11 or *Isthmian* 3) to the enormous *Pythian* 4, with 299 lines in 13 triads. Some, probably the less elaborate ones, were performed at the games immediately after the victory (e.g. *Olympian* 11), but most of those we have seem to have been composed for performance when the victor returned home. In origin, the epinikian is a variant of the encomium, which itself originated as a song for the revelry with which the symposium traditionally concluded, but came to refer to any song in praise of an individual (hence the modern English use of the word). It belongs, therefore, squarely within the aristocratic *milieu* of the kind of man for whom Pindar wrote: wealth, at least, if not necessarily aristocratic lineage, was effectively a prerequisite for athletic prowess. Pindar's clients came from all over the Greek world, and it is often assumed that Pindar was commissioned to write for them, for a fee. The question of whether or not a fee was charged is too complex to be discussed here; but it is largely based on the view propagated by Alexandrian scholars, in whose world the patron was a familiar and often essential figure (the view of the Athenians derived from vague references to the supposed fondness for money of, especially, Simonides; see 1e). We should note, though, that if Pindar was indeed an aristocrat himself, the question of payment would have been a sensitive one, and perhaps we should think of the relationship between patron and poet in terms of the ancient aristocratic tradition of *xenia* (guest-friendship), based on mutual gift-giving and hospitality, rather than as a cash transaction. This has the advantage of making sense of the assumption of familiarity and equality between Pindar and the men whose achievements he celebrates, which is evident from many references within the odes.

The format of the epinikian resembles that of choral lyric such as Alcman's *partheneia*, and it seems likely that they were performed by a choral group, perhaps of the victor's social equals (as in a symposium), perhaps with a solo element where appropriate. The accompaniment was that of the lyre, and in some cases the *aulos* (see 1c), and dance, to which Pindar frequently refers, was an essential component of the performance. An alternative and perhaps less likely view is that epinikia were sung by the poet himself, or a soloist representing him. Certainly on at least one occasion he composed epinikia for victors in the same games from Corinth and Rhodes, and cannot have performed both himself without undue delay to one or other of the celebrations. If this is the case, the poetic 'I' frequent in the epinikia will be a poetic convention – perhaps the poet's way of personalizing the gift; perhaps he reserved personal appearances for the victories of his particular friends, others having to make do with the gift of song itself – no mean gift, from the master of the craft.

Each epinikian is a unique composition (only two of Pindar's 45 have the same metrical scheme), but the overall structure is largely consistent: an opening section with references to the victor, interwoven with some moralizing or generalizing reflections; a middle section consisting of a myth or myths, usually connected with the victor's family or city; and a conclusion which returns to the victor himself with the same admixture of general and moralizing content. Apart from the overarching metrical scheme of each composition, however, there is little else regular or predictable. The Roman poet Horace (*Odes* 4.2) likened Pindar to a mountain torrent in spate, for the way in which ideas seem to come tumbling out one after another. There is indeed always an underlying logic, but the listener would have had to contend with ellipses of thought, sudden transitions and leaps of imagination, and, especially within the mythological section, a selective and allusive approach to the familiar stories. To a *reader*, especially a modern one, struggling to come to terms with Pindar's complexity of thought and allusiveness, it may seem extraordinary that a listener could have made any sense of the songs at all. But even to follow a more linear narrative (to which Bacchylides comes closer) in song, with music and dance, cannot have been easy, and it may be that the rapid succession of images with which Pindar presents us actually created a cumulative picture that could be grasped more readily and wholly by a listener than a more simplistic approach. *Reading* a text presents different challenges to listening to its performance; Pindar would hardly have been accorded such an elevated reputation if no one had been able to understand what he was singing about.

Pindar invariably opens with a striking image. To take three poems at random: 'Golden lyre, of Apollo and the Muses the shared possession' (*Pythian* 1); 'I praise you, lover of glory, fairest of the cities of men' (*Pythian* 12); 'Thrice-victorious-at-Olympia' (*Olympian* 13: a single polysyllabic compound adjective). He is fond of the *priamel*: 'Most excellent is water; gold, gleaming like fire in darkness, outshines the glory of lordly wealth; but if you wish, my heart, to speak of games, look for no shining star more bright by day in the lonely sky, and let us talk of no games but the Olympian' (*Olympian* 1). The imagery here is typically rich and complex, with a strong visual element. Pindar frequently refers to gold, not as the measure of a man's wealth, but as something closer to a metaphor for the immortal – and, no doubt, for its visual impact. Brightness and splendour are favourites too, not only, as here, descriptive of gold or the sun, but as metaphors for the glory of victory and its fame through the music and dance that celebrate it, and for the moment of exaltation in victory when a man seems to come close to the gods. Such moments, though – Pindar frequently warns – do not come by chance. A man who would be victorious in the games, as in other areas of life, must indeed have natural ability in full measure: noble lineage, perhaps a family tradition of athletic prowess and wealth wisely used all contribute, but sheer hard work and training are essential too – as they are for the poet, the conveyor of immortality, as much as for the athlete who is its recipient. Even so, none of this is of any avail without the favour of the gods. This must be sought, and not forgotten: even in the moment of victory, a man is not a god, and must respect the limits of mortality. He must avoid the envy of his fellow men, and the 'jealousy' of the gods: *phthonos*, a difficult concept to translate, meaning something like the sensitivity of the gods to a man over-reaching his proper status, linked to *hubris* and *nemesis*, excessive pride and its inevitable fall. Admonitions such as this seem to us perhaps incongruous, in the celebration of victory, but are quintessentially Greek.

It is impossible to do justice in a brief account to the richness of Pindar's thought and language. Translation can give only a superficial impression, and no impression at all of the complexities of his use of language – even the Greeks found him difficult. Horace's 'rushing torrent' image, however, is not the whole story. Sometimes, indeed, Pindar does seem to be intoxicated with words, but beneath the kaleidoscopic surface is a strict framework of metre, handled with the controlled assurance of complete mastery. We are constrained to appreciate this mastery through words alone; to have witnessed the spectacle and music of a performance of one of his compositions must have been an extraordinary experience.

Pindar's aristocratic milieu and his exaltation of its values quickly made him seem a representative of an older, vanishing, world, especially in the egalitarian atmosphere of fifth-century Athens, whence many of our critical approaches to Greek literature originate. That he was a Theban did not help; Thebes was Athens' traditional enemy, and had joined the Persian side during Xerxes' invasion, about which, significantly, Pindar had little to say – in contrast with his supposed rival, Simonides. But his status in poetic terms was not questioned: even those who were out of sympathy with his views admitted his stature: there is no one else quite like him.

Further reading

The standard texts are as follows: for Sappho and Alcaeus, see Voigt (1971); for the other lyric poets, see Page (1962; 1974); for iambus and elegy, see West (1989). Texts and translations can also be found in the Loeb series (Campbell, 1982–1993). On Greek lyric poetry generally (though there is information on various individual poets), see Budelmann (2009); Herington (1985); Miller (1994); Podlecki (1984); West (1974). Of the poets briefly discussed above, some have been treated individually. So, for Archilochus, see Burnett (1998); for Tyrtaeus, see the interesting article of Tarkow (1983). He is also mentioned in most histories that deal with Sparta (see the suggestions for further reading after the section on Archaic Greece). Theognis receives some detailed treatment in Figueira and Nagy (1985). For Alcaeus, see Burnett (1998) again. Sappho has probably excited most interest, especially in more recent times: Burnett (1998); DuBois (1995); Greene (1996); Williamson (1995); Wilson (1996). For Pindar, see Burnett (2008); Crotty (1982); Goldhill (1991: chapter 2); Kurke (1991); Lefkowitz (1991); Nagy (1990); Steiner (1986).

Interlude: Greek history in the classical period

Roy Hyde

All dates in this chapter are BCE unless otherwise stated.

UP TO THE END OF THE PELOPONNESIAN WAR

Greeks had been settled on the east coast of the Aegean – Ionia – for many years. By the middle of the sixth century they were subordinate to the kings of Lydia, but lived on reasonable terms with them. The defeat of Croesus of Lydia by Cyrus, king of the Medes and Persians, in 546, brought the Greeks new masters, who proved less congenial, and against whom they revolted in 499. The main result of the unsuccessful revolt was to bring the mainland Greeks into conflict with Persia, nominally because Athens had sent ships to help the Ionians, in fact, because of the expansionist policy of kings Darius and Xerxes.

An expedition against Athens sent by Darius was defeated (perhaps not quite as gloriously as the Athenians remembered, but still defeated) at Marathon in 490. A much larger one, led by Xerxes in person in 480, was repelled in 479, mostly through the efforts of Athens and Sparta. The Greeks resolved to drive Persia out of the Aegean altogether, and the Delian League was formed with this end in view: Athens, as a naval power, effectively headed the league, not least because of Sparta's reluctance to commit to overseas campaigns. Gradually, as the other member states preferred to provide money rather than ships and men, Athens came to dominate the alliance: by the late 450s the league treasury was moved from Delos to Athens, and the league had essentially become an Athenian empire. Tribute from the allies began to be used not only for military purposes (the Persian threat had by now almost disappeared) but also to adorn the city of Athens, under the auspices of the dominant political figure in mid fifth-century Athens, Pericles.

The other mainland Greek states were understandably concerned. Sporadic hostilities between Athens and Sparta took place, but stopped short of all-out war. Some of Sparta's allies were more vehemently anti-Athenian than Sparta herself; when open war did break out, in 431 (the Peloponnesian War:

431–404), it was probably as much a result of pressure from Corinth, a naval power, and consequently in more direct opposition to Athens, than as a result of pure Spartan hostility to Athens.

The first ten years of the war brought no decision, with Athens dominant at sea, and Sparta largely unchallenged on land. Pericles, whose strategy depended on control of the sea, died in the third year of the war, leaving no obvious successor; Cleon, after some success, and Sparta's most effective general Brasidas, were killed fighting against each other in 422, and in the Peace of Nicias (named after the moderate Athenian politician Nicias) of 421 Athens undertook to keep out of Spartan affairs, and Sparta recognized the reality of the Athenian empire: a qualified success for Athens.

Though diplomatic machinations and some fighting resumed almost immediately, the Peace was still nominally in force in 415 when Athens launched a major expedition against Sicily. It was a disaster: Alcibiades, the able but unscrupulous general most in favour of the expedition, went into self-imposed exile almost as soon as it reached Sicily as a result of the activities of his political opponents, leaving the aging and ailing Nicias in charge. Major reinforcements could not turn the tide; defeated in 413, Athens lost 200 ships and their crews, 4,000 Athenian soldiers, and far more allies.

Revolts began amongst Athens' ally states; Sparta went on the offensive, even taking to the sea; oligarchs at Athens for a time overthrew the democracy. But, extraordinarily, Athens survived, built ships and manned them, recalled Alcibiades, and held on to most of her allies. Both sides competed for Persian financial backing, while the Persians watched them wear themselves out, mostly in sea-fighting off Ionia, in a war neither side seemed to know how to win. Alcibiades was exiled again, and soon after killed in Phrygia; Spartan admirals bumbled; Persian satraps double-crossed both sides and each other. Eventually Sparta found an able commander in Lysander, and Athens shot herself in the foot; after a victory at Arginusae (406), the generals were prosecuted on a trumped-up (political) charge and those who did not flee were put to death. In 405, Lysander wiped out the Athenian fleet at Aegospotami; by 404 he was blockading the Piraeus. Athens sued for peace. Sparta's allies voted to destroy Athens and kill or enslave all her inhabitants.

Further reading

For good introductions to the period, see Buckley (1996); Cartledge (2002a); Davies (1993); Hornblower (2002); Munn (2002); Osborne (2000); Powell (1991); Todd (1996); and now Rhodes (2010). For a celebrated and distinctive history of the causes of the Peloponnesian War, see de Ste. Croix (1972). On the Athenian democracy, there is a large amount of good work. Here are some examples: Goldhill and Osborne (1999; 2006); Loraux (1986) (dense but interesting); Rhodes (2003b; 2004) (a good collection of some classic articles). Josiah Ober has made a number of important contributions to the study of the democracy (see 1989; 1998; 2001; see also 4a in this book). For a good collection of sources to do with the democracy, see Robinson (2003).

FROM THE END OF THE PELOPONNESIAN WAR TO THE DEATH OF ALEXANDER

At the end of the Peloponnesian War (404), Athens faced extermination. Sparta, however, resisted her allies' demands to destroy Athens; instead, Athens lost her empire and most of her surviving ships, and the Long Walls from the city to Piraeus were destroyed. A Spartan governor was installed, and a Spartan-backed puppet government, the 'Thirty Tyrants' established. The regime of the Thirty became a reign of terror: opponents were executed or exiled. The exiles regrouped, and civil war broke out; the democrats emerged victorious, and democracy was restored in 401.

On the whole, the Spartans let the Athenians get on with it, being more concerned with trying to control their own allies. The freedom of the Ionian cities had been sold to obtain Persian assistance at the end of the Peloponnesian War, and Sparta now tried to recover her reputation by campaigns in Ionia to restore that freedom. Cyrus, brother of the Persian king, recruited a mercenary Greek force (the Ten Thousand of Xenophon's *Anabasis*) in an attempt to usurp the throne. Even though Cyrus' attempt failed, the effectiveness of the mercenaries against Persian troops hinted at Persian vulnerability. Many of the Ten Thousand stayed on and fought alongside the Spartans and her allies during the 390s. Meanwhile in Greece, Athens was recovering, and joined Argos, Corinth and Thebes in an alliance against Sparta which resulted in a battle at Coronea in 394, which Sparta won.

The years after Coronea saw the always complex inter-state politics of Greece become even more complicated, with constantly changing patterns of alliances. Athens, with the help of Persian gold, rebuilt the Long Walls and for a time recovered some of her old influence in the shape of the Second Athenian Confederacy; Sparta became more and more isolated; by the 360s Thebes, under the dynamic leadership of Pelopidas and Epaminondas, was the major power in Greece and defeated the hitherto invincible Spartans at Leuctra (371) and again at Mantinea (362). But Epaminondas fell at Mantinea, and Thebes' hour of glory was over.

As the cities of central and southern Greece wore themselves out, the balance of power had begun to change. The northern states, Thessaly and Macedon, had long operated mainly on the fringe of Greek affairs. In the 370s, the expansionism of Jason, tyrant of Pherae, chieftain of a newly unified Thessaly, had briefly threatened to upset the balance, but his career was cut short by assassination. In 359, a far more serious threat appeared in the shape of Philip, the new regent, and soon king, of Macedon. By 352, Philip, having set about welding the Macedonian army into the most formidable fighting force in Greece, had absorbed Thessaly, and seemed set to move southwards.

His immediate aim appears to have been the unification of Greece under his control; his ultimate aim, probably, the conquest of Persia. Despite the efforts of Demosthenes in Athens to rally Greece against him, his manpower and military expertise were irresistible. Sparta was by now a spent force; Athens and Thebes combined were defeated at Chaeronea (338) and the formation of the League of Corinth (337) acknowledged Philip's effective sovereignty over Greece. Philip's ambitions came to nothing when he too fell victim to an assassin's blow in 336; if the Greeks hoped that his 18-year-old son and heir would prove more malleable, they were sorely mistaken: he was Alexander the Great. Hardly had Alexander established himself on the throne when Thebes rebelled: his response was swift and typical; Thebes, it is said, was razed to the ground, all but the house of the poet Pindar.

Philip was an extraordinary man, and had changed the face of Greece; Alexander, brutal, brilliant, romantic, insufferable, changed the face of a continent. When Greece was settled to his satisfaction, he set about fulfilling his father's ambition and his own: in 334 he crossed the Hellespont, in his own eyes a new Achilles, marching to avenge the long tale of Persian insults to Greece. By 326, with Darius III defeated and slain, Alexander, far into the north of India, was finally forced to abandon his relentless career of conquest, only because his men would go no further. He died at Babylon, on the return journey (323). His successors divided his empire between them, and their dynasties, for the most part, flourished. The Greeks continued to quarrel amongst themselves, but they were players on a small stage now: the age of the nation-state had dawned: the day of the *polis* was over.

Further reading

For good introductions to the period, see Buckley (1996); Hornblower (2002); Osborne (2000); Rhodes (2010).

Chapter 4

The drama of classical Athens

All dates in this chapter refer to BCE unless stated otherwise. Glossary items: *agōn; allegory; antilabē; aulos; boulē; chorēgia, chorēgos; distichomythiai; dithyramb; eisodoi; ekklēsia; ekkyklēma; epeisodia; kommos; komoi; liturgy; logeion; mēchanē; metic; monody; orchestra; parabasis; parodoi; parodos; philia; prologos; skēnē; stasimon; stichomythia; theologeion.*

THE ATHENIAN DEMOCRACY AND THE DRAMATIC FESTIVALS

Neil Croally

Most scholars now accept that very near the end of the sixth century – the date 508–07 is normally used, though with no guarantee of certainty – the Athenians established a form of government which had at least the outline of democracy. The Athenians themselves used the term *isonomia* (equality before the law), not coining the more familiar term until later (the first use we know is in Herodotus). The assembly (*ekklēsia*), which all citizens (free-born Athenian men over the age of 18; women were excluded) were entitled to attend, was the legislative body; the council (*boulē*) consisted of 500 citizens elected from the ten tribes sortitively (i.e. by lot), and was the executive body; the collection of law courts (the *heliaia*) was served by an annual roll of 6,000 jurors, who were not only sortitively elected, but arbitrarily assigned to particular cases.

What were tribes?

In the sixth century BCE, regional factions in Attica based around certain aristocratic clans tended to undermine the stability of the city. Whether the intention was to deal with the problem in principle or to obstruct particular aristocratic enemies, Cleisthenes' invention of the ten Athenian tribes looks, with hindsight, to be a masterstroke. Influenced perhaps by the new interests in mathematics and geometry, Cleisthenes divided Attica up into three regions: the city, the hinterland and the costal areas. Within each region he established ten trittyeis (trittyes means a thirtieth). Each of the ten tribes was made up of three trittyeis, one from each of the three regions. Thus – strange as it seems – tribes had no ethnic or regional identity.

Indeed, with the exception of the ten generals and some treasury officials, all the officers of the Athenian state were elected by lot. However, we should not think of the democracy as established fully-fledged by Cleisthenes in 508, but rather as an unprecedented system of government evolving throughout the fifth century. Ostracism, for instance, which was the mechanism by which politicians who seemed to threaten the stability of the city were exiled for a fixed period, may not have been introduced until the 480s. The reforms associated with Ephialtes and Pericles in the 460s and 450s arguably made the system even more democratic. And, while there were in the latter part of the century two oligarchic coups (412–11 and 404–03), for the most part Athenian democracy managed the inevitable tensions between the aristocratic elite and the majority with not inconsiderable success (Ober, 1989).

For our purposes it is important to note the ways in which the Athenian democracy was distinctive. In its reliance on sortition as its preferred means of election, the city did everything it could to ensure that every citizen was involved in the running of the city. Thucydides' Pericles famously asserted in the Funeral Oration that Athenians thought that the citizen who minded his own business had no business in Athens at all (Thuc. 2.46). Because the assembly was peopled not by elected representatives but by any citizens who chose to attend, classical Athens was a direct democracy. The assembly used its power as the dominant political institution to redistribute wealth.

All drama at Athens took place at festivals, and all festivals had a religious dimension. There were a number of dramatic festivals, established at various times and held in various parts of Attica, but the most important was that held at the Theatre of Dionysus in the centre of Athens. The evidence is not conclusive but it seems that this festival – called the Great or City Dionysia – was established during the tyranny of Peisistratus, probably some time during the 530s.

What did Dionysus have to do with tragedy?

The ancients themselves worried about the relationship between the god and the plays, but an answer to the question may be possible. Dionysus, while he was one of the Olympians, never seems to be quite part of that elite group. Mentioned only once in Homer, he seems to be a god never quite fixed, always leaving or arriving. Certainly we know of him as the god of wine, of the gift, of the mask, of theatre, and of the fig. I cannot explain the fig, but for the other areas we can say that they share a sense of not being oneself, of pretending to be someone else, or of being transported into unusual experiences. This Dionysus – the god of the other way of thinking – makes a very powerful and understandable god of the theatre.

It has been argued that, because the most important dramatic festival was founded before the establishment of the democracy, we should see the festival as broadly political rather than democratic (e.g. Rhodes, 2003a and 2003b). This argument misses the point that the democracy tended to adapt existing institutions, such as the assembly and the council, to its own needs: there is no reason to think that we should view the dramatic festival any differently. The festival took place annually in March at and around the Theatre of Dionysus. The position of the theatre in the very heart of Athens, together with the way the festival was funded and organized, suggest that the Great Dionysia was an extremely important event in the city's calendar.

The dramatic festivals

The Great Dionysia, the premier dramatic festival in classical Athens, occurred in March. It was organized by the *archōn epōnymos*, who selected the poets whose plays would be performed, and the *chorēgoi* who would pay for the cost of the productions. Before the festival began, the poets gave brief highlights of their plays in a ceremony called the proagon. After 440 BCE this took place in Pericles' Odeion. The statue of Dionysus Eleuthērios was taken out of the city and brought back to his sanctuary next to the theatre. The sequence of events at the festival is itself disputed. Two possible sequences are given below:

Day 1	Procession including citizens, metics and *chorēgoi*; dithyrambic contests with choirs of 50 men and 50 boys provided by each tribe.	Procession including citizens, metics and *chorēgoi*; pre-play ceremonies (described in the main text); boys' dithyrambic contest; first comedy.
Day 2	Pre-play ceremonies; five comedies (possibly reduced to three during the Peloponnesian War).	Men's dithyrambic contest; second comedy.
Day 3	First tragedian (three tragedies + one satyr play).	First tragedian (three tragedies + one satyr play); third comedy.
Day 4	Second tragedian.	Second tragedian; fourth comedy.
Day 5	Third tragedian.	Third tragedian; fifth comedy.

The tragic competition began in *c.* 533 BCE, the satyr competition in 520 BCE, and the comic competition in 486 BCE.

There were other dramatic festivals, but we know relatively little about them. The Lenaea in January or February was attended by Athenians only (Aristophanes *Acharnians* 501–8). The comic competition there, which almost matched that of the

(Continued)

(Continued)

Great Dionysia for prestige, began in 442 BCE; the tragic competition, for which the tragedians wrote two plays each, began about ten years later, but never achieved the importance of the competition at the Great Dionysia. Scholars also refer to the collection of dramatic festivals that occurred throughout Attica in December or early January as the Rural Dionysia but, apart from knowing that some urban theatrophiles liked to attend these festivals (Plato *Republic* 475d), we know little about them.

What was satyr drama?

We have one complete play (Euripides *Cyclops*) and some fragments of Sophocles' *Trackers*. Sommerstein (2002: 23) offers a recipe: 'Ensure that it [satyr drama] contains some of the following ingredients . . . : sex, babies, resurrection, athletics, new inventions or discoveries . . . Stir in a chorus of satyrs, together with their "father", Silenus . . . ' It seems as though satyr drama dealt with similar mythical stories as tragedy, but in a rollicking if not quite comic way.

The city of Athens was directly involved in selecting and funding the plays. The council selected those who judged the contests of both the playwrights and the actors. The selection of these ten judges was organized through the ten tribes, reflecting the formation of the state; and its method was sortitive, the electoral method basic to the democracy. A top state official called the *archōn epōnymos* chose the playwrights whose plays would be performed and the sponsors of the plays (called *chorēgoi*). The festival was funded by the city, either directly – through the fee paid to the authors – or indirectly, through a system of taxation called the *liturgy*. Liturgies, imposed on the rich, could be used to fund a variety of things, including the upkeep of triremes and financial provision for dramatic choruses. The cost of a *chorēgia* almost matched that of the upkeep of a trireme: a tragic chorus in 410 cost 3,000 drachmae, which is about one half of the cost of maintaining a warship. Given Athens' dependence on her navy, this suggests that the Athenians valued the production of their tragedies (almost) as highly as their imperial ambitions and the defence of their homeland. The festival was probably followed by a special assembly which judged the conduct of the officials organizing the festival. A special fund provided by the city called the *theōrika* was established, though we do not know when, to subsidize the cost of seeing the plays (two obols a day from the 440s onwards, when six obols a day was a reasonable daily wage; see Sommerstein, 2002: 5).

Most important, however, was the size of the audience which attended the plays. Modern estimates range from 14,000 to 17,000. While there were a few foreigners present, and there may have been women in the audience (the evidence is unhelpful), the vast majority of these thousands were citizens of Athens.

Were women in the audience?

If we take the Great Dionysia as a purely religious event, we would expect women to attend, as just about the only public role women had in classical Athens was presence at the city's religious rituals. However, if we take the festival as a political event, then one would expect women to be excluded, as they were from all other political institutions. Here is some of the evidence: *Life of Aeschylus* 9 and Pollux 4.110 both have the story of pregnant women in the audience of Aeschylus' *Eumenides* giving birth in terror at their first sight of the furies on stage. However, both pieces of evidence are late (fifth-century CE) and could be put down to a desire to describe the theatrical effect in an extreme way. The evidence of Plato – *Gorgias* 502b–d; *Laws* 817c – that tragedy was a rhetorical art form that appealed to slaves, children and women, could be understood not as confirmation of the presence of women, but rather as an insulting reference to a hypothetical audience of the least discrimination. Slaves were likely to have been present but not strictly as members of the audience; no doubt some metics were there. Ambassadors from the subject cities, who brought the tribute demanded by the Athenians, were there as well.

In the latter half of the fifth century, before the full effects of the Peloponnesian War of 431–04 were felt, the citizen population of Athens was probably between 30,000 and 50,000. So an audience of around 15,000 represents a very considerable proportion of the citizen body; and remember that plays were performed three or four days in a row, and it is unlikely that the same 15,000 turned up every day. It is also important to remember who these citizens were. A 40–50 per cent proportion of an electorate watching drama or a given programme is not something we find hard to imagine; it used to occur regularly with the big soap operas; now it tends to happen with celebrity or audience-participation shows. But the Athenian citizens in the audience were not just election fodder, people given the right every four or five years to elect a government. They were citizens of a direct democracy. That means that every citizen had the right to attend the assembly. The assembly met every ten days or so; every citizen had the right to speak and vote. Estimates of attendance at the assembly are around 6,000 (Hansen, 1976). To drive home the point about the power and responsibilities these citizens had, it should be borne in mind that, if they voted for war, they might, as members of a citizen army, have to go home to collect their weapons for immediate combat.

The ceremonies which preceded the performance of the plays also demonstrate the political nature of the festival. The generals, the highest officers of state, made offerings to the gods; crowns were awarded to citizens who had performed conspicuously well in the service of the state; the tribute from the empire was displayed on the stage; finally, there was a procession of orphans of war, educated at state expense as far as adulthood. This was a celebration of democratic ideology, a very public display of the power and wealth and all-pervasiveness of the city, a sort of mixture (in a modern analogy) of a royal wedding, a cup final, an Ashes victory celebration and the old celebrations of the October Revolution in Red Square in Moscow (Goldhill, 1990).

Tragedy was produced, then, in and by the city. The involvement of political institutions in its organization, the resources accorded the festival and the central position of the theatre all support that view. If we remember in addition the very distinctive city that Athens was, and the way in which it had adapted institutions that pre-existed the democracy, then we should accept that the theatrical festival was adapted too, both in the way its organization reflected important features of the democracy, such as in the use of sortition and the liturgy, and in the fact that the members of the audience were for the most part citizens in a direct democracy.

Further reading

For a collection of sources on the democracy, see Robinson (2003). For sources for the dramatic festivals, see Csapo and Slater (1994). On the democracy, see Goldhill and Osborne (1999, 2006); Loraux (1986) (dense but interesting); Ober (1989; 1998; 2001); Rhodes (2003b; 2004). On Greek political thought, see Cartledge (2009); Salkever (2009). The difference in scholarly opinion in relation to the festival is to do with whether the festival is (a) political and (b) democratic. For work that believes that the festival is both, see Croally (1994), Goldhill (1990; 2000), Seaford (2000) and a number of articles in Winkler and Zeitlin (1990). For work that accepts (a) but not (b), see Rhodes (2003a and 2003b). For a scholar who thinks that the festival is neither really (a) nor (b), see Griffin (1999a) (and also perhaps Heath (1986); though see his article in Griffin (1999b)).

TRAGEDY

Neil Croally

No literary genre from the ancient world, with the possible exception of epic, has rivalled the glamour of Greek tragedy. The plays of the three great Athenian tragedians – Aeschylus, Sophocles and Euripides – have influenced other dramatists and other artists, as well as critics and philosophers (note Aristotle's *Poetics* and Nietzsche's *The Birth of Tragedy*). There have been a large number of performances of tragedies in European and American cities in the past 30 years (Goldhill, 2007). But the apparent universality of Greek tragedy which these modern performances imply should not make us forget that tragedy arose in the city of classical Athens, and that all the plays that we have were performed during the period of Athenian democracy.

While we shall consider the formal literary characteristics of individual plays and individual playwrights, we should not forget that, for the Athenians, and for the Greeks more generally as well, the political and the literary were not mutually exclusive. The great philosopher Aristotle (who is named as the author of a fascinating text about tragedy – the *Poetics*) said both that man was a political animal (i.e. one who naturally operated in a city) and a being who learned through *mimēsis* (imitation or fiction: *Poetics* 1448b5ff.). That sense of a necessary relationship between the city and the fictions it watched on the stage of the Theatre of Dionysus seems to permeate and constitute tragedy.

We are less certain about the origins of drama and of tragedy than we are about the origins of the Great Dionysia. We could talk about *kōmoi* (songs of some sort) or *kōmasts* (performers of *kōmoi*); we might mention satyrs, the transgressive followers of Pan; or he-goat singers (*tragos* – he-goat; *aoidoi* – singers). However, even if we thought we could accurately understand these origins of drama and tragedy (and we cannot), this would not help us to understand the phenomenon of classical tragedy. Yes, drama seems to have originated out of singing and dancing in honour of a god (there is late seventh-century vase evidence for such komastic performances): tragedy, or rather its chorus, may have originated in a similar way. The first famous Attic tragedian, Thespis, possibly added an actor for performances at the new festival of Dionysus founded by Peisitratus in the 530s. But none of this mainly speculative information can help to explain fifth-century tragedy.

The texts themselves

Although all the extant tragedies come from the fifth century, the earliest manuscripts we have for these plays come from around the turn of the first millennium. At first sight a distance of 1,400–1,500 years between original performance and earliest text does not inspire confidence. However, when compared to earlier papyrus versions (where they exist) our texts seem relatively reliable. Indeed, some scholars argue that most of the damage done to tragic texts probably came in the first hundred years after their original performance. Why? The very popularity of the plays of Aeschylus, Sophocles and Euripides meant that there were probably a number of versions of the plays appearing in the late fifth and fourth centuries, both for reperformance at the smaller theatrical festivals (grouped under the name Rural Dionysia) and for recitation at symposia. However, because the book trade only started to function towards the end of the fifth century, most of these versions would have been passed on orally, allowing actors' interpolations, omissions and so on. According to Plutarch, the Sicilians were especially fond of Euripides, and would try to acquire new texts from any Athenians who passed through Sicily (Plutarch *Nicias* 29). Indeed, some of the Athenians who were captured by the Syracusans in 413, were freed by their captors because of their singing of songs from the plays of Euripides. Even someone as devoted to writing as Aristotle – he had the largest library in Athens – seems to have preferred to rely on his memory of poetry: most of the great philosopher's references to Homer are inaccurate. In an age when there was no definitive version of a play and in which there was no copyright it is no surprise that there was a great deal of variety in the texts of individual plays as they were performed.

The popularity of fifth-century tragedies can be seen in official measures taken to allow their reperformance: the Athenians voted some time after Aeschylus' death that his plays could be reperformed at the main theatrical festivals and, from 386, that old tragedies could be staged at the Great Dionysia. In *c.* 330 Lycurgus, an Athenian politician, sponsored a law that required official texts of the plays of Aeschylus, Sophocles and Euripides to be collected. Of course, we do not know what texts Athenian officials themselves worked from. But it does seem as though these Lycurgan texts were the same as those stolen by Ptolemy and deposited in the famous Library at Alexandria. These texts are the basis of the texts we have now which, with the possible exception of *Rhesus* and *Prometheus Vinctus*, are all by Aeschylus, Sophocles and Euripides. With Aeschylus known to be responsible for some 60 tragedies, Sophocles for more than 120 and Euripides for 92 and, as there were nine new plays performed in most years (making up to 900 tragedies in the fifth century), the three authors probably provided more than one quarter of all the tragedies performed at the Great Dionysia in the fifth century. Together they also won many of the playwright's prizes (Aeschylus, 13; Sophocles, up to 20; Euripides, 4): as the evidence of Aristophanes' *Frogs* confirms, the three playwrights were already regarded by the end of the fifth century as the greatest three tragedians.

Other tragedians

Earlier than or contemporary with Aeschylus: Choerilus, Phrynichus, Pratinas. Later authors: Aeschylus' son Euphorion, his nephew Philocles (who had two tragedian sons), Aristarchus of Tegea, Neophron of Sicyon, Ion of Chios, Achaeus of Eretria, Phrynichus' son Polyphrasmon, Pratinas' son Aristias, Sophocles' son Iophon, Agathon, Critias, Euripides' nephew, also called Euripides. So, with four known exceptions, tragedians were Athenian, and writing tragedies ran in the family.

That reputation provides one good explanation for the survival of the plays, first by oral reproduction and later by the collection and dissemination of the texts by Alexandrian scholars. Indeed it is often argued that we have the texts we do because they were copied so many times for school editions in the Byzantine period. It must be remembered, however, that we have only seven tragedies of Aeschylus extant (if we count *Prometheus Vinctus*), the same number by Sophocles, and 17 by Euripides (if we count *Rhesus* as not by Euripides and *Cyclops* as not being a tragedy). That means we have 31 tragedies, the earliest of which was performed in 472 and the latest of which was performed in 401. Those 72 years would have seen up to 648 new tragedies performed: that means that our extant plays constitute less than a 5 per cent sample. I suggest, then, that we should beware grand claims made about the nature of tragedy.

What did the audience see and hear?

The Theatre of Dionysus was situated underneath the Acropolis and was part of a complex that included a temple of Dionysus and, from about 440, the Odeion of Pericles. The archaeological evidence is not compelling but the early theatre seems to have been built of wood, though it was possibly replaced in the latter half of the fifth century with a stone building. The fifth-century audience would have been seated in a roughly semi-circular auditorium, possibly seated by tribe (thus further revealing the political nature of the festival), with some seats in the front row reserved for important officials, such as the Generals and the priest of Dionysus Eleuthērios. The plays were performed in four connected but distinct spaces (starting with the lowest): the *orchēstra*, the *logeion*, the *theologeion*, the *mēchanē*. The *orchēstra*, almost circular, was the space in which the chorus sang and danced (though some scholars argue that in the fifth century the *orchēstra* may have been an 'elongated, shallow quadrilateral space'; Sommerstein, 2002: 9); the *logeion*, possibly slightly raised above the level of the *orchēstra*, was mainly if not exclusively occupied by actors; the *theologeion* – used for heroes or gods – was on top of the *skēnē*, the hut which lay behind the *logeion* and which represented off-stage space indoors, allowing actors to change mask and costume (it is not clear when the *skēnē* was introduced); the *mēchanē* (a sort of hoist or crane) allowed the playwrights to show gods – or a Medea – towering above humans.

Some uses of theatrical space

Tragedians made use of the vertical axis (in ascending order: *orchestra, logeion, theologeion, mēchanē*) to reflect on the relative position of their characters. After Medea has murdered her children, she appears with their corpses in front of Jason on the *mēchanē*, where gods normally appear (hence *deus ex machina*). Has her murder of her children received divine support? That is not clear but she is literally superior to Jason. The god Dionysus in the *Bacchae* enters from the *skēnē*: this may stress that he is pretending to be human. Every time Oedipus enters the *skēnē* (representing his palace) in *Oedipus Tyrannus*, we are reminded that he should not be entering what is his mother's house in this way (i.e. as her husband).

Actors entered and exited the stage along passages (called *eisodoi* or *parodoi*): the use of specific entrances could signify where a character was going to or where they were coming from. There was also a piece of kit called an *ekkyklēma*. This was a sort of trolley on wheels and it was used to display dying or dead characters.

Thespis is said to have introduced the first actor, Aeschylus the second, and Sophocles the third. Having a maximum of only three actors means that in some plays various characters were played by more than one actor during the performance (Sophocles' *Oedipus at Colonus* is an example of this; there seem to be have been no limits on the number of mute characters). The actors were masked in what appears to be a fairly generic way. For instance, young men were not bearded, while older men were. The costumes were most likely to be splendid – remember the amount of money that went into these productions and the grandeur of the themes. Euripides' *Electra* is often noted as a sort of scandalous success because it was so keen on stressing how bad Electra's clothes were: this example would tend to suggest that tragic costume was normally grand. The spectacle must have been tremendous.

A peculiarity of Attic tragedy is the chorus. Originally numbering 12 and then 15 trained dancers and singers, the chorus had a number of roles. Its choral lyrics, involving singing and dancing accompanied by an *aulos* (we know little about the music), interrupted and commented on the action. Some choruses represent collectivity (as in *Antigone*), some do so less obviously; some are not much involved in the action; others are in our terms important protagonists (good examples would be *Eumenides* and *Bacchae*, two plays named after their choruses).

Early tragedy

We know that, with a few exceptions, almost all tragedies were based on stories inherited from a collection of mythical stories. These mainly concern a few cities: Troy, Thebes, Argos, Athens. Most of the audience, with their knowledge of Homer and other epic cycles (lost to us), would have known the stories already (even if tragedians could still spring surprises, such as Euripides' *Electra* and *Helen*). It is interesting that the earliest plays we know about, and the earliest complete extant play are not set in mythical time. In 493 Phrynichus' *Capture of Miletus* was performed. According to Herodotus (6.21.1–2), this play, which described the sack of Miletus by the Persians in 495, was banned by the Athenians as being too painfully close to home. (The other early plays we know about are Phrynichus' *Persians*, performed in 476 and Aeschylus' *Persians*, which survives complete and which was performed in 472.)

It is probable that between the 530s and 472 some of the formal characteristics of tragedy were established. The plays normally start with a prologue (*prologos*) or other speech which sets the scene. Then the plays alternate between episodes (*epeisodia*) and choral lyrics (the first choral lyric is normally called the *parodos*, sung as they enter the *orchēstra*; the other songs of the chorus are called *stasima* – literally 'standing songs', i.e. standing in the *orchēstra*). The episodes involve actors (including the leader of the chorus), are written in a metre (the iambic trimeter) as near to prose as a poetic metre can be, include both monologues and dialogue, in particular the type called *stichomythia*, when there is one line per character (there is also *distichomythiai*, where each actor has two lines and *antilabē*, where one actor interrupts another in the middle of a line). In episodes one also encounters solo songs sung by actors (*monody*), a particular form of which is the long lament, sometimes shared with the chorus (*kommos*). Choral lyrics are performed by the chorus, involve singing and dancing, use a variety of metres and musical accompaniment, and are characterized by dense poetic language and allusiveness; the choral lyrics can sometimes comment on the action by reference to other myths; one other common feature of the episodes is the set-piece debate (called the *agōn*).

The formal characteristics of tragedy are important, even though for a modern audience they can sometimes seem to obstruct understanding and enjoyment. We are not used to such long speeches (one messenger speech in *Persians* is 80 lines long, and the opening chorus is 154 lines; such a long speech is called a *rhēsis*) or to the interruption of the action that the choral lyrics represent. We no longer watch dramas with actors wearing masks, and with more than one actor playing the same role. What we can understand and enjoy, however, is the way that tragedy tackles a range of important themes, themes which both reflect the peculiar interests of the fifth-century audience and which also deal powerfully with what it means to be human.

Justice, the gods and fate

The first indisputable classic of Attic tragedy is Aeschylus' *Oresteia*, first performed in 458. It is a trilogy, a form which Aeschylus certainly used on at least two other occasions, but one not favoured by Sophocles or Euripides. The first play, *Agamemnon*, tells the story of Agamemnon's return from Troy to Mycenae, and his murder by his wife, Clytemnestra, and her lover Aegisthus. This is followed by *The Libation Bearers* (*Choephori*), which has two of Agamemnon's children taking vengeance for the murder of their father by killing both Clytemnestra and Aegisthus. The final play, *Eumenides*, starts with Orestes being pursued by the furies (the euphemistically named *Eumenides* or 'Kindly Ones' of the title) and ends with the very first jury (of Athenian citizens) in the very first trial finding Orestes innocent. It is apparent from this trilogy, as well as from Aeschylus' other plays, that Aeschylus was interested in the relationships between individuals and groups, and between humans and gods, and the setting he chose to dramatize those relationships was that of the city. In Aeschylus' *Oresteia* he seems particularly interested in the themes of the gods, revenge, and men and women, and how all these three themes relate to the (perhaps broader) theme of justice.

Clytemnestra pretends to welcome home her victorious husband, commanding her servants to spread red tapestries in front of him, so that justice may lead him into the house (*Ag.* 908–11). Agamemnon's response to this dramatic but ominous gesture is to reply that his wife treats him as if he were a woman or a barbarian or a god (*Ag.* 918–24). The scene is a rich and powerful one: Clytemnestra's talk of justice is suggestive and there is possibly dramatic irony; the red tapestries anticipate the bloody events that will soon occur inside the house, and Agamemnon's response nicely highlights the way Greeks thought in polarities. Clytemnestra's plan to kill Agamemnon by luring him into the inside of the palace exemplifies one of the ways that the relationship between men and women was dramatized in tragedy. In common with more prosaic ideological prescriptions, the tragedians tended to associate their women with inside rather than outside space. Inside space can become a dangerous place for a man: he might hear terrible, outrageous things, as Hippolytus does in *Hippolytus*; he might have his eyes stabbed out by women's brooches, as Polymestor does in Euripides' *Hecuba*; he might find himself sleeping and procreating with his mother, as Oedipus does. Or, as in *Agamemnon*, he will be ensnared and brutally murdered. Or, as in *The Libation Bearers*, Orestes will need his sister's help to murder his mother inside the palace (*Cho.* 554–5). Once Clytemnestra has committed the murder in *Agamemnon*, she commends the deed to the horrified chorus as the work of justice characterized as a sort of master craftsman (*Ag.* 1406). Her revenge is justified because Agamemnon killed (or sacrificed) their daughter Iphigenia so that the Greek fleet could reach Troy (*Ag.* 1417–18). Clytemnestra says that she herself has become the ancient, bitter avenging deity (*Ag.* 1501). For her, revenge and justice are the same thing.

Aegisthus, her lover, thinks the same: he is justified in killing Agamemnon because of what Agamemnon's father had done to his own father Thyestes (*Ag.* 1583ff.).

Thyestes' feast

Thyestes was the brother of Atreus (the father of Agamemnon and Menelaus). Thyestes had an affair with Atreus' wife, Aerope, and received from her the golden lamb, the owner of which could claim the throne of Mycene, a throne currently shared between Atreus and Thyestes. Thyestes thus took the throne but agreed to step down if the sun followed a reverse course through the sky. After Zeus arranged this (Euripides *Electra* 699ff.), Atreus banished Thyestes. When he later found out about the affair, he invited Thyestes to a banquet, pretending reconciliation. At the banquet he served Thyestes' own children to Thyestes.

Aegisthus' self-image is that he is 'the just weaver' of the murder (*Ag.* 1604), who has used the nets of justice to ensnare his enemy (*Ag.* 1611). When he first appears after the murders he memorably says (*Ag.* 1577–9):

> O happy light of a justice-bringing day!
> Now I may say again that the gods are the
> avengers of mortals . . .

Contained and conflated in these lines, then, are justice, vengeance and the gods. Such a conflation continues in the second play of the trilogy, where the children of Agamemnon think that they are similarly justified in taking vengeance on their mother and lover: their vengeance, too, is justified and supported by the gods (see, for instance, *Choephori* 142–4; 244ff.; 269–70 – Orestes talking of Apollo's support; 306–14).

But we might ask: when will the revenge-taking end? And on what possible basis? Might there be a different sort of justice? For Aeschylus, and for his audience, these were, of course, moral questions, but they were also political. For it was the city that determined how justice was to operate, and what its possibilities and limitations were. At the beginning of *Eumenides*, Orestes the matricide has returned to Delphi, to the oracle of Apollo, by which he had originally been instructed to take vengeance on his mother. He has almost been driven mad by the ghost of his mother and by the furies, who have been pursuing him because he has killed a blood-relative. (Had he not avenged his father's killers, he would have been pursued by the very same furies.) The furies accuse Apollo himself of being responsible for the murder. The action then moves from Delphi to Athens (this change of scene within a play is not common in tragedy), where a trial will take place, whereby Orestes' guilt or innocence will be judged by a jury of Athenian citizens, with the patron goddess of Athens, Athene, as the presiding judge (*Eum.* 487–9). The trial is represented as the very first, and so there is, of course, some sense that Athens is congratulating itself and referring to its fifth-century reputation as the home of the legal process. The trial takes place on a site in Athens called the Areopagus, where in myth the king of Athens, Theseus, had defeated the matriarchal tribe of the Amazons (this victory of men over women in the mythical past will be important later in the play). In the fifth century, the Areopagus was also the name of the advisory body of ex-archons whose power was diminished by the so-called reforms of Ephialtes in 461/460, just a few years before Aeschylus' *Oresteia* was performed. Scholars have argued over the extent to which *Eumenides* can be seen to support Ephialtes' reforms.

The furies' case is simple: Orestes is a matricide and must therefore be punished. Under cross-examination he states that he was instructed to kill his mother by Apollo, and that he remains unrepentant (*Eum.* 594, 596). He claims that his was a just act (*Eum.* 610). In an extremely interesting set of arguments Apollo then declares how appalling it is that such a noble man should have died at a woman's hands (*Eum.* 625–7). He claims, further, that a mother is not really a parent of a child, but a sort of nurse; it is the man who is the source of life, and he adduces as evidence the presiding judge herself, who was of course born of Zeus alone

(*Eum.* 658–73). The jury is split, but Athene casts her vote in favour of Orestes, stating (*Eum.* 736–9):

> No mother gave birth to me.
> I praise the male in all things, except for marriage.
> In my heart I am completely the child of my father.
> So I will not value more highly the death of a woman . . .

Once the verdict has been reached, Athene strives to accommodate the furies into a new civic order, one which now in part depends on the rule of law and legal judgement rather than revenge.

But what at first glance looks like the celebration of the city and its institutions, of the city's ability to intervene in the disastrous cycle of revenge staged in the first two plays of the trilogy, is perhaps not the resolution it seems. This new justice seems for men and against women. This is not perhaps surprising given the manner of Athene's birth and of the site of this first trial (the Areopagus, remember). But we should also note that the jury of the best of Athenian citizens is split (it is not clear whether Athene's casting vote makes the votes equal or not), so not all these jurors subscribe to this male-centred justice. Finally, it is not clear that law courts will stop or deter acts of revenge, even if they can pass judgement on the perpetrators. The new solution, the new order, then, fails to solve the problems of the first two plays, and raises new questions as well.

Gods, then, can play a significant role in determining what seems to be just. However, in some tragedies the gods are represented as less surely on the side of justice (however defined). The opening scene of Sophocles' *Ajax* has Athene explaining to Odysseus what she has done to the great hero Ajax. Angered by the decision of Agamemnon and Menelaus to award Achilles' arms to Odysseus rather than himself, Ajax has gone to seize the brothers and Odysseus. Before he can succeed, Athene – Odysseus' patron and supporter – has driven Ajax mad. Instead of attacking Menelaus and the others, he has instead been attacking and torturing sheep and cattle. Athene even speaks to Ajax in his demented state, playing him along. When Ajax returns into his tent, Athene says to Odysseus (*Aj.* 118):

> Do you see, Odysseus, how powerful the gods are?

She then warns him never to speak against the gods, and never to be arrogant. She concludes by saying (*Aj.* 132–3):

> The gods love those who are sensible but hate the bad.

It is not clear what it means to be 'sensible', except to honour the gods, however they behave. The world of *Ajax* seems characterized by arbitrary power, rather than by justice and the civilized institutions of the city.

In both *Hippolytus* and *Bacchae* a god appears at the beginning and tells us what is going to happen in the play. (This particular use of the prologue is a characteristic of Euripides.) In *Bacchae* Dionysus tells us that Thebes is the first city he has come to, having already established his religion in the east. He has chosen Thebes because the young king, Pentheus, refuses to accept the divinity of Dionysus. The god has come to demonstrate that he is a god, and he is prepared for violence (*Bacch.* 1–63). In the end, Pentheus is not persuaded, but he is destroyed. In *Hippolytus* the goddess who delivers the prologue is Aphrodite. She says that, as a powerful deity, she cannot allow Hippolytus to continue to dishonour her (Hippolytus does not like women or the idea of sex). She also explains her plans: she will make Phaedra fall in love with her step-son, Hippolytus. This illicit desire will set in motion a series of catastrophic events. She sums up (*Hipp.* 42–50) by saying that she will reveal the affair to Theseus, who will then destroy his own son, Hippolytus. Phaedra herself will die. Her enemies, Aphrodite says, must pay.

So, in both *Hippolytus* and *Bacchae* we see a world in which the gods wield extraordinary power, and in which human beings seem powerless. This impression is confirmed by the ending of *Hippolytus*. Here, as the dying Hippolytus is brought before a now contrite Theseus, the goddess Artemis explains that Hippolytus has been targeted by a vindictive Aphrodite. She then explains that she will pay Aphrodite back by taking vengeance on the mortal that she, Aphrodite, holds most dear (*Hipp.* 1420–2). Here, then, is a world in which humans seem to be merely the material used by the gods for their own amoral games of power.

Related to the gods is the idea of fate. It is never quite clear whether the gods create fate or are controlled by it, but in the tragic worldview fate becomes something which, like the gods, determines human lives, often in a destructive and bitterly ironic way. Perhaps the best example of this is Sophocles' *Oedipus Tyrannus*. The starting point for this most famous of stories is that Oedipus is predicted by the gods to be fated to kill his father and to marry his own mother. Everyone involved with Oedipus, and Oedipus himself, does everything in their power to avoid this fate. Yet the very steps they take ensure that the fate is achieved.

What's in a name?

Names from myth can be read in a variety of ways. First, Oedipus. This could be a play on *oidein* (to swell) and *pous* (foot): swollen feet – a name that points back to Oedipus' early days exposed on Mount Cithaeron. Alternatively, Oedipus' name could refer to the riddle that he solves (what has four feet in the morning, two in the afternoon and three in the evening?

(Continued)

(Continued)

Answer: man). Reading the name as *hoi* (to him) and *dipous* (two feet), we have 'he has two feet'. Or we can read *oida* (I know or understand) *pous* (feet). Some other punning names: Antigone as *anti* (contrary to, in place of) and *gonē* (generation) – an appropriate name for someone whose father is also her brother. Polyneices can mean 'much strife'; Pentheus is related to one of the many Greek words for grief; Andromache could have something to do with men and battle. The Greek for Ajax is *Aias*. In its vocative form – *Aiai* – this is the same as one of the words for 'alas'. Ajax mentions the connection himself (*Aj.* 430–2).

Oedipus, for instance, believes that, by leaving Corinth, where he thinks his real parents are, he will cheat his predicted future. Instead, of course, he finds himself in Thebes, his real home town, having killed a stranger who was in fact his real father, and married to the queen, who is in fact his real mother.

This brief survey of the way tragedy represents the gods, fate and justice suggests that the tragic view was a pessimistic one. There is a famous line in *Oedipus at Colonus* that sums this up (*OC* 1224–7):

> Not to be born wins every argument.
> But, once born, the next best thing
> is to go back to where one came from
> as quickly as possible.

The city and its institutions may be the only defence against the power of the gods and fate. But, as a guarantor of a good and untroubled life, the city is far from perfect. This is especially true when the life of the city, particularly a democratic city such as Athens, needs to be conducted in something as ambiguous and manipulable as language.

Language and rhetoric

The starting point of the many scholarly discussions on the subject of language and rhetoric in tragedy has quite rightly been the centrality of language and rhetoric in the Athenian democratic city, and the growing philosophical interest in the possibilities and limitations of language in the latter half of the fifth century, an interest normally associated with the sophists (see 6a and c). When criticism has focussed more on the tragedies themselves, critics have considered the powers of persuasion, the ambiguity and slipperiness of important terms and the formal set-piece debates (the *agōn*).

My treatments here are intended to give brief examples of the way tragedy is interested in language. (For lengthier treatments see Buxton (1982); Goldhill (1986).)

In Sophocles' *Philoctetes*, the problem faced by Odysseus and the Greek army at Troy is that they must seize Philoctetes and, with him, the bow he was given by Heracles, for it has been prophesied that Troy will not fall in Philoctetes' absence. The problem is compounded because the Greeks, at Odysseus' instigation, had left Philoctetes on the empty island of Lemnos ten years before, because of his injured and malodorous foot. Odysseus and Achilles' son, Neoptolemus, have been charged with securing the return of Philoctetes. Odysseus is in charge and he tells Neoptolemus that it is his duty to 'steal' Philoctetes away with words (*Phil.* 54–5); he goes on to instruct him in what he can and cannot say. In a concise and cynical expression of the view that the ends justify the means, Odysseus says to his young comrade (*Phil.* 79–85):

> I know, my boy, that it is not in your nature
> to say such things or to devise bad things.
> But it is a sweet thing to win, so be bold.
> We can show ourselves to be just later.
> Now for one little day give yourself
> shamelessly to me. Then for the rest of time
> be called the most pious of mortals.

It might seem odd that Odysseus, who in tragedy is often presented as an effective if not likable rhetorician, should use such arguments to the blunt and physical Neoptolemus. Indeed, Neoptolemus initially disagrees entirely, saying that he would prefer to use force rather than lie, and to fail nobly than succeed ignobly (*Phil.* 86–95). So, it looks as though Odysseus' attempt to persuade Neoptolemus to use a certain sort of persuasion has failed. But then matters are complicated further, as this exchange demonstrates (*Phil.* 100–03):

> Ne.:   So you are ordering me to do nothing but tell lies?
> Od.:   I am telling you to capture Philoctetes with deception.
> Ne.:   Why is it better to use deception than persuasion?
> Od.:   He won't be persuaded; and you won't take him by force.

So, there are now not only the two conventional options of violence or persuasion; a third term – deception – has been added. And, while Philoctetes does agree to return with the Greeks to Troy, it is not because he has been persuaded, deceived or compelled by anything suggested in the opening lines of the play. The play, if anything, presents the failure of language and rhetoric.

The influence of the sophists

Most obviously the sophists exercised their influence in the use and examination of rhetoric. Sophocles and especially Euripides were not immune to this influence. But sophists also thought about the nature of the gods, the distinction between nature and convention, and so on. Here again tragedians made use of and were influenced by sophistic provocations. Hippolytus' notorious claim that he had sworn an oath with his tongue but not his mind (*Hipp.* 612) seems a typically sophistic piece of slippery and rhetorical moral relativism. Whether nobility is innate or not is an important theme in Euripides' *Electra* and from time to time one hears a sophistic scepticism about conventional religion, as in Hecuba's prayer at *Tro.* 885–6 ('O Zeus, whoever you are, difficult to know, necessity of nature, or mind of mortals'). Tragedians had one important advantage over the sophists: what they said in their plays was licensed by the city and so, arguably, they could get away with more. Certainly, no tragedian is put on trial and executed (though Euripides may have been tried for impiety).

To hold to the idea that violence and persuasion were mutually exclusive, and that the latter was the civilized option, could be called naive. Certainly, Thucydides described Cleon, the most influential Athenian politician in the period after Pericles' death, as both the most violent *and* the most persuasive (Thuc. 3.36.6). The relationship between the two options is presented in a complicated way in Euripides' *Medea*. Medea, having lived with Jason for some years and having had two sons by him, discovers that he is to abandon her and marry a Greek wife. She is outraged at this betrayal and in her first encounter with Jason she vigorously argues that he is in the wrong, especially when she has done so much for him (*Med.* 465–519). He dismisses her claims. When she next talks with him, she pretends to have resigned herself to the new marriage, and offers gifts and the promise of assistance (*Med.* 869–905). In her first speech, she is aggressive, compelling and tells the truth about her view of the situation: most audiences will be persuaded by her arguments and appalled that Jason rejects Medea so casually. In her second speech she lies, and we in the audience are fully aware of it. Yet it is the second speech – falsehoods rather than the truth – that helps Medea to take her vengeance on Jason (which is a plan of exemplary and transgressive violence). So, persuasion can lead to rather than replace violence, and lies can persuade more effectively than the truth. It is persuasion as such in which the Athenian democracy must have faith.

We can see that tragedy also represents some crucial terms as slippery and ambiguous. One could look, for instance, at the term *telos* in Aeschylus' *Oresteia*, trying to read between its various meanings, such as end, goal, ritual, tax, and seeing all of those in the context of a trilogy that deals problematically with the idea of ending (is the verdict in the trial an ending, or just the start of a whole new set of questions? – see Goldhill (1984)). One could also refer to the problems that the characters in Euripides' *Hippolytus* face when trying to understand the meaning and effectiveness of such terms as *sophia* (wisdom) and *sōphrosunē* (self-control). Hippolytus, summing up the situation and his own and Phaedra's relations to *sōphrosunē*, comes up with a baffling couplet (*Hipp.* 1034–5):

> She practised *sōphrosunē*, without being *sōphrōn* (self-controlled).
> I possess it, but did not use it well.

One of the reasons that *Medea* is such an exquisite and powerful drama is the sharpness of the moral challenge posed by Medea's murder of her children. In the sense that Medea achieves all her goals – the murder of Glauke and the children, revenge on Jason, sanctuary and home in Athens – she must be seen to have won. Of course, her victory is morally questionable, but there is also the effect on Medea herself to be considered. And one of the ways that we see that effect is by looking at the language that Medea uses.

From line 1022 onwards Medea finds language difficult. This is the same Medea who, through most of the play, has been a masterful manipulator of language, successfully persuading both Jason and Aegeus to agree to her plans. Even when not successfully persuading another character, her description of the desperate life of a wife and her vehement attack on Jason's treachery are both examples of powerful rhetoric. However, in the speech at 1022ff. Medea comes unstuck linguistically as well as psychologically.

Medea's doubts are obvious as she veers between two different courses of action: to kill or not to kill. At 1022ff. it seems as though she will not in fact kill her sons. At 1044–8 she expresses her inability to carry out the murders (*Med.* 1044–8: 'I would not be able'). At 1049–55 she reasserts her need to kill, this time on the basis of a heroic desire not to be mocked. At 1056–8 she again draws back; this position is reversed at 1059–68; she possibly relents at 1069–73, but at 1073 her allusion to 'May you be happy there' (in death) and then the lines that follow tell us that she is still planning to perform the murders. This confusion is moving and dramatic, and Medea's increasingly frenetic changes of mind are psychologically plausible and are reflected in linguistic confusion.

From the very beginning of the speech we are aware of some split in Medea's self. The address to her own *thumos* (spirit, anger) at 1056 may be traditional, but it must also be viewed in the context of a Medea who seems uncertain of her self. Ordering herself (or rather her *thumos*) to spare the children at 1057 she then in 1058 talks of herself both as 'us/me' and 'you'. Then there is the famous couplet at 1078–9. These lines argue against the Socratic idea that virtue is knowledge. More interesting is the way in which Medea's references become unclear and contradictory, and what that inconsistency and lack of clarity might signify for the whole play. The couplet is:

> I understand that what I am about to do is wrong,
> but my spirit (*thumos*) is stronger (*kreissōn*) than my rational faculties (*bouleumatōn*).

At first sight we think we understand what Medea means: my plan to kill the children is wrong. I know that, but there is something inside me – a spirit, a passion, an anger – that compels me to carry out the deed.

However, the complications of the couplet lie in the ambiguity of two of the words Medea uses. First, her use of the comparative *kreissōn* (stronger). Clearly, to make sense of what Medea is saying this must mean 'more powerful'. But *kreissōn* can be used as the comparative of the Greek adjective *agathos* (good) and it can thus be used in a moral sense. If Medea can be taken as saying that her *thumos* is 'better, morally better' than her *bouleumata* (plans, rational faculties), then this contradicts what she had said in 1078. She would be saying:

> I understand that what I am about to do is wrong, but there is something in me (which is making me act the wrong way) which is *better* than those rational resolves which might stop me.

More problems reside in the noun *bouleumata*. This word is used more than in any other play by Euripides, and it is worth looking at the earlier appearances of the word. At 371–5 Medea, having just persuaded Creon not to banish her immediately, is talking to the chorus. The reference to 'plans' here (*bouleumata*) clearly refers to the plans to murder Creon, Glauke and Jason. After agreeing with Aegeus that she can live in Athens Medea says at 768–73 that that has provided a haven for her plans (*bouleumata*). Here it must refer to the revenge, but Medea is no more specific than that. However, she announces at 772 that she will tell the chorus her *bouleumata* (plans) and, given that by 792–3 she is announcing her plan to kill her children, I think that we must take *bouleumata* here to refer to all the murders, including those of the children. This more inclusive meaning is most obvious at 1044 and 1048 where she repeats the same two-word phrase to signify her new intention not to kill the children ('goodbye, plans'). So, when Medea uses *bouleumata* before lines 1078–9, she uses the word to refer to her plans to kill, sometimes specifically the children. But if the couplet at 1078–9 is to make any ordinary sense, then the *bouleumata* here must refer to some as yet unstated 'rational resolves' not to murder the children. That is, the word is strikingly and surprisingly used to refer to the opposite course of action to the one it has thus far referred to. And so, at the moment when Medea finally reasserts her desire and need to kill her sons, she does so in a way that shows her confusion and doubt continuing.

Medea explores the challenge that a woman makes to men's control of language, as well as their control of society more generally. The most particular challenge perhaps is to men's control and (ab)use of poetry to praise (themselves) and blame (women). The revenge that Medea achieves is one which strikes at the heart of a patrilinear society: she kills Jason's existing sons – one pair of future inheritors – and she murders Jason's new bride, thereby preventing the possibility of alternative inheritors. She thus destroys his future in two ways. As a method of undermining men's superior social status, political power and wealth, it is hard to think of anything more exemplary. In the speech on which I have been concentrating, Medea's quite understandable confusions and doubts about her planned course of action are extended and emphasized by the confusion in the words she uses and the things to which they refer. It is as if in this speech men, and the language which they seek to control, begin to fight back. The apparently dull point that this is a play written by a man, performed by and for men starts to take on a sharper outline. Can Athenian men allow Medea to wrest control of language (and thus of praise and blame) from men? Earlier in the play, at 540–1, during an argument about who has provided most benefits for the other, Jason says:

> If you were still living on the furthest boundaries,
> you would have no *logos*.

I have deliberately not translated *logos*. Some translators think it means 'reputation', but we cannot ignore the other meanings of the word: word, language, reason. It is in these latter senses that in her great speech at lines 1022ff. men seem to be withdrawing the gift of *logos*. As Medea approaches the moment when she must commit the awful infanticide, she becomes something else, her doubts and selves multiplying. At the same time, her language becomes an index of confusion and despair rather than the purveyor of persuasion. Her victory is not only morally questionable; it is not clear that it even makes sense.

As we know from Strepsiades' comment at Aristophanes' *Clouds* 208, Athens was (in)famous for its law courts and the delight its citizens took in sitting on juries (see Aristophanes' *Wasps*) and listening to speeches (Cleon contemptuously describes the Athenians as 'spectators of speeches': Thuc. 3.38.4). No surprise then to find in tragedy the formal debates called *agōnes*. Some scholars have wondered whether the debates contribute fully to the plays' dramatic effectiveness. Euripides' *agōnes* in particular have been criticized – wrongly, I would say – for dramatic irrelevance and self-indulgent rhetorical display.

We have already seen something of the debate in Aeschylus' *Eumenides*, in which Apollo defends Orestes' matricide on clearly patriarchal grounds. We could also mention the splendid debates between, first, Menelaus and Teucer (*Aj.* 1047–162) and, then, Agamemnon and Teucer in Sophocles' *Ajax* (*Aj.* 1226–315). The issue here is whether Ajax should be buried: the debates themselves do not resolve the issue; it takes the intervention of Odysseus to persuade Agamemnon to concede (*Aj.* 1316–73). There is also the fascinating debate between Oedipus and Teiresias in Sophocles' *Oedipus Tyrannus* (*OT* 316–462). What is very interesting about this exchange is the almost complete failure of communication. Teiresias actually reveals to Oedipus exactly the parricide and incestuous husband he is (*OT* 353; 362; 366–7). Of course – and this touch reveals Sophocles' deep psychological understanding – Oedipus cannot accept something so outrageous to be true, so he invents an alternative and (politically) plausible explanation for why Teiresias has spoken as he has, namely, that Teiresias is conspiring against him along with Creon (*OT* 380–403). So, even though language has revealed the truth, reasons outside language stop Oedipus from believing what he hears. The revelation comes when various pieces of evidence about the past are revealed by a stranger later in the play.

This theme of failed communication is also present in Euripides. We have already seen something of this in *Medea*, but it is also clear in *Hippolytus* and *Bacchae*. In the former, when Hippolytus is confronted by his father with Phaedra's lying suicide note, which claims that Hippolytus had attempted to rape Phaedra, Hippolytus is unable to defend himself because of an oath he had earlier sworn not to reveal anything when he was told about Phaedra's desire for him (*Hipp.* 902–1089). Forced to answer his father's accusations, without being able to express what he has heard, he is mired in an impotence that would be comic were the consequences not so lethal. Once again, language has failed a character. In *Bacchae*, on the other hand, Pentheus resolutely refuses to believe in the divinity of Dionysus and prepares to use troops against the frenzied maenads (*Bacch.* 778–809). Dionysus has been unable to persuade the young king. So, at line 810, in a unique line, he utters the single letter 'a'. From this point, Pentheus is transformed into an easy-to-manipulate, dreamy naif, whom Dionysus dresses in women's clothes so that he can watch the maenads without danger. (In fact, he is torn apart.) The god does not bother to debate: instead he imposes his will by other, appropriately theatrical, means.

For one of the most complex debates in Euripidean tragedy, though, we should turn to *The Trojan Women*. This play, performed in 415, has one of the most ominous and extreme settings of any tragedy: the scene is the tented accommodation of the newly enslaved Trojan woman. The imagined backdrop is the completely destroyed city of Troy. The tone and atmosphere of the play is grim and oppressive. However, just over halfway through the play, we are given a debate between Helen and Hecuba, as to who is responsible for the war (*Tro.* 895–1059). Surprisingly, Helen's defence seems to make use of some rather modish argumentation: she says in lines 895–965 that the war was not her fault, but rather was that of Hecuba herself, because she bore Paris, who in turn made the famous Judgement of Paris. Indeed, indirectly she has brought benefit to Greece. Her departure for Troy is blamed on Menelaus' absence and on Paris, because he was supported by the powerful deity, Aphrodite (a goddess who is indeed irresistible). So she had to go to Troy; she was also unable to escape once there, forced as she was into marriage. Some of these arguments surface in a piece called *The Encomium of Helen*, written by the sophist Gorgias. So Helen is, rhetorically at least, very much in fashion. Which is why Hecuba's response is all the more remarkable. For here, the Trojan queen, who throughout the rest of the play is constant reminder of the awful effects of war, a downtrodden and lamenting thing, becomes a spirited and highly rationalistic debater. In her speech in lines 969–1032 she dismisses Helen's account of the behaviour of the goddesses at the Judgement of Paris as irrational, accuses Helen herself of going out of her mind (Aphrodite is punningly adduced as a principle of irrationality at lines 989–90), of becoming too attached to barbarian ways and of being a treacherous wife who deserves to die (for more analysis, see Croally, 1994: 134–62).

What we see, then, in this debate is up-to-date argumentation; we also see irrelevant defences made, points not answered, points refuted that have not been made, and so on. It is a complex, interesting but highly flawed debate; but its flaws are not merely internal. When the Greeks used the word *agōn* to describe debates, they were using a word which meant contest, and which applied among other things to athletic competitions and war. To describe something as an *agōn* was to state that it was a contest, one which was regulated and which would produce a winner and a loser, as happened in wars, athletic contests and court cases. No such easy judgement can be made about the debate in *The Trojan Women*. It is, of course, up to the audience as to which of the speakers they prefer to believe (if any), but the play could itself show that either Helen or Hecuba has won. That it fails to do. Before the debate, Menelaus tells us he has decided to take Helen back to Greece and execute her there (*Tro.* 876–83). He only allows the debate because Hecuba persuades him that it is not really a debate at all and will have no effect on his decision to execute (*Tro.* 906–15). Once the debate is over, Menelaus judges Hecuba the winner, and says that he will execute Helen immediately, thus contradicting his earlier assertion (*Tro.* 1036–41). Following an appeal from Helen, he changes his mind again and says that he will take her back to Greece and execute her there (*Tro.* 1046–8). However, there is nothing in the text itself that tells us what actually happens to Helen. If we look outside the play to Homer's *Odyssey*, we find in book 4 that Helen is alive and well in Greece and living happily with Menelaus. So, in a play in which the Greek victory is powerfully questioned by the truth-telling prophetess Cassandra, we do not know who has won the debate and what effect any victory has had. It may very well be true that the most persuasive force during the whole debate is completely non-verbal: because of her looks, it may not matter what Helen (or Hecuba) says.

We have seen, then, that important moral concepts are unable to help the characters understand and deal with their predicaments; that persuasion sometimes does not work, or works for unexpected reasons or has unintended consequences; that formally organized debate can mislead and confuse rather than illuminate and resolve. In all these ways the language and rhetoric so central to the Athenian democracy's operation and self-image is problematic and unreliable.

War

Moses Finley once said that, during the fifth century, there was probably no day on which Athenian military forces were not in operation somewhere. This is one way of showing how central war was to the experience of classical Greeks. We could also note that the first poem of Greek literature was concerned with war (the *Iliad*), and that the development of politics through the seventh and sixth centuries went hand-in-hand with and/or was influenced by changes in military organization. Politics is the business of the city conducted within the city: war, as Vernant has said, is the 'city facing outwards' (Vernant, 1980). It should be no surprise then that war and its effects should be the backdrop and theme of so many plays we know about and of those that are extant. Of our 31 extant tragedies, 14 concern the Trojan War and its effects, and five concern the attack on Thebes by Polyneices and his six other heroes. Aeschylus also wrote *The Persians* about the Greek victory in the (historical) Persian Wars of 480–79. If tragedy examines some of the most important beliefs and values held by its audience, then it makes sense that it should use war as a setting. For it is in war that values, beliefs and political organization are most extremely put to the test.

In play after play the various ways in which the city tried to organize itself are shaken and undermined by war and its aftermath. So, even before the Trojan War, we see that the war requires sacrifice, as Agamemnon kills his own daughter so that the Greek fleet can sail (Aeschylus' *Agamemnon*; Euripides' *Iphigenia at Aulis*). In the plays set in or immediately after the war (Sophocles' *Ajax* and *Philoctetes*, Euripides' *Trojan Women*, *Andromache* and *Hecuba*), we see enslavement and complication of relationships: who is a friend and who is an enemy? We witness destruction and the violence of persuasion, and barbarians challenging Greeks about their Greekness. In the plays set after the return of the Greeks from Troy (Aeschylus' *Oresteia*, Sophocles' *Electra* and Euripides' *Electra* and *Orestes*), we see the breakdown of ritual order: people rather than animals can be sacrificed; marriage becomes corrupted, family life undermined; the relations between men and women complicated. War is a test. It is also an experience in which Athenian citizens (as well as other Greeks) confronted their enemies, or those they wished to exclude from their cities, and from having political and legal rights in their cities: war meant confrontation with the other. Tragedy examines the other against which the Athenians defined themselves.

The hero

People who approach Attic tragedy as students of English literature will sometimes do so through a reading of Aristotle's *Poetics*. One feature of this rather partial account of tragedy is an emphasis on the idea of the tragic hero. And so, without knowing all extant tragedy, one might assume that the tragic hero is a characteristic of Attic tragedy when, in fact, the picture is not that simple. The tragic hero is more a feature of Sophocles' than of other tragedies. That said, it is still a feature worth investigating, first by considering the literary and cultural context in which the Athenian audience watched the hero on the tragic stage.

Heroes pervade Homer's *Iliad*: Achilles, Odysseus, Ajax, Agamemnon, Menelaus, Diomede, Hector. While there is clearly mass fighting, the reader can easily have the impression that the Trojan War consisted of a series of individual combats between rugged, larger-than-life warriors. The heroes share values (sometimes called the heroic code): they aim through their deeds on the battlefield and in the assembly to achieve fame (*kleos*); they expect to be treated with proper respect and honour (*timē*). Generally speaking, they are characterized by their immense physical power, by their fearlessness and by the ruthless and selfish pursuit of their own interests. As Bernard Knox has said, the Homeric hero is not much aware of the gentler, domestic virtues; he may also lack any deep sense of communal feeling. It is this hero that tragedy inherits.

In *Ajax*, the hero is indeed well known from Homer. Set away from the battlefield in the Greek camp, *Ajax* tells the story of Ajax's response to the judgement of Agamemnon and Menelaus that the arms of Achilles (who had been the premier Greek warrior) should be handed to Odysseus rather than to Ajax, who is outraged that he has been treated with such disrespect. He attempts to capture and torture Agamemnon, Menelaus and Odysseus but, driven mad by Athene, he instead seizes and abuses sheep and cattle. Once he has emerged from his frenzy, the idea that he, one of the great Greek heroes, has wasted his anger and violence on animals is intolerable, most especially because of the mockery he will have to endure. To this point Ajax fits the Homeric template very well. However, this does not last through the play, for Ajax, in a famous speech (*Aj.* 646–92), accepts that he must be more flexible and accepting of change. This very unHomeric, unheroic proposal is then followed by Ajax's suicide. But should we take the suicide as consistent with the speech? Or should we see the suicide as confirming that the speech was an aberration? Was Ajax merely deceiving his wife and the chorus? Is the manner of death a return to the heroic values he otherwise represented in his life? Or an affront to the values of a Homeric hero? After Ajax's death the play concerns itself with the search for his body and then with the problem of his burial. Neither Agamemnon nor Menelaus is minded to allow their enemy a proper burial, until Odysseus persuades a reluctant Agamemnon. Some have argued that *Ajax* presents its audience with two competing types of heroism. Ajax, one example, is stubborn, resolute and, in the end, selfish; Odysseus, on the other hand, is more interested in persuasion than violence, and is flexible enough to see that former enemies can become friends. The former type is old-fashioned, mythical; the latter as more suited to the democratic world of the audience. Such a reading may appear too schematic. Also, there is the matter of how a hero could have fitted into the democratic city at all, except as a problem.

Heroes such as Ajax are rare in the extant plays of Aeschylus and Euripides, though Medea certainly shares some of Ajax's characteristics, not least her absolute determination not to be mocked; one might also make a case for Heracles in *Hercules Furens*. Other Sophoclean heroes include Antigone and Philoctetes in the eponymous plays, and Oedipus in *Oedipus Tyrannus* and *Oedipus at Colonus*. All share some of the qualities we have seen above in the case of Ajax: resolute, not susceptible to persuasion, certain of their rightness, and so on. Oedipus' heroism in *Oedipus Tyrannus* is an interesting case. First, his heroic qualities are not entirely physical: it is true that he has killed several people at the crossroads, but he has also demonstrated his intellectual acumen by solving the sphinx's riddle. And throughout the play he keeps asking questions, keeps investigating: one might almost see him as an intellectual (or a sophist) hero.

Self and other: places and times

Another feature of Oedipus' heroic investigation is that he eventually realizes that he is the person he is looking for. The cause of the terrible plague that has descended on Thebes is none other than himself. Two further points can be made about Oedipus' discovery of his self. The first is what it tells us about characterization – or rather the lack of it – in Attic tragedy. At the beginning of *Oedipus Tyrannus* Oedipus betrays the heroic characteristics of doggedness, persistence, arrogance and so on. At the end of the play, should we try to portray Oedipus in such psychologizing terms, it would be difficult to change what we said about him at the beginning of the play. That is to say, psychologically there has been no development at all – and psychological development is an important feature of characterization in modern literature – but there has been a significant change in his status: the saviour king has become an outcast parricide. (Euripides' Medea betrays some characteristics of inner indecision, but that is rare in extant tragedy.) Perhaps we should not be surprised that plays whose actors wore masks should not be so concerned with character.

Second, *Oedipus Tyrannus* makes much of the relationship between Oedipus' identity and various places. Vernant once argued that the original question asked by Oedipus – who killed Laius? – becomes a new question: who is Oedipus? That latter question can itself be redrafted as: where is Oedipus from? The play is set in Thebes, but it is clear that Oedipus believes that this is not his home city. Key events in his life before his (re)arrival in

Thebes are all related to specific places: his abandonment on Mount Cithaeron; his life in and then departure from Corinth; his encounter with the oracle at Delphi; his fateful encounter at the crossroads. As he tries to find out who the murderer is (who he is), Oedipus mentally retraces his steps through these places. Indeed, the very first time that Oedipus, rather than anyone else, begins to understand that he may not be who he thinks he is, comes when the crossroads at Phocis is described (*OT* 726ff.). It is no accident, then, that when Oedipus has seen who he truly is, and has blinded himself, he should call on three of the places – Cithaeron, Corinth and the crossroads – that marked his journey to Thebes, which ended up being his journey of self-discovery (*OT* 1391ff.).

Tragedy's dramatization of self-discovery does not always take the form described in the case of Oedipus. Both Hippolytus in the eponymous play and Pentheus in Euripides' *Bacchae* discover that their selves are too restrictive to accommodate aspects of human behaviour that they find distasteful. In Hippolytus' case this is represented by his refusal to worship Aphrodite: Hippolytus has no space in himself to accommodate sexual desire. Pentheus rejects another divinity, Dionysus. The two human characters experience a similar fate: both are torn apart by the very forces they had sought to repress. No doubt Aphrodite and Dionysus represented dangerous, irrational forces. Perhaps, though, the Athenian audience learned something about themselves from these plays: desire and Dionysus can be excluded only with catastrophic consequences for the self.

In an article originally published in 1986, Froma Zeitlin argued that, for the Athenian audience, tragedy was a form of self-examination. She further argued that the self was examined in mythical other-places and other-times. For Zeitlin, Thebes is the 'quintessential "other-scene"', a city 'imagined as a mirror opposite of Athens', where Athens 'acts out questions crucial to the *polis*, to the self, to the family and society' (Zeitlin, 1986: 117). While there are many attractive features of this theory, if taken broadly as it stands it is too schematic. Of known tragedies, the Theban cycle provides just under half as many plays as the Trojan War and its aftermath (33 as compared to 68): so how do we rate Troy as an other-scene? Also, the city of Thebes as it appears in the extant plays is itself variously represented. One can note, for instance, that while the Thebes of Sophocles is the site of a number of transgressions, the city in Euripides' *Bacchae* is one which is trying to resist the sort of frenzied rituals occurring outside the walls on Mount Cithaeron. Another difficulty with the privilege given to Thebes is: what about the Athens that is the scene of *Eumenides*, *Heracleidae*, *Supplices* and *Oedipus at Colonus*? Tragedy does set itself in a scene rendered other either in space or in time or in both, and it is peopled by characters obviously distinct from the Athenian citizens in the audience. But tragedy's other-scene is both more various and more complicated than Zeitlin's theory allows. She is arguably more persuasive when arguing that the men of the audience use tragic women as an other for the purposes of self-examination. And it is to women and some other others that we now turn.

The other: women, slaves, enemies and barbarians

Why should tragic women – played by men before a predominantly male audience – be such a potent other? The reason lies partly in women's legal and political status in classical Athens: they had no rights at all except by association with a male relative or husband. Another reason has to do with male ideology towards women: two powerful strands here are that there should be silence about and from women, and that their place was inside, rather than in the political and military spheres outside.

A famous article by Bernard Knox (1952) showed how, in Euripides' *Hippolytus*, the characters often face a difficult choice between speech and silence. In more recent critical work it has also been demonstrated that those mutually exclusive options are often tied to expectations of behaviour or other issues raised by gender. So, when Phaedra is first relating how she herself first responded to her desire for her step-son, one option is to keep silent, another is to ensure silence by suicide. Yet when she does commit suicide, she may be silent, but she leaves behind a note that incriminates Hippolytus with fatal results. It is the Nurse – a woman – whose speech starts the process whereby the fates of Phaedra and Hippolytus start to unravel. It is she who interrogates Phaedra about her worrying mental state (203ff.); who first explicitly utters the name of Hippolytus as the man whom Phaedra loves (310 – a line split three ways); who tells Hippolytus of Phaedra's desire, first ensuring Hippolytus' silence by making him swear an oath (611). Hippolytus, facing his step-mother's charges and constrained by his oath, can only be silent about what has really happened: if only the walls, who heard what the Nurse said, could speak, then all could be revealed (1074–5). These are some of the complications of the relationship between speech and silence, on the one hand, and men and women, on the other.

The other ideological strand is women's connection to the inside. We have already seen in the discussion of Aeschylus' *Oresteia* how Clytemnestra uses her command of the inside of the house to help her to kill Agamemnon (and some other examples were given above). In the cases of both Clytemnestra and Medea, their initial complaints against their husbands have most to do with the domestic inside. Clytemnestra has lost a daughter, who properly belongs inside the house, to a sacrifice in aid of a military expedition, launched to recover the famously transgressive Helen. Medea resents the fact that Jason has deserted her as his partner. Clytemnestra kills her husband inside, but then displays him on the *ekkyklēma*, outside on the stage. She is then often described as having in some way taken over the place of men. Medea's first words are (*Med.* 214): 'Corinthian women, I have come out of the house.' She does so to engage in the world of men, in those traditionally male pursuits of persuasion and violence (she is very good at both). In various ways both Clytemnestra and Medea become men. So, these women are a dangerous other: the inside space that they dominate is dangerous for men.

But the difficult thing for men is that they need women in order to produce the children, especially the boys, who will carry on their name. Both Jason (very briefly at *Med.* 573–5 and Hippolytus (at great length at *Hipp.* 616ff.) hope for a world in which women are not necessary for reproduction. Men's confusion and anxiety about all this is perhaps also demonstrated in the way that they use various words for bed (*lechos, lektra, eunē*): the bed can stand for marriage and the site of proper procreation, but it also can represent (dangerous and irrational) desire. Jason describes some of the dangers associated with the bed when he says at *Med.* 568–73:

> Nor would you say so, if the bed were not irritating you.
> But you have come to such a point that, if the bed
> is good, you women think you have everything,
> but if some disaster occurs to the bed,
> you make the best and most noble things
> the most hostile.

But bed standing for what? Sexual desire? Marriage? We cannot be sure. What we can say though is that, for men, the inside – where the bed is – is both necessary and frightening, and that these tragic women are a challenge to men and a call to self-examination.

Slaves, against whom the free distinguish themselves, are also represented on the tragic stage, though not as frequently as women. Indeed, it can be argued that the most important slaves in tragedy are those that we see in those plays of Euripides set in the immediate aftermath of the Trojan War, *Andromache*, *Hecuba* and *The Trojan Women*. In these plays, we see the former queen of Troy and her female relatives as slaves. This reversal of fortune allows some sharp consideration of the nature of freedom. No mortal is free, says Hecuba in the eponymous play. She continues (*Hec.* 856–7):

> Everyone is the slave of either money or chance,
> or the mob in the city or the writings of the laws
> compel them to adopt methods against their judgements.

It is hard to judge exactly what Hecuba is saying. She certainly seems be railing against all restrictions on behaviour (this became a fashionable nugget of sophistic thinking in the late fifth century; see, for example, Callicles in Plato's *Gorgias* 491e ff.), but in a baffling way. The existence of written laws was normally thought to guarantee freedom rather than taking it away; it was certainly used by the Greeks to distinguish themselves from the slavish barbarians (Hdt. 7.104). There is also a problem with these lines in the context of the play. As Hecuba realizes that she has been transformed from queen to slave, she understands that she has nothing to lose, and that she is therefore – paradoxically – free, and more free than the free themselves. She claims as much herself at line 869. But what is freedom then, if a slave possesses it to a greater degree?

Hecuba, as a slave, finds she has the freedom to destroy her enemies. But who exactly is your enemy is often a problem in tragedy. Again, we see here the Greek polarizing tendency – a world split into friends and enemies – called into question. Friendship or *philia* arose out of family connection, through marriage or political alliance. Even from this brief description it can be seen that tragedy is full of examples of people who should be friends becoming enemies. So, Agamemnon should be *philos* to Clytemnestra, but because he has killed his daughter – precisely because she was most *philē* to him – he has become Clytemnestra's enemy. Helen, in whichever play she appears or is referred to, is another example of someone who has herself ceased to be *philē* to those who should be her friends and who has caused a fatal disturbance in a world that is supposed to be clearly divided into friends and enemies. In *Antigone* we see how those who are one's *philoi* in a personal sense can still be enemies in a public sense (Oedipus' two sons have killed each other in single combat), and we see how honouring the demands of *philia* can make one an enemy of the city (Antigone herself).

Perhaps the polarity that tragedy is most keen on using and examining – with the exception of man/woman – is that of Greek/barbarian. This polarity had a strong significance in the fifth century because of the importance that the Greeks attached to their victory over the Persians in 480/479. The Athenians in the years that followed had many successes against the forces of the Persian empire, as they established and extended their empire. It is interesting to note, as Edith Hall does (Hall, 1989), that the Trojans we read about in Homer's *Iliad* are as Greek as the Greeks: in their language, customs, manner of fighting and so on, no distinction can be made. But the Trojans as represented in fifth-century tragedy are very definitely barbarians (as we shall see in some detail a little later).

We can only speculate about all the different ways that the Persian Wars affected the Athenians, but the fact that there were two tragedies in the 470s that dealt with the events of 480–79 would suggest that the cultural impact was immense. The first of the two plays – Phrynichus' *Persians* – is lost and may have been performed in 476. The second was *The Persians*, Aeschylus' earliest extant play, performed at the Great Dionysia in 472. This is in many ways a remarkable play. At some points the Persians are clearly referred to as slaves (241–4) but, at the same time, there is enormous imaginative sympathy for the Persians as they begin to hear the news of the extent of the calamities experienced by their forces. This is no simple representation of an alien and inferior race.

In tragedy it is an easy insult to call someone a barbarian, or to say of a character, as Agamemnon does of Teucer in Sophocles' *Ajax* (*Aj.* 1263), that what he says is incomprehensible, but tragedy tends to complicate the Greek/barbarian polarity. Medea, though a barbarian, demonstrates a rhetorical superiority – supposedly a Greek accomplishment. It is her skill in persuasion that allows her to achieve her murderous revenge. In *The Trojan Women* it is Helen – the Greek queen who has eloped to barbarian Troy – who has been seduced by barbarian manners (*Tro.* 991ff., 1020–1). This could be another example of Helen's transgression, until we remember that the character who criticizes Helen for going native is none other than the Trojan queen Hecuba. We must also remember that the criticisms are made in an *agōn*, which was a feature of Greek societies who liked to think that they were ruled by law, and that the rhetoric deployed by Hecuba is a startling example of sophistic rationalism. The question that remains, as with all of the other 'others' against which the Athenians in the audience defined themselves, is: who is the barbarian (slave, enemy, woman)? A line uttered by Andromache in *The Trojan Women* (764) starkly encapsulates some of the problems we have encountered:

O Greeks who have devised barbarian evils . . .

Tragedy in its second century: paradox, irony and self-reference

As the number of tragedies written and performed increased, so tragedy developed as a literary genre. We have seen how Aeschylus added a second actor and other innovations in staging, and how Sophocles added a third actor. But we can also see, especially later in the century, how tragedy starts to be more aware of its literary and cultural status, and more aware of its own past. This development – criticized often, though recently more celebrated – is usually seen as Euripidean. (Note that the extant plays of Sophocles come from very similar years to those of Euripides. The difference is that we have only seven tragedies of Sophocles and at least 17 of Euripides.)

Such self-consciousness in Euripidean tragedy is seen when we are confronted by an attitude to myth and to what is happening on stage that is paradoxical and self-referential. After Medea has persuaded Creon to allow her one extra day to stay in Corinth in order to sort out her affairs, the chorus sing an ode that has come to be known as the New Song (*Med.* 410ff.). In this ode the chorus declare that, from this point forth, poetry will change: it will no longer restrict itself to praising men; it will now praise women. What is the first example of this new, philogynist poetry? The answer surely is: Euripides' *Medea*, in which a mother murders her own innocent children in order to take vengeance on her husband.

When the chorus in Euripides' *Electra* are told about the golden lamb acquired by Thyestes and about Zeus' reversal of the movements of the sun

(*El.* 699ff.), they express incredulity, and assert that this is just the sort of bizarre and childish thing one would find in myth. When Heracles is consoled by Theseus and told that being driven mad by the gods and killing one's family is the sort of thing that has happened to other people in myth, Heracles replies that these are the lies promulgated by poets (*HF* 1346). In both instances, Euripides seems to question the status of his work, for it too is myth.

The sharpest paradox perhaps comes in *The Trojan Women*. There is a famous scene in this play in which Cassandra questions the victory of the Greeks in the Trojan War. The problem with this is that, if there is one undisputed 'fact' in the collection of stories called Greek myth, it is that the Greeks won the Trojan War. But one other mythical 'fact' has to do with Cassandra. This is that the Trojan prophetess always tells the truth, and that anyone who listens to her never believes her. At this point we, and the audience, seem very much stuck. Our sense of not knowing which way to turn is further complicated by the manner in which Cassandra introduces her heterodox analysis (*Tro.* 366–7):

> I may be possessed by god, but
> to this extent I shall stand outside my madness.

The first question then is: does Cassandra's attempt to distinguish what she is about to say from her more normal(!) utterances mean that we might be able to believe her? Or that she might not be telling the truth? The word I have translated as 'madness' is *bakcheumatōn*, a word clearly related to the god Dionysus. So, does truth-telling necessarily distance one from Dionysus? Cassandra puns on standing outside and ecstasy (*exō stēsomai*): does she suggest a new form of Dionysiac possession? Is Cassandra, as it were, simultaneously possessed by Dionysus and free from his power? Euripidean tragedy complicates its relationship to the stories it inherits but, in so doing, it also seems to question is own value.

Later, therefore Euripidean, tragedy can also be characterized as being increasingly ready to include elements that might earlier have been thought to be inappropriate, including the realistic, the grotesque and the comic. So here we could mention the rags that Electra wears in Euripides' version of the play (*El.* 184–5), and her rationalistic demolition of the Old Man's accounts of Orestes' return (*El.* 524ff.). There is also Orestes' terrible hair in Euripides' *Orestes* (e.g. *Or.* 223–4). We could mention that, in this area at least, Sophocles may have been influenced by Euripides. Certainly, the frequent emphasis on the bad odours emanating from Philoctetes' foot seems more typical of Euripides (see *Phil.* 473, 483, 783–4, 876, 809–1, 1032, 1378). Then there are the jokes. The most famous, and most inappropriate, is almost certainly this exchange between Menelaus and Hecuba in *The Trojan Women* (1049–50):

> *Hec.:* Do not let her [Helen] on the same ship as yourself.
>
> *Men.:* Why? Has she put on weight?

In what is otherwise a very grim play, it is difficult to pin down what effect this (very bad) joke has. But what we can say is that it is evidence of tragedy accommodating a tone that would in earlier times have been excluded. (For another joke, see Lyssa's exchange with Iris about driving Heracles mad at *HF* 843ff.: this joke plays around with ideas of madness and sanity.)

The play, though, that is most obviously and insistently self-referential is Euripides' *Bacchae*. There has been a good deal of excellent critical work on this aspect of the play (see, for instance, Foley, 1985; Goldhill, 1986: 244–86; Segal, 1982), so a brief survey will suffice. The play opens with Dionysus, the god of theatre, giving us, as it were, a synopsis of the play to come. He then proceeds to direct events so that they conform with that synopsis. The character Dionysus plays around with illusion: is he in mortal form (as he says at *Bacch.* 4), or is that merely what the characters on stage see? Does he destroy the prison or not (*Bacch.* 605–7)? Certainly, he uses what one critic calls 'theatrical weapons' when he lures Pentheus to his death. The young king is dressed up as a woman, so that he can go to watch the maenads dance around on the mountain. Instead of being a secure spectator, he becomes instead the object of the show, eventually torn apart by – among others – his own mother.

Over the course of the fifth century, then, tragedy developed into a genre that included a greater variety of characters, tones and plots. Certain critics argue that some of Euripides' late plays (such as *Iphigenia among the Taurians* and *Helen*) anticipate the more domestic genre of new comedy (see section d below). But, however it changed, what we cannot doubt about tragedy is that it was of the city: it was political.

Conclusion

One could argue about the ways in which tragedy was political. This section has tried to show that tragedy, along with the other institutions of the democratic city, performed an educative function for the citizens in the audience (Croally, 1994; 2005). Other critics have disagreed (Griffin, 1999a; Rhodes, 2003a; cf. Goldhill, 2000; Seaford, 2000). Still, it is worth stressing how directly tragedy can seem political. And, so it is with two sizeable quotations that I shall end. The first comes from Aeschylus' *Eumenides*, when Athene speaks just before the jury cast their votes. Within the play, Athene is of course addressing the jurors, but it is very easy to imagine the audience feeling that they too were the target of Athene's rousing rhetoric (*Eum.* 681–4):

> If you would now hear my law, people of Attica,
> as you judge the first case of bloodshed.

For the rest of time, and for the people of Aegeus,
this will be the council chamber of the jurors.

She goes on to say (*Eum.* 696–7):

I urge my . . . citizens to worship
neither anarchy nor tyranny.

This advice is overt, political and direct. In Euripides' *Supplices*, on the other
hand, we witness a debate between Theseus, the king of Athens, and a
Theban herald, which is famous partly because it is so anachronistic, but also
because its anachronism lies in the way that Theseus' defence of Athenian
democracy is so familiar, especially to anyone who has read Pericles' Funeral
Oration in Thucydides (see Easterling, 1985; Croally, 1994: 207–15).
Through this chapter we have seen that tragedy represents Athens, reflects it
back to the audience, mediates it sometimes through other places and people,
sometimes challenges its beliefs. In the following lines we see a more direct
representation and, perhaps, a more obvious celebration of the democratic
city. Euripides *Supplices* 404–7:

This city is not ruled
by one man; it is a free city.
The people rule, governing in turn in
yearly offices. The most power is not given to
the rich man; instead the poor man has an equal share.

Further reading

For a good general and factual introduction, see Sommerstein (2002).
However, the best critical introduction to tragedy remains Goldhill (1986);
other good collections of articles or introductions: Easterling (1997); Gould
and Herington (2009); Gregory (2005); Hall (2010); Pelling (1997);
Rabinowitz (2008); Segal, E. (1989); Silk (1996); Vernant and Vidal-Naquet
(1988); Winkler and Zeitlin (1990); Zeitlin (1986; 1995). On stagecraft and
tragic space, see Goldhill (2007); Rehm (2002); Taplin (1978); Wiles (1997;
2000). For the politics of tragedy, see Meier (1993); Carter (2007). On persuasion in tragedy, see Buxton (1982); for the idea of the barbarian in tragedy, see Hall (1989); on characterization, see Pelling (1990). For a collection
of articles on Aeschylus, see Lloyd (2006); see also Winnington-Ingram
(1983). On Aeschylus' *Oresteia* see Goldhill (1992); for Sophocles, see
Blundell (1989); Goldhill and Hall (2009); Griffin (1999b); Knox (1961 on
Ajax; 1964); Segal (1981; 1995a); Winnington-Ingram (1980). For
Euripides, see Foley (1985 concentrating on ritual and sacrifice); Knox
(1952 on *Hippolytus*); Michelini (1987) and the collection of articles in

Mossman (2003). On women in Euripides, see Powell (1990); on *Bacchae*, see Segal (1982). There is now a good series of monographs published by Duckworth. In this *Companions to Greek and Roman Tragedy* series there are now books on four of Aeschylus' plays, five of Sophocles', and ten of Euripides'. The Aris and Phillips editions, which include introduction and bibliography, text and translation, and commentary are also very useful. Fairly reliable translations are available from both Penguin, from the Oxford World Classics series (OUP), and from the University of Chicago series. For a good selection of modern views of tragedy and the tragic, see Lambropoulos (2006).

ARISTOPHANIC COMEDY

John Taylor

The rollicking and uninhibited comic drama of fifth-century Athens was called old comedy by ancient critics, to distinguish it from the tamer new comedy of the following century. Eleven plays survive, all by Aristophanes (about a quarter of his output). We know quite a bit about his predecessors and rivals from later quotations: these fragments show that Aristophanes worked within a tradition (other authors wrote broadly similar plays), but also tend to confirm the ancient verdict that he was its supreme exponent. Aristophanes represents the genre, and the genre represents the society that produced it: confident, competitive and endlessly inventive.

Like tragedy, comedy was staged at big public festivals dedicated to Dionysus. It was officially added to the City Dionysia (held each year in March) in 486, and to the January–February Lenaea probably some 40 years later. Both had very large audiences, but the spectators at the Dionysia included foreign visitors, whereas the Lenaea (where comedy came to assume a relatively greater importance) was a more local affair. Programme details are unclear, but at the Dionysia in the time of Aristophanes three comic writers entered one play each, and three tragedians each produced a set of three tragedies plus a satyr play. This last requirement indicates that writers of tragedy could turn their hand to humour (by burlesquing myth), yet it remained separate from comedy proper. Strikingly, no author wrote both tragedy and comedy: the possibility is raised in Plato's *Symposium* (223d1–5) only as a paradoxical fantasy. On the face of it, the two genres contrast strongly. Tragedy normally used for its plot a traditional myth, set in the distant past (and not in Athens), with a consistent dignity and distance of tone; comedy used a made-up story, set in the Athenian present, with a rollercoaster of linguistic register and a contrived spontaneity that seems to invite interruption and audience involvement. On closer examination the picture is more complex:

comedy often draws on myth or echoes its story-patterns, and tragedy may comment indirectly on contemporary issues. Over time the two genres tended to converge, yet stayed formally distinct. Comedy had a bigger chorus (24 rather than 12 or 15), and could use a fourth actor. Aristophanes shamelessly exploits the tragedians (particularly Euripides) for parody and comic effect: his drama is about contemporary theatre as well as contemporary life.

Aristophanes was born about the middle of the fifth century (as usual with ancient authors, we have little biographical information): the fact that he entered his early plays under their producer's name rather than his own probably indicates he was still young in the early 420s. Nine of his surviving plays were put on during the Peloponnesian War, which is a central theme in several of them.

His first extant play (and the oldest European comedy) is *Acharnians*, which won first prize at the Lenaea in 425. Its hero, Dicaeopolis ('Just City'), is an ordinary Athenian farmer. Frustrated by an impasse in the war and by demoralizing annual invasions, and failing to persuade the democratic Assembly to heed his plea for a negotiated peace, he arranges (with a bit of supernatural help and comic fantasy) a private peace for himself and his family. Denounced as treacherous by the pro-war chorus of men from Acharnae (a village directly in the Spartan firing-line), Dicaeopolis makes a dramatic speech parodying Euripides' lost play *Telephus* (whose hero defended the Trojans to Agamemnon as Dicaeopolis here defends the Spartans to the Acharnians) and finally wins them over. The rest of the play shows him enjoying the benefits of peace and the discomfiture of those who oppose it.

Aristophanes won another first prize at the Lenaea with *Knights* in 424. This play is an allegory: the household of the old man Demos ('The People') represents the city, with his slaves standing for its politicians. Havoc is created by a domineering new slave 'the Paphlagonian' (slaves were often named from their place of origin, but the name also suggests the Greek verb *paphlazein*, meaning 'to bluster'). He represents the populist democratic leader Cleon, flattering and manipulating Demos and making life difficult for the existing slaves (who stand for the more conservative politicians Nicias and Demosthenes). By oracular consultation and comic logic it is established that the usurper can be beaten only by someone more vulgar than himself, so a street vendor of sausages is recruited, and assured of the support of the upper-crust young cavalrymen who form the chorus. The sausage-seller duly triumphs, and Demos repents of his past gullibility.

Different in style is *Clouds*, which won third prize at the Dionysia in 423: this disappointing reception is referred to within the play itself, so the text we have must have been partly rewritten afterwards (though it may not have had a second official performance). The philosopher Socrates is satirized as a combination of a typical sophist (an independent provider of higher education) and a mad scientist. The main character Strepsiades has been reduced to debt by his son's expensive hobby of horse-racing. Socrates' reported ability to 'make the worse cause appear the better' (reflecting the allegation that sophists taught their pupils to win an argument regardless of right and wrong) seems to offer a way of bamboozling his creditors. Strepsiades proves a predictably inept pupil, but when his son is handed over by Socrates to a personified Wrong Logic for training, it misfires: he learns only arguments which justify beating his father. Strepsiades in disgust sets fire to Socrates' school, and the chorus of clouds (initially presented as objects of worship preferred by fashionable intellectuals to the traditional gods) are revealed as loyal supporters of Zeus.

Aristophanes returned to a political theme in *Wasps*, which won second prize at the Lenaea in 422. It satirizes the jury-courts, a key institution of democratic Athens. Large juries assigned to cases by lot offered an apparent safeguard against corruption, but in the eyes of conservative critics had an unfortunate bias: it was alleged that, dominated by the urban poor (who were drawn by the modest pay), they would sting wealthy defendants with heavy fines through class hatred and a desire to line the public purse and benefit from the resultant spending. The chorus are jurymen, but costumed as wasps to make this point: a metaphorical re-use of the old-comedy tradition of animal choruses. The main character is the old man Philocleon ('Lover of Cleon'), obsessed with serving on juries: the play again attacks Cleon, whom the jurymen ardently support. Philocleon's son Bdelycleon ('Hater of Cleon') tries various ploys to cure his father: imprisoning him in the house, arranging a mock trial, arguing that jurymen are exploited, and finally taking him for diversion into smart society; Philocleon remains his irrepressible self throughout.

In 421 Aristophanes won second prize at the Dionysia with *Peace*, named from an important non-speaking character. In the previous summer, about the time Aristophanes 'applied for a chorus' (a slot in the forthcoming festival), both Cleon – by now a general as well as a politician – and the Spartan leader Brasidas had been killed in action; this opened the way for a negotiated peace, brokered on the Athenian side by Nicias. Thus a play initially conceived as a wishful fantasy was reshaped by events as a celebration: the Peace of Nicias was ratified shortly afterwards. The main character Trygaeus ('Vintager'), suffering from wartime food shortage, flies to heaven on a giant dung beetle (parodying the winged horse Pegasus in a lost Euripides play) to remonstrate with the gods. They have moved out for the duration, leaving behind War, who has cast Peace into a deep cave. With the help of the chorus of Attic farmers, Trygaeus rescues Peace and restores her to Greece amidst general rejoicing (though in the real world fighting began again within three years).

These five plays of the 420s (together with two lost ones which preceded them) form a distinct group. Our knowledge of other playwrights confirms that this decade was a golden age of old comedy as well as the productive early maturity of Aristophanes himself. The themes of the plays intertwine, and introduce central critical issues. Aristophanes' first play *Banqueters* in 427 apparently portrayed a father with two sons, one educated traditionally and the other in modern sophistic style: here in embryo is *Clouds*. The two were taken into smart society, contrasting in behaviour: we think of the end of *Wasps*, a play which also reverses the generational conflict of *Clouds* by having the father as the quasi-adolescent tearaway. Something in *Babylonians* in 426 sufficiently antagonized Cleon that he tried (unsuccessfully) to prosecute and muzzle Aristophanes, for washing the dirty linen of the city in front of an audience including representatives of the allied states bringing to Athens their annual tribute (tax or 'protection money'): those states were perhaps represented as Babylonian slaves in a treadmill. But the enmity possibly went back to the playground: both Aristophanes and Cleon came from the deme of Kydathenaion, and so perhaps grew up in the same district of Athens.

In Athenian politics aggressive imperialism was a democratic cause and enjoyed strong popular support: Cleon was the heir of politicians who transformed an original anti-Persian defence league into an Athenian empire (whose existence provoked the Peloponnesians into war), and he favoured increasing the tribute to finance public spending in Athens. More conservative elements, including those with oligarchic sympathies, wanted peace with Sparta and criticized the ostentatious adornment of their own city from imperial revenue (even though some of them owned land in the empire and were happy to exploit it when it suited them). The plea for peace and the hostility towards Cleon (together with a traditionalist stance in education) may indicate that Aristophanes held consistently conservative views; but this is an area of controversy. Some critics question whether we can meaningfully discuss the personal views of ancient authors at all. Others deny a serious political purpose in comedy: for them, Aristophanes aims only to entertain the audience and win the prize. Cleon was elected to a generalship soon after *Knights* got first prize: unless the theatre audience represented a different cross-section of the population from the Assembly, or the complex judging procedure for plays failed to reflect audience opinion, this suggests that Aristophanes' attack on him was not taken too much to heart. Fragments of other old comedy writers give the impression that a conservative, traditionalist stance was a convention of the genre, though this may be partly because new ideas and institutions tend to invite satire. Critics observe that in the *agōn* (the contest or controversy within each play) Aristophanes typically satirizes both sides. Yet some people and issues are satirized more gently than others: in particular, conservative politicians such as Nicias escape lightly.

These plays also allow us to extrapolate a typical old-comedy plot, and recurrent traits of a comic hero. The Aristophanic main character is typically a middle-aged Athenian farmer: many members of the audience might identify with his dissatisfaction at a world run by more powerful interests. The hero conceives a fantastical scheme to right his wrongs. Despite encountering opposition, he is able to carry it through, with prosaic reality suspended. The chorus, having entered at the *parodos* (an entry song after the opening scene), now put aside their dramatic character and in the *parabasis* come forward to address the audience on behalf of the poet, sometimes about topical events but more often to advertise his talents and disparage those of his rivals. In the second half we typically see 'hostile intruders' vainly trying to spoil or usurp what the hero has achieved, while he and his friends enjoy its fruits. The play usually ends in an atmosphere of celebration (which might spill over to the audience, as a comedy usually ended the day). None of these elements is set in stone (*Clouds* has a notably dark ending) and Aristophanes increasingly varies them in his later plays, but there is enough to suggest a common template. Plot and character are often marked by discontinuity. Read in translation, the comedies seem fluid and informal, but Aristophanes inherited from his predecessors a complex structure dictating different metres for different sections of the play. Old comedy was paradoxically more formal than tragedy in this respect, though the two genres are broadly alike in alternating scenes of dialogue with choral songs. The Aristophanic hero is a jolly obverse of the tragic hero, who (particularly in Sophocles) also has recurrent traits, his awesome greatness of soul accompanied by prickly obsession and isolation.

There was a gap in Aristophanes' career after 421 (probably not just an impression created by the accident of what survives). His next surviving play is *Birds*, which won second prize at the Dionysia in 414. Its hero Pisetairos ('Persuader') and his friend Euelpides ('Hopeful'), dissatisfied with life in Athens, decide to join with the birds and found a new city in the sky. This motivates an unusually spectacular chorus entry, each of its members costumed and introduced as a separate species. Athenian theatre was a co-operation between the state (which provided the theatre and paid the actors) and private finance. When a playwright was 'granted a chorus', he was also assigned a sponsor who paid for props and costumes. Jokes are sometimes made about mean provision, but in 414 Aristophanes evidently had particularly generous backing. The birds are persuaded to join the two (now winged) Athenians in building 'Cloudcuckooland' (hence our name for a fantasy place). Hostile visitors are sent packing, and a dispute with the gods (suffering because the birds intercept the nourishing smoke of sacrifices) is satisfactorily resolved. *Birds* seems lighter and more free-wheeling than the earlier plays. Its fantasy may, however, be a veiled comment on the Sicilian Expedition launched by Athens the previous year in a bold attempt to extend her empire at a time when the Peace of Nicias, though nominally still in force, was precarious and clearly could not last. The campaign ended in disaster in 413. Athens had lost most of her fleet and was plunged into crisis: many cities in the empire took the opportunity to withhold their tribute, and a group of ten special magistrates was appointed, overriding the institutions of democracy.

In this climate Aristophanes produced *Lysistrata* in 411, probably at the Lenaea. Like *Acharnians* (but now surely to a more receptive audience) it is a plea for peace. The main character Lysistrata ('Dissolver of Armies') is a female version of the traditional comic hero. Her fantastical scheme is a sex-strike, by which the women of Greece hold their men to ransom until they make peace.

The suspension of disbelief here does not involve supernatural help but simply our willingness to ignore logical objections (alternative sexual opportunities, and the simultaneous complaint of the women that their soldier husbands are constantly away from home). The Athenian women occupy the Acropolis: an attacking semi-chorus of old men is repulsed by another of old women, and one of the ten magistrates who attempts to intervene is humiliated. An abandoned husband arrives to solicit his wife's favours but, though initially led on, is left in the lurch. After a herald reports similarly frustrating conditions in Sparta, Lysistrata presides over a general reconciliation. *Lysistrata* makes sex a central theme, but bawdiness and sexually explicit jokes are characteristic of old comedy. This may attest an original link with fertility rituals (like the procession carrying a model phallus in honour of Dionysus enacted in *Acharnians*); more obviously, it is a universal form of humour. Comic actors wore grotesque masks and exaggeratedly padded costumes, usually with a big leather phallus for male characters, to which attention is frequently drawn. The lack of inhibition in this area parallels the freedom with which politicians and other prominent individuals are insulted (often in sexual terms), and provides another contrast with serious literature. Sexual passion and jealousy are central to many tragedies, but physical detail is rigorously eschewed.

Acharnians and *Peace* drew on tragedy for individual scenes, juxtaposed with everyday reality. More extensive engagement with the grander genre is found in *Thesmophoriazusae* ('Women celebrating the Thesmophoria', an all-female festival of Demeter), also produced in 411, probably at the Dionysia. In this respect it foreshadows Aristophanes' next surviving play *Frogs*, but it also has similarities to *Lysistrata* (the poet was probably working on both simultaneously). Euripides learns that the women of Athens, angry because of the bad name given to their sex by his wicked heroines, are plotting his death (his ancient reputation was as a misogynist, in curious contrast to the modern perception of him as proto-feminist). He sends an elderly male relative in drag to infiltrate their festival. After trying to defend Euripides the old man is unmasked and put under guard. He tries to escape by re-enacting in parody scenes from the innovative 'escape' plays written by Euripides in the previous few years: the lost *Palamedes* and *Andromeda*, and the extant *Helen* (comparison with the original shows a level of detail in the parody which presumably few members of the audience could fully appreciate). Euripides finally agrees to stop slandering the women in return for the release of his relative.

Athens fought on for nine years after the Sicilian disaster, but the city was almost on its knees when Aristophanes won first prize at the Lenaea in 405 with *Frogs*, often regarded as his greatest play. The comic hero is here a god, Dionysus: Hermes was a character in *Peace*, and Poseidon in *Birds*, but Aristophanes would perhaps not so readily have brought Zeus on stage. Dionysus laments that there are no good poets any more – meaning tragedians (we are invited to reflect that one comic poet still thrives). In an opening dialogue with his slave Xanthias he describes his plan to go down to the underworld and bring back a dead poet (the death of Euripides was probably the inspiration for the play, perhaps conceived originally as a quest specifically for him, but the subsequent death of Sophocles necessitated broadening the theme). The effeminate god of theatre wears the costume of the great hero Heracles (a successful earlier visitor to the lower world) on top of his own. Later on the journey (when he is threatened by underworld inhabitants Heracles has wronged) he swaps costumes with Xanthias, and also appeals for help to 'his' priest occupying the seat of honour in the theatre of Dionysus. Such metatheatrical devices (drawing attention to the play as a play, and making us think about the nature of theatre) are characteristic of Aristophanic comedy: Trygaeus on his dung-beetle asks the crane operator to take more care, and at the beginning of *Wasps* the audience are invited (in pantomime style) to guess what is wrong with Philocleon. There is a remarkable parallel here with Euripides' posthumous masterpiece *Bacchae*, probably also produced in 405: the sinister Dionysus of that play (himself in disguise) uses overtly theatrical tactics by costuming his opponent Pentheus as a woman in order to lead him to destruction. It is possible that the earliest Greek plays dealt with stories of Dionysus himself: in both *Frogs* and *Bacchae*, we have a curious sense of coming full circle at the end of an era.

The themes of *Frogs* interestingly echo fragments of the other two famous poets of old comedy, Cratinus (a generation older) and Aristophanes' contemporary Eupolis. The theme of one character acting as another, specifically Dionysus as a mythical hero, has a parallel in Cratinus' *Dionysalexandros* ('Dionysus as Alexander', i.e. Paris of Troy): in that role he judged the beauty contest of the goddesses as Dionysus in *Frogs* judges the contest between Aeschylus and Euripides. A fragment of Cratinus coined the verb *Euripidaristophanizein* ('to Euripid-Aristophanize'), presumably referring to a perceived similarity in verbal ingenuity, implying fascination on Aristophanes' part with the target of his satire. In Eupolis' *Demes*, four great military and political leaders from the past return from the dead to advise the city in its hour of need: *Frogs* substitutes poets. In another Eupolis play, *Taxiarchs* ('Captains'), Dionysus is shown being instructed in the art of rowing, as he is by the ferryman Charon in *Frogs*. His underworld journey reminds us of lost literature in a broader sense. It includes all the 'traditional' features — but we know these from *Frogs* itself, and from later texts such as Virgil's *Aeneid*. There must have been underworld journeys in early epic, but they do not survive. (Similarly, the comic account of the Athenian Assembly in *Acharnians* is the best source for its procedure.) A play called *Frogs* had been written by Magnes, a still earlier poet: we know nothing about it, but the frogs in Aristophanes inhabit the marshes of the Styx. Critics have questioned whether the audience see them (would not frog costumes be too expensive in 405?) Their cry (*brekekekex koax koax*) is distinctive, but surely not satisfaction enough: it is inconceivable that a play called *Frogs* showed us no frogs — but it is entirely plausible that Dionysus himself, preoccupied with trying to row, cannot see them: again we think of panto-mime ('they're behind you').

A criticism of Aristophanes' early plays is that the story is essentially com-plete by half-time, with the later scenes inevitably anti-climactic. *Frogs* satis-fies modern taste by postponing the *agōn* into the second half: the great contest between Aeschylus and Euripides, traditionalist and modernist respec-tively, for the throne of tragedy (Sophocles modestly supporting Aeschylus). With Dionysus as referee, the two playwrights criticize each other's language, metre, music and (most importantly) characters: the grandly inspiring models provided by Aeschylean heroes, as against the ragged, crippled or depraved individuals in the debased tragedy of Euripides (felt perhaps to trespass on the territory of comedy). By the typical Aristophanic device of making imagery literal, verses from their plays are weighed in a balance; Aeschylus easily wins, and also offers better advice on how to save the city. Dionysus therefore takes him back to Athens. This seems to confirm the cultural conservatism we have identified already; yet the play's reading of Aeschylus is relatively crude, in contrast to the close engagement with Euripides. Further complicating our assessment, *Frogs* was (very unusually) given a second official performance, apparently for the advice in its *parabasis* to re-enfranchize citizens disqualified for supporting a brief oligarchic coup in 411. If Aristophanes really had been trying for years to influence opinion, perhaps he finally succeeded.

After 405 there is another long gap before *Ecclesiazusae* ('Assemblywomen'), produced about 392. Meanwhile Athens had lost the war and her empire, experienced another and harsher oligarchic regime, and seen democracy ten-tatively restored; but times were still hard (see the Interlude preceding this chapter). The play's title is a paradox, for women could not attend the Assembly. It moves away from the traditions of old comedy (for example by reducing the role of the chorus), but its main character, Praxagora ('She who gets things done in the Assembly'), is another Lysistrata. Deciding that women (experienced in domestic economy) could run the city better than men, she recruits, trains and costumes them to infiltrate the Assembly (reversing the theme of *Thesmophoriazusae*, with the additional metatheatrical joke that these women dressed as men are men anyway, as all actors were male). The ruse is successful, and power voted to women. Their regime (echo-ing the utopian theme of *Birds*, and curiously foreshadowing what Plato later prescribes for the class of 'guardians' in his *Republic*) proves to involve radical communism, both of property and of sexual partners.

Aristophanes' final play *Plutus* ('Wealth'), produced in 388, is more deci-sively different: a morality fable in which the hero Chremylus, disillusioned that the wicked prosper whilst honest men such as himself struggle in pov-erty, visits the Delphic oracle to ask whether it is worth bringing up his son to be virtuous. The god tells him to take into his house the first person he meets on leaving the shrine: this is a blind old man, subsequently revealed as Plutus, the god of wealth. Convinced by Chremylus that he will be able to distribute his favours more equitably if his sight is restored, he consents to visit a healing shrine of Asclepius. The goddess of poverty intervenes to argue that hardship has been the making of Greece (a theme we can trace back to Homer and Herodotus), but Chremylus is undeterred. The healing is successful, and a sequence of visitors (echoing the closing scenes of earlier comedy) dealt with appropriately.

These last works have their own interest and charm, but Aristophanes is best represented by the plays of the 420s, and by *Lysistrata* and *Frogs*. Old comedy belongs essentially to fifth-century Athens, a society sufficiently buoyant to take strong criticism. Whether or not Aristophanes is serious in the narrow sense of wanting to change political opinion, he is serious in pursuit of his art, in his handling of language, and in his criticism of literature and life. He is also great fun to read.

Further reading

For a collection of fragments of comedy, see Olson (2007). As a starter, one can consult Sommerstein (2002). For introductions to Aristophanes, see Cartledge (1990); Dover (1972); Lowe (2007); Macdowell (1995); Robson (2009). For some more detailed treatments, see Bowie (1993; 1997); Goldhill (1991: chapter 3); Reckford (1987); Silk (2000); Taafe (1993 on Aristophanes and women). For a good collection of articles, see Segal (1996b), and the relevant chapters in Segal (2001).

MIDDLE AND NEW COMEDY

Neil Croally

Middle comedy is the name we give to the plays that were produced between *c.* 400–385 to some time up to but not after the first appearance of Menander at a theatrical festival in *c.* 321 (see Table 4.1). Some scholars want to stress that the later plays of Aristophanes should be counted as middle rather than old comedy; others prefer to be more guarded. And, arguably, in this case being guarded is the safer option. Why? Because – if we remove the two late Aristophanes plays produced early in the fourth century – we have almost no middle comedy extant: papyrus fragments are rare, and most of the quotations from ancient authors are from Athenaeus, who has a particular interest in the symposium, which possibly affects what he chooses to quote.

It is reasonably clear, however, that middle comedy marks a transition between old comedy – characterized as civic, satirical, extravagant, obscene, grotesque – and new comedy, seen as domestic rather than civic, urbane rather than urban, and so on (see below). On the one hand, political and philosophical themes (and targets) are still present: Plato, for instance, seems to have been a common victim. On the other hand, it seems likely, if not certain, that middle comedy began to develop some of the plots and stock characters familiar from new comedy (e.g. in Alexis' *Agonis* from *c.* 340–30). Formally, the chorus becomes increasingly separate from and irrelevant to the action, and the five-act structure – typical of new comedy – is probably established. The extravagant and grotesque costume of old comedy seems to disappear, but it is not clear when. One important thing to remember is that it seems clear that, from post *c.* 380, the enormous increase in the productivity of the comic poets went hand in hand with a Hellenization of comedy. Increasingly, poets, actors, themes and audience were Greek rather than peculiarly Athenian. It is in this context that we should view new comedy.

Table 4.1 Known middle comedians

Name	Place of origin	Dates when active	Number of plays
Anaxandrides	Rhodes	385–348	65
Eubulus	Athens?	375–335	104
Antiphanes	Athens?	387–306	260
Alexis	Thurii	350–275	245
Timocles	Athens?	345–315	?

New comedy is associated firmly with the dramatist Menander, as only his plays are preserved (other known dramatists of the genre include Apollodorus, Diphilus, Philemon, Phillipides and Posidippus). Born in *c.* 344, Menander had his first play performed *c.* 321, a date sometimes (but implausibly) seen as the starting point of new comedy. He won first prize with *Dyscolos* ('The Grouch') in 316 at the Lenaea, and first prize at the Great Dionysia the next year. He appears to have won only eight victories during his career, which ended with his death in *c.* 290. The modern era, however, did not get to read any of Menander's plays in anything like full form until the twentieth century, when a number of codices were found, edited and published (including just about all of *Dyscolos*). As things stand, there are 19 plays with substantial fragments, of which there are seven with over half the text surviving (these seven are: *Aspis* ('The Shield'), *Dyscolos* ('The Grouch'), *Epitrepontes* ('Men Arbitrating'), *Misoumenos* ('The Hated Man'), *Perikeiroumene* ('Girl with cropped hair'), *Samia* ('Girl from Samos') and *Sikyonios* ('The Sicyonian')).

All the plays have a contemporary, domestic setting. While the actors continued to wear masks, the costume, developing changes introduced by middle comedy, was contemporary and ordinary as well. The main metre is the iambic trimeter, chosen perhaps because in this metre it is easiest to imitate the patterns and idioms of ordinary speech. All the plays have similar plot elements: there is always a love interest of one sort or another, in which a young man has to overcome various obstacles in being together with his inamorata. There are also deceptions, recognitions and reversals of fortune. These – along with some fairly long narrative speeches and divine prologues – show that Menander was influenced by and was adapting (mainly Euripidean) tragedy. A worrying feature for the modern reader is the extent to which rape is used as a plot device. Sommerstein (2002) argues that this not only reflects a very different gender politics than our own; it also allows Menander to have a young woman give birth to a child without making her unmarriageable. Menander further develops middle comedy's closet of stock characters. There are the already mentioned young lovers, the grumpy old men, the (often boastful) soldiers, clever slaves, courtesans, old nurses and cooks who just won't shut up. However, it is at least arguable that Menander does adapt some of these characters so that they become in his hands both more individual and more psychologically convincing. Thus, the boastful soldier in *Perikeiroumene* brags of the fine clothes his mistress wears rather than, as would be usual, his military derring-do.

Menander's reputation in antiquity was very high indeed. Two scholars several centuries apart – Aristophanes of Byzantium and Quintilian – rank Menander just below Homer (in their view the greatest poet). He certainly influenced the Roman playwrights, Plautus and Terence; indeed, some of their plays are direct adaptations of Menander. It is also true that we can see in the plays that the plotting is skilful and that the characterization is more than stock, but it is, I think, still difficult for us in the twentieth century to see what the ancients so admired. There is something of the soap opera in Menander, a sort of lightly enjoyable but not excessively impressive escapism with realistic touches. Menander may have been influenced by tragedy, but only formally: the power of tragedy is completely absent. He may also have been in a line of dramatists that stretched back to Aristophanes but his plays have lost the civic dimension, the linguistic verve and the surreal and grotesque imagination of the earlier poet. But the Greeks and Romans seemed to have admired Menander greatly and, given that he was a comic poet, we can take it that they found him funny. While this may seem strange to a twenty-first century reader, it is a view that should be respected.

Further reading

For an informative introduction, see Sommerstein (2002); also Lowe (2007). For a collection of comic fragments, see Olson (2007). On Menander, see also Goldberg (1980); Hunter (1985); Segal (2001: chapter 9; 2002); Webster (1974); Wiles (1991).

Chapter 5

Historical writing in the classical era

Roy Hyde

> All dates in this chapter are BCE unless stated otherwise. Glossary items: *analepsis; annalistic; apodexis; epideixis; gnōmē; nomos; physis; prolepsis.*

HERODOTUS

Candaules, descendant of Heracles and king of Lydia, was 'in love with his own wife', and continually praised her beauty to his bodyguard Gyges. Since Gyges seemed insufficiently impressed by what he was told, the king, 'who was fated to come to a bad end', said he would arrange for him to see the queen naked. Gyges was horrified at the impropriety of this suggestion, but Candaules insisted. One night, Gyges was concealed behind the door of the royal bedroom before the king and queen went to bed. The queen entered and took off her clothes. Having looked at her, as she turned to get into bed, Gyges slipped out, unseen – or so he thought. In fact the queen *had* seen him. The following morning he was summoned to her presence and offered a stark choice: having seen the queen naked, he must either die, or kill Candaules and become her king. Faced with yet another unpleasant dilemma, Gyges chose the latter alternative, killed the king and was proclaimed king in his stead.

Unsurprisingly, the Lydians at first rebelled against Gyges, but an appeal to the oracle at Delphi confirmed his position, adding the proviso ('which the Lydians and their kings took no notice of until it actually happened') that the descendants of Heracles would gain their revenge in the fifth generation. The relieved Gyges sent offerings to Delphi, 'the first of the barbarians of whom we know' to have done this. Despite this eventful beginning, Gyges ruled without much incident except a minor military success, 'but as no other great deed transpired during his reign of 38 years, we shall say no more about him' (summary of Hdt. 1.7–15).

This narrative occurs very near the beginning of Herodotus' *Histories*, a book which, as the author has already told us by this point, sets out to trace the history of the 'difference' between the Greeks and the 'barbarians'; the clash of east and west which will culminate in the defeat, in 479, of Xerxes' expedition against Greece. It is a big book (a commonly used English translation of it runs to more than 700 pages), almost certainly bigger than any book in prose that had been written before, and it is – arguably – the first history book. If we want to know what was happening in Greece and the near east during the couple of centuries before the Persian Wars, it is the book we must read: for most of what Herodotus tells us, there is no other available information. Yet, alongside the kind of material we would expect to find in a history book, it is full of narratives like the above, many of them even more apparently far-fetched and 'unhistorical' (in our usual understanding of the word), and of a great store of other information which might seem to be included for no better reason than Herodotus happened to know it.

Reading Herodotus, then, is – or may be – a rather different kind of activity for us than reading, say, Homer (the extent to which it would have been different for a Greek is another issue, which some of what follows should help to elucidate); we do not expect what Homer says Agamemnon said to Achilles to be what they actually did say – indeed, we do not necessarily have to believe that Agamemnon and Achilles actually existed at all. But we are inclined to believe – we are led to believe, because they appear in the pages of a history book – that Gyges and Candaules and, which is perhaps more important, Xerxes and Themistocles, existed. What they said and did are, in a sense, matters of historical fact. But did they say and do what Herodotus says they said and did? We can, of course, if we want, read Herodotus without asking such questions, and this approach is a perfectly valid and satisfying one. But if we read him as historians, we shall have other expectations.

We shall think about Herodotus as 'historian' later. For the moment I want to return to the Gyges narrative and to think about ways in which it is representative of Herodotus' *modus operandi*, and can be used to illustrate some of the approaches to reading Herodotus that are favoured by scholars today.

Folk-tales, history, sources

'Now this Candaules', Herodotus tells us, 'was in love with his own wife.' It might be the beginning of a fairy story or a folk-tale; it certainly is not what we would expect in a serious history book. In fact Gyges seems to have been something of a folk-tale figure, and at least two other versions of his accession existed.

What are folk-tales?

'Folk-tales' are not easy to define precisely, though we probably think we know one when we see one: roughly speaking, they are traditional stories passed down amongst 'ordinary' people, often about famous people or

(Continued)

(Continued)

types of people; they may have magical or outlandish elements, and they are not 'history', though they may do the job of history. The 'awful dilemma' is a recognized and frequently found folk-tale motif, as is the 'warner' – someone who advises a character in favour of a course of action, but is ignored: in this case, Gyges himself.

In one, he came to power by the use of a Tolkien-like ring of invisibility; the other is closer to Herodotus' version – the faithful servant Gyges falls in love with his king's new bride and faces a dilemma like that of our Gyges above. Two important considerations arise here: first, the fact that stories of this kind appear frequently in Herodotus and this has consequences for our view of him as historian (or not), and, second, the implication that Herodotus is having to choose which version of a story to include at any given point. (It is true that in this case we do not *know* that he has made a choice: he may have had access only to the one version. But in many cases it is certain that he did, as he tells us so himself.)

This second point is, of course, inseparable from writing history. Varying accounts of any event will inevitably exist, and part of the job of the historian is to weigh the probabilities of such accounts and present what he thinks is the true one, or, depending on the kind of historian he is, the one which best suits his purpose. Depending again on the kind of historian he is, he may or may not refer to accounts other than the one he favours. Sometimes Herodotus does, sometimes he does not; sometimes he tells us that there is another version, but that he will not be using it. He is, he says, 'not bound to believe everything' (7.152). More about this in due course.

This point interacts with the first point. A historian is, in terms of the factual content of his narrative, limited not only by his own preferences – unless he simply makes things up, which will seriously jeopardize his status as historian – but by the nature and extent of his sources. It is not easy to establish what history writing looked like before Herodotus: only disjointed 'fragments' of writers who seem to have been roughly his contemporaries have survived. It used to be thought that Herodotus may have had access to some written local histories and could have incorporated them into his narrative, but scholars now are more inclined to think that most of the writers of such accounts actually wrote *after* him, rather than before. Apart from anything else, this fact brings Herodotus' achievement into even sharper focus: the fact that the first attempt at written history is a book of such ambition, scale and complexity, is nothing short of extraordinary.

It also makes us think more deeply about what his sources of information were, and how he might have gone about synthesizing them. Gyges, for example, lived two centuries before Herodotus' time; Lydia, to the Greeks, especially those like Herodotus whose homelands lay on the coast of Asia

Minor, may have been less of a foreign land than at first appears – though its inhabitants were still barbarians – but his geographical scope extends far more widely; from one end of the Mediterranean to the other, into southern Russia, to India, to north Africa. He claims himself to have travelled extensively and, though these claims have been seriously challenged, the balance of scholarly opinion at the moment is that he did travel a good deal, though perhaps not quite as far as his narrative sometimes suggests. He lays claim to knowledge deriving from Persians, from Egyptians, from Phoenicians, and so on; occasionally he alludes to words in foreign languages, but shows no sign of real knowledge of any language but his own; he refers to the use of interpreters in the course of his investigations. Scarcely any of the material he incorporates can have been written down, and anything that was, in any language other than Greek, would have been accessible to him only through those same interpreters. Reliant as he was on orally transmitted information, much of it deriving from non-Greek sources, it is scarcely surprising that some material of a folk-tale nature has got into his narrative; it is, on reflection, more remarkable that Herodotus managed to collect anything of significance at all concerning some of the places and people and events about whom he writes.

It has often been remarked that when he embarks upon his narrative of the Persian Wars proper, the anecdotal content decreases, though it by no means disappears altogether: the story of how Alcmaeon became rich, for example, and the famous account of how Hippocleides 'danced away his marriage', which immediately follows it (6.125ff.) will hardly convince most readers that they are hard fact, but most readers would also probably rather have them than not. And what has been called the 'kaleidoscopic' nature of Herodotus' narrative – the constantly varied content, the changes of location, the variations in narrative focus – helps to serve a purpose beyond that of simply conveying factual information. We may not believe that the young Cyrus the Great was suckled by a bitch when abandoned in the mountains (1.122); nor does Herodotus, and he says so, though his preferred version seems scarcely more credible. But the fact that such stories attached themselves to Cyrus says something about what the Medes, or the Greeks, or Herodotus' informant – and indeed Herodotus himself – thought about Cyrus, and this is in itself worth knowing and worth thinking about.

Fame

The story of Cyrus' exposure at birth marks him out as a future hero (think, for example, of Romulus and Remus or Oedipus or, from another culture, Moses). Gyges, however, despite his enterprising beginning, turns out to be a disappointment as a hero, doing nothing worth recording for the rest of his 38 years. That Herodotus discards him and moves on to more worthy matters is in keeping with his declared aim: 'that the great and wondrous deeds, both of Greeks and barbarians, should not become without fame' (preface to book 1). The last, clumsy-sounding, phrase is hard to render exactly in English: literally, it means 'become fameless (*aklea*)', *kleos* being the Greek for 'fame'. Incidentally, the scope of these 'deeds' is extensive, and what is not covered by the word 'great' can be accounted for by 'wondrous'; he is interested in the whole range of human achievement, the actions men perform, their feats of engineering, the extraordinary customs of outlandish nations, and tells us about them. (He is also interested in the natural world and in animals and what they do, from crocodiles and hippopotamuses to monstrous ants that dig up gold.) Without any historical models to imitate, Herodotus had to create his own genre: though he wrote in the relatively new medium of prose, he looked to the poets, and to Homer especially. Homer, without question, created 'fame', not just for Agamemnon and Odysseus, but for the countless minor figures and their cities whose names punctuate the *Iliad*. Herodotus' Ionic dialect recalls Homer's; Homeric echoes show through his text, he is fond, as Homer is, of direct speech, and his narrative technique, especially his use of *analepsis* ('flashback') and *prolepsis* (anticipation of what is to come) probably owes something to Homer. Homer, of course, wrote about the heroes of the past. But poetry could praise the heroes of the present as well. Pindar and the lyric poets could exalt Olympic victors to the level of mythic heroes; more significantly for Herodotus' subject matter, Simonides had written a poem on the battle of Plataea, the culminating point of the Persian Wars and, almost, of Herodotus' book.

Cities, men and women

If Gyges is a disappointing hero, he is still a human motivator in the chain of events that link the distant, near-mythical, past with Herodotus' own time. Cities and peoples have their *kleos* too, though (to be in Homer was something to be proud of, and something from which political capital could be made), and Herodotus frequently presents actions in national terms ('the Spartans did this'; 'the Athenians say that'). He is also not unaware of political ideologies and developments, and their part in the shaping of history: it used to be considered that his approach to politics and constitutional matters was naive or simplistic, but recent work has shown that this is far from the case (Forsdyke in Dewald and Marincola, 2006: 224ff.). But anyone who reads a substantial portion of the *Histories* will be left in no doubt that, in Herodotus' world, individual human beings set events in motion and keep the wheels turning. Thus, for example, it is Candaules' foolishness (coupled with the inevitability of fate) that results in the change of dynasty in Lydia, and therefore sets in motion the chain of events leading to the Persian Wars, rather than (for example) economic factors or dynastic rivalry or any of the other forces which are more commonly – in the view of more recent and more ideological historiography – regarded as motivating factors in such occurrences.

Incidentally, in this case, another source identifies Gyges as the head of a noble family whose grandfather had been put to death by Candaules, so that from this viewpoint his usurpation of the throne (though still 'personally' motivated) fits into a more easily recognizable paradigm of dynastic struggle; Herodotus may not, of course, have known this version – or did he simply prefer the one he gives us?

In Herodotus' world-view, then, men are the motivators of events; men – and women too. Another glance at the Gyges story points up the fact that, in the end, the actual motivator of Gyges' accession is the queen. In much of Greek historiography, the contribution of women is negligible: Thucydides, for example, rarely refers to individual women, and the role he – or at least his Pericles – envisages for them in (Athenian) society is a passive and subordinate one (Thuc. 2. 46). In Herodotus, however, women figure not infrequently as personalities in their own right. Artemisia, for example, queen of Herodotus' own city of Halicarnassus, looms large in his account of Xerxes' invasion, as commander and counsellor, provoking by her (actually devious) actions in the battle of Salamis Xerxes' famous remark that 'his men had become women, and his women men' (8.88). We should not try to make of Herodotus some kind of proto-feminist – as a moment's consideration of this remark confirms – but we can at least suggest that his attitude to what remained in male-centred Greek thinking, especially historiography, decidedly the 'second sex', is a refreshingly open one.

Composition and publication; doctors and sophists

Towards the end of the *Histories* (9.108ff), Herodotus presents us with another love story, this time with Xerxes himself as protagonist, which results in the undeserved downfall and murder, at the instigation of Xerxes himself, of Xerxes' brother Masistes. Here again, a woman presents a man with an 'awful dilemma': Xerxes must either face public humiliation or hand over to his queen Amestris the mother of a woman with whom he has had an affair (and whom Amestris proceeds to torture horribly, once she has got her hands on her). The details of the story are not closely parallel, it is true, but there are more than enough similarities of phrasing to make it clear that Herodotus meant one story to echo the other. Such correspondences ('ring-composition', in this case) are too frequent throughout the whole book to be accidental, and give the lie to any image of Herodotus as an artless storyteller.

Narrative correspondences also emphasize the degree of control he exercises over his material, which, in an age without any of the aids to writing, memory and research which we take for granted, and when even basic writing materials were cumbersome and inconvenient, is remarkable indeed – and made the more remarkable by the fact that he does not seem to have had any precursors, at least in the medium of prose, to look to for guidance on how to marshal such a vast array of material.

He did, however, have the Homeric poems. We have already remarked on the Homeric model in the context of the creation and preservation of *kleos*, and the existence in Herodotus of linguistic echoes of Homer. The Homeric poems are in origin oral compositions, and the natural medium for their reception was the recitation or public reading. Though Herodotus may be seen as a product of an age in which orality was giving way to literacy, and to writing as the norm for literary composition, the oral element is still potent. As we have noted, most of his source material must have been orally transmitted, and there can be little doubt that the first public airing of his work would have come about by way of readings. Clearly such readings could not encompass the whole of a work of such dimensions and, to an extent, the nature of the book as it stands may be accounted for by this fact, and by the fact that different topics might be suited to different audiences: an audience interested in the habits of the Scythians, for example, might have less interest in the Cambyses and the Ethiopians or the reasons why the Nile floods. This is not to suggest (though some scholars in the past have considered it to be the case) that the *Histories* as a whole is no more than a patchwork of *logoi* (the plural of *logos*, meaning 'story', 'account', 'rationale'); there are indeed some sections, such as the long account of Egypt in book 2, that seem almost free-standing, but, as was said above, the resonances between the different parts of the work are such that it can hardly be seem as other than a unity. It may well be the case that Herodotus did compose some of his *logoi* independently of others: we cannot know what was his initial plan for the book as a whole, or indeed if he had one; but if he did, he at some point revised and unified the parts into a whole.

We do not have much information about public readings or lectures in Herodotus' time. There is a story that Herodotus read some parts of his work at the Olympic Games, and another that the young Thucydides attended one of his readings. That reading, if it happened, presumably took place at Athens, where Herodotus spent a good deal of time, and it would be in keeping with what we know of the intellectual climate of the time (not only of Athens, in fact, but of Herodotus' native Ionia) that he presented his work to the public there. Not only poets and rhapsodes (professional reciters of Homer) performed their works or advertised themselves in public. It was acceptable, for example, for a doctor to stand up before the Assembly at Athens and advertise himself for potential hire as a public physician (Thomas, 2000). In an age when there was no such thing as accepted 'scientific' medical practice, an individual doctor would have to convince potential patients that his methods were the best (and that he was, in Marcel Detienne's (1996) words, a 'master of truth'). This would no doubt entail criticizing the methods of rival practitioners, and specimens of medical writings survive (in the so-called Hippocratic corpus) which do precisely this.

Not only doctors did this: also familiar to Herodotus' contemporaries (that is, his audience) would have been the lectures of sophists, 'philosophers' – perhaps 'intellectuals' would be a better term – frequently itinerant around the Greek world, who made a career out of both teaching rhetorical skills and displaying their own. The reputation of sophists in much writing about Greek thought is not high (to a considerable extent as a result of the influence of Plato, who considered some of them to be a pernicious influence), but many of them were serious thinkers, concerned not only with what would be considered today philosophy, but with matters as diverse as natural history, ethnography and what may loosely be called science. Some became widely known, and (to judge, for example, from Plato's *Protagoras*), their visits and their lectures were eagerly awaited by their considerable number of followers. It is in the light of this intellectual *milieu* that Herodotus should surely be seen: like the sophists, his interests are broad, and cover much the same range of expertise; also like them, his discussions of – to take one example – 'scientific' matters, such as why the Nile floods, are polemical, designed not only to advance his own theory on the matter in question, but to refute, either specifically or implicitly, those of others. He also shows, incidentally, a considerable interest in medical matters and associated topics, such as climate and its influence on human life.

Display and demonstration

The Greek word for a (usually rhetorically sophisticated) exposition of a theory, such as those of the sophists, was *epideixis*. In the first sentence of his book, Herodotus uses a noun closely related to this word: *apodexis*. 'This', he writes, 'is the *apodexis* of the *historiē* of Herodotus of Halicarnassus . . .' *Historiē* means not 'history', but 'enquiry': 'research' or 'researches' perhaps conveys the meaning more fully. The root of the words *epideixis* and *apodexis* (the latter is the Ionic spelling of what would be in Attic Greek *apodeixis*), means 'show', 'display' and so forth. The word *apode{i}xis* later became the standard term for a philosophical proof: *apodexis* here is sometimes translated as if it meant nothing more than 'making public', but its close connection with *epideixis* strongly suggests that it may also carry the sense of 'display'. If we think of Herodotus as seeing himself as doing much the same as the sophists or the medical practitioners, putting forward their theories with the aid of the rhetoric of persuasion, we shall probably not be far wrong. At the same time, we should bear in mind the connotations of *apodexis* with 'proof': he is extremely fond of the verb with which this noun is cognate, *apodeiknumi*, and often uses it when he wants to demonstrate the rightness of his own views on controversial matters.

Prose and tragedy

Much could be said on this topic: the main point is that considerations such as this clearly indicate that Herodotus is far from being the naive storyteller that some have wanted to make of him; rather, he is very much working in the intellectual climate of his time. He is doing this, of course, in prose. We would not, now, expect historians – or indeed philosophers or medical writers – to express themselves in any other way, and would be somewhat surprised to find them writing their books or delivering their lectures in verse. Yet verse comes before prose: we have already noticed the centrality to the Greek world of the Homeric poems and the authoritative status of the poet as the maker of fame and a repository of truths about the past. Prose was not new in Herodotus' time, though it was much younger than verse, but it seems to be the case that it was in the fifth century that prose began to usurp the authority previously accorded to verse. Before Herodotus, philosophers such as Xenophanes and Parmenides had written in verse; Hesiod had written didactic poems on agriculture and on the gods; the Athenian constitutional reformer Solon had written politically charged verse; and so on. The establishment of prose as the medium for philosophy, history and the like, did not entirely put an end to the use of verse for such activities, but it is clear that, during the fifth century, Herodotus' lifetime, prose took on a new authority, which it has, of course, never lost. Why this is so is not entirely clear, but it has been reasonably suggested that it is connected with the rise of democracy and greater freedom of speech. Obviously enough, people speak in prose: the increased opportunities for political debate will have directed attention to making speeches and argumentation as persuasive as possible. Verse is clearly a restrictive medium for expressing complex ideas; at the same time as such political changes were coming about, speculation about the nature of the world was on the increase, as was the awareness of cultural variations between societies; ironically, the closer contact between east and west brought about by the Persian Wars may have stimulated this, just as it caused Herodotus to write about it. The natural mode of expression for the plethora of ideas thus generated would become the increasingly rhetorically refined medium of prose.

One literary genre which never exchanged verse for prose – and which during Herodotus' lifetime was reaching its apogee – was Athenian tragedy. Whether or not it is true that Herodotus was a friend of the tragedian Sophocles, he cannot have lived at Athens without being aware of the way that playwrights were at that time exploring the relationships between man and man, man and woman, mortals and gods, and the human condition in general. The story of Masistes referred to above is tragic in more than one sense of the word, and would have supplied a plot eminently suitable for tragic drama. As it happens, we know that the story of Gyges and Candaules *was* made into a tragedy, by an unknown author, probably later than Herodotus, and probably using Herodotus as the basis of his version. The moral dilemmas facing Gyges, the *hybris* of Candaules leading to his downfall, the intervention of a god in the shape of the oracle which confirms Gyges as king, the oracle's (disregarded) warning that vengeance would fall upon Gyges' descendants – all these are the stuff of tragedy. It would take a long time to catalogue the incidents in Herodotus that exhibit similar characteristics;

the fall of the fabulously wealthy Croesus, unwittingly doomed to work out the 'curse' incurred by Gyges (1.13), the (in this case almost verging on comedy) failure of the tyrant Polycrates to avoid his fate (3.40ff.), the story of Intaphrenes' wife (3.118), are but a few instances. Even the overarching theme of the book as a whole may be seen as tragic, seen from the point of view of the (flawed?) oriental monarchies whose court intrigues we meet first in the Gyges story, and operate still in the same manner at the end of the book in those of Xerxes and Masistes. It is not unreasonable to see in Xerxes himself a paradigm of the tragic hero – arrogant and despotic, yet oddly vulnerable and sympathetic, as when he weeps for the destruction that must befall many a man in his splendid assembled army of invasion, and doomed in the end to ignominious retreat, only to become the murderer of his own brother. It is probably not accidental that Xerxes *is* the tragic hero of the only Greek tragedy extant which is based on history rather than myth (and one of the very few known to have dealt with such a subject): Aeschylus' *Persians*, written and produced, in 472, by a man who himself fought in the war, and whose depiction of the Persians, the barbarians, is worth examining by way of contrast with that of Herodotus.

Barbarians and Greeks

Gyges, we are told, was the first of the barbarians known to have sent offerings to the Delphic oracle (1.14). A barbarian (*barbaros* in Greek) is essentially someone who speaks a language that one, as a Greek, does not understand. Originally it seems to have meant just that, without any derogatory overtones – in the *Iliad*, for example, the Trojans, who could have been characterized as barbaric, are not, and in fact are indistinguishable from their Greek antagonists in terms of behaviour and, conveniently, even language. The barbarian as not only non-Greek but as an inferior to the Greek, seems largely to be a creation of the fifth century and to make its first fully-fledged appearance in Aeschylus' *Persians*. It is quite likely that the Greek/barbarian dichotomy was already established as a way of thinking about the concepts of 'self' and 'other' – characterizing what one is not by reference to what others are – but there cannot be much doubt that the Persian Wars intensified it. At any rate, in the *Persians*, and in a good many later texts, barbarians (especially Persians – for the Greeks, the barbarians *par excellence*) are essentially characterized as effeminate, by contrast to the manly Greeks, and servile, by virtue of their willingness to submit to despotic rule, as opposed to the Greeks who, if not necessarily all free, in the sense of living in democracies, were at least conscious of the concept of freedom. Aspects of what later became the familiar paradigm of the barbarian certainly do occur in Herodotus, though he is in general pretty open-minded – perhaps his upbringing in Halicarnassus, a mixed Greek and Carian city, helped in this respect. Xerxes, for example, is unquestionably despotic and wilful, and capable of irrational brutality; on the other hand, as we noted above, he has a human side, and can even evoke sympathy. His soldiers, unlike the Greeks, who fight each man for his own freedom, have to be whipped into battle, but not all of them are cowards: one thinks of Mardonius, commander-in-chief at the battle of Plataea, mounted on his white horse and fighting to the death (9.63). King Cambyses may be characterized as insane, but Cyrus the Great lives up to his name until *hybris* overtakes him, and Darius, though cunning and at times also brutal, is nevertheless very much a king. Persian customs, too, and the administrative system of their vast empire, receive credit where it is due.

The converse is also true. The Greeks, despite – or perhaps because of – their love of freedom, are quarrelsome, and their disunity comes close to losing them the war. Leonidas and the 300 who die with him at Thermopylae are heroes whose names Herodotus sees fit to commit to memory, but the earlier Spartan king Cleomenes is as mad as Cambyses. Some of the Greek states come in for considerable criticism – the Corinthians, for example, especially their admiral at Salamis, Adeimantus. The Spartans are unqualifiedly brave, their military prowess essential to the Greek war effort; the constitution that produces such men is admirable (7.104), but their foreign policy is selfish (8.40, 9.8), and individual Spartans sometimes unstable and frequently grasping (3.148, 5.51, 6.72, 8.4). Thebes, which accepted Persian rule without a fight, is understandably vilified. But the Athenians, amongst whom Herodotus spent much time, whose democratic ways he admired (5.78) and whose role in the wars is duly (and no doubt rightly) acknowledged, are themselves sometimes disunited, and even their hero of Salamis, Themistocles, is a double-edged character. Some of this, no doubt, depends on the particular state, group, or individual from which or whom Herodotus was getting his information, as he is aware, but the fact remains that the picture of 'Greeks vs. barbarians' is by no means painted in black and white. It may be further coloured by the fact that Herodotus lived to see the league formed by the Greek states to keep the Greek world free from Persian interference become an Athenian empire: did he see the Athenians, subsequent to the war, as having cynically achieved what Xerxes had at least openly sought? Only some of the troubles that befell the Greeks in the years that Darius and his successors ruled in Persia were the Persians' doing, he says: the rest arose from contention amongst the leaders of the Greeks (6.98).

This must remain speculation. Another aspect of the Greek/barbarian polarity that can be more easily pinpointed, and which to an extent mitigates it, is that, according to some medical writings of the period (a reasonably accessible example is the Hippocratic *Airs, Waters, Places*) climate and environment have a decisive effect on national characteristics. Barbarians, that is to say, are different because they can't help it: if they are, for example, effeminate, it is because their environment allows them to be soft by making life too easy for them. Herodotus essentially subscribes to the same view: Libyans and Ethiopians, for example, he considers to enjoy especially good health because of the climate in which they live; in the very last chapter of his book, he records a story that tells how the Persians, when Cyrus combined their kingdom with that of the Medes, considered moving their homes to a land in which they would enjoy an easier lifestyle; Cyrus counselled against this, advising that they would be better off living in a hard land and being rulers than cultivating an easier one and being subjects, and the Persians agreed with him. (The fact that, in the context of the book as a whole, the Persians were not able to defeat the Greeks argues perhaps that, while sympathizing with such theories, Herodotus did not subscribe to them.)

This theory interacts with a common sophistic preoccupation of the time, the distinction between *physis* and *nomos*, that is, essentially, between 'nature' and 'custom', or perhaps 'convention': do we, or should we, obey the dictates of our nature as human beings, or is – as Herodotus himself puts it, quoting the poet Pindar – convention 'king of everything' (3.38)? His own stance on this question is that it is: the quotation comes at the end of a famous passage in which he recounts an experiment of Darius designed to illustrate the power of convention. Darius summoned to his presence some Greeks, whose custom was to cremate the bodies of their deceased parents, and some members of an Indian tribe, who were accustomed to eat theirs; the king asked each group what would induce them to do what the other customarily did, and each was duly horrified. What is important about this is not so much Herodotus' attitude, but the fact that, again, he can be seen to be very much a child of his intellectual time.

Causality, fate, gods

The Candaules and Gyges story illustrates yet another aspect of this. It is there to show how the ancestors of Croesus gained the throne of Lydia, which is important to Herodotus because, having given the reasons alleged by what he calls the *logioi* (plural of *logios*: what it actually means in this context is arguable; its basic meaning is one who deals in *logoi* – stories, accounts, explanations – it cannot mean 'historians' as such, as there do not seem to have been any Persian historians, so that it may mean no more than something like 'such of the Persians who have anything to say on the matter') amongst the Persians, he dismisses their views, stating that he *knows* who started the chain of events which led to the Greco-Persian conflict, and this man was Croesus.

At the very beginning of the book, Herodotus has told us that, as well as preserving the fame of the great and wondrous doings of both Greeks and barbarians, he intends to explicate the *reason* why they went to war against each other. Which is exactly what he does: throughout the book, though his narrative sometimes leaps ahead, sometimes harks back to the past, though he appears to digress (which, he says, he welcomes the chance to do: 4.30), he never loses sight of the great chain of events and the causality by which he sees it as linked. Past and present interact; one thing leads to another, and nothing is without its cause. Here again, Herodotus displays an intellectual preoccupation of his time. If there is one tendency which characterizes the intellectual endeavours of the mid-fifth century, that tendency is the search for causes. Why is the world the way it is? Natural philosophers (the forerunners of our scientists) search for the code by which the book of nature may be read. Why do men behave the way they do? Similar thinkers investigate customs and climate to explain the diversity of human activity. Why do we become ill? Doctors begin to analyse the causes and nature of diseases, laying the foundations of diagnostic medicine. Herodotus in his turn looks for, and finds, patterns of historical causality: later historians might not do this in precisely the same way, but it is still exactly what they do; if Herodotus is indeed the 'Father of History', it is perhaps for this manifesto that he chiefly merits the title.

If one thing leads to another, can that 'other' be avoided? The Delphic oracle, in confirming Gyges as rightful king of Lydia, warns that vengeance will come in the fifth generation. Oracles abound in Herodotus. Often his attitude to them seems to be non-committal, but, on the other hand, they usually turn out to be true. If prophecy is possible, fate cannot be avoided, though we may not see exactly where it is tending: Croesus, for example, notoriously falls victim to misreading the oracular statement that if he makes war on the Persians he will destroy a great empire, and destroys his own (1.53), despite his own previous experience that what will be will be (see the story of the wretched Adrastus and the preordained death of Croesus' son: 1.34ff.).

The lesson, if there is one, seems to be that more things happen in heaven and on earth than we mortals can account for. The gods, however, presumably can — whoever and whatever they are. Herodotus' attitude to religion and to the gods is notoriously problematical, and he has been seen as both a firm believer in conventional religion and as a religious sceptic. The answer probably lies somewhere in the middle. It is interesting, and surely significant, that he rarely names any of the Greek gods, or states that such-and-such a god is responsible for such-and-such an occurrence, usually preferring to refer to 'the god' or 'the divine'. 'Supernatural' and divine activity is frequent in his pages, and he is respectful towards it, though at times seemingly sceptical of such events as the phantom female figure that appeared to the Greeks before Salamis urging them to fight (8.84: 'it is said . . .', he says). But divine activity can be seen as underlying the way the world works, though with a proviso: 'the foresight of the god is wise, *as it seems* . . .' he says when discussing the nature of animals in book 2 (2.108). His reticence with regard to the gods as conventionally named by the Greeks may in part be accounted for in the light of his beliefs, expressed at some length in the same book, that the Greeks derive their ideas about the gods from Egypt and elsewhere (2.50–1). There is no doubt that Herodotus believed in the existence of god/gods, or of something divine; perhaps a reasonable approximation of his views (which are not necessarily fully worked out: he is not a theologian) is that there is undoubtedly a deity (or deities) of some kind, which takes (or take) an interest in human affairs; these deities are worshipped by different peoples in their own ways, each being as valid as any other, according to their *nomos*. The involvement of the divine in human affairs is not obvious and direct, though it can be dimly discerned through such media as oracles and dreams. But it underlies the workings of the world, maintaining order and balance, both in human affairs and on a cosmic level (Scullion in Dewald and Marincola, 2006: 208).

Reciprocity and polarity

Balance and order are integral to Herodotus' world-view, at all levels. Candaules comes to a bad end because of an excess – in his case, excessive love of his wife. Croesus and Polycrates suffer from an excess, in their case, of success, which, as they are told, is dangerous and cannot last for ever. Xerxes, and the Persian expedition as a whole, fail for similar reasons: as Themistocles is reported as saying, the gods and heroes did not see fit for one man to rule both Asia and Europe, especially an impious and sacrilegious man (8.109). Order does not necessarily mean stability; in fact, change is a key feature of the way the world works, and not only for men such as Croesus and Xerxes: 'for some [cities] were at one time great, but many of them have become small, and those that in my time are great formerly were small' (1.5). The concept of requital of good for good, bad for bad, by man to man as well as between gods and men – 'reciprocity' – has been identified as one of the most persistent features of Herodotus' text. Reciprocity maintains order, yet propagates change: an act which, for example, threatens the natural order (such as Xerxes seeking to bring both Asia and Europe under his control) brings forth another act which restores the balance; but this act in itself brings about further change, and so forth.

Akin to this is a mode of thinking which underlies not only Herodotus' thought, but many of the ways in which the Greeks (and not only the Greeks) saw themselves and their world: that of polarization – thinking in terms of opposites, or oppositions. We have already encountered a number of polarities in Herodotus' text: Greek and barbarian, male and female, *nomos* and *physis*, gods and mortals, for example. These, and others, are especially significant in the ethnographic sections, as their chief function is to place their user in his or her context in society and in the world, as an individual and as a member of a group: to identify the 'them' by reference to which we may know what we mean by 'us', to characterize 'self' by contrast with the 'other'. 'The Persians', Herodotus begins his chapters on Persian customs (1.131ff), 'I know to use the following *nomoi*: they have no images of the gods, or temples or altars'; the Greeks, of course, as Herodotus does not need to state, use all of these. Naturally, not all the customs of foreign nations, even Persians, can be seen as precisely the opposite of one's own. The Egyptians, however, in Herodotus' view, in respect of almost all their practices, 'do the opposite of the rest of mankind', and a list of some length illustrates this view (2.35ff). But the 'symmetry' thus achieved between Egypt and the rest of the world goes beyond customs: its climate is different from that of other places, and its river from rivers elsewhere; indeed, the shape of the world as Herodotus sees it reinforces the symmetry (2.34): the Nile itself flows into the sea diametrically opposite to the Danube, its counterpart in Europe, and the courses of the two rivers, each in its own continent, mirror each other in a similar fashion.

Some conclusions

It is impossible to do justice to a book like Herodotus' *Histories* in a few pages, such is its richness and variety: this account took as its starting point merely the story which Herodotus chooses as the real beginning of the series of events he means to narrate, yet even so we have seen illustrated in it or arising from it exemplars of almost every significant feature which marks the work as a whole. We can find in Herodotus geography, ethnography, some of the qualities of epic poetry and tragedy side by side with combative rhetoric and a sharp awareness of the intellectual climate of the day, a world-view at once polarized and simplified yet sympathetic and open-minded, a tolerant religious outlook alongside what could be – but never becomes – a deterministic cycle of vengeance for vengeance. But do we find in him what most readers expect to find: history?

The answer to this depends on what we think that history is. If, as was stated earlier, we expect a nineteenth-century history textbook, all about politics and battles, we shall be disappointed: there are plenty of both in Herodotus, of course; but there is much more besides. But is what he tells us actually *true*? Again, this depends. There are, without doubt, things in the *Histories* which were not as Herodotus tells us, and things that did not happen as he says they did. To an extent, this may be a matter of what he could find out: whether or not Herodotus really went where he said he did, he was always going to be dependent on others for information, just as he was when he was enquiring into events. Concerning, for example, political decision making, it may be reasonably doubted whether he was often in a position to question people who really *knew*; with regard to what actually physically happened, it may frequently have been impossible to tell – battles in the ancient Greek world, for example, were notoriously difficult to control, even for generals: even if Herodotus was able to talk to men who had participated in them, achieving any kind of over-view must have been well-nigh impossible. As far as historical 'facts' are concerned, we are in general not in a position to judge whether Herodotus' versions are 'true' or not, but it is interesting that when archaeological evidence is available to be compared with what he tells us, his reputation stands up pretty well.

Indeed, it could be argued that Herodotus is not really – or at least entirely – writing a history of facts. If we see one of Herodotus' main purposes as an attempt to define what it means to be Greek, if we accept that the way that Herodotus attempts such a definition is through a comparison of different peoples' *nomoi*, and if we further accept that one important *nomos* is the way in which a people or a culture sees, relates and celebrates its past, then we should be able to agree that, to some extent at least, Herodotus is not writing a history of the Persian Wars so much as a history of the Greeks' view of the Persian Wars. This might help to explain, for instance, the numbers given for the Persian forces (7.60), which are clearly impossible, although Herodotus comically parodies a scientific method of calculation. However, Herodotus' totals do sometimes match those given in earlier Greek writers (even if we have to rely on Herodotus himself for the evidence). Aeschylus in *Persians* (earlier and obviously independent of Herodotus) has a similar number for the Persian fleet (1207: *Persians* 341ff.), and Herodotus quotes an epitaph for the fallen Spartans contemporary with Thermopylae that has a similar number for the army the Spartans faced (4,000 vs. three million: 7.228). For the Greeks, their victory over the Persians was monumental, and the exaggeration of the numbers they defeated contributes to their celebration of their victory. Herodotus gives a history of that celebration.

In fact, it is questionable to ask whether the criterion of truth, in terms of 'exactly what happened and why' should be applied to Herodotus at all. Quite apart from the difficulty of defining precisely what historical truth is in any case, we should bear in mind not what we think he should have been doing, but – remembering that he was, in a sense, writing history before anyone knew what writing history was – what he thought he was doing himself. And that, as he says (preface to book 1; referred to above), was

> to make sure that the things done by mankind should not become forgotten over time, and that the great and wondrous achievements exhibited by Greeks and barbarians should not lack fame, including especially the reason why they went to war against one another.

It is hard to argue that he failed in his intention. The result was a book which is not so much the history of a war as a portrait of an age, and an endlessly fascinating one.

Further reading

There is a good collection of articles in Dewald and Marincola (2006). See also Gould (1989); Harrison (2000 on religion in Herodotus); Hartog (1988 on the 'other': very good, though quite difficult); Thomas (2000). Information can also be found on works concerned with historians and historiography more generally, such as Hornblower (1996); Marincola (1997; 2001; 2007); Pelling (2000); Woodman (1998a on rhetoric).

THUCYDIDES

It is hard to write constructively about Thucydides without referring frequently to his near-contemporary Herodotus, and a student who wants to get to grips with one can only really do so by reading the other. Anyone studying Thucydides, then, is advised to read some Herodotus, or at least to read the previous section in this book.

At first reading, the two writers may well appear to inhabit different worlds. In Thucydides we find no uxorious kings, no naked vengeful queens, no ants that dig up gold, no hippopotamuses or crocodiles or strangely-behaved Scythians – in fact, very little about the natural world and its other inhabitants at all. Instead, we find war and politics, and little else. Herodotus' book is finally, of course, about war and politics, but set in a wider landscape. For Thucydides, the Peloponnesian War is foreground and background, and little else is visible. In fact, the gulf between the two may not be as wide as it appears, but it is immediately evident that they are not doing history in quite the same way.

To a reader accustomed to history in the sense that the word was understood in the nineteenth and (much of) the twentieth century, Thucydides perhaps looks rather more familiar. Conventional history textbooks of this period concentrating on political machinations and on battles and warfare will probably be familiar: at first sight, Thucydides' *History* may look much like one of these. Rightly, in a sense, in that he is the forerunner of this kind of history; but to assume that Thucydides is therefore our contemporary, and is doing the same thing as these more modern historians, is a hazardous assumption, as much recent work on his text emphasizes.

Thucydides, like Herodotus, wrote one long book, on the subject of a war; in this case the Peloponnesian War, fought between Athens and Sparta and their respective allies (431–404: see the Interlude between chapters 3 and 4). An Athenian, and a wealthy man with aristocratic and even royal connections (in Thrace, where he owned goldmines), he served in the war himself as a general, before going into exile, in 424, apparently as a result of a military failure against the Spartan commander Brasidas. As he says, exile gave him the opportunity to collect information for his history – which he says he began to work on early in the war – from both sides. He returned to Athens after the war and probably died early in the 390s.

The reader (see below on readers and hearers) who turns to Thucydides from Herodotus is conscious immediately of entering a different world. Leaving aside for the moment his prefatory remarks (1.1–23), a glance at his narrative of the events which led up to the declaration of war (1.24–88) will serve to illustrate this. He begins with a few brief remarks on the city of Epidamnus, which was involved in one of the disputes that led to war. We are told of its legendary founder – as we would probably have been told by Herodotus – but only, we discover, because the city's foundation and the nature of its population are of significance for what happens next. The diplomatic and military operations that do happen next are related briefly, almost baldly: troops march here, ships sail there; 'the Epidamnians', 'the Corinthians' (*et al.*) do this or do that. The oracle at Delphi (one of Herodotus' favourite institutions) is called in and makes a decision; but in Thucydides it *is* 'the oracle' that replies, not 'the god'. (It may at this point occur to us that Thucydides has not yet mentioned 'god', or any of the gods.) Apart from the bare names of a few commanders, we encounter no individual who is remotely characterized, and no individual motivation is identified, until Archidamus, king of Sparta, makes a speech opposing the declaration of war (1.79). And all we are told of him is that he 'seemed an intelligent and sensible man'. No conversations are reported; of the five set speeches (three of them very long), three are attributed simply to 'the Corinthians' and 'the Athenians'; only that of the ephor Sthenelaidas, who never appears again, gives us any impression of the character of its speaker; we may suspect that this is more because Thucydides wants here to present us with a representative 'laconic' Spartan than because this is the way Sthenelaidas was, or because it is exactly what he said.

By the end of this longish episode (nearly 40 pages in a standard English translation) we have, we are inclined to think, been presented with facts, as they happened, without elaboration or digression, and as things like this – matters of war and politics – do happen in the real world, we are a long way from the folk-tale world of Herodotus' Gyges and Candaules. It is perhaps only on maturer reflection that we start to question Thucydides' authority. A Herodotean narrative presents us with digression, asides, deviations and variations: sometimes, indeed, at the expense of narrative clarity. Thucydides, by contrast, sticks to the point and makes sure we do not lose our way. But it is, of course, the point *as Thucydides sees it*: Herodotus, not infrequently, offers us alternatives: *x* says this, *y* says that; the choice is ours. Thucydides only very rarely does this: events proceed in an orderly, structured, fashion; but the order, the structuring, has been done for us. The picture we are presented with is 'photographically' clear, but we may miss the background and the frame that a narrative such as that of Herodotus offers us, and – most significantly in historiographical terms – we are allowed to view the scene through one lens alone rather than from varying angles.

Thucydides' objectivity used to be proverbial. More recently, without necessarily impugning his honesty, scholars have taken to scrutinizing more closely the ways in which he – perhaps unintentionally – shapes our perceptions of events. To return to the narrative of book 1: at 1.32, 'the Corcyreans' are given an extended speech, the first in the book. There have been opportunities to include speeches at other points – plenty of diplomatic activity has been going on – but Thucydides has waited until now, and chosen an unnamed ambassador to deliver it, which should at least make us think a little harder about what he is doing (see below on speeches). His narrative too is by no means as artless as it looks. By 1.88 we have reached the point at which the

Spartans declare war. But, having done so, they do not actually go to war; the action is postponed until 1.118. Instead – at this dramatic juncture – we are made to wait as Thucydides outlines (in flashback, of course) the events of the previous 50 years or so that, in his view, have contributed to the coming of war. In addition to this, Thucydides subtly invigorates his narrative. In the debate at Sparta that precedes the declaration of war, we hear first from ambassadors from Corinth, and from Athens. The Spartan king Archidamus then gives a measured response advocating caution. At this point the intervention of Sthenelaidas is decisive (1.86):

> I do not understand these long speeches . . . Spartans, vote for Sparta's honour and for war! Do not let the Athenians grow still more powerful, do not completely betray your allies, but, with the gods' help let us advance to meet the aggressors!

To make sure the point is driven home, Sthenelaidas (i.e. Thucydides: how much can he really have known what happened at this debate?) pretends he cannot make out from the reaction of the assembly whether the Spartans are for war or against it, so he makes them get up and move to one side of the assembly area or the other, depending whether they are for war or against it. This 'vignette', a brief but memorable image, in contrast to the way much of Thucydides' narrative proceeds ('25 ships went here, 1,000 hoplites went there . . .') is surely placed here so that the scene will still be in our minds when the story resumes, 16 pages later.

Thucydides tells us that he began collecting material for his book when the war started, in the belief that it was going to be a major conflict and worth writing about (1.1). He had not finished it when he died; book 8 is unfinished, and (though some scholars have disputed this) is almost certainly unrevised, as are some earlier sections. How Thucydides went about revising his work, and when, is a matter of controversy: he certainly wrote or rewrote some earlier sections after the war, as it is evident he knew its final outcome (e.g. 5.26). Whatever the truth about these matters, when he set about his task, he can have had only one model for such an undertaking: the *Histories* of Herodotus.

Thucydides never mentions Herodotus by name, but there is no doubt that he was deeply aware of the shadow of his predecessor, rival, and near-contemporary. That they were near-contemporaries can be obscured if Herodotus is – mistakenly – characterized as a naive and archaic storyteller, and Thucydides – no less wrongly – as a 'modern' historian. We do not know exactly when Thucydides was born, but if he was a general in 424 it is likely to have been before 460, and he may have been no more than 20 years Herodotus' junior. There is a story that the young Thucydides heard Herodotus give a reading from his work, and wept, though whether his tears were tears of admiration, emulation or disgust we do not know. Herodotus certainly lived through the early years of the Peloponnesian War into the mid-420s, and possibly longer. How Thucydides published his work is not known, though it would surely be unusual, in his time, if he did not first do so through readings (it has been suggested that certain set-pieces, such as the section on the plague at Athens at 2.47–55 or that on civil war at Corcyra, 3.70–84 may have been suitable for oral publication). Some scholars, then, have suggested that Herodotus may even have been influenced by Thucydides. This cannot be regarded as certain; the reverse, however, can.

The differences between the two may be more obvious than the similarities, but the latter should not therefore be discounted. To begin with, as enquirers into the past (even the very recent past), they are dependent on sources. In each case these must have been predominantly oral, and thus frequently conflicting and prone to confusion and prejudice. Since Thucydides' informants are likely all to have been Greek, he will not have had the problems of translation and interpretation that Herodotus had. And, as literacy levels at Athens towards the end of the fifth century increased and the practice of keeping and displaying public records became more prevalent, he may have had access to some – though unquestionably limited – written sources.

The intellectual *milieu* of Herodotus has been discussed in the previous section; that of Thucydides must have been markedly similar – the world of the early philosophers, of speculation into the nature of things and the questioning of conventional values. He does not show Herodotus' interest in the natural world, but this diagnostic approach is evident in his examination of the plague at Athens (2.47–55) and, indeed, in his book as a whole: an enquiry not only into historical and political causation, but a kind of natural history of war. Just as diseases recur and their progress can be predicted by observation and analysis of symptoms so, 'human nature being what it is', patterns of events will recur in future years, such that his book will be found useful by later generations.

The intellectual context of Herodotus and Thucydides was also characterized by rivalry. In an agonistic society like that of fifth-century Athens, even poetry, music and dance were competitive activities; rhetoric – persuading one's audience of the rightness of one's case, in politics or in law, or that one was a better practitioner in whatever field – was all-pervasive. Herodotus offers us a better account of history, or of natural phenomena, than his contemporaries; Thucydides must go one better still. Herodotus had written, after the event, the history of the largest-scale conflict that had hitherto afflicted the Greek world. Thucydides insists, in his preface (1.1) that the war he records (and had started to record from its beginning, thus exhibiting the quality of foresight he commends in others, by contrast with the hindsight of Herodotus) is in fact of greater consequence, and has affected almost all mankind (Thucydides is fond of superlatives, an interesting point to ponder for those who make much of his apparent detachment). The point is not which of the two was right, or on what grounds, but that Thucydides felt obliged to make the comparison, and to press it: early history (about which Herodotus wrote) was not of much consequence, either as far as warfare was concerned or anything else, he says, but he does nevertheless venture into it, perhaps by way of demonstration, in the so-called *archaeologia* (1.2–19), his very brief account of Greek history up to the Persian Wars. For the most part, his critique of Herodotus' approach to early history is implicit: according to Thucydides things happen for rational political, geographical and sociological reasons, not because, for example, (see above on Herodotus) kings are excessively enamoured of their wives. But, at the end (1.20), two corrections of minor points of Spartan military and political practice are both clearly (though not explicitly) addressed to Herodotus who, if Thucydides is right, had got them wrong (Hdt 6.57 on the voting of Spartan kings; 9.53 on the 'Pitanate *lochos*').

Some people, Thucydides warns us, may find his book less interesting because of its lack of *to muthōdes*: the 'mythical' or 'fanciful' element. Herodotus, in his preface (1.1), had specifically stated that 'wondrous things' were to be part of his brief: Thucydides' *archaeologia* is ruthlessly stripped of mythological content. His conclusions about early history, he tells us (1.21) will be more acceptable than those of the 'poets and *logographoi*', who are more interested respectively in exaggerating their subject matter and getting their audience's attention. Herodotus had claimed that his work would confer *kleos*, fame, as did the poets (specifically Homer), and is probably to be counted as a *logographos*, at least in Thucydides' estimation. (The word means 'writers of *logoi*', 'stories' and, in contrast with 'poets', may mean little more than 'prose writers'; it is not clear how Thucydides would have categorized himself, if at all.) Thucydides' own version, he says, is to be preferred because of the *akribeia* he employs. *Akribeia* is an important concept for Thucydides: literally it means 'accuracy', 'precision', 'exactness'. Here it seems to mean something like penetrating through the fog of myth and producing a sober businesslike account that satisfies Thucydides' criteria for the kind of things that are likely to have happened: in many respects an unimpeachable aim for a historian, but of course a subjective one; what seems likely to Thucydides may not seem so to all of us – or, indeed, be what actually happened. It is the same yardstick by which he appears to have established what he considers to be the truth of what happened in the rest of his book. He did not, he tells us (1.22) write down the first account of any event he happened to come across, but was either present himself at the events he narrates, and can thus vouch for the accuracy of what he says, or has checked the various account he has been given by other eye-witnesses, as he is aware that they may be biased or not remember clearly. We might want to question how many events he can have been present at in person (debates in Athens in the early years of the war, presumably, and some military campaigns), or whether he could really find eye-witnesses for everything he records; a more significant point is that his application of *akribeia* is, in the end, a personal one. Unlike Herodotus, who frequently offers alternative accounts and invites us to decide between them, Thucydides does our deciding for us. He was undoubtedly a formidably acute and intelligent man, and in many instances his explanations may well be correct, but in the end what he tells us is his own version of events. It has been said, with regard to the speeches he includes in his history (see below), that they are such as would persuade an audience of Thucydideses. The same might well be said of his history as a whole. Ancient historians wrote without the benefit of the kind of footnotes that their modern counterparts use to cite varying accounts. If we had the opportunity, which Thucydides denies us, to compare such variants, we might on occasion venture to doubt his judgement: it may be the case that his interpretations are generally right; it is most unlikely that they are always so.

The point about Thucydides' speeches and the 'audience of Thucydideses' is that it seems highly unlikely that the speeches he puts into the mouths of his characters could have been delivered in the form in which he writes them: they are too 'rational' (as opposed to rhetorical), too complex, and simply too unlike any other Greek speeches that have survived. They are certainly linguistically complex, and not only to us: Dionysius of Halicarnassus, a competent critic and, more important in this context, a native speaker of Greek, considered Thucydides' Greek to be excessively difficult. Since the language of his narrative is generally not hard to follow, it seems likely that he was referring to that of the speeches and those sections where Thucydides indulges in reflection or speculation, and his view cannot reasonably be contested. As far as the content of the speeches is concerned, Thucydides himself gives us some clues which, unfortunately, are by no means self-explanatory and need to be addressed as part of any assessment of Thucydides' achievement as a historian.

We have already noted that he is obviously selective in the speeches he chooses to include – and, indeed, in his decision to include speeches at all. Herodotus uses direct speech a good deal, often in situations when he cannot possibly have known what was said, but his direct speech consists mostly of conversations, with only a few set speeches, again without any real pretence that they reproduce the reality of what was said. Outside of his extended speeches, Thucydides rarely uses direct speech, reserving it for dramatic or significant moments: for example the remark of the Spartan ambassador Melesippus when his last-ditch peace mission fails: 'this day will be the beginning of great evils for the Greeks' (2.12). Herodotus has nothing to say about his methods as far as speeches are concerned: it is perhaps reasonable to suppose that he uses direct speech as Homer does, as a means of providing variety and focalization (see below), and does not expect us to believe that people really did say what he says they did, but rather to accept that they are *likely* to have said the kind of things he makes them say. Thucydides seems to have recognized the need to offer a rationale for the use of set speeches. Neither he himself, he says (1.22), if he was present, nor his informants could always remember exactly what a given speaker said. Therefore he has decided to write into his speeches the *xumpasa gnōmē* of what was said, along with *ta deonta* in the circumstances. *Xumpasa gnōmē* means something like 'the general sense', 'the gist', and *ta deonta* 'what was appropriate', 'what was required'. A great deal of scholarly energy has been expended on this statement; most probably now agree that the two cannot be satisfactorily reconciled, and that Thucydides' practice will vary from one speech to another. In some cases he may have known in some detail what a speaker said, and what he writes may be reasonably close to this (though the wording is Thucydides' own: the style of the speeches is rarely individualized). In others, where he cannot have known (how much can he really have found out about, say, debates inside Syracuse?), he will compose a speech appropriate to the circumstances, and to the speaker's stance, if he knows this. This means, of course, that the speeches in Thucydides should not be read literally as historical documents, though this does not mean that they have no historical value or validity. For example, the speeches of Archidamus at Sparta (1.80ff.) and Pericles at Athens (1.140ff.), even if they were not delivered as Thucydides suggests, nevertheless discuss strategies for the coming war which must have been talked about by the war leaders at this time.

Speeches can also foreshadow – as these two do – later events, whilst responding to earlier ones, and thus help to bind together the fabric of the overall narrative: some scholars see an important theme of Thucydides' book as being the interplay of *logos* and *ergon*: not just 'word' and 'deed', as *logos* includes 'rational thought', and perhaps any kind of attempt to make sense of the world and of men's actions (*erga*), and how to respond to events and plan one's own actions for the future. Thus, to take a very obvious example, Pericles in the speech mentioned above discusses the possibility that the Spartans, if war breaks out, may establish a permanent military base in Attica (1.142). Sixteen years later, when such a base had still not been set up, we find Alcibiades – an Athenian, at that time in exile at Sparta – recommending the policy in a speech at Sparta (6.91). The following year, it is at last carried out (7.19), and proves to be a dangerous threat to the security of Athens: did Pericles really consider it as a possibility? We do not know, but we are inclined to respect his prescience; when we read Pericles' speech, we perhaps know (if we were Athenians reading it in the 390s, we knew only too well) that the strategy was in the end put into practice. When we come to the later passages, we (may) remember the earlier ones, such that the resonances serve to unify the book; and we are perhaps encouraged to compare Pericles, the admired leader, and Alcibiades, who might have become a 'second' Pericles, but, through his own fault and the failings of democracy, did not. Interestingly, in this case, the *logos* is an Athenian one, but the *ergon* is carried out by Sparta.

On a basic level, speeches provide narrative variety, as we noted above, simply by offering a different voice. Instead of the authorial voice of the historian, the retrospective voice of hindsight, we are offered the opportunity to view events from – ostensibly – another, contemporary, angle. This focalization, seeing events from the point of view of participants, or from one other than that of the historian, is also happening whenever an author says something like, 'Nicias, thinking that . . .': how often does the author *really* know what someone was thinking before they acted? Is he not rather making an assumption which may not be justified? No doubt in many cases he is right; but we must not automatically assume so. For the most part, Thucydides is much less present in his narrative than Herodotus, who frequently tells us what he thinks, in his own person. From time to time, he will give an opinion (see below) but, for the most part, if we want to try to find out what he really thinks we have to read between the lines. The speeches may give us some clues: for example, the famous funeral speech of Pericles in book 2 (2.35ff.) is ostensibly Pericles' vision of what Athens was and should be. Many think that it is as much Thucydides' vision as Pericles', and we cannot, in the end, establish the truth of that. But other considerations may affect how we see the nature and function of the funeral speech: it appears that such a speech was made every year during the war, to commemorate the dead, yet Thucydides does not mention any of the others, or who delivered them. Furthermore, the funeral speech is immediately followed by Thucydides' description of the plague at Athens, from which Pericles died. Arguably, Pericles' vision died with him; the juxtaposition can surely not be accidental. (Note also that Pericles is the one speaker in Thucydides whose speeches are never responded to or refuted in a debate, as if what he said could not be challenged.)

As we noted above, Thucydides' apparent objectivity and the veracity of his account of the Peloponnesian War were at one time regarded as exemplary. In the nineteenth century, for example, when a positivist – and optimistic – view of historiography suggested that accurate reconstruction of what happened in the past was a realistic possibility, Thucydides was inevitably seen as the pioneer of this kind of scientific history. To impugn Thucydides' objectivity or to belittle his overall achievement would be crass: every historian writes from some sort of individual or cultural standpoint; and to have collected and synthesized such a mass of material into a coherent whole, given the difficulties he must have encountered in simply obtaining material, is a remarkable feat. There are, inevitably, omissions; and there are places where his judgement seems less than sound, and others where he simply seems to be wrong. The latter are few, but might of course be more if we had other reliable sources to compare with his account.

Some of his faults are sins of omission: things that Thucydides leaves out that we would like to know but which, for whatever reason, did not seem to him important. In general, for example, although he fully appreciates the economic aspects of war, he never gives us much in the way of detailed information. We know, for instance, from archaeological evidence, that in 425 the

Athenians substantially increased the tribute imposed on their allies; shortly afterwards, the Spartan Brasidas is found to have considerable success in causing Athenian allies to defect: it may not be as simple as cause and effect, but it seems unlikely that the two sets of events were wholly unconnected, and we feel that Thucydides should have had something to say about them. He also has little to say about the internal politics of states involved in the war, even about those of Athens in its earlier years, when he must himself – as he was elected *stratēgos* – have had some involvement in politics. Furthermore, what he *does* tell us seems undoubtedly to be coloured by his own experiences and preferences. He approves, for example, of Pericles, whom he considered to have led the democracy (of which Thucydides was certainly somewhat suspicious: see 8.97 on his approval of the moderate oligarchy of 411) effectively, and this admiration seems to cloud his judgement both of Pericles' strategy, which was perhaps not as foolproof as Thucydides would like us to believe, and of that of his successors, especially Cleon, who may have been responsible for his exile, and whom he plainly dislikes ('most violent . . . and most persuasive amongst the people at that time': as damning a judgement as Thucydides makes throughout the book; 3.36). Thucydides' military judgement, too has been questioned. He fails, for example, to do justice to Demosthenes, one of the ablest Athenian commanders in the war – perhaps because he was associated with Cleon, though this cannot be proved – and, for a historian to whom the qualities of intelligence and rationality, not to mention success, are of high importance (see, for example, his brief judgements on Antiphon, Brasidas or Alcibiades), he is surprisingly sympathetic to the ultimately indecisive and unsuccessful Nicias.

Sometimes it appears that the importance of an episode may be exaggerated or diminished for artistic as well as historical reasons. He was clearly much affected by the disastrous Athenian invasion of Sicily and its importance in the context of the war as a whole (disaster though it was, as Thucydides himself makes clear, Athens did in fact recover remarkably quickly, and could still have won the war): it occupies two books out of eight, though it took only two of the 20 years he had written up at his death. And it hardly seems accidental that the expedition to Sicily immediately follows the Melian Dialogue, a grim exploration of the politics of power at the end of which the Athenians slaughter or enslave the whole population of Melos (5.84ff.): just over two years later the Athenians themselves are fearing a similar fate (8.1). The dialogue itself is unique in Thucydides: unnamed representatives of Athens and Melos debate *in camera* the fate of the Melians, who have refused to join the Athenian alliance and subsequently assisted Sparta of which Melos was a colony. It cannot have taken place in the form in which it is written: it is presented in the manner of an early Platonic dialogue, and is actually the first extant piece of writing in this form, which is not to say that it was the first written (this evaluation depends in part on the date of the *Dissoi Logoi*; see 6c); dialogue and dialectic are the natural media for philosophical discussion, and Thucydides may have had some model in mind. Its subject is the nature of power and how it is exercised, but this is more than philosophical enquiry: its outcome will decide if the Melians live or die.

The relationship of Thucydides to other literary genres is less evident, but is there nevertheless. According to Thucydides' Pericles, Athens needed no Homer: the words of poets offer transient pleasure, but the memory of Athens will survive through the more tangible memorials the Athenians leave behind (2.41). In theory, the *erga* of the Athenians need no *logos*. In practice, of course, Thucydides hopes that it will be through his *logos* that Athens will be commemorated, though transience is far from his intentions (see below). He was fully aware of the power of the word in preserving the past (see, for example, 3.104 on the festival at Delos) and, despite his condescending attitude to the poets, he is not immune to their influence. It has been observed, for example, that his treatment of the great Spartan general Brasidas, including some of the language he uses about him, has resonances of the Homeric hero. Certainly Brasidas seems to have possessed the qualities of intelligence, foresight and energy that Thucydides admires (and he was 'not a bad speaker for a Spartan': 4.84); he was also the man responsible for Thucydides' own military failure at Amphipolis, and hence his exile.

Echoes of tragedy appear in Thucydides, too. In a sense the whole book is, or becomes as the war unfolds, the tragedy of Athens, the reversal in their fortunes redolent of the demise of the heroes of tragic drama. The vision of Pericles may have been a glorious one (from the Athenian point of view), but in the nature of things, as Thucydides knew (1.22), it could not last. He lived to see Athens' defeat, though not to write it. But he did complete his account of the Sicilian expedition, the progress and destruction of which in a sense mirrors that of the war as a whole, and the reversal in Athenian fortunes. As noted above, in the context of the whole book, the account of the Sicilian expedition is disproportionately long, and clearly engages Thucydides' interest and emotions. It is, apart from the odd divergence to recount other events in the same years (Thucydides uses the annalistic technique of narrating all the events of one year before moving on to the next, which can be seen as interrupting narrative flow, but may also make for suspense, and for juxtapositions such as that of the Melian Dialogue and the Sicilian expedition), and the almost tangential digression on Harmodius and Aristogeiton (6.53ff), which seems to be included to add an extra dimension to the story of Alcibiades, almost a monograph in itself, with its own introduction, and its tragic consummation. The expedition is launched (6.30–2) with extravagant hopes: a demonstration of Athenian power, 'the finest looking force ever to set out from a Greek city'. The whole population of the city crowds the Piraeus to see it off: when the men are aboard, a trumpet sounds, and the crews in unison offer up their prayers; the triremes, beautifully equipped, race each other as far as Aegina as they pass out of sight. But notes of foreboding have already been sounded. We know from the account of the debate about the expedition that one of its commanders, Nicias, has serious doubts (6.9ff); and that another, Alcibiades, sails under the cloud of prosecution for impiety (6.27ff). Even in the euphoria of departure, the families of those about to sail suddenly realize the magnitude of the task, and it occurs to them that they may never see their loved ones again. Very few will: the seeds of doubt have been sown, and we know, as surely as we anticipate at the beginning of Sophocles' *Oedipus Tyrannus* the reversal that will leave the great king a blood-ied wreck, that those who survive as long as the desperate debacle of the final retreat (end of book 7), will perish in the horror of the stone-quarries of Syracuse. The tragedy of Athens in Sicily is further concentrated in the person of one man, the general Nicias. Reluctantly in command and already in late middle age, his vacillations, together with illness, political machinations at home and the energy of the Spartan Gylippus in command of the Syracusan forces, bring about the disaster we know will come. Nicias seems to have none of the qualities Thucydides habitually admires: he is no Pericles or Brasidas. At a vital moment, when a swift retreat might have saved his belea-guered army, his superstitious refusal to move after an eclipse effectively sentences to death himself, his men and his abler colleague Demosthenes. Yet somehow the fate of Nicias touched Thucydides: Demosthenes receives no 'obituary' (see above for Thucydides' judgement of him), whereas Nicias 'of all the Greeks of my time least deserved to meet such a fate' (7.86). He was a good man, but goodness is not always enough.

That Nicias evokes Thucydides' sympathy is the more surprising in that it is his religious scruples (or superstitions) that in the end precipitate his downfall, for religion is one of the areas in which Thucydides shows little interest – thus, unwittingly perhaps, underestimating the considerable role played by religion in the Greek world, both on the personal and the civic level. Occasionally he acknowledges the latter: the Peisistratid tyrants meet with his approval for performing all the proper religious sacrifices (6.54); but the gods are nowhere represented as active agents in human affairs, though chance, especially in warfare, is a significant factor. Individual speakers do, indeed, make references and appeals to them – it is safe to assume that no general's speech before battle would have been complete without the latter – but usually to no effect: the gods, as characterized by the Athenian speaker in the Melian Dialogue, are not comforting figures (5.105: rule when you can). If we can risk a conclusion on Thucydides' stance on religious matters, it may be that religion is indeed a force in human affairs, but more by virtue of its psychological and social effects than because there are gods who interest themselves in the activities of mankind.

Not only the gods are missing. Very few women appear in Thucydides, in keeping with the advice Pericles has for the women of Athens: not to be talked about by men, for good or ill (2.46). The (unnamed) wife of a Molossian king helps the suppliant Themistocles, in a passage about earlier history with something of a Herodotean flavour about it (1.136). Women are found helping out in defence of their homes, on one occasion with courage 'beyond that characteristic of their sex' (3.74). One woman who is mentioned twice is Chrysis, priestess of Hera at Argos; first, because she is useful for the dating of events (2.2), and again when she accidentally sets fire to the temple and has to run away (4.133). Thucydides makes no comment: in view of his prevailing silence as far as women are concerned, it would probably be superfluous.

Thucydides' world is a man's world, and a narrowly focussed man's world, at that. It has been remarked that, on the evidence of Thucydides, no one got drunk during the Peloponnesian War: there is, that is to say, almost no evidence in Thucydides of activities outside the spheres of war and politics. The type of history he pioneered became the standard model for historians especially in the nineteenth and earlier twentieth centuries, when it was optimistically believed, for a time, that scientific history – rediscovering with complete accuracy what happened in the past – might be possible. Thucydides himself, indeed, may have believed that the truth about the past might be established; he cannot, however, if he was honest, have envisaged the telling of this truth wholly without personal involvement. Certainly, however high accuracy may have been on his list of priorities, he himself was engaged by his subject in a way that goes beyond the purely factual. He has been set up as a model of objectivity; in ancient times he could be seen (Dionysius of Halicarnassus again) as the historian of emotion. We might remember his epitaph on Nicias (7.86; and above); his compassion for the victims of the plague at Athens (2.47ff); or his description of the horrors of civil war at Corcyra, and his consequent sense of the erosion of human values (3.82ff). Frequently, Thucydides' own opinion is expressed in passing; on some Athenian hoplites ambushed and killed by Aetolians, 'the best men from Athens who died in this war' (3.98); and on the slaughter by Thracian mercenaries of the whole population – every man, woman and child, even the children in school – of the small town of Mycalessus, for no particular reason, 'a calamity second to none of those experienced in the war' (7.29ff).

Such things, Thucydides knew, happen in war, and will happen again. If justification for writing about war is needed, this is it. He set out to create – concerning what was, in the light of history, undoubtedly a rather small-scale conflict in a chronically war-torn peninsula – 'something to be possessed for ever' (*ktēma es aiei*: 1.22). It is for qualities such as this that his book has, so far, achieved this aspiration.

Further reading

Thucydides has not perhaps received the critical treatment he deserves. See, however, Cartwright (1997) for a companion to the Penguin translation; also Connor (1984); Dover (1973); Greenwood (2006); Hornblower (1987); Kagan (2009); Morrison (2006); Rood (1998); Zagovin (2008). Most impressive, though, are the several essays on Thucydides in Macleod (1983): these really get to grips with the complexity of Thucydides' rhetoric. Information can also be found on works concerned with historians and historiography more generally, such as Hornblower (1996); Marincola (1997; 2001; 2007); Pelling (2000); Woodman (1998a on rhetoric). On more purely historical issues, see Cawkwell (1997).

XENOPHON

Since his *Hellenica* takes up the history of the Peloponnesian War at the point at which Thucydides' unfinished history breaks off, and he has thus conventionally been regarded as the third of the triad of classical Greek historians (after Herodotus and Thucydides), it is reasonable to include him in a chapter about historiography. In fact, as we shall see below, the *Hellenica* is a rather different kind of book, and Xenophon a very different kind of writer.

In a long life (*c.* 430–*c.* 355) Xenophon wrote a good deal. At least one of the books formerly attributed to him certainly is not, the so-called *Constitution of the Athenians*, nowadays usually referred to as the 'Old Oligarch', a critical account of Athenian democracy written during the Peloponnesian War by an unknown writer whose political sympathies were probably not dissimilar to those of Xenophon himself. It is not clear when Xenophon wrote most of his books. His early years were spent at Athens during the Peloponnesian War where, as a young man from a wealthy family, he appears to have served as a cavalryman and to have been involved, on the anti-democratic side, in the civil war in which the regime of the Thirty Tyrants came to an end. As a supporter of the oligarchic faction, as well as of Socrates, whose association with prominent oligarchs such as Critias, the leader of the Thirty, was to a considerable extent responsible for his execution in 399, Xenophon probably found life in Athens uncongenial under the restored democracy, and in 401 joined the expedition of Cyrus, younger brother of Artaxerxes of Persia, in an attempt to usurp the Persian throne. When the campaign came to an abrupt end with the death of Cyrus and the subsequent murder of the generals of the Greek contingent by the satrap Tissaphernes, Xenophon was elected general and, with others, helped to lead the Greeks out of Persian territory (see below on the *Anabasis*). As commander, at first, of the so-called 'Ten Thousand', he then remained in Persia and served in the Spartan campaigns there during the 390s, becoming a friend of the Spartan king Agesilaus. When Agesilaus was recalled to Greece in 394, Xenophon went with him, and may well have fought against his fellow-countrymen at Coronea in that year. Either at this point or earlier, he was formally exiled from Athens. The Spartans gave him an estate at Scillus, where he remained until the Spartan defeat at Leuctra in 371 and the consequent upheavals in the Peloponnese. He seems then to have gone to Corinth, where he probably died, though at some time the decree of exile was revoked, and some believe that he may have returned to Athens at the end of his life. If he did not, he was at any rate still interested in his native city: his short book *Poroi*, datable to 355, is concerned with the Athenian economy and how to increase its revenues; and his two sons fought – and one died – as cavalrymen in the Athenian contingent with Sparta against Thebes at Mantinea in 362.

Most of Xenophon's other books are less easily datable. It seems unlikely that he can have had time to write much during his years of active service, and some prefer to date all his literary activity to the very last years of his life. It seems reasonable, however, to suppose that he began to write whilst at Scillus as well as enjoying there the life of a 'country gentleman', farming, riding, hunting and entertaining his friends (see *Anabasis* 5.3).

Xenophon's writings reflect the interests of his eventful life. Three of them concern Socrates. The *Symposium*, an account of a *symposion* attended by Socrates and including a speech by him on love, is perhaps a more realistic depiction of a *symposion* – and conceivably of Socrates – than Plato's book of the same name. The Socrates presented by Xenophon in the *Memorabilia*, supposedly a record of various conversations of Socrates, and the *Apology*, concerned, like Plato's *Apology*, with Socrates' trial and defence, is also a rather more down-to-earth figure than the one more familiar from Plato's dialogues. They are interesting from that point of view, if not from a philosophical one: Xenophon was by no means a stupid man, but no philosopher. Socrates also appears in the *Oeconomicus*, where for once he mostly listens, to an Athenian gentleman called Ischomachus (whom one may suspect to be Xenophon in disguise) talking about how to manage an estate and how to run a house – or rather how to train one's wife to run it. It is more interesting than it sounds, not least for the light it sheds on the relationship between husband and wife in Xenophon's world.

A prevalent theme in the *Oeconomicus* is order and discipline, and this characterizes also Xenophon's three books on two lifelong passions of his, hunting and horsemanship. The *Cynēgeticus*, probably not wholly by Xenophon, deals not only with methods of hunting and keeping hounds, but with the usefulness of hunting as training for military discipline. The *Peri Hippikēs* is about buying, training and riding horses, and is well regarded by experts in equestrianism, whilst the *Hipparchicus* deals with the duties of a cavalry commander, especially in the context of the Athenian cavalry corps and is, no doubt, based on Xenophon's own experiences as cavalryman and as general.

Also based on his own experience is the *Lakedaimoniōn Politeia* (Constitution of the Spartans), which is actually more concerned with the workings of the Spartan social and educational system, in which Xenophon had his sons brought up. More political is the *Hierōn*, a fictional dialogue between Hieron, tyrant of Syracuse, and the poet Simonides, which discusses the nature of tyranny; unusually, in the tradition of Greek writings about tyrants, Hieron is a not unsympathetic character.

Xenophon's *Agesilaus* is a biography – the first extant biography in Greek literature – of his friend King Agesilaus. It is historically based, but selective, devoting a considerable amount of space to Agesilaus' Persian campaigns, in which Xenophon took part, and is excessively favourable to Agesilaus, whose virtues are commemorated at length without reference to his failings or failures. The *Cyropaedia* is also a biography, this time an obviously fictional one, purporting to describe the upbringing and career of Cyrus the Great of Persia, who is represented as the perfect monarch presiding over a utopian realm. Despite his omnipresence in the narrative, Cyrus does not emerge as a clearly defined character, but some of the minor figures are more memorable; especially sympathetic are Abradatas and Pantheia, whose love-story is important as a forerunner of the Greek novel which emerged as a literary genre in the Hellenistic and Roman periods.

To the historian, Xenophon's most important book is the *Hellenica*, which takes up Thucydides' account of the Peloponnesian War more or less at the point that Thucydides breaks off. Having reached the end of the war by book 2.3.10 (the book and chapter numbers are not Xenophon's own, hence the odd numbering), he goes on to cover events down to 372. Stylistic analysis indicates very strongly that the two parts were written at different times. Unlike Thucydides or Herodotus, Xenophon presents us with no manifesto as to his aims, his sources or the nature of the book, which is the only continuous account we have of the period. Important though it is because of its unique status, it raises as many questions as it answers: it is uneven in its coverage, shows little indication that Xenophon has compared or unified different sources and, when his version can be checked against others, he tends to come off worse. (Parts of another history that continued Thucydides have been discovered on papyrus fragments from Oxyrhynchus in Egypt; the *Hellenica Oxyrhynchia*, or Oxyrhynchus Historian, whose name is unknown, clearly provided a far more balanced and superior account, but is infuriatingly incomplete.)

The truth is that the *Hellenica* is not really history, and that Xenophon was not practising history in the same way as Herodotus and Thucydides. His omissions and distortions can be accounted for by his own interests, contacts and whereabouts. There is, for example, much on the internal history of Athens in the first part, when he was in Athens and involved in events there; in the second part, when he was not, there is almost none. Here, he writes almost wholly from a Peloponnesian, and indeed Spartan, point of view: during these years Thebes, under the inspired leadership of Epaminondas, effectively broke Sparta's domination for ever; Xenophon cannot entirely ignore him, but his account of one of the greatest generals in Greek history is grudging, to say the least. Xenophon's friend Agesilaus similarly receives more favourable coverage than he seems to deserve. Such examples could be multiplied.

The nature of the book might be explained if we knew its purpose. There is no sign of oral composition, or of any performance context such as that of

Herodotus, and perhaps Thucydides. Xenophon may, of course, have read parts of his work to his friends, but shows no ambitions in terms of posterity. The book seems to be a compilation of what he remembers and what he has heard about the events of his lifetime: it is, as George Cawkwell says, not history but 'essentially memoirs', perhaps put together as much for his own satisfaction as anything else. Memoirs, then, but not valueless ones in historical terms, being those of a man who witnessed and took part in events of great consequence, or knew men who had.

Much of Xenophon's writing in the *Hellenica* is matter-of-fact, but the book contains some memorable scenes: the trial of the generals after the battle of Arginusae (1.7ff); how the news of the defeat at Aegospotami reached Athens and how one man told another so that the wailing went up from the Piraeus to the city, and no one slept that night (2.2.3); the appeal of Cleocritus, herald of the Mysteries, with his splendid voice, to the warring factions to end the civil war at Athens.

Xenophon's most-read book – one of the most-read books in Greek literature, indeed – contains some similarly memorable pictures. For most readers, the climax of the *Anabasis*, Xenophon's first-hand account of his participation, first as soldier, then as general, in the expedition of the 10,000 Greek mercenaries who fought for Cyrus against his brother for the throne of Persia comes halfway through the book, in the shape of one of the most famous scenes in Greek literature. Having fought their way past Persian armies, barbarous natives, hostile terrain and the elements, the Greeks, foot-slogging their way up yet another mountain, catch sight of the sea and know that salvation is at hand; rushing helter-skelter to the summit, shouting '*Thalassa! Thalassa!*' ('Sea! Sea!'), they embrace each other, weeping for joy, and build cairns to commemorate the moment; their native guide goes home a rich man.

Some might say that the *Anabasis*, in more ways than one, goes downhill the rest of the way (the word means 'going up', inland from the sea). Disputes about leadership, negotiations with Greek cities in the area, struggles for provisions, can be less than enthralling, and the frequent speeches tedious. Even here, though, there is more than meets the eye. The Ten Thousand, complete with slaves, concubines and camp-followers, have been likened to a *polis* on the march, and Xenophon even suggests, to no avail, that they stay in the Bosporus region and found a real *polis*. This may be seen – as is the democratic, argumentative but effective way in which the soldiers re-establish a structure of command after the deaths of Cyrus and their generals – as a potential assertion of the concept of Greekness in the face of the barbarian 'other' that permeates the book. The achievement of the Ten Thousand in keeping together in the midst of this 'other' evokes another theme found elsewhere in Xenophon and in other contemporary writings: a kind of utopianism centred on the concept of 'Panhellenism' – the unity of all Greeks. Greece, except perhaps in the Persian Wars, and even then only to a limited extent, had never been a unity, but in the fourth century some, including apparently Xenophon's hero Agesilaus, dreamed that such a thing might come about, under the leadership of Sparta, and crystallize in a victorious campaign against Persia. In a sense this did, in time, happen; but only through the enforced unity imposed on Greece by Philip and Alexander of Macedon. Another theme of the *Anabasis* is leadership, especially that of Xenophon himself. The *Anabasis* may well have been written in response to other accounts of the expedition, which gave Xenophon (in his view) less credit than he deserved: that Xenophon ended up in command seems to be the case, but for much of the time the commander-in-chief seems to have been the Spartan Cheirisophus, which is not immediately obvious from Xenophon's version.

The *Anabasis* may be read on various levels, including the simple one of a young Athenian who joined up in search of adventure and riches, and found both – and perhaps himself – on the way. Even in the *Anabasis*, Xenophon does not foist his personality on us (he is a more subtle writer than he is sometimes given credit for). But throughout his varied *oeuvre* we can clearly detect something of his personality and preoccupations. He believed in order, training, and discipline in all areas of life (that Sparta, or his personal image of Sparta, was his model *polis* is not accidental). He was interested in leadership and in great men who possessed the gift of leadership. He was a profoundly and conventionally religious man – no leader, he believed, prospered without respecting the gods and his religious duty but, as perhaps a commander of mercenaries must, he had a ruthless streak: he would beat a man for ill-discipline (*Anab.* 5.8) and – not to mention the many villagers people to whose homes and lands his men laid waste on their march – enrich himself by an unprovoked attack on an innocent man and his family (*Anab.* 7.8). Behind the bland facade of his clear and straightforward Greek lurked a sharper intellect than is immediately apparent: as a literary figure he was a pioneer in the genre of biography, and indeed of prose fiction. But to a 'conservative', and a lover of order, the political chaos of the Greece of his time must have been bemusing: in the end, even his beloved Sparta let him down. The end of the *Hellenica*, which he must have written in old age, shows him a disappointed man: the battle of Mantinea (362), he says, was expected to resolve the chaos; in fact, all it did was make matters more uncertain and chaotic than before: 'so let this be the end of my account. Perhaps someone else will deal with what happened afterwards' (*Hell.* 7.5.27).

Further reading

For a good introduction, see Anderson (1974). On *Hellenica*, see Dillery (1995). See also Tatum (1989). Information can also be found on works concerned with historians and historiography more generally, such as Hornblower (1996); Marincola (1997; 2001); Pelling (2000); Woodman (1998a on rhetoric). On the *Anabasis*, see the collection of articles in Lane Fox (2004).

LATER GREEK HISTORIOGRAPHY

Almost none of the Greek historical writing of the two centuries after Xenophon has survived, which is particularly regrettable in the cases of the two major historians of the fourth century, Ephorus of Cyme, who wrote a 'universal' history encompassing the history of the eastern peoples as well as of the Greek world, and Theopompus of Chios, who wrote a continuation of Thucydides which was more detailed than that of Xenophon, and a universal history which focussed especially on the rise of Philip II of Macedon. These two historians represented trends in Greek historiography which became prevalent in the Hellenistic period and which are related to the change in the political shape of the Greek world with the domination of Philip and Alexander and their successors: recognition that the history of Greece could only be understood in a wider, international, context; and a more strongly biographical tradition in the writing of history resulting from the historical significance of important individuals. An interest in the wider world opened up by the conquests of Alexander resulted also in the attention paid to ethnography and geography in the Hellenistic scholarly world in general, and by historians in particular.

The reign of Alexander spawned a large number of histories, all of which, again, have perished, though much of their work was incorporated in that of later writers whose books have survived. The name of Alexander's personal historian, Callisthenes, nephew of Aristotle, who accompanied him on his campaigns, survived in connection with the 'Greek Alexander Romance', which became extremely popular during the Roman imperial period, but is almost entirely fantasy (see 12d). Other lost Alexander historians included Cleitarchus, Aristobulus and two of Alexander's officers, the admiral Nearchus and Ptolemy (later king Ptolemy I of Egypt).

The intrusion of Rome into Greek and Macedonian affairs introduced a further new element for historians to reckon with. The first six books of the history of Polybius (c. 200–c. 118), which dealt with the rise to domination of Rome in the Mediterranean world, survive almost intact, along with considerable fragments of later books. Polybius is an important historian, and our chief source for the period his work covers: his rigorous historical method makes him far superior to the credulous and moralizing Roman historian Livy, though his literary style is much inferior. One of the few ancient historians to whom content was more important than style, he may perhaps be considered the only true successor to Thucydides, like whom he was a soldier and politician and he writes with especial insight into these areas, as well as into geography as a factor in history.

No other Greek historical writing survives for a century or so after Polybius, although the stoic philosopher Posidonius, who spent time at Rome and, like Polybius, travelled widely, wrote an influential continuation of Polybius' book covering the period from 146 to the 80s. Greek interest in

Rome is also attested by the work of Diodorus Siculus, Dionysius of Halicarnassus and Strabo (all late first century), all of whom lived in Rome at least for a time. Diodorus, author of an enormous universal history of which a good deal survives (and which incorporates Roman history alongside Greek), has not generally been highly regarded as a historian: recent work has attempted to restore his reputation, but it must be admitted that he is frequently uncritical and confusing, and his chief historical value lies in his preservation of the work of important earlier historians such as Ephorus. Dionysius, a literary critic and rhetorician as well as a historian, wrote on the early history of Rome and about half of his book survives. He was an enthusiast for the traditional virtues of Rome, and saw Rome as emphatically belonging to the Greek world. The historical work of Strabo, another Greek admirer of Rome, is lost, but his large book on geography survives and contains a good deal of historical information.

There is another gap in the Greek historiographical tradition for a century or so after the time of Augustus, though the biographies of Plutarch (before 50–after 120 CE) contain much useful historical information and there is an interesting new departure in Greek historical writing in the shape of the Jewish historian Josephus (born 37/8 CE). Josephus was involved in the Jewish revolt of 65–70 CE, but later became a friend of the emperor Vespasian who, with his son Titus, was largely instrumental in suppressing the revolt. Having written a book about it in Aramaic, for a Jewish readership, he then wrote a longer one in Greek, as well as a history of the Jews in Greek, usually known as the *Jewish Antiquities*, which included an autobiographical section defending (against his Jewish critics) his conduct with regard to Rome. Another book, *Against Apion*, attempts to demonstrate the antiquity of Jewish culture in response to anti-Semitic criticism.

A figure of major importance for our knowledge of Greek history, and an important man in his own time, is Arrian or, more correctly, Lucius Flavius Arrianus (*c.* 86–160 CE). A philosopher and friend of the emperor Hadrian, who became consul at Rome and a provincial governor, Arrian is chiefly known for his *Anabasis*, an account of the life and expeditions of Alexander the Great. The *Anabasis* is a readable and interesting book – Arrian is as interested in style as he is in content – and, though it cannot be relied on as a whole as a source for Alexander, is nevertheless the first extant full account of him in Greek (the date of the Latin one by Curtius is not known, and may be from around the same time), and is based on contemporary accounts, especially those of Ptolemy and Aristobulus. Arrian also wrote a brief account of India, the *Indikē*, which similarly preserves earlier Greek accounts of India.

Not to be confused with Arrian is Appian (died 160s CE), who wrote a long book on the history of Rome down to the time of Trajan based on both Greek and Latin sources which, like that of Cassius Dio (*c.* 164–after 229 CE), another provincial from the Greek east who became consul at Rome, is useful as a historical source for certain periods not covered by extant earlier writings.

Both are primarily literary men rather than historians, and their evidence must therefore be used with care.

The nature of Greco-Roman life and society was radically changed by the coming of Christianity. So, of course, was that of literature, and in the early fourth century CE we encounter the first Christian Greek historian, Eusebius, whose *Ecclesiastical History* is an attempt to synthesize Christian and pagan history and to show that all of history is part of God's plan for mankind. Eusebius was also the biographer of the emperor Constantine, whose contemporary he was, and whose establishment of Constantinople as the capital of the eastern empire changed the nature of the empire as a whole. The subsequent history of Greek historiography is essentially Christian, and based in the eastern empire. After the fall of the western empire in 476 CE, Greek cultural life centred on Constantinople, but never forgot its classical roots: indeed, as far as literature and literary language was concerned, it became unhealthily conservative. The major figures in Byzantine historiography continued to write in Attic Greek, or what they considered to be Attic, and for the most part, although valuable as historical sources, are of little literary interest. Exceptions – translations of whose work are readily available – are Procopius (sixth century), who wrote an official history of the wars of the emperor Justinian and a much more entertaining and satirical account of Justinian, the *Secret History*; Michael Psellos (eleventh century); and Anna Comnena (twelfth century), daughter of emperor Alexius I, who wrote up her father's achievements in her *Alexiad*.

Further reading

On Polybius, see Walbank (1972); on Josephus, see Bilde (1988); on Plutarch, see the collection of articles in Mossman (1997); Russell (1972); Stadter (1992); on Arrian, see Stadter (1980); on Cassius Dio, Millar (1964). On later historians, see Rohrbacher (2002). Works on ancient historians and historiography can also be useful: see Hornblower (1996); Marincola (1997; 2001, 2007); Pelling (2000); Woodman (1998a on rhetoric).

Chapter 6

Rhetorical and philosophical writing

All dates in this chapter are BCE unless stated otherwise. Glossary items: *akribeia; allegory; apeiron; aporia; aretē; ataraxia; catharsis; crasis; dialectic; doxographer; elenchus; elision; eristic; eudaimōnia; forms; logographoi; mimēsis; nomos; nous; phronēsis; physis; Presocratics; Socratic irony; sophists; syllogism; technē.*

LAW COURTS, RHETORIC, THE SOPHISTS IN CLASSICAL ATHENS

Neil Croally

In his play *Wasps* Aristophanes superbly satirizes the relationship in democratic Athens between the law courts, their juries and politicians, such as Cleon, whom he held to be demagogic in his (ab)use of the courts for political purposes. In another play, *Clouds*, when the rather ignorant farmer Strepsiades is shown a map of the Greek world and the location of Athens, he expresses his disbelief as he can see no law courts (*Clouds* 207–8). Cleon himself, at least in Thucydides, berates the citizens attending the assembly for being obsessed with rhetoric rather than policy: they have become, he says, 'spectators of speeches' (Thuc. 3.38.4). The rule of law can exist without democracy, but the latter rarely exists without the former (certainly, the rule of law existed in Athens before the Cleisthenic introduction of democracy in 508). But democracy and the legal process have something extremely important in common: both depend on 'faith in public argument' (Buxton, 1982). In a variety of ways Athens developed a love for the persuasive word: *peithō* – the Greek for persuasion – was honoured as a deity, and rhetoric became one of Athens' most important interests.

It is not clear how exactly the Athenian legal system functioned in the sixth and early fifth centuries, though most scholars would probably agree that the democracy developed and adapted some procedures which had been established by Solon. But first things first. Who made law in democratic Athens? The only institution capable of this was the assembly, which passed law by majority vote. In the earlier years of the democracy it seems that little or no effort was made to distinguish between laws which were meant to be permanent (*nomoi*) and decrees which contained specific decisions about specific matters (*psēphismata*). During the fourth century efforts were made to clarify any existing confusions, and decrees were not allowed to overrule any law. The assembly continued to decide on decrees, but lawmaking was carried out by citizens in smaller groups (these were called *nomothetai*).

It is often said of Greek law that it lacks the distinction we have between civil and criminal law: it is true that the city of Athens never acted as the prosecutor; all cases were brought by individual citizens. However, a distinction was made between private and public actions. In the former, the wronged individual had to bring the case and, if he won the case, might receive compensation. In public actions – of which there were various types – any individual acting on behalf of the city could bring the case and all fines were paid to the city. A famous example of a public action was the trial of Socrates. All trials, though, were presided over by an elected magistrate. For instance, the Polemarch was in charge of trials involving non-Athenians; the Archon Basileus dealt with murder trials and trials to do with religion. It is important to understand, however, that, while the magistrate presided, he did not act in the way a judge in a modern British court acts: he did not advise the jury on points of law and he did not sum up before the jury went to decide on its verdict.

There were a number of different courts, only some of which had specific functions. The Areopagus, for example, was used only for homicide trials, and the Heliaea was presided over by the thesmothetai, who dealt with a wide variety of cases. Trials were held sometimes in other places, such as the Odeion (next to the Theatre of Dionysus), or the Painted Stoa. On occasion, the assembly itself acted as a court. Another distinctive feature of the Athenian legal system were the juries. To serve as juror, one needed to be a citizen over the age of 30. At the beginning of each year a jury list of 6,000 citizens was drawn up. A payment to serving jurors of two obols per day was introduced by Pericles in 451 and in *c*. 425 Cleon had this raised to three obols. This amount had an effect on the make-up of juries because it did not match even a fairly low daily wage and thereby encouraged a disproportionately large number of older citizens to volunteer. It is the number of jurors making up a jury in each trial that is most surprising to us, as it was normally in the hundreds. At Socrates' trial, for instance, there were 500 jurors, and there is evidence for even larger juries. The juries not only decided on a verdict; they also voted on the sentence (when the penalty was not laid down by law).

Trials normally followed this pattern: the prosecutor spoke first, the defendant second. There was a time limit on speeches, which were supposed to be given by the litigants themselves (see below on speech writers or *logographoi*). Evidence and other laws could be adduced; witnesses could be called and interrogated (though in the latter part of the fourth century witnesses sent in written statements which were read out to the court). The evidence we have of actual court cases seems to suggest that many defendants did not limit themselves to using evidence and relevant witnesses; they often appealed to the juries in much more emotional ways (which would be not be allowed in a modern court).

The problem with Athenian trials, according to some scholars, is that a clever rhetorician could easily sway a jury, even when the facts of the case were against him. In the middle of the fifth century this was one of the areas in which the sophists – travelling teachers – became important in Athens. Protagoras' famous claim that he 'could make the weaker argument win' suggests a demand for rhetorical training that would improve performance both in the assembly and in the courts. Gorgias' description of the power of the word in his *Encomium of Helen* is worth quoting in this context (*Encomium of Helen* 8 and 14):

> Speech is a powerful master . . . It can stop fear, relieve pain, create joy, and increase pity . . . The power of speech has the same effect on the disposition of the soul as the disposition of drugs on the nature of bodies . . . words: some cause pain, others joy, some strike fear, some stir the audience to boldness, some benumb and bewitch the soul with evil persuasion . . .
>
> (Gagarin and Woodruff, 1995: 192–3)

Being taught rhetoric by a sophist was one way to ensure political and legal success. Another way, more specific to the courts, was to get a good rhetorician to write your speech for you. And it is to these speech writers – and the other famous orators of the fourth century – that we now turn.

(Suggestions for further reading are given at the end of the section on oratory; on the sophists and rhetoric, see also 1g and 6c.)

CLASSICAL ORATORY

Neil Croally

The speech writers and orators that I shall discuss here come from a period of a little less than 100 years, from *c.* 415 until *c.* 320. My ordering is chronological.

Antiphon (c. 480–411)

Not all scholars are agreed that this Antiphon – the first Attic orator – is the same as Antiphon the sophist. But, from the evidence of the speeches that have been preserved, the orator does seem to have been influenced by the sophists' approach to rhetoric. We have extant three courtroom speeches for clients (all to do with murder) and three *Tetralogies*, which deal with speeches for and against hypothetical cases. The contrasting arguments deployed in the

Tetralogies reveal sophistic influence, as does the use of arguments from probability. Some scholars argue that Antiphon's style lacks ease and clarity, but one could also say that he was an influential innovator in the writing of Attic prose (he may have taught Thucydides). The most obvious characteristic of his style is his use of antithesis, which again reveals some sophistic influence. One speech it would be interesting to have in its entirety is the speech Antiphon gave to defend himself when charged with treason (he was one of the oligarchs involved in the coup of 412–11). Thucydides says that it was probably the best speech he had ever heard (8.68).

Lysias (c. 459–c. 380)

Lysias is arguably the most famous of the Attic speech writers. We have 34 of his speeches extant, though we know of a further 130 he may have authored. The ancients themselves speculated that he may have written over 400. One problem here, as was pointed out by Dover, is that Lysias may have to varying degrees co-written his speeches with his clients. It can certainly be argued that Lysias, perhaps more than any other speechwriter, manages to tailor the style of individual speeches to the individuals who would have to deliver them in the court. He wrote speeches for both private and public cases: the best example of a private speech is arguably Lysias' most famous speech, the first, in which a husband argues that his murder of his wife's lover is justifiable (at least one scholar argues that this speech was not delivered as a courtroom speech, but published as an advertisement for Lysias as speechwriter; Porter, 1997; cf. Pelling, 2000: 301 n. 89). The public speeches are both more numerous and more varied. Lysias is generally praised for the relaxed quality of his writing and for the clarity of his narrative organization. As someone who may have been taught by the Sicilian rhetorician Tisias, Lysias also demonstrates a shrewd understanding of his various audiences, using variously charm, humour, self-deprecation and suspense to win juries over.

Lysias led an eventful life. He left Athens in the 440s to go to the new colony at Thurii in southern Italy (Thurii's constitution was probably drafted by the great sophist, Protagoras), but was forced to leave there in 412. He returned to Athens in 412 and found himself at odds with the Thirty Tyrants in 404/3. They arrested both Lysias and his brother, and confiscated their property. While Lysias managed to escape, his brother was killed. His Speech 12, *Against Eratosthenes*, is an attempt to prosecute Eratosthenes for the murder of his brother, but we do not know whether Lysias was successful. It would seem, then, that Lysias was opposed to the oligarchs, but there is a problem with such a characterization, because his Speech 25 was written for someone who was accused of supporting the Thirty Tyrants. Various critical views have been advanced, but we shall probably never know whether Lysias was an inconsistent hypocrite, an ambitious businessman or someone who believed that everyone deserved a defence.

Andocides (c. 440–390)

Andocides is an intriguing figure. He was implicated in the mutilation of the Herms which occurred on the eve of the departure of the Sicilian expedition in 415. He seems to have confessed that he was involved in the mutilation, as well as in what was taken to be a profanation of the Eleusinian mysteries, but that confession may have been motivated in part by his wish to ensure that both he and his father were freed. The allegation of involvement continued to hound him and he left Athens in 414, but returned in 410. His first extant speech (*On My Return*) is his attempt to argue his case, but he failed. A second attempt at defence in 403 (*On the Mysteries*) was more successful. From this point on Andocides played a full part in Athenian politics. His third speech (*On the Peace*) was delivered in 392/1 on the terms offered by the Persian king. There is a fourth speech which is sometimes attributed to Andocides (*Against Alcibiades*), but most scholars think that it is not authentic. Andocides has not been very highly regarded, either in antiquity or in more modern times. He has been seen as a writer who cannot stick to the point, who prefers the digressive and the parenthetical. But while the standard of argumentation may not be particularly high, there can be a rude charm and expressiveness to Andocides' style.

Isocrates (436–338)

Isocrates is not well-known for his oratorical performances; his reputation was achieved by the influence he had on other orators, which he achieved through an educational system which privileged rhetorical training. He himself received a top-class education in rhetoric, having both Prodicus and Gorgias as teachers. Although he tried his hand at speechwriting (Speeches 16–21), he preferred to teach rather than provide rhetoric, something that is very much in the spirit of the sophists. Some of his 15 extant non-courtroom speeches deal with a number of the major political problems faced by Athens and other Greek cities in the fourth century. So, in the *Panegyricus* (380) Isocrates argued for a panhellenist ideal, in which Athens and Sparta would together lead the Greeks against any threat from the Persians. Towards the end of his life he was more concerned with how to deal with Philip of Macedon, and in the *Philippus* (346) he appealed to Philip to take the lead against the barbarians.

Isocrates was a slightly older contemporary of Plato, and his system of education – which we mainly know about from his speech *Antidosis* – was in competition with and in contrast to the education offered at Plato's Academy. What marks out Isocrates' system is its concern with the practical rather than the abstract philosophizing associated with the school of Plato (see the criticism of Isocrates at *Phaedrus* 279a). Isocrates clearly learned from the sophists but also distinguished himself from them: so rhetoric had an important but not an all-important place. Given Isocrates' interest in the more pragmatic approach to private and public affairs, it seems inconsistent that the style of his own speeches is so elaborate. He makes uses of certain metrical combinations, and he likes to build up long, complex sentences. He seems to have tried hard to avoid such things as anaphora, elision and crasis. Modern readers do not always find Isocrates easy to follow or to their taste and, at the time of writing it can be safely said that he appears rarely as an author used in public examinations.

Isaeus (c. 420–c. 340)

Less is known about Isaeus than some of the other orators. Indeed, we cannot be sure whether he was Athenian or from Euboea. He may have been taught by Isocrates, seems to have studied Lysias and was a teacher of Demosthenes. Of the 64 speeches that were attributed to him in antiquity (of which probably 50 were genuine), 11 have survived. All the speeches were written for clients in cases to do with inheritance. For that reason, it is historians of Athenian society and family who have found Isaeus most useful. As far as his style is concerned, it sits somewhere between the clarity of Lysias and the elaboration and fastidiousness of Iscorates. He had a reputation for using innuendo and emotion skilfully.

Aeschines (c. 397–322)

Aeschines was a prominent orator and politician in fourth-century Athens, whose name is always tied to his rival and critic, Demosthenes. The two orators reveal the difficulties that Athens had in working out how to respond to the growing power of Macedon from the 350s onwards. The enmity between the two men arose first from a legation both served on to negotiate peace terms with Philip of Macedon. The details are argued over, but it seems as if a tactical disagreement about how best to secure peace for Athens – Aeschines argued for a common peace for all Greeks; Demosthenes preferred an alliance between Athens and Macedon – allowed or prompted Demosthenes to cast Aeschines as too friendly with the Macedonians. From that point, the two rivals engaged in prosecution and counter-prosecution, of each other and of each others' associates. Aeschines continued to be involved in diplomacy and negotiation until Demosthenes' famous speech *On the Crown* effectively ended his political career in 330.

It is conventional that Demosthenes' rhetorical skills were the superior. But this judgement – which is difficult to argue with – has probably affected, in turn, the judgement of history of Aeschines' role in trying to protect the interests of Athens. It is certainly plausible that he was as patriotic as Demosthenes. The three speeches that survive do not, indeed, match the splendour of Demosthenes, but it is clear that he was often successful in persuading his audience, which was his main purpose, and which he succeeded in doing with one of his extant speeches, *Against Timarchus*, which attacked one of Demosthenes' associates. By all accounts Aeschines displayed a good knowledge of poetry, with liberal use of quotation, and he also seems to have used his training and experience as an actor to project himself when he spoke.

Demosthenes (384–322)

For someone who came to be regarded as Athens' finest orator in both political and judicial speeches, it could be argued that Demosthenes' childhood and young adulthood were not necessarily the best preparation. Suffering from bad health and a speech impediment, he also had to endure the death of his father when he was seven, and the loss of his inheritance after his father's estate was mismanaged by the trustees. His early career, which began in the late 360s, was the by now conventional one of speech-writer. However, from the mid-350s onwards he began to take on a more public role. In his first public speech – *Against the Law of Leptines* (Speech 20) – he is already using the theme which he would so often expound in his later speeches; namely, that the Athenians are not worthy of the distinguished achievements of their forebears, preferring inaction instead. By the time of the *First Philippic* (351), his first direct attack on Philip of Macedon, he is not only characterizing the Athenians as apathetic and selfish, he is also contrasting their sloth with the energy and insolence of their Macedonian enemy (Speech 4.9). The language of Demosthenes' polemic is certainly vivid – there is the famous comparison of Philip to a barbarian boxer – but it is not at all clear that Demosthenes' rearmament and other military proposals were achievable in what was a dire financial situation in Athens. In a further three speeches, the *Olynthiacs* (Speeches 1–3), Demosthenes continued his criticism of Philip's expansionism. In the mid and late 340s Demosthenes moved between further attacks on Philip (the *Second* and *Third Philippics*; Speeches 6 and 9), and an unsuccessful prosecution of Aeschines (*On the False Embassy*; Speech 19).

The defeat of the Greeks by Philip at Chaeronea in 337 and the subsequent imposition of terms seem to have put Demosthenes in a far weaker political position. Nevertheless, some would argue that his greatest speech was *On the Crown* (Speech 18), in which he responded to Aeschines' attempt to prosecute Ctesiphon (Aeschines Speech 3), who had proposed in 336 that Demosthenes should receive a golden crown in recognition of his efforts on behalf of Athens. This speech shows all the rhetorical qualities associated with Demosthenes; arguably, it displays a greater range as well. Demosthenes can be as apparently simple and clear as a Lysias and occasionally as high-flown as an Isocrates. His arguments are generally clear, though he is not beneath covering up weaknesses with a sort of rhetorical white noise (as Cicero would also do 300 years later). He is capable of both rousing, patriotic statements – the sort of tone Churchill aspired to in his Second World War speeches – and what seems to us dismally degrading personal invective. Aeschines is variously criticized for his status (his father was allegedly a slave), for his alleged collaboration with the Macedonians and for being an actor. While this sort of material may now be fairly distasteful, though we all still love an amusing political insult, it seems clear that, like all good rhetoricians, Demosthenes was a good judge of his audience. His judgements, therefore, of when to use simile or insult, high-flown or ordinary language, were often vindicated. And he not only persuaded his audience; he also impressed later orators and writers, from Cicero, who called his polemics against Mark Antony *Philippics* in imitation of Demosthenes, to Tacitus, Quintilian and Longinus.

Further reading

For law and the law courts in Athens, see Macdowell (1986) and Todd (1993). A *Cambridge Companion to Ancient Greek Law* (Gagarin, 2005) is currently available that contains a number of interesting articles. There is a large bibliography on rhetoric now available. See, for instance, Buxton (1982); Goldhill and Osborne (1999); Gunderson (2009); Habinek (2005); Hesk (2000); Kennedy (1963; 1972; 1994); Russell (1983); Wardy (1998); Worthington (1994; 2007); Yunis (1996).

Antiphon: the text can be most easily found in Maidment (1941 with translation); for Lysias, there is an OCT (Carey, 2007); see also Dover (1968); for an interesting article on Lysias 1, see Porter (1997). For the text of Andocides, Maidment (ibid.), and for some interesting discussion, Missiou (1992); for the text of Isocrates, see the Loeb edition (Norlin, 3 vols., 1968); on Isocrates' rhetoric, see Too (1995), and on his importance in education, see Jaeger (1945) and Marrou (1956). For the text of Isaeus, see Maidment (ibid.); for the text of Aeschines, see Adams (1919), and Harris (1995) for some interesting discussion. For the text of Demosthenes, there is a recently published OCT in 4 volumes (Dilts, 2002–09). For Demosthenes as orator, see Macdowell (2009); Pearson (1976) and, as politician, Sealey (1993); see now Worthington (2000).

EARLY GREEK PHILOSOPHY

Jonathan Katz

The beginnings of western philosophy emerged with the speculations of proto-scientific thinkers – the first of the Presocratics (those who either lived before Socrates or were his contemporaries but were uninfluenced by him). By the first part of the sixth century the eastern Greek world of Ionia had enjoyed considerable contact with the cultures of Asia Minor, the near east, Persia and Egypt. Scientific, religious and cosmological ideas from these cultures must have influenced the Ionian Greeks. Increasing literacy, and perhaps a growing political consensus that rested on notions of rules and laws, encouraged not only new speculations about the nature of the world and man's place within it but also the search for the (rational, non-arbitrary) laws that govern nature.

The first fruits of this new intellectual era are traditionally seen in the figures of Thales (fl. 585) and his successors Anaximander and Anaximenes, natives and residents of the Ionian city of Miletus in the early and middle decades of the sixth century; they are regarded as the first philosophers. Being convinced that there was a comprehensible order to be found in the universe, these Milesians departed from the tradition of mythological explanations (as found in Homer and Hesiod) and were concerned to explain the basic substance from which everything is formed, and the principle by which the world proceeded from this material.

Of Thales we have no original surviving words at all, nor any certainty that he actually wrote anything; our earliest major source for his thought is Aristotle (fourth century), and later writers claimed to have had access to some of his ideas through texts now lost. Thales was, from the earliest days, associated with the belief that everything came into being from water (though the precise meaning of this is much contested), and it is likely that he was influenced by near Eastern perceptions of the world as enlivened and sustained by water. Anaximander and Anaximenes were known to have written prose works, but nothing has survived of these except through paraphrase, or possibly quotation, in fourth century and later writings. Both posited an 'infinite' first substance as origin of the physical and finite world, Anaximander's being called *apeiron* ('unbounded'). For Anaximenes the infinite origin was air, and he appears to have applied a method of 'empirical' thought based on evidential observation – an important mark of rational argument.

Pythagoras, born an Ionian on the island of Samos in around 571, spent the greater part of his life in Croton, Magna Graecia. There he founded a community of like-minded devotees who followed strict dietary rules, believed in the reincarnation of the soul and shared a preoccupation with a mystical view of the universe that depended on mathematics; the important Pythagorean discovery of the precise relation of numerical proportion to musical acoustic intervals led to a more general conviction that the universe was to be understood in terms of number and ratio.

Another Ionian, Heraclitus of Ephesus (born *c.* 540), whose aphoristic writings survive only in fragments quoted by later authors, has been associated since at least Plato's time (fourth century) with the idea of universal flux (*panta rhei* – 'all things flow'), a doctrine hard to assess independently of what Plato and his successors made of it. Famously, he also propounded a doctrine of universal tension between opposites, the *logos*, a principle that holds the world in its present form, and he seems to have suggested that mankind is naively deceived by the appearance of the physical world, whereas true knowledge is to be achieved only by understanding the fundamental order of the *logos*.

Xenophanes, an older contemporary of Heraclitus, was born in Ionian Colophon in around 570, and through voluntary or compulsory exile emigrated to Sicily and Magna Graecia, where as an accomplished poet he became known for his attacks on superstition and on the absurdities of anthropomorphizing the gods. He favoured instead a monotheistic view of an all-powerful, non-personal entity. He was also said to have used his observation of fossil remains to reach deductive conclusions about the history of the physical world (on Xenophanes, see also 3c).

Two other important Presocratics of southern Italy are Parmenides of Elea and his disciple Zeno. Parmenides (fl. *c.* 500), in some ways the single most significant philosophical predecessor of Plato, was the author of a poem of which substantial portions survive. Most importantly, it represents views on the unity of 'reality' and the distinction between true reason and those beliefs obtained through the senses. Zeno (first half of the fifth century) most likely derived his famous paradoxes from the Parmenidean notions of the indivisibility of reality.

Mention should be made of some major cosmological thinkers nearer to Socrates' time in the mid-fifth century. Anaxagoras, born in Ionian Clazomenae *c.* 500, moved to Athens and developed a theory of transformation from an unlimited mass of ingredients to the ordered physical world through the agency of *nous* ('mind'). Empedocles was born at Acragas in Sicily. Parts of two of his philosophical poems survive, and recent publication of further fragments has promised possible reassessment of his ideas in philosophy of nature, including four fundamental elements of water, air, earth and fire and a theory of the origins and natural evolution of living species.

The age of the Presocratics provided some important elements for the future development of western philosophy. The record of these thinkers' original words and writings is sketchy, and we rely on careful interpretation of the works of later writers who claimed to quote, or at least describe, their predecessors' ideas; but these later accounts are sometimes biased towards an attempt to fit the early thinkers into some scheme. Aristotle and his followers, for instance, wished to identify early signs and origins of their own methods of systematic thought; the result was a somewhat anachronistic depiction of Presocratic achievement, ascribing to the early thinkers ideas and intentions which they could not have had. And yet, though it would be inaccurate to claim for the Presocratics a fully developed system of scientific or philosophical investigation, there are certainly more general signs of an impressive intellectual system, in which reasoned argument appears to have been valued as a means of attaining truth and conviction, and a comprehensible order of things in the universe was sought to be identified and explained.

Among the last Presocratics was Democritus (*c.* 460–371) from Thracian Abdera. His name, along with that of his teacher Leucippus, is always associated with the doctrine of atomism. Democritus was, in fact, a contemporary of Socrates and outlived him by nearly 20 years. His extensive writings do not survive intact, but more is preserved in fragments, and what are claimed by later writers to be quotations, than from any earlier philosopher. Diogenes Laertius, the third century CE doxographer, or writer on the works and ideas of the philosophers, ascribes numerous works in many different fields to Democritus, and his extraordinary breadth of active intellectual interests (including scientific, literary, musical, psychological, mathematical, moral and others) was probably unparalleled before Aristotle.

Two areas above all should be noted. As an atomist, Democritus argued against the position of Parmenides and the Eleatics, whose doctrine of the unity and motionlessness of reality rested on the conviction that empty space, or 'nothingness' does not exist. With an insight that obviously prefigures much more recent theories, now backed up by experimental observation, atomism saw the real world as composed of tiny indivisible (*atomos*) material elements, which are separated by equally existent void space and collide and connect with each other to form larger physical entities. Perception of these composite elements through sight is fallible and uncertain, and touch is a surer sense but, like the Eleatics, though for different reasons, the atomists drew the distinction between knowledge and (deceptive) belief as obtained through the senses. True knowledge, they said, was only of the atoms and space, while our perception of physical entities is fallible and changeable. The distinctions, drawn in different ways, between knowledge and perception, and between appearance and reality, were themes which came to be of the utmost importance and were much debated in the later fifth century.

Democritus apparently wrote much also on ethics. The surviving fragmentary utterances are somewhat aphoristic, and some appear dogmatic; that is, of course, in the nature of exemplary quotations which have probably been removed from their context and from any argumentation that may originally have supported them. Considering the detail and intellectual force with which the atomist doctrine was elaborated (the 'crown of Greek philosophical achievement before Plato' as one modern writer describes it), it is likely that the ethical writings were also grounded in rigorous thought. Occasional, and so far not very convincing, attempts have been made to link the ethics and the atomism. It is tempting to imagine that there was indeed a system of thought which supported both; this would have been a precedent to Plato's application of epistemology (theory of knowledge) to moral questions, which was probably already suggested by his teacher Socrates. Curiously enough, though Aristotle wrote about Democritus and took both his atomism and his ethics seriously, while agreeing with him in neither, Plato makes no mention of him. According to Diogenes Laertius, Democritus did visit Athens as a young man and complained that he was unknown there even to Socrates, whom he claimed to have met. Plato's silence was explained by some as a deliberate attempt to remove a threateningly convincing rival system of thought.

If there was an intellectual Presocratic revolution starting in the sixth century, then a second important wave of new thought must be identified in what is often termed the 'Greek Enlightenment' of Athens in the mid-fifth century. In this period there is a shift of primary focus from matters of cosmology and the nature of the material world to that of the individual and personal role played within the world by its inhabitants. Political and social conditions help to explain the preoccupations of the itinerant teachers known collectively as the sophists, who are normally taken to be among the most characteristic markers of this era. The turning of philosophy towards moral and political concerns was due to them.

The increasing confidence of Athens as a political power and its growth in prosperity after the end of the Persian wars made this city an attractive destination for highly employable educators from all over the Greek world. In the democratic system it was possible for young citizens to rise in influence if they could exercise their powers of persuasion and rhetoric; it was prose rhetoric above all that the sophists taught, though they effectively practised their skills in fields such as politics, ethics, science and literature; the sophist Hippias boldly claimed there was no subject in which he could be wrong-footed. The persuasive use of language in argument (*logos* in a broad sense) was their trade. As a group they have had a generally unfavourable reputation because the towering influence of Socrates and his pupil Plato, in this respect followed by Aristotle, rests partly on their contempt for the concerns and methods of the sophists. But the word 'sophist' (Greek *sophistēs*), originally meaning a 'practitioner of wisdom, (*sophia*), but coming to mean nothing very different from 'professional teacher', was not always the negative term it became through Plato's hostility to these rhetoricians, leading to our term 'sophistry' in the sense of 'fallacious quibbling'. It can be argued that Socrates himself, though clearly distinguished in important ways from the sophists, with whom he apparently engaged in discussion and debate, was able to make his unique contribution partly thanks to them, for it was in his arguments with them and opposition to their principles and methods that he expressed some of his most seminal and celebrated ideas.

Once again, as with all the philosophers before Plato, we are dealing with a small number of surviving primary sources; the most famous names are most familiar from the philosophical dialogues in which Plato pits them against Socrates – Gorgias of Leontini in Sicily (*c.* 480–380), Protagoras of Abdera in Thrace (*c.* 490–20) and Hippias of Elis in the Peloponnese (a later contemporary of Protagoras). But citations and references to these and others are found in a number of other authors; nearer to their time were Xenophon and (in the next generation) Aristotle, and later authorities include philosophers, historians, physicians and bibliographers.

Generally, the sophists stressed human autonomy, subjectivity, the absence of universal truth and the importance of personal experience in reaching judgements. The observation that different cultures followed different customs had invited the conclusion that no one set of customs was more valid than any other. But certain characteristics and tendencies in mankind are apparently innate. An important old distinction that became particularly popular in the fifth century was that between *physis* (nature) and *nomos* ('law' or 'convention'). The distinction was argued by some sophists in matters of morality to support the idea of relativism. But it could also be used in other fields, for instance in language, in the debate as to whether words naturally and necessarily represent the ideas they stand for or are essentially conventional and therefore in a sense arbitrary, and in political issues such as the definition of justice or the legitimacy of one kind of government over another.

The value of being competent to argue one's own case obviously follows from these principles; Protagoras was famous for claiming that there were two opposing arguments about everything. The influence of such thinking is to be seen in the closely argued debates in some of the famous tragedies of Euripides and Sophocles, in the various sorts of arguments in both Herodotus and Thucydides, in forensic rhetoric used by orators like Antiphon (*c.* 480–11) and Isocrates (436–338), and even in the method of explanation and inference used in the scientific and medical writings, known as the Hippocratic corpus, starting in the later fifth century.

Of Protagoras, clearly an immensely influential figure who was a friend of Pericles and was entrusted by him with important duties, we have only two surviving original utterances. One is the beginning of an essay *On the Gods*, in which is the famous 'Man is the measure of all things, of things that are that they are, and of things that are not that they are not'. Lacking the full context, we cannot be sure of the precise meaning, but it can be assumed that Protagoras was at least arguing for the subjectivity of knowledge and perception, and thereby supporting the crucial role of rhetoric in influencing others and persuading them to follow one's (subjective) judgements.

Gorgias was the author of a treatise *On What Is Not*, a philosophical argument in logic and language that survives in two summary versions, and he offers us an intriguing glimpse into his florid style and method in surviving specimens of speeches, such as the brief but complete *Encomium of Helen*; this is an exercise of defence of Helen of Troy against the conventional accusations on the grounds that, acting as the result of some compulsion – fate, or the will of the gods, or irresistible persuasion by another, overpowering passion – she was not to be blamed for causing the Trojan War. A free-thinking, though perhaps cynical, questioning of traditional morality is thus implied. In his closing words to this little essay Gorgias notes that through *logos* (surely meaning here both 'verbal discourse' and 'argument') he has fulfilled his undertaking at the beginning of his *logos* (speech) and has not only exonerated Helen of the unjust blame she has traditionally suffered, but also provided himself a *paignion* (playful diversion).

Other exercises are seen in a surviving anonymous treatise *Dissoi Logoi* ('Double Arguments'), a collection of short essays each illustrating opposing or controversial but tenable positions on moral and epistemological subjects. The treatise is of doubtful date, but possibly comes from the late fifth century.

The arguments as such are not all impressive or even very coherent, but the very existence of the work is of interest as illustrative of the kind of practice attacked and caricatured in the comedy *Clouds* by Aristophanes in the 420s. Relativism, and the subordination of truth and moral values to mere clever argument, are depicted by the playwright to be ruining young Athenian minds. The specific personal target is 'Socrates' or rather a character of that name who is a satirical caricature of the real person. Aristophanes' charge could well be meant only humorously; it is possible that he and Socrates actually knew and respected each other. But at the same time it may reflect the unease of conservatives in Athenian society at what they would have seen as collapsing moral standards – a particularly sensitive issue at a time when Athens had to face the threat of losing the war with Sparta, and when democracy and a more authoritarian oligarchy were serious rivals as political options.

Further reading

Original Greek sources for the Presocratics are most conveniently gathered and annotated with translations for English readers in Kirk *et al.* (1983). A useful introductory selection of texts with notes is Lesher (1999). Selected translated texts with introduction and notes are in Barnes (2002) and Waterfield (2000). An excellent first introduction to ancient philosophy is Cornford (1932). Good general introductions to the Presocratics are Hussey (1972) and Barnes (1982); see now Osborne, C. (2004) and Warren (2007). There is also a *Cambridge Companion to Early Greek Philosophy* (Long, 1999) that is worth consulting, as is Wright (2009). For a magisterial work on why the intellectual revolution occurred in Greece, and occurred in the way that it did, see Lloyd (1979) (see also Gill, 1995; Goldhill, 2002). Selected sophistic writings can be found in Waterfield (2000); for the sophists, Guthrie (1971b) and Kerferd (1981) are good introductions.

PLATO AND ARISTOTLE

Jonathan Katz

An account of philosophical literature should deal primarily with authors and their philosophical works. For Socrates, arguably the most famous philosopher in the history of western thought, this is impossible, as he did not write. We meet him rather as a character in the literature, and we cautiously piece together the evidence of different sources if we wish to picture him as an independent figure. Our major source is Socrates' own disciple Plato. Other sources are his contemporary and close acquaintance the historian and general Xenophon (whose interests were more anecdotal and less philosophical than Plato's), Plato's pupil Aristotle (who offers, presumably on the basis of close acquaintance with Plato, a brief but important delineation of the difference between the views of Socrates and Plato), and a few surviving fragments of the writings of Socrates' followers such as Aeschines of Sphettus (who wrote Socratic dialogues that were considered faithful to the character of his teacher). The 'Socratic question' is concerned with who and what was the real Socrates; it remains largely elusive, and his philosophy is, in the meantime, to be read cautiously through the 'Socratic' parts of Plato's published works.

If we take Plato's and Xenophon's accounts seriously, we may say that Aristophanes' portrayal of Socrates in *Clouds* was a grotesque distortion. In this comic portrayal Socrates takes fees for teaching dishonest techniques of argument, and he concerns himself with arcane questions about the physical world. The Socrates of Plato and Xenophon is concerned only with human and moral issues, and if he did once as a young man have an interest in physical questions he soon came to regard them as sterile and unsatisfactory. From Aristotle on, Socrates was seen as the crucial figure in the history of thought for having brought philosophy, as Cicero later put it, 'from heaven to earth'. In Plato's dialogue *Phaedo* Socrates, as an old man on the eve of his death, recalls the initial excitement and subsequent frustration he felt as a youngster who studied the works of Anaxagoras, especially in relation to the ordering of the world through the guiding power of *nous* ('mind'), only to find that Anaxagoras' explanation was limited to physical, material origins and stopped short of 'reasons' in the sense of *why* things should be or become what they are. The moral and intellectual integrity of Socrates is taken for granted by Plato and Xenophon; he took no fees, and even claimed to have no 'teaching' for which he could charge anyway. His relentless questioning and refutation of the arguments or assertions of others was aimed at the pursuit of truth and the betterment of the moral self. Perhaps most famously of all he taught that virtue and knowledge are the same, and that accordingly no one willingly acts wrongly.

Taking Socrates, then, as we find him in the available sources, we have just a few essential and generally uncontested facts. He was born near Athens in 469, the son of a sculptor and a midwife. He left Athens only for military service in the early part of the Peloponnesian War. He attained fame, and incurred both love and hostility, for his acute and challenging exchanges and debates with alleged experts, including sophists, and for encouraging the young to question fundamental assumptions (including political convictions) and to think boldly and independently. In the last phase of the war (in 406) he courageously stood out against majority demand for an illegal procedure in prosecuting jointly, rather than separately, eight generals, and during the suspension of democracy and rule of the Thirty after the end of the war (in 404–3) he refused to obey an order to arrest a condemned citizen. In 399, the restored democratic regime put him on trial for not recognizing the gods of the state, for introducing new divinities, and for corrupting the youth. He chose to conduct his own defence in a boldly provocative style, was convicted and sentenced to death, and refused to escape when the opportunity was provided, preferring to remain true to his principle that the laws of the state must be observed. His argument for so doing is powerfully presented in Plato's (probably early) dialogue *Crito*, which together with the *Phaedo* gives a deeply moving impression of Socrates' final conversations with his friends. Still, regarding his attitude towards the law, we cannot ignore the contrast between the *Crito* and his more bullish stance in Plato's *Apology*, where he reminds his hearers that he was more than capable of resisting unreasonable authority. It is a thought-provoking exercise to try to reconcile, or somehow explain, the two.

Xenophon (*c.* 430–355) left four Socratic works among his voluminous writings. The *Symposium* is an account of a dinner party which Socrates attended in 421, written after, and probably under the influence of, Plato's work of the same title. It portrays Socrates the man, a social being, and in a generally light-hearted context offers a serious speech supposedly delivered by him in praise of spiritual (a superior to physical) love. The *Oeconomicus*, a treatise on estate-management, has the form of a dialogue between the philosopher and an acquaintance Ischomachus. Though mainly representing Xenophon's own ideas rather than Socrates', there are some telling moments at which the method of argument and choices of imagery appear to accord with what Plato tells us of his teacher, including a suggestion of the famous 'Socratic irony' ('I know that I know nothing') and the idea that learning is recollection (see Guthrie, 1971a: 15ff.). The *Apology of Socrates* (*Apologia Sōkratous*) is a short work on the trial, both its circumstances and the content of some of the defence. The *Apomnēmoneumata* ('Reminiscences'), four books of recollections of Socrates, are usually known under the Latin translated title *Memorabilia*. Most are in the form of conversations between Socrates and his acquaintances, including Xenophon himself, about religion, the good life, friendship, education, justice and other matters; the variety of topics is noteworthy, as is the social and educational range of the characters with whom Socrates is shown to have conversed. In this work Xenophon's stated aim is to show the injustice of the accusations he faced, and the benefit he brought to society.

Plato (*c.* 427–347), like Xenophon, clearly aimed to refute the charges against Socrates and reinstate him as a figure of both brilliance and integrity. Through the Socratic dialogues of Plato there is a sustained, if complex, portrayal of Socrates' intellectual preoccupations and his methods of questioning, arguing and probing, and puncturing of cant and pretension. These dialogues form the first phase of the work of one of the great masters of European prose writing; Plato was also the initiator of much of what is now regarded as western philosophy, though he must also be seen as inheriting some of the achievements of his successors, especially Parmenides and his Eleatic followers.

Born into an aristocratic family in Athens during the early years of the Peloponnesian War, Plato came under Socrates' influence as a young man, and was thus approaching 30 when Socrates was executed. Details of his life beyond this are uncertain, and have been much disputed. If we accept some traditional accounts, and if one of the letters (the seventh) attributed to him is at least substantially genuine as a brief autobiography, when Socrates died Plato left Athens in disillusion and travelled, perhaps to Egypt and more certainly to Sicily and Magna Graecia where he was to some extent influenced by Pythagorean circles. Returning to Athens in his early forties he founded a school, the Academy (named after the grove, sacred to the hero Academus, in which it was placed), dedicated to philosophical discussion and teaching. On later visits to Sicily he was invited to attempt to put some of his ideas to practical use in tutoring the young ruler Dionysius II, but he failed in this endeavour and returned to Athens and the Academy for the last 15 years of his life. The legacy of the Academy, where Plato was said to have taught also some doctrines not found in his writings, survived under his successors until the mid-first century, and a Neoplatonic school in Athens is said finally to have been closed down by the emperor Justinian in 529 CE.

It is believed that we have all of Plato's writings – the first major surviving corpus of philosophical works in western literature, and a remarkable contrast to the fragmentary nature of everything that survives from before his time. The works cover a great range of philosophical issues in epistemology, metaphysics (problems in the nature of 'being'), ethics, politics and language. They are mostly in the form of dialogues, a lively dramatic medium which reflects Plato's conviction, presumably derived at least partly from his experience of Socrates' method, that philosophy is most effectively practised through the exercise of conversation, in which minds can work together towards a common purpose. The spoken word, we are told, and not the written, is the proper means to progress. The dialogue *Phaedrus* ends with such an assertion; Socrates gets his young interlocutor to agree that 'dialectic' – the process of collaborative endeavour through discussion – allows questioning and the consequent modification of views and statements, whereas writing is by its nature static and cannot be so questioned. The dialogues are for the most part carefully structured, with dramatic scene-setting, suggestive and 'leading' introductory comments that prepare the reader, sometimes subtly and subliminally, for major topics to come. In some dialogues we start with a number of characters as the *dramatis personae*, but once the argument settles into a serious mode the conversation is normally limited to two of them, typically Socrates and a single interlocutor, at a time.

Plato keeps himself out of the dialogues, preferring to project ideas and arguments through his characters. By this means he achieves a certain open-endedness, for he seems to want his readers to experience, and ponder, the thought processes at first-hand, not merely accepting an argument handed to them on his authority. Sometimes the arguments are incomplete or apparently unsatisfactory, for instance some of those concerning the definition of justice in the first book of the *Republic*, and here it seems likely that Plato knows exactly what he is doing and is encouraging us to read critically, evaluate and judge the fairness of statements and rebuttals. But above all he stresses, often explicitly, that dialectical progress is quite different from *eristic* – combative verbal dispute of the kind championed by some sophists and aimed at simply winning, by fair means or otherwise, an argument. Philosophy is the common pursuit of truth, eristic debate the pursuit of victory for one side. The medium of the dialogue is particularly well suited to the treatment of topics in Plato's earlier works, while in some of the later writings it seems to have become more of a convention, and is used more to break or punctuate the monotony of longer passages of argument.

There is some irony in the fact that Plato, a master stylist of Greek prose, at times allows his Socrates to appear fundamentally suspicious of the use of style at all. In his *Gorgias*, a dialogue in which the rhetorician and his associates are challenged by Socrates first on the use of rhetoric itself and then on some crucial ethical issues that arise, Plato shows himself a highly adept mimic in parodying Gorgias' style, and then has Socrates beg Polus, the hotheaded young student of Gorgias, to spare him the eloquent long speech and indulge rather in the dialectical business of question and answer. But some of the most impressive and moving passages in the dialogues, and increasingly so in later works, are in fact in speeches by Socrates himself, which come either as responses to clarifications achieved through this process of dialectic, or else represent a more discursive summation and extension of these clarifications. In the *Symposium*, Plato's account of a banquet supposedly held at the house of the poet Agathon, each of the guests delivers a speech, markedly individual in character and style, on the subject of love, its nature and definition and status. In this context Socrates, here (as often) disclaiming independent knowledge on his own part, recalls how a holy woman named Diotima taught him that love is essentially the desire for wisdom and beauty, and that is beauty itself, which transcends any particular body or person or object that is the bearer of beauty. The initiate to her understanding of love gradually ascends a ladder, passing through and beyond the stage of erotic and physical attraction and into an appreciation of Beauty as such. This, then, is what should be meant by Platonic love – not, indeed, a disavowal of erotic desire but a way to realization of a transcendent quality.

Plato's writings are commonly placed in three groups or periods, though there is still disagreement over where some of the individual dialogues fit in. Such consensus as there is rests partly on understandings, or interpretations, of Plato's development as a thinker, and partly on grounds of stylistic development in his language. In the first group, in addition to the *Crito* (see above) and possibly *Phaedo* (on the immortality of the soul, a work which may, on grounds of subject and interest, be better assigned to the second group), there are some dozen other early Socratic dialogues, including the *Apology*, a speech which Plato invites us to believe was given by Socrates in his own defence when on trial before the Athenian Assembly. Plato was present at the trial, and here records, perhaps with imaginative elaboration, Socrates' eloquent answer to the charges of impiety and corruption of youth – the story of his search for a wiser man than himself, and his conclusion that his only knowledge consisted in his acknowledgement of his ignorance. Here also is his famous proposal that he be rewarded, not punished, by the state.

In many of the dialogues in this first group – such works as the *Laches* (on courage), *Lysis* (on friendship and love) and *Euthyphro* (on piety) – ethical problems are raised through the pursuit of definition of moral terms. Being 'aporetic' (coming to an 'impasse' – *aporia* – and stopping well short of proposing a definitive solution), their value is in the exposing of the problem itself. Here we see in action the Socratic technique of *elenchus*, a refutation of an answer to a question, in order to show the ignorance of the one who offers this answer and the need for another approach. The *Meno*, a dialogue on whether *aretē* (virtue) is a thing that can be taught, and the *Protagoras*, a vigorous debate with the sophist on the nature of virtue and how it is to be acquired, are also generally assigned to this group, as is the first part of the *Republic*, afterwards incorporated as the first book of that later work.

The second group of works contains, in addition to the *Symposium*, some of the greatest and philosophically weightiest dialogues – the major part of the *Republic* (Plato's monumental treatise on the nature and management of the ideal political state, starting from a consideration of the definition of justice), *Parmenides* (examining the Eleatic philosophers' views on the unity of reality), and *Theaetetus* (the major work on the philosophy of knowledge and perception). In this group also are *Phaedrus* (on the use and validity of rhetoric) and perhaps the *Cratylus* (on language, its origin, and how it relates to reality), but the latter is considered by some scholars to be a later work.

In this second group we also see the development of Plato's theory of 'Forms'. 'Theory' suggests, wrongly, that there is a single systematic doctrine to be teased out of the texts, whereas Plato's perceptions and uses of the idea seem to vary considerably. It is, however, an assumption fundamental to some of the dialogues that what the philosopher aims to grasp is the true reality that lies behind the diversity of the material world which we experience through the senses. Beyond the reach of the senses is the true 'form' of Beauty itself (the aim of the philosophical lover of the *Symposium*), or Courage itself, or Piety, attainable ultimately only through the intellect. The *Republic* presents the ideal state as one governed and led by philosopher-rulers who have been through the demanding educational and spiritual process leading to an understanding of the only true objects of 'knowledge' as opposed to sensory perceptions and beliefs. Here Plato develops, with supreme literary genius, the famous images of the nature of the soul and its cognitive capabilities, the hierarchical divided line of reality, with the illusory sensory world at one end and the truly intelligible world at the other, and the great allegory of the Cave, in which unenlightened mankind is trapped in a world of illusion and imperfect understanding, but out of which there is, through philosophical training, a way to the outside world up above, and ultimately to true realization of the way things are, and the ability to contemplate, without being dazzled, the sun as source of true illumination, the form of the Good.

It is in the *Theaetetus* (especially sections 148 to 151, but intriguingly extended beyond this passage) that one of the most beautiful and evocative of Socratic images is elaborated. Here Socrates, the son of the midwife, presents himself as a 'midwife' of men, preparing and attending the 'birth' of wisdom and ideas from others, while being incapable himself of giving birth because he has no wisdom of his own. In this case the midwife ministers to the brilliant young mathematician Theaetetus in 'delivering' insights into the nature of knowledge.

In the third group are some challenging works which bring together philosophical issues of epistemology with ethics, education and problems of existence and reality. There appear here some subjects which had not engaged Plato's interest in his middle phase. In the *Timaeus* a philosopher of that name gives an account of the origin and nature of the created universe, its relation to higher reality, and the status of living creatures within it. Plato has here returned, in his own way, to cosmology, a subject which he rejected in its more physical, material guise in the *Phaedo*, and introduces the image of the 'demiurge', the divine craftsman as creator of the material world. The *Sophist*, a subtle and humorously ironic analysis of how a 'sophist' must be defined, elaborately uses the method of collection and division to locate the sophist as a properly existent being – a necessary aim if he is to be pinned down and effectively opposed and refuted. The method of first collecting together the multiple members of a class or genus and then dividing the class into rational sub-classes and constituent members, here enables a gradual and rigorous classificatory definition of the sophist as a particular kind of mercenary and manipulative teacher and trickster. The *Politicus* ('Statesman') also uses this method to define the politician and his art and to explore how the pursuit of politics relates to judgement (*phronēsis*) and expertise (*technē*). There was probably to be a third work defining the Philosopher, but we are left to imagine, from what Plato did write, what would have been the distinctions between this category and the others.

The *Philebus* and *Laws* are further works in this final group. The *Philebus* argues the rival claims of the pursuit of pleasure and that of knowledge as the essential ingredient in the good life, concluding that the true Good transcends them both and governs the fruitful mixing of the two. The *Laws*, a massive and somewhat forbidding work which may have been left unfinished by Plato at the end of his life, relates in subject matter to the *Republic*. Its dramatic setting is Crete, and an Athenian stranger (Socrates does not figure here) converses, while on a pilgrimage, with a Spartan and a Cretan about what laws are desirable in a state, and how they should be drawn up and applied as a systematic and coherent code. Here we see at the end of Plato's career a more dogmatic, perhaps normative, approach to ethics and politics.

The dialogue form remains, but has tended to become less 'dramatic' in the later works, and the probably unrevised prose of the *Laws* can be ponderous. In its content, however, the work is revealing as the product of the author's long experience of life and ideas.

A broad chronology of the dialogues of Plato

Early period (up to c. 380)	Middle period (c. 380–60)	Late period (c. 360–47)
Apology	Phaedo	Sophist
Charmides	Republic books 2–10	Statesman
Crito	Symposium	Philebus
Euthydemus	Parmenides	Timaeus
Euthyphro	Theaetetus	Critias
Gorgias	Phaedrus	Laws
Hippias Major		
Hippias Minor		
Ion		
Laches		
Lysis		
Protagoras		
Republic Book 1		
Cratylus		
Menexenus		
Meno		

There are signs in the later phases of Plato's writings that his enthusiasm for the doctrine(s) of Forms may have been challenged, and perhaps even to some extent undermined. His most distinguished pupil, Aristotle, later rejected, on logical grounds, his teacher's separation of the Forms from material reality as independent (indeed the only true) entities, claiming to know that Socrates himself had spoken in terms of Forms but it was Plato who had developed the theory of their separate world. This was not the only matter in which Aristotle went his own way, but he would have willingly admitted his indebtedness to Plato, and his work in many areas must be seen as a brilliant continuation of, and advance on, the traditions not only led by Socrates and Plato but originating with the Presocratics. It is clear from his own words that he insisted on the value of learning from predecessors, and he probably saw his own scientific advances as part of a continuum. As a brilliant young student of Plato it is even possible that he influenced his teacher, but he did not succeed him as leader of the Academy, though he remained there as long as Plato lived.

Aristotle was born in Stagira in northern Greece (Chalcidice) in 384. He was the son of a physician at the Macedonian royal court, who died while Aristotle was a child. His guardians sent him to Athens to join the Academy at the age of 17 in 367. After 20 productive years of studying, teaching and writing, he left in 347 and travelled to Asia Minor with another disciple of the Academy. In Assos, in the southern Troad, he worked for a few years in a group of former members and associates of the Academy. He then moved for a short while to Mytilene on the island of Lesbos. During this time he probably built practically on some of the scientific interests in biology, natural history and classification that he may have developed at the Academy and which stayed with him throughout his life. In 343 he was invited back to Macedon by Philip II to tutor his young son, who became Alexander the Great. In 335 he returned to Athens and opened his own school at the grove of the Lyceum; this school of philosophers became known as the *Peripatetics*, so called because of Aristotle's habit of 'walking about' on the *peripatos* (a covered walkway) as he conversed with pupils. He created the first substantial library, large enough to require a classification system that became a model for the organization of the Alexandrian Library of the Egyptian kings. When Alexander died in 323 there was anti-Macedonian feeling in Athens; Aristotle was caught up in this, and retired to Chalcis on the island of Euboea, where he died in 322.

The relation of literary to philosophical qualities in Aristotle is very different from that in Plato's work, and it is hard to assess him as a great writer. This is not because he never wrote creatively – indeed in antiquity he was highly praised for his skills – but because the enormous corpus of his works which have survived, in a bafflingly huge range of disciplines, represents a different kind of writing. A very early distinction was made between his *exoteric* writings, intended to be 'accessible', and the *esoteric*, which were for specialists and needed close studious attention and, in most cases, supporting comment or elucidation.

The *exoteric* category included dialogues in the Platonic style (though apparently including himself as a 'player'), and there were also a substantial treatise *On Philosophy*, some treatises on narrower subjects such as Plato's Forms, and a *Protrepticus*, an invitation to 'turn' to the philosophic life; this last text was particularly popular and influential in antiquity, and Cicero modelled one of his own works on it. The dialogue form had been an imitation of Plato, but Aristotle's preferred form was the prose treatise. What we have, except for small fragments of these works, is all of the *esoteric* category, and often the style is dense, compressed, even elliptical, suggesting notes for lectures rather than self-sufficient continuous discourse. To offset the loss of the *exoteric*, on the other hand, Aristotle's technical work on literature and aesthetics in the form of his treatises on rhetoric, and even more so his masterpiece the *Poetics*, has been among his most influential, and has inspired confidence in him as a literary thinker of distinction and of the highest importance.

While Plato had been predominantly concerned with higher reality – abstractions, Forms, principles beyond or above the material world experienced by the senses – Aristotle came to a quite different standpoint, which governed his interests and his eventual turning away from Platonism. For Aristotle the starting point is the world around us. The difference between the two philosophers is famously represented in Raphael's Vatican painting, the *School of Athens*, in which Plato points up to the sky and Aristotle has his hand down towards the earth. Plato, it might be said, at least in his later work brought philosophy from earth to heaven. For Aristotle, the 'here and now' of the world, including the views and theories which have been formed about it, are to be welcomed and thoroughly investigated, understood and classified. That said, it is equally clear that the methods of systematic thought encouraged by Plato must have given impetus to Aristotle's own practice, however independent his priorities and focus were to become.

Aristotle seems to embody the principle he suggests at the beginning of his work now called the *Metaphysics*:

> All men by nature desire knowledge. And this can be seen in the pleasure we take in our senses; even aside from their usefulness they are loved for themselves; and above all others the sense of sight. For it is not only when we wish to act, but also when we do not intend to do anything, that we value seeing above everything. This is because sight, more than any other of the senses, makes us clearly aware of the many differences between things.

Observation, then, and analysis of what we see, are primary.

Knowledge itself is observed and analysed, and the analysis of knowledge and its various fields becomes the intellectual map of Aristotle's works. The arrangement of his *oeuvre* now commonly used is due to the early nineteenth-century edition of the German scholar Immanuel Bekker, but its roots may be in the ordering of a collection put together by early editorial hands in the first century. Broad divisions are under the headings *Organon* ('instrument' of learning, i.e. methods of reasoning, or logic), natural sciences (including physics, biology, zoology and psychology), *Metaphysics* (a post-Aristotelian term, used by the editors simply to mean what was placed by the editors 'after the Physics', for what he himself called 'First Philosophy', namely treatises dealing with the nature of being and reality), moral, political philosophy and aesthetics (ethics and political principles being considered closely related by Aristotle, as human beings are essentially members of society and it is in the context of society that ethical virtues are acted on).

The influence of Aristotle was long felt in most of these major areas, and he remains one of the most important figures in the history of European thought. Among the subjects of the *Organon* are works exploring the very principles of reasoning, and it was Aristotle who identified, and first formulated, the structure of arguments – logic itself – introducing the syllogism and studying, in his works *Prior* and *Posterior Analytics*, the nature of valid reasoning and its procedures and its application in the sciences so as to deliver properly based understanding. The doctrine of the 'Four Causes' (Material, Formal, Efficient or Moving, and Final) is developed in the context of the sciences to explain change, the nature and status of substance, and also ways in which we understand, and should classify, occurrences involving consequence. He rejected Plato's independently existing Forms in favour of a concept of the essence, the fundamental nature of things which inheres in them and to which they ultimately tend. In ethics Aristotle, like other Greeks, was a 'eudaemonist', identifying the good that we aim for as *eudaimōnia*, 'happiness'; but this itself has to be defined, and his *eudaimōnia* is different from mere pleasure and gratification and is rather found in contemplation, namely the contemplation of truth through the appropriate activity of the intellect. His aesthetic theories in the *Poetics* included his famous principles of *mimēsis* (imitation) and *catharsis* ('cleansing'), disputed in their meaning but productive of much later investigation of art and literature in terms that blend psychology, morality and structural analysis of genre and works.

In Hellenistic times Athens retained its central importance for philosophy. The Academy passed into the hands of 'Sceptics' under Arcesilaus of Pitane (*c.* 316–242). On the basis of the inconsistency of sense perceptions, sceptics denied the possibility of knowledge, and consequently of judgement. Our major source for their writings and doctrines is the later philosopher and physician Sextus Empiricus (second century CE). Arcesilaus had previously been a pupil of Theophrastus (*c.* 371–287), Aristotle's chosen successor as head of the Lyceum, a scholar and thinker of wide interests in sciences, philosophy and the arts but best known for his acutely observed sketches of human types in his *Characters*.

A school of Cynics flourished for a while in the third century; these followers of Diogenes of Sinope (who famously expressed his contempt for social conventions), and more distantly of Socrates' pupil and friend Antisthenes (*c.* 445–360), stressed the sufficiency of virtue for human happiness. Their contribution to literature was most importantly in socially critical satirical writing which strongly influenced the 'Menippean Satire' of the Roman author Varro (116–27) and the Greek satirical dialogues and other works of Lucian (second century CE).

The major Hellenistic schools of Epicureanism and stoicism applied, in different and opposed ways, physical doctrines to moral ends; both schools were founded in Athens at the end of the fourth century, and both were centrally interested in the question of how to live well. Epicureanism, founded by Epicurus and later eloquently transmitted to Roman readers by the poet Lucretius (our principle source for understanding the doctrines), used a modified form of the Democritean atomistic theory to argue that the soul is material and disintegrates at death; hence fear of punishment after death is irrational, and death itself should not be feared. A principle aim of philosophy should be the achievement of *ataraxia* – freedom from anxiety. The stoic school, founded by Zeno of Citium, was interested in logic and epistemology, and developed in its long history and several phases an elaborate doctrine of the world as a complex of physical and divine elements, producing an ethical system which gave much thought to man's living in harmony with nature while maintaining a detached independence. Stoic doctrines were attractive to Romans in republican times, and greatly influenced the younger Seneca (first century BE) and the Roman emperor Marcus Aurelius (121–80 CE).

Further reading

Recent scholarship on ancient philosophy is covered in excellent essays and extensive bibliographies in the *Cambridge Companion to Plato* (Kraut, 1992), *Aristotle* (Barnes, 1995) and *Greek and Roman Philosophy* (Sedley, 2003); see also Gill and Pellegrin (2006). There are four works in the *Very Short Introduction* series published by OUP that are useful: Annas (2000) on Ancient Philosophy; Taylor (2000) on Socrates; Annas (2003) on Plato and Barnes (2000) on Aristotle. For a very short introduction (which is a not *A Very Short Introduction*) to Plato by a very good modern philosopher, see Williams (1998); see also Hare (1986). Those who want to read more about Socrates can consult Burnyeat (1994); Guthrie (1971a); Vlastos (1991); about Plato, Kahn (1996); Rowe (1995; 2007); Rutherford (1995); Szlezak (1999); and, most recently, McCoy (2008) and Mason (2010); about Aristotle, Ackrill (1981); Lloyd (1996).

Chapter 7

Alexandria and beyond

Robert Shorrock

All dates in this chapter are BCE unless stated otherwise. Glossary items: *ecphrasis; elegiac couplets; epyllion; hexameter; iambic.*

ALEXANDRIA, GREECE AND ROME

The death of Alexander the Great in 323 brought the grand narrative of Greek hegemony to a sudden and dramatic halt. Alexander's empire was broken apart and slowly refashioned by his former generals into a number of competing power bases, each vying for political and cultural superiority in a contest to be the true successor to Alexander: Antigonus established himself in Macedonia, homeland of Alexander, as ruler; at Pergamum (in Mysia, close to the island of Lesbos) the Attalids came to power; Egypt came under the sway of the dynasty of the Ptolemies who ruled from the city of Alexandria; Seleucus and his descendants dominated Asia from Anatolia to Iran.

It was Alexandria, the city founded by Alexander himself in 331 on the southern shore of the Mediterranean – where his remains were finally laid to rest – that would become the dominant cultural, political and economic force within the Greek world. In many respects, Alexandria resembled a traditional Greek *polis* complete with *ekklēsia* and *boulē* and a citizen body divided into demes. It even had a history that could be traced back to Homer: Pharos, the island at the mouth of the harbour of Alexandria (location of the famous lighthouse) was said to have been the home of Proteus, the old man of the sea with whom Menelaus wrestles in *Odyssey* 4. From the outset of his reign Ptolemy I Sōtēr actively strove to enhance the image of Alexandria as a beacon of Greek culture.

Central to Ptolemy's cultural project was the establishment of the Museum and Library of Alexandria (overseen, it is said, by a former pupil of Aristotle). Ptolemy's plan was quite simply to bring the whole of Greek literature to Alexandria, to recentre the Greek world in the former land of the Pharaohs. A new home was prepared for the Muses of Greece far from the mountain top of Helicon in Boeotia. Book rolls by the thousand were collected from all over the Greek-speaking world. This was a project on an unprecedented scale, with a seemingly inexhaustible budget. According to one celebrated account the 'original' copies of the plays of Aeschylus, Sophocles and Euripides were borrowed from the Athenians on payment of a large sum of money to ensure their safe return. The works were duly copied, but it was the copies that were then returned to Athens and Ptolemy III Euergetēs happily lost his deposit of 15 talents. The story may well be a later fabrication, but it clearly tells something important about how the Library was perceived. At its greatest extent, it is estimated that the Library (which appears to have survived at least until the fire caused by Julius Caesar's attack on the city in 48) contained almost half a million book rolls.

In order to initiate and manage such an ambitious project, an elite community of scholars was recruited. They were accommodated in the Museum and spent their time cataloguing, collecting, commentating on and arguing about the texts that continued to pour into the Library. It was at this point that literary scholarship can be said to have been born: the text of Homer was debated and established by scholars of the Library like Zenodotus and Aristarchus; it was here that Homer was divided up into 24 books and that the *logoi* of Herodotus were divided into nine books, each named after one of the nine Muses; here literary genres were established, the canons of poets and orators were codified, literary biographies were compiled.

Alexandria's fully-funded research facility became a magnet for the foremost intellectuals. Its official librarians – who were also responsible for the education of the royal heir – were some of the most important names in the literary history of the age (the first three librarians were Zenodotus, Apollonius Rhodius and Eratosthenes of Cyrene). The majority of those occupied with the Library were not simply prolific scholars but also active poets. A comparison is sometimes made with Philip Larkin who combined the roles of poet and Hull University librarian. Larkin, however, was a poet who needed to work to earn a living; for the scholars of Alexandria there was not such a sharp divide between their work as poets and as scholars.

The model for the scholar-poet was in fact already established before the creation of the Library and Museum by Philetas of Cos. Philetas was appointed as tutor to the second Ptolemy (Ptolemy II Philadelphus) who was born on the island of Cos; he is said to have been the teacher of the first librarian, Zenodotus. He was the author of a scholarly work on unusual words in Homer but his later reputation is founded on his poetry. Little of his work survives, but his reputation as an elegist endures (his poetry appears to have had a profound influence on Callimachus; he is invoked with reverence by Propertius and Ovid in their own elegies).

The vast holdings of Greek literature that were acquired and preserved in the Library at Alexandria established a clear link and sense of continuity between the Hellenistic present and the classical past. Paradoxically, the accumulation of the literature of classical and archaic Greece also served to underline the distance between past and present. One such point of distance and difference between the Hellenistic and classical worlds was that of performance. Although performance was still an important aspect of Alexandrian culture this was profoundly different from the performances of Greek tragedy in fifth-century Athens or the civic festivals at which bards performed the works of Homer. The traditions of oral poetry that was performed before a vast citizen body had now given way to a more exclusive literary culture, a self-consciously intellectual exercise centred around the court of the all powerful patron. Orality versus literacy, democracy versus monarchy, Greece versus Egypt – the city of the Ptolemies is characterized by a dramatic tension between sameness and difference, tradition and innovation. For all its Greekness, Alexandria remained a profoundly unGreek city.

Even after the fall of the Ptolemies and the transformation of Egypt into a Roman province, Alexandria retained a powerful cultural prestige. Horace memorably declared that 'captured Greece made a captive of her fierce captor and brought culture to rustic Latium' (*Epist.* 2.1.156–7) but it is important to realize the extent to which his understanding of Greece had been shaped not by Athens but by Alexandria. The scholar-poets of Alexandria stand squarely between the worlds of Greece and Rome. It is hardly an exaggeration to say that everything that the Roman world knew about the poetry and literature of Greece derived from the carefully ordered bookstacks of the Library. The Augustan poets read their Homer in editions that were established in Alexandria; they take lessons in literary aesthetics from Callimachus; and they look to the poet-scholars of the Ptolemies for a model of how to produce literature under the shadow of a dominant patron.

Further reading

This era has not received as much critical treatment as it deserves (though there are difficulties with evidence). However, for good introductions, see Malcolm Errington (2008); Shipley (1999); Walbank (1981). There is also Fraser (1972) – which is something of a classic – and Green (1990 and 2007), both on the history and politics of the era.

HELLENISTIC LITERATURE

In the modern canon of Hellenistic poets three names stand out above all others: Callimachus, Apollonius and Theocritus. In different ways they all exemplify the spirit of the age: self-consciously intellectual, boldly innovative and unrepentantly (sometimes almost agressively) difficult.

Callimachus was born in Cyrene (a Greek colony in north Africa) and probably moved to Alexandria as a schoolteacher. From there, under the patronage of Ptolemy II Philadelphus (who ruled from 285 to 246) he made his way to the Museum. Although Callimachus was never appointed as official Museum 'librarian' (a job which often included responsibility for tutoring the king's son), his influence on the cultural and administrative life of the Museum was profound. He is said to have produced over 800 books in both poetry and prose (of which only a tiny fraction has survived). One of Callimachus' most astonishing endeavours was a 120-book catalogue of the whole of Greek literature (or at least that work deemed worthy of the name): the *Pinakes* ('Tables', 'Catalogues'). This catalogue was divided according to genre, with poets listed alphabetically within each section. For each author a brief biography was supplied, followed by a list of works. The opening line of each work was also recorded (a convention used to this day in the bibliographic referencing of manuscripts) along with the number of lines. Most of the biographical snippets that we now have for Greek poets are likely to have been derived from this unparalleled bibliographical resource. In addition to his work on the catalogue, Callimachus also wrote scholarly books on a diverse range of subjects from rivers and fish to foundation myths and lexicography.

Alongside his work as an academic ran his work as a poet. Perhaps the most influential and celebrated of all his poetical works was the *Aetia* ('Origins', 'Causes'). This poem, concerned with the origins (mythical or otherwise) of Greek customs and rituals, was written in elegiac couplets in four books and is likely to have totalled more than 4,000 lines. Books 1 and 2 were published first as a complete poem. It begins with a version of the famous scene of poetic inspiration described at the start of the *Theogony* when the shepherd Hesiod encounters the Muses on Mount Helicon and becomes a poet. The scholar-poet Callimachus arrives on the top of Helicon in a dream and uses the opportunity to interrogate the Muses (who have perfect knowledge of the past, present and future). The question and answer session between the poet and the Muses provides the framework for the first two books. From what can be gleaned from surviving fragments, part of the first book was taken up with the story of the *Argonautica* (material that appears to have been used by Apollonius Rhodius in his own epic account of the voyage of the Argo). The focus of Book 2 was probably a series of episodes relating to the foundation of Greek colonies in Sicily. Books 3 and 4 appear to have been added at a much later point in Callimachus' career, following the accession to the throne of Ptolemy III. The Muses of books 1 and 2 find no place here. Instead, Callimachus draws poetic inspiration from Berenice, Ptolemy's new queen: book 3 begins with an account of a victory in a chariot race at the Nemean games of a team of horses belonging to Berenice; the fourth book ends with the account of the 'lock of Berenice' (famously 'translated' by Catullus as poem 66). This was not just an act of flattery towards the new king – Berenice, like Callimachus, came from the city of Cyrene.

One of the striking features of the *Aetia* is its rejection of traditional narrative form in favour of a relatively brief series of discontinuous episodes.

The challenges presented to the conventions of narrative clearly disconcerted many contemporary readers. The prologue (not original to the *Aetia*, but added when the book was expanded to include books 3 and 4) makes explicit reference to certain unnamed critics of Callimachus who have been muttering about his poetry precisely because 'it is not one continuous poem'. These same critics also attacked the length of his poetry and the fact that it is not written about conventional (epic) subjects such as kings and heroes.

Callimachus uses the prologue as a platform for a (typically discursive) presentation of his own poetic credo. The poet is to keep off the beaten track, to drive the chariot of poetry on narrow and unfamiliar paths. Callimachus' words have been readily interpreted as a self-conscious reaction against traditional poetic forms, most especially the Homeric-style epic (long in extent, short in substance). When Callimachus says that, 'it is not my place to thunder, but that of Zeus', it is hard not to think that he is distancing himself from the 'thunder' of epic poetry. His aim (to pick up another of his images) is to sing like a cicada, not bray like a donkey. Poetry, he goes on to say, should not be judged in terms of its length, but in terms of its artistic merit (*technē*). In other words, quality is more important than quantity. He gives further illustration to his point by relating an encounter with Apollo, the god of poetry (another replay of Hesiod's encounter with the Muses on Mount Helicon) who tells him to keep his victim fat, but the Muse slender.

Callimachus' aesthetic preference for novelty does not mean that he steers away from conventional poetic genres. Rather, he chooses to approach traditional material in an untraditional way. He tackles the epic genre head on in his hexameter poem, the *Hecale*. The story of Theseus and his attempt to tame the bull of Marathon is promising material for a conventional epic poem but what Callimachus provides is far from conventional. Theseus is eclipsed within the poem by an old woman Hecale who offers hospitality to the hero after a sudden rainstorm. The prototype for this scene of rustic hospitality is clearly recognizable in the *Odyssey* when the herdsman Eumaeus welcomes the disguised Odysseus, but whereas the Eumaeus scene forms just one of many episodes in the *Odyssey*, the hospitality of Hecale dominates Callimachus' epic. Released from the demands of a grand narrative that sweeps the epic reader along in eager anticipation of the next scene, attention is turned onto the ordinary and overlooked aspects of the story and the simple rustic hospitality offered by an old woman. As with the *Aetia*, the story is more than *just* a story. When Theseus returns to the hut following his victory over the Marathonian bull he finds that Hecale has died and in her memory he creates an Attic deme that bears her name and founds a sanctuary to Zeus Hecaleius.

Much as the Ptolemies had attempted to replicate the cultural experience of Greece in Alexandria, producing something that was both familiar and yet profoundly different, so Callimachus' engagement with traditional Greek literary forms exhibits the same tension between tradition and innovation and transformed them into something quite different. Elegiac poetry had never before been pressed into such serious service as it was in the *Aetia*, nor had epic poetry ever looked quite like the *Hecale*. The same dialectic between similarity and difference was clearly in evidence throughout Callimachus' *Hymns*. Six Hymns survive, clearly recalling the longstanding tradition of the Homeric Hymns which turn the spotlight onto a variety of gods in the Greek pantheon: Zeus (1), Apollo (2), Artemis (3), Delos (4), Athena (5), Demeter (6). Once again we have a demonstration of the way that Callimachus takes familiar material in new and often startling directions. Hymn 1 to Zeus (probably written in the 280s at the start of Ptolemy Philadelphus' reign and early on in the Alexandrian career of Callimachus) provides an opportunity to exploit connections between Ptolemy and the king of the Gods (coins of the early Ptolemies display the eagle of Zeus holding a thunderbolt on one side with the head of the ruling Ptolemy on the other); the Hymn to Athena takes the genre in a new direction on account of its rejection of the traditional hexameter form in favour of (doric) elegiacs.

A series of 13 *Iambi* further serve to illustrate Callimachus' seemingly inexhaustible capacity for innovation and variety. Written in a number of different iambic metres these poems engage provocatively with the tradition of invective poetry that looks back to Archilochus. Nor is that the end: numerous epigrams have been preserved in the *Greek Anthology* within the selection of Meleager, on a range of traditional themes from erotic to sepulchral.

Apollonius Rhodius was the second of the royal librarians (*c.* 270–45) appointed to oversee the running of the Museum (in succession to Zenodotus) and tutor to the future Ptolemy III Euergetēs. Though born in Alexandria, his epithet 'the Rhodian' presumably relates to a period of his life spent on the island of Rhodes or perhaps even to a family connection, but we have nothing to go on beyond ancient biographical speculation. Like so many of the intellectual community that flourished in Alexandria under the Ptolemies, Apollonius appears to have moved effortlessly between the worlds of scholarship and literature. In addition to a prose treatise written in response to the work of Zenodotus on the text of Homer, he produced epigrams and a number of poems on the foundation of cities (including both Alexandria and Rhodes). He is most famous, however, for his extant *Argonautica*: a mythological epic concerning the voyage of the Argo, the world's first ever ship.

The journey of the Argo was a story already known to Homer and probably formed a part of the original epic cycle; aspects of the story would have been very familiar from the *Medea* of Euripides and other tragedies. It is a story full of magic, darkness and despair. Book 1 begins with the catalogue of the Argonauts and their departure from Iolchus in northern Greece bound for the mysterious land of Colchis beyond the eastern shore of the Black Sea. The Argonauts advance through the Clashing Rocks and spend time with the formidable Lemnian women; they are initiated into the mysteries on Samothrace and manage to lose Heracles (who disappears in search of his young lover Hylas who has been abducted by water nymphs). In book 2 the

Argonauts journey as far as Bithynia where they liberate the blind Phineus from the foul and polluting assaults of the bird-like Harpies. Phineus gives them prophetic advice about the second stage of their journey and they proceed up the river Phasis to Colchis, via an encounter with the terrifying Stymphalian birds. Book 3 begins with a new proem (addressed to Erato as the muse of love) and describes how Jason achieves the aim of the mission to capture the golden fleece with the help of the king's own daughter Medea who uses her dark magic to help Jason yoke fire-breathing bulls, sow dragon's teeth and kill the armed men who spring from the ground. The final book sees the escape of Jason and the Argonauts with Medea in tow. In order to frustrate the pursuit of the Colchians, Medea's brother Apsyrtus is lured into a trap and cast into the sea in pieces so that the Colchians have to stop to pick up his remains. The Argo next finds itself in the territory of the *Odyssey* and we meet Circe (Medea's aunt), Alcinous and Arete the king and queen of the Phaeacians (on the island of Corcyra/Corfu); in a final adventure before landfall at Aegina, Medea's powerful magic destroys the bronze giant Talos on the island of Crete.

According to the biographical tradition Apollonius had been a pupil of Callimachus, but a quarrel had taken place between them. It has been suggested that the two poets fell out over the *Argonautica*, a poem that appears to be everything that the *Aetia* is not: a continuous Homeric-style narrative in many thousands of verses. Such a hypothesis is, however, hard to defend. Apollonius' poem, for all its traditional narrative trappings, is more closely allied to the poetic principles of Callimachus than is sometimes imagined. Though it is a continuous narrative told over four books, it is also episodic and at just under 6,000 lines it is probably no longer than Callimachus' own four-book *Aetia*. In keeping with the principles of Callimachean poetry this is no derivative or formulaic work, but a playful and self-conscious attempt to rewrite Homeric epic for a new Hellenistic present. It should come as no surprise that Apollonius took inspiration from the *Aetia* and that one of Callimachus' *Hymns* shows signs of the influence of Apollonius.

The *Argonautica* exhibits a clear interest in the enlightenment atmosphere of the Hellenistic world in terms of discoveries in science and geography. The return journey from Colchis in book 4 parades the poet's knowledge of geography as the Argonauts sail up the Ister, Eridanus, Rhodanus and into the Ionian Sea. The epic also steers its readers into unfamiliar territory most especially in the concentration on the pathology of love in book 3, where we are given unparalled access to the workings of Medea's mind. Many earlier poets from Homer onwards had portrayed the effects of love, but Apollonius dramatizes the experience of love from the inside out (powerfully reprised by Virgil in his dramatization of Dido in *Aeneid* 4). One of the most distinctive and disturbing aspects of the epic is the fact that this is an epic without any real moral compass. There is no great destiny that drives Jason to Colchis, nor any sense of triumph in his journey home with the darkly powerful Medea. From the very start of the Argonautica Jason emerges as an epic failure – leader of the Argonauts only by default after Heracles had turned down the position for himself. The shadow of failure and weakness stays with Jason throughout the epic. The heroes of Homeric epic have analagous moments of self-doubt, anxiety and failure, but never to the extent that it dominates their characterization. Odysseus used techniques of manipulation and sexual exploitation on his journey back to Ithaca as a means to an end; for Jason such techniques become ends in themselves. For Jason there is neither a Penelope nor a Patroclus to give certainty or direction to his story. Ultimately, the ambivalent characterization of Jason may reflect a broader point about the relationship between the Hellenistic world and the Greek classical past – a sense of anxiety and inferiority that forces poets and heroes alike to engage with the world anew.

Theocritus is the third major figure of Hellenistic poetry. He was born in Syracuse on Sicily in the early third century and was active from the 280s onwards. He appears to have flourished in Alexandria but, unusually for poets of this age, he seems to have had no connection with the academic life of the Museum and Library of Alexandria. Surviving works attributed to Theocritus include only works of poetry: nearly 30 epigrams, a pattern poem in the shape of a flute (an early form of 'concrete poetry') and 30 *Idylls* (of which 22 are regarded as genuine). It is hard to characterize the collection of *Idylls* given the great diversity of subject matter and tone, but the term 'Callimachean' is not inappropriate: this is small-scale experimental poetry – highly allusive and ironic – that treats familiar subjects from unusual angles, elevating themes that might otherwise be deemed to be below the dignity of proper poetry.

Theocritus was credited in antiquity as the inventor of the pastoral (or 'bucolic') genre – poetry that conjured up a world of shepherds, singing contests and goats (famously taken up by Virgil in his *Eclogues*). The poems are mostly short hexameter pieces written in Doric – a Sicilian dialect that would have sounded rustic and jarring to the sophisticated audience of Alexandria. Central to the construction of this illusionistic pastoral word is love. As in the *Argonautica*, however, this is not love as a benign positive force, but as a harsh and painful part of life. In *Idyll* 11 (and also *Id.* 6) we are given a glimpse of the Sicilian Cyclops ('my countryman', says Theocritus) like we have never seen him before – not as the flesh-eating ogre of Homer's *Odyssey*, but as a youth madly in love with a nymph Galatea (11. 9–11): 'he was just now getting a beard around his mouth and temples. He loved not with apples nor with rose nor with ringlets, but with real fury'. Any sympathy we may feel for his predicament is wittily undercut by the fact that, unlike the Cyclops, we have read our Homer and know how the story continues. When, for example, he boasts that he can play the pipes 'like none (*outis*) of the Cyclopes in this place' (*Id.* 11. 38), his words cannot fail to recall the name that Odysseus calls himself during his encounter with Polyphemus: Nobody (*outis*). And there can be no greater irony than when the young Cyclops invites Galatea to burn his one eye 'than which nothing is sweeter to me' (*Id.* 11.53).

Other surviving poems include encomiastic poetry clearly designed to win patronage for his poetry (*Idyll* 16 to Hieron of Syracuse appears to have been less successful than *Idyll* 17 to Ptolemy Philadelphus). Several idylls reprise themes that appear to have been inspired by their treatment in Apollonius – the story of Hylas (*Id.* 13) and the boxing match between Pollux and Amycus (*Id.* 22). The contrast between the world of rustic simplicity and urban sophistication – an implicit feature of so many of Theocritus' poems – is explicitly dramatized in *Idyll* 15 when two Syracusan women provide a gossipy commentary on an Alexandrian festival. The boorish nature of the Syracusan women stands as an ironic counterpart to the self-conscious sophistication of the Syracuse-born poet at the court of Ptolemy. Certainly poetic self-consciousness is a prominent feature elsewhere in the collection: in *Idyll* 1 the description of scenes carved on a wooden bowl has clear implications for the way that the poetry itself is to be viewed (highlighting themes of eroticism, *labor* and *mimēsis*); *Idyll* 7 in part reworks Hesiod's poetic initiation on the top of Mount Helicon and has important implications for our understanding of Theocritus' own poetic programme.

It would be misleading to think of Hellenistic literature only in terms of Callimachus, Apollonius and Theocritus, just as it is misleading to think of fifth-century Athenian tragedy only in terms of Aeschylus, Sophocles and Euripides. For one thing, no mention has been made of prose. This is largely because so little survives. The one exception is the remarkable work of Polybius from the mid-second century whose 40-book history (books 1–5 survive) engages with the rise of Rome from the perspective of a Greek (see 5d). Poetry endured and proliferated in a diversity of forms and metres, at times inspired, ingenious and even incomprehensible. The genres of elegy, epigram, didactic, drama and dithyramb flourished alongside the sophisticated vulgarity of mime. Moschus of Syracuse (his name means 'calf' in Greek) was celebrated as a bucolic poet second only in repute to Theocritus. He is best known today as the author of the *Europa*, a miniature epic (or so-called *epyllion*) in only 166 lines that tells the story of the abduction of Europa by Zeus in the guise of a bull. Even within the brief confines of the narrative, Moschus still finds room for that most self-conscious of poetic devices, the ecphrasis – in this case a 26 line description of the golden casket that Europa took with her to the sea-shore. The poet Aratus (*c.* 315–*c.* 240: born at Soloi in Cilicia, educated in Athens and latterly occupied at the court of the Macedonian king Antigonus at Pella and at the court of Antiochus in Syria) produced the *Phaenomena*, a poem in over 1,000 verses about the constellations of the night sky (based on a prose work by one Eudoxus of Cnidus). The poem was in the tradition of didactic epic, following the model of Hesiod's *Works and Days*). It was an outstanding success and became one of the most popular poems in the history of classical literature. Cicero and Tiberius' nephew Germanicus both found time to produce versions in Latin; the poem was read and imitated by Virgil in his *Georgics*; it was even translated into Arabic. Those looking for patterns in the stars would certainly have appreciated the patterns of Aratus' own Greek text, most particularly the use of the adjective *leptē* (slender) at 783 – a key word for Callimachean poetic 'refinement'. Aratus added his own further refinement by reproducing the word as an acrostic in lines 783–7. Those who tried to use the work as an astronomical manual would, however, have been confronted with its many serious errors; but as an exotic form of poetry it clearly appealed and endured.

Nicander of Colophon (a prolific epic poet and scholar active in the later part of the third century) took didactic epic into the territory of venomous creatures (*Thēriaca*) and remedies for their bites (*Alexipharmaca*). Nicander took his inspiration from prose works of Apollodorus of Alexandria. This was not poetry that could be relied upon as a practical guide to toxicology and zoology, yet there was clearly a readership (including both Virgil and Ovid) which was ready to appreciate the transformation of a technical treatise into literature. Aratus may have produced one of the most popular of all poems from the classical world; perhaps the most obscure and difficult of all poems was produced by Lycophron. The *Alexandra*, written in the wake of the battle of Cynoscephalae in 197/6, is a recitation in iambic trimeters by the prophet-ess Cassandra. It takes a Callimachean fondness for allusion into a new and almost incomprehensible dimension. The witty (if inevitable) sting in the tail of this allusive *tour de force* is Cassandra's declaration after nearly one and a half thousand lines that her prophetic performance has been in vain.

Further reading

For a collection of Hellenistic poetry, see Hopkinson (1988). Generally, see Bing (1988); Easterling (1989); Fantuzzi and Hunter (2004); Gutzwiller (2007); Hutchinson (1988); Zanker (1987). On Apollonius, see Beye (1982); DeForest (1994); Goldhill (1991: chapter 5); Hunter (1993). On Theocritus, see Burton (1995); Goldhill (1991: chapter 4); Gutzwiller (1991); Hunter (1996). On Callimachus, see Cameron (1995); for a commentary on Callimachus' *Hymn to Demeter*, see Hopkinson (1984). On Hellenistic philosophy, see Inwood (1988); Long and Sedley (1987).

Chapter 8

The early republic

THE EARLY REPUBLIC: AN HISTORICAL INTRODUCTION

Terry Edwards

The republic which the early writers experienced had grown up over a period of 250 years through a sequence of, at times, violent events. Meanwhile Rome was being challenged externally by the peoples of central Italy, and it is mark of her resilience and flexibility that she met those challenges successfully.

Traditionally the reigns of the kings ended in 507, and this was followed by what is known as the 'The Struggle of the Orders', between the patricians and the plebeians. The patricians were *patres* (fathers) or senators, selected during the reigns of the kings – an hereditary aristocracy. The plebeians included both urban and rural rich and poor. Plebeians were, however, excluded from the privileges enjoyed by the patricians. In addition, debt had led to effective slavery for many. Political, social and economic oppression of the majority by the minority resulted in series of general strikes (secession – between 494 and 287) in which the plebeians exacted concessions from the patricians. What is remarkable is that there was no violent revolution, but a series of peaceful changes to the constitution.

Assemblies were an important institution in republican political organization. The centuriate assembly (*comitia centuriata*) was essentially a military organization, initially based upon the division of the army into centuries, but assuming a major role with legislative and elective powers. The division into 193 centuries, voting in units, was dominated by the aristocratic rich. The plebeians, however, created their own assembly, the plebeian assembly (*concilium plebis*) which was organized by tribes rather than centuries. Their own magistrates, the tribunes of the people, protected individuals from oppression. By 449 they numbered ten, with the right of veto and *sacrosanc-titas*. By 287 the plebeians had access to the magistracies, the priesthoods, marriage to patricians and the senate and their decisions had the force of law; so there arose a new patrician-plebeian aristocracy. An assembly of the whole people (*comitia tributa*) was instituted based upon the 35 tribes which took some of the duties of the centuriata (see Table 9.1 in the next chapter).

The magistracies also evolved over this period. The censor was created *c.* 443. The consuls were the executive officers of the state. The praetors performed civil and judicial roles for citizens and foreigners. Quaestors acted as administrative and financial assistants. Aediles administered public services. This division of duties provided checks and balances to prevent one person gaining supreme power. The senate guarded the constitution, having a customary practice of being consulted on legislation, and few magistrates would annoy a body they wished to join. The senators were a rich, aristocratic and privileged group who maintained a continuity in the status quo (the *mos maiorum* – the customs of the ancestors) through patronage and *clientelae*. Ultimately there was the sovereignty of the people and the right of appeal of any citizen to the people in the assemblies (see Table 9.2).

By 250 Rome's control had expanded far beyond Latium. The confederacy of Latin states in time had become a Roman dominated league. Rome struggled with peoples surrounding the city – the Etruscans, the Sabines, the Aequi and, of course, the Volsci, enlivened by the story of Coriolanus (491), who opposed the people, left Rome, and returned with an army of Volsci, only to leave at the pleading of his wife and mother. The Aequi episode is romanticized with the dictator Cincinnatus' simple loyalty to Rome (458). Such stories mitigate Rome's setbacks. In the hundred years of fighting Rome learnt much about the art of war and strengthened her armies and allies. The defeat of Veii in 396 by the heroic Camillus set the seal on Rome's dominance of central Italy. However, the capture of Rome by the Gauls in 390 undid much of this; yet, by 338 Rome had recovered and established her control over the Latins after the Latin War. Instead of treating them as conquered peoples, Rome invited them to join a confederacy that held out the privileges of citizenship as a prize.

The strength of this confederacy was shown during the next 150 years. The Romans survived three Samnite Wars, closely followed by the invasion of Italy by Pyrrhus in 280 and 276–5, including the defeat at Heraclea. The confederacy established a political, economic, social and military unity in which the citizen body reached 300,000 with an equal number of allied troops to call upon by the end of the third century. The first Punic War (264–41) added Sicily, Sardinia and Corsica to Rome's possession and saw the first application of *provincia* to an overseas command. It was also the emergence of Rome as a sea power with a number of victories over Carthage at sea. The confederacy again enabled Rome to withstand the defeats inflicted by Hannibal, most notably at Cannae in 216. It resulted in Rome's acquisition of two Spanish provinces and Rome's status as a world power. War with the Macedonian Philip began almost before the war with Carthage ended. Whether this was motivated by imperialism or philhellenism is a matter of debate. It ended in 196 with peace terms for Philip and a declaration of freedom for the Greeks by Flamininus at the Isthmian Games. Conflict with Antiochus of Syria followed and victory at Thermopylae in 191, and again at Magnesia in 189, gave Rome possession of Asia Minor. Yet from both Greece and Asia she removed all her troops – Rome had no intention to occupy either as yet. However, in 171 Rome was at war with Macedonia. Less sympathetic to Greek cities this time, Rome imposed her authority by some brutal acts of retaliation. One of these was to deport 1,000 Achaeans to Rome, among whom was Polybius. The final act came soon. In 148 Macedon became a province and in 146 the capture of Corinth ended Greek independence.

Horace credits Livius Andronicus, by tradition a Greek slave, with the beginnings of Latin literature, but it was based upon Greek models. Those who followed – Naevius, Ennius, Plautus, Terence – continued this practice. With the influx of wealth and slaves from the Hellenistic east, Roman aristocrats could be patrons of the arts, as Scipio was to Polybius. The expansion of Rome's authority brought them into contact with the literature and art of other civilizations, most obviously that of the Greeks, for which the aristocratic class acquired a taste. An educated Roman was expected to be familiar with the epic poems, drama and histories of the Greeks; they would have some knowledge of Greek language, history and philosophy; they would read the speeches of the Greek orators in learning rhetoric. While they grew to have little respect for Greek politics and military achievements, they fully absorbed Greek culture.

Changes were taking place socially also. The people who constituted the ruling class were proportionally getting fewer, while the population of Rome increased. Rome's increased possessions and the extension of citizenship brought this about as Rome filled up with freedmen, whose sons could claim full citizenship. However, rural citizens were also coming into Rome as they found farming no longer provided a living, since the influx of slaves offered cheap labour to the holders of large estates. The voters in the assemblies were becoming difficult for the nobility to control by the end of the second century. Furthermore, men who were newly rich from the empire – business men, holders of tax-contracts, Italian nobles – were beginning to take an interest. They too were challenging the accepted order. Holding onto the means of power would be difficult for the nobles as they faced the challenges of Tiberius and Gaius Gracchus, Saturninus, Marius and Sulla (between c. 133 and 80), and, of course, the demands of the ordinary citizens of Rome.

Further reading

For tables outlining the assemblies and magistracies of the Roman republic, see the end of 9a. There are many good histories and collections of articles about the Roman republic. See, for instance, Cornell (1995); Flower (2004); Rosenstein and Morstein-Marx (2010).

EARLY LATIN POETRY

Jonathan Katz

For the Romans themselves Latin literature had a beginning, namely the staging by Livius Andronicus of one of his own plays in 240. Of course there were antecedents; the Latin language already had a long history, and we have some fragmentary evidence of its being used creatively in religion and ritual as well as more official writings and perhaps secular narrative. But Livius' work was accepted by later tradition as something Roman, a successful blending of Greek and Italian elements. A freed Greek slave from Tarentum in southern Italy, he composed tragedies and comedies on mythological subjects and translated, or adapted, Homer's *Odyssey* into Latin *Saturnians* – a stress-based metre which was prevalent in the Italian tradition before the hexameter was adopted from Greek. Livius' epic was studied by schoolchildren until the time of Augustus, and while his literary merits may not always have been very highly regarded in the republican and Augustan periods he enjoyed the reputation of having provided the essential link between Greek and Latin literature.

Livius' contemporary Gnaeus Naevius, probably a Roman citizen born in Campania, was also active in the second half of the second century as a playwright and poet. His best known work, and that of which we have the most surviving remains, was again an epic in the Saturnian metre, on the first Punic War, in which he himself fought. It was thus the first epic on a Roman subject. The story was taken back to Aeneas and his bringing the *penates* from Troy to Rome. Here was a precedent and source for some ideas in Virgil's *Aeneid*, and in its own right there is enough evidence in the fragments quoted by ancient grammarians and commentators to show that Naevius was a bold experimenter not only in narrative but also with vivid and colourful language, delighting in alliteration and other rhetorical flourishes.

The greatest name in early narrative poetry, and one that remained great in later Roman tradition, is that of Quintus Ennius, born in 239 in Rudiae near the present-day Lecce in the southern Italian region of Puglia. He was trilingual, being brought up with Greek as the language of education, Oscan as the local vernacular and Latin as his adopted cultural medium. He served in the Roman army in Sardinia and, coming to Rome when he was around 40, worked as a teacher and playwright (of successful tragedies and comedies). He was rewarded with citizenship for his services to the Roman cause, probably most of all in a work celebrating the campaign in Aetolia, which he accompanied in 189. What secured his reputation was his epic poem, the *Annales*, a work admired and routinely studied until, and even after, the *Aeneid* had replaced it in eminence.

Ennius' title brings to mind a historical chronicle based on priestly records, rather than a creative narrative epic, and the work did indeed aim to record history, if we may judge from the mere 600 or so lines that survive from what is believed to have been a monumental composition in 15 books, each containing 1,000 lines or more. There is enough in what survives to show the author's brilliant creativity with language and imagery. We must bear in mind that most of the fragments, especially the shorter ones, have survived for reasons other than illustrating stylistic qualities. Not only later poets, but grammarians, antiquarians and historians took an interest in the language and content, and even an author who appears to have thought particularly highly of Ennius' style may happen to quote him on some point of information which has nothing to do with poetry as such. Thus Cicero, who admired Ennius and is our source for many lines, as often cites him for historical or political interest as for literary merit. Cicero is one of over 30 authors to whom we owe the haphazard surviving collection of lines, from a work which for long was standard reading for Roman teenagers and more mature scholars.

A telling indicator of Ennius' standing in the republic and early principate is the fact that no lesser poets than Lucretius and Virgil quoted him in phrases or whole lines; it is likely that we have not picked up all of these echoes and borrowings in the later works, but those that we can identify with certainty in the *Aeneid* are enough to put Ennius among Virgil's most revered sources, used by him especially at moments when he wished to represent the grandeur of Roman antiquity. Famously, for example, he celebrates the old hero of the Punic War, Fabius Cunctator, in the crowning moment of the pageant of heroes in book 6, by quoting almost verbatim Ennius' line, 'one man by his delaying restored for us our State' – almost verbatim, but not quite, for he heightens the reference by apostrophizing the old hero himself: 'you are that great (Maximus) one, who as one alone restored for us, by delaying, the State' (*Aeneid* 6.845ff.). Thus the celebration of Fabius becomes also a celebration of Ennius. Lucretius honours the old poet by name in the proem of his *De Rerum Natura* (1.12ff.), referring to some great verses depicting the underworld. It seems that Lucretius modelled his poetic style partly on the grandiloquence of his predecessor.

The content and structure of the *Annales* were themselves monumental. The books were arranged in five groups of three each. Each group covered a historical period, starting with the fall of Troy, Aeneas' journey and arrival in Italy, and the period of the kings. In his version of the legend, Ilia, mother of Romulus and Remus, is the daughter of Aeneas himself. The next 'triads' take us through Rome's conquest of Italy and the war against Pyrrhus, the Punic Wars, the Syrian wars of the 190s, and finally the other campaigns which Rome pursued during Ennius' own lifetime.

The work was undoubtedly original in its compass – this was almost certainly the first epic to cover a national history comprehensively, and here was an outstanding source of legends, heroic stories and moral *exempla* which dominated the Roman imagination – but just as importantly in its technique, for to Ennius goes the credit for bringing the quantitative dactylic hexameter into Latin poetry, adapting the Greek model and effectively completing the process, probably started by Plautus, of refashioning Latin verse on the Greek model of long and short syllables. The result, if one considers the pioneering nature of the poem, is a remarkably polished form of verse which became an effective precedent for the whole narrative hexameter tradition even beyond the Augustan and into the Silver age.

Still, it is easy to apply anachronistic standards to this verse. An ear tuned to Ovid and Virgil can be disturbed by apparent roughnesses in Ennius. The later poets developed conventions and preferences which did not occur to him. To Augustan readers his lines had a primitive, rugged, even crude character, and such impressions have stuck even with some modern critics. But taken on their own terms the fragments repay close study. Restrictions in the allowable syllable patterns (excluding, for example, a single short between two longs) encouraged Ennius to create new words and to imitate Greek diction. The conventional invocation of the Muses with which the *Annales* opened (the first line survives: *Musae quae pedibus magnum pulsatis Olympum* – 'O Muses, who with your feet beat great Olympus') is known to have been extended by the report of a dream, in which the spirit of Homer appears and tells the poet that he is reincarnated in him. This grandiose turning of an idea first found in Hesiod's *Theogony*, and also used by Callimachus, is one of the many flavourings which, alongside the metre itself, helped to transfer Greek and Hellenistic techniques into the Roman tradition.

Descriptive passages can rise to great rhetorical heights with much use of alliteration, assonance and anaphora and a clear, if fascinatingly un-Virgilian, attention to rhythms within the lines and sentences, interplay between metrical accent (the pulse felt at the beginning of each foot) and the natural accentuation of the Latin words and phrases themselves. Alliterations balance and answer each other in powerful imagery – *viresque valentes / contundit crudelis hiems* ('stout strength crushed cruelly by winter'); *hastati spargunt hastas; fit ferreus imber* ('spearman scatter their spears; iron rains down') – often providing inspirational models for Virgil (e.g. *ferreus imber* in *Aeneid* 12.284). The longer surviving fragments show considerable skill in building tension through both sound and depicted action, such as a dramatic passage in the first book in which Romulus and Remus take the auspices to discover who should rule the new city (Warmington 1935–40, vol. 1: 30), and there is evidence of strong character portrayal in a description of a nobleman of gentle and civilized manner (Warmington, ibid.: 78), thought by some ancient commentators to be a description of the poet himself!

Ennius was also a satirist, though little of his four books of *saturae* survives. Satire was a genre in which the personality of the poet played a greater role, and the few fragments we have hint at character sketches and moral comment on social and political types and stereotypes (some perhaps in a dramatic stage form). We cannot identify any direct political or personal targeting. Naevius had fallen foul of political enemies, and had been exiled for his indiscretions.

Ennius, whether through tact or unimpeachable eminence, survived, and died in modest respectability in 169. His nephew and pupil Marcus Pacuvius won some distinction as a tragedian, mainly in the Greek mould of plays, and his work was later highly rated by Cicero. It incurred the scorn of the satirist Gaius Lucilius (180–02), the last great figure to be considered in early republican poetry and, though not the first socially critical and humorous Latin writer, in the eyes of later satirists the true founder of the genre. Of his 30 books of poems we have fewer than 1,400 lines, once again tantalizingly fragmentary, but enough to indicate a bold critical spirit and some prowess in iambic, trochaic and hexameter verse, even if a century later it was considered by Horace somewhat rough and ready, and was indeed already admitted to be so by Lucilius himself. Eventually settling on the hexameter, he established this metre as the standard for the genre.

A middle-class Latin from Suessa Aurunca on the Campanian border of Latium, Lucilius appears to have been well-connected in Roman society, and to have written from a position of comfortable security. Impressions of the subject matter of his poems, which he called *sermones* ('discourses') are hard to confirm, such is (as with Ennius) the haphazard nature of the fragments we have; but he was perhaps the first Latin poet to make his own individual attitudes and reactions the focus of attention, and he thus sets a precedent not only for critical satire itself but for the intense personal tone of the Latin love elegists. He ploughs a broad furrow, at one time describing a journey from Rome to his estates in Sicily (a model for Horace's *Journey to Brundisium* and *The Bore* in his first book of *Satires*), at another parodying or ridiculing a literary work by Ennius, or again humorously lampooning some contemporary figure in private or public life. Though clearly a Hellenist in his cultural interests, he nevertheless stands out as an authentically Roman Latinist, using the colloquial language and common idiom.

Further reading

Texts with translations are in the Loeb series, Warmington 1935–40. Warmington's edition of the *Annales* of Ennius was superseded by Skutsch (1985), a major commentary and reassessment of the sources. Ennius' tragic fragments are edited with full notes in Jocelyn (1967). Evidence for the careers and works of the major early writers is set out with good bibliographies of editions, translations and secondary studies by Williams and Gratwick in Kenney and Clausen (1983: 53–76 and 799–807), in part 1 of Conte (1994). Williams (1968: 443–523) discusses Lucilius in a chapter called 'Interest in the Individual' and offers a critical analysis of the longer fragments of the *Annales* in the chapter 'Thought and Expression: Language and Style', especially pp. 684–99. Early Latin poetry and drama are discussed in the literary-historical context by Goldberg in Harrison (2005: 15–30), and as literary and social history by Leigh in Taplin (2001, pp. 4–26). Feeney (2007: 99–128) is an examination of Naevius' and Ennius' use of the gods in mythology and theology. For the early metres, see Raven (1965). For some general introductions to early Roman epic and Ennius, see also Boyle (1993); Goldberg (1995).

ROMAN COMIC DRAMA

Jonathan Katz

The oldest complete and substantial surviving works of Latin literature are the comic plays of Plautus (*c.* 250–184) and Terence (*c.* 195–59). With these authors came the culmination of classical comedy and, in addition to their vibrant, eloquent language, they give us our only major sources for anything like a colloquial Latin style in the republican era. Livius Andronicus, Naevius and others had already been active as comic playwrights. Like Plautus' contemporary Ennius, these had also written tragedies and narrative poetry; but Plautus and Terence made their names solely through their comedies. Though only small fragments of the pre-Plautine works survive, we know the names of a number of them, and some must have been familiar to Plautus when he came to Rome from the provinces.

Under the label Latin comedy should be included a number of forms which are known to have thrived in Italian tradition even well before Plautus' time. Livy (7.2) tells us that *ludi scaenici* (theatrical shows) were set up in 364 to placate the gods when Rome was struck by plague. Imported Italian (Etruscan) dances were featured at these performances, and the tradition continued, so that by the latter part of the third century there were frequent *ludi scaenici* staged at times of public and religious festivals. It was at such a festival in 240 that Livius Andronicus (see above) staged his own Latin version of a Greek play.

The *ludi* also contained performances of mime, farce and gladiatorial contests as well as tragedies. Among traditional Italian forms of entertainment were the so-called Atellan Farces (*Fabulae Atellanae*), originally associated with the town of Atella in Campania. They represented scenes in provincial life and used a number of stock characters – Bucco the fool, Doscennus the glutton, Maccus the clown and others – of a kind that became familiar in the later Italian *commedia dell'arte*. The plays were a few hundred lines long and, if we may judge from the few surviving lines of them, were in iambic and trochaic stress-based (i.e. not quantitative) verse. They may have contained some literary play, occasionally perhaps parodying the style and sentiment of tragedy. Italian traditions also included more *ad hoc* forms such as the 'Fescennine' verses, a kind of improvised and no doubt scurrilous poetry of humorous mockery, used at weddings and other social functions.

All of these Italian forms must have fed into the character of an art theatre as championed by Plautus, but the most important influence by far was the

Greek theatre, in the form in which it either migrated from Attica to Italy or grew up in the culturally Greek towns of Magna Graecia itself. What is normally meant by the very term Roman comedy is the *fabula palliata* ('play in Greek dress'), an adaptation of Greek new comedy as found in the works of Menander (*c.* 344–291) and his contemporaries Diphilus, Philemon and others; almost all of the 20 surviving plays of Plautus and the six of Terence (all that he composed) are such adaptations, though the two writers dealt rather differently with their Greek models, and in matters of style, language and humour they are also different, and highly distinctive (see 4d).

Another type of Latin derivative of the Greek theatre, the *fabula togata* ('play in a toga') survives only in fragments. This form flourished in Rome in the second century; it appears to have favoured a higher degree of Romanization of themes and settings. Because so little evidence survives for the precise nature of these plays, but perhaps more because of the towering reputations and importance of Plautus and Terence, the *palliata* became the leading drama in Roman tradition. The first Roman theatre, as a more or less permanent structure, was built in 55 by Pompey. In earlier times the staging was erected for a production and dismantled afterwards. It is likely that masks were used, enabling actors to take more than one part each. The temporary staging arrangements did not necessarily prevent colourful and sometimes elaborate performances.

Titus Maccius Plautus is somewhat mysterious in his origin and even his name. According to an account relayed to us by the first-century CE writer Aulus Gellius, he worked in some capacity in theatrical productions when he first came to Rome; relying on an uncertain ancient tradition, the provincial Umbrian town of Sarsina claims he was born there. His name suggests a humorously derived Roman-citizen form, 'Maccius' being a name based on 'Maccus' (the fool of the Atellan plays), and 'Plautus' meaning perhaps something like 'flatfoot'. Gellius also reported the story that he lost his money in his theatrical ventures and worked in a mill before returning to his favoured profession; in this last phase of his life he composed the plays which were to immortalize him.

The plays continued to be performed and transmitted through the second century and well into the first. There was common agreement that 21 plays were unquestionably by Plautus himself, and these were later selected by the first-century grammarian and antiquarian Varro. Over a hundred others were of doubtful authorship even if Varro himself accepted some as genuine. It is thanks to Varro that the 21 survived, and the manuscript tradition preserved 20 of them, plus fragments of the last (the *Vidularia*), right through to the renaissance.

Not many of the plays are precisely datable, but there is some evidence in the early *didascalia* (production notices), which were preserved through manuscript-copying, that Plautus' *Stichus* was first produced at the Plebeian Games in 200, and the *Pseudolus* at a temple dedication festival in 191.

The *Casina* must have been produced, at least in the form in which we have it, after 186, because it refers to an event in that year.

The surviving plays run from little more than 700 lines to nearly 1,500. The majority have prologues, as appears to have been common, if not universal, practice in the Greek new comedy, probably influenced by earlier Greek dramatists such as Euripides and by a tendency of comic writers to parody the tragic form. Plautus and Terence sometimes use a special *prologus* (prologue-deliverer) to catch and inform the attention of the audience, giving away enough of the forthcoming plot to allow for irony or surprise and playing on a kind of interaction with the spectators. In the opening of Plautus' *Captivi* ('The Captives') the *prologus* points, presumably after the raising of the curtain (or rather lowering, as the normal practice was for a curtain to be brought down into a slot at the front of the stage), to two prisoners chained to a pillar, explains their identity, jokes about their present condition, then cajoles the audience into following him further:

> *iam hoc tenetis? . . . optume est.*
> *negat hercle ille ultimus. accedito.*
> *si non ubi sedeas locus est, est ubi ambules,*
> *quando histrionem cogis mendicarier.*
> *ego me tua causa, ne erres, non rupturus sum.*

> You get me? Excellent! By god, that fellow at the end there says he doesn't. Come nearer. What, no room to sit? Then take a walk outside, rather than turning an author into a beggar. You won't find me busting myself just to stop you missing the point!

Often changing the titles of his originals, Plautus appears to have been fairly free with his adaptations, summarizing or expanding the original. What remained of the dancing chorus, essential in Old Comedy, in the Greek new comedy, has now gone completely. But Plautus introduced more singing in the form of *cantica* – lyric passages delivered by individual actors – and probably, in accordance with popular taste, much of each play apart from the iambic dialogue and speeches was sung as a kind of recitative in more elaborate metres and accompanied by a flute. The *cantica* are used sometimes to heighten emotion, to divert the audience, or to introduce a new dramatic element, such as the arrival of two shipwrecked girls in *Rudens* ('The Rope'), a scene in which the combined poetry and music could have moved the audience considerably before the comedy returned to defuse the tension.

Apart from structural changes that Plautus made to his Greek models the plots combined predictable type-situations, familiar from the originals, with inventive variety of detail. The use of standard situations and type-characters in practice creates the possibility of surprise, irony and variation in the individual case. Typically confusions of personal identity are resolved, lost items and persons found, hopelessly separated young lovers eventually reunited, rivalries settled, villains discomfited. Many details in the superficially Greek settings are Romanized (see Williams, 1968: 285ff. and Segal, 2001: 186ff.), and Plautus' achievement was above all in his virtuosity in language (Gellius was to call him the 'glory of the Latin tongue') and in comic situations involving brilliantly conceived characters – slave-dealer, boastful soldier, parasite and the innovative Plautine speciality of the clever slave who facilitates and complicates the plot, sometimes profiting personally but characteristically showing a sophisticated or ironic appreciation of situations and human reactions.

It is often said that Plautus aims above all at fun, and does not moralize. But in the strange workings of chance and fate, in the rewarding of virtue and the observation of good and bad faith in human behaviour, in such plays as *Rudens* and *Pseudolus*, there are striking moments in which the audience would be forced to ponder moral issues, sometimes with considerable irony and playful undermining of conventional wisdom.

The work of Caecilius Statius, an Insubrian Gaul from Milan and close friend of Ennius at the beginning of the second century, is lost except for a few scattered lines; but his plays and their plots were much praised in republican times, sometimes even above Plautus. In his more than 40 *palliatae* he is believed to have respected the integrity of his Greek originals more than Plautus. He was undoubtedly an important influence on Terence, who met him and shared with him some painful experience of professional rivalry and opposition from other playwrights.

Plautus' own term for his 'adapting', *vertere* ('turning'), was also used by Terence for his elegant and finely written *palliatae*, which were studied and admired for many centuries both for the beauty of their Latin language and for their stories and moral lessons. The life recorded in the first century CE by Suetonius and transmitted to posterity by the fourth century commentator Aelius Donatus states that Terence was born in Carthage in the first quarter of the second century and came to Rome as a slave; when freed he became Publius Terentius Afer, the second element in his name being taken from his former master Terentius Lucanus. According to the same source he died in 159 while on a journey to Greece. From the surviving early production notes we know that the six plays were first produced between 166 and 160, and the author was said in ancient times to have had powerful Roman supporters.

For Plautus, deliberately Greek elements left in the plays could even be an exotic feature. He playfully used the term *pergraecari* (perhaps something like 'Tomgreekery') for 'carousing' or 'merry-making'. Terence's approach to the Greekness of his originals was purer, more scrupulous, and went beyond merely keeping the original Greek titles. His prologues assert as much; he tells us, sometimes defensively in reply to criticism as in the *Adelphoe* ('The Brothers', adapted from a play by Menander) that, even if he has combined elements from different plays or transferred characters from one plot to another, he has remained faithful to the spirit of the originals. This may be in part a symptom of changing taste after the battle of Pydna (168), when a significant new wave of Greek culture came to Rome as a result of the political appropriation of Greece.

The prologues are interesting in themselves for another reason. No longer used as synopses of the ensuing dramatic plots, they speak of the author himself, his professional difficulties, and the charges (of plagiarism, for example, or *contaminatio*, the 'mixing' and perceived 'adulterating' of materials from different sources) which he has to answer. The plot will unfold *in agendo* – in the actual process of the play, which therefore will place a different demand on the attention and intellect of the audience.

Terence indeed caters for a more sophisticated and educated, Hellenized taste; he favours linguistic elegance, moral comment and psychological depth over popular bawdy, slapstick and situation comedy. The plays deal with the same kinds of characters and situations as those of Plautus, but he uses his material to explore human nature as revealed and tested by circumstances. Plays such as the *Heautontimoroumenos* ('The Self-Tormentor') and *Eunuchus* ('The Eunuch') and *Phormio* (named after its brilliant principal character, an attractive, wily and complex parasite and facilitator), and above all the *Adelphoe*, an intriguing and moving study of tension between generations and between different and conflicting principles of bringing up youngsters, are still eminently performable, and they exerted a long and powerful influence on later traditions of European (French, English, Spanish and Italian) classical comedy.

Further reading

For full texts and parallel translations of the plays of Plautus, see Nixon (1916) and for Terence, see Barsby (2001): both are in the Loeb series, as are fragments of Livius Andronicus and other early authors in Warmington (1935–40). Fluent translations of four Plautus comedies are in the World's Classics series (Segal, 1996a), as are those of Terence (Brown, 2008). Editions with commentaries are available for a number of plays, and a good list is to be found in the bibliography to Leigh (2004, see below).

Two classic older studies of comedy are Fraenkel (1922, now available in English (2007)) and Duckworth (1994); there is also Konstan (1983). Excellent detailed surveys of the authors and of secondary literature are in Gratwick in Kenney and Clausen (1983: 77–127) and Conte (1994: 49–67 and 92–103). Further valuable studies are Barsby (1991); Beare (1964); Hunter (1985); Leigh in Taplin (2001: 4–26); Segal (1987; 2001: chapters 10–12). An important new examination of the comedies in relation to Roman social and political history is Leigh (2004). For a recent interpretation of Roman comedy, see Sharrock (2009), and for one that deals particularly with slaves and masters in the plays, see McCarthy (2000). For Roman theatre and the plays in performance, see Beacham (1991); Moore (1998); Slater (1985). For early Roman tragedy, see Boyle (2006); Erasmo (2004).

Chapter 9

The late republic

All dates in this chapter are BCE unless stated otherwise. Glossary items: *allegory; anaphora; archaism; Asianism; asyndeton; Atticism; cursus honorum; ellipsis; Epicureanism; epyllion; exordium; hexameter; metonymy; mos maiorum; neoterics; novus homo; personification; propemptikon; recusatio; reductio ad absurdum; stoicism.*

THE LATE REPUBLIC: AN HISTORICAL INTRODUCTION

Terry Edwards

The final century of the republic was, from one viewpoint, one of violence, disruption, greed and the victory of individual ambition over the welfare of the state. Alternatively, it was the inevitable outcome of the failure by the patrician-plebeian aristocracy to exercise the flexibility and tolerance which had characterized the evolution of the republic in its early days. By 100, Rome had become the mistress of much of the Mediterranean, either as provinces, such as Spain or Africa, or as client states, such as the kingdoms of the east.

Her soldiers had fought numerous wars. Despite setbacks, they had triumphed, partly by excellent leadership and partly by luck and the mistakes of their enemies. Wealth had flowed into Rome or, more accurately, into the ample treasure chests of a few individuals. Meanwhile, by judicious use of citizenship grants, the Romans had brought their conquered peoples into the system and bound them in loyalty to the state. Their armies were citizen armies, but no longer landowners, after Marius' reforms which opened recruitment to any citizen. Dependent on their generals for pay and a share in victory spoils, soldiers became a means by which ambitious politicians could manipulate the assemblies to achieve their goals.

The urban populace was by 100 a mix of many nations: migrants into Rome from the growing empire attracted by the economic prospects of the city; freed slaves brought to Rome and their descendants who became full citizens; Italians unable to make a living in the countryside or looking to make a name for themselves in the capital. Since voting in assemblies took place in Rome, the urban population was the focus of politicians seeking popularity and, ultimately, office and a rich province. And if they could not do this legally, there was always bribery, corruption and violence.

Marius and Sulla had set the pattern. Violence in Roman politics did not begin with either of them. Tiberius and Gaius Gracchus, and their supporters, were murdered between 133 and 122 by the right-wing hard-core aristocracy protecting what they saw as the *mos maiorum*. The republic's history had enough examples of assassinated politicians accused of seeking kingship, dominance or dictatorship. The excuse had always worked, since nothing appeared worse than the prospect of a single ruler in Rome. The excuse was useful propaganda for those who found no legal way to get what they wanted. Marius and Sulla went a stage further and involved not a single assassin but a whole legion or more.

The self-interested perspective of the typical Roman aristocrat is shown in the Social War of 92–88. Drusus, who wanted citizenship for Italian communities, was murdered and this sparked the very revolt he was trying to avoid; Rome effectively granted what Drusus had proposed in the end, although the politicians, as always, were slow to keep the promises. In Asia, meanwhile, king Mithridates was making war on Rome's possessions. In 88, Sulla was granted command in Asia and the glory of war. However, Marius, wanted this last shot at glory himself. The tribune Sulpicius engineered a change of command. Sulla, arguing that this was for the good of Rome, chose to ignore the vote of the people and marched his army on the city. When he left for Asia, Marius took over, and instituted a bloodbath, which only ended when he died (of natural causes!). Six years later Sulla returned (without having decisively defeated Mithridates, who was to cause Rome trouble for another 20 years).

His entry into Rome and his dictatorship was bloody and ruthless. He instituted proscriptions – arbitrary lists of 'outlaws' to be killed on sight and their property confiscated and auctioned usually at a low price to some supporter of Sulla. Cicero's speech *Pro Roscio Amerino* highlights dramatically this feature of Sulla's dominance. Both Marcus Licinius Crassus and Julius Caesar felt it wise to be absent from Rome during his dictatorship. Sulla died in 78, but he left behind reforms to stabilize the republic under the protective guidance of the senate (increased to 600). He weakened the tribunate by removing its veto and right to further office; he restricted governors in provinces and regulated the ages for holding magistracies; he ended the subsidized corn dole, altered qualification for entry to the senate, organized the seven courts and even tried to limit expense on parties. Much of this was either ignored or repealed because the senate was too weak and not willing to make it work. By 70, Pompey (the Great) was consul, six years too young, having held no other magistracy, but having waged wars successfully in Africa, Sicily and Spain. He had shown that laws and constitutional regulations were no match for someone with military success, the backing of an army and popular appeal.

Rome's received history is dominated by the heroic, loyal individual servants of the state – Cincinnatus, Camillus, the Scipios, Appius Claudius, Flamininus, Cato the Elder. Roman politics had always been about individual success, and

Rome's top families had always seen the supreme magistracies and army commands as theirs; they struggled against each other with the occasional new entry from an unknown family. With their clients and loyal support, they used patronage and wealth to maintain their position. The wealth-dominated *centuriata* ensured their control of the praetorship and consulship. These families continued to hold the offices regularly, govern provinces and occupy the senate. However, a small group of military dynasts could take control whenever they wanted through their vast popularity and military strength. The constitution continued to function – with elections, assemblies and laws passed. But power was shifting away from the senate. In addition, corruption seemed to be everywhere. Cicero's Verrine orations, while exaggerated, vividly portray the bribery of republican juries and the corruption of governors.

In 67 and 66, Pompey, by means of a tribune, got the plebeian assembly to grant him military commands, first against the pirates, then against Mithridates. Crassus, his rival, organized political support in Rome, chiefly among the equestrians (businessmen, knights), the wealthy middle class and the Italian aristocracy. Julius Caesar became aedile in 65 and praetor and pontifex maximus in 63, building support among the people.

Cicero achieved the consulship in 63 despite being from an Italian town (Arpinum) and a *novus homo* (a man whose family had no previous consul). The high point of his career was the Catiline conspiracy. Catiline's attempts at the consulship were thwarted by Cicero and the nobles in 64 and 63, and he turned (apparently, if one accepts Cicero and Sallust) to violent revolution with the aid of Etrurian farmers and peasants in debt. There was undoubtedly a serious debt problem which the ruling class had failed to solve by their ineptitude, self-interest and corruption. How serious it was is open to question. But it showed that violent revolution lay just under the surface of Roman politics. Cicero executed five conspirators without a trial, and in 58 was exiled for it.

Within two years, thwarted by the senate, led largely by Cato the Younger, Pompey, Crassus and Caesar combined their forces in the first triumvirate. Caesar got the consulship and the governorship of Gaul; Crassus and Pompey gained rewards for their supporters. The 50s saw Caesar gain glory and a well-trained army in Gaul; Crassus died in defeat at Carrhae in 53 trying to do the same; Pompey stayed in Rome and, after getting Cicero back from exile, battled to gain control and the support of the nobles. Clodius, tribune in 58, made street violence into a political weapon, along with Milo, until his murder on the Via Appia by Milo in 52.

The desire for glory, wealth, popularity, fame, to be the first man in Rome, thus led to the civil war of 49 between Pompey and Caesar, or – apparently – between conservatism and revolution. In reality, self-interest was at the root of it. The excuse for Caesar was the treatment of the tribune Mark Antony: he could claim that he was defending the republic. For Pompey and the aristocrats, Caesar's refusal to lay down his command was illegal. For Cicero the real cause of the civil war was that neither Pompey nor Caesar could stand to have a rival. The battle of Pharsalus settled little except the end of Pompey (he died in a boat off Egypt). Caesar went on to fight four more battles ending with Munda in Spain in 45. The real end came when, after establishing his dictator-ship for life (six months was normal!) and ignoring the tribunes he swore to protect, he was assassinated on the Ides of March 44 with his assassins using the age-old excuse of his wanting to be king.

The next 14 years saw a repeat of these events with the names changed. Octavian, Lepidus and Antony split the world up between them, and then fought each other for sole control. The second triumvirate of 42 saw proscrip-tions like Sulla's. Cicero was killed and mutilated; Lepidus fell in 36; Octavian consolidated the west and Italy with his general Agrippa; Antony made futile attempts on Parthia. He was more successful with Cleopatra but lost the propaganda war in Rome. The republican constitution still func-tioned, but all under the control of the man with the army. The writing was on the wall for the republic.

Further reading

For some good introductions to the world of the late republic, see Beard and Crawford (1985); Davies and Swain (2010); Flower (2004); Rosenstein and Morstein-Marx (2010); Wallace-Hadrill (2008); Wiseman (1985). For the very late republic, in particular, see Goodman (1997) but, for a classic account of how the republic ceased to be, see Syme (1939). For a more obviously cul-tural history, see Rawson (1985). On the importance of oratory, see Morstein-Marx (2008); on the importance of the plebs, see Mouritsen (2007).

Table 9.1 The assemblies of the Roman republic: summary of their roles during the early and late republic

Assembly	Formation	Functions	
comitia curiata	division of citizens into 30 curiae	originally conferred imperium on magistrates; function gradually limited by the centuriata	
comitia centuriata	division of citizens into 193 centuries	enacting of laws; election of magistrates (consuls, praetors); declaration of war and peace; court for charges requiring the death penalty	met in Campus Martius; summoned by the magistrate
comitia tributa	division of citizens into 35 tribes	elected quaestors, curule aediles, tribunes of the soldiers; enacted laws; minor trials	consuls or praetors presided
comitia plebis	division of plebeian citizens into 35 tribes	decisions of the assembly given force of law in 287 BC; elected plebeian tribunes and aediles; minor trials	summoned by the tribunes

Table 9.2 The magistrates of the Roman republic: summary of their roles during the early and late republic

Magistrate and number	Functions: areas of control	Term	Elected by
censors (2)	census (list of citizens); public morals; revision of list of senators; public contracts (buildings, roads, tax collections, etc.)	18 months (every 5 years)	comitia centuriata
consuls (2)	army commander; presided over assemblies, the senate and elections; executive authority	1 year	comitia centuriata
praetors (6) (8 after 81 BC)	judge; army commander; presided over assemblies; issued edicts	1 year	comitia centuriata
curule aediles (2) plebeian aediles (2)	regulated the streets and traffic in Rome; water-supply, public buildings, markets, weights and measures; public festivals and games	1 year	comitia tributa plebeian assembly
quaestors (8) (20 after 81)	finance and treasury officials; public records; financial assistants to generals and to governors of provinces	1 year	comitia tributa
tribunes (10)	protection of citizens; right of veto; presided over the Plebeian Assembly	1 year	plebeian assembly
dictator (1) magister equitum (master of the horse) (1)	power over all other magistrates in a time of crisis dictator's deputy/second in command	6 months	appointed by consul after a proposal by the senate

CICERO

Neil Croally

> *O happy fate for the Roman state was the date of my great consulate.*
>
> Had Cicero always spoken thus, he might have laughed at the swords of Antony.
>
> (Juvenal *Satires* 10)

One image of Cicero is that he was a pompous bore, a self-absorbed social climber, a man obsessed with his own importance. The awful line of his poetry quoted above seems to bear this view out. But Cicero was also known in his own times as a great wit, and a patron of literature and philosophy. This is the image I shall be advancing as I consider the enormous range of Cicero's work: his speeches are not only outstanding examples of high-flown rhetoric; they can also be extremely funny. The letters show a man of great humanity and practical wisdom; the philosophical and rhetorical works reveal a very good if not an original thinker. Yet, the great Roman historian of the nineteenth century, Mommsen, wasted little time in trashing Cicero's reputation. Syme, arguably the greatest Roman historian of the twentieth century, damned Cicero as largely irrelevant to Roman politics, certainly by comparison to a Pompey, a Caesar or an Octavian. But both views underestimate the complexity of Cicero's self-presentation, the ways in which he is a distinctive Roman politician, and his abiding belief in the power of language to persuade and encourage.

Life and career

Born at Arpinum, south-east of Rome, in early 106, Cicero first made his name as an orator with his defence of Roscius in 80. He spent the years between 79 and 77 in Athens and Rhodes furthering his education. He was quaestor in Sicily in 75, successfully and amazingly had Verres convicted in 70, served as praetor in 66 and in 63 became the first non-aristocrat (*novus homo*) to become consul for 30 years. As he made his way up the *cursus honorum*, Cicero achieved all the posts (quaestor, praetor, consul) at the youngest possible age. His year as consul was the high point of his political influence, his main achievement being the suppression of the conspiracy of Catiline. Scholars have argued about how threatening this conspiracy actually was and many have ridiculed Cicero for his frequent self-praise for his role in ending the conspiracy. A more moderate view is that Cicero himself was not always as certain as he seems about his behaviour during what was at least a minor political crisis: in so often stating how important he had been and how effectively he had acted, Cicero was actually trying to convince and reassure himself. Such fragile self-confidence sits uneasily with the more conventional view of Cicero.

Still, as a result of his illegal execution of some of the conspirators, Cicero was himself exiled in the early 50s. Recalled in 57, he languished without reliable political influence for the next 13 years, though there was a governorship of Cilicia in 51 (some good evidence provided by Cicero here for the nature of Roman provincial administration). The reason for Cicero's relative lack of influence in these years is that his sort of political beliefs – the primacy of the republic, the harmony of the different classes within the Roman body politic, faith in reason and persuasion – were all swept aside by a confirmation of power politics that was brutal and stark even by Roman standards. The first triumvirate of Caesar, Crassus and Pompey in the 50s and the second of Antony, Lepidus and Octavian of the 40s both stressed power backed by force of arms. In this context, Cicero's respect for constitutional politics, belief in the importance of the word and his lack of military experience all counted against him. After the assassination of Julius Caesar in 44, Cicero's political career briefly flared again, as he sought to persuade his fellow citizens of the pernicious nature of Antony's character (in a set of speeches – *Philippics* – named after Demosthenes' attacks on Philip of Macedon). However, in attacking Antony he badly misjudged the character of Octavian, by whom he was blandly betrayed: executed by Antony's soldiers, his head and hands were displayed in the forum.

The quantity and range of Cicero's works are extraordinary. There are 58 speeches, evenly split between the legal and the political. There are about 900 letters, most of which are addressed to his friend Atticus, but also to his brother Quintus, and to Brutus (the murderer of Caesar). There are also a number of philosophical and rhetorical works, which have been extremely influential. Cicero was also a poet but, as the line quoted at the beginning suggests, this may not have been his strongest area. Still, we know that he wrote an epic poem about Marius (who was also from Arpinum) and that he translated nearly 500 lines of Aratus' *Phaenomena*. All in all, Cicero was a literary man, as well as a politician and lawyer, and it is this that distinguishes him from his contemporaries. And the way that he is a literary man, as well as a politician, helps us to understand the difference between Greek and Roman culture.

The speeches

In the law courts Cicero was successful; in the senate and in front of the people of Rome he achieved much. So it seems as though we might have to accept Cicero's own judgement that he was the best orator in Rome. However, we have little with which to compare him; we also cannot see how he actually delivered the speeches. (One suspects that Cicero was a good actor, and that his pacing, his pauses, his passion were all used to good dramatic effect.) We should also note that the texts of the speeches that we have were in one way or another edited for publication. Indeed, some of the speeches were never delivered, such as the later *Verrines* (because Verres chose not to defend himself), or were published as pamphlets, such as the *Second Philippic*. As we will never know the extent to which Cicero amended his speeches (or indeed his letters) for publication, it is wise to acknowledge the fact of editing, but not to become obsessed with it. We have 58 speeches in all, though they are not all complete. They are evenly split between speeches delivered in court cases and political speeches. In order to see a little of Cicero's rhetorical mastery, I shall look briefly at an example of each type of speech.

My first example is the opening, or *exordium*, of Cicero's first speech criticizing Catiline. The exact date of the speech is uncertain, but it likely to have been delivered in late 63 when Cicero was consul. It was published – though again the exact date is not sure – sometime in 60 or the next year. I will break down the *exordium* into manageable chunks.

quo usque tandem abutere, Catilina, patientia nostra? quam diu etiam furor iste tuus nos eludet? quem ad finem sese effrenata iactabit audacia?

For how much longer, Catiline, will you abuse our patience? For how long now will that frenzy of yours elude us? To what end will your unbridled recklessness flaunt itself?

In this speech, delivered in the senate, one might expect the senators themselves, who are, after all, the audience that needs to be persuaded, to be the addressees. But no. Boldly and unusually, Cicero addresses his enemy, Catiline, and he does so in the fifth word. By addressing Catiline in this way, Cicero can also move with speed to characterize the man he believes to be such a dangerous threat to the republic. With marvellous economy, Cicero indicates exactly what it is about Catiline that makes him so dangerous: he is frenzied (*furor*) and marked by unbridled recklessness. One would expect the adjective perhaps to follow the noun, but the position of *effrenata* (unbridled) is both emphatic and suspenseful. What is it about Catiline that is unbridled? Ah! It's recklessness. Of course. The opening is also arresting because Cicero deploys three rhetorical questions in a row, and those rhetorical questions are subtly varied. All begin with an interrogative, but that is slightly different each time (*quo . . . quam . . . quem*). The subject of the first question is 'you, Catiline', but of the latter two questions the subject changes to his bad qualities, frenzy and recklessness, stressing again and in a different way that Catiline's character is the threat. Cicero then continues with a more elaborate rhetorical question.

nihilne nocturnum praesidium Palati, nihil urbis vigiliae, nihil timor populi, nihil concursus bonorum omnium, nihil hic munitissimus habendi senatus locus, nihil horum ora vultusque moverunt?

Does the nightly garrison of the Palatine, the city guards, the fear of the people, the gathering of all good people, this heavily fortified place for the convening of the senate, the faces and expressions of these people here, do none, do none of these things move you?

The main characteristic of this question is the anaphora of *nihil*. It is very striking (and difficult to match in English translation). The emphasis on 'nothing' also suggests an association between Catiline and, say, annihilation: his effect will be to reduce the republic to nothing. But there are other ways in which this question is careful and arresting. Once again, Cicero places an adjective before the noun it describes. One might expect *praesidium nocturnum* but, by putting the word for nightly first, Cicero not only creates for himself the opportunity for a double alliteration (*nihil nocturnum/praesidium Palati*), which may very well have been easy to deliver with some passion, he also suggestively associates Catiline with the night, with all its associations of secrecy and darkness (of a moral kind as well, of course). Note also how in the second part of sub-questions, Cicero keenly stresses the urgency of the matter with his use of *hic* (this) and *horum* (of these people): the conspiracy must be dealt with here and now. Let us move on.

> *patere tua consilia non sentis, constrictam iam horum omnium scientia teneri coniurationem tuam non vides? quid proxima, quid superiore nocte egeris, ubi fueris, quos convocaveris, quid consili ceperis quem nostrum ignorare arbitraris?*

> Do you not realize that your plans are obvious? Do you not see that your conspiracy is now constrained by the knowledge of all these people here? Do you think that any of us do not know what you did last night and the night before, where you were, whom you summoned and what plan you devised?

Cicero continues his use of rhetorical questions, but with a different aim. Having stressed the threat of Catiline, he now moves to ridicule him by showing that the conspiracy is no longer secret. The position of *patere* (lie open, are obvious) is clearly emphatic; the position of *constrictam* (constrained) underlines the same point. Presence and urgency are again underlined by *horum omnium* (of all these people). Then Cicero uses five quickfire indirect questions, deploying the same sort of variety as in his opening (*quid . . . quid . . . ubi . . . quos . . . quid*/what . . . what . . . where . . . whom . . . what). Cicero suggests that Catiline should know: the game is up. This might appear to be a risky rhetorical strategy, having started by characterizing Catiline as a threat. But it is in fact a clever move, as it allows Cicero to move into his next section.

> *o tempora, o mores! senatus haec intellegit, consul videt; hic tamen vivit. vivit? immo vero etiam in senatum venit, fit publici consili particeps, notat et designat oculis ad caedem unum quemque nostrum, nos autem fortes viri satis facere rei publicae videmur, si istius furorem ac tela vitemus.*

> O the times, O the values! The senate understands these things, the consul sees them. Yet this man is still alive. Alive? No, he even comes into the senate, takes part in public discussion, indicates and singles out with his eyes each one of us to be murdered. But we brave men seem to do enough for the republic, if we avoid the frenzy and weapons of that man.

Cicero made the first exclamation famous. He knew it was good: he used it elsewhere on three occasions. At this point in this speech, though, it broadens our view. The problem may not just be with Catiline; there may be a more general moral decline. Cicero uses this often-stated view of late republican writers as an implicit explanation of the strange current situation. Catiline should have accepted that the game was up, because everyone knows. But something else is happening instead. Note how Cicero registers his shock. He starts with the two short phrases – the senate understands these things, the consul sees (them) – then adds in astonishment (note *tamen* – yet) that Catiline is still alive. The shock of this state of affairs is rendered powerfully by the repetition of *vivit*, the second time as a question. It is said as a question because there is worse. Cicero is saying: Catiline's just being alive is bad enough, but he is still an active politician. Note here, though, how quickly Cicero moves from the general statement 'takes part in public discussion' to once again stressing the direct and personal threat posed by Catiline ('. . . us to be murdered'). Before his final remarks, Cicero indicates the passivity of his fellow senators.

> *ad mortem et, Catilina, duci iussu consulis iam pridem oportebat, in te conferri pestem istam quam tu in nos omnes iam diu machinaris.*

> You should a long time ago, Catiline, have been led to your death by the consul's order, and that destruction you have been planning against all of us for a long time now should have been visited on you.

Cicero concludes with a nicely balanced and economical statement of what should be the case. The word for 'death' is emphatically placed at the beginning, and a verb which describes Catiline's machinations wraps up the paragraph.

If these were the words that Cicero uttered in the senate in 63, we can imagine the stunning effect they may have had. What we can see on the page is a masterly use of various rhetorical and stylistic techniques. The most recent commentator provides a nice summary: '. . . a masterpiece of concentrated innuendo and vituperation, based upon a limited stock of themes and images, skilfully interwoven and subtly varied' (Dyck, 2008: 61). Cicero made his name, though, as an orator in the courts. And it is to one of the extant judicial speeches – *Pro Caelio* (In Defence of Caelius) – that we now turn.

M. Caelius Rufus was charged with a wide variety of crimes, including the murder of an Alexandrian envoy and the attempted poisoning of a now notorious aristocratic lady called Clodia. Clodia was the sister of the populist politician and enemy of Cicero, Publius Clodius Pulcher. Caelius seems to have had an affair with Clodia (as the poet Catullus may have done), and then rebuffed her advances. Cicero's advocacy relies on the same sorts of rhetorical techniques which we have already seen deployed, but the tone is less high-brow than in his senatorial speeches, and he is more ready to use humour, digression and literary models. One of his main tactics in this speech to is to render any evidence provided by Clodia unreliable by attacking her character: she is presented to the court by Cicero as a promiscuous courtesan with a fragile hold on the truth. Such a figure was not unusual in Roman comedy, so it is no surprise to see Cicero also making some use of quotes from such authors as Terence. In order to criticize Clodia, Cicero imagines what one of her early and far more austere ancestors (Appius Claudius Caecus) would have said to her; for an alternative view he also conjures up the thoughts of Clodia's younger brother. Such use of literary techniques goes hand in hand with the suggestion and innuendo that are once again to the fore, as in this comic list (*Pro Caelio* 35):

> Indeed the prosecutors are throwing around such things as orgies, flirtations, adulteries, Baiae, beach parties, dinner parties, drinking parties, singing, concerts, boating picnics, and they claim that they are saying nothing without your permission.

Cicero uses the list to drive home the idea of the sort of crowd Clodia moves with, neatly sliding over the fact that Caelius shares the same sorts of friends. The use of the metonymy Baiae is suggestive and amusing: Baiae was a celebrated or notorious pleasure ground of the rich on the bay of Naples. We might achieve a similar effect by using Nice or the Côte D'Azur metonymically.

Perhaps one of the most amusing sections of the speech comes when Cicero deals with Clodia's accusation of attempted poisoning. The section to which I refer (*Pro Caelio* 56–69) is too long to quote in any detail, but the way in which Cicero treats Clodia's accusation of attempted poisoning by a superb series of *reductiones ad absurdum* marks out this section of the speech as a fine example of they way Cicero can use humour to devastating rhetorical effect. Cicero's tactic in this section is clear from the start (*Pro Caelio* 56.1–6):

> So there remains the charge of poisoning. I cannot find where this began nor where it was supposed to lead. What reason was there why Caelius should want to give poison to that woman? So as not to return the gold? Surely she didn't ask for it? So that the [other] charge might not stick? Surely no one thought that it did?

Cicero goes on to ridicule the prosecution's claims that Caelius had an accomplice in the poisoning, the role played by slaves, the provenance and power of the poison, the meeting in the public baths, and so on. Cicero characterizes Clodia's circle in the most unflattering terms (*Pro Caelio* 67). The Latin is worth quoting here:

> *vigeant apud istam mulierem venustate, dominentur sumptibus, haereant, iaceant, deserviant; capiti vero innocentis fortunisque parcant.*

Let them flourish with that lady with their style, let them lord it with their extravagance, let them stick close to her, lie at her feet, serve her. But let them spare the life and fortunes of an innocent man.

These lines contain comic invective, irony, a certain dramatic quality and – in the final exhortation – a deadly seriousness, which achieves weight by what immediately precedes it. Clodia herself is finally roundly condemned as the sort of woman whose reputation makes believable every story involving promiscuity and (unspecified, here) base sexual behaviour (*Pro Caelio* 69).

Cicero was very probably the culmination of an oratorical tradition in republican Rome. It is true that his style, elaborate as it is, is not always to twenty-first-century tastes. After all, we live the world of the sound-bite, and we prefer our political and judicial oratory plain. Cicero may indeed have been part of a dispute in his own day about whether the florid and elaborate rhetoric (normally referred to as *Asianism*) was inferior to the plainer, crisper style associated with Lysias (which was called *Atticism*; there is some scholarly dispute about whether these were clearly defined schools of rhetoric in Cicero's day). What we can say about Cicero's rhetoric is that it is marked by a certain exuberance and musicality, with a sure command of rhythm and tone. Cicero also displays considerable erudition, whether in his use of Greek rhetorical models, his digressions on Roman history, or in his extensive quotation from Greek and earlier Latin literature. He makes clever use of digressions, humour, quick character portraits and emotional appeals. The speeches are well-structured but allow for variety. Certainly, for a later educationalist such as Quintilian, Cicero's writings were a good source of exemplary material.

Approaching Cicero from a literary point of view, it is his speeches which we will most often encounter. But it is important to note that he wrote a number of theoretical works about oratory, a variety of philosophical works and a large number of letters. There are several minor works on oratory which need not concern us, but most scholars would regard *De Oratore* (55), *Brutus* and *Orator* (44) as important contributions to the Roman theory of rhetoric. The figure of the orator as presented in the earliest work is of a liberal, erudite master, concerned not just with rhetorical niceties, but also with literature, philosophy and politics. *Brutus* is a helpful history of Roman rhetoric, while *Orator* deals with more technical matters. As to his philosophical work, this can be divided into that which deals with questions of political philosophy and with those mainly concerned with ethics. In both areas he was much influenced by Plato and Aristotle; in the latter area by the stoics (he found Epicureanism not at all to his liking). Cicero's philosophical writings have been very important in the history of European thought, as they convey much of Greek thinking that would otherwise have been lost. It may be true that Cicero himself was not a thinker of the first rank, but he has a good understanding of argument and is a good explicator of others' ideas. Perhaps most important among his philosophical works were *De Re Publica* (On the Republic), which was perhaps inspired by Plato's *Republic* and which, in its proposals, strangely anticipated the principate, and *De Officiis* (On Duties), which remains one of our most important texts expounding stoic ideas.

The letters have Cicero presenting himself in a slightly different way. While still sometimes conceited, the Cicero here can be self-deprecating and ironic; he can also express concern as to whether he has done the right thing.

In conclusion, there may be a number of ways in which Cicero does not appeal to us now. But if we wish to understand the late republic, we will have to confront this masterly rhetorician, ambitious politician, recorder of important political events, interesting but not original thinker, notorious self-advertiser, and champion of *humanitas*. What is clear is that politics was central to Cicero. The writings that were theoretical were – almost without exception – written when his political involvement was, for one reason or another, limited. Nothing could more obviously distinguish classical Rome from classical Athens. For the Athenians, philosophy made no sense unless it occurred within the *polis*; for Romans, one engaged in philosophical thinking in exile or retirement.

Cicero's *Pro Caelio* and his relationship with Caelius reveal much about the nature of the Roman political elite. Caelius had connections with Cicero going back to adolescence, but in 59 he prosecuted C. Antonius Hybrida, who was Cicero's consular colleague in 63. His opponent in the courtroom was none other than Cicero himself; Caelius won. They faced each other again in 56 in the case of L. Calpurnius Bestia, on which occasion Cicero was the victor. In defending Caelius (and the *Pro Caelio* was also delivered in 56 as well), Cicero found himself having to explain away the fact that his young client was at one time associated with the very Catiline whose character he had so memorably assassinated in the *First Catilinarian*. In the later speech, Catiline has been transformed into an attractive, though dangerous figure, who possessed many virtues (*Pro Caelio* 12.2–4), and who, though complex and many-sided, still had supporters who were good men (ibid., 14.1–4). The circles that Cicero and Caelius moved in were made up of a relatively small number of men. When crafting a speech, Cicero would have had to remember that his opponent one day could be his client the next.

Further reading

Cicero wrote so much that his extant writings take up 15 volumes of the Oxford Classical Text series. There are various commentaries on individual speeches, philosophical and rhetorical treatises, and the letters. There are various translations: best to check Penguin and Loeb first. Cicero has variously been considered as a politician, an orator, a political commentator and a philosopher. The following works all contain some consideration of at least some of these various activities: Douglas (1968); Mitchell (1991); Murrell (2008); Rawson (1975); Steel (2005; 2006); Stockton (1971). On the speeches and Cicero's place within ancient rhetorical practice, see now Booth (2007); Gildenhard (2010); Habinek (2005); Powell and Patterson (2006); Usher (2008); Vasaly (1993); on the letters, see Hutchinson (1998); on Cicero as philosopher, see MacKendrick (1989); Powell (1999). On his role in the republic, see Wiedemann (1998). The two recent novels of Robert Harris (*Imperium* and *Lustrum*) capture well the ruthlessly competitive nature of Roman politics, and Cicero's place within that culture.

CAESAR

Roy Hyde

As consul in 59 Gaius Julius Caesar (100–44) was appointed to the command of the provinces of Gaul, both Cisalpine (south of the Alps), and Transalpine (what is now France). The latter was not yet Roman territory, but signs of military activity amongst the Helvetii, which could be construed as threatening the Cisalpine region, justified his mission and led to a full-scale war of conquest which brought the whole of Gaul under Roman rule. Caesar's command was not a regular proconsular appointment, but a move in the power game between himself, Pompey and Crassus, the three great political figures of the day. The Gallic command might be hoped to bring Caesar wealth, prestige and power – the latter in the form of a trained and loyal army which was to prove decisive in the civil war which broke out on his return to Italy.

It would also mean absence from Rome for at least five years (in fact it was ten, as his command was extended in 55). Caesar's associates in Rome would keep his reputation in the public eye; but the *commentarii* he wrote on his activities whilst in Gaul, and sent back apparently annually, would serve as a more tangible reminder that he was still a major player on the Roman stage. These reports constitute what are now known as the *Gallic War*; seven books of them, with the eighth added by Caesar's officer Aulus Hirtius after Caesar's death. His other extant work is the *Civil War*, written in similar format – with important differences – and dealing with the war which broke out between him and the adherents of Pompey in 49. The three books of this do not, for some reason, cover the whole war; the remainder of it was written up as the *Alexandrine War*, probably by Hirtius, the *African War*, perhaps also by him, and the *Spanish War*, by an unknown officer of Caesar. Caesar wrote other books which are lost, including one on grammar which he dedicated to Cicero, who regarded him as the most eloquent speaker of his time (Quintilian thought him the greatest Roman orator after Cicero; none of his speeches survive).

Commentarii originally meant 'notes', memoranda for private or public consultation. By Caesar's time the word had taken on a further, more literary, sense, of autobiographical material supposedly intended for historians to write up. (See Hirtius' remarks in his preface to *Gallic War* book 8.) Cicero had written some (lost) on his consulship in 63, and thought Caesar's to be admirable in style (*Brutus* 262), describing them as elegant and 'naked' – that is, without rhetorical adornment – and so good that no one with any sense would use them in a history because they could not be improved on. (Incidentally, Cicero's remark may also be seen as suggesting that he saw them as in some respects approaching closer to historiography: see below.) Stylistically, they are indeed a model of clarity, so much so that until recently they have been extensively used as school text-books, much to the detriment of their reputation. In terms of content, it must be said that they are of interest mostly to military historians; though the *Civil War*, as an account of a seminal conflict of western history, by its victorious protagonist, holds an intrinsic interest that the *Gallic War* lacks. But it is instructive to read the one in the light of the other.

Throughout the *commentarii*, Caesar refers to himself in the third person: 'Caesar thought this, Caesar did that'; the name springs out from every page, and the effect needs no elaboration. Xenophon had done the same in his *Anabasis*, but as he seems to have published this first under a pseudonym he had no alternative: whether it was the custom in Roman *commentarii*, we do not know. The impression it creates of Caesar as the epicentre of events, and as somehow distanced from the implied narrator, is reinforced when he occasionally does use a first person: '*Caesar*, for the reasons *I* have given, had decided to cross the Rhine' (*BG {= Gallic War}* 4.17.1) In the *Gallic War* the desired effect seems to be to identify Caesar with Rome itself; near the beginning of the book, after a brief account of the geography of Gaul and the warlike preparations of the Helvetii, he says: 'when Caesar [first word in the Latin] found out that they were trying to march through our province, he hurried to set out from the city' (*BG* 1.7.1). No indication that he is acting on behalf of the republic; and the 'our' is significant. Caesar customarily refers to his soldiers as *nostri*, 'our men', which in the context of the Gallic War is unimpeachable (though, of course, furthering the Roman reader's inclination to identify with Caesar); when he refers to 'our men' in the *Civil War*, meaning 'his' men, the word clearly takes on an additional shade of meaning.

Other features seem to go beyond what might seem to be appropriate in *commentarii*. Ethnographic details such as those about Gaul and the Gallic way of life, for example, would not seem to be central to *commentarii*, though geographical facts might be important in a military report designed to be of use to a general's successors. (It is interesting that Caesar does not generally give such details in the *Civil War* when he is describing events in Italy, presumably assuming that his readers will be familiar with them.) The use of direct speech, too, would seem out of place. In fact, Caesar does not use direct speech much in the *Gallic War*, but he does frequently report speeches, his own and other people's, in indirect speech. When he reports what he himself said (or thought), we can allow ourselves at least to accept its reasonableness: if it is not exactly what he said or thought in the heat of the moment, it is at least Caesar interpreting Caesar to us. When he reports, occasionally in direct speech, more often indirect, what a Gallic leader said to another in a Gallic camp, we may reasonably be sceptical, and suggest that Caesar the politician and Caesar the near-historian for the moment have the upper hand over Caesar as the writer of *commentarii*: the imputation of thoughts and words to individuals where they cannot possibly have been known is characteristic of ancient historiography, and perhaps of all historiography; and, to a man whose life was for the most part spent in the speculative world of politics, interpretation of political motivation must have been second nature. A couple of instances of direct speech interestingly come in passages of the *Gallic War* when Caesar is dealing with the heroic actions of ordinary soldiers (*BG* 5.44; 7.50): perhaps this is to show people at home that our brave boys in Gaul are doing their job for the state; more cynically, but perhaps more realistically, it is also making a point of their loyalty to their general. Also interestingly, in the *Civil War*, Caesar gives two direct speeches in succession to his loyal but foolhardy officer Curio (*BC* {= *Civil War*} 2. 31–2), not long before he falls into a trap and gets himself and his men killed.

The reason for the prominence of the unsuccessful Curio emerges in his final words (in indirect speech): he would rather die, he says, than return to Caesar without the army Caesar has entrusted to him (*BC* 2.42.4). He does so: loyalty is all. Throughout both the *Commentarii* the qualities prized by or disapproved of by Caesar are evident, overtly or by implication, but more significantly in the *Civil War* in obvious justification of his own position. In the *Gallic War*, though Caesar's opponents can be devious and unpredictable, they are brave and resourceful, posing strategic and tactical problems that require Roman (that is, Caesarian) ingenuity and courage to overcome: although we need not doubt the essential truth of this, it is equally obvious that to appear to have routed a disorganized horde of cowardly barbarians would hardly have increased Caesar's all-important reputation. In the *Civil War*, on the other hand, the disorganization, duplicity, cruelty, cowardice and over-confidence of the Pompeian commanders are constantly reinforced, by contrast with Caesar's superior strategy and organization, his generosity to the defeated and the loyalty shown by his followers. No doubt these virtues, along with the toughness of his battle-hardened Gallic veterans, went a long way towards winning the war; they were also, of course, ones which Caesar would have wanted to exhibit and to emphasize in the post-war world in which he was writing his account, and was king in all but name.

There is no reason to doubt the basic factual accuracy of the *Commentarii*: Cicero's judgement, referred to above, is a stylistic one, but (as an opponent of Caesar in the Civil War) if he had considered them merely falsified propaganda, we would expect him to have said so. Of course, they *are* propaganda, or in the case of the *Civil War*, justification: but what general's or politician's memoirs are not? They are not (quite) history – clearly they are not history as Cicero, and the prevailing Greco-Roman view of history, saw it – but they come close to it by virtue of the skill with which Caesar marshals his material, as well as the lucid fluency of his Latin: style, as much as content, was a prime consideration of the Roman historian. We might wish that such a pivotal figure in the history of the Western world *had* written a history, or at least left us an autobiography. At least, though, by reading between the elegant lines of Caesar's *Commentarii*, we can get some kind of insight into the actions and the thoughts (insofar as he allows us) of the man: the clarity of thought, the single-mindedness of purpose, the complete assurance, the ruthlessness that destroyed the lives of so many and a charm and charisma such that even his bitterest enemies found it hard to dislike him.

Further reading

For a classic account of Caesar's political career, see Gelzer (1968). On his murder, see now Woolf (2006). On Caesar as narrator, see Welch and Powell (1998). For a challenging approach, see Henderson (1998: chapter 2).

SALLUST

Neil Croally

Before Sallust decided to try his hand at history, he had been a practising politician in one of Rome's most turbulent eras. He was a tribune of the people in 52, in which role he acted against both Cicero and Milo. In 50 he was expelled from the senate for alleged immorality and became in the next year the commander of one of Caesar's legions in Africa. As praetor in 46 he was appointed the governor of the newly created province of Africa Nova. He was charged with misconduct on his return but escaped prosecution, it seems, only because of Caesar's intervention. At this point Sallust retired to write history. Before we go on to look more carefully at his works and their characteristics, it is worth noting that Sallust was criticized in antiquity for being a moralizing historian who had himself been involved in corruption and immoral behaviour. Given the way Roman politicians deployed every possible charge against their opponents, there is finally no way of knowing whether Sallust was guilty as charged. There is an intriguing moment, though, near the beginning of *The War of Catiline* (3.4–5), where he says that, while he himself rejects greed and similar vices, he was seduced by ambition when young.

There are two extant works written by Sallust, *The War of Catiline* which was published *c.* 42 and *The Jugurthine War* which appeared a year or so later. We know that he also later wrote a work called *Histories*, which seems to have begun with Sulla's death in 78 and gone on to some point in the 60s (the last fragment concerns 67). A number of other works were attributed to Sallust, but they seem not to be genuine.

The first interesting feature of Sallust's work is that, for his first work (*The War of Catiline*), he chose not to write a history of a period in annalistic form, but a monograph which concerned itself with one, limited episode. True, he is keen, as most Greek and Roman historians were, to stress the importance of his subject matter (*Catiline* 4.4), but not because his war lasted more years than others (as Thucydides argues about the Peloponnesian War), but because the threat posed by Catiline to the Roman state was so great. In choosing the monograph form, he may have been influenced by the work of L. Coelius Antipater, who wrote an account of the second Punic War in the late second century. Cicero himself is known in 56 to have asked an acquaintance to write an account of Catiline's conspiracy in monograph form, but that never appeared. So, while there were some precedents for the form of history that Sallust chose to write, for us he remains the first exponent of the historical monograph in Latin.

Anyone who reads either *The War of Catiline* or *The Jugurthine War* will be struck in particular by two things: Sallust's highly distinctive style and his fiercely expressed view that there is something rotten in the Roman body politic. If we take the latter feature first, we can also see that Sallust has a powerful theory about the causes of the moral degeneration of the Roman political class. This is expressed most succinctly in *The Jugurthine War* (41), where he states that, after the destruction of Carthage, factions arose in Rome. He further argues that, with Carthage no longer around to constrain the actions of Rome's politicians, all the vices associated with prosperity and untrammelled power flourished, that the aristocrats began to enrich themselves and oppress the people and that, as a result, there was civil dissension and eventually civil war. As he puts it in *Catiline* 5, Sallust is interested in how the Roman republic changed from being the finest and the best into the worst and most depraved. Sallust does his best to prove this very interesting historical hypothesis by concentrating fiercely in both his extant works on the nature of *virtus* (virtue, courage) and on the more particular moral deficiencies of his leading characters. Perhaps the most famous of his analyses of moral corruption is that of Catiline (*Catiline* 5; I paraphrase):

> Catiline was of noble birth, but was vicious and depraved, enjoying turbulence, bloodshed and discord. He possessed considerable physical endowments, most particularly a remarkable stamina. Mentally, he was daring, subtle and unscrupulous. From the time of Sulla's dictatorship, he desired power and cared not at all how he achieved it.

This seems to be an unambiguous picture of the dangers of ambition unrestrained by any moral considerations. However, Sallust does allow for some complexity in his portrait. The final speech which Catiline makes (*Catiline* 58) has persuaded some critics to view Catiline as something like a tragic figure. We may not want to go that far, but we can say that Catiline's depravity is seen to exist in an interdependent relationship with the moral decline of the republic as a whole.

In taking as his theme the degeneration of the Roman republic, Sallust was travelling down a similar path to that of Thucydides and of Cato the Elder. Thucydides, of course, believed that, after the death of Pericles, the Athenians were led by politicians who were more corrupt, more venal, less intelligent and, as a result, responsible for the terrible decision to attack Sicily that, in Thucydides' view, led to Athens' eventual defeat. Cato the Elder was an austere, stoic-influenced politician, who – ironically, given Sallust's view – strongly and unflinchingly proposed the destruction of Carthage. But Thucydides and Cato both clearly had an important influence on Sallust's method and style.

When Sallust chose to write a monograph about an important recent historical event, he may very well have been influenced by Thucydides. Thucydides had been an Athenian general until his exile in 424; Sallust too had a high-level military and political role in a republic dramatically affected by the events of 63. Having made the choices they did, both Thucydides and Sallust were choosing recent history, which meant that they could rely on the oral evidence of those who actually participated in the events they describe and analyse. (In this sense, then, Sallust is to Livy as Thucydides is to Herodotus.) Thucydides' use of speeches to characterize the main personalities, to crystallize issues and to provide a dramatic view of events is also a feature of Sallust (there are, for instance, four speeches in *Catiline*, two by Catiline, with the others by Caesar and Cato). Another Thucydidean aspect of Sallust's method is to concentrate on particular episodes in order to illustrate larger themes. One might argue that the whole of *The War of Catiline* is an account of an episode that illustrates the moral decline of Rome, in the same way that Thucydides uses the Melian Dialogue and the Sicilian Expedition to illustrate the decline of political leadership in Athens. Near the beginning of *The Jugurthine War* Sallust makes it very clear that he has chosen this (rather more distant) war, because it was the first time that there was any popular opposition to the aristocrats (*Jug.* 5.1).

Cato the Elder, while he may have influenced the critical and moralizing tone adopted by Sallust, is probably more of an influence on Sallust's style. At *Brutus* 65ff. Cicero argues that those wanting to adopt a simpler, plainer style than that favoured by orators could do worse than look at the *Origines* of Cato the Elder. For Sallust, who wanted to write, as it were, Thucydidean Greek in Latin, this suggestion seems to have been one that he was eager to follow. Sallust's style, following Cato, is first of all characterized by brevity. This is sometimes achieved by ellipsis (e.g. *Catiline* 7.2); sometimes by asyndeton (e.g. ibid., 5.3–5). In particular, Sallust likes to use historical infinitives, often in an elliptical way, as in this example from *The Jugurthine War* (41.5):

namque coepere nobilitas dignitatem, populus libertatem in lubidinem vortere, sibi quisque *ducere trahere rapere*.

For the nobility began to turn dignity, and the people freedom, into lust, and everyone appropriated, carried off and plundered for themselves.

In fact, this one sentence illustrates a number of features of Sallust's style: it is elliptical, it makes use of historical infinitives (in italics), and there are also archaizing elements (*vortere* rather than *vertere*; *lubidinem* rather than *libidinem*). (For other such archaisms, note: *-undus* rather than *-endus* for gerundives; e.g. *vivos* and *vivom* rather than *vivus* and *vivum*.) There is also a fairly liberal approach to word order, sometimes referred to as *inconcinnitas* or awkwardness. A good example of this is the reversal of the normal order in the phrase *maria terraeque* (seas and lands: *Catiline* 10.1; there is a good set of examples of Sallust's distinctive features in Ramsey, 2007: 10–14).

Sallust's style was both admired and criticized in antiquity, but both admirers and critics agreed on the essential characteristics of that style. For Seneca (*Letters* 114.17) Sallust wrote in a style in which 'phrases had bits chopped off, words ended unexpectedly, and obscure brevity was taken as elegance'. For Quintilian, on the other hand, Sallust was a superior writer to the Herodotean Livy, with his diffuse and elaborate style (Quintilian 2.5.19; 10.1.101), even though his sort of brevity should not be employed in oratory. Perhaps, though, Sallust's most important achievement was to be an influence on Tacitus, in both style and approach.

Tacitus, like Sallust, makes his theme, especially in the *Annals*, that of corruption and decline, in his case caused by the advent and then establishment of the autocratic system known as the principate. In a classically Sallustian and elliptical way Tacitus describes the behaviour of the political class at Rome following Tiberius' succession (*Annals* 1.7):

> *At Romae ruere in servitium consules, patres, eques.*

> And at Rome consuls, senators and knights rushed into servility.

One suspects Sallust would have enjoyed this sentence. In another Sallustian way, Tacitus is well aware that ambitious men thrive in amoral times, although his understanding of moral dilemma and political pressure is altogether more complex and ambiguous. His portrait of Sejanus, however, owes a lot to that of Catiline which we saw earlier (*Annals* 4.1):

> His body was tolerant of hardship; his mind was daring. Secretive about himself, but an incriminator of others, [he was] a mixture of flattery and arrogance; on the surface a well presented modesty; inside a supreme lust for power.

Tacitus may have wanted to alert his readers to the Sallustian echoes by starting the *Annals* with a brief discourse on Roman history, which not only imitates the brief history given by Sallust in *Catiline* (6–13), but starts with the same two words (*Urbem Romam*). However, Tacitus marvellously outdoes his own model in brevity: Sallust takes eight short paragraphs to cover Roman history; Tacitus takes a mere eight lines.

Sallust, then, plays an important role in Roman historiography. His choice of the monograph form, his moralizing tone and his archaizing and elliptical style are all important. But his main achievement may be more particular. The great Roman historian, Ronald Syme, wrote one of the masterpieces of Roman historiography when he produced his two volume work *Tacitus* in the late 1950s. Some 15 years later he published a single volume and eponymously titled work on Sallust. As one playful critic observed, as Sallust is no Tacitus, *Sallust* is no *Tacitus*. True, the latter historian is in many ways far superior. But Sallust's greatest achievement may have been this: without Sallust, no Tacitus.

Further reading

For a commentary on *Catiline*, see Ramsey (2007); on *The Jugurthine War*, see Watkiss (1984). Syme (1974) remains one of the best books. See also Earl (1961); Feldherr (2009); Kraus and Woodman (1997); Marincola (1997); on Thucydides' influence, Scanlon (1980).

LUCRETIUS: THE POEM AND THE WORLD

John Godwin

Lucretius did not set his sights low. His poem *De Rerum Natura* ('On the Nature of the Universe') seeks in six books of epic verse to explain quite simply everything – and to do so in language which is both philosophically and scientifically accurate and also poetically beautiful. He seeks, as he tells us in the proem to book 4, to 'coat everything with the honey of the Muses' in order to persuade the reluctant reader to be led to drink the bitter draughts of the science because of the sweet taste of the poetry.

In terms of content, the poem does pretty well what it sets out to do given that the title means literally 'On the Nature of Things'. It describes the world of the invisible atoms and explains their nature and movement in the first two books: in the middle books 3–4 Lucretius goes on to describe human beings – the nature of death in book 3 and the way the senses work in book 4. The fifth book looks at the way in which human society evolved, while the final book examines a range of other phenomena such as the weather, the flooding of the Nile, the workings of the magnet and finally the cause and pathology of the plague which hit Athens just after the beginning of the Peloponnesian War (431). The poem thus ranges from the microscopic to the telescopic, from the random mutations of atomic compounds to the issue of how and why we fall in love, embellished with detailed observation from his own day of such ordinary things as clothes hanging out to dry, the noise of the traffic or the nasty experience of biting a piece of stone baked in a loaf of bread.

In terms of structure the poem is beautifully arranged: it begins with the theme of birth and ends with the theme of death, and within these two parameters the poet divides up his material like an expert tutor into modules which follow on from one another. So the first principles come first – what is everything made of? – followed by the ways in which atomic compounds behave, leading to the highly interesting atomic compound called mankind and then on into society at large and finally into the skies. In each case the theory is stated and then démonstrated in a range of examples and analogies which allow the reader to visualize the process at work. When he tackles the fear of death in the third book he does so with 27 arguments which seek to prove that 'we' do not survive bodily death: the poet then finishes off the book with a rousing set of speeches to convince our hearts of what (he hopes) our heads are now persuaded – namely that *nil igitur mors est ad nos* (death is nothing to us).

That Latin tag just quoted was in fact not originally thought up by Lucretius but is a direct translation from the Greek of Epicurus, the philosopher who lived from 341 to 270 and who was highly influential on many thinkers who came after him. Lucretius' theories are all based on the thinking of Epicurus – in fact it has recently been persuasively argued that Lucretius was a fundamentalist when it came to the teaching of the Greek master. The essence of Epicurus' philosophy is that there is nothing which is not material in composition; there is matter and nothing (empty space, vacuum). Everything that can be said to exist must be made up of matter, and this matter is made up of the invisible, indivisible building blocks which he called 'atoms' (the word deriving from he Greek for 'indivisible'). Atoms cannot be created or destroyed, and they have a finite number of different sizes and shapes, for the apparently logical reason that if there were an infinite range of atomic shapes then there would have to be an infinite range of sizes – and this would have produced atoms of infinite size (2.476–99). As no atom can be seen, then it follows that there is a limited range of sizes. This line of argument – the so-called *modus tollens* – is one of Lucretius' favourites and can be summarized thus:

if P, then Q (if infinite range, then we would see huge atoms)
but not-Q (we do not see huge atoms)
therefore not-P (there is not an infinite range)

It is itself a line of argument which we use all the time without thinking too hard about it. How do I know that it rained last night while I was asleep? Because the grass would not be wet if it had not. It is very useful for proving what we cannot see (such as the shape of atoms) on the basis of the visible and probable consequences of different theorems. As such it is useful also in mathematics to prove such theories as whether there is an infinite number of primes. What makes Lucretius' argumentation especially appealing and more obviously poetic than a page of algebra is the way in which he unpacks the theory into concrete examples. So, for instance, his theory that atomic shapes vary is shown by the wonderful illustration of the mother cow searching for her lost calf. The poet begins with the clear observation that all atoms are not alike, as otherwise we would not be able to tell any one thing apart from any other. So far so good. The example he chooses however gives him the freedom to indulge his poetic effects to the full (2.352ff):

> For often in front of the glorious shrines of the gods a calf falls down slaughtered beside the incense-burning altars, breathing out a hot river of blood from his breast. Yet the bereaved mother-cow roams through the green glens searching for the footprints on the ground pressed down by his cloven hooves, gazing everywhere with her eyes to see if she can spot her lost baby anywhere. She stops moving and fills the leafy grove with her laments and keeps going back to the stall, stabbed with longing for her calf.

The 'reason' for this behaviour is that other calves will not do – she recognizes her own calf as being atomically different from others. He later turns the image round with the less harrowing image of lambs running to the correct udder to feed from their own mothers and not other sheep.

One thing which is at once obvious about the above passage is the dig at religion – the cow has lost her beloved calf to a religious sacrifice at 'incense-burning altars'. Elsewhere (4.1236–41) Lucretius mocks the pathetic impotent man who makes offerings to the gods to help him get his wife pregnant:

> They spatter the altars with lots of blood in their sad state and set up burnt offerings on them, to get their wives big with abundance of sperm. It is all a waste of time their tiring out the power of the gods and wearying of the magic lots. They are just barren.

What they need, he hints with a typical verbal joke, is not *numen* (the power of the gods) but more *semen* (sperm) to do the job.

Lucretius does refer to the gods in his poem, and he does not preach atheism as such. His attitude towards them, however, is the classic Epicurean position that the gods do not care about us and so are not worth praying to. The reasoning is (again) *modus tollens*:

> If the gods listened to all our myriad prayers they would not be 'blessed gods'.
> But the gods are 'blessed' (i.e. happy) gods.
> Therefore they cannot listen to our myriad prayers.

We can be sure that the gods did not create the world as it is for our benefit, as he argues in a glorious piece of rhetoric (5.195–234): most of the world is uninhabitable and the place is teeming with beasts who are all equipped with teeth, claws and the strength to eat us for their dinner. If this is done for the benefit of anyone it is perhaps done for the sake of the animals but not for us.

Elsewhere (3.322) he tells us that we can live 'a life worthy of the gods' (*dignam dis degere vitam*) if we cultivate the divine serenity and practise a life untroubled with cares, in particular the twin fears of death and the gods. If the gods do not notice us then all the old tales of divine anger avenging slights to divine honour must be untrue and we do not need to worry that gods will punish us here or hereafter. They cannot punish us hereafter as there will be for us no 'hereafter' to be punished in.

For many people the third book of the poem is puzzling. The poet seeks to disabuse us of the unhealthy fear of death by showing that we do not survive it but that rather the atoms of which we are made disperse and go on to make other things. We 'borrow' matter for our span of life and then give it back at the end like a library book. Lucretius' arguments take the form of such considerations as that we were dead before we were born and that was fine, for all that the world was in turmoil with Rome facing Hannibal in the Punic wars – after death will be no different and so we need not fear what we will not experience. We are, in that sense, the dead on a brief holiday. This does answer the fear of torment in the underworld – either the tedious disembodied boredom of the 'strengthless heads' in the eleventh book of Homer's *Odyssey* or more imaginative suffering such as the fables of Tantalus and Sisyphus who were made to pay for their wrongdoing with eternal pain. It is less consoling to twentieth-century mankind who does not want to cease existence.

The ethical side of the poem is essential and Lucretius takes pains to set out his programme for the enlightenment of his addressee – the Roman political figure Gaius Memmius who was also the provincial governor of Bithynia whom Catullus served and described in highly unflattering terms. Lucretius is – it seems – seeking to persuade the reader to change his attitude to life by a mixture of scientific argument and ethical exhortation. The science is used to justify the ethics by proving that the world and we ourselves are made up of temporary atomic compounds. We cannot be happy unless we live in accordance with nature: Lucretius therefore needs to tell us what Nature is like so that we can live in accordance with it and so be happy.

The ethics also justifies the science – to anyone who might ask what was the point of all that dry technical information about the nature of the atom or the physics of magnetism Lucretius can thus reply that science shows us how to be happy. There is, however, more to it than naturalist ethics depending on scientific data: for Lucretius the science is itself part of the lasting pleasure of life and worth doing for its own sake.

Epicureans have always had a bad press when it comes to pleasure. They were said to be devoted to physical pleasure and the modern English word 'epicure' comes to mean one who cultivates bodily pleasures, often of a rare and fastidious kind. This is a million miles away from the teachings of Epicurus and Lucretius on the subject. For, while it is true that they both argued that what we actually seek in life is pleasure (and the avoidance of pain), they both stressed that once the pain of want has been satisfied then the pleasure cannot be further increased. So the hungry man will enjoy his dinner while the one who has already eaten would not, however tasty the food. 'Kinetic' pleasure of this sort – food, drink, sex – is a matter of atomic balance being restored by the ingestion of food and drink or the expulsion of sperm. Anything will do if one is hungry and one is in fact better off *not* cultivating a taste for luxury if one wishes to avoid hunger. Epicurus himself was famed for eating bread, cheese and olives rather than expensive cuts of meat, on the principle of *parvum quod satis est* (the little that is enough). The same goes for sexual release in that the romantic lover who rejects the available partner in favour of the idealized unavailable partner is literally stoking up trouble for himself and dooming himself to painful frustration. In the last section of the fourth book Lucretius writes a lengthy tirade against romantic love; after his explanation of the biology of healthy sexual contact and human reproduction he shows us the unhealthy attitude which is both painful and embarrassingly shocking. The conclusion to be drawn from this passage is of general application to the whole poem: the healthy person sees the truth while the unhealthy person indulges in make-believe. The lover believes that his beloved is perfect when she is obviously not and even her maids giggle at her behind her back as they have access to what he cleverly calls (4.1186) the 'backstage aspects of life' (*vitae postscaenia*). Lovers make up silly nicknames to turn the faults of the beloved into good qualities (4.1160–2):

> The dirty and untidy girl is lovely disorder, the green-eyed girl is the image of Pallas, the skinny wooden one is a gazelle while the little dwarf is one of the Graces.

Lovers also, like foolish gamblers, throw all their money away in the quest to impress this skin-deep heartless fantasy: and even if they get their hearts' desire they are still not happy (4.1133–40):

> From the very centre of the spring of their joy rises a taste of bitterness to torture him amid the flowers: either he is biting himself in guilty remorse at the way he is wasting his life and wrecking everything in brothels, or because she has left him after shooting a word of ambiguous intent at him, a word which sticks in his heart and grows like a fire, or because he thinks she is making eyes and gazing at another man and in her face he sees the traces of a smile.

In contrast to that we see the healthy life: one of marriage and children, one of avoidance of stress and enjoyment of life, above all one of the pleasure of seeing the world and enjoying the spectacle.

The attitude of Lucretius towards society in general is most properly described as apolitical. He sees the pursuit of political power in much the same terms as he sees the pursuit of the idealized lover, as a course to disaster. Courting the fickle populace for the illusion of power is bad for the politician and also for society (3.59–63):

> What is more, greed and the blind lust for honours make unhappy men cross the boundaries of what is right. Sometimes as allies and agents of crime they will strive night and day with excessive toil to get to the top.

This creates envy (that that man has power, is gazed on, is walking in the glare of public honour, while they complain they are rolling around in the darkness and the mud 3.75–7) and leads men to wear out their whole lives 'for the sake of statues and a name'. Epicurus famously led his friends out of Athens to the garden where they lived a life of communal support and philosophy; the world in which Lucretius was born was one of internecine strife as the old republic struggled with less and less success to harness the power of the army commanders whose rivalry would tear the Roman world in two, and he must have felt the same disillusion with politics as many other people in the generation where, as Cicero was to claim, 'weapons are out and the laws keep silent'. The wise man will avoid contact with stress – except in the position of a passive viewer of the turning world around him.

The classic statement of Lucretius' ethical stance is the opening of book 2 (lines 1–4):

> It is a pleasure, when the winds are battering the waters on the high seas, to look on the great toil of another man from the land. Not because it is a joyful pleasure for anyone to suffer, but because there is pleasure in seeing the ills that you do not have to share.

This again sounds like *Schadenfreude* and is unattractive as it stands. What the poet is doing is clear from what follows, where he spells out the folly of mankind pursuing wealth and power when real happiness is available for nothing to those who 'possess the lofty serene temples, shored up with the teaching of the wise'. Every word counts here: the only temples to cultivate are the ones of philosophy and not of unheeding gods, 'serene' is the state of mind aimed at by the wise person who will avoid the stress and excitement of life in favour of a balanced contentment midway between pleasure and pain; and the 'wise' clearly refers to Epicurus, whose teachings have (according to the prologue to book 5) done more for suffering humanity than the fabled labours of Hercules.

Hercules, after all, only rid some bits of the world of some troublesome monsters, leaving the rest of us to suffer now that he has gone, while Epicurus has given us all the key to happiness.

Further reading

The classic edition of Lucretius is that of Cyril Bailey (3 vols, 1947). There are translations of the whole poem by Latham and Godwin (1994), Melville (1997), Slavitt (2008). For good introductions to Lucretius, see Gale (1994; 2001); Godwin (2004); Johnson (2000); Sedley (1998); Segal (1990); West (1969). On didactic poetry more generally, see Volk (2002).

CATULLUS: THE POETRY OF PLEASURE AND THE PLEASURE OF POETRY

John Godwin

> *Hedgehog and the fox. Knows many things or one thing. . .*

Of all the writers of the ancient world Catullus is one of the easiest to read and the hardest to pigeonhole in any or genre or style. Some writers always write history, others comedy or satire. Some writers produce a large body of work which embraces a variety of styles. Catullus is unusual in that his surviving output is tiny and yet his range is huge. Catullus moves from the sublime to the absurd, from the tragic to the comic, from the sentimental to the scatological, in the time it takes to move from one poem to the next. His poems range from the tiniest two-line epigram (poem 85):

> I hate and I love: why do I do that, you perhaps ask?
> I don't know – but I feel it happening and it's torture

to the sustained mini-epic poem 64. The one common feature of all of his poems is their dedication to poetry itself as a source of power and pleasure.

Ancient poets sometimes divided their poetry into the 'useful' and the 'delightful', with romantic lyric giving delight and didactic epic giving instruction. Even poets who are not explicitly didactic still sometimes pay lip service to the 'useful' qualities of their verse if only in the sense that one can learn history or mythology from them. Catullus' poems, on the contrary, are dedicated to pleasure: the celebration of different sorts of pleasure (love, friendship) and the pleasure of poetry even when – especially when – the social pleasures are lacking. What the poet often does is to foil the expectations of the learned reader with the constant use of surprise and ingenuity. Take poem 64 for instance: this poem, at 406 lines, is by far the longest poem in the collection and is concerned with its magical evocation of the wedding of the mortal Peleus and the sea-nymph Thetis after their surprise encounter in mid-ocean. The wedding is arranged and the gods all arrive bearing their divine gifts: the marriage bed is described and its coverlet allows the poet to indulge in a 'digression' as long as the surrounding narrative, a digression about the abandoning of Ariadne by her faithless lover on Naxos. The shock value of this is enormous: not only the formal shock of having a digression – if it is a digression – as long as the framing narrative, but also the tasteless nerve to show such a testament to male faithlessness at a wedding celebrating romantic love. So also perhaps is the prophecy of the Fates which follows on from the digression: the old ladies with their white hair and their almost toothless mouths sing of the future offspring of Peleus and Thetis, the great Greek hero Achilles. To be told that one's child will grow into a great hero is one thing, but to be told that he will mow down his enemies like grass, choking the stream of the river Scamander with heaps of slain bodies – this is perhaps taking things too far. The poem ends with a moralizing epilogue whose ostensible purpose is to explain why it is that such mixed marriages of mortals and gods no longer happen because of human wickedness repelling the gods (poem 64.397–408):

> After the earth was soaked with evil crime
> and everyone scattered justice from their lustful thoughts
> brothers wet their hands with brothers' blood,
> the son stopped grieving for his deceased parents,
> the father longed for the death of his first-born son
> so that he might be able to enjoy the flower of a new young wife;
> the wicked mother laying herself underneath her unwitting son,
> wicked woman showed no fear of adulterating family gods.
> Everything both speakable and unspeakable, mingled together in wicked madness,
> has turned the righteous mind of the gods away from us.
> That is why they do not deem our gatherings worthy of visiting,
> and do not allow themselves to be touched with the clear light of day.

Poem 64 then is a surprising poem in many ways. We constantly find our expectations foiled by the poet: what seems to be a poem about the voyage of the Argo – the first ship to sail and the vessel which would most plausibly introduce mariners to sea-nymphs – turns out to be about a wedding. The wedding is interrupted by the lengthy description of the coverlet which shifts the optimism of the wedding to the pessimism of love betrayed, only to shift the despair of Ariadne with the prospect of her salvation at the hands of her divine lover Dionysus. The god-mortal theme thus comes full circle – Peleus the mortal corresponds to Ariadne, while Dionysus corresponds to Thetis – with the pairs of lovers contrasted in gender. The poem has immense variety – from narrative to descriptive passages to the song of the fates. Above all the poem is a kaleidoscope of poetic and sensuous pleasure.

The poem immediately before this one (63) is an equally shocking account of the self-castration of Attis when he is in a state of religious frenzy worshipping the Great Mother Cybele; the two poems which follow it (65–6) are dedicated to a translation of a poem by the highly influential Greek poet Callimachus. There then follows a scabrous tale of tabloid qualities: poem 67 is a dialogue between the poet and a door which is encouraged to tell the scurrilous gossip which it has access to – in this case a tale of impotence and adultery which would do justice to the lowest gutter press hack. The last of the long poems (68) is sublime and is perhaps the best poem which our poet ever created. It also typifies his work.

Here again Catullus blends the personal and the mythological, romance and tragedy. The setting is the poet's love-making with his married lover, but the 'gleaming goddess' is never described except in terms of her effect on the poet. The relationship of the poet and his mistress reminds him of the love of Protesilaus and Laudamia, a love which was doomed to frustration when Protesilaus was killed in the Trojan War. This then reminds him of the death of his brother who has died in northern Turkey – close to the site of ancient Troy. Weaving these themes – Catullus, his brother and the legend of Troy – the poet creates a web of poetic analogy which relies heavily on the device of the simile. This poem in fact uses the simile to such an extent that there are more lines of simile than there are of 'straight' narrative, and again the effect is one of kaleidoscopic poetic pleasure, whereby the male poet is equated to the female lover Laudamia. The poem is constructed in a form of ring-composition and shows beyond all doubt that poetry for Catullus is born of hard work and detailed planning rather than any mere outpouring of emotion. The emotion here is channelled through lines of metrical and linguistic sophistication which links past and present, sorrow and joy, beauty and the repellent ugliness of death.

So much for the longer poems: but Catullus is better known for the short poems which many meet for the first time at school and which convince them that Latin was once spoken by real people and not militaristic robots. Take poem 5 for example:

> Let us live, my Lesbia, and let us love
> and let us count the gossiping of strict old men
> as all being worth one penny.
> The sun can set and rise again:
> but when our little light has set
> there is but one long night to be slept through.
> Give me a thousand kisses, then a hundred:
> then another thousand, then a second hundred:
> then at once another thousand, then a hundred.

Then when we have many thousands of kisses
we will throw the accounts into confusion, so we don't know the number
and so no bastard can give us the evil eye
when he knows we have so many kisses.

The poem falls into two neat sections: lines 1–6 are a meditation on the tran-
sitory nature of life and the need to make the most of what little we have
before eternal death takes it and us away. Lines 7–13 follow this with a lover's
demand for a multitude of kisses. Lurking behind the romantic love is a rejection of traditional, older Roman values, seen in the 'strict old men' and the
'bastard' who gives the young happy lovers the evil eye.

The identity of the poet's lover has been the subject of speculation ever
since Roman times. Whatever her real name, it was almost certainly not
'Lesbia' – that was clearly a light pseudonym and had the double senses of
'bluestocking' and also 'sexually adventurous' – both derived from the island
of Lesbos which was home to the most famous woman poet in antiquity,
Sappho (see 3c). The soubriquet was partly a compliment and partly a teasing
joke; it was also a highly literary choice.

Who was Lesbia?

Critics and readers unworried by the biographical fallacy have made
strenuous efforts to identify the real woman behind Catullus' Lesbia. Most
have settled on Clodia, one of the sisters of P. Clodius Pulcher. Clodia's
lifestyle and promiscuity were notorious, and were much mocked and
criticized in Cicero's defence of one of her lovers, Caelius (see section b
in this chapter). Even if Catullus did have an affair with Clodia, we can never
know whether the Lesbia poems accurately reflect the relations between
the lovers: Catullus wrote poetry not a diary. However, it is important to
be aware of changes in the lifestyles of the social elite in the late republic.
In particular, a new type of intelligent, educated and – yes – racy woman is
apparent: Clodia is representative of this new type. (On the demi-monde
of the late republic, see Lyne (1980).)

The Lesbia poems appear to document the ups and downs of the poet's
relationship with this mysterious woman. There are the happy moments –
such as poem 5 above – and the poems of venomous hatred toward her when
the poet feels betrayed by her infidelity (11.17–24):

Let her live and thrive with her lovers
whom she grips in her embrace three hundred at a time
loving none of them truly but again and again
breaking the balls of them all.

Let her not look back as she once did to my love
which has fallen down thanks to her wickedness, like a flower
at the edge of the meadow, after it has been touched
by the passing plough.

Then again there are the poems which celebrate the beauty of the poet's girl when contrasted to other girls such as Ameaena, the girl with a whole check-list of faults (poem 43):

Greetings, girl, whose nose is not small
whose foot is not pretty, eyes not black,
fingers not long, mouth not dry,
tongue which is not over-elegant by any means,
girlfriend of the bankrupt from Formiae.
Is it you whom the locality claims to be pretty?
Is our Lesbia compared with you?
What a lack of wit and taste in this generation!

The fair sex for Catullus is not always female: there are passionate poems addressed to a certain young man called Iuventius, whose 'honeyed eyes' the poet would love to kiss hundreds of thousands of times (poem 48). Yet the language of homosexual abuse is also much used in the more ribald and scathing poems directed even at the rich and politically famous (poem 57):

They make a good pair, the shameless perverts
Mamurra and his bumboy Caesar

or the less famous (poem 33.8):

you cannot sell your hairy buttocks for a penny . . .

The language of satire is not far away from poems such as 59:

Rufa, the wife of Menenius, sucks off Rufulus.
You have often seen her in graveyards
snatching her dinner right off the funeral pyre,
running after a loaf that has rolled out of the fire
and getting banged by the stubbly cremator.

Or the throwaway remarks about men who brush their teeth with urine (poem 39) or who shit pebbles (poem 23).

Catullus is certainly unbuttoned in his choice and use of language. When occasion dictates, he can be as offensive as anybody in Roman literature. His poems convey a power which can be directed for good or for ill, and he uses his verses as missiles more than once: he even addresses his verses as if they were troops lined up to attack his enemies in poem 42, where a 'foul tart' with the 'face of a dog from Gaul' has taken his writing tablets and refuses to return them. The poet summons his verses to shame her into surrender.

Many of his most effective poems are in fact about poetry. The joy of composing verses is conveyed in a lovely light-hearted reminiscence (poem 50) while the criticism meted out to him that he must be a louche individual because he writes 'naughty verses' makes him compose a spirited defence of the writer against the documentary (or biographical) fallacy (poem 16.1–6):

> I'll bugger you and fuck your mouths
> Aurelius the pansy and Furius the pervert:
> you thought on the evidence of my little poems
> that I lacked purity because they are a bit louche:
> the decent poet ought to be pure himself
> but not his little poems . . .

Further reading

For introductions to Catullus, see Ferguson (1988); Fitzgerald (1995); Godwin (1996; 1999; 2008); Hurley (2004); Wiseman (1986). See also Kennedy (1993); Lyne (1980), most especially for Catullus' contribution to what would become love elegy. And note the challenging piece by Henderson (1999: chapter 3).

VIRGIL: *ECLOGUES* AND *GEORGICS*

Caroline Butler

Publius Vergilius Maro (70–19 BCE) is without question the most influential Roman poet of them all. The *Eclogues*, the *Georgics* and the *Aeneid* rapidly came to define the genres of pastoral, didactic and epic, and have remained consistently at the centre of the classical canon, their reputations enhanced by their importance to the poetry of (among others) Dante and Milton. The *Eclogues* deal – on one level, at least – with the lives and loves of shepherds in an idyllic, imprecise landscape; the *Georgics* (apparently) with the practicalities of Mediterranean agriculture. Both are located firmly in a very particular literary and political context, and both are written in a highly sophisticated language which makes significant demands of the reader.

Both the *Eclogues* and the *Georgics* were written during what is known as the triumviral period, the years between the assassination of Julius Caesar in

44 and the defeat of Antony and Cleopatra by Octavian (later the emperor Augustus) at the battle of Actium in 31. Virgil's ancient biographers state that his family lost ancestral estates in the confiscations. We do know that he was one of the poets who formed the circle of Maecenas, a close associate of Octavian. This association brought Virgil into close contact with the inner circle of power and led him, like Horace and Propertius, to write poetry that engaged closely with the political issues of the time.

But equally important is the literary context. In common with the vast majority of Roman poets, Virgil looks to the Greek literary tradition for his models. Moreover, the first half of the first century saw a generation of poets, the 'neoterics' or 'new poets' (of whom only Catullus' work has survived in any quantity). Their work was modelled on the Alexandrian or Hellenistic poets of the third and second centuries, of whom Callimachus was probably the most celebrated. The characteristics of Alexandrian poetry included the rejection of epic and tragedy in favour of shorter, more concise forms and the parade of scholarship (which the Romans called *doctrina*). This encompassed obscure examples from mythology, sophisticated vocabulary, and the display of historical and scientific knowledge. And it is in the *Eclogues* and *Georgics* that we see Virgil at his most Hellenistic (see 7b).

The direct inspiration for the *Eclogues* was the work of Theocritus, who flourished in the third century. Probably a Sicilian who subsequently worked in Alexandria, his *Idylls* ('Images') or *Bucolica* ('Poems of Cowherds') are credited with the invention of the genre of pastoral poetry. Theocritus' great innovation was to take situations from contemporary country or city life and to impose on these an extremely polished literary language (the exclusively poetic Doric dialect) and metre (the dactylic hexameter, traditionally used for the 'high' genres of epic and didactic poetry). Most important for Virgil are the conversations and singing competitions between shepherds and cowherds, the love-song of the Cyclops Polyphemus, the lament over the dying shepherd Daphnis and, more generally, the detailed evocation of the Mediterranean landscape.

It is this vividly-described landscape which perhaps proves the most accessible aspect of the *Eclogues*. In *Eclogue* 2, for example, we hear the love-song of the rough shepherd Corydon for Alexis, a slave-boy. The poem, set in Theocritus' native island of Sicily, begins with him wandering among the thick, shadowy canopy of beech-trees, crying to the mountains and woods. He talks of the searing heat, as flocks make for the shade and the cool, as the lizards hide in the thorn-bushes, and women pound garlic, thyme and other fragrant herbs to make a meal for the exhausted harvesters, while he hears the harsh cries of the cicadas coming from the bushes under the blazing sun. The heat, sounds and smells of a Mediterranean summer are immediately recognizable.

Other poems in the *Eclogues* bring the world of contemporary Rome more obtrusively into the pastoral landscape. *Eclogue* 1, for example, is a dialogue between the herdsmen Tityrus and Meliboeus (both Theocritean names). It opens with a familiar pastoral description of Tityrus playing his reed-pipe beneath the shade of a beech tree. But as early as line 2 Meliboeus says that he must leave his *patria* (fatherland), a situation which immediately suggests the land-confiscations of the triumviral period.

Throughout the poem, the names and the rustic scenarios are all familiar from Theocritus, but with a constant and unsettling admixture of contemporary Rome. Tityrus, we discover, is a slave who has visited Rome and successfully petitioned a young man, to whom he expresses his gratitude with divine honours – details which are too specific to suggest anyone but Octavian. It is difficult to appreciate just how jarring a Roman reader will have found the naming of Rome, or the use of the political catchword *libertas* (freedom), both in emphatic positions at the beginning of their lines, in a book of poems apparently located in the highly literary and stylized world of Theocritean pastoral.

The allusions to the confiscations have led some scholars to identify Tityrus with Virgil himself. The poem also possesses wider significance as a discussion of the repercussions of the recent political upheavals on Italian country life, where the apparently eternal seasonal round was being violently disrupted. And yet it is equally difficult to read the first *Eclogue* as an allegory of contemporary events: the 'fit' with Theocritean pastoral is too close, the details of Tityrus and Meliboeus too specific, for the reader to ignore the literary or the individualized character of the poem. Virgil compels the reader to consider his poetry through both a contemporary and a literary lens: there is no single key or meaning.

References to contemporary political events occur elsewhere in the *Eclogues*. In *Eclogue* 5 an apparently Theocritean lament for the death of Daphnis is now widely accepted as alluding to the assassination of Julius Caesar. Interestingly, the shepherd Menalcas identifies himself as the author of the *Eclogues*, though the extent to which he can be said to act as a 'mouthpiece' for the poet is far from straightforward. The confiscations again appear in *Eclogue* 9, as does Menalcas, though once again the details are too ambiguous to permit a clear identification with Virgil.

Eclogue 4 is perhaps the most famous of the collection. The poet begins by declaring that he will sing of things 'a little greater' (*paulo maiora*) and proceeds to anticipate the birth of a child that will usher in a new golden age. Creatively misread by medieval scholars as foretelling the birth of Christ, the poem in fact owes much to the Roman books of Sibylline prophesies which were in turn influenced by near-eastern apocalyptic writing. Attempts to link the poem conclusively to any specific historical event have all been unsuccessful, and it seems most likely that Virgil is exploring the images and ideas associated with the golden age theme which can be traced back to the Greek poet Hesiod as well as the Roman tradition of the age of Saturn.

Eclogue 6 is important in introducing to Roman literature the poetic conceit of the *recusatio* (literally 'refusal'). Here, Virgil imagines himself to have been on the point of writing epic ('kings and battles') when Apollo tweaked his ear (addressing him, interestingly, as 'Tityrus') and told him to stick to pastoral. This idea of the poet's course being redirected by divine intervention is found in Callimachus and is later deployed by Horace, Propertius and Ovid. It is also in this *Eclogue* that we find Virgil engaging most widely with contemporary Latin literature: addressed to the epic poet Varus (whose works are now lost), the poem also includes the character of the elegist Cornelius Gallus, who appears again in *Eclogue* 10.

Gallus is generally regarded as a key figure in the development of Roman elegy, though all that survives of his work is a single line plus a 16-line papyrus fragment whose authenticity has been doubted. In the final poem of the collection, Virgil imagines him wandering alone in a cold, rocky Arcadia very different from the sultry landscapes of conventional pastoral, and singing of his unrequited love for Lycoris (whom we know to have been the mistress addressed in his own poetry). It is, of course, impossible to know how this poem relates to Gallus' work; no doubt it is significant, however, that Virgil chooses to end the collection in this inhospitable and barren landscape, before declaring that the day grows cold, the shadows lengthen and it is time for him to take his goats home and end his song. The farewell to pastoral is unmistakable.

The *Georgics* similarly have their roots in the Greek literary tradition. Here the overt model is Hesiod, who wrote in the seventh century BCE and whose surviving works, the *Theogony* (on the genealogy of the Greek gods) and the *Works and Days* (on farming) are our first examples of didactic poetry (see 3b). Written like the *Eclogues* in dactylic hexameter, didactic poetry – named from the Greek word for 'teaching' – purports to instruct the reader and tends to be addressed to an individual. But didactic poetry also appealed to the Hellenistic desire to show off knowledge, and examples of the genre such as Callimachus' *Aetia* (on the origins of Greek religious customs) and Aratus' *Phaenomena* (on the weather) are an important influence on Virgil (see 7b). Unlike the *Eclogues*, though, the *Georgics* also have a Roman predecessor, Lucretius' *De Rerum Natura* ('On the Nature of the Universe'; see section e in this chapter). Written in the 50s, this is a didactic poem on Epicurean philosophy, and the concern shared by both poems with the relationship of human beings to their physical environment has led some scholars to see the *Georgics* as a stoic reply to Lucretius.

If the *Georgics* are to be viewed primarily as a didactic work, one must ask first what they purport to teach. The immediate answer – farming – is by no means unproblematic. Certainly they contain much detailed information about the growing of crops and the care of animals: book 1 deals with cereal crops and weather signs; book 2 with trees and vines; 3 with animal husbandry, and 4 with bee-keeping. Indeed, the quantity of technical detail about different types of soil in book 2, or the training of cattle in book 3, can seem exhaustingly dry to a modern reader. And yet the work contains much that is, at best, of tangential relevance to this theme: the description of the supernatural portents surrounding the death of Julius Caesar that ends book 1, for example, or the lengthy narration of the story of Orpheus and Eurydice in book 4. Moreover, as a practical manual the *Georgics* are at best patchy and at worst misleading.

One traditional interpretation of the *Georgics* is to view them as a metaphor or even an allegory of the human condition. Thus the farmer equates to the individual, struggling through *labor* – hard work – to prosper by taming a hostile environment. Natural disasters – the storm in book 1, the devastating plague that ends book 3 – equate to the seemingly random events that can make all these human endeavours fruitless. Some commentators have seen in the society of the bees in 4, with their well-ordered hives led by a king, a metaphor for the monarchical rule of Augustus and the message that only he can save Rome from the catastrophes that have engulfed it.

But this reading ignores the fact that much of the detail of farming is minutely and lovingly realized. The personification of the bees (in, for example, the description of the swarm in 4.67–87) is almost Beatrix Potter-like in its precise blend of the human and the animal. Equally, the behaviour of the different birds in book 1 is sharply delineated and individualized in a way that encourages the reader to see them as birds, not metaphors.

A further problem with an allegorical reading of the *Georgics* is that its message is far from clear. At times the poet appears to be promoting *labor* (work, toil) as the path to success (see especially 1.145–6), but he is under no illusions as to the grinding and dreary nature of this *labor*. And elsewhere he is explicit about the ease with which the fruits of *labor* can be swept away by random events. He is also pessimistic – in the story of the plague in book 3 – about the value of religious observance in ensuring prosperity. The eulogy of the simple life of the farmer that closes book 2 and Aristaeus' regeneration of his hive at the end of book 4 strike a note of optimism which contrasts with the gloom that concludes the other two books.

The reader in search of political allegory encounters similar difficulties. Book 1's closing account of the natural world's reaction to the death of Julius Caesar would seem to promote Octavian, Caesar's heir, as the man equipped to restore order to a world turned upside-down. Going one step further, the poem's emphasis on the human taming of nature has been read as endorsing Octavian's restoration of peace after the civil wars. In the same way, the *laudes Italiae* (praises of Italy) of book 2 can be seen as a celebration of the Italy that Octavian has brought into being. But the darkness elsewhere in the poem and the metaphors of violence used to depict the process of taming nature (see, for example, the pathetic picture of the birds displaced by deforestation in 2.207ff.) rather undermine this optimistic reading.

Equally problematic are the interlocking stories of Aristaeus and Orpheus which close book 4. The narratives themselves belong to the genre of *epyllion* – 'little epic': the miniature mythological narratives which the Hellenistic poets proffered as their more refined and polished alternative to classical epic. They tell how the shepherd and bee-keeper Aristaeus pursued Eurydice, wife of Orpheus, leading her to tread on a poisonous snake in her flight, with fatal consequences; how Orpheus journeyed to the underworld in an ultimately unsuccessful attempt to bring her back; and how Aristaeus, punished by the loss of his bees, ultimately regained them by the bizarre practice of *bugonia*, regenerating the hive from the corpse of a slaughtered ox.

Interpretations of the epyllion are many and various. Some commentators see the generation of the bees as a positive, optimistic ending to the *Georgics*, emphasizing the triumph of *labor* and human endeavour over hostile nature; others stress instead Orpheus' grief and failure, pointing to the explicitly miraculous (and hence impossible) character of the *bugonia*, and argue that Aristaeus' undeserved success is emblematic of a dark reality. Other readings contrast Orpheus' passion – *amor*, portrayed elsewhere (book 3) as a destructive force – with Aristaeus' practical following of instructions, and see the regeneration of the hive as endorsing a problem-solving, technological approach to the struggles of human existence. Also relevant is the violence necessary to slaughter the ox, which can be read as symbolic of the bloodshed necessary for Augustus to restore peace to Italy.

Most modern commentators agree that a straightforward reading is too simplistic, and that the ambiguities and opacities of Virgil's poetry encourage the reader in an exploration of the questions raised without ever providing an answer. And, indeed, this is arguably true of the work as a whole: the *Georgics* discuss the farmer's engagement with the natural world as a means of exploring the human condition, with its inherent contradictions and tensions. While at first sight the wealth of technical detail can seem forbidding to the modern reader, further acquaintance with the *Georgics* gradually uncovers the astonishing complexities of this extraordinary poem. Rooted in the practicalities of farming, vigorously engaged with both Hellenistic and Roman literary predecessors and referencing contemporary Roman politics, the *Georgics* nonetheless succeed in debating and exploring issues of universal significance.

Further reading

There is a good translation of the *Eclogues* by Lee (2006), and of the *Georgics* by Wilkinson (2005). For commentaries on the former, see Clausen (1994); Coleman (1977); on the latter, see Mynors (1990). For good introductions to Virgil, see Griffin (1986); Martindale (1997). On the *Georgics* in particular, see Farrell (1991); Gale (2000); Volk (2002). For a challenging piece on *Eclogue* 3, see Henderson (1999: chapter 6).

HORACE: THE EARLY POETRY

Caroline Butler

During the political upheavals of the 30s, a freedman's son, who had served with distinction on the losing side at the Battle of Philippi in 42 and was working as a scribe in the treasury, began to attract attention. His quasi-autobiographical poetry coupled moral and political reflection with obscene invective in the manner of the Greek poet Archilochus. The poet was Quintus Horatius Flaccus, and his adoption in about 37 into the circle of Maecenas heralded one of the most fruitful patron-poet relationships of western literature.

Horace's poetic career begins with book 1 of the *Satires* (probably 35 or 34), followed by the *Epodes* and *Satires* 2 in about 30. The apparently comfortable moralizing of the *Satires* and the violent abuse of the *Epodes* have attracted less critical attention than his more grandiose later poetry (see 10d). But more recent scholarship, by examining the poems more closely in their cultural and literary context, has done a certain amount towards their rehabilitation.

Uniquely among Latin poetic genres, satire claims no Greek precedent. Horace's avowed model for his *Satires* (referred to by the poet himself as *Sermones* – 'conversations') is Lucilius (180–102), whose work survives largely in quotations by other authors. Lucilius' poetry is wide-ranging in subject-matter and metre, but he was most prized by the Romans themselves as a writer of scathing attacks on contemporary society and individuals (see 8b). Horace adopts Lucilius' metre (the dactylic hexameter); perhaps because of the political uncertainties of the times, or perhaps because of his own somewhat insecure position, his polemic is less vitriolic. Instead of prominent individuals, Horace targets stock figures (or indeed himself), and the poems appear enthusiastically to support moderation and the Aristotelian 'Golden Mean'. In this way, he aligns himself broadly with the Epicurean school of philosophy, though not without the occasional nod to stoicism.

Traditionally, much of the appeal of the *Satires* has lain in the engagingly direct autobiographical detail they contain. They convey a portrait of a bluff and genial poet who will gently point out the failings of others while remaining sensitive to his own foibles. Though he may rub shoulders with the great, he seems keenly aware that his own political importance is minimal. In *Satires* 1.6 we are told the story of Horace's freedman father, whose success as an auctioneer enabled the poet to be educated at Rome instead of in the local school with the oafish sons of centurions. We are given the charming picture of the cash-strapped father, instead of the usual slave, accompanying his son to school, swinging the boy's satchel from his shoulder. We learn too about his military service with Brutus prior to the catastrophic defeat at Philippi in 42, his promotion to the rank of military tribune, and about his introduction by Virgil to Maecenas. In 1.5 Horace gives a characteristically self-deprecating account of his journey to Brundisium in order to attend a crucial meeting between Octavian and Antony. In 2.6, a poem celebrating his country estate in the Sabine hills (generally supposed to be a gift from Maecenas), he compares himself to the country mouse in the fable to emphasize his separation from city life and politics; in 2.7 he allows his slave Davus to lecture him on freedom.

This self-portrait is clearly built up with considerable care. Even in the turbulent times of the civil war, the rise of a freedman's son to the rank of commander of a legion was a startling one. It is significant that Horace chooses to emphasize both his modest origins and his father's homespun Roman moral instruction (in 1.4) and to mention the military promotion almost in passing, in a poem (1.6) which stresses his lack of ambition and enjoyment of the simple life. In discussing his involvement with Maecenas' circle he is careful to portray himself as a tentative but grateful newcomer (1.6) and to deny himself any political importance (1.5), while in 1.9 he lampoons a bore who accosts him in the hope of being introduced to Maecenas. No doubt there were vulnerabilities in Horace's position as a freedman's son and adherent of the losing side in the Civil War who nonetheless enjoyed the patronage of one of the most powerful men in Rome. We can read the deliberate self-effacement of the character who emerges from the *Satires* as a concerted attempt to anticipate the criticism to which he felt exposed.

Horace's self-deprecation is also apparent in his choice of the genre of satire, which lacked the status afforded by a Greek model. Equally, Horace criticizes Lucilius for the virulence of his attacks (in 1.4 and 1.10) and for his style, which he describes as careless. In book 2, however, he is at pains to stress his inferiority to his predecessor. His relationship with his predecessor is a complex one; but we can discern the younger poet's attempt to establish himself as the supreme exponent of a Roman satire that combines Lucilian freedom of expression with a Hellenistic polish.

Horace's next work was the collection of 17 *Epodes*, published about 30. Here he explicitly took as his model the seventh-century Greek poet Archilochus, whose poetry addressed political themes as well as abuse – often obscene – of contemporary men and women (see 3c). Like Archilochus, Horace adopts the iambic metre (where the basic unit is a short syllable followed by a long one). Indeed, in the ancient world the poems were known as *Iambi*.

The vigour of Horace's invective has led the *Epodes* to be treated as something of a footnote to his *oeuvre* as a whole. Certainly, poems 8 and 12, which discuss in minutely itemized detail why precisely the poet fails to find certain women attractive, seem crudely misogynistic to the modern reader. Nonetheless, his darkly atmospheric poems about the witch Canidia (*Epodes* 5 and 17) have a certain gothic appeal, with their gruesome potions and nightmarish incantations (Canidia also appears in *Satires* 1.8 and 2.1).

The aspect of the *Epodes* that has received the most critical attention is Horace's depiction of his relationship with Maecenas, explored in 1 and 9. *Epode* 1 begins with an expression of concern for Maecenas as he prepares to join Octavian for the battle of Actium; 9, in a theme developed later in *Odes* 1.27, portrays the battle itself. In 1, Horace takes as his starting-point the conventional form of the *propemptikon*, a poem written for a friend about to embark on a journey, but subverts it, insisting that he will follow Maecenas to the battle and stating explicitly that he does so not in the hope of favour but out of loyalty and friendship. Given that by this time Horace had received considerable largesse from Maecenas, including his Sabine estate, it is difficult not to read the poem as a defence of Horace's poetic independence in the face of a powerful patron.

In *Epode* 9, however, we see a conventional Augustan response to Actium. The battle is described as a war against a foreign enemy, and a woman at that, with an army of emasculated barbarians. Antony is largely airbrushed out of the picture, enabling the poet to evade the uncomfortable reality of civil war.

Written during a period of tremendous turbulence, Horace's early poetry provides a powerful insight into his development of both a political and a poetic standpoint. From the resolutely apolitical stance of the *Satires*, written by a poet cautiously feeling his way in a regime which he had initially vigorously opposed, Horace progresses to the triumphal Augustanism of *Epode* 9. And in contrast to the literary diffidence of the *Satires*, which claim as their model only the Roman poet Lucilius, he progresses to a Greek form in the *Epodes*, paving the way for his confident claims to poetic immortality in the *Odes*.

Further reading

For a classic introduction, see Fraenkel (1957); see also Hills (2005); West (1967). For good collections of articles, see Harrison (1995; 2007); Rudd (1993). On Horace as satirist, see Anderson (1982); Braund (1992; 1996); Coffey (1976); Freudenburg (1993; 2001; 2005); Henderson (1998, chapter 3); Hooley (2006); Schlegel and Rosenmeyer (2003); Sullivan (1963). For other analyses of early Horace, see Houghton and Wyke (2009); McNeill (2001); Oliensis (1998). For an interesting reading of *Epode* 8, see Henderson (1999: chapter 4).

Chapter 10

The Augustan age

Glossary items: *auctoritas; ecphrasis; elegiac couplet; hexameter; imperium; militia amoris; pentameter; peripeteia; periphrasis; procinsulare maius imperium; servitium amoris; topos; tribunicia potestas.*

THE AUGUSTAN AGE: AN HISTORICAL INTRODUCTION

Terry Edwards

Octavian's defeat of Antony and Cleopatra at the naval battle off Actium in 31 BCE settled the future of Rome and the empire. Octavian was looking forward to enhancing his image by leading Cleopatra in his triumph in Rome but she and Antony committed suicide in Alexandria. He now stood alone with the name of Caesar, a name which ensured the loyalty of over 50 legions and an oath of allegiance from the whole of Italy. He was to make a great deal of the name and his status as the son of the god Julius.

However, Octavian did not intend to go the same way that his great-uncle had gone. In truth, the situation was considerably different. The old patrician-plebeian aristocracy was smaller in number, and he had married into the Claudians. The majority were fed up with civil war and the disruption it caused. Tacitus tells us bluntly how he bought off, with gifts, corn, political appointments and other delights of peace, any remaining opposition. His one real problem, however, was that his legal and constitutional position was somewhat uncertain. There was resentment and ill-feeling among the senatorial class, despite a senate filled with his men. The empire was not without problems, and employment, food and amenities in Rome needed vast resources. Octavian could learn from Julius Caesar's mistakes, both in what he did and in the presentation of his position and actions.

Octavian was not going to retire like Sulla, nor invent some post such as life-time dictatorship. He intended to 'restore the republic', whatever that was intended to mean. Certainly, he would establish the rule of law and constitutional stability. He knew he could not hide from fellow senators where real power lay, but he could make it advantageous to accept him through the enormous patronage he held; he could, above all, bring peace and security to the vast majority. Perhaps the most important and significant monument of his principate (and there are a lot of monuments!) was the Ara Pacis (the Altar of Peace) built between 13 BCE and 9 BCE. It presents images of Aeneas, the Mother Earth of Italy, the senators and Octavian's family among the priests of Rome, in the act of a ceremony – the past, the present and the future benefits of the Augustan age in visual imagery which all could understand and appreciate. It is a piece of propaganda but also indicates, much like the *Res Gestae* (Augustus' autobiography), a perspective on his 44 years in charge of Rome and its empire. It re-interprets history to present his principate as the culmination of one age and the beginning of another. Virgil will take the story of Aeneas and link it to the Augustan present. Augustus' own forum will link the Augustan achievements to the past heroes of Rome. His temple to Mars Ultor (the avenger) will proclaim his religious and filial duties. Horace's *Carmen Saeculare* will celebrate the family values promoted in Augustus' social legislation of 18 BCE (despite the question mark over their success). Writers, artists, sculptors, architects and engineers will work under Augustus' patronage make his a regime appear a 'golden age', in the words of Virgil (*Aeneid* 6.793).

In August 29 BCE Octavian celebrated his three triumphs for his victories in Illyricum, at Actium and in Egypt. He then began the process of normalizing the situation. He reduced the legions to 28 and settled the rest in colonies in Italy and the empire. He closed the gates of the Temple of Janus to signal that war had ended and there was now peace. He also revised the list of senators in this year and his name was placed at the top as chief member of the senate (*princeps senatus*).

In January 27 BCE he gave up all his powers in a carefully staged event; the senate immediately granted him proconsular power over the provinces where problems remained and the armies were stationed – Gaul, Spain, Syria and Egypt. Egypt became the emperor's private province – no senator was allowed to enter without permission – since it provided much of the grain for Rome and a great deal of wealth for Augustus' projects. He continued to be elected as consul every year. This gave him power inside the city boundaries; he appears also to have been able to override the decisions of other magistrates. This is barely republican in a traditional sense, although the titles and powers were constitutional and granted by the senate. Yet it was clearly not ideal, especially since he was absent from Rome for much of the next three years, but still dominated the city through his agents, especially his political advisor and cultural minister, Maecenas. He was also given a new name – Augustus.

In 24 BCE Murena and Caepio organized a conspiracy against Augustus. His annual consulships restricted their opportunities, and his apparent interference in the province of Macedonia, leading to the trial of Primus, created ill-feeling. His power was all too obvious. In the same year, he fell seriously ill. In 23 BCE he gave up the consulship but received in return *proconsulare maius imperium* which seems to have been a grant of proconsular power greater than that of other magistrates. The senate renewed it regularly, giving it an appearance of constitutional validity. In addition, perhaps for life, the senate granted him the power of a tribune (*tribunicia potestas*). This provided him with a veto over other magistrates, but also the power to propose laws, summon the senate, and protect citizens. He dates his principate from this point, giving it a public significance, while keeping his proconsular *imperium* in the background (his tribunician power is mentioned in the *Res Gestae*; the proconsular power is not). He now had control within Rome and in the empire which could not be challenged.

When there was food shortage in Rome shortly after this, he refused a demand from the people that he take up the dictatorship; this was too much like his adopted father and, as far as his image was concerned, not what he wanted. He did receive the right to sit with the consuls and speak first before the senate, perhaps as part of being granted the imperium of a consul anyway. At a later date (12 BCE) he became Chief Priest (*Pontifex Maximus*) having waited patiently and constitutionally for the death of Lepidus, although already an augur, a duty he took seriously. In 2 BCE he was given the title Father of his Country (*Pater Patriae*).

As princeps he proceeded to reform all aspects of the administration of Rome and the empire. He eventually reduced the senate to 600, and gradually it acquired the right to make law. It acted also as a court, but Augustus' influence (*auctoritas*) overshadowed all its actions. Augustus took over from magistrates the administration of the corn supply, the water supply and the giving of games, as well as major roles in finance such as the minting of gold and silver coinage.

Although the senatorial class lost much of their power and responsibility, he used his patronage for the advancement of senators: he nominated and recommended them for office; he appointed them as his legates in provinces; he placed them on commissions for the corn supply or the treasury; he could bring men into the senate or the patrician order. With so much patronage at his disposal he could ensure loyalty and support from many who grew up under his rule and knew nothing of the old republic, as well as those who had lived through the civil war. Another class whom he patronized were the equestrians; he provided specific administrative posts for them – the two major ones, which he could not trust to give to senators, were the Prefect of the Praetorian Guard and the Prefect of Egypt. In binding a large group of wealthy Romans to his regime, he also weakened senatorial power.

He worked just as hard to gain the trust and popularity of the ordinary people of Rome and the provinces. As patron of the armies in 6 CE he created the military treasury to fund pay and retirement grants to the soldiers. Efficient management of the corn supply, gifts of land and money, the creation of a fire-brigade and a police force of sorts, opportunities for employment on public works, and overseas colonies were means to ensure the support of the Roman populace. Augustus was their patron and he used patronage to add further solidity to his position. No one had ever given games and entertainments as splendid as his – it was not until Trajan that they were surpassed in numbers and expense. He combined his public works with religion in promotion of his regime as traditional, maintaining a continuity with the past. He emphasized all of this in his own *Res Gestae* and contemporary writers largely, but not entirely, present Augustus as Rome's saviour. Velleius Paterculus was to say that the ancient, traditional form of the republic was restored (*History of Rome* 2.89.3). An exaggeration, but life for the majority was certainly better under Augustus than during the previous 50 years of Rome's history.

Further reading

There are a number of good introductions to this period. See, for instance, Davies and Swain (2010); Eck (2007); Galinsky (2005); Goodman (1997); Wallace-Hadrill (1993; 2008). Syme (1939) remains the classic account of how the Roman republic changed into the principate; see also Habinek and Schiesaro (1997). On the Augustan aristocracy, see Syme (1987).

LIVY

David Woodhead

Titus Livius (59 BCE–17 CE) was born in Patavium (now Padua in northern Italy) and in the very first sentence of his history pays discreet homage to his home town by linking Aeneas, legendary founder of Rome, with a less well-known Trojan: Antenor, founder of Patavium. The historian was a close contemporary of the emperor Augustus (63 BCE–14 CE) with whom he was acquainted but from whom he seems to have maintained a certain independence. We cannot be sure whether he was a supporter or critic of the new Augustan regime (there is some suggestion that he was a closet republican); but we are told that he encouraged the young Claudius to write history, and this would suggest a degree of imperial approval. About 25 BCE he began to publish his *magnum opus*: a history of Rome 'from the foundation of the city' (*Ab Urbe Condita*). The work took him the rest of his life and contained 142 books, beginning with Romulus in 753 BCE and ending with the death of Drusus in 9 BCE. Of these 142 books, only 1–10 and 21–45 survive, although we do have brief summaries of almost every book. Livy appears to have divided the work into sections of five or ten books (known as pentads and decades): for instance, the fifth book ends with a significant event in the history of early Rome, the sack of the city by the Gauls *c.* 390 BCE, and there is a new preface at the beginning of book 6; the entire third decade (also with a preface of its own) is taken up with the war with Hannibal. Since the work was so large, it is likely that pentads and decades circulated separately, and such a theory would go some way to explaining exactly why these particular books have survived. Livy was unusual for an ancient historian in having no experience of public life; Roman historians were usually retired soldiers and politicians (Sallust and Tacitus are typical examples) who knew at first hand how history was made. Livy, however, had no such experience and his accounts of battles and senatorial debates are more literary than realistic. Indeed, when we compare the *Ab Urbe Condita* with the *Annals* of Tacitus, for instance, Livy's narrative often appears rather naive; although on the one hand his history contains a vast quantity of important historical data (for which we have no other source), on the other hand Livy seems far more concerned to moralize, to dramatize and to romanticize than to provide a coherent historical analysis. He has been compared with historical novelists (such as Sir Walter Scott) and the comparison is a useful one; the Roman novel had yet to be invented and it is easy to imagine Livy's contemporaries deriving the same sort of pleasure from the *Ab Urbe Condita* as we might from a historical novel by Sebastian Faulks or William Boyd.

Before we look more closely at Livy's history, it is worth while to consider one or two significant differences between ancient historiography and its modern counterpart. To begin with, a modern historian would lay much greater emphasis upon primary sources than upon secondary; we might therefore expect Livy to have discovered new documents, to have consulted inscriptions, to have travelled to battle sites. However, this was not Livy's way, at least not in general. On the contrary, he chose a small number of secondary sources (i.e. previous historians) and constructed his narrative almost solely from them. At places in the fourth decade, Livy's text is so close to that of his source (the Greek historian Polybius) that we, with our laws of copyright, would undoubtedly accuse him of plagiarism. Furthermore, inconsistencies sometimes arise in Livy's narrative when he switches from one source to another; he is certainly guilty of carelessness here and there. That said, reading Livy and Polybius together does make one thing very clear: the Roman historian has far greater literary qualities.

Livy's narrative is also a very good example of the ancient practice of annalistic history; as the word suggests, it is a year-by-year account whereby the historian records the names of the new consuls and the various events of the year, both at home and abroad. Livy's account of events which have not run their course by the end of the year is broken off and not resumed until the following year (with its new consuls) has been introduced. Such a 'horizontal' analysis often makes for a rather disjointed narrative.

The general preface: history as moral instruction

Whichever part of Livy's history you may be reading, it is important to read the general preface as well (attached to book 1), for a number of things are made clear there. One is Livy's strong moral purpose. Whereas a modern historian would concentrate on a scientific discovering and recording of fact and leave the reader to pass any moral judgement, Livy makes plain how important a part of his purpose is moral instruction. In the preface he addresses his reader directly and urges him/her to choose, from the examples contained within his history, what best to imitate and what best to avoid. An important part of a young Roman's education was to shadow a senior figure and learn by example, by watching the elder man carry out his duties (such an apprenticeship was known as a *tirocinium fori*); in some ways Livy can be seen as providing a literary equivalent of such training and his narrative is full of *exempla*. Also clear in the preface is Livy's disillusionment with contemporary Augustan Rome; he believed that the growth of Rome's power and wealth had corrupted the Roman nobility with greed and with love of luxury (his words can seem to resonate strongly with twentieth-century readers, too). There is a touch of pessimism when he declares that his fellow Romans can endure neither their vices nor their cures; and a hint of escapism when Livy says that his recollection of the good old days allows him to avert his gaze from contemporary troubles.

The most important moral qualities, in Livy's view, are the following (they read like a roll-call of Victorian values): *pietas* (respecting the gods); *fides* (respecting treaties and promises); *disciplina* (respecting authority); *virtus* (courage); *pudicitia* (sexual probity); *continentia* (self-restraint) and *prudentia* (care and forethought). For Livy, if a Roman commander was to succeed, he needed the *moral* high ground as much as any other; without it, he was doomed to failure. Time and again, in the *Ab Urbe Condita*, both Romans and non-Romans come to grief because of some moral failing. A good example would be Hannibal's first victory, after he had crossed the Alps, at the battle of Trebia in 218 BCE; in Livy's narrative, the most important factor in the Roman defeat was the arrogance and recklessness (the lack of *prudentia*) of the consul Sempronius.

The importance of character

Next to a modern historian, therefore, Livy may appear somewhat naive. Historians today seek exactitude of chronology and topography; economic and political factors are believed to far outweigh the contribution of mere individuals. Livy, by contrast, sees history *primarily* as a matter of individuals, their characters and their moral worth. He would regard the war in Iraq, for instance, very much as he saw the Carthaginian War: dominated by personalities (George W. Bush and his father against Saddam). The characters of Gordon Brown and Tony Blair would figure very largely in any Livian version of late twentieth-century British politics. Hand in hand with this emphasis upon character is Livy's strong interest in human emotion. The critic Quintilian, writing about 100 years after Livy, says that no writer surpassed him in the description of human emotion. Joy and grief, fear and anger, pity and pride – indeed the whole gamut of human passion appears in Livy's pages; how human beings, large crowds or whole communities react when faced by extraordinary circumstances, are of deep interest to Livy and he has a gift for re-creating these emotions for the reader. If there is one omission in Livy's description of human behaviour, it would be humour; he seems to feel that wit and laughter somehow detract from the dignity of a true Roman noble. You do see a smile on Livy's face from time to time, but seldom (if ever) on the faces of Rome's great heroes. Livy believed that making Roman history was a serious business and that *gravitas* was as important a moral attribute as any other; jokes were definitely *infra dignitatem*.

Roman chauvinism

Throughout his history, Livy is guilty of serious Roman chauvinism (so-called after Nicolas Chauvin, a fanatical French patriot, famous for his blind devotion to Napoleon). Livy's strong patriotism leads him always to be firmly biased in favour of the Romans, to such an extent that he will deliberately omit details of Roman barbarity. Similarly, although Scipio Africanus is known from Polybius to have had a weakness for women, Livy does not allow any suggestion of this to intrude into his narrative (his portrait of Scipio is an idealized one, designed to provide an edifying example for Roman readers). What is more, his description of other races is rather crudely drawn: Carthaginians are untrustworthy, Greeks can talk a good battle but are hopeless when it comes to actual fighting; and, as for the Numidians, they are only interested in one thing – sex.

Speeches

The feature of Livy's history which strikes a modern reader perhaps more than any other is the prominence given to speeches. Livy's characters seem always to be delivering long speeches, either through direct statement or indirect. In fact, the composition of speeches was a traditional part of ancient historiography; it goes as far back as the Greek historian Herodotus, the 'father of history', writing in the fifth century BCE (see 5a and b). The ancients attached enormous importance to the art of public speaking, rhetoric was an essential part of a child's education and powerful speakers who could move and persuade an audience were widely admired; it is important for us to remember this, especially since the word 'rhetorical' is often used these days as a derogatory term to mean 'false' or 'deceptive' (see 1g; 6a). In the modern world, thanks to the spread of literacy, we privilege the written word, whether we access it through books, newspapers, computer screens or even our mobile phones. In the past, however, when the percentage of illiterate people was much greater (see 1b), the spoken word was the more important; oral communication, word-of-mouth, was paramount. In such a world, therefore, people developed a strong taste for rhetoric and, when historians included speech after speech in their narratives, they were responding to this taste. Strange as it may seem to us, therefore, in Livy the natural culmination of a dramatic episode is a speech, often indeed a pair of speeches where two antagonists argue their cases.

In point of fact, Livy (in common with all ancient historians) regularly invented speeches, even when a record of what was actually said existed. His purpose was twofold: he wished to add his own Livian brand of eloquence but he wished, in particular, to suggest aspects of the speaker's character. Motives, feelings, lines of reasoning – all these were explored and expressed through the medium of the speech. Livy attempts to 'get inside' the speaker and to convey, through his or her words, the essence of the personality.

Drama

In order to make his history more readable, Livy often seeks to add drama to his narrative. A device for which he shows particular fondness is known by the Greek word *peripeteia*; it means a 'change to the reverse of what was expected'. Aristotle, writing about Greek tragedy, used the term to describe the sudden twist where the plot of a tragedy turns decisively. In the *Oedipus Tyrannus* of Sophocles, for example, the *peripeteia* occurs when the king suddenly realizes his true parentage; in *Othello* when the Moor suddenly begins to suspect Desdemona. So, in Livy, Romans will often snatch victory from the jaws of defeat, soldiers caught in desperate circumstances will suddenly be rescued by reinforcements at the eleventh hour. There is often a strong hint of Hollywood in his battle descriptions. Moreover, Livy often uses tragic effects to arouse pathos and sympathy in his readers; thus, when great kings are humbled by the Romans, Livy will dwell upon the scene and draw out the various human emotions involved: the humiliation of the victim, the pity of the onlookers. At the linguistic level, too, we often see Livy seeking to dramatize events. He has a vast array of resources at his command but it is astonishing, for instance, how frequently you meet the adverb *subito* (often combined with *cum* in an 'inverted when' clause). Verbs are very often used in the historic present to add a sense of immediacy; direct speech allows us to hear characters speaking *sua voce* (the same effect is achieved in Ken Burns' TV history of the American Civil War when actors read the letters or speeches of participants, be they private soldiers, generals or presidents); particularly common is *repraesentatio* whereby, in indirect speech, Livy retains the tenses actually used by the speaker in the direct statement. Furthermore, in order to enhance his description, Livy will often choose to dramatize events through particular characters: we see not through the objective eyes of an onlooker but rather through the eyes of the characters involved. So, for example, when the Romans are besieging a town, Livy in his narrative will so far enter into the hearts and minds of the besieged that the Romans become the enemy and Livy actually uses the word *hostes* (enemy) to refer to the Romans. The reader is thus led to empathize very strongly with the characters.

Livy and women

It might be thought that a history of ancient Rome would be a record of exclusively male endeavour. However, Livy reveals (as part of his preoccupation with human psychology in general) a strong interest in female characters. I do not wish to suggest that Livy was some sort of proto-feminist but there are, within the *Ab Urbe Condita*, a number of women (Lucretia and Sophonisba are only the most famous examples) whose courage and nobility evidently hold a strong appeal for Livy. Furthermore, the quality of Livy's writing is such that the sexual outrage done to Lucretia, on the one hand, and the sexual allure of Sophonisba on the other are both powerfully conveyed. Sophonisba's story is told in little more than three or four pages, but it is such a potent mixture of sex, race and courage in the face of death that numerous writers since have been inspired to produce their own versions. Such literary homage is testament to the power of Livy's storytelling. In the Boxing Day tsunami of 2004, television pictures were broadcast showing the giant wave approaching a beach; all the locals and holiday-makers were desperately fleeing the wave and heading inland. To the astonishment of TV viewers, however, one person was seen striding out *towards* the wave – a tall blonde woman, a mother (one assumed) searching for her children. Within days, the woman was identified by journalists and found to have survived with all her children. This is just the sort of heroine who would have appealed very strongly to Livy. That said, the 'fair maid' motif also crops up and here we see the more overtly romantic side of the historian. During the Hannibalic campaign, for instance, Scipio's troops bring before him a captive girl so beautiful that she turns heads wherever she goes. The soldiers expect their commander to exercise his *droit du vainqueur*; Scipio, however (at least in Livy's version of events), informed that the girl is engaged to a prince of the local tribe, nobly returns her intact to her fiancé. Scipio summons the young man and, as we have come to expect, makes a fine speech in which he asks that the prince bring his tribe into alliance with the Romans.

Episode

This is perhaps an appropriate point at which to examine a particular episode from Livy's history and to see how it exemplifies the characteristics identified above. At the beginning of book 23, during Livy's narrative of the Hannibalic War, the historian relates how in 216 BCE the city of Capua (100 miles south of Rome in Campania) revolts from the Roman alliance and transfers its allegiance to Hannibal. Hannibal has just inflicted upon the Romans (at the battle of Cannae) the heaviest defeat which they had ever suffered; the Romans are thus at their lowest ebb and Hannibal is able to cajole or intimidate a number of Rome's allies into joining him. Livy makes clear, from the very beginning, that the defection of Capua is hardly surprising, since its population have been corrupted by wealth, luxury and over-indulgence. The Capuans send envoys to the defeated Roman consul Varro, and in an eloquent speech Varro demonizes the Carthaginians and powerfully argues the case for the Roman alliance. The Capuans, nevertheless, see an opportunity not only to re-establish their independence but also to supplant Rome as the pre-eminent power within Italy; they strike a deal with Hannibal and the great Carthaginian general enters Capua. Within Capua, however, there remains one man who still continues to champion the Roman cause and to resist the Carthaginians: a certain Decius Magius. This man bravely stands up to Hannibal; he has virtually no adherents, but one person *does* support him, a young man who happens to be the son of Pacuvius Calavius, leader of the pro-Carthaginian faction.

In a vivid episode of carefully constructed drama and suspense, the tensions between the Roman and the Carthaginian factions come to a head at a dinner party given by two Capuan brothers in Hannibal's honour. Calavius senior attends, having persuaded Hannibal to overlook his son's errant ways and to offer an invitation to the young man. The dinner is a lavish affair, typical of Capuan luxury and extravagance; one of the guests, however, refuses wine – the young Calavius. In the garden, during an interlude, we discover why: the son informs his father that he has a plan, reveals that he is armed with a sword and announces that he intends to re-ratify the alliance with Rome by shedding Hannibal's blood. Horrified, Calavius senior makes an impassioned speech and begs his son to reconsider. He reminds him of the agreement struck only hours before with the Carthaginian and of their obligations thereto. He warns his son that, whether he kills Hannibal or not, he will certainly die himself; and he concludes his speech by asserting that he (Calavius senior) will defend Hannibal: if he is to kill Hannibal, the young man's sword will have to pierce his father's chest first. The son bursts into tears; he is embraced and kissed by his father, and finally prevailed upon to abandon his plan, not before making a final bitter speech in which he asserts that he has remained faithful to his father, if not to his fatherland.

This episode exemplifies a number of typically Livian features. Note first the emphasis upon morality; Livy draws a clear correlation between the lax morality of Capuan society and their readiness to abandon the alliance with Rome and join Hannibal. The dilemma of the Capuans is dramatized by having a father and his son represent the two conflicting choices; and the romantic in Livy responds readily to the notion that Hannibal came so close to being killed by a noble youth. The description of the dinner party is a *tour de force*: the discomfort of the young man is contrasted with the ease and relaxation of the other guests; Livy carefully builds the suspense so that the reader is almost as shocked as the father by the sudden revealing of the sword (hith-erto hidden beneath the young man's toga); the passionate speeches are packed full with rhetorical fireworks; and the emotional climax, when the son finally relents, is capped with one final dramatic gesture: in a flourish of Ciceronian rhetoric (Livy was great admirer of the orator), the young man addresses his own fatherland, tells it to accept his sword and then throws the weapon over the garden wall.

Such, then, is a typical episode from the *Ab Urbe Condita*. It should be pointed out that Livy is our only source for these events in Capua and we may, if we wish, cast doubt upon the historicity of the story; what is not in doubt, however, is the quality of the storytelling. It is all too easy to denigrate Livy's abilities as a historian and, to a modern historian seeking to make sense of the Hannibalic War, Livy is just as much a source of frustration as he is of fact. That said, his literary credentials are not in doubt. He is a brilliant literary artist, one of the three or four greatest masters of Latin prose, and as such he continues to delight the general reader.

Further reading

For good introductory material, see Dorey (1971); Kraus and Woodman (1997). For more detailed treatments of Livy, see Feldherr (1998); Jaeger (1997); Walsh (1961). For a provocative piece, see Henderson (1998: chapter 8). See now the relevant chapters of Feldherr (2009).

VIRGIL: THE *AENEID*

John Godwin

If Homer and Plato are two good reasons for learning Greek, then Virgil is an excellent reason to learn the Latin language. All poetry is in a sense untrans-latable, but the music and the beauty of Virgil's verse can only be fully appre-ciated in the original. He of all the ancient poets comes closest to Homer in his mastery of sound and sense, in his ability to narrate a story and also move his readers. His works were regarded as classics within a very few years of being composed and most epic poets who came after him paid him the high-est compliment of imitating both his style and his subject matter. The *Aeneid* is indeed the great Roman epic which both reflects and expresses the private and the public faces of empire, of conquest and of duty, but Virgil did not start out as a epic poet. His first published work (of 37 BCE) was a set of ten pastoral poems called The *Eclogues*; his second (30 BCE), this time imitating the Boeotian poet Hesiod and more recent Roman poet Lucretius, was a didactic poem in four books on the theme of agriculture (see 9g). However, the great work for which the poet is best known is the 12-book epic of Rome's origins, the *Aeneid*. Virgil had already announced his desire to compose a military epic in the preface to *Georgics* 3 and it is fascinating to see the ways in which he managed to compose a piece exploring the glory of empire while also being honest about the cost of such a mission.

The tale narrated in this monumental epic is inherently simple. 'Arms and the man I sing' is how the poem begins: the narrative begins with the Trojan hero Aeneas being blown off course in his journey from Troy after the Greeks have destroyed his home city: he is blown to Carthage, where he is met by the lovely queen Dido – a remarkable lady in many ways who had also fled her Phoenician home after the murder of her husband. The second and third books of the poem are Aeneas' own first-person narrative to Dido of the fall of Troy and the journey to Carthage. Book 4 tells the tale of the doomed love of Dido for Aeneas – a love consummated during a storm while they were out hunting and then condemned by the gods as interfering with Aeneas' duty to leave Carthage and found his new homeland in Italy. Aeneas leaves his lover and she, in anguish, commits suicide. When Aeneas meets her again as a spirit in the underworld she will not respond to his emotional pleas and turns in angry silence back to her first love Sychaeus – the two of them reunited in death and leaving Aeneas hurt and alone. The descent to the underworld was a fairly common feature of the lives of great ancient heroes – one thinks of the similar encounter between Odysseus and the dead in the eleventh book of Homer's *Odyssey* – along with the legendary heroes such as Heracles and Theseus who made the same journey. The purpose of Aeneas' going to Hades is to visit the spirit of his father Anchises and to consult him for advice and guidance. The aged parent shows his son a vision of the future greatness of Rome and thus galvanizes his courage. The first half of the poem ends with the vision of Roman greatness and we see our hero land quietly on the shore of his future home.

If the first half of the *Aeneid* evokes the *Odyssey* (a series of fantastical adventures leading to a return 'home'), the second half of the poem – with its war around a (new) settlement, heroes fighting each other in single combat, gods intervening and so on – is more akin to the *Iliad*. Virgil himself, though, tells us that he regards this second half as a 'greater work' (7.44) than the first half. The poem now describes the arrival of Aeneas and his Trojan followers in their new home: asylum-seekers and refugees from a war zone, but also men sent by the gods to found a great race. At first things go very smoothly: the omen which stated that they would have found their home when they found themselves eating the tables is fulfilled when young Iulus notices that their food is being eaten off square table-like cakes. The embassy to local king Latinus meets with success and Aeneas is at once betrothed to Latinus' daughter Lavinia. What could go wrong?

Juno now intervenes and sends her fury Allecto to incite war-fever among the local population. The peasants rise up when one of the Trojans inadvertently kills a deer belonging to a local girl, and Allecto breathes fury into the breast of the Rutulian chief Turnus. Aeneas' hopes to marry the local princess and integrate into the local population will not be fulfilled easily and he will need help.

Book 8 begins with the god of the river Tiber telling Aeneas to seek help from King Evander of Pallanteum. Evander – whose name means 'good man' in Greek – is the father of a young warrior called Pallas and his city occupies the site of the future city of Rome. This allows Virgil the freedom to explore the poignancy of Aeneas seeing the city of Virgil's readers but without having seen the greatness which it would one day achieve. Evander is also celebrating the rites of the hero Hercules who was said to have visited Pallanteum – which gives the king the chance to narrate the tale of Hercules defeating the monster Cacus and thus once again give Aeneas the sort of heroic *exemplum* which he needs to maintain his nerve. The book ends with the forging of new armour for Aeneas on the orders of his divine mother Venus. The shield is described in detail as was the shield of Achilles in Homer's *Iliad* and it culminates in a vision of the battle of Actium in which Aeneas' distant descendant Augustus would defeat the forces of eastern disorder led by Cleopatra and Antony. Once again the hero loves the image but does not understand the full import of what it depicts as he lifts onto his shoulder the 'glory and the destiny of his descendants'.

Book 9 narrates the events which take place while Aeneas is away visiting Pallanteum. Juno inspires Turnus to attack the Trojan camp and when this provokes no response the Italians attempt to burn the Trojan ships – only for the goddess Cybele to turn the ships into sea-nymphs. Turnus is powerless for the moment against the forces of divine magic-making. His men do however capture and kill two young warriors Nisus and Euryalus who make a sortie from the camp by night to try to bring word of the Italian attack to Aeneas. The murderous activity of the two young men followed by their grisly deaths is an episode of realism in what has so far been a faintly unbelievable book. The grief of Euryalus' aged mother in particular is a moment of real pathos. Aeneas returns to his camp at the start of book 10 accompanied by Pallas, the young son of his host Evander – a boy whom he had promised to protect. Within a few hundred lines the boy is dead, killed by Turnus. Aeneas is in turmoil: for all that Pallas met an honourable death in combat against a man he sought to kill, Aeneas is blinded with rage and grief and guilt. Turnus' stripping of Pallas' corpse of his armour – again, a normal feature of heroic warfare – will cost him his life at the close of the poem. Meanwhile Aeneas gains some temporary release by killing an equally young and worthy Italian named Lausus. The situation is something akin to that in the *Iliad*, where the death of Patroclus changes everything for the hero Achilles, who now directs his famous anger away from Agamemnon and towards Hector; from now on the fighting is more personal than it had been before and when the two men meet in the end of the poem the personal anger is the deciding factor. Book 10 ends with the heroic death of the anti-hero Mezentius – one of many surprises in this poem. Mezentius was arrogant, a scorner of the gods and hated by his own people who have expelled him. He has allied himself with Turnus but comes over in the book almost as a free-lance warlord, a lonely anti-hero. His death, however, is heroic: he accepts the fact of his death and bravely refuses to surrender.

The Trojans have regained control of the battlefield by the start of book 11 and the Latins now call a council of war. The debate reminds us of the issues at stake and the options open to them: make peace, as Latinus suggests, arrange a single-combat duel between Aeneas and Turnus (the proposal of Drances and the one which finally happens) or just continue the war as before, as Turnus wishes. The talking ends when news arrives of a fresh Trojan attack and the book concludes with the fighting and death of the Amazon-like Camilla.

Turnus announces at the start of the final book that he will fight Aeneas in single combat. King Latinus and his queen Amata attempt diplomatically to dissuade him from this suicidal course of action, but in vain. His semi-divine sister Juturna is more successful at removing Turnus from danger as she impersonates his charioteer and drives him away from Aeneas and to tempo-rary safety. It is a long time before Turnus realizes what is going on and makes his determined way back to face his death. There is a final debate among the gods in which the wrath of Juno is finally laid to rest and the scene is set for the climax of the poem. Turnus is soon reduced to submission and begs for his life. Aeneas is tempted momentarily to spare his opponent until he sees the sword-belt of Pallas whom Turnus had killed in book 10, and in a moment of boiling rage he dispatches the soul of Turnus to the shades below.

As with the *Eclogues* and the *Georgics*, the *Aeneid* is a text which looks back to Virgil's Greek literary predecessors: most obviously the epic poet Homer, but also the Greek tragedians, various Hellenistic poets and Ennius. The poem is dense and allusive and, in that sense, counts rather as a Hellenistic poem than a straight imitation of Homer. However, what is distinctive in Virgil is his narrative technique, which is extremely visual and what one might call cinematic. A good example of this technique is the description of the hunters, hunting dogs and horses gathering in advance of the hunt during which Aeneas and Dido will begin their affair (4. 129–50).

Virgil sets the scene with a brief description of the sun rising (4.129). He then cuts to describe the young men with their equipment, the Massylian horsemen and the hunting dogs (intriguingly described in the phrase 'strong scent of the hounds'; 4.130–2). He then cuts again to the Carthaginian nobles waiting for Dido as she hesitates in the bedroom, and a horse in purple and gold, straining at the bit (4.133–5). At last (*tandem*) we see Dido herself, accompanied by a large crowd (including Trojans), with a golden quiver, gold in her hair, and a golden clasp holding her purple garment (4.136–41). Then we see the object of her affections, so handsome and golden that he is com-pared to Apollo (4.141–50). In its spectacular changes of perspective, in its zooming in and out, and in its gorgeous physical detail, the passage could easily act as a storyboard for a film director.

The story of the *Aeneid* is as follows: the first six books draw extensively from the *Odyssey* in their tales of the adventures of the hero as he makes his way from Troy to a homeland: while the second half of the poem draws on themes and storylines from the *Iliad*. Some of the plot devices and even the wording of the text are so close to Homer that Virgil's readers will have spotted the correspondence at once. The very last line of the poem for instance, describes the life of the dying hero Turnus leaving his body:

> His life with a groan flees angry to the shades . . .

Compare these lines describing the death of Hector in the *Iliad* (22.361–3):

> As he spoke thus the ending of death covered him
> and his soul flew from out of his limbs and went to Hades
> groaning at its fate and leaving his manliness and youth behind.

The same lines are also used of the death of Patroclus at the hands of Hector at lines *Il.* 16.855–7.

What is interesting here is the irony that Hector suffers the same fate as his victim: but more interesting for our purposes is the fact that both Hector and Patroclus are highly sympathetic characters: Virgil thus injects huge intertextual pathos into the death of Aeneas' enemy. This means that, if Turnus is Hector, then Aeneas must be Achilles, the hero whose insatiable wrath forms the overarching theme of the *Iliad*. The link between Turnus and Hector is strong: the death of Aeneas' young protégé Pallas at Turnus' hands reminds one of the death of Patroclus in the *Iliad* at the hands of Hector. One feels that, just as in the sixth book of the *Iliad*, the sympathy is being extended towards the innocent wife and child and parents of the doomed Hector, so also the formerly happy engagement of Turnus to the local princess Lavinia is something which it is a shame to see broken by this Trojan interloper. The breaking up of a sound relationship by the sudden arrival of a Trojan prince is an obvious reference to the tale of Paris, whose seduction of Helen caused the Trojan War in the first place. For Aeneas to resemble Achilles is fine, but for him to be compared to the effeminate cowardly Paris is something very different and less glorious.

For Aeneas may be the hero of the poem which bears his name but his behaviour is far from uniformly heroic. His destiny commands that he leave the burning shell of his home city of Troy and find a new home for the remnants of his people far over the seas. He arrives in Italy as a seeker of a new home and his fate soon forces the local people to accept him as their future ruler – a pattern of imperial domination which is at once questioned and shown to carry a price for the local peoples, who dismiss him at one point as an 'effeminate Phrygian with his hair curled with hot iron and soaking with perfume' (12. 99–100).

His dalliance with the fragile and charismatic queen Dido in Carthage is full of pathos as well as literary and historical resonance. Seen in one light she is the *Aeneid*'s equivalent of the divine Calypso in book 5 of Homer's *Odyssey* – a lovely woman who wants the male hero to be her husband but whom he ultimately leaves for his wife and home. Seen in a historical context she is a reminder to Virgil's readers of another African queen whose dalliance with a Roman general caused mayhem and immense upheaval – Cleopatra – as well as a way of bringing in the enmity of Rome and Carthage which found expression in the three long Punic Wars in one of which the great Carthaginian general Hannibal almost defeated the might of Rome. All three are powerful forces at work in this episode, but all three fail to measure the depths of the pathos which this book conveys. For Calypso the departure of Odysseus is a disappointment and a cause of anger towards the gods, but she is not able or keen to commit suicide as Dido does. What gives the incident its peculiar power is the way in which Virgil explores the psychology of the agents involved in it and makes it clear that Aeneas' duty is going to be hard to put into practice. In the *Odyssey* Homer has the god Hermes visit Calypso and tell her to release her captive Odysseus who is weeping with longing for his wife and homeland. Virgil does things differently: Aeneas is the one who receives the divine visit and Dido knows nothing of this. One can only sympathize with her scepticism when her partner tells her that he has been commanded by the gods to leave her shores. Her pleas to him to stay a while longer fall on deaf ears – in one of his many effective similes, Aeneas is like a huge tree buffeted by strong winds which, however, refuses to budge. For all her begging, his mind is made up (4.449):

mens immota manet, lacrimae volvuntur inanes

The mind stays unmoved, the tears roll down in vain.

Dido had a lot to lose in surrendering herself to Aeneas as she did in the fatal hunting expedition. Gossip – brilliantly personified (4.173–90) as a winged creature with as many eyes as mouths and as many mouths as feathers – conveys the tale of the new liaison between Aeneas and Dido to the African prince Iarbas who angrily prays to his father Jupiter, complaining that this woman who has rejected his offers of marriage has now taken up with this 'Paris with his half-man companions' (4.215). Jupiter listens to his son and sends Mercury to hurry Aeneas away from his tomfoolery, and the words of Mercury are harsh in the extreme – both in what he says to Aeneas himself (calling him 'uxorious') and also in the monstrously unfair generalization he utters about women in the second visit to Aeneas. Dido now learns that her lover is going to leave and her whole world collapses. She cannot abandon her city and go with him, but neither can she regain the respect of her people now that her 'sins' have been discovered. We feel nothing but sympathy for her – as a widow she was perfectly free to form a new marriage and the poet delicately brings out both her charisma and also her vulnerability.

Seeing the end towards which we are working is not granted to many of us. Aeneas is lucky in that he goes down to the underworld to visit and consult the soul of his dead father Anchises, and while there he is given a glimpse of the future greatness of the Roman people. Virgil, writing this poem in the 20s BCE, can look back on heroes and events which are, for Aeneas, far in the future, and the reader is thus invited to review the glories of his city. What is history for the reader is news to the hero and the device offers freshness and excitement to the telling of the tale.

The ending of the poem is, of course, an important moment in determining what the text is in some ways all about. The ending of the *Aeneid* is wonderful and disturbing. The final book of the poem, as we saw, shows the two main protagonists clash. History is, of course, against Turnus and, in the closing pages, Aeneas' superior power overcomes his adversary, leaving the future and the girl to the Trojan. The war is ended and Roman history can now begin.

So far, so simple: but, of course, there is a lot more to it than that. In the first place, there is the Homeric parallel to consider, which disturbs any cosy idea we might entertain of Aeneas as the conquering hero with justice on his side. The equivalent scene in Homer is the duel between the aggrieved lover Menelaus and the Trojan seducer Paris. In Homer the scene is one of almost comic proportions: Paris arms himself with all the self-regard for which he is renowned but almost faints with fear when he comes face to face with his Greek opponent. He is compared to a man who has trodden on a snake and who turns green with fear: in the duel which ensues he is only saved from death by the intervention of Aphrodite who whisks him away from the battlefield. If Aeneas is the Paris of this tale, then he is far from the hero of the narrative. Second, the duel proceeds in the usual manner with missiles flung followed up by close fighting at the end. Turnus ends up subdued and offers to surrender: Aeneas has won and he will go back to his father and never trouble anyone ever again. For a moment Aeneas wavers: he has after all been instructed by his father in the underworld that the imperial arts of the Roman will be to 'impose custom on peace, to spare the conquered and to war down the arrogant' (6.852–3). But when he sees that Turnus is still wearing the belt which he stripped from the corpse of Aeneas' protégé Pallas, clemency seems to be the last thing on his mind, for the pain of that boy's death still rankles. Aeneas, far from killing his opponent in a mood of clinical principle, lashes out verbally at him (12.947–9):

> You are to escape from me, you dressed in the spoils of my people? Pallas is sacrificing you with this wound, Pallas is enforcing his punishment from your wicked blood.

This is, of course, disingenuous: stripping spoils from the dead enemy was nothing new or reprehensible in itself and Trojans had done it in the past – think of Hector stripping Patroclus of the arms of Achilles. Moreover, the language used is deliberately oblique and self-justifying: it is not Aeneas who is doing the killing but Pallas, and the killing is not a murder but either a sacrifice (*immolat*) or an execution ('he exacts vengeance from your criminal blood'; *poenam scelerato ex sanguine sumit*). Aeneas seems to be hiding behind this veil of excuses when all he needs to do is to carry out the coup de grâce.

When the blow falls, then, it is in anger and madness (12.950–2):

> Saying this he buries the weapon beneath the chest facing him
> boiling with rage: that man's limbs are freed with cold
> and his life flees with a groan, angry, to the shades.

The ending is right – Aeneas has to win the contest and the future of Rome can now proceed as destiny has ordained – but the manner of the ending is disturbing. As Eliot has it in *Murder in the Cathedral*:

> The last temptation is the greatest treason
> to do the right deed for the wrong reason.

The political angle of the poem has aroused a lot of controversy over the centuries. For older scholars the purpose of the poem was simple: its aim was to 'glorify Rome and Augustus'. Later scholars find the parts of the poem which glorify Augustus somewhat embarrassing – as if they show the poet paying homage to a brutal regime. The picture of Virgil as a paid hack producing propaganda dies hard in some quarters – and it is worth examining the relationship between poet and patron before returning to the text for a brief discussion of this important issue.

Much of Roman literature was addressed to somebody specific (see 1e). Lucretius dedicated his great didactic epic to the Roman politician Gaius Memmius, Catullus dedicated his little book of poems to Cornelius Nepos and most of Horace's *Odes* and *Epistles* have their named addressees. When a writer is composing for a known recipient then the writing will be tailored to that person's personality – Trebatius, for instance, who was well-known for being a strong swimmer, is the addressee of Horace *Satires* 2.1 where the poet suggests 'swim the Tiber three times' as a solution for his insomnia. Patronage, of course, means more than this: in a world where the book trade was even less likely to make authors rich than it is today, the patron could be important in securing the writer's freedom from financial worries. As such, the writer is just one among many *clientes* of the richer man – 'friends of slender means' – and so received hospitality, gifts and support. They could, however, offer the patron something which he craved, namely fame and praise. Lucretius mentions the name of Memmius several times but does not give him the full-blown panegyric which some politicians craved. The emperor was the patron of all patrons, and it is difficult to imagine that any poet working under the Augustan regime – while accepting that this was no strong-arm censorship – was free to write material openly critical of the regime. Virgil was writing a poem which was in many senses political, and it was therefore essential that his words should reflect the political milieu of their composition.

Some parts of the poem seem to go much further than that. There are three major passages of praise for the emperor: the prophetic speech of Jupiter in book 1, where he foresees the future of the Julian family and announces that he has granted the future Rome *imperium sine fine* (power without limit). There is also the parade of future heroes of Roman history in book 6, where Aeneas is shown the glorious future towards which his own efforts are directed – a parade which culminates in the figure of (6.792–3):

Augustus Caesar, son of a god, who will bring back the age of gold.

And then there is the shield of Aeneas in book 8. Achilles in the *Iliad*, it may be recalled, lost his weapons when they were stripped from the corpse of his friend Patroclus. He needed new arms and so had a set made for him by the gods, and the set-piece description of the scenes depicted on the shield started a literary trend known as the *ecphrasis*. Aeneas is not in the same position: when his mother Venus arranges for him to have new weapons made it is to facilitate the poet's use of this poetic device. The difference between the Homeric and the Virgilian shields is also instructive: where Homer depicts the world of peacetime Greece complete with village life and ordinary life, Virgil makes his shield a pageant of military glory culminating in the battle of Actium where the future emperor Augustus defeated the forces of Antony and Cleopatra. The tone is one of chauvinistic triumphalism – we see the shame of Antony and his barbaric hordes led by a woman and worshipping animal deities set against the forces of right and superior strength led by our hero Augustus. The civil war between the two former Roman allies is turned into a battle between east and west, Rome and Egypt, good and evil. How can we explain or understand this apparently shameless propaganda for the regime?

In the first place, each passage has to be set in its context. The pageant of heroes in book 6, for instance, is all calculated to inspire courage and strength in a wavering son. Anchises is making his son focus on the great glories of Rome in order to galvanize him into action. He even acknowledges this when, at the end of the saga, he says (6.806–7):

And do we still hesitate to extend our prowess with our deeds? Does fear stop us from settling on Italian soil?

The pageant is to Aeneas a shimmering vision which he does not understand fully – how could he? – and we can see that Aeneas needs this shot in the arm if he is to press on towards an unseen goal of glory. In book 8 again the hero is in need of encouragement, which the depiction of the shield affords him. The dramatic irony is here again manifest – we can see the full meaning of the imagery on the shield while Aeneas sees merely a picture. The passage tellingly ends with Aeneas picking up the shield at which he gazes in wonder, ignorant of the facts but delighting in the image (8.730–1):

> lifting onto his shoulders the fame and the destiny of his descendants.

This does not answer the critics who see Virgil as in some ways selling out to the regime: it is all very well to plead dramatic necessity or dramatic irony within the plotting of the narrative, but the Roman reader still hears a fulsome and partial account of Roman history being relayed as if it were the sole truth. The ancient critics were in no doubt that the poem's purpose was to produce a national epic and to glorify the emperor. One could point out plausibly that Virgil may well have felt nothing but gratitude to the regime which brought an end to almost a century of civil strife and that the rhetoric of imperialism was a price worth paying to celebrate peace. Coinage of the period shows an ear of corn with the word *pax* ('peace') together on one side and the image of Augustus on the other – a neat illustration of the association of peace and prosperity which is reflected in the language of 'golden age' which Virgil uses of the Augustan regime (6.791–3). The poem is also acting as the conscience of the nation, giving the emperor the sort of ideal which he is being urged to live up to – as Plato had hoped to give to Dionysius II of Syracuse. Far from being the poodle, Virgil is thus more like the chaplain of the ruler, giving advice which is both uplifting and also soberingly at odds with the reality. Within the economy of the poem itself Aeneas himself is constantly being given this sort of advice – in the pageant of heroes, the shield, the many visions of gods and omens – but he conspicuously fails to act on this good advice and once again we see the typical Virgilian gap between the dream and the reality. Aeneas knows that it is his duty to seek Italy but he ends up dallying in Carthage and is roused to leave by the vision of an angry Mercury: he is told to be restrained in his anger and to make peace the way of life but still kills young Lausus in a mindless fit of rage after the death of his friend and protégé Pallas (10.802–20). The final book of the poem begins with Aeneas a calm and civilized warrior insisting on the duel which is only fair, while Turnus, his opponent, rages like a bull: but after endless delays and frustrations our hero loses his composure and ends up acting on emotional rather than ethical grounds, killing his enemy in a fit of rage.

An important line of criticism – the so-called Harvard school – sees the poem as multi-layered, with the praise of the regime on the surface but with more critical voices clearly audible beneath it. So, for instance, the heroic future of the imperial family as shown to Aeneas in book 6 ends not with the glorious and the victorious, but with the tragically early death of the emperor's nephew Marcellus. The tale of Aeneas is one of sadness, bitterness and no great happiness – he is widowed when his city is destroyed, his love for Dido is doomed to suicide and misery, his fulfilment of the gods' orders is only achieved at the immense cost of lives and happiness belonging to the native Italians whom he has to conquer first. Time after time he puts his duty before his inclination. We are told that he will only live for three years after all this is over and he will die long before any of the future glory is achieved. In personal terms he dies having lost an enormous amount.

Furthermore the human agents of this sorry tale are also the victims of the gods. Aeneas has a divine mother Venus who joins forces in this case with Aeneas' divine enemy Juno to promote the love of Dido for Aeneas. Venus wanted her son to be warmly received in Carthage and Juno was hoping that he might be prevented from ever founding the Roman people who would one day destroy her beloved Carthage. Neither of them cared about Dido – gods only care about themselves and their own families – and so Dido suffers with no respite and no divine help, while Aeneas is given help at many stages to achieve his destiny. Any temptation we might have to blame Dido – or Aeneas for that matter – is offset by the plot which demands that we make allowances for the 'bigger picture' which treats all of them as in some senses means to an end which is greater than any of them can see.

The main source of the difficulties faced by Aeneas is the goddess Juno. If one took away Juno from this poem, for instance, the 12 books would instantly shrink down to a mere few hundred lines of verse. She it is who causes the storm which makes his ships sail off course to Carthage, who joins with Venus to make Dido fall in love with the Trojan stranger, who causes her fury Allecto to inspire rage in the native Italians and in Turnus in particular. Some critics like to see the poem as a conflict between *furor* (frenzy) and *pietas* (piety), with Juno's victims, Dido and Turnus, representing respectively the frenzy of love and the madness of war. Pious Aeneas must overcome Juno and her pawns in order to fulfill his destiny. And it is his struggle with Juno, who – in the memorable words of the American critic W.R. Johnson – makes us think that 'hell is a possibility', which gives the poem much of its grandeur and epic quality. However, not all the gods oppose Aeneas. His mother Venus often acts to help him and the Trojans, and Jupiter (king of the gods) looks on with all the impartiality he can muster, trying to referee this violent divine squabble. Why did Virgil use this divine machinery? He could have written a story without gods – storms at sea do happen, queens can fall in love and indigenous peoples can hate incoming invaders without needing to bring in quarrelling gods. So why have what Quinn calls the 'fairytale' of the gods?

One reason is simply the weight of the epic tradition. An epic poem without gods would be unthinkable and no ancient poet – with the possible exception of Lucan (see 11d) – ever did attempt one. Even that anti-religious didactic poet Lucretius still feels the need to begin his poem with a hymn to Venus. A more impressive reason is that the mythology of the gods in this poem helps to support the twin ideas that humans here are acting towards a cosmic purpose but also that they are not wholly to blame for what is happening to them. Dido falls in love – as did Phaedra in Euripides' *Hippolytus* and as Gorgias famously explored in his speech in defence of Helen – because the goddess of love forced her to do so. She is not therefore to blame but is rather a victim deserving sympathy than a selfish woman deserving contempt. Equally, Aeneas' decision to leave her was motivated by commands from a higher being and not because he was fed up of her – his feelings being beautifully conveyed in the one word 'sweet' in 4.281 where his urgent need to obey the gods and 'escape' is counterposed by the delights of staying where he is:

> he burns with longing to go in flight and to leave behind the sweet lands.

The source of the fighting between the Trojans and the native Rutulians in book 7 is fascinating in the way Virgil has blended the natural and the supernatural. The fighting starts because a Trojan has shot a pet deer belonging to a native girl called Silvia ('the woodland girl' is the meaning of her name) and sympathy for the distraught child and her pet – which manages to limp home to die in her arms – quickly turns to lynch-mob justice. All that Allecto had to do was ensure that the stray arrow hit the deer and human psychology did the rest. Just before this, the urbane Turnus has to be goaded into fighting Aeneas: Allecto dresses up as an old woman urging war, only to be rebuked by an impatient Turnus who tells her rudely that war is man's business and she had better get back to working in the temple. She loses her temper and infuses him with the full power of her rage (7. 460–2):

> Mad he roars for weapons, looks for weapons in the room and in the house:

> the passion for steel rages, and a criminal madness of war and anger also . . .

Virgil has his heroes acting on the orders of the gods and in the interests of a supernatural end which they often cannot see, but he was praised above all for his quality of *humanitas*. This is the characteristic which still wins him new admirers today: the ability of the poet to show us people behaving not well but plausibly; the pathos of the death of old Priam in book 2 at the hands of the wicked Pyrrhus is saved from melodrama by the subtle hint that old Priam was once the arrogant ruler of the whole of Asia (2.556–7) and so in his younger days was something of a Pyrrhus himself. The point is made gently and not hammered home – for all his immersion in rhetorical education Virgil knew how to use understatement and his nuances are more eloquent than the bombast of most of his epic successors.

Further reading

Modern English translations of the *Aeneid* include those of Fagles (2007) and West (2003). R.D. Williams produced a commentary on the whole of the *Aeneid* in two volumes (1972–3). For introductions to Virgil and to the *Aeneid*, see Boyle (1993); Cairns (2006); Gransden (1984; 1990); Gransden and Harrison (2003); Griffin (1986); Hardie (1989; 1998; 1999); Harrison (1990); Jenkyns (1998); Lyne (1987); Martindale (1997); Otis (1963); Williams (1968). There is also material on the *Aeneid* in Feeney (1998; 2007); Hinds (1998); O'Hara (2007). For a collection of articles that deals with the idea of the *Aeneid* as propaganda, see Powell (1992). For poets in Augustan society more generally, see White (1993).

HORACE: THE LATER POETRY

Neil Croally

> The first three books of the *Odes* were published together in 23 BCE; book 4 and the *Carmen Saeculare* were both probably published in 17 BCE. *Epistles* I was published in 19 BCE and the dates of publication of the rest of Horace's work is infuriatingly imprecise: *Epistles* 2 and the *Ars Poetica* could have been published at any point between 20 and 10 BCE.

A contemporary of mine at school once began an essay with the comment: 'Horace was a man of about 43'. At the time we all found in this limpid but impossible observation an essential truth: there is something insufferably middle-aged, smooth, jaded, unexcited and smug about Horace (remember: we were only 17 years old). However, we may have to accept that there is something more to this central Augustan poet. We have already seen in an earlier part of this book (9h) that the Horace of the *Satires* could be apolitical and self-deprecating, and that in the *Epodes* he could be vigorous, obscene and insulting. We also saw that in the *Epodes* that he had begun to develop his attitude towards the regime of (the then) Octavian (see especially *Epodes* 1 and 9). But if the Horace of the early poems had already demonstrated an interestingly various poetic persona, then the poet of the *Odes*, the *Epistles*, the *Ars Poetica* and the *Carmen Saeculare*, demonstrates a wholly new sort of variety: technically, thematically and tonally. But Horace, with his dazzling technical virtuosity, also faces the world as a very particular Roman, representing a very particular sort of Romanness. Born in 65 BCE as the son of a freedman (who was still most likely to have been Italian), Horace benefited from his father's career as a public auctioneer. The money his father earned allowed Horace to be educated in the manner of an aristocrat, first in Rome and then in Athens. Indeed, the way that Horace confronts and adapts earlier Greek poetic models is one of his most distinctive features, and he himself is explicit about the centrality of the relationship between Greece and Rome. His advice to Roman poets in the *Ars Poetica* (268–9; 323–4) includes the following:

> Turn [or use] Greek examples in your hand by night; turn them every day. The Muse granted the Greeks talent, and the ability to speak with rounded tongue . . .

Most famously, Horace describes a certain ambivalence about Rome's relationship with Greece (*Epistles* 2.1.156–7):

> Greece, once captured, captured its feral conqueror
> and brought the arts to boorish Latium.

Arguably, it was part of the aspiration of Augustan Rome to match the cultural as well as the military achievements of the Greeks. In this project, Horace, the son of a freedman who ended up counting Maecenas and Augustus as well as Virgil as his friends, had a central role to play. He may not have been interested in becoming an epic poet (see *Odes* 1.6; 2.12; 4.15). It was left to Virgil to (try to) match Greek epic; Horace's chosen ground for the same contest was much less regular and predictable, but in his later work it was mainly in the area of lyric poetry.

And how that lyric poetry begins! In the first nine poems of the first book of the *Odes*, each poem is written in a completely different metre. Given that the turn to the Greek hexameter was barely 100 years old and that, alone of earlier poets, Catullus had used the Sapphic metre, this is an astonishing technical *tour de force*. Of the hundred or so odes contained in the four books, 37 are in the Alcaic metre, 26 are in the Sapphic metre. In the first poem of the first book of the *Odes*, Horace is keen to put himself explicitly among the Greek lyric poets (*Odes* 1.1.35–6):

> But if you count me among the lyric poets,
> I shall strike the stars with my head held high.

At *Epistles* 1.1.21ff. Horace claims to have been the first to have adapted Archilochus, Sappho and Alcaeus into Latin verse. He elsewhere mentions Sappho and Alcaeus by name (*Odes* 2.13.24–5) and, in *Odes* 4.9, he puts himself in the company of Pindar, Simonides, Alcaeus, Stesichorus and Anacreon. The influence of, and Horace's engagement with, Greek lyric poets has been noted by scholars in a number of the odes: Anacreon (1.23); Pindar (1.12; 3.4; 4.2: on this complex poem, see Hills, 2005: 116–19); Sappho (1.13). Alcaeus is the most pervasive influence, however (see 1.9; 1.18; 1.32; 1.37; 3.12): as

Horace himself says in his ironic portrait of two poets placing themselves in the poetic tradition (*Epistles* 2.2.99):

> According to him, I end up as Alcaeus . . .

There is some pride when Horace talks of his poetic achievement, a pride that has to do with both technical difficulty and his own lowly origins (*Odes* 3.30.12–14):

> Poor-born but capable
> I was the first to match Aeolic [Greek] music
> to Italian rhythms.

Horace, however, does not only address earlier Greek poets and claim to be their Roman inheritor; he also, on occasion, imitates particular poems. One famous example is *Odes* 2.7, in which Horace describes his experiences at the battle of Philippi in 42 BCE, when he fought on the losing side. In particular, Horace mentions dropping his shield on the battlefield. To his knowledge-able audience and readers, this would have been an obvious reference to a poem in which Archilochus described leaving his shield behind a bush but saving himself. At the same time as Horace makes the reference, he is also writing a rather different poem. There is first of all the delicate matter of having fought against (the future) Augustus. There is also a variety of tone in the poem: doom, killing, retreat, broken courage and the wildness of war dominate the first half of the poem. In the second half, there is joyous relief that his friend Pompeius has returned alive: now we have wine, sweet-smelling oil, myrtle and parsley. The ending is even mildly light-headed, apparently overwhelming the ignominy of retreat and loss of shield (*Odes* 2.7.26–8):

> I will rave no more sanely
> than those Thracians: it is sweet for me to go mad
> when a friend is restored.

So, even as Horace admits his debt to his earlier Greek models, he does so in a way that also demonstrates his own distinctiveness (on all the Greek lyric poets mentioned above, see 3c).

One reason which might explain why Horace is both similar to and different from the Greek lyric poets is that, like all Romans, he absorbed his Greek culture from Alexandria. Horace may explicitly ally himself with Alcaeus and Archilochus, but the language of the *Odes* (and of the *Epistles* as well) is sophisticated, dense and allusive. That is to say, the style of the *Odes* – and even some of the themes (see *Odes* 1.5, 28 and 30) – is reminiscent of Hellenistic poetry (see 7b). Indeed, in his imitations and adaptations, Horace does not limit himself to early Greek lyric poets. In *Odes* 1.20, for instance, in which he invites his rich and powerful friend, Maecenas, to come to his house to drink some cheap wine. The opening two words – *vile potabis* (you will drink a cheap [Sabine]) – allude to Catullus' invitation to his friend Fabius (poem 13), which begins with the words *cenabis bene* (you will dine well). In Catullus' poem the joke is that he starts by saying that 'you will dine well' but then proceeds to explain that that will only happen if his friend brings everything himself, as Catullus himself has run out of money. Horace, by contrast, starts with *vile* rather than *bene*, but then goes on to explain that, while his wine may be cheap, there is something splendid about it, as he stored the wine on the day that Maecenas recovered from illness and was applauded in the theatre. Horace's poem, while alluding to that of Catullus, moves, as it were, in the opposite direction.

However, Horace does not only allude to individual poets; he also on occasion alludes to one poet's allusion to another. Using Catullus again, we can see that Horace *Odes* 1.22 alludes clearly to Catullus 51.1–5. In the latter poem Catullus talks of his envy of the man sitting opposite his loved one, able to hear her 'sweetly laughing' (*dulce ridentem*). These lines are clearly an imitation of Sappho fr. 31 (see Campbell, 1982, vol. 1), where she talks of a lover listening to his loved one 'talking sweetly' and 'laughing delightfully'. Writing in the same metre as Catullus (Sapphics), in *Odes* 1.22 Horace says he will love Lalage 'sweetly laughing' (*dulce ridentem*) and 'sweetly talking' (*dulce loquentem*). In adding the 'sweetly talking' Horace puns on Lalage's name (which means something like 'babbler'). Something else is going on, though, as Philip Hills points out (2005: 46): '[Horace] is both nodding at Catullus' earlier allusion to Sappho and then "correcting" it by including the reference to sweet talks which is there in the Sapphic original but omitted by Catullus.'

When I spoke of Horace's pride in his poetic achievement in bringing Greek lyric poets into Latin verse, I quoted some lines from *Odes* 3.30.12–14, in which Horace said he was the first to 'match' Aeolic music to Italian rhythms. The verb I translated as 'match' (*deduxisse*) refers to the sort of vocabulary that the Alexandrians used to describe the kind of dense and allusive poetry which they preferred. So, as Horace explicitly casts himself as the Roman successor to Alcaeus *et al.*, by his choice of vocabulary, he shows that he is a Hellenistic poet at Rome.

It should be no surprise, then, that the variety of Horace's relationships with his Greek models and of his metres is matched by a similar variety in subject matter. In the late poetry of the *Odes* and the *Epistles* we encounter poems about politics, about poetry (both treated separately later in this section); we see hymns (such as *Odes* 1.30; 3.22); we read poems about friendship, especially about friendship with Maecenas (*Odes* 1.1, 20; 2.12, 17; 3.16, 29). There is conviviality, as in the famous opening of *Odes* 1.37 ('now we must drink': *nunc est bibendum*; see also 3.14). And there is, of course, love. But

Horace the love poet is once again rather distinctive. While Horace uses some of the devices familiar from the other love elegists, such as the *militia amoris* (see *Odes* 1.6; 3.26), he does not, as Catullus, Propertius, Tibullus and, even, Ovid do, concentrate on writing about his relationship with one woman. Indeed, he mentions both boys and girls as the objects of his affection and, of the girls, there are at least five mentioned between one and four times. Horace is less eager to write his own feelings than the other love poets and, in relation to sexual desire, he is more moderate. He tends to present himself not so much as a young man swept away by the tides of desire but more as an older man (43?!) enjoying the odd tryst and maintaining at all times an amused, slightly wry attitude (see *Odes* 1.5, 6, 8, 13, 23, 33; 3.12; on the love elegists, see the next section in this chapter).

As the subject matter is varied, so is the tone and the persona. We have already seen how in *Odes* 2.7 Horace can move from bleak descriptions of the effects of war to joyful, lightheaded celebration of a friend's safe return. Such variety is present both within and between poems, and is sometimes emphasized by the order of the poems. Thus *Odes* 1.5 is a lovely poem addressed to Pyrrha, wondering about who her lover is, the delusion under which he is bound to be operating, and the poet's own experience of failure in love. The next poem seems much more serious, beginning as it does with references to epic poetry and, by implication, Augustus' great deeds. The second stanza, though, rather changes the tone. I am no epic poet, says Horace, and am unable adequately to praise Caesar's achievements. Ironically, perhaps, he describes his talent as far from perfect and liable to tarnish Augustus' reputation. The last two stanzas describe first the inability of poetry to describe epic deeds and, second, Horace's desire to write about love, passionately or otherwise. The persona presented in this poem – polite but not interested, capable both of passion and levity – is also part of the variety that is so central to Horace's poetry. The wry and ironic detachment of the slightly older lover is another aspect of Horace's *persona*, as *Odes* 3.26 well demonstrates. But Horace is also capable of serious ethical and political engagement. And it is to Horace's relationship with the Augustan regime and to his concern with the ethical dimension of poetry that we now turn.

In *The Roman Revolution*, published in 1939, Sir Ronald Syme argued trenchantly and against the prevailing orthodoxy that Virgil was not a great poet, as he had put his art at the service of a ruthless dictator. This problem of whether great poetry can also be propaganda is perhaps even more acute in the case of Horace, because his celebration of the Augustan regime is arguably more pervasive and – at least on occasions – apparently more direct than anything to be found in Virgil. Certainly, Horace's relationship to his patron, Maecenas (along with Agrippa, one of Augustus' most important advisers) is open, as the number of (grateful) poems addressed to Maecenas demonstrates (see e.g. *Odes* 1.1, 20; 2.12, 17; 3.16, 29). However, it is worth considering again the extent to which we would like to adopt Syme's opinion in relation to Horace.

In the first two books of the *Odes*, if we count the number of poems that address Augustus' regime and aims, there is relatively little. The penultimate poem of book 1 does, though, seem to be explicit in its celebration of Augustus' defeat of Cleopatra. But this celebration is framed by the beginning of the poem – which famously asserts that now is the time to drink – and by the later lines, which seem to praise Cleopatra for her courage. Although she is described as a 'fatal monster ' (*fatale monstrum*: *Odes* 1.37.21), she is also shown seeking a better (*generosius*: ibid., 21) way to die. As she considers the ruins of her own kingdom, her expression is said to be serene (ibid., 26), while she herself is 'brave' (*fortis*: ibid., 26). Finally, she refuses to give Augustus what he wants by appearing in his triumph (ibid., 30–2). Horace seems to be at pains to praise both Augustus for his defeat of Cleopatra and the queen for her behaviour in defeat. It is difficult, however, to be sure whether to call this a generosity of spirit, a nuanced or even implicitly critical approach to Augustus' rule. The description in *Odes* 2.1 and 2.7 of the sadness and destructiveness of civil war – to which Augustus has happily put an end – does nothing to undermine the opinion that Horace's view of the regime (if not of Maecenas) is not quite straightforward.

The best test of this view, though, is to consider the first six poems of book 3 of the *Odes*, which are indeed sometimes known as the Roman Odes. Generally speaking, most critics accept that the poems seek to praise old Roman customs and morality (with some stoic attitudes thrown in), and that those values are consistent with Augustus' policy aims (especially in relation to the Julian laws, eventually passed in 18 BCE). The first of these six poems champions reverence of the gods and being satisfied with having what one needs rather than giving way to the desire to have more. Wealth is definitely not celebrated. In the second poem, Romans are asked to learn endurance and perseverance. Such sentiments are comfortably general, and could easily be appropriated by propagandists like Maecenas and Augustus. There is, however, some mild discordance. While poem 1 disparages the importance of wealth, Augustus himself was by far the richest man in Rome and had come to power, and then maintained it, by judicious but often generous use of the money to consolidate support and buy off rivals and critics. In poem 2, Horace writes the famous line:

dulce et decorum est pro patria mori.

It is a sweet and noble thing to die for one's fatherland.

This compact but dangerous idea – learned by generations of English schoolboys in the nineteenth century before they went off to run the British empire and later decried in the first World War as a lie by Wilfred Owen – perhaps does not sit so happily with the Horace who fought against Augustus at Philippi (*Odes* 2.7), who perhaps thought he was fighting for his *patria* then, but who threw away his shield.

Odes 3.3 and 5 seem more direct in their approach to Augustus' regime. *Odes* 3.3 is highly religiose in tone, thanks Augustus for ending the civil war and claims that he will be deified (he is compared to Hercules and Pollux). In 3.5 Augustus is compared to Jupiter and will be hailed as a god. His imperial destiny is lauded, and he is depicted as the champion of *virtus* (courage, manliness). We might feel a little queasy as we read these poems. In 3.6, a more general tone is again adopted and the addressee is *Romane* (Roman). In this poem reverence is again praised, but there is also a troubling emphasis on moral degeneration, as the last three lines make clear (3.6.46–8):

> Our grandfathers produced weak children; their
> children were even weaker – us, who will give birth
> to a more degenerate offspring.

Later in book 3 in 3.14 Augustus is again praised for what he has been doing in Spain, and is once again compared to Hercules. But the poem ends with Horace recalling his more hotblooded and anti-Augustan youth, precisely located in time by the last two words – *consule Planco* ('in the year of Plancus' consulship', i.e. 43/2 BCE, the year of Philippi).

The fourth book of the *Odes* contains less nuance and more direct praise of the emperor. In poem 4 Caesar is championed as the epitome of *pietas* and proper parenting. In the fifth poem, which is addressed to Augustus, the emperor is twice invoked as *dux bone* ('good leader'); he is seen as like the sunshine and as the source of Rome's security from dangerous foreigners. The impression that, as Augustus' regime became more established, criticism – even of the nuanced and probably deniable sort we have already seen – became less possible is confirmed by the *Carmen Saeculare* (Centennial Hymn), which Horace was commissioned to write for a national festival held in May 17 BCE. In this poem – religiose, pious and pompous – Augustus is seen in the line of rulers of Rome going back to Aeneas and Romulus, whose regeneration of Rome is sanctioned by Diana, Apollo, Ceres, Venus and Jupiter. In an interesting echo of Anchises' famous injunction to Aeneas to 'spare those who have been conquered' (*Aen.* 6.8.), Augustus is seen as 'lenient to the defeated foe' (*iacentem/lenis in hostem*: line 51–2). Little room in this context for sly digs and wry observations: Horace seems to confirm that the Augustan regime increasingly stifled different voices. Horace may have been an unwilling propagandist but the fact remains that he did serve the interests of Augustus' regime in the *Carmen Saeculare* and at least in some of his *Odes*. It is perhaps no surprise that the poet sought some consolation in a consideration of the function and effects of poetry.

While it is mainly in the *Epistles* and the *Ars Poetica* that Horace examines poetry, there is running through the *Odes* a strong sense of his status as a *vates* ('seer': see e.g. *Odes* 1.1.35). As a poet-seer, Horace can express his specialness in a Callimachean dismissal of the masses (*Odes* 3.1.1):

> *odi profanum vulgus et arceo.*
>
> I hate the profane masses and stand aloof from them.

In *Epistles* 1.19 Horace argues that poets should avoid slavish imitation, while acknowledging the importance of poetic tradition. He himself is, of course, an excellent example of someone who has adopted and adapted but in the end done his own thing. In *Epistles* 2.1, addressed to Augustus, Horace claims that Romans do not always have an intelligent attitude to poetry, ignoring sometimes the ethical benefits that poetry can bring. That said, he still urges Augustus to be a patron of (the right sort of) poetry. In *Epistles* 2.2 he again stresses the importance of being self-critical. His most detailed treatment, though, of poetic function and effect is in the *Ars Poetica*. In this tract – not much read now, but often raided for quotable phrases (e.g. *sub iudice*: 78, *in medias res*: 148) – Horace insists that a poet should be aware of tradition, should use a style that is appropriate to this theme and characters, should be realistic and clear, and – in a fairly Aristotelian way – should mix instruction with pleasure.

   The consolation that is most important to Horace, however, is surely that his poetry will grant him a sort of immortality. This becomes something of a *topos* in Augustan poetry (perhaps especially in the case of Ovid) but Horace perhaps makes more of it than any other poet. While he is fully – and beautifully – aware of the passing of time and the necessity of change (see the famous *Odes* 4.7: *diffugere nives* – snows have gone . . .), Horace is sure that he can immortalize what he writes about. This is clear from his poem about the Bandusian spring (*Odes* 3.13), but is even more explicit when he asserts – to Maecenas no less – that he will not die as others do (*Odes* 2.20.7–8). The most complete statement of his immortality comes in the last poem of the third book of the *Odes* (3.30.1–2, 6):

> I have built a monument more lasting than bronze,
> Higher than the royal site of the pyramids . . .
> I shall not completely die . . .

Horace, then, was a poet of great technical accomplishment. His appropriation and reinvention of Greek poetic models for Roman audiences and uses is analogous to that of Virgil, though he adapted lyric rather than epic. In so doing he demonstrated a distinctive (Roman) poetic persona, one which encompassed technical, thematic and tonal variety. As he moves from metre to metre, Horace also moves between serious literary criticism and ironic detachment, between gentle hedonism, blurred stoicism and pompous propaganda. Less celebrated than Virgil in his own times, he was still, according to Juvenal (7.225ff.) read eagerly by schoolboys. His reputation declined during the early Christian era, as his obvious paganism, humanism and hedonism were deemed not quite the thing. After the renaissance he was rehabilitated, influencing in the seventeenth-century Jonson, Herrick and Marvell. The high points of his influence in the modern era were probably in England in the early 1700s, a so-called Augustan age, in which poets such as Dryden and Pope championed the poetic values laid out in the *Ars Poetica*. Later, in the late nineteenth century, he became the acceptable poetic face of imperialism and was used for that reason in English education. It may be true that he is a poet not much read these days but he lives on at least – as he said he would – in those famous quotations: *nunc est bibendum*, *carpe diem*, *dulce et decorum est* . . .

Further reading

For introductions to Horace, see Fraenkel (1957); Hills (2005). For magisterial commentaries on the first two books of the *Odes*, see Nisbet and Hubbard (1970; 1978); on the third book, Nisbet and Rudd (2004). For a commentary on the *Epistles*, see Brink's three volumes (1963–82). For good collections of articles, see Anderson (1999); Costa (1973); Harrison (1995; 2007); Rudd (1993); Woodman and Feeney (2002). For more detailed analyses of the Horace of the *Odes* and the *Epistles*, see Houghton and Wyke (2009); Lowrie (1997); McNeill (2001); Oliensis (1998); Santirocco (1986); West (1967). On *Odes* 2.1 in particular, see Henderson (1998: chapter 4). For a collection of articles that deals with the idea of Augustan poetry as propaganda, see Powell (1992). For poets more generally in the Augustan age, see White (1993).

LOVE ELEGY

Caroline Butler

Latin love elegy is full of contradictions. Written in the first person and ostensibly dealing with the poet's relationship with his beloved, it is nonetheless poetry of the most stylized and mannered kind; although a uniquely Roman genre, it is dense with allusion both to Greek literature and to Greek mythology; while self-consciously eschewing Roman politics and political life, it engages closely with the Augustan social and moral agenda. From seeds planted by the erotic personal poetry of Catullus, it came fully into being with the now lost books of Cornelius Gallus (probably published in the late 30s BCE), reached its height in the work of Propertius and Tibullus (roughly 30–16 BCE), and was then thoroughly dissected in the elegiac works of Ovid. Other contributors to the genre include Sulpicia, contemporary with

Propertius and Tibullus (her five elegies are included in Tibullus' third book), and the only female Roman poet whose works survive.

The elegiac metre – a hexameter followed by a pentameter – first appears in the work of archaic Greek poets (see 1c). Writers of the seventh and sixth centuries such as Callinus, Tyrtaeus, Mimnermus, Solon and Theognis use elegy as a vehicle for poetry on a wide range of subjects – martial, philosophical, political and personal. Archaic Greek lyric poetry (such as that of Sappho, Anacreon and Ibycus) also provides thematic material through its depiction of Love as a consuming force – a disease, a fire, a north wind – or an opponent – a boxer, a blacksmith (see 3c). But it is the Hellenistic elegists, notably Callimachus and Philetas, whom the Roman poets claim as their models, despite there being relatively little overlap in subject matter (see 7b). Most important for Roman elegy is their self-conscious scholarship and their declared preference for concise and polished poetry over the heroics of epic and tragedy. While some Hellenistic elegy on personal themes survives in papyrus fragments, it is epigram – short poems in various metres – which, by developing the themes found in the personal poetry of the archaic lyricists, provides the Roman elegists with many of the images and stock situations which they choose to develop, together with the poetic persona of the love as victim of the beloved or of Love – Eros – itself.

Roman literature also feeds into the genre. While never explicitly acknowledged, the comedies of Terence and Plautus give the elegists characters such as the unfriendly doorkeeper, the compliant slave-girl and the *lena*, the procuress. However, the genesis of Latin love elegy can most clearly be seen in the poetry of Catullus, who flourished in the late republic (see 9f). Catullus is the first surviving poet in western literature to produce a sustained group of poems relating to a single beloved. His Lesbia poems, in various metres, range in tone from the ecstatic to the despondent and embittered, and his depiction of her as a promiscuous and capricious mistress proves hugely influential for the elegists. Most importantly, he wrote a number of personal poems in elegiac metre, two of which are particularly significant in the development of the genre. Poem 76, which reflects on the end of the affair, and the ingratitude of the mistress who has betrayed the countless kindnesses and acts of friendship shown her by the poet, lays the foundations for the elegiac lover's sense of injustice, which can border on the masochistic. Poem 68, and most particularly its second half, often regarded as a separate poem and referred to as 68b, explores at length the story of the mythological lovers Protesilaus and Laudamia as a parallel to the poet's relationship with Lesbia, something developed further in the extensive use of Greek mythology by the elegists, particularly Propertius.

Between Catullus and the 'canonical' elegists (Propertius, Tibullus and Ovid) lies Cornelius Gallus, of whose work there survives only a single line, plus a fragment of eight lines and uncertain authenticity. The reason for the loss of his work almost certainly lies in his spectacular fall from grace: a distinguished military commander under Octavian, he was given the plum job of prefect of Egypt in 29 BCE, but was condemned by the senate to confiscation and exile after some foolishly monarchical behaviour, and committed suicide in 26. We know little of Gallus' work beyond the name of his mistress (Lycoris: generally regarded as a pseudonym for the actress Cytheris), but Virgil so admired him that he made him the central figure of the tenth *Eclogue*, where Gallus wanders in a bleak and frozen landscape, lamenting his separation from his beloved.

Sextus Propertius was born in about 50 BCE in Assisi in Umbria, to a wealthy equestrian family. It appears that, like Virgil and Horace, the family lost property in the confiscations of 41 BCE, but, unlike them, he seems to have retained financial independence: although a member of the circle of Maecenas by the time of the publication of book 2, the relationship as depicted in the poems is notably less dependent than that of Virgil and Horace.

His first book of elegies, published around 29 BCE and known as the *monobiblos*, is dedicated to his friend Volcacius Tullus, and focuses on his relationship with his mistress Cynthia and on the dominant position this relationship holds in his life. Book 2, which appeared no later than 25, may well have originally been published as two books. Poem 2.1 is addressed to Maecenas, and poems such as 2.31, on the dedication of the temple of Palatine Apollo, show an increased engagement with public and political themes, but Cynthia and the life of love still hold the primary position. In book 3 (*c.* 23 BCE), Propertius proudly lays claim to be the Roman Callimachus, aligning himself with the anti-epicism of the Alexandrians, and claiming a literary pedigree for his personal, elegiac poetry. Love-poems are interspersed with praise of Maecenas, celebration of Augustus' military campaigns (3.4) and a lament for the dead Marcellus (3.18), Augustus' nephew and putative heir. The book ends with a farewell to Cynthia and a declaration that he has recovered from his passion. Accordingly, Cynthia makes only brief appearances in book 4, once from beyond the grave (4.7). This final book of elegies (*c.* 16 BCE) represents a more concerted attempt to assume the mantle of Callimachus through poems on the origins of Roman customs and traditions in the style of the earlier poet's *Aetia* ('Causes'). The date of Propertius' death is uncertain, but a reference in Ovid's *Ars Amatoria* shows that he was no longer alive by 2 BCE.

Roughly contemporary with Propertius was Albius Tibullus (*c.* 55–19 BCE). Little is known of his life beyond his association with his patron, the general Valerius Messalla Corvinus, whom he may have accompanied on campaigns to Aquitania and the east. Unlike Propertius, Tibullus does not have a single mistress: Delia and the boy Marathus provide the focus of book 1, and the sinister Nemesis features in book 2. Characteristic of Tibullus' elegies is a longing to retreat to the simplicity of the countryside, coupled with a fascination with the violence of lovers' quarrels and the dominant status of the beloved.

The poetry of Tibullus has come down to us in a manuscript form of three books, of which the first two are attributed to Tibullus. The third consists of poems written by members of the circle of Messalla: as well as six poems by one 'Lygdamus' addressed to a mistress called Neaera, we find five short elegies by the female poet Sulpicia, who may well have been the niece of Messalla himself. It is quite possible that Sulpicia's poems were written for publication, in which case her proud declarations of love for the apparently low-born Cerinthus are remarkable.

Ovid's life and works are discussed in the next section in this chapter. His contribution to the genre of elegy consists of the early works *Amores*, *Ars Amatoria*, *Remedia Amoris* and *Heroides*. The *Amores* were published in five books around 20 BCE and revised into the present, three-book edition around 1 BCE. They form a playful exploration of the stylized conventions of love elegy as found in the works of Propertius, Tibullus and (presumably) Gallus. The dating of the *Heroides*, letters from Greek mythological heroines to their faithless or absent lovers (including the lovers' responses to three of them), is problematic, but they were probably completed in the last decade BCE. The *Ars Amatoria* and *Remedia Amoris*, dating from about the same time, are didactic poems, the *Ars* in three books, the *Remedia* in one. The former purports to instruct the would-be lover, the latter to offer cures to the lovesick. It is the *Ars* (though it was published some years earlier), with its cheerful lessons in the techniques of seduction, which is widely regarded as being the *carmen* which precipitated Ovid's banishment in 8 CE. (Some critics prefer to stress the importance of the *error* Ovid claims he made, though he never tells us what exactly the *error* was.)

Distance, separation and alienation form some of the primary characteristics of the persona of the elegiac lover. Propertius and Tibullus seem to revel in their lack of engagement with Roman political life, in stark contrast to the grand public poetry of Virgil and Horace. Tibullus, though he may have accompanied Messalla to Aquitania in 30 BCE, consistently expresses his longing to escape with Delia to a rustic idyll. Both poets, concerned with the temptations afforded by city life, regard the country as morally superior to the city (see e.g. Propertius 2.31, Tibullus 1.10). Propertius' attitude to political matters is detached to the point of subversion: as well as declaring himself unworthy to write about Augustus (e.g. 3.9), he says that he will observe the triumphs of Caesar from the arms of his mistress. In 3.11, he sets an apparently conventional attack on Cleopatra in the context of a declaration of his own subjugation to a powerful woman, thus calling into question the standard Augustan view of female rule as unnatural and even monstrous. More generally, the elegists' proud adoption of a life of love outside wedlock is profoundly at odds with Augustus' social legislation, which included rewards for marriage and procreation.

While Virgil, Horace and Ovid allude frequently to contemporary Roman politics, the poetry of Tibullus and of Propertius 1 and 2 has a much vaguer, more obviously literary setting. Tibullus' longing for the simple life of the countryside (see e.g. 2.3.1ff) is not contrasted with the urban whirl in the way that Horace, for example, compares the lives of the town mouse and the country mouse in *Satires* 2.6, and while Propertius does include the occasional poem about the contemporary urban scene (e.g. 2.31), the majority of his poetry is set in an interior landscape, within the essentially closed dynamic of the relationship with Cynthia, or, particularly in book 4, in the past. Contemporary politics and the contemporary scene hold little interest for the elegiac lover; the elegiac poet both explicitly and implicitly eschews engagement with the regime whose patronage was so important to Virgil and Horace.

Two stock themes in love elegy reinforce this alienation from the norms of upper-class Roman masculinity. The first of these, called *militia amoris*, 'love's military service', depicts the lover as a soldier, sometimes laying siege to his mistress as though to a beleaguered city, sometimes battling with Love himself. The image is found in Hellenistic epigram and again in Roman comedy, but it is with elegy that it becomes a commonplace. Thus Tibullus in 1.1 contrasts the military campaigns fought by Messalla with his 'military service' among the battles of love. In the same way, Propertius in 1.6 leaves his friend Tullus to make war, while he experiences the *militia* of love. And the crucial difference between *militia* as experienced by young Roman aristocrats and the *militia amoris* is that the latter is – of course – not really war at all. 'Love is a god of peace', proclaims Propertius at the beginning of 3.5, and in 2.7 he announces that no one of his blood will be a soldier, though he will happily follow the camp of his mistress. The topos is taken to its extreme, as so often, by Ovid. In *Amores* 1.9, he proclaims that 'militat omnis amans', 'every lover is a soldier', and proceeds to explore every possible point of comparison between love and military service. The best lovers and soldiers are young, they endure physical hardships, go on long journeys over hostile terrain, spy on the enemy or their rivals, make secret nocturnal expeditions, are engaged on missions with uncertain outcome and so on, as some commentators have felt, *ad nauseam*.

Servitium amoris, 'love's slavery', is the term given to the elegiac lover's depiction of himself as in thrall to a dominant mistress. It is difficult for a modern reader to grasp fully just how shocking this image would have been to a Roman audience, accustomed to view servitude as an inherently degrading state and to regard male control of women as very much the natural order of things. For a man to glory in a woman's power over him to the extent of considering himself her slave represented a level of emasculation and self-abasement utterly abhorrent to traditional Roman values.

This idea of the lover as slave is one of the dominant themes of Tibullus' poetry: 2.4 opens with a defiant proclamation of his servitude to his mistress, and goes on to describe himself as held in chains which Love will not relax. In the closing lines of 1.2 he calls himself the slave of Venus – 'always my mind, dedicated to you, is your slave'. Elsewhere his attention to the detail of torture and punishment can strike the modern reader as grotesquely masochistic, such as 1.5, where he asks that a burst of outspokenness be punished by burning and torture. Propertius, too, revels in his servitude, even envisaging for himself an epitaph describing him as *servus amoris*, 'the slave of love' (2.13.36).

Other stock themes and characters feature regularly in love elegy, often themselves derived from Hellenistic epigram or Roman comedy. One such is the *paraclausithyron* ('beyond a closed door'), which depicts the lover denied access to his mistress, often due to the presence of a hostile janitor (see e.g. Tibullus 2.6, Ovid *Amores* 1.6). Propertius 1.16 goes a step further in having as its narrator the door itself, which complains of having to listen to the laments of the excluded lover. All the elegists at various times find themselves in competition with a rival, be it a husband or another lover (e.g. Propertius 1.5, Tibullus 1.6, Ovid, *Amores* 2.2) and are forced to deal with separation from the beloved and with her infidelity (e.g. Propertius 1.8A, Tibullus 1.5, Ovid, *Amores* 2.6). Stock characters, as well as the door-keeper, include the slave-girl, who may be helpful or not (e.g. Ovid, *Amores* 2.7–8) and the sinister *lena* or procuress (e.g. Propertius 4.5). These stylized characters and themes create a tension with the intense emotional tone of the *militia* and *servitium topoi* and force the reader to ask whether the poets are primarily writing about actual, experienced love-affairs at all.

These questions become all the more urgent when we examine the figure of the elegiac mistress. Can we ground the elegists' poetry in any plausibly reconstructed relationship? The emotional power of Catullus' love poetry, at least, has led many readers to view it as directly autobiographical, and Lesbia herself has been often – though not always convincingly – identified with the aristocratic and immoral Clodia of Cicero's *Pro Caelio* (see 9b and f). However, the order of the poems in the form that has come down to us does not present the affair in any sort of chronological order, and attempts to reconstruct the course of the relationship from the surviving poems have invariably foundered. Much of the love poetry, too, has very clear literary antecedents: poem 51, often read as referring to Lesbia though she is not mentioned by name, is a translation from Sappho; and 3, on the death of Lesbia's sparrow, has as its model the Hellenistic tradition of epigrams mourning a favourite pet.

These warnings against a straightforwardly autobiographical reading of Catullus' poetry make us approach the writings of the elegists with similar caution. Although Apuleius, writing in the second century CE, identifies Propertius' Cynthia with a certain Hostia, and Tibullus' Delia with one Plania, he gives no historical form to Nemesis or Marathus, or to Ovid's Corinna, whose status as a literary construct has never been seriously questioned. Broadly speaking, the characteristics of the elegiac mistress are fairly standard. Elegiac poets have girlfriends who are tall, blonde, elegant, materialistic, capricious, hot-tempered, fickle and well-read. They wear too much make-up for their lovers' tastes and take excessive pride in personal adornment. Their interest in the lavish social scene at Rome and in notorious fleshpots such as Baiae causes their lovers considerable concern; and they can be sharp-tongued and even violent in the inevitable quarrels which plague the affair.

In the nineteenth and early twentieth century, scholars meticulously reconstructed the trajectory of the various affairs and attempted to draw detailed pen-portraits of Lesbia, Cynthia and Delia, based on details in the poems themselves. In the later decades of the twentieth century, the tendency was to look at the poetry in the context of a supposed *demi-monde* of lavish entertainments and glamorous, highly-educated courtesans, and to see Cynthia and Delia, in particular, as real figures operating within this milieu.

Modern scholarship has radically revised this reading of love elegy, most notably in the work of Maria Wyke, whose *The Roman Mistress* (2002) argues compellingly for the futility of attempting to construct a 'real' woman lurking beneath the surface of the text. Indeed, far from representing an actual girl-friend, the elegiac mistress stands in many ways for the genre of elegy itself, and the relationship depicted is essentially that between the poet and elegy. This can be seen most clearly in Ovid *Amores* 3.1, a contest between elegy and tragedy. Elegy is described as having perfumed hair which is bound up; her figure is *decens*, 'attractive'; her clothing very finely-woven (*tenuissima*) – all attributes of the elegiac mistress from Cynthia to Corinna.

In this context, the emphasis all the elegists place on the hope that the power of their poetry to win over the mistress (see e.g. Propertius 2.34, Tibullus 2.4) is realigned: if the mistress is to a great extent a symbol of the genre of love elegy, the attempt to woo her through the writing of elegiac poetry can be seen as the elegiac version of the ambition, common in Roman poetry (see, especially, Horace) to be viewed as the supreme exponent of that particular genre. Elsewhere, we find the poet celebrating the fame conferred on the beloved by his poetry (e.g. Propertius 2.1, Tibullus 1.4.61ff), again foregrounding the poetry itself over the relationship (let alone the woman) that allegedly inspired it.

Nonetheless, whatever the relationship of the poetry to reality, it is the emotional power and passion of love elegy which is its most immediately attractive quality, and it is perfectly possible for the reader to respond to this emotional impact without needing to adopt a forensically biographical approach. Propertius 1.3, for example, depicts the poet returning home from a party, somewhat the worse for drink, to discover that Cynthia has fallen asleep while waiting up for him. He tiptoes around her, fighting the temptation to wake her, tentatively draping around her neck the garlands he is wearing, and placing in her hands the fruit he carries. Eventually the bubble bursts: moon-beams strike the window and wake her up, and she subjects him to an eloquent and vitriolic tongue-lashing of the kind that only the elegiac mistress (or, per-haps, the harridan of Roman comedy) can deliver. With characteristically sophisticated use of mythological parallels – Cynthia is compared to the aban-doned Ariadne, to Andromeda rescued from the sea-monster, to the devoted Penelope – the poem clearly owes much to the tradition of Alexandrian *doctrina* and is a highly literary piece. But it is one of the great strengths of elegy that it can speak so powerfully at both an intellectual and an emotional level.

Ovid's contributions to the genre of love elegy have traditionally been regarded as fundamentally different from the work of his predecessors. Critics have searched in vain for the apparent emotional sincerity and spontaneity of earlier elegy, and in exasperation have accused Ovid of destroying the expressiveness of the genre. More recently, however, the emphasis by scholars on the literary character of the work of Tibullus and Propertius, and the re-examination of the 'realistic' nature of their poetry, have led Ovid's self-conscious exploration of the stock themes and *topoi* of love elegy to be seen as a natural progression from the work of his predecessors.

Ovid begins the *Amores* by telling how, when on the brink of composing an epic, Cupid surreptitiously stole a foot from the verse – turning the six-footed hexameter metre into the hexameter plus five-footed pentameter of the elegiac couplet. Thus he defines himself first as an elegiac poet: the elegiac mistress does not appear until 1.3, and is not named until 1.5. This is in stark contrast to Propertius, who begins his first book of elegies with the words 'Cynthia prima' – 'Cynthia was the first'. Elsewhere, too, Ovid plays knowingly with the ambiguous status of the elegiac mistress as part real girlfriend, part literary inspiration – or even literary construct. In 1.5, for example (his account of a siesta-time visit by Corinna with predictably steamy consequences), he teasingly invites the reader to contemplate her body from shoulders to thigh, before breaking off to ask 'Who does not know the rest?' And the dream-like quality of the whole episode, with Corinna appearing as Ovid reclines half-asleep, compels the reader to question whether the poet is describing an actual event or a fantasy – and, finally, whether this is a question one is entitled to ask of poetry.

Ovid shows himself acutely conscious of the function of his poetry in realizing the figure of his mistress. In 2.17, for example, he remarks that many women want to have a *nomen* ('name', but also 'reputation', 'fame') through him; but most telling is 3.12, a discussion of the outcome of Corinna's immortalization in his verse, where he complains that his poetry has made her a whore and himself her pimp, when in fact his own poetic licence has significantly exaggerated her charms.

Throughout the *Amores*, Ovid explores the stock themes and characters of earlier elegy in a way that has often been described as parodic, but which arguably does no more than expose the inherent artificiality of the genre. The theme of the lover's disapproval of his mistress' reliance on cosmetics is played out in 1.14, where Corinna's over-dyed hair has fallen out; that of the mistress' illness in 2.13 and 14, where Corinna is recovering from an abortion; the Catullan (and Hellenistic) theme of the death of the mistress' pet in 2.6, the famous elegy on the death of Corinna's parrot – and so on.

Ovid's degree of self-consciousness is significantly greater than that of Propertius and Tibullus. Also different is his lack of fidelity to a single mistress – even Tibullus is serially monogamous. Ovid in *Amores* 2 presents a pair of poems (7 and 8) in which he reveals himself to be having an affair with

Corinna's maid Cypassis; in 3.7, he proclaims his recent conquests of Chlide, Libas and Pitho. Ovid can certainly portray himself as unsuccessful in his attempts to win his object of desire – see, for example, 1.4, where he recognizes that a dinner-party attended by all three participants in the love-triangle may well terminate in sex between the girl and his rival. However, it is the persona of the *bon viveur* and man-about-town which he develops in his ventures into didactic elegy, the *Ars Amatoria* and *Remedium Amoris*.

Although the hexameter had previously been the preferred metre for Latin didactic (in Lucretius' *De Rerum Natura* and Virgil's *Georgics*), there were Greek precedents for didactic elegy. In particular, Callimachus' *Aetia*, poems explaining the origins of religious festivals and customs, had provided an explicit model for Propertius' fourth book. Ovid could thus trace the pedigree of his didactic elegy through Propertius back to the Hellenistic poets.

In the *Ars Amatoria*, Ovid presents himself as the *praeceptor amoris*, the 'teacher of love', who confidently advises his reader in the techniques which will ensure him success with the opposite sex (female in books 1 and 2, male in book 3). In a marked shift from earlier elegy, the setting is explicitly that of contemporary Rome. Very early in the *Ars Amatoria* (1.67–88), Ovid takes his reader on a tour of Rome's most splendid monuments, recommending them as locations for picking up girls. Elsewhere, he advises the would-be lover to go on the hunt in the Circus Maximus or at the theatre and at 3.113ff. he rejoices in the sophistication of the great modern city.

The *Ars Amatoria* instructs the reader in how to be a successful elegiac lover, deploying many of the themes common to elegiac poetry. He explains how to communicate with the beloved at a dinner party in the presence of a rival (1.571ff.); he advises against excessive violence in the quarrels that bedevil an elegiac love-affair (2.169ff); he advises against over-praising the beloved (1.739ff) in terms ruefully reminiscent of *Amores* 3.12. The *Remedia Amoris* takes this persona a step further. Here, Ovid – drawing on Greek didactic poems on medical or pharmacological themes, such as those of Nicander – presents himself in part as a doctor, capable of 'curing' elegiac love. The poem has been read as Ovid's renunciation of love elegy before moving on to the 'greater' themes of the *Metamorphoses*. More recently, scholars have questioned the ingenuousness of its purpose: given Ovid's own emphasis on the motivating power of Love in driving both emotional and (crucially) literary activity, can an effective 'cure' ever really be achieved?

Roughly contemporary with the *Ars* and *Remedia Amoris* are the *Heroides*. Routinely dismissed as monotonous and unrealistic by nineteenth- and twentieth-century critics, they are only now attracting renewed scholarly attention. Modern critics are intrigued by the poems' status as letters, addressed to an actual mythological recipient but in fact read by the far more knowing Ovidian reader; and by the way in which their purported immediacy can reinvent the 'canonical' versions of the heroines' stories. Thus Ovid's Dido (*Heroides* 7) presents the possibility that she may be carrying Aeneas' child (133–4) and – in contrast to Aeneas' own account of the loss of his wife Creusa in *Aeneid* 2 – depicts him as heartlessly abandoning her in the burning Troy. But in the context of the genre of love elegy, the most significant achievement of the *Heroides* is the transfer to its female subjects of the emotions, imagery and situations of the male elegiac lover. Ovid's heroines are abandoned by capricious or faithless lovers (Medea, Ariadne); they communicate optimistically but probably ineffectually by letter (especially Penelope and Ariadne); they may be enslaved by love (literally, in the case of Briseis); while Ovid's Sappho unhappily contrasts the fame of her poetry with its failure to move the object of her love. Whether Ovid is deliberately empowering a female voice or – perhaps more plausibly – merely revelling in his effective subversion of a well-established genre is still open to question.

Ovid's two didactic elegiac works, together with the *Heroides*, mark (as far as we can tell) the end of the development of the genre. Nothing survives of the few poets reported to have written in the style of the elegists; nor – unlike Cornelius Gallus – can their influence be detected in the work of others. With a mere half-century elapsing between Catullus' love elegies and the *Remedia Amoris*, the brief flowering of Latin love elegy encapsulates a remarkable poetic and emotional range.

Further reading

Good introductions to love elegy can be found in James (2003); Keith (2000); Kennedy (1993); Lyne (1980); Miller (2002); Veyne (1988). Commentaries on 17 love elegies by Catullus, Propertius, Tibullus and Ovid can be found in Booth and Lee (1999). There are some very good articles as well in Griffin (1985), and Wyke (2002) is an interesting work on the importance of the figure of the Roman mistress (so essential to elegy). For Propertius, see Cairns (2009); Hubbard (2001); Stahl (1985); Sullivan (1976). For Tibullus, see Cairns (1979); Lee-Stecum (1998). For Ovid, see Armstrong (2005); Boyd (1997); Davis (2005); Hardie (2002). For a collection of articles that deals with the idea of Augustan poetry as propaganda, see Powell (1992). For poets more generally in the Augustan age, see White (1993).

OVID

Caroline Butler

For much of the twentieth century, Publius Ovidius Naso (43 BCE–*c.* 17 CE) attracted relatively little critical attention. Ovid's delight in language for its own sake, his fascination with the incongruous and the grotesque, his self-conscious reworking of the works of his predecessors (including, occasionally, himself) and his apparently flippant approach to affairs of the heart all failed to appeal to an age often preoccupied with 'authenticity' in poetry. All too frequently, Ovid's poetry was dismissed as superficial and regarded as a precursor to the 'decadent' style of, for example, Seneca, Martial and Lucan – the so-called Silver Latin Age – in contrast to the 'Golden' Augustan poets who preceded him.

Recent scholarship, however, has done much to rehabilitate Ovid and to restore to his poetry some of the stature it enjoyed in western culture from the renaissance to the eighteenth century. Postmodernism, the critical movement which flowered in the closing decades of the twentieth century, has found much to enjoy and engage with in Ovid's self-reference and his literary self-consciousness. Ovid's use of female voices in the *Heroides* and the *Metamorphoses*, and the prominence, unique in Roman poetry, given to female experience, has benefited from the development of feminist criticism. And the publication in 1997 of Ted Hughes' *Tales from Ovid* brought the poet into the cultural mainstream in a way not seen since the renaissance.

Ovid was born to a wealthy equestrian family in Sulmo in the Abruzzo region of Italy in 43 BCE. He and his elder brother studied rhetoric in Rome, probably with a view to embarking on a political career. His brother died young, and Ovid himself, after holding some minor official posts, abandoned politics in favour of poetry. It is difficult to reconstruct the exact chronology of the writing and publication of Ovid's poetry from what he himself tells us. However, it seems that his first works, the *Heroides* and *Amores* appeared some time between 25 and 15 BCE. He lived in Rome, writing and interacting with the literary figures of the day, until in 8 CE he was exiled by the emperor Augustus to Tomis, on the Black Sea. The reasons for his exile are obscure: Ovid himself alludes to a *carmen* (poem) *et error* (in *Tristia* 2.207). It is possible that the *carmen* was the racy *Ars Amatoria* (even though the poem was published several years before the banishment), which offered advice on the seduction of married women, and the *error* may have been an association with the emperor's daughter Julia, herself exiled in the same year. By the time of his exile, Ovid had substantially completed his masterpiece, the *Metamorphoses*, and six books of the *Fasti*, as well as the lost tragedy *Medea*; the *Tristia*, *Epistulae ex Ponto* and the curse-poem *Ibis* were written in Tomis, where he died in 17 or 18 CE.

Ovid's poetry, therefore, was produced in a very different milieu from that of his immediate predecessors. Unlike Virgil, Horace or Propertius, he was not financially dependent on a patron, and was able to write primarily for a wider public. This, together with the fact that he experienced civil war only as a child, helps to explain why engagement with contemporary politics – though by no means absent – is given less urgent foregrounding in his work prior to his exile, and is approached somewhat tentatively in the *Tristia* and *Epistulae ex Ponto*. Finally, while the poets of the previous generations were trailblazers, bringing to Latin literature the polish and erudition of the Hellenistic tradition, Ovid inherited a mature Roman poetic tradition, which casts a powerful shadow over his own work.

His first published works, the *Heroides* and the *Amores*, like the later *Ars Amatoria* and *Remedia Amoris*, both explore and subvert the genre of elegiac poetry which had flourished so spectacularly in the preceding generation, notably in the work of Propertius and Tibullus. As such, they are discussed in detail in the section on love elegy (10e). The *Fasti*, a work in elegiacs which deals with the Roman calendar and its religious festivals, clearly owes much to Propertius book 4, in which the poet explicitly takes as his theme the origins of Roman customs and place-names, and lays claim to be the Roman Callimachus. But it is in the *Metamorphoses* that we see Ovid at his most intertextual. In a poem whose stated subject is that of spirits (*animas*) turned into new bodies (*in nova corpora*, 1.1–2), Ovid also takes the full gamut of literary genres, including epic, tragedy, comedy, elegy, didactic and rhetoric, and turns it into something entirely his own.

Traditionally, scholars have found it difficult to assign so complex and shifting a work to a particular genre. Ovid himself, by describing the *Metamorphoses* as a *carmen perpetuum* (continuous poem) in 1.2, encourages the reader to view it as an epic. As a hexameter poem which deals with gods and heroes, it would seem to qualify as such. Unlike the *Iliad* or the *Aeneid*, however, wit and play are never far from the surface, leading some critics to label the work not only superficial but also amoral and to classify it as a mock-epic, a comic epic, or even anti-epic. Most recently, however, scholars have emphasized both the *Metamorphoses'* universal theme (from the creation of the world up until Ovid's own time) and the strong interaction with Virgil's *Aeneid* and with Homer.

Ovid begins his work with a description in epic style of the creation of the world – itself a process of change from chaos into order – and proceeds to narrate two apparently uncomplicated stories of divine retribution: the punishment of mankind through the flood and the transformation of the wicked Lycaon into a wolf. The next story concerns the heroic slaying of the python by Apollo. While the literary allusions are manifold (encompassing Hesiod, Lucretius and the *Eclogues* of Virgil), the themes and tones are firmly epic, with the creation narrative owing much to *Iliad* 18. Similarly, it is with Homer and Virgil that the work ends, with books 12–14 being taken up with the events of the *Iliad*, *Odyssey* and *Aeneid*, and 15 culminating in a heroic and epicized account of the triumphs of Augustus.

In between, despite the astonishing range of tone and subject-matter, epic is never far from the surface. When Ovid moves in book 1 to tell of Apollo's passion for Daphne, in one of the work's best known stories, the switch from the heroic to the erotic has been viewed as a move away from the epic into love elegy. And yet Apollo is wounded by an arrow shot by Cupid in *saeva ira* (fierce anger) – the very phrase used to describe Juno's hatred of Aeneas in *Aeneid* 1. And there are plenty of stories which have an appropriately epic theme, such as the battle between the jilted suitor Phineus and the hero Perseus at the beginning of book 5, or the – admittedly exaggerated – heroism of the Calydonian boar hunt in book 8.

The *Aeneid*, while owing its greatest debt to Homer, nonetheless successfully incorporates the Hellenistic and the tragic. Ovid pushes this inclusivity still further, achieving a literary universality together with the cosmic universality of his subject matter. We have already seen that the opening lines of the poem, with their proclamation of a *carmen perpetuum*, lay claim to epic; but the verb that Ovid uses to describe this process, *deducere*, to draw down, roots the *Metamorphoses* equally in the tradition of Callimachus. The very familiarity to modern readers of many of the stories which Ovid makes his own (Apollo and Daphne, Echo and Narcissus, Pan and Syrinx) can blind us to their relative obscurity to a contemporary audience: in true Alexandrian style, Ovid is parading his scholarship by this display of mythological learning as well as by his delight in allusion and periphrasis. From Callimachus, too, comes his frequently surprising reworking of well-known myth: see for example how in book 8 he despatches Theseus' slaying of the Minotaur in a mere two lines (172–3), focusing instead on the abandonment of Ariadne. And Callimachus' long narrative poem the *Hecale*, which survives only in fragments, provides a starting-point for Ovid's own complex interlocking and internesting narrative structure, where stories of metamorphosis are often put in the mouths of characters who are themselves players in someone else's speech.

It was, of course, as a love poet that Ovid first made his name, and the transforming power of love, or lust, or desire, is a major thread in the *Metamorphoses*. This transforming power takes many guises. At one extreme, we see the conjugal fidelity and simple morality of the elderly couple Philemon and Baucis earning them the reward of transformation into perpetually intertwined trees (book 8); or in book 11 the inability of Ceyx and Alcyone to endure life apart leading to the gods taking pity on them by turning them into birds. In other stories, unrequited love leads to transformation, as when Clytie, constantly watching the path of the sun in fruitless longing, becomes a heliotrope (book 15). But love has its violent aspects too. Whether from a protofeminist or sado-masochistic or merely voyeuristic standpoint, Ovid depicts some 50 rapes or attempted rapes. And so we see Jupiter turned into a bull in order to abduct Europa; Io becoming a cow so that she can be hidden from jealous Juno; Daphne and Syrinx transformed into a laurel tree and a bank of reeds in order to escape a violent pursuer – and so on. The violence of love can even lead to a change of sex: thus the girl Caenis becomes Caeneus after an aggressive rape by Poseidon leaves her praying never to have sex with a man again.

Ovid's portrayal of sexual violence is far from straightforward. On the one hand, he can invite a voyeuristic response from the reader by dwelling on the erotic allure of firm flesh revealed by the ripping of garments – see, for example, the rape of Proserpina in book 5, or Apollo's pursuit of Daphne in 1. On the other hand, the horror experienced by the victim and by onlookers rather stands in the way of the temptation to dismiss the violations as unreal and mythological. Thus the nymph Cyane, after remonstrating ineffectually with Dis for taking Proserpina against her will, pines away until she merges with the water of the fountain she inhabits. One aspect of Ovid's genius is his ability effectively to project actions and emotions from the everyday world onto the stylized tales of mythology, and we can see a refusal to put these potentially troubling stories into a comfortable box labelled 'myth'; also important is his interest in making the familiar strange, in telling a story from a different angle, which leads him to focus on the perspectives and reactions of characters usually treated as passive players in the drama.

It would be wrong to discuss the *Metamorphoses* without looking at the brilliance of Ovid's wit, whether in his coruscating wordplay, his relish for the comic potential of situations, or his subtle sending-up of the more stylized conventions of his literary predecessors. This wit was often dismissed as superficial cleverness by critics who unfavourably compared Ovid's lightness of touch with the portentous gravity of Virgil or the tragic intensity of Homer. Much of Ovid's humour can simply be enjoyed at face value, such as the deliberations of the princess Scylla in book 8, in love with Minos, leader of a besieging army. Scylla talks herself into betraying her city in a speech redolent of the agonizing thought processes of a Medea, but one which combines self-conscious epic posturing ('I would go through fire and the sword') with an egotistical rationalization ('He will win anyway . . . the gods hate a coward').

Postmodernism, with its interest in the nature of writing itself ('textuality') and the relationship between art and life, has offered new ways of looking at Ovid's self-conscious fictionalization of his stories. Thus Pirithous' questioning of the truth of stories of metamorphosis in book 8 is not merely the predictable response of a *spretor deorum* (despiser of the gods, lines 612–13), but can be viewed as a reminder to the reader of the suspension of disbelief that Ovid himself has encouraged. Again, his frequent departures from the received versions of myths not only pay tribute to the inherently shifting and metamorphic nature of these traditional stories but also draw attention to their fictional nature.

Ovid's narrative technique has never failed to excite admiration. Across 15 books and within a broadly chronological framework stretching from the creation of the universe to the reign of Augustus, Ovid succeeds in weaving together an astonishingly diverse collection of stories through an equally wide-ranging spread of narrative devices. In book 11, for example, he opens (1–66) with the death of Orpheus, and proceeds to tell the story of Bacchus' punishment of the Maenads who caused his death (67–84); uses the absence of Silenus from Bacchus' train to tell the famous story of Midas and the golden touch, followed by his growing of ass's ears as a punishment from Apollo (85–193). Apollo is the link to the next story, which deals with his and Neptune's involvement in the building of Troy, the king's failure to honour his promise and the sacrifice of his daughter to a sea-monster, ending with her marriage to Telamon, brother of Peleus (194–220). Peleus' marriage to the reluctant Thetis forms the next episode (221–65), and his exile after the murder of his half-brother brings him to the court of Ceyx, who narrates the metamorphosis of his brother Daedalion, (291–345), before Peleus' prayers result in the turning to stone of a monstrous wolf (346–409). The tragic love of Ceyx and his wife Alycone, turned into kingfishers after Ceyx's death at sea, is dealt with at 410–748; and finally a bystander is inspired by this metamorphosis to tell the tale of Aesacus, turned into a sea-bird. Minor characters from one story provide links to the next, whether as protagonists (Peleus) or tangential figures (Silenus); stories are inset into the main narrative as speeches from one of the characters (Daedalion); they may be narrated at breakneck speed (the building of Troy, Laomedon's treachery towards Apollo and then Hercules, the rescue of Hesione crammed into just over 25 lines) or with lingering detail (Ceyx and Alcyone); the metamorphosis may be lovingly described (the Maenads) or brushed over in a single line (Ceyx).

In the two closing books of the *Metamorphoses*, 14 and 15, Ovid reworks the events of the *Aeneid* and brings his narrative up to the present day with the death and apotheosis of Julius Caesar and the rule of Augustus. Contemporary political events are thus brought sharply into focus in a work which hitherto has seemed firmly (if not entirely straightforwardly) in the world of myth. With the shift across the 15 books from the beginnings of the universe to the present, and from east to west, Ovid appears to be presenting the principate as the culmination of the process begun with the first emergence of order from chaos. That this process is divinely ordained is strongly suggested when he announces that, while Jupiter rules the heavens, Augustus has power over the earth: 'each is father and governor' (15.858–60) – a statement which comes very close to presenting Augustus as a god. On the other hand, the behaviour of the gods throughout the *Metamorphoses* is violent, lust-crazed, vengeful and capricious – hardly the qualities one would desire in a ruler. Again, Julius Caesar's final appearance in the poem shows him watching his (adopted) son, Augustus, whose achievements are even greater than his own (850). The stress on the dynastic succession of power, so contrary to the ethos of the Roman republic, strikes another jarring note. Clearly it would be wrong to describe the *Metamorphoses* as apolitical, and over-simplistic to label them as 'anti-Augustan'. But while the final scenes of the work present Augustus' Rome as the summation of the immense chain of metamorphoses which form the body of the poem, that picture is not without its ambiguities and undercurrents.

Written apparently concurrently with the *Metamorphoses*, the *Fasti* take as their theme the Roman calendar. Until recently they represented almost the most neglected part of the Ovidian corpus, dismissed as a merely antiquarian undertaking; and while the last two decades have seen a renewed interest in their dialogue with the Augustan regime and with their engagement with narrative authority, they still remain at the margins of Ovidian scholarship. Ovid himself describes the *Fasti* (in the *Tristia*) as unfinished: while it is uncertain how much of the poem was originally completed, what survives is the account of the first six months of the year, in six books. He claims to have written (*scripsi*) the second six by the time of his exile, books which would have begun with the heavily Augustan months of July and August; but, in the absence of any firm evidence of the date of their composition, scholars have questioned the absolute truth of this assertion. Quite possibly the project, with its strongly Roman theme, was derailed by his exile from the capital; the theory that he abandoned the work out of boredom seems unlikely.

Literary precedents for the *Fasti* exist in the form of Greek didactic works, most notably Callimachus' *Aetia*, which looked at the mythological origins of religious customs and beliefs, and the *Phaenomena* of Aratus, on astronomy. In the generation preceding Ovid, Propertius (who himself laid claim to be the 'Roman Callimachus') had opened his fourth book of elegies with a declaration of intent to write about 'sacred matters, days, and the ancient names of things' (4.69). Also important is the Roman antiquarian prose writer Varro (116–27 BCE), whose works included treatises on Roman religion and institutions. Furthermore, many prose *Fasti* were produced during the reign of Augustus, most notably that of Verrius Flaccus. And, as with the *Metamorphoses*, Virgil is never far away, particularly when Ovid recasts and reworks stories of Roman origins from the *Aeneid*.

In contrast to the *Metamorphoses*, the *Fasti* engage in constant dialogue with Augustan ideology. The Roman calendar had been reformed under Julius Caesar and, in 8 BCE, the month Sextilis renamed Augustus in honour of the princeps. Moreover, during the reign of Augustus, the official calendar expanded to include an increasing number of commemorations of Augustus and his family. Augustus' promotion of traditional religion and his rebuilding of temples is well known; recent scholarship has emphasized how Augustus used the calendar to underpin the authority of his reign: a good example is his immense sundial, the Solarium Augusti, whose shadow pointed towards the Ara Pacis on Augustus' birthday, reinforcing his role as bringer of peace. By writing on the calendar, then, Ovid had chosen a subject closely aligned with Augustus' own interests. It is brought even closer to the imperial family with its dedication to Germanicus, grandson of the princeps' wife Livia and prominent military commander.

The word *Fasti* was used by the Romans to mean merely 'calendar', but in fact it is an abbreviation of *dies fasti*, literally 'speakable days': days of good omen on which business could be transacted. Their opposite was *dies nefasti*, 'unspeakable days' which were regarded as ill-omened. So a poem titled *Fasti* refers not just to the calendar, but to the fact that its subject matter is something that can be talked about. Recent scholarship has seen a link with a shift in Augustus' later years towards a more autocratic and dynastic style of government, in which freedom of speech was increasingly curtailed. Denis Feeney (1992) has demonstrated how Ovid connects the *Fasti* with speech early in book 1 (45–52), where he talks about the rules governing days on which it is permitted or forbidden to speak, and highlights a preoccupation with speech and silence throughout the poem, whether in Ovid's narrative of the stories of (for example) Lucretia and Tacita (whose name means 'silent'), or his own authorial interjections. An example of this can be seen in book 4, where a moment of nostalgia for his home town of Sulmo is broken off with an invocation to his Muse to curtail his laments.

But Ovid's characteristic playfulness is never far away. This can be seen most clearly in his adoption of the persona of the antiquarian scholar. Throughout the *Fasti*, Ovid is both diffident (as when he describes the work as *timidae* in the opening address to Germanicus) and keen to display his assiduous research and the wide range of his sources, referring to himself as *operosus*, 'painstaking'. But, as Carole Newlands has pointed out (1995: 66ff.), very few of his sources are written, and he frequently quotes his (oral) sources verbatim. This introduction to the work of multiple narrators invites the reader to question their reliability, particularly as he rarely commits himself to evaluation or criticism. The confident authority of the narrator of the *Metamorphoses* and the *praeceptor amoris* ('teacher of love') of the *Ars Amatoria* thus dissolves into the hesitant and indiscriminate antiquarianism of the *Fasti*.

Ovid's elegiac exile poetry, the five books of *Tristia*, the four of *Epistulae Ex Ponto*, and the curse-poem *Ibis* were long dismissed as self-indulgent and inferior productions, with some scholars even speculating that the exile was merely a poetic conceit and that the poet remained in Rome throughout. While the poems have benefited from the late twentieth-century renaissance in Ovidian criticism, they still remain relatively unexplored.

His place of exile was Tomis (modern Constanza) on the Black Sea. The region makes its first appearance in classical literature in the work of the fifth-century BCE historian Herodotus, for whom it marks the very edges of the world. For Herodotus, the territory north and east of the Black Sea was inhabited by the Scythians, an historical people whom Herodotus depicts as an archetypal 'other'. Roman writers, including Virgil, deploy them as representing the antithesis of civilization, a primitive people inhabiting an icy landscape which the Roman empire has yet to pacify (see e.g. Virgil, *Georgics* 3.339–83). Tomis itself, however, was originally a Greek colony and by Ovid's time, although situated in an area populated by the Thracian tribe of the Getae, it was most probably still Greek in its language and culture. Ovid nonetheless chooses to depict his exile as taking place in an inhospitable region, where the complete absence of Graeco-Roman culture is made all the worse by the constant incursions by hostile tribes and the overwhelming cold. An exile caused by his poetry is effectively ending his career as a poet (he claims) by eroding his familiarity with the Roman literary scene and with the Latin language itself – see, for example, *Tristia* 3.1.13–18; *Pont.* 4.13.

There is no explicit literary precedent for Ovid's exile poetry; unsurprisingly, however, the work of earlier writers provides a number of important intertexts. The influence of Herodotus has already been mentioned, and there is an irony inherent in Ovid's determined location of his actual exile in the kind of territory used as an imaginary situation for marginalized or displaced figures such as Gallus in Virgil's tenth *Eclogue*. Odysseus, desperately seeking his wife and his home through years of wandering, is an important parallel (see *Tristia* 1.5.57–84 and *Pont.* 1.4.23–46). It is significant in this context that Ovid's wife makes her only appearances in the exile poetry. Also relevant are the *Ars Amatoria* (the alleged cause of his exile), whose blamelessness forms a plaintive and recurring thread throughout, and the *Heroides*, whose epistolary form and reproachful content provides a model for the *Epistulae ex Ponto*.

Throughout the exile poetry, Ovid pleads with Augustus for his recall, alternating between flattery of the emperor's reputation for clemency and defence of his own poetry. A more subversive tone can be detected in his assertion that Augustus must have been far too busy to have read the *Ars Amatoria* in any case (*Tristia* 2. 225–32); and at 3.7.47–52 he claims that the stature of his poetry is such as to have won him fame beyond the control of Caesar.

Ovid's poetry encompasses a glittering diversity of subject matter, a remarkable range of style and tone, and a dazzling wit that never ceases to remind the reader of the astonishing poetic *ingenium* that we see at work. His dialogue with and reworking of his literary antecedents is no less powerful than that of his Augustan predecessors; to a lesser extent, he engages with the imperial regime and the questions of government and free speech that it raises. More than any classical poet before or since, he is concerned with the process of writing poetry and with the inherently fictional quality of literature.

Further reading

There is a good collection on many aspects of Ovid's writing in Hardie (2002); see also the same author's learned and interesting work on Ovid's 'Poetics of Illusion' (Hardie, 2007). For Ovid's (strained) relationship with the Augustan regime, see Barchiesi (1997); Davis (2005); see also Powell (1992) on propaganda more generally. For a work which interprets a number of works by Ovid, see Barchiesi (2001). On the *Metamorphoses*, see Fantham (2004); Galinsky (1975); Hardie (1993); Solodow (1988); Wheeler (1999). There is also material in Feeney (2007) and Hinds (1998). On *Heroides*, see Lindheim and Rosenmeyer (2003) and Verducci (1985). On *Tristia*, see Williams (1994). On *Fasti*, see Newlands (1995). For poets more generally in the Augustan age, see White (1993).

Chapter 11

The early empire

The dates in this chapter are CE unless otherwise stated. Glossary items: *a bibliothecis; a studiis; ab epistulis; allegory; apostrophe; aristeia; ataraxia; hendecasyllables; imperium; mores; pietas; recitatio; reductio ad absurdum; senatus consultum; stoicism; topos.*

THE EARLY EMPIRE: AN HISTORICAL INTRODUCTION

Terry Edwards

After the death of Augustus in 14 CE, for the next 54 years Rome enjoyed ('suffered' in Tacitus' view) the reigns of the Julio-Claudians. While some emperors of this period, and later in the century, tried to maintain that delicate balance of republican forms and imperial/military power, others could barely be bothered to keep up the pretence. These latter emperors displayed both their power and their contempt for the senatorial class. It may be that only Vespasian and Nerva died natural deaths during this century. The emperors who made a show of their power died violently. The middle of the century was disrupted by a civil war and a year in which four emperors ruled (69). This war ended the assumption that the senate chose the emperor in Rome; the armies on the frontiers, along with the praetorians in Rome, chose these emperors; and none was related to the Julio-Claudians in the slightest.

In the republic, many writers – Fabius Pictor, Cato the Censor, Caesar, Cicero, Sallust – were active politicians; even Catullus spent some time in the provinces. However, the emergence of imperial power and the patronage which the emperor could wield meant that everyone, to some extent, was dependent on the favour of the most powerful man in the world. The benefits could be worthwhile, as Horace and Virgil learnt. At the same time, a writer might, like Cremutius Cordus in 25, find himself in court on a charge of treason for opinions which went counter to the views of Tiberius. The more paranoid the emperor, the more dangerous was the existence of writers. Tacitus waited until Domitian was dead before embarking on his career as a historian. Both he and Pliny survived his reign by keeping their heads down (or on!) and saying nothing. They both felt guilty afterwards. Others were less lucky, or braver. Lucan fell foul of Nero, as did Petronius and Seneca: they committed suicide. (At least Augustus only sent Ovid into exile.) Pliny the Elder seems to have lived through and prospered in the same period. Later, Juvenal may well have been exiled by Domitian for some minor criticism, leaving him destitute on return. Martial left Rome for Spain rather than continue the struggle for imperial patronage (although he had Pliny's support).

The emperors certainly spent money on literature, art and architecture, admittedly for propaganda purposes more than from a desire to promote the arts. Tiberius, an efficient administrator, had a prosperous and peaceful reign but added only a little to the splendour of Augustus' achievements. Claudius himself had written histories, of the Etruscans for example, before he became emperor. According to Suetonius, he was a keen attendant at recitals. Furthermore, Cluvius Rufus and Fabius Rusticus both were active during the middle of the century and wrote histories of Nero's reign. Nero personally participated in performances of poetry and chariot-racing competitions. Domitian, like Gaius, had an enthusiasm for chariot racing and games. Vespasian set up a chair of rhetoric in Rome.

Claudius was murdered in 54 by Agrippina, Nero's mother. The historians characterize Claudius as ruled by his wives and freedmen, a weak emperor, drunk much of the time. It is a largely biased and unfair portrait: he invaded Britain, brought Gauls into the senate, began the enlargement of Ostia, and maintained peace, order and prosperity. Nero, supported by his praetorian prefect, Burrus, and his tutor, Seneca, began well, even with the shadow of his domineering mother looming over him. Corbulo eventually ended the Armenian problem. The northern frontiers were largely peaceful. Even Britain, despite Boudicca's revolt in 60, was consolidated under a series of sensible governors. Nero's early years were generally undisturbed, apart from Agrippina's meddling.

Agrippina harassed Nero over Acte, his freedwoman lover, voiced support for Britannicus, Claudius' son, and interfered in politics. Britannicus died in 55 – or was murdered by poisoned mushrooms, later Nero's self-proclaimed favourite dish. Nero then fell in love with Poppaea, wife of Otho. Agrippina opposed Nero's wish to divorce his wife, Octavia, Claudius' daughter, to marry Poppaea. Nagged by Poppaea (according to Tacitus) in 59 Nero staged a shipwreck on the bay of Naples to make his mother's death look accidental. The plan failed. He sent a freedman, Anicetus to kill her in her villa. He was now free to fulfil his wish to perform on stage and race in chariots.

His Greek games and entertainments pleased the common people. He patronized artists and wrote poetry himself. He encouraged the performance of plays and music. But it was his own appearance on a public stage which shocked some Romans and provincials. In 64 he performed on stage in Naples, before performing in Rome the year after. Then he set off to tour Greece and its festivals while in Rome the opposition grew.

The death of Burrus, the retirement of Seneca, the divorce and death of Octavia and marriage to Poppaea, all in 62, signalled the change. Ofonius Tigellinus became his closest advisor. The deaths of Sulla Felix and Rubellius Plautus followed, and relations with the senate deteriorated. The great fire of Rome in 64 simply made matters worse. Nero did not start the fire, nor fiddle as it raged; however, his rebuilding of the city, especially his Golden House, was a political miscalculation. The plot of Piso in 65 revealed the senatorial opposition (and this included Lucan). Even so, it was a Gaul, Vindex, who began the revolt, followed by Galba, and others. On return from Greece, Nero was abandoned and forced to commit suicide in a villa outside Rome in 68. His effort at cultural revolution had failed. The army was once again marching on Rome.

Galba, Vitellius and Otho lasted only a few months each. Vespasian established a new dynasty, the Flavians. In 79 his son Titus succeeded him, but 18 months later Domitian was emperor. Suetonius, Tacitus, Pliny, Martial and Juvenal are among the writers who lived through his reign. Domitian did not intend to be polite and respectful to the senate. He liked to be addressed as *dominus et deus* (master and god). He may have felt insecure, since, much like Claudius, he had had little experience before his accession. Yet the damning accounts we have hide the fact that he had some success against the tribes in the north and the Dacian king Decebalus. His building projects were considerable. His administration was efficient – Nerva retained many of those who served him. The economy of the empire was stable, and finances were well organized. He tried to control the spread of non-Roman cults; he banned and banished stoic and Epicurean philosophers from Rome and Italy (in 89 and 95 respectively). Meanwhile he sought to revive old Roman morality and religion. The magnificent temple of Jupiter Capitolinus with a roof of gold, and the rebuilding of temples to Janus, Castor and Apollo were witness to his objective. However, the portrait of his final years with the senate house surrounded by armed men and the slaughter of senators (Tacitus *Agricola* 45) has some truth in it. It is not surprising that the upper class hated him and he became paranoid about conspiracies. In 89, Saturninus, a governor, failed in an attempt at revolt. In 95, Domitian executed his cousin Flavius Clemens and his two praetorian commanders. However, the assassination originated not from the senate, who suffered most, but from his own household. His wife and the new praetorian commander were in the plot along with Parthenius, his chief steward.

Nerva, himself chosen by the senate as a dependable stopgap, adopted Trajan in October 97. Trajan was a career soldier, acceptable to the army, capable and sensible. He was, however, a Spaniard, a logical development from Augustus opening up the magistracies to men from Italy and Claudius admitting Gauls into the senate. Needing to establish his credentials, like Claudius, he began a series of foreign conquests. In two wars, in 101–02 and 105–06, he defeated Decebalus and the Dacians and added Dacia to the empire. The immediate result was an influx of gold, silver and slaves which financed Trajan's building and welfare projects and increased popularity.

Table 11.1 List of emperors (the early empire)

27 BCE–14 CE	Augustus
14–37	Tiberius
37–41	Gaius (Caligula)
41–54	Claudius
54–68	Nero
68–69	Galba
69	Otho
69	Vitellius
69–79	Vespasian
79–81	Titus
81–96	Domitian
96–98	Nerva
98–117	Trajan

Next he annexed the client kingdom of Arabia Petraea in 106. This was preparation for the invasion and conquest of Parthia begun in January 114. He added Armenia, Mesopotamia, Assyria and Parthia as provinces to his conquests by 116. However, success was illusory; his resources might conquer these lands but could not hold them. A Jewish revolt arose in Mesopotamia and in Cyprus, Cyrene and Egypt. Before Trajan could organize his forces he died at Selinus in August 117. Tacitus and Pliny present his reign as a golden age (in contrast to Domitian's). Even allowing for the customary exaggeration, Trajan's personality appealed to the classes and peoples of the empire; above all, his dealings with the senate resembled the days of Augustus; he was respectful, he consulted the senators, he provided them with positions and roles. His buildings were magnificent: the baths and theatre on the Campus Martius, his magnificent forum, including the basilica Ulpia, two libraries and his famous column. Like Augustus in this, as in other ways, he was a master of patronage in the interests of propaganda.

Further reading

There are a number of good introductory histories to this period. See, for instance, Alston (1998); Goodman (1997); Wallace-Hadrill (2008); Wells (1984); Wiseman (1985).

SENECA (c. 4–65)

Roy Hyde

Although none of his speeches has survived, Seneca rose to prominence at Rome by virtue of his oratory. By 39 he was important enough somehow to have offended the emperor Caligula; by 41 he was sufficiently involved in court life to be accused of adultery with Caligula's sister Julia, and was exiled to Corsica by Claudius, who was now emperor. He was recalled in 49 as tutor to the future emperor Nero at the instigation of Nero's mother Agrippina, now married to Claudius. When Nero succeeded in 54, Seneca, along with Burrus, prefect of the praetorian guard, became effectively ruler of the Roman world, and remained so until Burrus died in 62. By now Nero seems to have come to resent Seneca's eminence: Seneca went into voluntary retirement, but Nero believed him to be involved in the conspiracy against him headed by Piso in 65, and ordered him to commit suicide; Seneca's death is recorded by Tacitus (*Annals* 15.62ff.).

Some of the extracts made by Seneca's father (who was deeply interested in rhetoric, but probably not, as tradition has it, a teacher of rhetoric himself) from the declamations of famous orators of his day have survived. The elder Seneca says (*Controversiae* 1, *Preface* 23) that his sons were obsessed with rhetoric, and especially with the *sententiae* of famous speakers. A *sententia* is a brief pithy statement, often of a generalization: *animum debes mutare, non caelum*, the younger Seneca says ('you need to change the way you are, not where you are'; *Letters to Lucilius* 28.1). As the English translation here shows, the natural conciseness of Latin is particularly suited to such devices. Seneca's writings, poetry and prose, are full of *sententiae*, and his style throughout is marked by brevity, abrupt transitions, memorable metaphors and paradoxes; the antithesis of the 'periodic' style of Cicero with its long sentences, balanced clauses, and smooth transitions. The style pervades the literature of Seneca's time (see, for example, the poetry of Lucan, Seneca's nephew): writing within a generation of Seneca's death, Quintilian, who as a Ciceronian deeply disapproved of it, whilst admitting Seneca's stature as a writer, observed that young writers and orators were obsessed with him and with imitating the seductive brilliance of his style (*Institutio Oratoria* 10.1.125ff).

Ten verse tragedies are attributed to Seneca. One, the *Hercules Oetaeus*, is almost certainly not by him. Another, the *Octavia*, is certainly not, but is interesting as the only surviving *fabula praetexta*, a drama on Roman historical subject matter: it deals with the story of Octavia, the wife whom Nero rejected in favour of Poppaea. Seneca is himself a character in it, and it shows Senecan influence but seems to refer to events after Seneca's death. The remaining eight are, with the exception of the *Thyestes*, on themes dealt with by the three great Greek tragedians (*Oedipus*, *Agamemnon*, *Medea*, etc.), and have suffered by comparison with them. Such comparison is unhelpful: considered as works in their own right, they contain scenes of great rhetorical power and their characterizations are by no means derivative. But they are undoubtedly episodic, and lack the unity of the Greek dramas, and their gothic dwelling on gruesome details is not to all tastes. It is uncertain whether they were meant for performance or for recitation.

A minor work generally agreed to be by Seneca is the *Apocolocyntosis*, a 'Menippean satire' (see 12c) on the attempt of the dead emperor Claudius to be accepted as a god by the other Olympians. The title means 'being turned into a pumpkin': Claudius does not in fact turn into a pumpkin, so presumably the word is simply a pun on *apotheosis*, 'being turned into a god', which was officially supposed to happen to emperors when they died. Witty and full of parody, its authorship has been doubted on the grounds of its questionable taste: but as Seneca had no reason to be grateful to Claudius, and it must have been written by someone of great literary skill with an intimate knowledge of court life, there is no other obvious candidate.

It is arguable, though, that Seneca is best known for his philosophical writings. These include the *Quaestiones Naturales*, on natural phenomena such as earthquakes, comets and the Nile floods. As well as their scientific interest as representing the stoic view of the universe, the book contains passages of considerable literary power and a sense of the grandeur of the natural world. The *Quaestiones Naturales* touches also upon stoic ethics: man's place in the universe, the futility of resisting the inevitable, and therefore the necessity of accepting stoically, as we say now, what must be. Seneca's more specifically ethical essays deal at greater length with such matters. These are the *De Clementia* ('On Mercy'), addressed to Nero and a discussion of the duties of a benevolent monarch, the *De Beneficiis* ('On Good Deeds'), concerning man's duty to do good to his fellow man just as the divine powers (more abstract in stoic thought than the usual gods) provide for man through the cosmic order, and the 12 essays known as the *Dialogi*, though they are not in fact dialogues. These deal with issues of general and of particularly stoic interest: anger, leisure, the shortness of life, the good life and peace of mind; the fortitude of the stoic sage (the *sapiens*); and three essays of consolation, one addressed to his mother on the occasion of his exile. All these issues, and others, arise also in the collection of 124 Letters (really short philosophical reflections) supposedly addressed to Seneca's disciple, Lucilius. The short format suits Seneca's style perfectly: in a page or two, the brilliant rhetoric which palls when extended to greater length enhances the thought rather than obscures it. And the wit and humour with which Seneca makes his point, as well as his genius for evocative description, enable him to teach without seeming to preach: we read, for example, about Seneca going to sea in a small boat, getting caught by a storm and having to struggle ashore in his soaking overcoat; eccentrics who choose to live their lives by night, and sleep by day; habitual drunks who nevertheless held down responsible jobs (their example is not recommended); the excesses of the vulgar rich and witty put-downs addressed to them; and much more. Seneca is at pains to point out that he speaks not as a perfected stoic *sapiens* but, like Lucilius, simply a man trying to find out the best way to live. The stoic concept of the brotherhood of all men is discussed: we should never forget that slaves, too, are men like us; Seneca is disgusted by the slaughter of the gladiatorial arena – even convicted criminals deserve better. Friendship is a frequent theme; and when one loses a friend to death, one should not grieve excessively, but (against a sterner stoic view), to grieve with restraint is permissible, and only human. Illness and old age figure: Seneca goes to his country estate and complains to his steward that some trees need better looking after; informed that they are very old, he remembers that he planted them himself. Abstinence from rich living and taking exercise (the daily run and cold bath) make for a sound mind as well as a sound body: if illness or circumstances become intolerable, the stoic accepts his fate and takes his own life uncomplainingly. Though it is best to avoid crowds, it is a duty to take part in public life: the good man can preserve his equilibrium come what may.

As a writer and as a man, Seneca has been a figure of controversy since his own time. Stylist without substance, or stoic sage? A millionaire, preaching about hard mattresses, cold baths, and abstinence; tutor to the monstrous Nero, did he turn a blind eye to the assassinations of Claudius, of Britannicus, of Agrippina? Early Christian writers characterized him as a pagan saint; many others read him as a rank hypocrite. Accusations are many: for the defence is that the years in which he effectively ruled Rome were seen by many as a golden age; that he never claims perfection, only that a man must live as best he can in the circumstances in which he finds himself; and, per-haps, that – though it was forced upon him – in the end, he died according to his creed.

Further reading

Seneca poses particular problems for the bibliographer, as he variously presents himself to the reader as philosopher, letter-writer and dramatist. For an introduction, see Costa (1974). On Seneca the philosopher, see Griffin (1976); Veyne (2003). As dramatist, see Boyle (1997; 2006); Erasmo (2004); Harrison (2000a). As a letter-writer, see Henderson (2004).

PERSIUS, MARTIAL AND JUVENAL

Neil Croally

The first thing to be explained here is why these three authors have been grouped together. Partly the reason is chronological: all had their poetry published in the latter half of the first century or in the first third of the second century. We shall also see that there is some commonality in tone and approach between the three poets, though Martial is not normally referred to as a satirist. Which brings me to my next point: what is satire?

Satire held a special place in the hearts of Roman literati, as they could reasonably claim it to be the one genre with no definite earlier Greek model (see 9h). Quintilian (*Institutio Oratoria* 10.1.93) can boldly state that 'satire is completely ours'. However, there were some disagreements as to what exactly satire was. A late grammarian, Diomedes, says this (Keil, 1857: 485):

> Satire is said to be the poetry among the Romans that is nowadays abusive and composed to criticize the vices of men in the manner of Old Comedy, as was written by Lucilius, Horace and Persius. But, in the past, poetry which was made up of various poetic items was called satire, such as was written by Pacuvius and Ennius.

The idea of variety seems to have been the most dominant explanation of satire. There are references in the critical literature to the *lanx satura*, which was a mixed dish; to *satura*, which was a type of stuffed sausage with many ingredients; and, finally, to the *lex satura*, which was a name given to a law which contained a variety of provisions in a single bill. Certainly, the three authors we are considering in this chapter each present us with a variety of subject matter, tone, style and persona.

Persius

Aulus Persius Flaccus was born in 34 and died young in 62. He was connected to the stoic opposition to Nero, though we cannot say whether that led to his death. There are six poems extant, totalling about 650 lines of hexameter verse, along with an introduction in the choliambic metre (see below). The poems were published posthumously and may not be complete.

Persius was clearly familiar with the work of Lucilius and Horace; nevertheless he produced a distinctive type of satire through the persona he developed. The relatively easy-going and detached persona developed by Horace is completely absent. And this is immediately apparent from the prologue, both because of the metre used (choliambic or scazon, normally used by Greek poets such as Hipponax and later Callimachus for bitter or aggressive poetry) and because of what he says in the opening lines (*Prologue* 1–3):

> I did not wet my lips in the Hippocrene spring [made by the horse Pegasus on Mt. Helicon],
> nor do I remember having dreamed on Parnassus with its double summit that I would suddenly come forth in this way as a poet.

Most Roman poets are keen – in their opening or programmatic poems – to stress their vatic status and their place in the poetic tradition; not so Persius. This picture of a rather different, rather alienated persona is further emphasized in line 6 of the prologue where the poet describes himself as 'semipaganus', which means something like a semi-citizen or, perhaps, a semi-rustic. The persona of distance and alienation is repeated in the opening lines of the first *Satire*, where the poet expresses a lack of surprise that no one is likely to want to read his verse (1.1–3). The final satire – in the form of a letter sent from the Ligurian coast – geographically stresses the distance of Persius' persona. In short, then, Persius presents a persona of a bitter, cynical, angry and alienated young man.

The subject matter of the six poems fits happily with such a persona, as the targets are such things as: stupidity, self-deception, hypocrisy and various forms of diseased thinking. Arching over all these criticisms is an interest in stoicism. Thus *Satire* 1, in its relatively programmatic way, lays out what is wrong with contemporary poetry: it has none of the vigour and moral probity of a Lucilius, being feeble, spluttering drivel. The second satire criticizes the hypocrisy of those Romans who pray and sacrifice in an ignorant and debased way. *Satires* 3–6 all in their different ways have stoicism as their theme, whether in the dialogue between the lazy student and his tutor in the third satire, in the dialogue between Alcibiades and Socrates (the theme here is the importance of self-knowledge), in the homage to Persius' own tutor Cornutus in the fifth satire, or in the reflections on how to view wealth in the final satire.

Persius' language matches the bitterness of his self-presentation. In *Satire* 1, when Persius condemns contemporary poetry for its moral feebleness, he alludes to Horace's description of the moral exertions of Lucilius (1.106; cf. Horace *Satires* 1.10.70):

it [modern poetry] does not bang the desk, or taste of bitten-off nails.

Such concentrated language is sometimes used in tandem with very physical imagery, as at *Satire* 3 (19–24), when a lazy student is being criticized:

Why do you
whine these evasions? The move is yours. You're flowing away mindlessly,
you are rejected: an earthen pot of green mud not quite cooked
responds badly when hit and betrays its flaw.
You are wet and soft clay, now, this instant, you must be
moulded endlessly on the swift wheel.

Persius then is a minor original, whose most telling contribution was to develop the persona described above, thereby having considerable influence on the later and greater Juvenal. The opening couplet of *Satire* 1 could stand as a summary of at least the opening poems of Juvenal:

O the cares of men! O how vast is the emptiness in human affairs!

Martial

Martial was born *c.* 40 in Spain and died *c.* 101. We know from his own *Epigrams* that he came to Rome in 64 (10.103.7–9). He was supported by Seneca and Lucan. He lamented the latter after his death (7.21) and remained friendly with the poet's widow. From the mid-80s he became a popular poet, one increasingly perceived to be close to the emperor Domitian. His earliest work was a *Book of Spectacles*, published in 80 to celebrate the opening of the Flavian Amphitheatre (or the Colosseum). Between 83 and 85 he produced two works – *Apophoreta* and *Xenia* – which deal with various types of gift. Finally, and between 86 and 101, he published the 12 books of *Epigrams* for which he became most famous.

Martial's epigrams are most characterized by variety, and that in relation both to style and to subject matter. Thus we encounter funerals, parties, gladiatorial games, patronage, sex, Rome itself, praise of the emperor, physical problems and deviant sex. These subjects are described in various metres, including elegiac couplets, hendecasyllables and scazons. Martial likes paradox, comic surprises, *reductiones ad absurdum*; he displays verbal ingenuity and likes also to mix the realistic with the fantastic and the grotesque. His language may have been influenced by Horace and Ovid, but the most important influence is most surely Catullus. One of Catullus' most famous poems is 85, the *odi et amo* poem (I hate and I love . . .). It must be one of the most famous couplets in Roman poetry. Here is Martial *Epigrams* 1.32:

> *non amo te, Sabidi, nec possum dicere quare:*
> *hoc tantum possum dicere, non amo te.*

> I don't love you, Sabidius; and I cannot say why.
> This only thing I can say: I do not love you.

Without quite fitting into any particular generic tradition, Martial straddles the gap between the late republican Catullus and satire as produced by its greatest exponent. For Martial, in his relentlessly critical depiction of the hypocrisies and absurdities of Roman society, is an important influence on Juvenal.

Juvenal

We know little about the life of Juvenal and, unless we are willing to overlook the biographical fallacy and raid the poems themselves for biographical detail, we shall have to remain satisfied with our state of ignorance. We do know, however, that between 110 and 130 Juvenal published 16 satires in five books (book 1 is made up of *Satires* 1–5; book 2 is *Satire* 6; book 3 is *Satires* 7–9; book 4, *Satires* 10–12; book 5, *Satires* 13–16). Juvenal puts the city of Rome, and the characteristics of urban living, at the heart of his poetry. While he is clearly aware of, and indeed knowledgeable about, the earlier satirists, his particular brand of verse satire has probably been the most influential.

The very lack of biographical detail allows us to grasp more readily an idea that is central to a sophisticated understanding of Juvenal: the satirist's persona. In the first two books, namely *Satires* 1–6, the persona is characterized by a relentless but observant anger. The relentlessness can be comic; it is certainly often outrageous and outraged. The angry satirist, while cast as someone absolutely certain of his own moral positions, can be partial, inconsistent and incoherent. The satiric poet, who derides the possibility of any poetry but satire, cannot convince in the end that only the one genre will do. In order to see this first persona at work, it is worth looking at the first, programmatic satire in a little detail.

The beginning of the first satire encapsulates the poet's concerns. A series of angry rhetorical questions about having to listen to bad epic poetry starts us off (1.1–6); sharp criticism of the dullness of epic follows (1.7–21). A series of outrages in contemporary Roman society is then described (1.22–78): so bad has society become that the only possible poetic response is an angry one (1.79):

If natural talent stops me, indignation will make my poetry . . .

The subject of this poetry seems easy to define (1.85–6):

Whatever men do, their vows, their fear, their anger, their pleasure, their joys, their distractions, that is the mash of my little book.

Actually, not everything will appear in Juvenal's poems. The retrograde, the immoral, the cynical, the scandalous: all these have pride of place. Near the end of this first satire, Juvenal remarks how safe it is to write about Aeneas and Turnus, Achilles or Hylas: no one gets hurt that way (1.162–4). Satire is altogether more effective – and dangerous (1.165–8):

But whenever a fiery Lucilius bellows as if with sword drawn, the listener blushes, his mind cold with his crimes; inside he sweats with his secret guilt. Thence anger and tears.

Thus does Juvenal appropriate the high tone of epic, while disparaging its relevance as a poetic form that can deal with Rome's moral degeneration (he does something similar with tragedy: *Satire* 6.634–61). The other poems for the first two books continue in the same vein. In *Satire* 2 passive homosexuals (or pathics) are derided. *Satire* 3 explains from his point of view why

Umbricius is leaving the unruly and degrading metropolis Rome has become. Poor honest men have been replaced by the dishonest and the parasitic, both of which are exemplified by Greeks (see 3.58–125). This tirade is long, and keeps going even when the reader may have had enough: perhaps the effect can be comic. Anyway, the moral position of Umbricius is less clear cut than one might have expected: he admits he has tried what the Greeks do; it's just that they are better at it (e.g. 3.92–3).

Satires 4 and 5 persist with the same indignation: 4 criticizes the misuse of power, while 5 critically describes the breakdown of the client/patron relationship. It is *Satire* 6, however, that stands out as perhaps the high point of Juvenal's invective. Given that this poem attacks women at a length of 661 lines (not dissimilar to the length of a book of an epic), it is not always a poem with which the modern reader has much sympathy. The poem takes the form of advice given to a certain Postumus as to whether he should marry or not. A total of 661 lines is an awfully long time in which to say 'no' but, as ever with Juvenal, the delight (if any) is in the detailed descriptions. We should also be aware of how literary the poem is. Note the beginning (6.1–2, 5–8):

> I believe that Chastity lingered on the earth during
> Saturn's reign and was seen for a long time . . .
> when the mountain-born wife spread her bed
> with leaves and straw and the skins of her
> neighbours the beasts, not like you, Cynthia, nor you,
> whose bright eyes the dead sparrow disturbed.

It is telling that Juvenal chooses to compare the hardy and virtuous wives of the Golden Age (one literary conceit) with the poetic inamoratas of first Propertius and then Catullus. This highly literary and allusive opening belies the apparently straightforward moral criticism of women, and especially so when we remember that Catullus and Propertius described adulterous relationships. Even for Juvenal, then, the rot set in some time ago. For a flavour of the poem, one might look at the following description of Messalina, the notorious wife of the emperor Claudius (6.116–17, 121–4):

> When the wife realized her husband was asleep,
> she dared to prefer a mat to a bed on the Palatine . . .
> she entered the brothel warm with old quilts,
> an empty room, hers; then she showed herself
> naked with gilded nipples, under the fake name 'Wolf-Girl',
> she showed your belly, noble Britannicus.

There is lots more of this sort of thing – and more extreme. Indeed, so extreme is this poem that one critic at least (Sue Braund) has argued that Juvenal had used up all the possibilities of the indignant, critical persona. So in the poems of books 3–5 (*Satires* 6–16) the persona is slightly more gentle. It is still critical but is more detached, cynical, ironic and superior. For instance, the mockery of, in turn, power, eloquence, military success, longevity, beauty and the power of prayer in *Satire* 10 is almost Horatian in tone, and in *Satire* 13 (175ff.) anger is explicitly rejected as an appropriate reaction. Furthermore, there is arguably a more concentrated literary quality in the these later poems. Consider, from the famous *Satire* 10 describing the vanity of human affairs, this description of Hannibal (10.154–62):

> Now he holds Italy, yet he moves to go further:
> 'Nothing has been achieved,' he said, 'unless with Carthaginian force
> we break down the gates, and I plant the standard in the middle of the Subura.'
> What an image, worthy of what sort of picture,
> when the Gaetulian monster carried the one-eyed general!
> So what was his end? O glory, the same man is defeated
> and he flees headlong into exile and there the great and
> marvellous man sits as a client in the residence of the king,
> until it pleases the Bithynian tyrant to wake up.

This is a superbly condensed piece of narrative, using such epic techniques as apostrophe and direct speech, which still has space to make Juvenal's rhetorical points about vanity.

So, the early Juvenal of *Satires* 1–6 is an angry persona, who has an apparently black-and-white view of the world. The angry rhetorical questions, the exaggerations and exclamations are all characteristic of such a persona. But the length of some of the poems, the inability or lack of desire to let something go, can also be seen as a lack of control. And, with these earlier poems, we are left with this challenging question: is the object of the satire the things complained about or the angry person doing the complaining? After all, the picture Juvenal presents of Rome could be said to be partial, if we compare it, say, to that contained in the *Letters* of the Younger Pliny. The persona changes slightly, as we have seen, in the later poems but all the poetry betrays certain stylistic similarities. Juvenal's is a grand style, self-conscious and full of mordant observations. The sharpness of his rhetorical technique can also perhaps be seen in how often he comes up with a memorable phrase: *quis custodiet ipsos custodes?* ('who will guard the guards?': 6.347–8), 'bread and circuses' (10.81), 'a healthy mind in a healthy body' (10.356) are three that come to mind.

Conclusion

So, Roman verse satire of the first and second centuries seems to have the following things in common: the author adopts a (more or less) angry persona through which to criticize; the events and people satirized are normally urban; it entertains – through witty allusion, verbal dexterity and playful fantasy – and moralizes as well; a variety of subjects are treated in a way that deploys the fantastic, the absurd and the grotesque. The powerful, the corrupt, the feeble, the parasitic are derided and variously rendered absurd. It is perhaps more arguable whether satire tends to reinforce social norms. However, we can say that Roman verse satire has had an enormous influence on English literature. Dr Johnson's poem *London* (1738) was based on Juvenal's third satire; the same author's *The Vanity of Human Wishes* (1749) is based on Juvenal's tenth satire. Juvenal's spirit can also continue to be seen in our tradition of political satire, embodied in the UK by, say, *Private Eye* and in the USA by *The Onion* and Jon Stewart.

Further reading

For good introductions to satire as a genre, see Anderson (1982); Braund (1992; 1996); Freudenburg (2001; 2005); Hooley (2006); Keane (2006); Plaza (2007); Rudd (1986); Sullivan (1963). On Persius, see Bramble (1974). On Martial, see Sullivan (1991). For more particular work on Juvenal, see Braund (1988), which deals with the third book of satires; Henderson (1997), which examines the eighth satire; Henderson (1999) and Martin (1996).

LUCAN, STATIUS AND OTHERS

Roy Hyde

The instant success of the *Aeneid*, especially perhaps its use as a school text, meant that almost every later Latin poet had to come to terms with Virgil. Still within the lifetime of Augustus, Manilius' *Astronomica*, a didactic poem on astronomy and astrology, shows his influence, as well as that of Lucretius. Manilius was a good poet, and when he was not wrestling with the difficulty of expressing technical matters in verse, wrote some fine passages, but the nature of his theme means that his work is not much read. Another didactic poem, probably of the mid-first century, the *Aetna* (Etna), on volcanoes, is less successful, but not without interest. Around the same time the agriculturalist Columella wrote a manual on agriculture, of which one book is in verse, after the model of Virgil's *Georgics*: Columella was a better farmer than poet, but his efforts at versification say something about the seriousness with which didactic poetry could be taken. Virgil's *Eclogues*, too, had their imitators: two indifferent poems known as the *Einsiedeln Eclogues* date from the Neronian period, as do the seven rather better *Eclogues* of Calpurnius Siculus, who may also be the author of the *Laus Pisonis*, in praise of a

Calpurnius Piso who may be the man who headed a conspiracy against Nero in 65.

Naturally, though, it was in the field of epic that Virgil's achievement especially had to be reckoned with. Roman epic, from its earliest manifestations in the persons of Naevius and Ennius, had – unlike Greek – a predominantly historical slant: Naevius had written about the first Punic War, and Ennius about the whole of Roman history down to his own time. Such poems continued to be written: about, for example, Caesar's campaigns in Gaul, by Varro of Atax, and Germanicus' northern campaigns, by Albinovanus Pedo. Both of these poets also wrote on legendary subjects, but it seems to have been left to Virgil to combine the two traditions, extending 'epic time' down to his own by means such as the prophecy of Anchises in *Aeneid* 6. Reference to a poet's own time necessarily involved political considerations; all the four epics which survive from the first century, in one way or another, engage with these two factors: the influence of Virgil, and the politics of the principate.

Of their four authors, Lucan (39–65) came to prominence first, winning a prize at the Neronia festival in 60, and publishing some of his *Bellum Civile* (or *Pharsalia*) by 62/3. Valerius Flaccus' birth date is unknown, but he seems to have been writing his *Argonautica* by the 70s, and to have died in the early 90s. Silius Italicus (*c.* 26–*c.* 101) was the oldest of the four, but probably wrote his *Punica* mostly after he retired from a successful public career (consul 68) in the late 70s. Statius (*c.* 45–*c.* 96) pubished his *Thebaid* around 90–91, and had started on an *Achilleid* when he died.

Valerius' epic is the most traditional: a version of the legend of the Argonauts, indebted to but not a translation of the *Argonautica* of Apollonius of Rhodes. It is incomplete, breaking off in the eighth book, when Jason and Medea are fleeing Colchis with the golden fleece. Stylistically Valerius owes a debt to Virgil, but there are reminiscences too of Ovid and Lucan, as well as intertextuality with other versions of the legend. His material is derivative, but treated with some originality, and there are some fine passages. Although set in the epic past, there are links with the present: the poem is dedicated to Vespasian (with a mention of the poetic skill of his son Domitian), and there are references to the 'future', and to Rome, as in the prophecy of Jupiter in book 1. Some scholars have seen more significant contemporary allusions, for example in the joint suicides of Jason's parents, which could be taken as referring to the suicide of Caecina Paetus and his wife when Paetus was accused by Claudius of conspiracy.

Valerius was not a great epic poet, but he was not a bad one: of Silius Italicus, however, few have good words to say. His 17-book *Punica* is an account of the second Punic War, so is traditional Roman historical epic in the manner of Ennius, but with all the trappings of Homeric epic, such as a descent to the underworld (by Silius' hero, Scipio), and much intervention from the gods. The ultimate theme is the invigoration of Rome to combat the threat of Hannibal (who nevertheless comes close to being the hero of the poem by contrast with the insipid Scipio), and her consequent rise to world domination. Though he conventionally bemoans the decline in Roman *mores*, he is clearly not at odds with the imperial ideology to which he accommodated himself so ably. Silius was a politician skilful enough to live through turbulent times without giving fatal offence to anyone, except perhaps those invited to attend the readings of parts of the *Punica* which he gave when enjoying an affluent retirement and living the life of a connoisseur, but as a poet he is mediocre. The influence of Virgil, whom he revered, is evident on every page; imitation, however, does not guarantee inspiration.

To read a poet's work by reference to his life, and vice versa, is a hazardous activity. But in the case of Lucan it is inescapable. Lucan was the nephew of Seneca, the orator, stoic philosopher, controversial literary stylist, and mentor and ultimately victim of Nero. At first a friend of Nero, Lucan subsequently offended him to the extent that Nero 'silenced' him by banning him from publishing poetry or practising in the law courts. Implicated in the conspiracy of Piso in 65 which also brought about the downfall of his uncle, Lucan was ordered to commit suicide. He was 26.

Such factors can be seen as going towards the making of Lucan's one surviving work, the *Bellum Civile* or *Pharsalia*, an epic on the theme of the civil war between Caesar and Pompey which effectively marked the end of the Roman republic. It was unfinished, and had reached the tenth book by the time of his death. The *Bellum Civile* (*BC*) has been criticized as being rhetorical, and it is: Lucan, like Seneca, is fond of striking phrases and *sententiae*. Quintilian, who disapproved of Seneca's style, necessarily disliked Lucan's, whilst admitting his power: 'more suitable to be imitated by orators than by poets' (*Inst. Orat.* 10.1.90). But Quintilian was swimming against the tide: styles change; the poetry of Lucan's period, indeed almost all literature, is similarly rhetorical, and it is of no more use to berate Lucan for not being Virgil than to complain that Seneca is not Cicero. To a considerable extent, the rhetorical style is a product of the practice of authors reading out their works before an audience (*recitatio*), which seems to have become widespread only in the Augustan age (unlike early Greek literature, which was designed for performance, earlier Latin literature was generally written down). *Recitatio* itself, in the early empire, can be thought about within the context of show or spectacle: orators showed off by declaiming, emperors and the rich showed off through architecture and the visual arts; 'shows' (the word for one was *spectaculum*) took place in the arena, where Romans could watch people killing each other. (Lucan's penchant for descriptions of violent death would seem to evoke the arena: see below.) It is not, then, surprising if poetry, too, became showy and all the epic writers of the period exhibit the same rhetorical tendencies, to a greater or lesser degree (except Silius, whose backward-looking Virgilianism was a dead end).

Another stick to beat Lucan with was his use, or non-use, of the gods in his poem. Parallel action on the divine as well as the human plane was a stock element in mythological epic and appears to have been carried over by Roman epic writers into their historical epics: Silius' use of divine apparatus exemplifies this well. An interesting gloss on this topic are the lines given by Petronius, Lucan's contemporary, to his poet Eumolpus in the *Satyrica* (119) on the topic of the civil war, which are fully equipped with divine apparatus, and have been seen as an admonishment to Lucan in the form of 'this is how it should be done'. The gods are not absent from the *BC*; they are frequently referred to (and there is plenty of other supernatural paraphernalia: omens and prophecies and necromancy) and apostrophized. (As are the fates, which Lucan seems to use as interchangeable with the gods.) But they do not appear in person, they do not take sides; we do not see, for example, Jupiter expounding his reasons for bringing the war about as we do in Silius (though we are given a reason: see below on this and on how seriously we are to take it). Rather, however, than seeing the absence of gods as a weakness, it might be seen as a strength, and as part of Lucan's overarching reading of the civil war: how, after all, could the gods of Rome be justifiably seen as countenancing, let alone conniving at, Rome's self-destruction? Their apparent withdrawal, and the consequent struggle of various characters in the poem to try to make sense of events or to foresee their outcome, is one of the many ways in which Lucan subverts or inverts or invests with irony the conventions of the epic: if his version of epic reality departs from the epic norm, it is because his theme demands a new vision of that reality.

The *BC* is not only an epic without gods, it is an epic without heroes. A simplistic reading of the civil war as a prelude to the principate could have taken Caesar as the hero; Lucan chooses to see him as the motivator of the war, his famous swiftness to act transmuted into frenetic egocentric activity. A republican stance (to which Lucan is closer) would have heroized Pompey: Pompey does indeed have fine qualities, but with his indecisiveness and weak leadership he is a shadow of the young conqueror he had once been. Cato comes closest, but his brand of heroism is as self-defeating as it is self-righteous. With an irony that is surely deliberate, one of the few characters allowed to die a hero is Domitius, a man whom other accounts reveal as duplicitous and cowardly; he was an ancestor of Nero. In a war fought between *cognatas acies* ('armies of [rival] kinsmen'), when *ius datum sceleri* ('legitimation is given to crime'), acts of bravery become acts of evil: a soldier of Caesar, Scaeva, is given a Homer-like *aristeia*, but what do his deeds amount to other than murder of his fellow-countrymen (6.144ff)? When Caesar's men hesitate to march on Rome, the decisive voice is that of the centurion Laelius, a man who had won the highest military decoration – for saving the life of a Roman (1.355ff.).

Such inversions abound; the world is turned upside down, and the gods seem uninterested: the priestess of the Delphic oracle has to be forced to prophesy, and all she can reveal to her questioner Appius Claudius is a veiled response as to his personal fate, which he still fails to understand (5.64ff). Aeneas had descended to the underworld to receive guidance as to the future; Pompey's son Sextus has recourse to a loathsome cannibalistic witch, who revives for him a dead soldier, in a scene of pure Gothic horror, and receives scant enlightenment (6.507ff). Even Lucan's syntax has been seen as echoing the inversion and chaos of civil war (Bartsch, 1997: chapter 1), and his own voice – which is ever-present in the poem, apostrophizing characters and interpreting his own text – mirrors its uncertainty with its combination of 'cynical detachment and intense involvement' (ibid.: 101). The self-dismemberment of Rome too may be read in the frequent and grotesque mutilations and spectacular (in more than one sense: see above) slaughter: what seem to be the poem's shortcomings and inconsistencies when measured against the canon of earlier epic are precisely its strengths.

Was Nero's response to Lucan no more than the petty jealousy of a bad poet towards a better one, as it is trivialized by some versions? Or was Lucan's political involvement greater than we know? There is no clear answer. But we can read Lucan's dedication to Nero (1.33ff): the crimes of the civil war, heinous as they were, in the grand scheme of things were nevertheless worth it – if they were necessary in order that Nero should reign. Whether these words were in the version of the poem that Nero read or heard we do not know: critics have been reluctant to take them as ironic, but – having read the *BC* – can we really think that Lucan meant them at face value? Or doubt that Nero can have misunderstood Lucan's import?

Statius' 12-book *Thebaid* tells the story of the 'Seven against Thebes'. Polynices, son of Oedipus, deprived of his share in the kingship by his brother Eteocles, gathers an army to reassert his rights. In the end, the brothers kill each other: Creon, their uncle, now king, forbids the burial of Polynices and his Argive followers; Theseus of Athens defeats and kills Creon.

The *Thebaid*, then, is a dark tale. Its first words, *fraternas acies* ('brothers' armies') set the tone, evoking Lucan's *cognatas acies* of the Roman civil war. After a dedication to the emperor Domitian, the poem proper begins in multi-layered darkness: Oedipus, self-blinded and hiding from the light in the recesses of the palace of Thebes, curses his sons, calling on the gods for vengeance (1.46ff.). In particular, he calls upon Tisiphone, the spirit of vengeance, who hears his prayers sitting by the river Cocytus in the underworld (1.88ff.). Tisiphone immediately rises to the upper world, terrifying the bright horses of the sun: all nature recoils at her coming. She sets the brothers at enmity (1.97ff.). Meanwhile, Jupiter, wearied by the crimes of mankind, in particular those of the royal houses of Thebes and Argos, resolves to destroy them, despite the objections of Juno. He sends Mercury to summon the ghost of Laius, Oedipus' father, from the underworld to bring about rivalry between the brothers (1.197ff.). We see Polynices in exile, alone and wandering in search of allies. A storm of truly epic proportions breaks over him by night, and he finds his way to Argos, attracted by the lights (1.312ff.). Another exile, Tydeus, soaked by the same storm, arrives at the same time; for no good reason, a bloody fight breaks out, terminated only by the arrival of king Adrastus of Argos (1.401ff.). Adrastus calms them, and entertains them at a meal at which they meet his daughters, who are destined to be their wives (1.438ff.). Adrastus tells them about the origins of the festival he is celebrating, and asks them who they are; Polynices is reluctant to admit his ancestry, but when he does, Adrastus is by no means deterred from offering his hospitality (1.557ff.).

The above summary of book 1 illustrates most of the themes of the *Thebaid*, and Statius' methods. Unlike Lucan, Statius sets his action on three levels: on earth, amongst the gods above – and the gods below. It is noteworthy that Tisiphone here acts on her own initiative; elsewhere, Dis, king of the underworld, appears as more a rival to Jupiter than a colleague – he nods his assent like Jupiter (8.82–3) and thunders (11.410–1); Tisiphone can prevent prayers reaching the celestial gods (11.207ff.). The powers of the underworld were not usually seen as evil by the ancients: they simply do their job; the dualism that Statius at times approaches may go some way to explaining Statius' popularity in the Christian middle ages, as a kind of 'proto-Christian', like Seneca. Another tendency developed (though not invented) by Statius also had a long subsequent history, that of personifying allegorical figures such as Pietas or Clementia; his Mars, too, seems to approximate at times more closely to the spirit of bellicosity rather than being an individual whose general responsibility is warfare. It has been said with considerable justice that Statius' allegories are more like gods, and his gods like allegories. His Jupiter, however, is beyond question the chief of the gods; his word is equivalent to fate, and he brooks no opposition – even Juno must simply accept his word as law.

The worlds of gods and men interact closely: the crimes of the House of Thebes offend Jupiter, and affect the cosmic order (an essentially stoic view) and must be righted before he can recover his *ataraxia* (stoic again). The intrusion of Tisiphone into the world above reflects this, and sets the world into confusion. The darkness that surrounds her, like the darkness and the storm in which we first encounter Polynices, are more than literary evocations of atmosphere – though they certainly do create atmosphere: Statius is a master of gothic, and clearly relishes exercising his powers on scenes of horror and violence. His subject in the *Thebaid*, of course, is especially adapted to this: as in Lucan, heroes are few and far between, until the appearance of Theseus. Amphiaraus, the seer who knows his own fate but cannot avoid it is a sympathetic figure, as is the peaceable Adrastus, whose ordered world is devastated by the appearance of Polynices and Tydeus: stoicism may be invoked with reference to him too, as he appears first as something like the enlightened stoic monarch; but the stoic knows that order is not guaranteed to last, and that he must accept his fate. On the other hand, the gods must take responsibility for what men become: Tydeus throughout is a man of violence, but the brothers seem to be trying to work out a *modus vivendi* before Tisiphone enters, and Oedipus has become what he is through no choice of his own.

Statius' world is not all darkness. For example, the long account of the Lemnian women in book 6, gruesome as it is in parts, is an illustration that *pietas* is still alive; and at the end of the poem Clementia is instrumental in restoring order through Theseus. The Lemnian narrative seems a digression, as do other episodes not directly related to the tale of the Seven: it has been suggested that the practice of *recitatio* encouraged episodic composition, and there is no doubt some truth in this. Statius' digressions are in fact less digressive than they at first appear; and they also provide a welcome change of atmosphere. It does, indeed, take Statius a long time to reach the climactic duel between Polynices and Eteocles, but it is arguable that the delays in the action (which Statius implicitly acknowledges: Jupiter intervenes in book 7 because he thinks things are moving too slowly towards his purpose) contribute to the overall tension.

Statius explicitly recognizes his debt to Virgil (12.816ff.), and his own inferiority, and there are indeed echoes of Virgil not only in his poetic technique but in structural aspects of the book (book 1, for example, broadly resembles the opening of the *Aeneid* in plan), but he is indebted to other predecessors in various ways, especially Seneca, of whose tragedies verbal echoes can be found, as well a flavour of stoicism less fully worked out than Seneca's, but evident nevertheless. His theme in the *Thebaid* obviously has resonances with the *Bellum Civile* of Lucan, but Statius is less flamboyantly rhetorical, and the *Thebaid* shows an overall integrity that the (unrevised) *Bellum Civile* ultimately lacks.

It is also clearly less politically driven: Statius dedicated it to the notoriously paranoid and dictatorial Domitian, and critics have tried to discover contemporary allusions within it, without much success. (Suggestions that the relationship between the brothers echoes the tensions between Domitian and his brother Titus are unconvincing; reference to the more overt ones between Nero and Britannicus, whom Nero poisoned, carry more weight, but were history by now.) There is indeed much in the poem about the nature of monarchy (apart from the earthly kings, Jupiter, for example, is an absolute monarch in a more blatant fashion than Virgil's Jupiter); but if Statius was a critic of Domitian, he conceals the fact exceedingly well. Publishing anything under a totalitarian regime is a risky activity, and might invite imperial displeasure; but it is bad monarchy, not monarchy per se, that Statius deplores, and there is no reason to suppose that he thought Domitian was a bad monarch, even if other people did.

Statius had written a book and a half of an epic on the life of Achilles, the *Achilleid*, when he died. It has been seen as lighter in mood, more Ovidian than the *Thebaid*, and so it is. But the completed section deals only with Achilles' early life, and the remainder might well have proved less light-hearted.

Statius was a professional poet; son of a schoolmaster-poet, he needed to rely on patronage, from the emperor downwards, to afford the leisure to write. A lost poem on Domitian's military activities reinforces (if it does not wholly confirm) the impression that he did not altogether disapprove of the emperor, as do some of the poems in the collection of shorter poems known as the *Silvae*. These (there are 32, in five books) are mostly occasional poems, written for a variety of patrons and friends, including Domitian and his own wife. Most are in hexameters, but some in hendecasyllables and lyric metres. Some are ecphrastic, on works of art (such as a statue of the emperor) and buildings or places. One is about a tame lion, one on a parrot. Others are more serious: in memory of his father; on the loss of his son; to the widow of Lucan on Lucan's birthday. The range, wit, technical skill and delicacy of the *Silvae* underline Statius' stature as a poet, which in the middle ages was extremely high, but has since declined, although in recent years a revival in interest has, justly, begun to restore his reputation.

Further reading

There has been increased interest in so-called silver Latin in the past 20 years, and Lucan in particular has benefitted from sophisticated critical treatment. For a good introduction to later epic, see the relevant sections in Boyle (1993); Dihle (1994); Feeney (2007); Hardie (1993); Leigh in Taplin (2001). Foley (2005) has a good collection of articles. For Lucan, see Ahl (1976); Bartsch (1997), and her chapter in Foley (2005); Johnson (1987); Leigh (1997); Masters (1992); Morford (1996). For some particularly challenging work on Lucan, see Henderson (1998: chapter 5). There is some material on Statius in Hinds (1998), which is concerned with the important topic of intertextuality. On Statius' *Achilleid*, see Bernstein (2008); Heslin (2005); on *Silvae*, see Newlands (2002); on the *Thebaid*, see Augoustakis (2010); Bernstein (2008); Henderson (1998: chapter 6); Lovatt (2005); Vessey (1973). There are some articles on Valerius Flaccus and Silius Italicus in Foley (2005); on the former, see also Herschkowitz (1998); on the latter, see now Augoustakis (2010); Bernstein (2008); Tipping (2010).

TACITUS

Seb Wakely

P.(?) Cornelius Tacitus was provincial in origin, born *c.* 56 in either Narbonese or Cisalpine Gaul. He enjoyed a successful political career under the Flavian emperors (especially Domitian), rising to the suffect consulship in 97. He could therefore write about Roman politics with an insider's insight. In 77 (*Agricola* 9) he married the daughter of Cn. Julius Agricola, another rising provincial. Under Trajan, Tacitus served as proconsul of Asia in 112–13. Indications in his last work, the *Annals*, suggest that he died in 118 or later and indeed some critics see coded criticism of Trajan's successor Hadrian in the *Annals'* portrayal of Tiberius.

Tacitus was the author of five works. The earliest, published in 98, was a biography of his father-in-law Agricola, a successful governor of Britain under Domitian. In the same year he published the *Germania*, an ethnographic treatise on the tribes of Germany. The last of his minor works, the *Dialogus*, is usually dated to 101–2, although it may have appeared as late as 107; it is a discussion of the role of oratory under autocratic rule. It was not until *c.* 105–6 that Tacitus began to collect material for the historical works upon which his current reputation largely depends. In *c.* 109–10 he produced the *Histories*, an account in 12 or 14 books of Roman history from the year of the four emperors in 69 to the death of Domitian in 96. Only the first four and a half books survive. Tacitus' last and greatest work, the *Annals* (probably composed between 113 and 120 – certainty is impossible), looks back to an earlier period which, unlike the subject matter of the *Histories*, predates Tacitus' own life – the reigns of the Julio-Claudian emperors from Tiberius to Nero. Again, only part of the work has survived, but it was probably divided into three hexads (a series of six books): the first covered the reign of Tiberius (most of book 5 is now missing); the second (of which only half of book 11 and book 12 survive) dealt with Gaius Caligula and Claudius; and the third (our text of which breaks off half way through book 16) described Nero's reign. Despite the loss of key parts, enough of the *Annals* survives to give a good view of its overall structure and to provide us with the fullest demonstration of Tacitus' mature talent. For this reason consideration of the *Annals* will form the basis of the discussion that follows.

Tacitus opens the *Annals* with a thumbnail sketch of Rome's history (specifically, the city of Rome), tracing the evolution of government from the kings to the republic and then, through a succession of warlords, to Augustus. A parallel account of the decline in Roman historiography follows. During the republic, authors could freely write what they thought; initially this was true under Augustus but gradually sycophancy took over and freedom of speech became impossible. Hatred infected accounts of the reigns of recently deceased emperors. From the start, therefore, we are introduced to the dominant themes of the work – the nature of political power under the emperors, the difference between appearance and reality (suggested by the implicit contrast Tacitus draws between the term Augustus used of himself – *princeps* – and the real nature of his power – *imperium*) and the corrosive impact of autocratic government on its subjects, affecting even the language they use.

Tacitus and *sententiae*

As a moralizing historian and accomplished rhetorician, Tacitus includes *sententiae*, pithy and memorable statements apparently applicable outside their immediate context, within his work. They form part of what Mellor calls Tacitus' 'rhetoric of exposure', peeling away the layers of dissemblance to reveal the unpalatable truth. A notable example is Calgacus' statement in the Agricola (*Agricola* 31) that the Romans 'falsely rename robbery, butchery and rapine empire, and where they create desolation they call it peace'. However, in Tacitus context is everything – Calgacus' speech is no simple indictment of Roman imperialism and is immediately answered, if not refuted, by Agricola's address to his own troops. *Sententiae* help to give Tacitus' work its moralizing and pessimistic tone but the whole text suggests a more complex and messier judgement.

Tacitus ends his preface by outlining his subject matter – he will give a short summary of Augustus' rule before describing the reigns of Tiberius and his successors. He claims that he himself is able to write of the era without anger or partiality, unlike his predecessors (*Annals* 1.1). How seriously are we to take such a bald (and simplistic) claim to neutrality? The Augustan system of government survived the end of the Julio-Claudian dynasty. Although Tacitus claimed in the Agricola (*Agricola* 3) that Nerva had blended the long-incompatible principate and liberty and that Trajan daily increased the happiness of the times (and he repeated the sentiment in the *Histories* (1.1), remarking that under Trajan one could think what one wanted and say what one thought), the fulsomeness of the praise undermines the sentiment. Can the reign of Nerva, who was forced to adopt Trajan in the aftermath of an attempted coup, really be described, without irony, as the beginning of a most happy age? Tacitus' failure to praise the current regime at the start of the *Annals* is suggestive. His analysis of the operation of power under the Julio-Claudians remained pertinent in his own day and it is open to question how far away he really could hold the causes of anger and partiality (*Annals* 1.1).

Tacitus' professed neutrality does not survive a sentence as he launches immediately into the promised short survey of Augustus, tracing the destruction of all opposition and Augustus' accumulation of political power in his hands, under the guise of constitutionality, in a few devastating sentences. Augustus is dead by the end of chapter 5, yet we have to wait until Augustus' funeral (*Annals* 1.8–10) for an evaluation of the first emperor. Tacitus does not simply give us his own view of Augustus but instead provides two divergent opinions of the late princeps, current (he says) at the time of Augustus' funeral. The first is largely positive (and at odds with the tone of Tacitus' account of the reign), defending Augustus' behaviour during the civil war and arguing that he brought stability to the Roman world; the second presents the opposite argument, seeing the Augustan regime as a thinly disguised autocracy destructive both to its opponents and the constitution. This presentation of opposing views is typical of Tacitus. He is careful to support neither himself but, by presenting the longer, hostile view second, he ensures it forms the reader's abiding impression of Augustus' reign. In his depiction of the Julio-Claudian emperors, Tacitus frequently contrasts appearance with reality, forcing the reader to look behind the facade. His provocative claim to write without 'anger and partiality', undercut immediately by his acerbic portrayal of Augustus, invites us to apply the same level of scrutiny to the historian.

But Tacitus is a difficult historian to read. Compressed, poetic, deliberately archaic, Tacitus' style looks back to the work of Sallust. The opening sentence of the *Annals* is modelled on the start of Sallust's *Catiline* ('in the beginning the Trojans . . . held the city of Rome'; cf. Sallust *Cat.* 6.1; see 9d). It is no mere artistic adornment to the content but an important vehicle for the author's thought in its own right. A superficial reading of Tacitus can leave a misleading impression of clarity; further consideration often confuses the issue, to which there is no definitive answer.

Tacitus constantly seeks variety and innovation, subverting typical sentence structures. In most Latin prose authors complex periodic sentences (sentences with one or more subordinate clauses) tend to conclude with the main clause; in Tacitus this process is often reversed – the sentence opens with the main clause to which two or more subordinate clauses are appended. This brings the relationship between the main and the subordinate clauses into sharper focus – do the subordinate clauses offer a causal explanation of the main clause, flesh out the context in which it took place, or do they undermine and call into question its apparently simple statement of fact? The interpretation of an event or statement can turn on the relationship assumed between the syntactical units in a sentence. Woodman devotes a whole article to the simple word *quod* at *Annals* 3.65.1 (Woodman, 1998b: 86ff.): is it a conjunction (because) or a relative pronoun (which), in which case: what is its antecedent? The meaning of the sentence depends on the reader's answer. Tacitus further complicates matters by seeking compression of thought and avoiding balance. His style demands the active involvement of the reader at all times – the absence of connecting particles in the *Annals'* opening sentences forces us to consider for ourselves the connection between the successive phases of Rome's history and the different words for power Tacitus employs (*consulatus, potestas, ius consulare, dominatio, potentia, imperium*).

The murder of Agrippa Postumus (*Annals* 1.6) will serve as example of Tacitus' method and his exploitation of the interplay between first impressions and a more considered reading of the text:

> The first act of the new reign was the murder of Agrippa Postumus, caught unawares and unarmed, whom a centurion, although resolute, had difficulty in finishing off. Tiberius did not discuss the matter in the senate: he

pretended that his father [Augustus] had issued the orders, instructing the tribune in charge of his guards not to delay Postumus' death when Augustus himself should have met his end. Augustus undoubtedly complained often and savagely about the young man's behaviour and had seen to it that his exile was ratified by a resolution of the senate: but he had never been so hard-hearted as to kill any of his own family and it was not believable that he should endure the death of a grandson in order to free his stepson from concern. [It is/was] closer to the truth to suppose that Tiberius and Livia, the former motivated by fear, the latter by the hatred typical in stepmothers, had hastened the death of a young man they suspected and hated. But when the centurion announced, as is the custom in the army, that he had carried out his orders, Tiberius replied that he had given no orders and that a proper account of the deed would have to be submitted to the senate. After Sallustius Crispus, an accessory to secrets, found this out (it was he who had sent the note to the tribune), he warned Livia that the secrets of the palace, the advice of friends, the services of soldiers should not be divulged and that Tiberius should not unravel the power of the principate by referring everything to the senate: he said it was a condition of giving orders that an account would balance only if it was submitted to one man.

The opening of the passage is startling as it sets the scene for Tiberius' principate with the claim that political violence will be the order of the day. In fact, the first decade of Tiberius' reign, as Tacitus himself recognizes (*Annals* 4.6), was a period of comparatively good government. Nevertheless, Tacitus seems keen to colour Tiberius' rule with the spectre of murder from the beginning. Our negative impression of Tiberius is enhanced by the description of the victim's vulnerability ('caught unawares and unarmed') and Tiberius' failure to mention the matter in the senate, pretending instead that the orders came from Augustus. The implication seems to be that Tiberius was himself responsible but wished to shift the blame to Augustus, his (adoptive) father, a most unfilial act. Tacitus apparently endorses this view, commenting that Augustus had never killed any of his family in the past and was unlikely to have done so now simply to help his stepson (note the contrast between 'real' family (grandson) and the relationship by marriage (stepson)). But a careful rereading of this sentence gives the reader pause for thought – the second half of the sentence is not Tacitus' opinion but a view current at the time ('and it *was* not believable'). We are no longer so sure where Tacitus stands on Tiberius' culpability.

The next sentence has no main verb and its interpretation depends on whether we supply *est* (making it Tacitus' opinion) or *erat* – or indeed *esse* – (indicating that Tacitus is continuing to report contemporary opinion). The statement itself is an appeal to psychology, balancing the earlier remark about Augustus' reluctance to kill his own family – Tiberius wanted Agrippa dead out of fear, Livia through a step-mother's malevolence (a phrase more redolent of folk-tale than history). For the time being the matter is unresolved and Tacitus is able to continue to exploit the studied ambiguity.

Tiberius' reaction, given the impression created so far that he was guilty, comes as a surprise – he denies responsibility and wants the matter reported to the senate. This seems to exonerate him. Surely, if he had issued the order, he would not have risked exposure and embarrassment in the senate? But we already know (from the opening of the passage) that Tiberius said nothing in the senate. Is Tiberius' reaction sincere? The behaviour of Sallustius Crispus (who, as the passage shows, was well-placed to judge) suggests it was. He takes the matter to Livia and, in words that echo/parody Tiberius' high-minded talk of rendering an account to the senate, argues that Tiberius is endangering his rule and does not yet understand the nature of autocracy.

Tacitus has artfully constructed a narrative sequence that gives the impression that Tiberius is responsible for the murder. However, several details jar and force us to reassess the incident. The true interpretation of the crucial sentences exonerating Augustus and condemning Tiberius and Livia is unclear. Tiberius' reaction undermines our confidence in his guilt and the behaviour of Sallustius Crispus strengthens our doubts. We realize that Tiberius' failure to mention the matter in the senate, promoted to the beginning of the narrative and seemingly indicating his guilt, temporally belongs at the end – it is a reaction to Crispus' visit to Livia. Responsibility, Tacitus hints (but never explicitly says) lies with Crispus and Livia. At the start of Nero's reign (*Annals* 13.1), Tacitus deliberately recalls this passage in his description of the murder of Junius Silanus but there Agrippina's guilt is stated as fact. The beginnings of Tiberius' and Nero's reigns are compared but the differences are as important as the similarities.

The incident also raises deep questions about the operation of government in the early principate. What role is there for the senate under autocracy? Who is really in control – Livia or Tiberius? Despite the doubts the passage raises over Tiberius' guilt, it is hard for the reader to shake off the abiding impression of his complicity. Tacitus consistently characterizes Tiberius as a ruler who misreads situations and characters and is himself misread (at times communication becomes impossible, as in the accession debate at *Annals* 1.11–13) but Tacitus' own words are easy to misread. Innuendo and suggestion create an impression at odds with the meaning revealed by closer scrutiny. To read Tacitus is to engage in a sort of intellectual archaeology.

So far, Tacitus' view of Roman politics might seem wholly negative but his analysis is neither simplistic nor unitary. In the *Agricola* (*Agricola* 42), Tacitus gives a spirited defence of Agricola's career, remarking that even those who celebrate opposition should recognize that a good man can lead a life of service even under a bad emperor (there is more than a hint of self-interest in Tacitus' argument here – his career prospered under the Flavians, as he acknowledges at *Histories* 1.1). Tacitus praises the early parts of the reigns of both Tiberius and Nero (*Annals* 4.6 and 13.5), for the relative freedom and prestige of the senate. At times he seems to acknowledge the inevitability of the principate, if not its desirability (*Histories* 1.1; 2.37).

Tacitus is a consummate literary artist, trained in rhetoric (where presenting both sides of an argument was an essential skill) and with an eye for the dramatic. It is difficult to pinpoint his own views with any certainty. He puts trenchant criticism of Roman imperialism in the mouths of Rome's barbarian opponents (e.g. Calgacus' speech in the Agricola – *Agricola* 30–2), and speaks with admiration of the customs of her barbarian opponents, contrasting the simple and honourable ways of these noble savages with the corruption of contemporary Roman morals (*Annals* 13.54; *Germania* 14–19). Elsewhere, Germans are objects of fear and Rome's failure to conquer Germany a matter of regret (*Germ.* 37), as is the abandonment of Agricola's conquests in Britain (*Histories* 1.2). In the *Histories*, Cerialis gives a strong speech defending Roman imperialism (*Histories* 4.73) and Agricola is praised (*Agricola* 19–21) for his enlightened administration, which included encouraging acculturation among the natives. Here, characteristically, Tacitus' description has a sting in the tail – it was called civilization among the untutored [Britons], when it was part of their slavery. Each remark must be weighed carefully in its context and undue weight should not be attached to remarks considered in isolation.

Tacitus' sources

Tacitus is the first historian of note whose work survives after Livy, who died around 17. We know of a number of writers who wrote of the early principate but they only survive in fragments. This makes it difficult to assess Tacitus' dependence on them. Tacitus himself acknowledges his debt to his sources and gives the impression that he drew on a number of them for his account (*Annals* 13.20), claiming that he will only mention them when they are at variance. But Tacitus' mention of his sources are few (the implication, of course, being that the tradition is uniform and his account conforms to it). His allusion to Cluvius Rufus and Fabius Rusticus on the subject of Agrippina's alleged incest with Nero (*Annals* 14.2) is instructive. After mentioning Rufus' and Rusticus' accounts, he sides with the weight of tradition and discounts their testimony. In typical fashion, Tacitus has coloured his narrative with a story that he subsequently discredits. The allegation is included for Tacitus' rhetorical ends rather than to point up disagreements in the tradition. Tacitus may also have made use of the senate's own records, the *acta senatus* (*Annals* 3.65 and, more conclusively, 15.75), but the evidence is scanty. Ultimately, Tacitus follows the standard practice of ancient historiography and presents his account as a seamless whole, unless it suits his purpose to allude to one of his sources. Unless archaeology can fill the gaps in the literary record, the precise relationship between Tacitus and his likely source material remains largely a matter of conjecture.

Despite Tacitus' claim to write 'without anger and bias', many critics have cast doubt on his reliability. Although truth was supposedly of prime importance in Roman historiography (Cicero *On the Orator* 2.62), there are good reasons to be sceptical of the veracity of many ancient historians. These criticisms go far beyond accusations of bias, unreliable sources or even the presence in the text of obviously invented speeches, and point to the rhetorical roots of Roman historical writing. Forensic rhetoric in Rome aimed above all at persuasion and what was plausible often passed as truth. A certain amount of elaboration (we would call it invention) was part of the discipline. Enjoyment was an important part of history's appeal (Tacitus' catalogue of disasters in *Histories* 1.2 not only sets the pessimistic tone for the whole work but also whets the reader's appetite for the drama to follow) and some invention was permissible to improve the dramatic impact of the narrative. But Tacitus goes further than merely elaborating details – how did he know, for example, of the conversation between Crispus and Livia? It is unlikely to have been preserved in official records and the participants would hardly have courted witnesses. Tacitus here may well be presenting rumour, inference or outright invention as fact and it is not an isolated example (cf. *Annals* 13.57). Some critics argue that, while much of Tacitus' narrative may be factually accurate, the problem is identifying when he is keeping close to the facts and when he is elaborating. They point to the repetition of similar incidents for dramatic or rhetorical effect – for instance, Tacitus twice uses the *topos* of combatants' deaths at the hands of close relatives to bring out the horror of civil war (*Histories* 3.25 and 3.51). Can we have any faith in the historicity of either incident? Leaving aside the question of his accuracy, he has other limitations, especially his lack of interest in provincial events (apart from when they impact upon central government) and his cursory treatment of military actions, especially in the *Histories*. It is impossible to recreate with any confidence the course of campaigns or battles based upon Tacitus' narrative.

Tacitus and the annalistic form

Tacitus' use of the annalistic form, with its emphasis on consular years and the machinery of constitutional government, seems to put his history firmly in the tradition of republican historiography. In actuality, it enables Tacitus to highlight what is particular about his subject: he keeps the norms of republican government constantly before the reader, even as he charts the subversion of Roman politics by the principate. To begin with, the consular year determines the form of Tacitus' history as, during Tiberius' principate, the ends of books and consular years coincide. But this pattern breaks down as the principate progresses and the senate becomes increasingly subservient. Finally, in Nero's reign Tacitus seems to lose patience with the genre he is writing in (*Annals* 13.31). Annalistic history fails with the republic.

Many of these criticisms are well made but they do not necessarily force the reader to discard any notion of Tacitus as an historian and treat him only as a literary artist. Tacitus' lack of interest in the provinces and his shortcomings as a military historian are certainly irritating for anyone interested in these aspects of Roman history but they are not fair criticisms of Tacitus. The *Histories* is concerned with more than merely the movement of armies and the *Annals* sets out its subject in the opening line – the city of Rome. All historians have to limit their subject matter and Tacitus is no different. Tacitus' tendency to include material whose veracity he could not possibly have proved is a more serious criticism, as is his tendency to embellish his account with *topoi*. We should remember that, whatever the limitations of the discipline when compared to modern historiography, history in the ancient world did routinely purport to give a true record of events (whatever true may mean here) and sought to distinguish itself from other genres partially through this claim. We are fortunate to be able to check Tacitus' account of two incidents against other records. The actual text of the *senatus consultum* condemning Piso for his actions after the death of Germanicus in 19 has come down to us. Germanicus' death and its aftermath is a key incident in Tacitus' account of Tiberius' reign (*Annals* 3.10–17). While Tacitus' version is highly dramatic and a little selective, it agrees largely with the senate's text and his analysis stands up to scrutiny. At *Annals* 11.24, Tacitus gives his version of Claudius' speech to the senate on the admission of Gallic senators. By chance, an inscription bearing the text of the actual speech has survived. A comparison of the two shows that Tacitus keeps close to the substance of the argument, while improving it in parts and removing infelicities of style. Where Tacitus' version can be checked against independent evidence, his credibility is largely enhanced. Ultimately, the view we take depends on our understanding of ancient historians' claim to record the truth. Is the claim merely conventional or do some ancient historians strive to give a largely accurate portrayal of the past within the limitations of their genre? At the very worst, Tacitus stands as a witness to the attitudes and concerns of his own time, even if we despair of him as an historian of the Julio-Claudian era.

Tacitus is a complex and dense writer who rewards close attention. The *Histories* and the *Annals*, whatever their limitations as history, are excoriating analyses of the operation of power and politics under autocratic rule, analyses which are enlivened and deepened by their author's consummate mastery of the fusion of style and content.

Further reading

Both Penguin Classics and Oxford World Classics produce translations of Tacitus' works. There are a number of academic commentaries on his work. The Cambridge Greek and Latin Classics series are usually excellent. There is some good introductory material on Tacitus in Kraus and Woodman (1997). The fullest and best introduction to Tacitus is still Syme's (1958) monumental survey; Ginsburg (1981), Martin (1981), Mellor (1993) and Ash (2006) have attempted briefer treatments. Woodman's articles (many of which are collected in Woodman, 1998b) offer detailed analyses of key passages (including the death of Agrippa Postumus) and a clear appreciation of the difficulties in reading ancient historiography; see also Luce and Woodman (1993). Henderson (1998: chapter 7) gives a characteristically dense reading of the Tacitus' writing in the *Annals*. O'Gorman (2000) and Ash (1999) discuss the difficulties of reading Tacitus; see also Haynes (2003). The *Cambridge Companion to Tacitus* (Woodman, 2010) provides the student with a good overview of recent scholarly thought. See also now the relevant sections in Feldherr (2009).

PLINY THE YOUNGER

Hilary Goy

Gaius Plinius Caecilius Secundus was 17 when Vesuvius erupted in 79. He sat studying at Misenum while his uncle sailed on a rescue mission into the seething bay of Naples (*Letters* 6.16). He describes the eruption, the cloud like an 'umbrella pine' over the mountain and its effects, the darkness and the panic. His uncle (and hero) died, overcome by sulphur fumes, on the shore. Pliny was adopted by his uncle in his will, gained a fourth name, extensive lands and substantial wealth.

We know about his life from his ten books of letters and from inscriptions, notably one over the baths in his home city, Comum. Pliny gave a benefaction for the baths (the kind of gift expected from noble Romans); in return he required his achievements to be recorded. From the inscriptions we have a clear idea of his progression through the Roman political career structure. He started as a minor court official, having practised in the centumviral court which dealt with wills since he was 18; he served in the army, as he was expected to do; then moved up the ladder of political offices to become quaestor, tribune of the plebs, praetor and finally consul for two months in 100. In between, he held positions in the military treasury and the treasury of Saturn. Then he undertook a vital job administrating the bed and banks of the Tiber and the city drains. He was good with finance and practicalities, so it was no surprise that he was sent to the troubled province of Bithynia and Pontus in 110 as a special legate of the emperor Trajan to deal with financial and administrative irregularities. It is believed that he died there in 111, a loyal official to the end.

Of Pliny's writings we have the *Panegyricus*, a speech thanking Trajan for the consulship, and the ten books of letters covering a range of topics reflecting his public and private life. The letters are in a literary tradition, not one as well represented as other genres. Letters are written in a less formal style than history or oratory. There are two main precursors of Pliny as letter-writer: Cicero, who gives us a sense of the immediacy of political life in the late republic, and Seneca, who by contrast uses the genre to present and examine philosophical issues. Pliny's letters, while apparently in an informal and relaxed style, are often careful, artfully and even poetically constructed with an eye to publication and self-advertisement.

There are 247 letters in books 1–9 which he prepared for publication himself. They are written to a variety of people: writers like Tacitus, young men needing advice, friends from Rome and Comum, family, people who want help and whose help he wants. Book 10 is different: it was published after his death. He did not prepare it himself. It consists of correspondence with the emperor Trajan, overwhelmingly about Bithynia. It contains 121 letters.

We appear to have a mirror of his life in these letters. In the public sphere he writes about legal cases, for example when the Bithynians prosecuted their govenor, Varenus (7.6). Pliny goes into detail about aspects of protocol and enumerates which of the senators spoke for or against. There is the case of the fearful lawyer Nominatus (5.4), absent at the second hearing for the people of Vicetia who were trying to stop a market on a senator's land. His excuse was that he realized he risked senatorial disapproval; a vivid picture is given of him throwing himself on the court's mercy. Pliny makes it clear that he knew members of the stoic opposition to imperial rule in his vindication of Helvidius Priscus after Domitian's death. His work with the centumviral court was considerable; he mentions a case where he spoke for five hours and the emperor expressed his concern about the physical strain Pliny was experiencing; it may be tempting for the reader to feel that respite for the audience was also in Trajan's mind.

Pliny has reverence for men of standing, such as his uncle, Pliny the Elder, and Verginius Rufus. He recounts how Verginius Rufus has an inscription on his tomb stating that in defeating Vindex he acted for his country not himself (9.19). He praises men of modesty and good character like Acilianus (1.14), a prospective bridegroom for Mauricus' niece, but he values money and is concerned for reputation and standing. He is committed to literature and the fame and immortality brought by writing and being written about. He is proud of being bracketed with Tacitus by an unknown spectator at the games (9.23). He is nervous about giving public readings, but does it anyway because he wants constructive criticism. He revises his speeches for publication to the point where the extra material is noticed by a reader. He is indefatigable in sending work to friends for their opinion and in giving his on theirs. He not only writes letters and speeches, but also poetry; interestingly, this has not survived.

Pliny often complains of his time-consuming commitments in town, so he cannot go to the country for literary pursuits. Yet when he is there he finds the affairs of his farms are pressing, with tenants' problems and decisions such as whether to buy an adjacent property with economies of scale but doubled risks. He owned various estates, most notably in Laurentum and Tifernum on Tiber. He writes lyrical descriptions of two of his villas (2.17; 5.6) and also the stream of Clitumnus (8.8). Estates were business; he is distressed by the poor grape harvests and the effect on his income. He is involved in his native city of Comum, also the home of his third wife.

Roman society operated on patronage at town and personal level. There are numerous letters recommending men for posts in politics and the army, and to Trajan asking for citizenship for individuals such as a doctor who treated him (10.5). He gives readily himself, referring to building a temple in Tifernum on Tiber (4.1) and endowing baths and a school at Comum (4.13). He mentions getting Robustus promoted to centurion and giving him money (6.25). He regularly helps young men: both ones he knows and those recommended to him by his grandfather-in-law, Fabatus.

Private life is also represented. Although it is difficult to be convinced by a highly literary love letter written to a teenage Calpurnia, Pliny seems to direct the reader to applaud his style rather than show spontaneous emotion. He wants to express his love for her and in a letter to her aunt, Calpurnia Hispulla, praises his wife's virtues, their mutual love and Hispulla's matchmaking skill. He is devastated when Calpurnia miscarries; he longed for children and the grant of the 'ius trium liberorum' (a law giving privileges to fathers of three children) by Trajan as an honour cannot compensate for inability to pass on the reputation of the family to posterity. He hardly knows how to tell Fabatus that he has lost a great-grandchild with all that it could have meant (8.10). Fabatus is an important man in Comum and Pliny is wary of him, seeking to avoid confrontation, but irritated by him – for example, when he upbraids Pliny for selling land cheaply to a friend (7.11). His slaves and freedmen matter to him. He does not question their status, but worries about them. He sends his freedman Zosimus to Egypt and Paulinus' estate in Forum Iulii, hoping for a cure for Zosimus' lung disease (5.19). He is upset when his slaves are ill or die and lets them make quasi-wills which he upholds. Yet there is a feeling that he centres on his own reactions and emotions in these letters. However, he is horrified by the murder of Larcius Macedo, a 'cruel and proud master' and feels that no one is safe (3.14).

Daily life is here. Pliny dislikes the host who graded dinner parties with fine food for the nobles and cheaper fare for the others (2.6). He prefers a simple approach with a reading as entertainment not dancing girls. He despises the races and intelligent people's support for teams rather than the drivers' skill – he uses the time to write (9.6). The same thing happens when he hunts; the quiet by the nets is perfect for inspiration (1.6).

Book 10 is concerned with correspondence between Trajan and Pliny. The latter's financial expertise is used as he 'shakes out' the accounts of Prusa on his arrival (10.17a). He wants to investigate fraud in building and redeem disastrous projects such as the theatre at Nicaea (10.39). His interest in public welfare is shown when he asks Trajan if he can cover a stream in Amastris (10.98) which is like an open sewer; he discusses the engineering problem of joining a lake to the sea by canal to aid transport (10.41) and the need for a fire brigade in Nicomedia (10.33). Administrative problems also abound; he encounters slaves enrolled in the army (10.29), prisoners guarded by public slaves, the condemned released from punishment (10.19) without due paperwork and lack of opportunity to invest public money (10.54). He is always subservient to Trajan and flatters him.

Through the letters we come to see a serious-minded, hardworking man, tireless in his profession, loyal to his friends and community, a loving husband and a caring master. On the other hand, he seeks approval (especially in the unrevised letters to Trajan), and he is ambitious: it is all very well being compared to Tacitus, but one wonders what Tacitus made of the comparison. Pliny, like other orators, revised his speeches for publication: he must have revised his letters also. He gives us the image of himself he wants us to see. To find the real Pliny we need not ask what kind of man wrote these letters but what kind of man wanted us to have this image of him.

Further reading

For text and commentary, see Sherwin-White (1966). For works dealing with Pliny's letters, see Gamberini (1983); Henderson (2002); Hoffer (1999); Marchesi (2008). On literary letter-writing in antiquity, see Morello and Morrison (2007). There is also interesting material on Pliny in Bartsch (1994) and Fantham (1996).

SUETONIUS

Stephen Kern

Gaius Suetonius Tranquillus is well-known as the author of *The Lives of the Caesars* but he is less familiar for the other areas of his scholarly pursuits. He was probably born at Hippo Regius in north Africa around 70, trained and practised as an advocate, and was a beneficiary of the patronage of Pliny the Younger. He held three important posts within the imperial household, according to an inscription from Hippo: *a bibliothecis* (in charge of the imperial libraries); *a studiis* (in charge of the emperor's own archives); *ab epistulis* (in charge of the emperor's correspondence). His scholarly output was prolific, and he apparently wrote on subjects as diverse as clothing, Roman games and spectacles and the partly-surviving *On Famous Men* (*De Viris Illustribus*). However, his only complete extant work is *The Lives of the Caesars* (*De Vita Caesarum*). By the time he wrote this he had another patron, the praetorian prefect Septicius Clarus, who was the dedicatee of both Pliny's *Letters* and

Suetonius' *Lives of the Caesars*. According to one later source, albeit somewhat unreliable, both Septicius and Suetonius were dismissed in 122 as a result of an impropriety involving Sabina, the wife of the emperor Hadrian.

The Lives of the Caesars are biographies of the first 12 emperors from Julius Caesar (not strictly an emperor, of course) to Domitian. A biographical approach naturally looks at an individual's parentage, date of birth, education, family, achievements and death. But the emperors received more extensive treatment than the *Viri Illustres*, and Suetonius continued to build on an existing literary tradition to which he himself alludes. His principal literary precursors were the *Imagines* of Varro in the first century BCE (700 portraits of famous men, international in scope), and another work, slightly later in date, the *De Illustribus Viris* of Cornelius Nepos who himself gives a low ranking to biography, and is conscious that he is writing not for historians but for the general public. The *Foreign Generals* of Nepos had widespread popularity as a school book, principally for their morality and simplicity rather than accuracy and erudition. The main biographer of Suetonius' own era was Plutarch, a polymath from Boeotia, with wide-ranging intellectual interests and productivity. After writing some initial *Lives*, he conceived a huge plan to compare parallel Greek and Roman lives, very much a product of the Greco-Roman empire of the second century, and principally concerned to foster moral edification, where a phrase or jest could reveal more about character than great deeds. This work was dedicated to Sosius Senecio, a friend of Pliny the Younger.

Suetonius' tenure of the three posts within the imperial household would have provided him with access to useful sources of information. There has been speculation as to the effect Suetonius' dismissal, if genuine, had on his access to the material he wanted. Certainly the quality and length of the individual *Lives* declines over the series, with the *Lives of Julius Caesar* and *Augustus* being the most detailed, the rest of the Julio-Claudians being somewhere in the middle, and the last six *Lives* being rather slighter.

How did Suetonius' approach to his subject matter differ from that of contemporary historians? G. B. Townend (2002) comments that the biographical method, very different from the year-by-year annalistic tradition even with modifications, makes it difficult to compare him with other ancient writers or assess his value as an historical source, although both genres had an interest in character and its consequences. Since the *Life of Julius Caesar* is one of the fullest examples of Suetonius' techniques and interests, it is a good place to start our examination of his biographical style.

The opening chapters of this *Life* are missing but sufficient remains of the account of Caesar's youth and the early stages of his political career to demonstrate how Suetonius incorporates a number of anecdotes and incidents that appear to anticipate the subsequent development of the young man into a brave, determined and ambitious careerist. When captured by pirates, Caesar organizes a plan for his own ransoming, and follows it by the rapid dispatch of a fleet to arrest the pirates, retrieve the money and crucify the criminals. He is prepared to resort to massive bribery and subsequent indebtedness to make his bid to become *pontifex maximus* (chief priest) successful. The first triumvirate is dealt with expeditiously at the end of chapter 19, and the consulship of 59 BCE is covered in a few chapters. Despite the length of Caesar's command and campaigns in Gaul, only a short section is specifically devoted to that period, with the focus on a few achievements, such as the construction of the bridge over the Rhine and a brief reference to the expeditions to Britain. The civil war is also treated very economically and in a matter-of-fact way, but the scene on the bank of the river Rubicon, in the run-up to Caesar's fateful decision to cross into Italy, is given a melodramatic character with an apparition of superhuman size, whose trumpet-blast is the signal for Caesar to demonstrate his resolve. After the account of the civil war, the writer looks at the various reforms and projects started or anticipated by Caesar prior to his assassination, and then returns to look at his character and mode of life before dealing with his death.

Before the drama of the death-scene, we have some impressions of Caesar's appearance and mode of dress, his places of residence and passion for luxuries, some insights into the management of his household, and his behaviour as a magistrate and as a general. This provides the opportunity for some presentation of his character and some psychological insights into his personality. He is appreciated for his successful handling of his troops and their bravery arising out of their loyalty towards him, his magnanimity in victory and his famous *clementia* (mercifulness). This leads to a reappearance of the pirate episode, in which Caesar's decision to have the pirates strangled prior to crucifixion is taken as testimony to his *clementia*. Much is made of titles and awards. Remarks with political implications are also mentioned, such as Caesar's dismissal of the republic, or his comment on the folly of Sulla in resigning his dictatorship.

We come to the scene of Caesar's murder. Once again attention is given to portents that appeared to prefigure this event, and the actual assassination is vividly expressed with the different actions of individual conspirators and Caesar's attempt to die with some dignity. The scene of his body being carried away by some young slaves, with the arm of the victim dangling down from the bier, is a strikingly visual demonstration of Caesar's downfall. There is vividness, too, in the scenes of the funeral, with the public manifestations of grief and anger on the part of the crowd, but the final comments are somewhat perfunctory: the closure of the room where the assassination took place, the renaming of the ides of March, and the fates of the various conspirators, some of whom were alleged to have committed suicide with the very daggers with which they had murdered Caesar. The overall impression is of an assemblage of dramatic and exciting material, rather than any analysis of its significance.

When we come to the *Life of Caligula* (Gaius) the writer regales us even more with peculiar details. This *Life* opens with a eulogistic treatment of

Caligula's father, Germanicus, including a number of portents associated with his death, and there is apparent concern for factual accuracy in the attention paid to Caligula's birthplace; but there is anecdotal material as well with focus on his cruelty, ruthlessness and sexual depravity, all of these contributing to the presentation of his corrupt character, and bizarre and unbalanced frame of mind. The prodigies presaging his assassination are also described, and there is yet another dramatic death-scene, followed by the apparition of ghosts near his tomb. The account concludes with a brief section on the state of the times and the incredulity with which news of the assassination was greeted.

In the final *Life*, that of Domitian, corruption and lack of self-discipline manifest themselves even more rapidly. Some military campaigns are dismissed as unnecessary, as attempts merely to emulate his brother Titus. Domitian bribes the soldiers and is obsessed with shows, adding two new factions to the racing teams at the Circus Maximus. He promotes himself through building projects bearing only his name. But Suetonius' own longer accounts of some military campaigns attest to their being genuine responses to critical military situations. Domitian could be severe in traditional religious practices, unpredictable and cruel in punishments meted out to senators, and a source of terror to all. Ultimately he was killed in a conspiracy including his wife and other trusted people. Once again an assassination is prefigured by portents and predictions. Death this time is only a short dramatic scene, regarded by the plebs with indifference, by the soldiers with dismay.

An obvious issue concerning a writer of short biographies, such as Suetonius, is the matter of the historical value of the episodes referred to. How do they compare with their treatment by more conventional historians, how much credibility do they have ? A couple of incidents may illustrate the problem even if they do not solve it. Both Suetonius and Tacitus write about the withdrawal of the emperor Tiberius to Capri. Tacitus (in *Annals* 4) focuses on how the remoteness of the island climate appealed to Tiberius. He ceased to be absorbed in state affairs and instead spent time in secret orgies and malevolent thoughts. There is some overlap with Suetonius but there the principal subject matter is the depravity and sexual misconduct indulged in by the emperor with voyeuristic descriptions of his perversions and obscene pleasures. Concerning the great fire of Rome in Nero's reign, Suetonius ascribes relatively little space to it but holds Nero responsible, with the bizarre scene of the emperor in tragic costume, singing of the fall of Troy, orchestrating the deliberate destruction of buildings. By contrast, Tacitus' treatment is much lengthier and less melodramatic, focusing on areas of destruction with some empathetic description of the experiences of ordinary people, and emphasizing Nero's immediate response to the disaster and implementation of programmes of relief.

Suetonius provided the model for the subsequent biographies of the *Historia Augusta*, and even later works such as Einhard's *Life of Charlemagne* and now Hamilton on American presidents. The subject matter and its arrangement can sometimes frustrate those who are trying to create a more obviously conventional history, but Suetonius preserves anecdotes and vignettes which help us to obtain an impression, albeit at times brief and bizarre, of the activities and personalities of the imperial court in the first century. Much of what we think of as characteristic of imperial Rome (and subsequent adaptations of it as in Robert Graves' *I Claudius* and *Claudius the God*) comes from these pages.

Further reading

There is no OCT of Suetonius, though there is a Teubner text. The texts of all the individual lives (except for Claudius and Titus) – with introduction and commentary – can be found in the Bristol Classical Press series, by various editors; there is an Aris and Phillips edition of the lives of Galba, Otho and Vitellius (ed. D. Shotter). For a good introduction, see Wallace-Hadrill (1983); see also Baldwin (1983) and, for an investigation into the sources used by Suetonius, see Dennison (2009). Interesting material can also be found in various works on Roman historians, such as Feldherr (2009); Kraus and Woodman (1997); Marincola (1997); Woodman (1998a). A recent historian of American presidents has consciously imitated Suetonius, as the title – *American Caesars* – makes clear (Hamilton, 2010).

Chapter 12

Greece and Rome come together: later literature

Roy Hyde

All dates in this chapter are CE unless stated otherwise. Glossary items: *Asianism; Atticism; ecphrasis; epideictic; paradoxography; stoicism.*

LATER ANTIQUITY: AN HISTORICAL INTRODUCTION

The reigns of Trajan, Hadrian, Antoninus Pius and Marcus Aurelius (collectively 98–180 CE) were for the most part years of peace and prosperity for the Roman empire. Partly this was because each of them was appointed on merit by his predecessor, with senatorial approval, rather than according to hereditary principles. Unfortunately, Marcus Aurelius chose to succeed him his unstable son, Commodus, on whose assassination (192) a civil war broke out. The victor, Septimius Severus (193–211), instituted a more militaristic, anti-senatorial regime which outlasted his dynasty, though the temporary stability he had restored did not. Severus' son Caracalla, Caracalla's murderer Macrinus, Macrinus' successor Elagabalus and Elagabalus' successor Alexander Severus were all, one after another, assassinated or put to death (between 217 and 235).

The empire's problems were not only political and internal. Its north-western and eastern frontiers had rarely been stable and required a continual military presence. For some 50 years (235–84), warfare against the Sassanian dynasty of Persia in the east, and against various barbarian tribes to the north-west, had been practically continuous. The empire also faced serious economic crisis, with rapidly increasing inflation, in part brought about by the need to fund all this military activity. A succession of 'soldier-emperors' arose, one after another, usually elected by the legions, on the frontiers, on the demise of their predecessors, or sometimes in rivalry with them. Most of these short-lived emperors have received a bad press, from the (mostly inadequate) sources that record their activities, which tend to be biased towards the senatorial class: many were not senators, but career soldiers, often of obscure ancestry; some rarely, if ever, saw Rome, and had little time for the niceties of senatorial politics. But many were fine soldiers – Claudius Gothicus, Gallienus, Aurelian, for example – and lived and died in the service of the empire.

And the empire, by virtue of their efforts, survived; many parts of it, indeed, continued to thrive, despite all its problems. Some measure of stability was restored by Diocletian (284–305), an able soldier and great administrator who attempted economic reforms, reorganized the provinces and their governance, and heightened the dignity, and remoteness, of the imperial office. Most significantly, he acknowledged, in his appointment of three co-emperors with power nominally almost equal to his own (the Tetrarchy), that the empire could not effectively be centrally ruled by one man. Until Diocletian abdicated, his own authority ensured that the system worked. But it depended on mutual trust, which the Tetrarchy's successors lacked, and further civil wars eventually resulted in the emergence of Constantine I (306–37) as sole ruler. Diocletian had ruled the empire from the east (he visited Rome only once). Constantine's establishment of Constantinople as a second capital, like his own recognition, in the appointment of his three sons as co-rulers, that an emperor could not function alone, was a further and perhaps decisive step in the division of the empire into east and west which Diocletian had foreshadowed, and which was hastened by the continual pressure from barbarians on the vulnerable frontiers between the eastern and western portions. The extent to which Constantine was a genuine Christian is debatable; Christianity had spread widely through the empire in the preceding two centuries, despite sporadic persecutions (most recently by Diocletian, and in general less dramatic than conventionally depicted), occasioned essentially because the refusal of Christians to accept other gods beside their own was seen as socially and politically divisive. But he certainly, at the very least, validated the official status of Christianity within the empire, and attempted, at the Council of Nicaea (325) to reconcile the various branches of Christianity into a coherent whole: an empire-wide religion riven by its own divisions would be more destabilizing than a whole range of mutually tolerant faiths. (In fact, heresies dogged the Christian church for centuries to come, and the division between the Roman branch and the orthodox Christianity of the east persists to this day.)

Paganism by no means died out, especially amongst the old senatorial families at Rome, but after Constantine only two pagan emperors ruled at Rome, and neither for very long: the philosopher-emperor Julian (361–3), many of whose interesting writings survive, and Eugenius (western emperor 392–4). But ostensible religious unity did not lead to political unity: on the death of Theodosius I in 395, his two sons became joint rulers, Honorius in the west and Arcadius in the east; the Roman empire was never thereafter ruled by one man. The sixth-century emperor at Constantinople, Justinian, made determined efforts to recover some parts of the western empire, and enjoyed some success, but his achievements were not lasting. The story of the demise of the western empire and the survival of the eastern one is complex and cannot be dealt with in any detail here. In the fourth and fifth centuries both were threatened by barbarian tribes from the north-west; the eastern empire's power-base was further away from these threats, so that its survival was perhaps more assured. In any case, the situation was by no means as simple as barbarians v. Romans, with one group inside the empire trying to preserve it and another outside trying to destroy it. By the time of Honorius and Arcadius, many of the barbarian tribes were already established within the boundaries of the empire, and were no more barbaric than other subject peoples. In particular, the Roman armies depended largely on these peoples for their manpower, so that frontier wars were frequently fought between, for example, hostile Gothic forces and Roman armies, which themselves were largely made up of Gothic soldiers. To Romans of the west, one of the great traumatic events of the last years of the empire was the sacking of Rome by the Goth Alaric in 410; but what Alaric seems to have wanted, apart from sustenance for his nomadic people, was official status within the empire. Honorius' commander-in-chief, who had conducted earlier campaigns against Alaric, Stilicho, was himself of Vandal descent. At the same time, in the east, Honorius' brother depended for a time on a Gothic general called Gainas, despite incursions into his territory by other Gothic groups. Only by abandoning simplistic concepts such as 'Roman' and 'barbarian' can we make sense of the events of the fifth century.

The date generally given for the end of the Roman empire in the west is 476, when the boy emperor Romulus Augustulus was deposed by the German leader Odovacer, who was subsequently recognized as king of Italy. But Odovacer himself probably simply saw himself as succeeding to the office as western emperor; and it appears that the eastern emperor of the time, Zeno, accepted him as such. The Ostrogothic king Theoderic, who subsequently deposed Odovacer, was no uncultured barbarian, but had received a Roman education. His minister, the scholar and monk Cassiodorus, was a major figure in the preservation of classical culture, and in his time the influential philosopher Boethius, though a Christian, was still imbued with the traditions of classical thought. The western Roman empire shrank, and the new states of the medieval world grew from its parts, but the classical tradition, or at least the Latin branch of it, never entirely perished. In 800, Charlemagne, king of the Franks, at whose court a brief renaissance of classical learning took place, and who consciously pursued a policy of reviving the empire, was crowned emperor of the Romans. The Holy Roman Empire, which was a lineal descendant of Charlemagne's ambitions, survived until 1806.

But to the surviving, essentially Greek, half of the empire, there was in 800 already a Roman emperor; we talk now of the Byzantine empire, centred on Constantinople, but the Byzantines called themselves Romans, and did so until the fall of Constantinople to the forces of the Ottoman Sultan Mehmed II in 1453. Legend had it that the last emperor, Constantine XI Palaiologos, who led his army in the final battle against Mehmed, and whose body was never found, had survived and would come again to restore his people. During the last years of the empire, scholars from Byzantium migrated to western Europe, bringing with them their learning and their books. The renaissance that their coming inaugurated brought together again the Greek and the Latin traditions that the division of the empire had sundered: the emperor may not have survived, but the classical tradition did.

Further reading

Good introductions to the world of late antiquity can be found in Bowersock *et al.*, (1999; 2001); Brown (1989); Cameron (1993a; 1993b); Collins (1999); Goldhill (2001); Jones (1986); Mitchell (2006); Treadgold (1997); Wells (1984).

Table 12.1 List of emperors – the later empire (all dates are CE)

117–38	Hadrian
138–61	Antonius Pius
161–80	Marcus Aurelius (co-ruled with Lucius Verus 161–9)
180–92	Commodus
193	Pertinax
193	Didius Julianus
193–4	Pescennius Niger
193–7	Clodius Albinus
193–211	Septimius Severus
212–17	Caracalla
217–18	Macrinus
218–22	Elagabalus
222–35	Severus Alexander
235–8	Maximinus
238	Gordian I and II
238	Balbinus and Pupienus
238–44	Gordian III
244–9	Philip the Arab
249–51	Decius
251–3	Gallus
253–60	Valerian
254–68	Gallienus
268–70	Claudius Gothicus
270–5	Aurelian
275–6	Tacitus
276–82	Probus
282–5	Carus, Carinus, Numerianus
285–c. 310	Diocletian
295	L. Domitus Domitianus
297–8	Aurelius Achilleus
303	Eugenius
285–c. 310	Maximianus Herculius

(Continued)

(Continued)

285	Amandus
285	Aelianus
286?–297?	British emperors (Carausius 286–93; Allecto 293–7)
293–306	Constantius I Chlorus
293–311	Galerius
305–13	Maximinus Daia
305–7	Severus II
306–37	Constantinus I
306–12	Maxentius
308–9	L. Domitius Alexander
308–24	Licinius
314?	Valens
324	Martinianus
333–4	Calocaerus
337–40	Constantinus II
337–50	Constans I
337–61	Constantinus II
350–3	Magnentius
350	Nepotian
350	Vetranio
355	Silvanus
361–3	Julianus
363–4	Jovianus
364–75	Valentinianus I
375	Firmus
364–78	Valens
365–6	Procopius
366	Marcellus
367–83	Gratian
375–92	Valentinianus II
378–95	Theodosius I
383–388	Magnus Maximus
384–8	Flavius Victor
392–4	Eugenius
395–423	Honorius [division of the empire – Honorius' brother Arcadius ruled the east 395–408]

	Western empire		Eastern empire
407–11	Constantine III usurper	408–50	Theodosius II
411–21	Constantius III		
423–5	Johannes		
425–55	Valentinian III	450–7	Marcian
455	Petronius Maximus		
455–6	Avitus		
457–61	Majorian	457–74	Leo I
461–5	Libius Severus		
467–72	Anthemius		
468	Arvandus		
470	Romanus		
472	Olybrius		
473–4	Glycerius	474	Leo II
474–5	Julius Nepos	474–5	Zeno
475–6	Romulus Augustulus	475–6	Basiliscus
		476–91	Zeno (restored)
		491–518	Anastasius I
		518–27	Justin I
		527–65	Justinian I

LATER LITERATURE: A BRIEF INTRODUCTION

Conventional approaches to Greek and Roman literature (and courses in classics based on them) tended to classify the literature into more or less strict periods: for Greek, the archaic period up to the early fifth century BCE, followed by the classical, consisting of most of the fifth and fourth centuries, with the Hellenistic age extending down to the coming of Rome. At Rome, a somewhat vaguely conceived period of early literature preceded the golden age of Latin – Cicero and Livy in prose, Virgil and Ovid in verse – of the late republic and early empire, which was succeeded by the silver age, lasting until roughly the end of the first century. Implicit in this classification was a set of value judgements: the best Greek was the Attic written around 400 BCE, and the best Latin that of the age of Cicero. To a considerable extent, this view represented that of the Greeks and Romans themselves (more on this below), and it may be the case that, to many readers, Virgil (for example) seems to be a better writer than Lucan. But literary judgements are, in the end, subjective: supposing that (for the sake of argument) Dickens were universally acknowledged to be the greatest writer of novels in English; this would not prevent other people from continuing to write them, nor would it be a reason not to read these, or not to read novels written before Dickens' time.

As far as Greek and Latin are concerned, we have rather less choice, in that the literature that has survived tends to be that which Greeks and Romans, rightly or wrongly, judged to be the best. But, one way or another, a good deal of other writing, especially from the period of the Roman empire, *has* survived. As far as beginnings are concerned, Greek literature starts, for us, with Homer and Hesiod, and Latin with Ennius. Latin literature of a recognizably classical type was still being produced during the last days of the western empire (the last Roman emperor in the west was deposed in 476), and beyond; in the east, where Constantinople became the capital of the Byzantine emperors who considered themselves heirs of the Caesars, classical Greek was studied and written until the fall of Constantinople in 1453. This chapter cannot go as far as that, but it is meant to serve as an introduction to some less familiar material which is nevertheless well worth reading.

One reason for reading some of the Greek and Latin literature from the Roman imperial period is that, after many years of leading largely separate lives, Greek and Latin began to come together in new ways. Latin, of course, had been influenced by Greek from the beginning, not only in literary terms but because there were many Greek-speaking communities in Italy with which Roman expansion had necessarily brought contact and conflict. But early Latin literature would not have come about without Greek: for example, the poet Livius Andronicus (third century BCE) adapted and translated into Latin the *Odyssey*, as well as writing tragedies and comedies in the Greek style; in the late third and early second centuries BCE, the founding father of Latin poetry, Ennius, and the playwrights Plautus and Terence began to forge a Latin tradition based on similar material. And the first Roman historians, Fabius Pictor and Cincius Alimentus, around 200 BCE, actually wrote in Greek. This was not simply a literary device: Rome's increasing role in Greek affairs required mediating to the Greeks themselves, and since very few Greeks at this date will have understood Latin, this had to be done through their own language.

To begin with, there is no sign of the infant Roman literature affecting Greeks, and we should not expect it: the prevalent Greek attitude to Rome was probably one of intimidated disdain. But Greeks did come to Rome, in increasing numbers. Livius Andronicus himself is said to have taught Greek to the sons of Roman aristocrats, and Roman diplomatic and military activity in the Greek world (culminating in Greece becoming a province of the Roman empire in 146 BCE) accelerated such contact. Greek art had been coming to Rome since the early third century; by the second century, Greek philosophy, rhetoric and literature had followed, brought by the practitioners of these arts themselves. They came, no doubt, mostly attracted by the prospect of employment and patronage, but some, such as the stoic philosopher Panaetius, were eminent figures in their fields. Presumably Panaetius spoke some Latin; the historian Polybius must have, as he spent a considerable time

at Rome, first as a political hostage and subsequently as an associate of Scipio
Aemilianus, who was also the patron of Panaetius. Polybius may be said to
represent something of a new departure in the Greek attitude to Rome, and
his *History* charts the rise of Rome 'in a period of no more than 53 years' to
its position of dominance in the Mediterranean world. But, although he used,
amongst others, Fabius Pictor as a source, he wrote very much in the Greek
historiographical tradition.

Every Latin poet who wrote during the first two centuries BCE was influ-
enced by Greek poetry, yet it is a curious phenomenon that very little
Greek poetry has survived from this period (and that what was produced
does not seem to have been especially good): between the death of
Apollonius of Rhodes, *c.* 215 BCE, and the Roman imperial period, perhaps
the only substantial figures are Moschus (mid-second century BCE) and
Bion (probably a little later), who wrote pastoral poetry in the tradition of
Theocritus, and Meleager (fl. 100 BCE), who collected elegiac epigrams,
including his own, in the anthology known as the *Garland of Meleager*.
Other poetry was written: it would be interesting to have some of the work
of Archias (mid-first century BCE) – who was defended in court by Cicero
and is known to have written in celebration of the victories of Roman
generals – in order to see a Greek poet working with specifically Roman
material. And, exactly at this same time, those Roman poets who created
what quickly became the Latin classics were at work. The concept of classicism is perhaps partly responsible for this situation. Greeks were very
conscious – over-conscious, perhaps – that their classics had already been
written: the Homeric epics, the Attic tragedies, the comedies of
Aristophanes, and so on. These classics were still read, learned, acted and,
since the Hellenistic period, exhaustively written about, analysed and
annotated. The Romans, however, were equally consciously setting about
creating a classical literature of their own: thus Virgil, beginning as the
Roman Theocritus in the *Eclogues*, and continuing as the Roman Hesiod in
the *Georgics*, eventually became the Roman Homer with the *Aeneid*. (Similar
ambitions are clear in the case of other poets.) Perhaps what was happening, simplistically expressed, was that amongst the Greeks those people
who might have created new literature were busy writing about the old;
whereas the Romans were actively creating their own.

Certainly we know that, from Hellenistic times onwards, a great deal of
scholarly writing in Greek was being produced about literature. To Greek
and Roman scholars, writing about any kind of literature was essentially
writing about rhetoric. The wealthy Romans who, in increasing numbers
during the last two centuries BCE, went to Athens to study philosophy and
rhetoric, or had their sons educated in their own homes by Greek teachers,
were interested first and foremost in rhetoric as an instrument by which to
achieve political influence. (Though their interest in philosophy may well
also have been genuine: Cicero's certainly was, and he set about introducing

Greek philosophy to a wider Roman readership, with great success.) Thus, whilst there may have been little incentive for literary Greeks to produce poetry, teaching rhetoric and producing books about it seems to have become something of a growth industry in this period, and a common interest in rhetoric to have been one of the factors that tended to unite Greek and Roman.

There is other evidence of the drawing together of Greece and Rome during this time. One of the Greeks who spent time at Rome was the important stoic Posidonius. Amongst a large literary output, mostly lost, he wrote a history of the Mediterranean world in the second and early first centuries which, obviously, dealt with Rome as well as the Greek world. He was followed (and used as a source), not much later, by Diodorus Siculus, who wrote a vast compendium of history of which a considerable amount survives. Diodorus is an erratic historian, who tends to follow his sources closely and thus to lack direction: the point here is not the accuracy or otherwise of his work, but the fact that in it, as in Posidonius, the history of Rome is placed alongside the history of Greece, by a Greek writer, on an equal footing. The Greek geographical writer Strabo, our most important source for Greek knowledge of and theory about geography, visited Rome several times during the reign of Augustus, and readily accepted the beneficial effects of Roman rule throughout the Mediterranean. Another Greek writer much interested in Rome, and also in literary theory and rhetoric, was Dionysius of Halicarnassus, who was in Rome for more than 20 years in the time of Augustus. Not only did he write a long (extant) account of early Roman history, but he specifically states that he learned Latin in order to be able to read Roman sources on the subject. Dionysius was also interested in the long-standing theoretical dispute between 'Atticists', who favoured a more restrained literary style modelled on the language and style of orators such as Lysias, and the more florid 'Asiatic' style: in one of his literary critical works, he expresses the hope that the good taste of the aristocratic Romans who now take an interest in rhetoric will help the cause of his preferred Atticism (see 9b on this in relation to Cicero).

Thus, by the start of the imperial period, the Greek and Latin literary worlds were beginning to come together, even if it was still the case that literary influences continued to be one-way. Greece was, of course, subject to Rome, and no doubt this fact rankled with some Greeks; but the stability brought to the eastern Mediterranean (most of which was by now Greek-speaking) can only have been conducive to literary output, as can the greater ease of travel and communications resulting from it. In 67, the emperor Nero proclaimed Greece free from Roman taxation and administration, and this – along with the later philhellenism of Hadrian (reigned 117–38) – has been seen as a factor in the revival of Greek culture and literature which began in the later first century BCE and continued for the following two centuries or so. The Roman writers of the first and early second centuries CE are dealt with elsewhere, with the exception of one who was an exponent of a literary genre not generally associated with Greece and Rome, the novel: Petronius.

THE LATIN NOVEL: PETRONIUS AND APULEIUS

Several books survive in Latin which may reasonably be characterized as novels. One is from the fifth or sixth century, *Apollonius, King of Tyre*, which is either a translation or a paraphrase of a Greek original, and another of the fourth century, a Latin version of what is usually called the *Greek Alexander Romance* by Julius Valerius. There are also two prose versions of the Trojan War story, attributed to participants in the war, Dares, probably from the fourth century, and Dictys, probably somewhat later: the latter seems to have been a translation of a Greek original, and the former may well have been. All of these were popular in the middle ages, but there is not room to discuss them here. Two earlier ones, Apuleius' *Metamorphoses* (often called *The Golden Ass*), and Petronius' *Satyrica*, are of much greater literary importance, and should be read by anyone interested in the literature of the Roman empire.

It is generally thought that Petronius was the man of that name mentioned by Tacitus (*Annals* 16.18ff.) as an able provincial governor who preferred a life of luxury. He became a close associate of Nero, and was regarded by him as *elegantiae arbiter* – the man to whom all questions of good taste were submitted. Having offended Nero, he was forced to commit suicide, which he contrived to do in a leisurely manner which looks like a parody of the stoic suicide forced by Nero on his counsellor Seneca. There is no incontrovertible evidence that this man is the author of the *Satyrica*, but if he was not, his character suggests that he ought to have been.

The name of the book indicates what it is about: Greek prose fictions often bore titles like *Milesiaca* – 'things to do with Miletus/Milesian tales'. *Satyrica* therefore means 'things to do with satyrs' (though not literally), satyrs being the bibulous and sexually omnivorous creatures associated with the god Dionysus; the title also puns on the Latin word *satura*, which came to mean much the same as our 'satire'. (*Satyricon*, by which name the book is often called, is almost certainly incorrect, and is a Greek genitive plural: manuscripts would begin 'The *x* books of the *Satyrica* of Petronius'). It is written mostly in prose, with some interludes of verse, and thus sometimes characterized as belonging to the genre of Menippean Satire, a type of book in both prose and verse originating with the third century BCE cynic philosopher Menippus, of which the first-century BCE Roman writer Varro produced versions. Menippean satire seems to have combined humour and social comment, and is thus a very respectable ancestor for the *Satyrica*. Seneca's *Apocolocyntosis*, which pokes fun at the deification of the late emperor Claudius, was in similar form, though much shorter, and may have influenced Petronius, whose near-contemporary he was (see 11b on Seneca).

The *Satyrica* was a very long book, and most of it has not survived. The original may have been as long as 20 books (or even 24, in imitation of the *Odyssey*: see below), and we appear only to have most of books 14–16. The story is told by the first-person narrator, Encolpius, and what survives consists largely of three episodes which are to some extent self-contained (especially the second one), but which also refer to previous episodes and include some subsidiary self-contained narratives as well as pieces of verse which are connected more or less loosely with the rest. The plot is complex, and a summary of it will help to illustrate the nature of the book: in the following summary it should be borne in mind that some parts even of the more continuous narrative are missing, and the connections between sections are therefore sometimes unclear.

The first episode opens with Encolpius in conversation with a teacher of rhetoric called Agamemnon, who talks at some length about the shortcomings of contemporary education and by whom, it later emerges, he and his friend Ascyltos have been invited to a dinner party (which looks ahead to the next episode). Ascyltos has slipped away, and when Agamemnon is besieged by a group of students wanting to argue with him, Encolpius follows him. Back at their lodgings, Encolpius' boyfriend Giton complains that Ascyltos has tried to rape him, and Enclopius and Ascyltos agree to part company, but not until after the dinner party. A slightly confusing interlude follows in the market-place, involving a tunic which Encolpius and Ascyltos have filled with money stolen in a robbery, and subsequently lost. (No doubt the affair would be clear enough if we had the complete text.) Again at their lodgings, they receive a visit from a woman named Quartilla and her two maids; we discover that Encolpius has somehow offended the god Priapus and is consequently impotent. A fragmented sex-scene follows, involving the three men and the three women and a male homosexual prostitute.

The second episode begins at the baths, where Encolpius and his friends see an old bald man playing ball with some slaves: it turns out that he is Trimalchio, at whose house they are to dine that evening. A long description of the dinner party follows. Each course of the meal, and the entertainments offered, is described in detail: everything is carefully orchestrated by Trimalchio; his freedmen friends talk, gossip and tell stories, as does Trimalchio himself, reminiscing, berating his slaves, philosophizing, insulting and throwing a cup at his wife, and finally enacting his own funeral. Towards the end, another friend of Trimalchio's, Habinnas, comes in drunk, with his wife. Eventually the party generates so much noise that the fire brigade break into the house under the impression that it is on fire; Encolpius and his friends, who are desperate to get out, take the opportunity to escape.

At the beginning of the third episode, Encolpius and Ascyltos do part company; much to Encolpius' distress, Giton chooses to go with Ascyltos. While Encolpius is looking at some paintings in a gallery, he runs into Eumolpus, a distinguished looking but shabby elderly man who turns out to be a (bad) poet. Eumolpus tells Encolpius an amusing story about his sexual adventures with a young man in Pergamum, then goes into a diatribe about the decline of the arts through greed. They look at a painting which inspires Eumolpus to recite a long poem on the fall of Troy, which is so badly received by some other listeners that they start to throw stones at him. Escaping to the baths, Encolpius meets up with Giton again, and makes off with him while Eumolpus recites more poetry. Somehow Giton contrives to disappear again, which distresses Encolpius so much that he attempts to hang himself in his lodgings. Eumolpus and Giton come back in the nick of time, whereupon Giton stages what turns out to be a mock suicide of his own. The ensuing chaos brings the landlord to investigate, and a fight breaks out which is only stopped when the manager of the lodging-house, who is a friend of Eumolpus, turns up. It then emerges that Ascyltos is offering a reward for the recovery of Giton, whom Encolpius hides under the bed until Ascyltos has gone, only for Eumolpus to threaten to betray them and claim the reward. Somehow a reconciliation is effected, and Encolpius, Giton and Eumolpus decide to go away together by ship. Unfortunately the ship turns out to belong Lichas, and on board it is a woman called Tryphaena, with both of whom Encolpius has had affairs and offended, and from whom he has been trying to escape. Despite disguising themselves, Encolpius and Giton are recognized (Lichas recognizes Encolpius by his penis), and another fight ensues. When an uneasy truce breaks out, Eumolpus entertains the ship's company by telling them the story of a widow of Ephesus. A storm then blows up, and the ship is wrecked; when they get ashore, the friends discover that Lichas has drowned. They find that they are near Croton, which is said to be rife with legacy-hunters who ingratiate themselves with rich people in the hope of gaining bequests in their wills. On the road to Croton, they hatch a plan: Eumolpus is to pretend to be wealthy, childless and ill, and Encolpius and Giton to pose as his slaves. To while away the rest of the journey, Eumolpus recites a long poem on the Roman civil war. In Croton, the plan seems to be working well, when Encolpius meets an apparently wealthy woman called Circe, who is sexually attracted to slaves, which she believes Encolpius to be. When Encolpius is again afflicted by impotence, he seeks the help of a witch and a priestess of Priapus, but only manages to offend the god again by inadvertently killing a goose sacred to him. The end of the surviving section of the book is another fragmentary sex scene involving Eumolpus, Encolpius and the son and daughter of a female legacy hunter, though it is apparent by this time that their deception is wearing thin.

It is obvious that the plot of the *Satyrica* owes a good deal to that of the *Odyssey*. Like Odysseus, Encolpius is constantly on the move and has offended a god; not, in his case, one of the Olympians like Poseidon, but the minor fertility god Priapus, whose effigy, complete with oversized phallus, was frequently to be found in gardens. The reference to the beguiling Circe is an obvious one; less overt but fairly clear is that Encolpius' visit to Trimalchio evokes the traditional epic *katabasis*, a descent to the underworld; the episode is full of references to death and Trimalchio's household operates very much as a world of its own, with Trimalchio as its 'king' (the name Malchus was a common slave name, and ironically means 'king': Trimalchio is thus 'three times a king'). Our heroes also find it extraordinarily difficult to get out of his house: Odysseus does not actually enter the underworld, but Virgil's Aeneas does, and is warned by the Sybil that anyone can go down to the underworld: the problem is getting out again. This is not to say that the *Satyrica* is a slavish parody of the *Odyssey*: Petronius is too subtle a writer for that; rather there are unmistakable resonances with the *Odyssey*, somewhat as James Joyce's *Ulysses* evokes the *Odyssey* without specifically imitating it.

Other genres are apparently similarly parodied. The standard plot of Greek novels (see below on the Greek novel for possible influences on Petronius) involved a pair of chaste and faithful heterosexual lovers who, after various vicissitudes (including shipwreck and attempted suicides: see plot summary), are ultimately reunited. The bisexual Encolpius and Giton are anything but chaste, except insofar as Encolpius' Priapic affliction inhibits his activities, and we do not know what happens to them in the end, but they do keep getting back together and, in their fashion, remain faithful to each other.

The poetry that regularly recurs in the text is clearly parodic. Eumolpus' poem on the civil war can only evoke Lucan's epic on the same theme; and that on the fall of Troy seems fairly certainly to parody the style of Seneca's tragedies. If Petronius was Nero's *elegantiae arbiter*, he will have known both of these men. It may also be significant that Nero is said to have sung about the fall of Troy during the fire that ravaged Rome in 64. It has indeed been suggested (perhaps not altogether convincingly) that the tasteless and extravagant Trimalchio himself, who also composes bad poetry and is excessively fond of music, is a satire on Nero: we should need to know more about the doings of the imperial household to be able to pursue this parallel further. Trimalchio's dinner party, though, is undoubtedly a parody of symposium literature, such as that by Plato: like Socrates and his friends, Trimalchio and the other freedmen tell stories and reflect on life (on a rather different level); the entry of Habinnas, drunk, recalls that of Alcibiades in Plato's *Symposium*.

As I noted above, the title *Satyrica* evokes not only satyrs, and makes us think about sexual activity and drinking, of which there is a good deal in the book; it also evokes the idea of satire. There are in it plenty of the regular objects of Roman satire, such as legacy hunters, wealthy freedmen, lecherous women and bad poets. But Petronius' satire is of a rather different nature from that of, for example, Juvenal. Trimalchio, Eumolpus and the rest are offered to us as figures of fun, to be laughed at, and indeed sometimes with, rather than targets to be shot at. They are, for all their vices and absurdities, human. Eumolpus is pompous, long-winded and deceitful; but he does not, in the end, seem to be a bad man. And Trimalchio, ostentatious, superstitious, tasteless and maudlin as he is, is nevertheless oddly sympathetic.

Perhaps it is because Petronius appears to us to be observing and reporting rather than preaching that he was able to create in Trimalchio arguably the greatest comic figure in classical literature: for all his excesses, he remains human, and therefore believable.

One way in which Petronius distances himself from the censoriousness that can easily come to dominate satire is in his choice of narrator. We see everything that happens through the eyes of Encolpius, who is hardly within his rights to be censorious about anything. Although clearly an educated man and interested in rhetoric and the arts (the conversations he has with Agamemnon and Eumolpus about these subjects have been seen by some as reflecting Petronius' own views: but they too are surely meant to be read as parodic), he is a thief and a sponger, sexually amoral and even apparently a murderer (of a man named Lycurgus, during a robbery, the circumstances of which are not clear): an anti-hero rather than a hero, in a world where there are no heroes. His is by no means the only voice we hear in the book, but it is he who holds the narrative together. And it is one of Petronius' great achievements that the narrative does hold together. It is interspersed with other stories, with the speeches and musings of a great range of other characters, and with references to what has gone before, and it is a tribute to Petronius' mastery of his art that, even though perhaps less than a quarter of the whole book survives, we can not only make narrative sense of what we have, but also largely reconstruct what must have happened at least in the earlier parts of the book.

The movement of the narrative is helped by Petronius' style. Encolpius' narrative voice is clear, elegant and unmannered, and it is reasonable to suppose that it approximates to the way an educated but not especially literary man would have told such a story. Other characters speak in appropriate registers: the literary criticism offered by Agamemnon and Eumolpus is rhetorical; the speech of Trimalchio and the freedmen is colourful and lively, though not coarse. The extent to which it represents the way such people really spoke is controversial, but it seems likely that Petronius' ear for variations in speech register was reliable, and that they are reasonably realistically represented: the freedmen are, after all, if not educated, nevertheless men who have succeeded in business, and not to be thought of as stupid, even if their good taste may be faulted. Petronius is a competent writer of verse and no more: when writing as Eumolpus, of course, it would be contrary to his aim to produce verse of high quality.

The *Satyrica* used to enjoy an unfortunate reputation as a dirty book. It is not. There is, it is true, a good deal of sex in it, and the characters are hardly models of ethical behaviour. But it is never coarse: the sex is described in a matter-of-fact or humorous manner, not pornographically. It is an aspect of the life of a man like Encolpius, and is neither glossed over nor especially emphasized. It has been suggested that, in contrast for example to the idealization typical of the Greek novel, Petronius is presenting life realistically, even though the situations and characters might be described as larger than life. The *Satyrica* certainly introduces us to a side of Roman life rarely encountered elsewhere in Latin literature, and presents it unforgettably. Petronius is one of the original geniuses of classical literature, and it is a source of great regret that his book has not survived intact.

Although less original than the *Satyrica*, the other great surviving work of Latin prose fiction, the *Metamorphoses* of Apuleius (*c.* 125–after 170) is also a fascinating book, and its author himself a remarkable man. He was born at Madauros in north Africa and educated at Carthage (then a considerable centre of culture), Athens and Rome. He eventually seems to have returned to Carthage and to have been figure of some consequence there. Apuleius may best be described as a sophist, like his mostly Greek contemporaries of the second sophistic: that is, he lived by practising and teaching rhetoric; Stephen Harrison (Harrison, 2000b: v) characterizes him accurately as a 'professional intellectual and display orator' – a definition which fits most sophists of the period. Many books now lost were attributed to him, on subjects as diverse as medicine, history and natural history. Apart from the *Metamorphoses*, three other works survive, *De Deo Socratis*, on Platonic philosophy, apparently a speciality of his, the *Florida*, extracts from his speeches presumably collected to demonstrate his virtuosity, and the *Apologia*, a version of a speech delivered by him in court when prosecuted by relatives of his wife, who was older than him, and wealthy, on the grounds that he had persuaded her to marry him by means of magic (which was taken seriously in the ancient world).

The *Metamorphoses* is the story of a young man called Lucius, of literary and philosophical interests but inquisitive and credulous. On a visit to Thessaly, generally regarded as a hotbed of witchcraft, he learns that Pamphila, the wife of his host, is an accomplished witch. He embarks on an affair with her maid, Photis. One evening, returning drunk from a dinner party, he is attacked by robbers, whom he kills, and is consequently put on trial. He uses all his rhetorical skills in his defence, only to find that his is a mock trial, set up as part of the town's festival of Laughter, and that the supposed robbers were in fact wine-skins. But it turns out that the wine-skins had been magically animated by Photis in a piece of magic that had gone wrong. He persuades Photis to let him watch Pamphila practising magic, and sees her turn into a bird. He persuades Photis to do the same for him, but she manages only to turn him into an ass. Before the antidote (roses) can be administered, he and the other domestic animals are stolen by robbers, and he remains an ass until the last book of the story (which consists of eleven books). While with the robbers, he hears the story of Cupid and Psyche (which takes up more than two books, and is often read separately), told by an old woman who works for the robbers to a girl whom they have abducted, Charite. Lucius escapes from the robbers when Charite's boyfriend Tlepolemus turns up disguised as a robber, gains their confidence, then drugs their drink. For a while he works, in ass-form, on Tlepolemus' farm, but Tlepolemus and Charite both die, and the slaves run away, taking him with them. He is then owned by various people and undergoes various sufferings, until one of his owners notices that he can do various un-ass-like things, and he is put on show as a curiosity. A rich woman takes a fancy to him, and has sex with him in his ass-form, which prompts his owner to offer him to do the same with a condemned female poisoner, in the arena. Appalled at this prospect, he manages to escape. Waking on the beach at Cenchreae near Corinth and seeing the moon, he prays for deliverance. She appears to him as the goddess Isis, and undertakes to transform him back at her festival, which is about to be celebrated. Back in human form, he becomes an initiate of Isis, and eventually a priest of her cult at Rome.

The story is not original. A condensed version of it, the *Ass Romance*, is included in the works of the Greek writer Lucian (see below), though clearly not by him, and it is known that a longer form of this existed, either by Lucian or by an earlier writer. Apuleius' version seems to be longer still, and much more complex. The basic narrative is much extended by his inclusion of other stories, which Lucius hears from various people: the Cupid and Psyche episode is only the longest amongst many. Lucius, or the ass, narrates it in the first person, and the narrative voice is itself complex: the Lucius narrator appears to have many of the characteristics and interests of Apuleius himself, and the last book has been seen as referring to his own 'conversion'; Isis tells Lucius that his transformation was a result of his devotion to pleasure and foolish curiosity. It is not necessary to go as far as this: Apuleius was certainly interested in religion and the occult, and appearance and reality (an important feature of Platonic philosophy) and it may simply be that, finding the ass story a congenial vehicle for his abstruse form of storytelling, he decided that it was necessary to explain why Lucius had to undergo such an ordeal (no explanation is given in the Greek version).

Stephen Harrison has called the *Metamorphoses* 'a sophist's novel' (Harrison 2000b: chapter heading), which is a fair description. It contains a good deal of learning and rhetoric, though the learning is not obtrusive and the rhetoric does not hinder the narrative drive of the book. There are echoes of Homer, of Plato, of Greek tragedy, of the Greek novel, of forensic oratory. There is a strong vein of satire, on man's inhumanity to man (and to asses), on sexual morality, on venality, on gullibility – perhaps even, at the end, on religion. Overall, though, perhaps it should not be taken seriously: a sophist enjoying himself. At the beginning of the narrative proper, Apuleius says *lector, intende; laetaberis*: 'reader, get on with the story; you'll enjoy it.'

Further reading

The texts of Apuleius and Petronius can be found in the Loeb series. For general introductions and collections of articles on the novel, see Hagg (1983); Harrison (1999); Hoffman (1999); Holzberg (1994); Tatum (1994); Whitmarsh (2007). There has been a lot of work on both Petronius and

Apuleius in recent years. On Petronius, see Connors (1998); Conte (1996); Courtney (2001); Slater (1990). For Apuleius, see Finkelpearl (1998); Harrison (2000b); Winkler (1985).

THE GREEK NOVEL

Until fairly recently, the Greek novel has been a neglected genre. Scholars were mostly preoccupied with its origins rather than with the novels themselves, which were considered to be an inferior class of literature. The latter seems to an extent to have been the opinion of the Greeks themselves: other genres of literature, from epic poetry to historiography, were written about by critics extensively; novels get only the occasional, uncomplimentary, mention. Yet they were read a good deal – as the preservation of manuscripts of them, and the number of papyrus fragments which turn up, testifies. Attempts to preserve the dignity of the Greek reading public were made by suggesting that novels were read by people of an inferior level of education, or by women or children (which, by implication, was the same thing). But to read a text as long as even the shorter novels would require a high degree of literacy, if not of literariness: even the least ambitious of them presupposes a knowledge of other literary genres; there is nothing in the novels particularly likely to attract a young readership, and to argue that a woman who managed to attain the level of literacy required to read an extended text would then be satisfied with an inferior product is clearly nonsense. (The argument that women might read novels because their heroines are often women of some character who think and act for themselves is a better one, but not ultimately convincing.) The subtext of all this was that Greeks, being serious people, only read Great Literature, and the novels are not great literature. Both of these premises are faulty. Most readers would probably agree that, if we are to think in hierarchical terms, the Greek novels are not as great as, say, the *Iliad*. But they are not bad: the plots are generally carefully worked out, they are often entertaining, some are very well written, some require a considerable degree of literary sophistication to comprehend fully. And no one finds it odd nowadays that the same person will one day read a serious book, and at another time read a crime novel or science fiction. Of course, such a reader may insist that he or she really prefers the serious stuff: no doubt the Greeks said that too, but the evidence suggests that they read the novels all the same.

The question of origins arises because the novel – that is to say, an extended work of fiction, in prose – is something of a latecomer on the literary scene: as far as we can tell, the genre as we know it does not get going until (probably) the first century BCE, and only becomes popular somewhat later. The typical novel plot is not unlike the typical plot of new comedy; the wanderings, and eventual homecoming, of many characters in novels evoke the *Odyssey*; some of the novels had historical or pseudo-historical settings; the emphasis on romantic love is reminiscent of some Hellenistic poetry; the plots of some novels show decided similarities with narratives known from other near-eastern literatures. But this does not mean that the genre is a direct descendant of any of these. The most direct ancestor is perhaps Xenophon's *Cyropaedia*, a fictional biography of Cyrus the Great, but more fiction than biography. No fewer than three novelists were known as Xenophon, which seems, as John Morgan says, 'two too many to be a coincidence' (Morgan and Stoneman, 1994: 5), suggesting that the name may have been used as a pseudonym, and that the novelists regarded themselves as working in the tradition of Xenophon. But this does not mean that the novel tradition descends from the *Cyropaedia* alone: it is merely one influence amongst many.

It does, however, certainly seem surprising that it took so long for a tradition of writing extended prose fiction to become established. After all, we all tell stories, and we tell them in prose. And there is no lack of prose narrative in earlier Greek literature: plenty of episodes in the Greek historians read like fiction (and some of them probably are); and when a forensic orator like Lysias presents a jury with an account of events relevant to his case, he is doing something not very different from what a novelist does in shaping his narrative. One factor militating against the development of prose fiction was no doubt the tradition of storytelling in verse. The Greeks were highly genre-conscious: prose was used for some purposes, verse for others; particular metres within the verse context were again linked with particular subject areas. The accepted medium for epic, because of the historical fact of the existence in early Greece of a class of highly skilled storytellers in verse, was hexameter poetry, and, for epic subject matter of high seriousness such as the *Iliad*, continued to be. But the *Odyssey* is much closer to the world of imaginative fiction (Odysseus himself is a formidable creator of fictions), both in terms of its plot and of its combination of the mundane and the fantastic, which has echoes in perhaps all the Greek novels. At some point, we may conjecture, the first Greek novelist, whoever he was, realized that such material could as well be presented in prose as in verse. It is probably not accidental that the novel appears to be a creation of the late Hellenistic period when, as I pointed out above, verse seems to have been somewhat in decline. Furthermore, the production of novels seems to have reached its height during the period known as the second sophistic, which especially privileged prose over verse: there are many passages in the works of the sophistic display-orators which read like condensed novels; some of the novels we have may actually have been written by sophists.

How many Greek novels survive depends rather on what we define as a novel. If our definition is simply to be 'a work of imaginative prose fiction', we are spreading our net quite widely. There is, however, a smaller group of five fully extant works which are more closely connected by similarities in plot (their dates are often uncertain: those given here represent as nearly as possible the general consensus of scholars as it stands at the moment): *Chaereas and Callirhoe* by Chariton of Aphrodisias (first century BCE or CE); the *Ephesiaca* of Xenophon of Ephesus (mid-second century); *Leucippe and*

Clitophon by Achilles Tatius (late second century); *Daphnis and Chloe* by Longus (*c.* 200); and the *Aethiopica* by Heliodorus (third or fourth century). We know of a number of others either from fragments or through references in other writers.

There is no room here to summarize or discuss each of them. They can be grouped together because of a broad similarity in plot, which is roughly as follows: a handsome young man and a beautiful girl meet and fall in love; they get separated and pass through all sorts of vicissitudes and threats to their fidelity and to their lives – pirates, robbers, storms at sea, other people falling in love with them and so on; despite all this, they remain faithful and in the end, having often travelled long distances, they are reunited and, we assume, live happily ever after. Obviously there are considerable differences in the authors' treatment of their stories, characterization and style. Some have a more or less specific historical and/or geographical setting: Chariton, for example, starts his off in Syracuse just after the defeat of the Athenian invasion – Callirhoe is the daughter of the general Hermocrates, who actually existed. Some of the plots are more complex, and their authors' narrative techniques more ambitious, than others: Heliodorus' is much the longest, and told in an imaginative and sophisticated fashion, in highly literary language by contrast, say, with that of Xenophon of Ephesus. Achilles Tatius uses a first-person narrator, the story being supposedly told to the writer by its protagonist; the other four are told in the third person; *Daphnis and Chloe* purports to be take as its starting point a painting the author has seen in Lesbos – a greatly extended example of the rhetorical device of *ecphrasis*, a description of a scene or a work of art. The characters of the protagonists obviously vary considerably: Longus' Daphnis and Chloe are naive young country folk, and their adventures are to do with their journey to maturity rather than geographical journeyings (and they turn out, surprise surprise, really to be the children of aristocrats). Longus may have been a sophist, and Achilles Tatius too; the latter's (highly rhetorical) take on the novel may be seen as ironic. Achilles and Heliodorus are both said by Christian writers to have abandoned the writing of frivolous literature and become bishops, which is pretty surely wishful thinking designed to alleviate the guilt feelings of the pious in wasting their time reading such nonsense: some of our information about the novels comes from Photius, a ninth-century patriarch of Constantinople, who rather disapproved of them, but read them nevertheless.

If, as I said, we choose to spread our net more widely and include other types of imaginative fiction, we can extend our list of novels considerably. We have a summary of the plot of Antonius Diogenes' *Wonders Beyond Thule* (perhaps second century), which seems to have been highly complex and to have concentrated on the travel theme rather than love interest. Fictitious travel narratives had a long history in Greece: we know of examples from the early Hellenistic period by Euhemerus and Iambulus, both of which contained a utopian element which may derive from more or less fanciful accounts of faraway places such as India which became current in the wake of Alexander the Great's expeditions. Alexander himself became the subject of an enormously popular story, told in Greek (in various versions) and translated into Latin and many other languages, the *Alexander Romance*. Travel books were parodied by Lucian (second century) in his amusing *True Story* (often know by its Latin title of *Vera Historia*), in which his travellers get as far as the moon (he considerately warns us at the beginning that none of this is true). Travel is an important ingredient in the *Life of Apollonius of Tyana* of the sophist Philostratus (early third century CE), a fictionalized biography of a (real) wonder-working Pythagorean magus of the first century. The tradition of fictionalized biography went back to Xenophon of Athens, as mentioned above, and some purportedly genuine biography verges on the fictional – Xenophon's own *Agesilaus*, for example: fairly obviously apocryphal material could be tolerated in the context of the genre for its exemplary or didactic function. In the same way, fiction might have a purpose beyond mere entertainment. Euhemerus' utopian fiction, mentioned above, clearly did, and there is evidence that Apollonius of Tyana was elevated by some pagans into something like a rival to Christ, whose followers were becoming a major force by the time Philostratus wrote. Although their attitude to pagan literature remained equivocal, Christian writers of any degree of education had necessarily been trained in pagan literary traditions, and their writings reflect this: thus some early Christian writings – the *Shepherd of Hermas*, some of the *Apocryphal Acts of the Apostles*, for example – fairly clearly exhibit characteristics derived from the novel, appropriately Christianized.

Since well educated Latin speakers would generally know Greek as well, it is not surprising to find Apuleius, the Latin sophist, adapting a Greek novel (see the previous section in this chapter). All other surviving Latin novels similarly depend on Greek originals, apart from the *Satyrica*. The relationship between Petronius and the Greek novel is less clear. According to conventional chronology, the Greek novel was in its infancy at the time Petronius wrote. On the other hand, of course, he only needed to have read one to have been inspired to create a Latin counterpart: a fragment of a novel by Iolaus has recently been discovered, which appears to have had a similar low-life setting, and to have used verse as well as prose. He may also have been influenced by the *Milesiaca*, Milesian tales, of one Aristides, apparently short erotic prose pieces contained within an overarching narrative, which were translated into Latin probably not long after they were written in the early first century BCE. Apuleius knew them, and the stories of the Widow of Ephesus and the Pergamene Boy in the *Satyrica* are generally considered to be examples of the genre.

Further reading

The texts of Chariton and Achilles Tatius can be found in the Loeb series; for the text of Longus, see also Reeve (1994). For the text of Xenophon of

Ephesus, see Dalmeyde (1962) and Papanikolaou (1973); for the text of Heliodorus, see Colonna (1938); Rattenburg *et al.*, (1960). Translations of the novels are collected in Reardon (1989). For a good introduction to later Greek literature, see Dihle (1994); Winkler and Williams (1982). Recent years have seen a growth in critical work on the Greek novel; see, for instance, Goldhill (1995, concerned mainly with sexuality); Hagg (1983); Holzberg (1994); Morgan and Stoneman (1994); Swain (1999); Tatum (1994); Whitmarsh (2007). On Longus, see Hunter (1983); MacQueen (1990). On Lucian, see Bracht (1989); Jones (1986). On Achilles Tatius, see Morales (2004); Whitmarsh and Morales (2003).

THE REVIVAL OF GREEK PROSE LITERATURE

An important aspect of the revival of Greek literature during the early Roman empire was the movement known as the second sophistic. The original, mostly itinerant, sophists of the fifth and fourth centuries BCE had been teachers of rhetoric, and sometimes philosophy. Their reputation was mixed – serious philosophers often disapproved of rhetoric as it has no necessary regard for truth – but they fulfilled a need in providing a kind of higher education, which was otherwise largely unavailable, and they may be seen as forerunners of the literary scholars of the Hellenistic period and of the Greek teachers to whom rich Romans sent their sons to train in rhetoric. (Rhetoric had become more respectable since the fourth century, to a considerable extent as a result of Isocrates' redefining of it as an educational discipline, with emphasis on moral issues rather than mere persuasion; Plato still disapproved, however; see 1g, 6a.)

Higher education in the early Roman empire consisted essentially either of rhetoric or philosophy: some young men studied both. Either could, of course, be studied nearer home, but a wealthy student (Greek or Roman, or indeed from anywhere in the empire) would go, for philosophy, to Alexandria or to Athens, where the 'schools' founded by the great classical philosophers still flourished. For rhetoric, major centres were Ephesus and Pergamum, as well as Athens: Greek culture, influential in the west, was universal in the east, with contacts between its centres facilitated by the stability of the *pax Romana*. It is sometimes maintained that the domination of Rome (and, earlier, that of Macedon and the Hellenistic kings who succeeded Alexander) devalued oratory in the Greek world. It is certainly true that the new breed of sophist was much devoted to *epideictic* oratory – display oratory designed to show off the speaker's skill rather than for any practical purpose. And some sophists were undoubtedly prima donnas whose principal concerns were to further their own reputations (and undermine those of their rivals) and to entertain their (frequently large) audiences. But there were still plenty of opportunities for the practical application of rhetoric: in the law courts, in town councils, at civic ceremonies, and so on, and sophists can be found in action in all of these spheres. Many, indeed, were important figures in their own communities; unlike some of the earlier sophists, they were often men from influential backgrounds, and frequently rich: Herodes Atticus, for example (c. 101–77), the Athenian sophist, was fabulously wealthy and used his resources to erect some fine new buildings at Athens and in other parts of Greece. Herodes became consul at Rome in 143, along with the Latin sophist Fronto, whom he knew – an interesting illustration of the coming together of Greek and Latin cultures – and was a friend of the emperor Marcus Aurelius (whom Fronto had tutored as a young man). He was also arrogant and quarrelsome, but well exemplifies the status to which sophists could now aspire, as well as their important function as intermediaries between the Greek world and its Roman masters. Apart from their public activities, most sophists spent much of their time on their traditional occupation of teaching: official recognition of their importance came when the emperor Vespasian (69–79) allowed teachers of rhetoric tax dispensations, and also established 'chairs' of rhetoric at Rome (one for Greek, one for Latin). Similar privileges were extended to teachers of rhetoric in many cities of the empire, an acknowledgment of their importance in providing, along with the schools of philosophy, a higher education which was a distant ancestor of the medieval university education, and thus of today's universities.

The period of the second sophistic is generally regarded as extending from the late first century to c. 230. But the terminal date is defined only by the lifetime of Philostratus, a sophist himself, who in his *Lives of the Sophists* was the first to identify the second sophistic as a literary phenomenon. In fact, sophists continued to be important figures until the fourth century and beyond: a large number of speeches and letters of Libanius of Antioch, who died c. 393, for example, survive and show that he was still doing much the same things as the sophists of two centuries previously, except that by now rhetoric was employed in the service of Christianity; Libanius was in fact a pagan, but two of his students, John Chrysostom and Basil of Caesarea, were important figures in the early church.

Not very much of the writings of Philostratus' sophists has survived, apart from a good deal of the output of the remarkable Aelius Aristides (117–after 181), in the shape of speeches, hymns to the gods (in prose, significantly, in an age which privileged prose over verse), and the *Hieroi Logoi*, an account of Aristides' religious experiences whilst receiving treatment for illness at the temple of Asclepius at Pergamum, and a unique document of pagan personal religiosity, as well as of Aristides' hypochondria. Although his ill health prevented him from playing as large a part in public life as some sophists, we find him fulfilling the typical sophistic role of intermediary between the Greek and Roman worlds in an appeal to the emperor Marcus Aurelius for aid for the city of Smyrna after an earthquake; his speech delivered at the Panathenaic festival reveals an intimate knowledge of classical Greek history, and another in praise of Rome emphasizes the unity of Greco-Roman culture in his day, and the role of Rome as facilitator of the spread of Hellenism. All of this, of course, is expressed in classical Attic Greek.

Aristides was not much interested in philosophy. One travelling rhetorician who was, was Dio of Prusa (Dio Cocceianus, or Dio Chrysostom: *c.* 40/50–after 110). Dio was a man of some importance in his native city who studied philosophy, and practised as a rhetorician at Rome. Exiled by the emperor Domitian, he spent some time travelling and lecturing (and, by his own account, impoverished) before being restored to imperial favour under Trajan. He later returned to Prusa. Many speeches survive, on all manner of subjects, generally with some didactic, rather than simply epideictic, purpose: evidently he thought of himself as a teacher of men rather than simply an entertainer, though this does not mean that he is universally serious – one of his most agreeable works, the *Euboicus*, describes his adventures after being shipwrecked on Euboea and looked after by the local people, whose unspoilt way of life he contrasts with that of the urban poor. Dio himself is critical of sophists and their love of display, but, to the outside world, he must have looked very like one.

Dio, like most sophists, wrote Attic Greek and was interested in the Greek past whilst acknowledging the political realities of his time. Another important figure who looks superficially like a sophist, but in this case certainly is not, is Plutarch (before 50–after 120). He did indeed study rhetoric, and some epideictic declamations of his survive, but he was not an Atticist, and his main achievements were in the fields of philosophy and biography. Like many sophists, though, he travelled – from his home in Chaeronea in Greece, to Athens, to Rome, to Alexandria and Asia, and back to Chaeronea – and was friendly with important Romans. His biographies are an important source of historical information, though they can be frustrating for the historian as Plutarch's prime interest is in character rather than deeds. Their subjects include famous Greeks from the classical and more recent past, as well as Romans: many of them are arranged in pairs, for the purposes of comparison; there is no doubt that, for Plutarch, Greece is the true home of civilization, and that he viewed Rome from the point of view of an outsider, but also accepted that their histories were now inextricably interwoven. His philosophical works, known as the *Moralia*, are not serious or innovative philosophy, but rather the practical application of philosophy in everyday life – in the family, for example, or within marriage. Many are in the form of dialogues, and are by no means restricted to philosophy: Plutarch shows interest in almost all areas of life, from the natural world to constitutional matters to literary criticism.

Another writer of the period who cannot be considered a sophist, despite his antiquarian subject matter and interest in writing classical Greek, is Pausanias (fl. 150), whose *Journey through Greece* is the only guide book to classical Greece that has survived, though it belongs to the tradition of the *periēgēsis*, a type of writing listing the coastal towns and features which would be encountered on a sea-journey from one place to another. There is some useful historical information in Pausanias, and his book has also been of use to archaeologists excavating sites that he discusses, and art historians interested in recreating works of art he describes in the course of his travels.

A more important literary figure of the period is Lucian (c. 120–after 180). He too travelled extensively. He was born in Syria, and tells us that Greek was his second language – both of which facts testify to the international nature of Hellenic culture under Rome in his time, as does his later appointment to a post on the staff of the praefectus of Egypt. His Greek is strictly Attic – as good as that of any of the sophists – though he mocks the pretensions of the purist Atticists, and presumably made his living as an orator and teacher of philosophy, to which he says he was converted in middle age. But he mocks philosophers too, and indeed he mocks just about everything, including religion, and especially anyone he considers false or pretentious. Lucian wrote in a wide variety of forms, including dialogue, Menippean satire (see above), and even a parody of the novel (the *Vera Historia*). His knowledge of classical literature was vast, but he wears his learning lightly; his satire is cutting, but not bitter, and he is often genuinely funny.

A brief mention should be made of a younger contemporary of Lucian who, while by no means solely a sophist, nevertheless shared with them an interest in rhetoric and language, and philosophy, and is one of the major figures of all time in the history of his field: the physician Galen (c. 130–early third century). Galen was born in Pergamum, studied in Alexandria, and spent much time in Rome, eventually as court physician to Marcus Aurelius. He wrote on all aspects of medicine, and also found time to write on grammar, rhetoric, philosophy and psychology; a man of great energy and intellect, he is a key figure in the transmission of Greek medical theory and practice to the middle ages.

The Philostratus whose *Lives of the Sophists* was responsible for identifying the phenomenon of the second sophistic has already been mentioned, both for this and for his novelistic biography of Apollonius of Tyana. Either he or another Philostratus (the name ran in the family, and there may have been at least three Philostrati), around the beginning of the third century, put together a collection of descriptions of paintings supposedly seen in a gallery at Naples: the description of a work of art – *ecphrasis* – as a literary genre went back to Homer's shield of Achilles, and as description of all kinds was a regular exercise in the training of an orator. The writer of these *ecphraseis*, then, is putting on an exhibition of his rhetorical skill, and incidentally giving us a rare insight into how an educated Greek might 'read' a work of art. Perhaps about the same time that Philostratus was documenting the second sophistic, an otherwise unknown writer, Diogenes Laertius, was putting together a series of biographies of famous philosophers; these are of indifferent quality, but preserve a considerable number of quotations from earlier writings, and are valuable for that. Two other important compilers were at work around the same time: the Egyptian Greek Athenaeus' enormous *Deipnosophistai* purports to be an account of conversations at a dinner party at which various erudite guests (Galen is one) discuss at great length everything conceivable to do with food and drink, and other things; it is a valuable repository of quotations from and references to authors and works otherwise lost (see 1k on texts and fragments). The other was Aelian, who compiled a *Historical Miscellany* (*Varia Historia*), which is what it says: a collection of anecdotal extracts from all manner of historical sources, with no apparent purpose other than entertainment; and a longer book *On the Characteristics of Animals*, which is similar in construction, or lack of it. The latter is in the tradition of *paradoxography*: a *paradoxon* is something 'contrary to what one would expect'; paradoxography probably started with Aristotle and his school, in the form of collections of facts that needed scientific explanation, but had evolved into a minor genre of its own in the Hellenistic period and later – a sort of *Guinness Book of Records* type of literature. (A collection by Phlegon of Tralles, a freedman of Hadrian, contains, amongst other things, some accounts of ghosts, notes on people who spontaneously changed sex and a list of people who lived to be more than a hundred.)

Further reading

All authors, except Phlegon, referred to in this section can be found in the Loeb series. Phlegon's *Book of Marvels* is translated by Hansen (1996). For a good introduction to later Greek literature, see Dihle (1994); Winkler and Williams (1982). On the second sophistic, see Anderson (1993); Bowersock (1969); Whitmarsh (2005). On rhetoric, see Kennedy (1994); Worthington (2007).

LATIN PROSE LITERATURE OF THE LATER EMPIRE

An interesting point about Aelian is that, although an Italian born and bred, he chose to write in (Attic) Greek. The second sophistic, since it was centred on the revival of Attic, necessarily did not extend to Latin, though there were Latin sophists too: Apuleius has already been mentioned. Another man who might reasonably be regarded as a sophist, being a rhetorician, a notable orator and lawyer, as well as grammarian and teacher, is Cornelius Fronto (c. 95–c. 166), some of whose speeches have survived, as well as a good number of letters, many addressed to Marcus Aurelius (emperor 161–80). Fronto could write Greek, but usually used Latin; Marcus Aurelius himself, whose tutor Fronto had been, choose to write his *Meditations* (as it is usually known) in Greek. His book is not much read nowadays, but has been enormously popular at various times, and is an interesting document: his philosophy (essentially stoic) is not original, but the reflections of a serious thinker who happened for 20 years to be the most powerful man in the world cannot be without interest.

Fronto seems to have known another man who can be seen as a Latin sophist, Aulus Gellius (born *c.* 125). Gellius had an impeccable sophistic pedigree, being a student of Favorinus, who was himself a student of Dio of Prusa, and a friend of Herodes Atticus. His one book, the *Noctes Atticae* ('Attic Nights': he started it, he says, when he was studying at Athens), is an interesting compilation of extracts from his reading, encompassing history, philosophy, grammar and anecdotes of various kinds. Atticism, in its literal sense, could have no meaning with regard to Latin, but Gellius (amongst others) shows that Roman scholars engaged in similar debates with regard to Latin: Gellius is an enthusiast for Sallust and earlier Latin, as opposed to that of the Augustan period.

A similar book of extracts, apparently for the use of orators seeking anecdotes with which to illustrate their speeches, dates from much earlier in the imperial period: Valerius Maximus' *Memorable Deeds and Sayings*, dedicated to Tiberius (emperor 14–37). These can be tediously moralistic, but preserve material from earlier writers that would otherwise be lost. The father of the philosopher and statesman Seneca, Seneca the Elder (*c.* 50 BCE–*c.* 40), preserves in his writings, supposedly compiled for his sons, some interesting material from the orators of his generation, as well as some poetic extracts. A fuller account of the training and education of the orator comes from the practising teacher of rhetoric Quintilian (*c.* 35–90s), who, like Seneca, originated from Spain. His *Institutio Oratoria* is a storehouse of information on rhetorical theory and practice, as well as more general literary criticism; in the educational tradition of Isocrates (see above), Quintilian insists on the need for an orator to be a good man as well as a good speaker: *vir bonus, dicendi peritus*.

The major historian of the early empire, Tacitus, the polymathic Suetonius and the younger Pliny, are discussed elsewhere (see 11e, f, g). Apart from Tacitus, the tendency of historians of the period seems predominantly to have been to produce summaries of earlier works. To an extent, this was probably a result of the cost and difficulty of keeping large books in many volumes: Livy's 142 books were summarized at least as early as the third century, and Florus' extant *Epitome of All the Wars of 1200 Years*, largely based on Livy, was probably written in the middle or late second century. A history produced in the time of Tiberius by Velleius Paterculus covered most of Roman history in just over one book, but the rest of the second of its two books is more detailed, and valuable as the work of a man who held important military commands under Tiberius. Little historical writing except Tacitus' survives from the early imperial period, apart from a history of Alexander the Great by Quintus Curtius, perhaps the man of this name who was consul in 43. Curtius' book is highly rhetorical and uncritical, but preserves some traditions about Alexander that would otherwise be lost.

Most later historiography consists either of summaries, such as those of Festus (fourth century) and Eutropius (probably of the same period), or is

largely in the biographical and anecdotal tradition of Suetonius and his late
republican predecessor, the superficial Cornelius Nepos (c. 110–24 BCE).
Such are the works of the fourth-century Aurelius Victor, and the *Historia
Augusta*. This, a collection of biographies of emperors from Hadrian onwards,
purports to be the work of several authors, and to include contemporary
documentary evidence; scholars now think it is all by one author, probably of
the later fourth century, and that most of the 'documentation' is bogus. One
distinguished exception to the poor quality of imperial historiography is
Ammianus Marcellinus (c. 330–95). Ammianus' first language was Greek,
which probably explains his complex and sometimes idiosyncratic Latin. He
was a high-ranking officer under the emperors Constantius II and Julian, and
participated himself in some of the campaigns he describes. Books 14–31 of
the original 31 survive. Ammianus is a powerfully descriptive writer and one
of the few reliable sources for later Roman history: if he had written about a
period more commonly studied, he would be considered one of the great
historians of the classical world.

Further reading

Translations and texts of all the authors here mentioned are available in the Loeb
series, except Aurelius Victor, whose text is available in Pichlmayr and Gruendel
(1970), a translation of which can be found in Bird (1994). In general, see Dihle
(1994); Kennedy and Clausen (1983). On Aulus Gellius, see Holford-Stevens
(1988); on Ammianus, see Kelly (2008); Matthews (1989); on Seneca, see
Fairweather (1981). On rhetoric as discussed in this section, see Dominik and
Hall (2006); on historiography, see Marincola (2007); Rohrbacher (2002).

LATER GREEK AND LATIN POETRY

The period of the second sophistic is generally regarded as an age which
privileged prose over verse, and to an extent this is true, both of Greek and
Latin. Of course, in both languages, poetry was still written, and while it is
true that not a great deal survives from the second and third centuries, all the
familiar classical genres continue to be represented (alongside some more
innovative productions) well into the late imperial period, and even, in Latin,
after the fall of the western empire (476) and, in Greek, under the Byzantine
empire. This account can only mention some of the major figures who are
particularly worth investigating.

Shorter poems in both languages continued to be written. The reign of the
philhellene Hadrian saw a brief revival of poetry, with the emperor himself at
the centre of a group of *poetae novelli*. One of Hadrian's freedmen, Mesomedes
of Crete, wrote lyric poetry in Greek for which, for once, some specimens of the
musical accompaniment survive. Throughout the second sophistic, collections

of epigrams, often written in the first century, like the *Garland* of Philip of Thessalonica (*c.* 40) and the influential work of the satirist Lucillius (*c.* 60), were garnered and circulated. Didactic poetry continues to be represented. In the second century, perhaps during the reign of Hadrian, one Dionysius, known as *Periēgētēs* (which means 'guide'), produced in Greek a versified geographical description of the world. (Other poems sometimes attributed to the same Dionysius include the very fragmentary *Bassarica* (stories about the god Dionysus), which may have influenced the later Nonnus, *Lithica* (on stones and gems, and involving Orpheus), *Ornithiaka* (on birds) and *Gigantias*.) Towards the end of the same century, two Greek didactic poems on fishing (*Halieutica*) and hunting (*Cynegetica*) respectively are both attributed to Oppian, though they are fairly clearly not by the same author; the *Halieutica* is surprisingly interesting, the *Cynegetica* less well written. A curiosity of around the same period which has not survived was a bizarre 'lipogrammatic' version of the *Iliad* by one Nestor of Laranda: book 1 is written without the letter alpha, book 2 without beta, and so on; some kind of Latin parallel can be found in the somewhat later (period of Constantine) word-game poems of Optatianus Porfyrius, whose collection includes acrostics, metrical games, poems in the shape of objects, and so on.

More serious, epic, verse was still being written. Probably in the third century Quintus of Smyrna wrote a 14-book continuation of the *Iliad* known as the *Posthomerica*, an interesting work influenced by Hellenistic epic, tragedy, and perhaps Latin epic, as well as Homer. Somewhat later, from Triphiodorus, an Egyptian (who also wrote a lost lipogrammatic *Odyssey* and a historical epic on the battle of Marathon), there survives a short epic on the capture of Troy. Two other short epics in Greek survive from around 500, one by another Egyptian, Colluthus, on the abduction of Helen, the other by the otherwise unknown Musaeus, on the story of Hero and Leander. These two poets were both influenced by the somewhat earlier epic by the important Nonnus, of Panopolis in Egypt, the *Dionysiaca*, one of the more remarkable (and one of the longest, at 48 books) poems to survive from the ancient world. This chronicles the career of Dionysus, culminating in his acceptance by Zeus as a deity. Nonnus uses and adapts to his own purposes all the techniques of Homeric epic, as well as incorporating (amongst other things) the psychological element and the learning characteristic of Hellenistic poetry, and influences from pastoral poetry and the novel. His language is exuberant and baroque. The result is not to everyone's taste, but repays attention. Nonnus may have been influenced by *Bassarica* (mentioned above and possibly by a Dionysius); he may also have looked at the *Heroic Marriages of the Gods*, composed in a staggering 60 books in the early third century by Pisander, the son of the aforementioned Nestor. (Another possible epic poem of late antiquity is the so-called *Orphic Argonautica*, in which Orpheus narrates the story of the argonauts.) Historical epic is also found, even after the end of the western empire: the Latin poet Corippus, from north Africa, wrote at Constantinople epics on the emperor Justinian and one of his generals, which survive, and

Christodorus, from Egypt, wrote epics in Greek on contemporary events, which do not. There are also some fragments of an early fifth-century epic, the *Blemyomachia* (*Battle against the Blemmyes*), which is sometimes attributed to Olympiodorus of (Egyptian) Thebes.

Perhaps the greatest Latin poet of the late empire was also, curiously, a Greek-speaking Egyptian, Claudian (died *c.* 405). He wrote some Greek poetry, but most of his output was in Latin – of such a classical type that it has been said that if we did not know his date, he might easily be taken as a poet of the early empire. Claudian was effectively the court poet of the emperor Honorius, and more especially of Honorius' counsellor and general Stilicho. Much of his poetry is thus celebratory or polemical, and of historical importance, but three books of an epic on the abduction of Proserpina, and the beginning of a *Giagantomachy*, survive, unfortunately incomplete. About the same time, one Avianus was writing fables in Latin elegiacs modelled on the Greek ones of Babrius (second century), and probably a little earlier the similarly named Rufius Festus Avienus was translating Greek didactic poems into Latin: the *Phaenomena* of the Hellenistic Aratus, on astronomy, and the geographical poem of Dionysius mentioned above; he also wrote an interesting *Ora Maritima*, describing the coasts of the Mediterranean, Black Sea and Atlantic Europe, of which some of the latter survives and preserves some important earlier material on exploration and geography. A younger contemporary of Claudian was Rutilius Claudius Namatianus, who wrote a description of a journey from Rome to his estate in Gaul, *De Reditu Suo*. Written not long after the sack of Rome by Alaric the Goth (410), and after Namatianus' own estates had suffered from the depredations of barbarians, it has not survived whole: what remains, in fine elegiacs, includes a splendid and, in the circumstances, moving eulogy of Rome; others after Namatianus wrote in the classical Latin tradition, and could still do it well, but it is hard not to read his poem as an epitaph on the dying empire of the west. The barbarians are within the gates; the glory has departed.

Further reading

There has been a great deal more critical work on later Greek poetry in recent years. See, for instance, Bowie (1990); Cameron (2004); Dewar in Taplin (2001); Dihle (1994); Hopkinson (1994); Paschalis (2005); Shorrock (2001); Whitby (1994); Whitmarsh (2001). For a good introduction to later Greek literature more generally, see Winkler and Williams (1982). The classic studies by Raby (1927 and 1934) are still invaluable for later Latin poetry.

CLASSICISM AND CHRISTIANITY: PROSE AND VERSE

Namatianus disliked Christians – or monks, at any rate. If he regarded Christianity as a major factor in the decline of Rome, he was not alone among the pagan aristocracy of his time. But such were now in a minority. Claudian may have been a pagan, but the imperial court at which he worked was emphatically Christian. Nonnus, however, despite the decidedly pagan nature of the *Dionysiaca*, also wrote a version of St John's Gospel in hexameters (normally called the *Paraphrase of St. John's Gospel*), which presumably indicates that he was a Christian, but saw no difficulty in moving between the two traditions.

Christianity had been on the increase in the empire from the first century. To begin with, most of its adherents came from the less well educated classes: the Greek New Testament Gospels, and the writings of St Paul, although clearly not the products of men of no education at all, show little influence from the classical tradition. But as Christianity spread, and permeated the higher classes of society, Christian literature came to be written, both in Greek and Latin, by people educated in the classical rhetorical tradition who, necessarily and in many cases no doubt unconsciously, wrote in a manner and style shaped by that tradition. Thus, by around 200, we find Clement of Alexandria, in Greek, and Tertullian, in Latin, both men educated in the classical tradition, using the rhetorical skills they had acquired through this education in the service of Christianity, in efforts to convince their contemporaries of the truth of the Christian faith. Many others followed the same path: Lactantius, the 'Christian Cicero' (*c.* 240–*c.* 320), a very fine and innovative writer of Latin prose, should not go without mention. Clement and Tertullian were also well versed in classical philosophy, which, especially in the form of neo-Platonism, continued to flourish and indeed – as Christian writers clearly recognized – constituted among the educated classes perhaps the chief rival to Christianity, with which it had some affinities: a Christian who reads, for example, Plotinus (205–69/70), the major neo-Platonist of late antiquity, will find much that is familiar. The battle between pagan and Christian, once joined, was waged long and vigorously, despite the considerable philosophical common ground; as late as the sixth century the emperor Justinian was sufficiently concerned by the persistence of classical philosophy to have found it necessary to close down the schools of philosophy at Athens – which, therefore, must still have been finding adherents. Sometimes the lines between the combatants were not clearly drawn: the writings of the important Christian thinker Origen (184/5–254/5), who defended his faith against the Platonic philosopher Celsus in his *Contra Celsum*, were later condemned as heretical by the church.

In the end, though, for the most part, the older classical tradition and the new Christian one came not only to co-exist, but to feed off each other, such that classical rhetoric (especially in Latin) came to be the vehicle of Christian thought, and Christian influences opened up new directions for the traditions of classical literature. Some, of course, in any case took their Christianity more seriously than others. Relations between Ausonius, the fourth-century poet, rhetorician and politician from Gaul (whose classicizing poetry, especially a poem on the River Moselle, is still worth reading) and his pupil Paulinus of Nola, who became a bishop, can be seen through their correspondence gradually to have cooled: Ausonius' Christianity, perhaps, was of a more superficial kind; Paulinus was prepared to follow his faith further. A contemporary of Paulinus' exemplifies the conflict between classicism and Christianity, and also some kind of resolution of it: Eusebius Hieronymus, or St Jerome. Classically educated, and a great lover of classical literature, as well as a devout Christian, monk and prolific writer, Jerome relates a dream in which he is challenged by the Lord with being less of Christian than a Ciceronian. As a result he gave up reading classical literature for a time, though he apparently returned to it later: true to this dual nature, when in his monastery at Bethlehem he heard the news of the sack of Rome by the Goths (410), he lamented it by reference to the biblical destruction of Moab — and to the fall of Troy.

A masterpiece of Latin prose, Jerome's great work was the translation of the Christian scriptures into Latin, the *Vulgate* which became the standard Latin text of the Bible, and for which he learned Hebrew and Aramaic to go with the Greek he already knew. His contemporary St Augustine, another great prose writer, produced two of the major achievements of later Latin literature, the autobiographical *Confessions*, relating his conversion to Christianity, and the *City of God*. Christians and pagans alike were much preoccupied with the relationship between their religion and the Roman empire, some of the latter maintaining that it was the coming of Christianity that had led to the empire's decline. More simplistically minded Christian historians, such as Augustine's contemporary Orosius in his *Historia contra Paganos*, attempted to rewrite history in Christian terms. This idea did not go away — as long as the Roman empire at Byzantium survived, it was customarily seen as the empire of God on earth, and the emperor as the elect of God — but for Augustine, the true city of God was no earthly city, but its manifestation in the hearts of Christian believers.

Not only prose was used for Christian purposes. In the sixth century Agathias from Asia Minor (whose debt to Nonnus is well established) produced a seven-volume *Cycle* of epigrams, in which traditional classical themes were explored alongside poems with explicitly Christian content on topics such as the birth of Christ and the annunciation. In the later fifth century, the Gallic bishop Sidonius Apollinaris and the north African Dracontius were writing both traditional poetry and Christian works in classical Latin metres. Christian poetry of this type was not new. As early as the third century the Spanish poet Juvencus produced a Latin version of the Gospels in Virgilian hexameters; a Greek rendering of the Psalms into Homeric hexameters may date from the same period and be the work of Apollinaris or Apollinarius, bishop of Laodicea. In the late fourth century, the major Christian poet to have written in classical forms was thought to be Prudentius, whose enormous output, which survives, uses classical metres of all kinds, and contains many echoes of pagan poetry.

Classical poetry was written in quantitative metres (see 1c). Although some such poetry continued to be written even into the middle ages (in Latin, though somewhat less so in Greek), there is evidence as far back as the third century in Christian poetry of both languages of attempts to accommodate classical metres to the ways in which their pronunciation was changing, in a Greek hymn by Methodius, and in the very un-classical Latin hexameters of Commodian. Augustine wrote verse based on word-stress and the number of syllables in each line, which was of course to become the regular form for European poetry, particularly in an ecclesiastical context. By the sixth century, the Byzantine priest Romanos was producing a large *oeuvre* of such poetry for liturgical use. And in the west, Venantius Fortunatus, bishop of Poitiers, who has been described as the last classical poet and at the same time the first medieval one, as well as writing in traditional metres, wrote quantitative hymns, translations of some of which are still used in catholic worship today, as are those of Romanos in the Greek orthodox church.

Paganism was the past, and Christianity the future. But, as the above paragraphs suggest, classicism in literature was transmuted in the service of Christianity, rather than being replaced by it. Not only classical forms, but much classical learning too was preserved, both in western Europe and in Byzantium. For a long time, large-scale compilations of knowledge somewhat like encyclopaedias had been produced. Hellenistic scholars had been interested in collecting and recording information of all sorts, and the practice passed to Rome. The first century BCE scholar Varro, most of whose works have not survived, wrote on almost every conceivable sphere of human activity, and in the first century the elder Pliny's extant *Historia Naturalis* came close in conception to the modern encyclopaedia. Pliny's book was enormously popular in the middle ages, as were similar encyclopaedic compilations, such as the probably third century one of Solinus, the *Saturnalia* of Macrobius from the early fifth century and that of the north African Martianus Capella, probably from the end of the same century. Not only pagan writers were interested in the preservation of classical learning and information: the encyclopaedic works of the seventh-century bishop of Seville, Isidore, were of equal importance in transmitting information to later generations. Compilations of similar form were made in the Greek east too; epitomes of some of the work of Stephanus of Byzantium (sixth century) are of value to scholars today, as are the summaries of now lost books made by the ninth-century patriarch of Byzantium, Photius, and the tenth-century encyclopaedia known as the *Suda*.

Further reading

In general, see Dihle (1994). On Christianity, see Hopkins (2000); Lane Fox (1986). On philosophy in this era, see Armstrong (1967).

RECEPTION: A FEW WORDS

It is, of course, on material preserved in this and other ways from the Greek and Roman past that classicists now work. But what do we do with it? What does it mean to us? It is evident (and, indeed, obvious) from reading Macrobius on Virgil, or the contemporary commentary on the *Aeneid* by Servius, that already by 400, when the Roman empire still stood, and while Latin was still a living language, a good deal of what Virgil had written required explication and interpretation. That is to say that it *meant* something different to Macrobius than it had meant to its original audience; and, for that matter, given that no two individuals' personal life experiences are identical with each other, it will have meant something different even to every single reader or hearer, even in Virgil's own time. Virgil, as a man and as a writer, was a product of a particular period in time, with the preconceptions of his time, and furthermore with a life experience different from that of any other particular individual, even within that time. His contemporaries will at least have shared some of the external features of Virgil's life: they will know what it is like to live under the regime of Augustus, for example, or perhaps recognize in the *Aeneid* references to other authors that escape us. Even so, there will be in any author's work things which are so personal and individual – the resonances of certain words, perhaps, or reminiscences of situations known to no one else – that it may well be the case that in a very real sense we cannot claim to know what an author meant. Some literary critics, indeed, believe that meaning in a text is brought to it only by the reader or hearer: though to deny that an author means something when he or she constructs a text seems to be an extreme and scarcely tenable position. It is, however, vital to remember the possible multiplicity of responses (any or all of which may be valid) to a text whenever we are tempted to say 'this is what Virgil is trying to do . . .'.

It is with reference to such considerations that the term reception is used. As soon as any work of literature is heard or read by anyone other than its author, it is undergoing reception. Some of the authors we have discussed in this book wrote more than two and a half millennia ago, and have thus been received by individuals and audiences with (even if we leave aside their own personal circumstances) necessarily very different life experiences, even down to the most basic considerations, such as the material conditions under which they lived. For example, it is immediately evident that an audience watching a play by Sophocles, performed for the first (and supposedly only) time, at a religious festival, in the open air, in Greek, in Athens, during the Peloponnesian War, will have a different experience from one watching the same play, translated into English, in a theatre in the West End of London in 2010. And their experience will be different again from that of a schoolboy at Constantinople in 900 studying the play as part of his school curriculum, or a scholar of the Italian renaissance reading it in the fifteenth century when

Greek literature was still being rediscovered in western Europe. This may seem fairly obvious. And we may feel that some of the ways in which classical literature has been received are no longer valid and, indeed, sometimes rather silly. For example, in the middle ages, Virgil was popularly supposed to have been a wizard, as well as a kind of proto-Christian (his fourth *Eclogue* was thought to prophesy the coming of Christ). Fairly clearly, then, a medieval reader approaching the *Aeneid* was doing so with a very different mind-set from, say, a nineteenth-century public school educated Englishman for whom the empire of Augustus might seem to be analogous to the empire of queen Victoria, or from us, reading it now in postcolonial times, when imperialism might seem not to be such a good thing after all.

The history of the reception of classical literature is a vast field, and cannot be explored in any detail here. Perhaps its chief lesson is to beware of assumptions: knowing how earlier generations have read the *Aeneid* should make us wary of saying that we know what it means, and aware, too, that whatever we think about it, future generations will read it differently. It has been perceptively said that every age gets the classics it deserves: we must remember that ours will not be the last word.

Glossary

a bibliothecis   secretaryship within the Roman imperial administration, concerned with imperial libraries

a studiis   secretaryship within the Roman imperial administration, concerned with giving advice on literary matters

ab epistulis   secretaryship within the Roman imperial administration, concerned with correspondence between the emperor and his officials

aetiology   reflection on the origins of things. Often used to refer to myths that tell the story of, for example, the first law court

agōgē   the name given to the education of young Spartans

agōn   Greek for 'contest', applied to a variety of activities, including war, athletic games and rhetorical contests; in tragedy it is used to refer to set-piece debates

aischrologia   Greek for 'scurrility'; 'scurrilous verses'

akribeia   precision in expression; an important term in Plato

Alcaic   a metre, associated first with the poet Alcaeus (3c), then taken up by Horace (10d)

allegory   symbolic narrative

alliteration   words beginning with the same letter or sound beginning two or more words in sequence, e.g. *veni, vidi, vici*

analepsis   the narrative technique of 'flashback'

anaphora   words, phrases, clauses or lines beginning with the same word or phrase

annalistic   historical writing that uses years as its organizing principle (see 5b)

antilabē   a feature in Greek tragedy in which a line is split between two actors

aoidos   Greek for 'singer'

apeiron   literally 'unbounded'; used by Anaximander to describe the infinite first substance of air

apodexis   Greek for 'display' but also, in a more philosophical sense, 'proof'

aporia   being at a loss, completely flummoxed, snookered or at sea

apostrophe   an address to a specific person or group

archaism   the use of older words, spellings or phrases

aretē   Greek word for 'excellence' or 'virtue'

aristeia   a sequence of individual combats in which one hero excels. There are a number of such *aristeiai* in the *Iliad*

Asianism   a style of rhetoric, in which Roman orators of the late republic were seen to be imitating elaborate, Greek models

assonance   the same sound repeated in words close to each other

asyndeton   lack of conjunctions between phrases or clauses

ataraxia   the desired Epicurean state in which one can remain indifferent to all external media and stimulation

Atticism   used to refer to a style of Greek, associated with (mainly Athenian) prose authors of the classical period, and imitated by some Roman orators

auctoritas   Roman word meaning 'influence' or 'prestige'

aulos, aulētris   *aulos* is a musical instrument something like an oboe used to accompany the performance of poetry; *aulētris* is the player of the instrument

boulē   'council'. In democratic Athens the *boulē* consisted of 500 citizens sortitively elected; see 4a

cantica   lyric passages delivered by individual actors in Roman comedy

catharsis   'purification', 'purging' or 'clarification', most famously used by Aristotle in his *Poetics* when describing the effect of tragedy

choliambic   similar to an iambic trimeter, but the last foot is a spondee (two long syllables) rather than an iamb (a short followed by a long syllable)

chōra   literally: 'country' or 'region'. Used to refer to the land in which a *polis* (city) was situated and over which it had control

chorēgia, chorēgos   a *choregos* was a rich individual who, in democratic Athens, was charged with paying for the production costs of tragedies or comedies performed at one of the dramatic festivals; *chorēgia* was the name of the tax; see 4a

clientelae   literally 'clientage'. In Rome the relationship between patrons and clients was a feature of social organization: some scholars think it was essential, others marginal. A patron could be as powerful as an emperor and as ordinary as an ordinary free man

contaminatio   the mixing of material from different sources, something of which Terence is sometimes accused

crasis   when two vowel sounds are forced together to make one syllable

cursus honorum   the career path for Roman politicians; see 8a; 9a

dialectic   collaborative intellectual enquiry through discussion; important in Plato

distichomythiai   an arrangement of lines in tragedy in which each character in a dialogue says two lines

dithyramb   hymn sung in honour of the god, Dionysus

doxographer   writer on the works and ideas of the philosophers (e.g. Diogenes Laertius)

ecphrasis   literally a 'description', but often used to refer to descriptions of artistic objects

eisodoi   one of the entrances onto the tragic stage or into the *orchēstra*

ekklēsia   Greek for 'assembly'; in democratic Athens the sovereign body which all citizens could attend

ekkyklēma   a sort of trolley used on the stage in Attic tragedy to display dead or dying characters

elegiac couplet   a metrical scheme in which a hexameter line is followed by a pentameter; see 1c

elenchus   refutation of an answer to a question; important in Plato

elision   when one word ends in a vowel and the next word starts with a vowel it is common in Greek and Latin verse for the second vowel to disappear (or to be elided)

ellipsis   the omission of a word or words normally required for a phrase to make complete sense

encomium   poem in which a person is praised for his exploits. Pindar is a celebrated composer of *encōmia*

epeisodia   the parts of tragedies in which actors spoke to each other or made speeches, for the most part in iambic trimeter. Tragedy moves between such episodes and choral lyrics (or *stasima*)

epic cycle   the lost collection of stories which tell the stories of the heroic age, which later poets used and adapted

Epicureanism   philosophy derived from the writings of Epicurus. The ideal state for an Epicurean was one of *ataraxia*, namely, a state of complete indifference to all stimuli or a state of being completely undisturbed

epideixis   'display', often used to refer to the rhetorical displays given by some sophists in late fifth-century Athens

epinikian   a type of poetry –most closely associated with Pindar – in which someone's victory is praised; see 3c

epithets (stock)   many Homeric characters are routinely described in the same way with one adjective. Odysseus, for instance, is very often *polymētis* (meaning 'with many resources' or 'with much intelligence')

epyllion   a miniature epic poem

eristic   combative verbal dispute performed by some sophists and aimed at winning an argument (rather than showing something to be true)

eudaimōnia   'happiness': an important term in Aristotle's ethics

exordium   the opening of a speech

fabula palliata   a play in Greek dress, such as the plays of Plautus and Terence

fabula togata   a play with characters dressed in togas

fabulae Atellanae   Atellan farces (Atella was a town in Campania where the farces originated)

forms   forms (or ideas) are what, for Plato, constitute the real world and include such abstract concepts as 'justice' and 'truth'. The perceivable world is an imitation of the world of forms; see 6d

gnōmē a proverbial statement, an aphorism or a maxim

hendecasyllables a verse line of 11 syllables

hexameter a verse line of six feet; the meter of epic poetry; see 1c

hyporchēmata hymns sung in honour of Apollo, generally of a happy nature

iamb, iambic an iamb is a metrical foot in which a short syllable is followed by a long

iambic trimeter a verse line of six feet (or three *metra*) dominated by the *iamb*; the most common meter in Attic tragedy

imperium Latin for 'power', 'command', 'empire'

Judgement of Paris mythical event in which Paris, the Trojan prince, judged which of Aphrodite, Athene and Hera was the most beautiful goddess. He chose Aphrodite, with devastating consequences (the Trojan War, Hera's hatred of Troy, etc.)

kleos Greek word for 'fame'. Homeric heroes are eager to achieve such fame by their deeds

kommos in Greek tragedy a lament shared between the chorus and a character

kōmos a riotous procession with a ritual dimension involving revellers (called *kōmasts*) singing, dancing and drinking. Some scholars think that there is a relation between the *kōmos* and comedy

leschē room attached to a smithy where men would gossip; important in Hesiod

liturgy the name given to the direct taxation of rich Athenian individuals during the period of the democracy. The most famous liturgies paid for the upkeep of a trireme for a year or for the costs of the production of a tragedian's plays in a year

logeion the area in front of the *skēnē*, possibly raised above the level of the *orchēstra*, on which actors spoke in Greek theatres

logographoi writers of speeches for delivery by prosecutors and defendants in Athenian law courts

mēchanē a theatrical device used in Attic tragedy. Something like a hoist or crane, it showed characters – often gods – high up in the air

melos Greek for 'song'

metic normally used to describe a free non-Athenian resident in Athens

metonymy a form of metaphor in which one term (e.g. a part) is used for another (e.g. a whole). An example: 'Whitehall announced today . . . '

militia amoris a feature of Latin love elegy, in which the lover's attempt to capture the heart (and more besides) of his loved one is described in the terms of a military campaign

mimēsis Greek word for 'imitation', used by both Plato and Aristotle to describe works of literature (and art more generally)

moira (aisa) Greek words meaning 'fate'

monody a solo song

mores   Latin for 'customs' or 'values'

mos maiorum   Latin for 'custom of the ancestors'. Romans – who claimed to love tradition – often used it to evaluate policies or ideas

Muses   the nine gods in charge of creativity

neoterics   the name given to the group of Latin poets in the 50s BCE, who paraded an interest in Hellenistic and otherwise clever verse. The most famous is Catullus

nomos   Greek word for 'custom', 'convention' or 'law'

nostos   Greek word for the 'return home'; a dominant theme in the *Odyssey*

nous   Greek word for 'mind' or 'intelligence'

novus homo   a man who, in republican Rome, achieved election to the consulship without being a member of either the patrician or plebeian aristocratic families

orchēstra   the area in a Greek theatre – normally held to be almost circular, in which in tragedy the chorus sang and danced

paean   originally the name of the doctor to the gods, then an epithet of Apollo. It then comes to mean a hymn to Apollo (or Artemis) and, more generally, a song of thanksgiving or triumph

Panathenaea   festival held in honour of Athene every four years in classical Athens. There were competitions in the recitation of Homer

parabasis   the name given to the speech delivered by the leader of a chorus in an Athenian comedy in which – it is normally assumed – the views of the author are expressed explicitly

paradoxography   writers who dealt in the unexpected, the unbelievable or the marvellous

parodoi   one of the names given to the entrances and exits in a Greek theatre, situated either side of the *logeion*

parodos   in tragedy the first song sung by the chorus as they enter the *orchēstra*

partheneion   choral lyric performed by a chorus of girls on a religious occasion. Alcman, Pindar, Simonides and Bacchylides all wrote *partheneia*

penates   one Latin word for 'household gods'

pentameter   a verse line of five feet; usually the second line in an *elegiac couplet*

peripeteia   Greek for 'reversal [of fortune]'; an important idea in Aristotle's theory of tragedy as outlined in his *Poetics*

periphrasis   literally: speaking around, i.e. circumlocution

personification   a form of metaphor in which a thing or idea is represented as a person

philia   literally means 'friendship', but used to refer to all sorts of relationships, whether between family members or political allies

phronēsis   perception, practical wisdom

physis   Greek word for 'nature'

pietas   Latin for 'piety' or 'reverence for the gods'; important as a characteristic of Aeneas in the *Aeneid*

polis the Greek word for 'city' and 'city-state'; the most important unit of social and political organization in the archaic and classical periods in the Greek-speaking world

Presocratics the group of thinkers in the sixth and early fifth centuries who sparked the intellectual revolution in Greece; the shared title implies no similarity of beliefs or ideas

priamel literary term for a sort of list, as in Sappho's 'some like x, others y, but I like desire . . . '

proconsulare maius imperium Latin phrase meaning 'greater proconsular authority'. Governors of Roman provinces governed by virtue of the proconsular authority granted to them by the senate. In 23 BCE Augustus received the greater version of this authority, thereby allowing him to govern – through governors or his own legates – all the provinces of the empire

proem an introduction, prelude or preface

prolepsis the narrative technique whereby future events are anticipated one way or another

prologos the first speech, or prologue, in a tragedy

propemptikon normally a poem that hopes that a friend who is leaving will have a prosperous journey

provincia Latin for 'province'

recitatio recitation of a work by the author himself

recusatio refusal; sometimes used to refer very specific refusals, such as that of Horace when he refuses to write an epic poem

reductio ad absurdum literally 'reduction to absurdity', a technique used to rubbish an opponent's argument

rhapsode a professional reciter of Homer

sacrosanctitas inviolability; normally used to refer the religious protection granted to tribunes of the people in the Roman republic

Sapphic a metre employed by the poet Sappho, later used by Catullus and Horace

Saturnians a stress-based metre common in Latin before the adoption of the Greek hexameter

senatus consiltum decree of the (Roman) senate

servitium amoris literally 'the slavery of love'. A stylistic technique associated with love elegy whereby the poet claims that his love for his girl is akin to slavery

skēnē the sort of hut that sat behind the *logeion* (stage). It was used practically to allow actors to change costumes and masks and symbolically to represent off-stage space indoors

Socratic irony Socrates claimed to know that he knew nothing. He often uses this apparent ignorance to probe his interlocutors' beliefs and arguments, hoping to get his interlocutors to see the contradictions in the positions they adopt

sophists   the group of heterogeneous intellectuals and paid teachers who became prominent n the latter half of the fifth century BCE

stasimon   in tragedy, a stanza of a choral lyric

stichic metres   composed in recurring lines of the same type, such as *hexameters*

stichomythia   actors in tragedy speaking one line each in alternation

stoicism   ancient school of philosophy founded by Zeno of Citium (*c.* 300 BCE), named after the *stoa poikilē* (a painted colonnade in Athens where Zeno lectured). In stoic theory, virtue and knowledge are intertwined, and the virtuous are indifferent to reversals of fortune and to pleasure and pain

strophic metres   composed in stanzas

syllogism   a term in logic: an argument where two propositions (or premises) which contain a common term lead to a third proposition or conclusion

syssitia   the messes in which Spartan warriors were organized

technē   Greek word for 'skill', important in Plato

theologeion   the space on top of the *skēnē* used for the appearance of gods (the word means something like 'divine speaking place')

timē   'honour' or 'respect': Homeric heroes desire this

topos   literally 'place'; used to refer to what – in literary criticism – we would call a 'theme' or a 'commonplace'

triadic   verse in which a pair of stanzas in the same metrical form are followed by a third in a related but not identical form

tribunicia potestas   literally: tribunician power. Tribunes had the power to summon various assemblies, including the senate

trochaic   a foot in a metrical scheme consisting in a long syllable followed by a short

xenia   the code or informal set of rules which governed hospitality

Maps

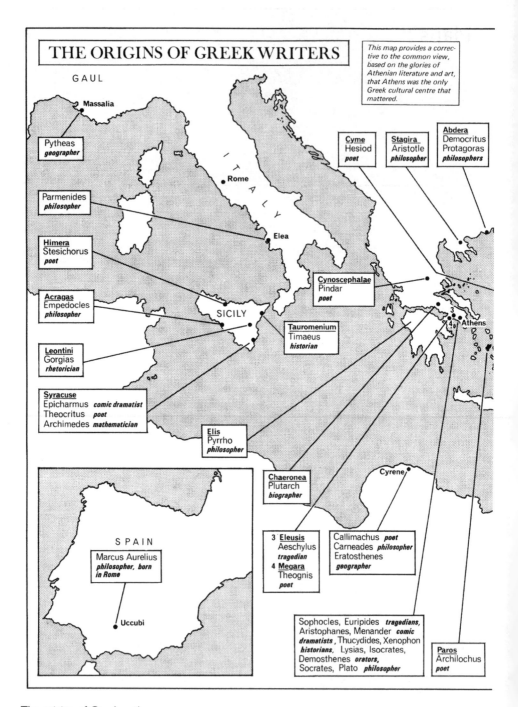

THE ORIGINS OF GREEK WRITERS

This map provides a corrective to the common view, based on the glories of Athenian literature and art, that Athens was the only Greek cultural centre that mattered.

GAUL

Massalia

Pytheas
geographer

Parmenides
philosopher

Himera
Stesichorus
poet

Acragas
Empedocles
philosopher

Leontini
Gorgias
rhetorician

Syracuse
Epicharmus   *comic dramatist*
Theocritus   *poet*
Archimedes   *mathematician*

Rome

Elea

SICILY

Elis
Pyrrho
philosopher

Cyme
Hesiod
poet

Stagira
Aristotle
philosopher

Abdera
Democritus
Protagoras
philosophers

Cynoscephalae
Pindar
poet

Tauromenium
Timaeus
historian

Athens

Chaeronea
Plutarch
biographer

Cyrene

S P A I N

Marcus Aurelius
philosopher, born in Rome

Uccubi

3 Eleusis
Aeschylus
tragedian
4 Megara
Theognis
poet

Callimachus *poet*
Carneades *philosopher*
Eratosthenes
geographer

Sophocles, Euripides *tragedians,*
Aristophanes, Menander *comic dramatists*, Thucydides, Xenophon *historians*, Lysias, Isocrates, Demosthenes *orators,*
Socrates, Plato *philosopher*

Paros
Archilochus
poet

The origins of Greek authors

Source: Grant, M. *The Routledge Atlas of Classical History* (London, 1971), pp. 37–8.

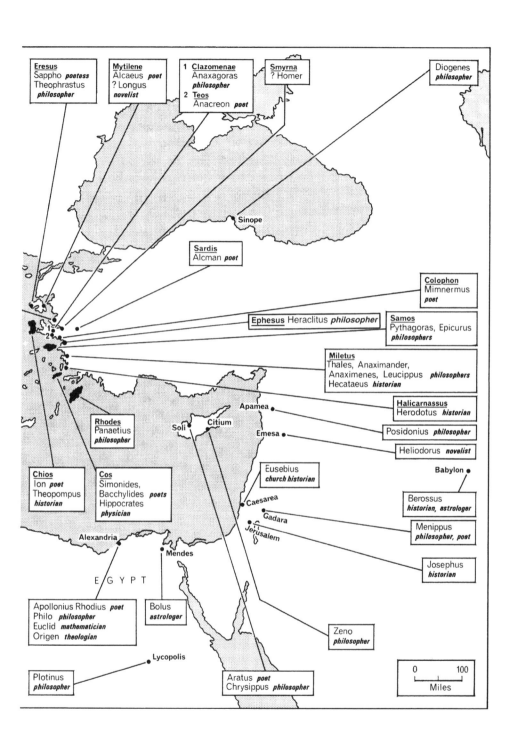

Eresus
Sappho *poetess*
Theophrastus *philosopher*

Mytilene
Alcaeus *poet*
? Longus *novelist*

1 Clazomenae
Anaxagoras *philosopher*
2 Teos
Anacreon *poet*

Smyrna
? Homer

Diogenes *philosopher*

Sinope

Sardis
Alcman *poet*

Colophon
Mimnermus *poet*

Ephesus Heraclitus *philosopher*

Samos
Pythagoras, Epicurus *philosophers*

Miletus
Thales, Anaximander, Anaximenes, Leucippus *philosophers*
Hecataeus *historian*

Apamea

Rhodes
Panaetius *philosopher*

Soli   Citium

Emesa

Halicarnassus
Herodotus *historian*

Posidonius *philosopher*

Heliodorus *novelist*

Babylon

Chios
Ion *poet*
Theopompus *historian*

Cos
Simonides, Bacchylides *poets*
Hippocrates *physician*

Eusebius *church historian*

Caesarea

Gadara
Jerusalem

Berossus *historian, astrologer*

Menippus *philosopher, poet*

Josephus *historian*

Alexandria

Mendes

E G Y P T

Apollonius Rhodius *poet*
Philo *philosopher*
Euclid *mathematician*
Origen *theologian*

Bolus *astrologer*

Zeno *philosopher*

Lycopolis

Plotinus *philosopher*

Aratus *poet*
Chrysippus *philosopher*

0   100
Miles

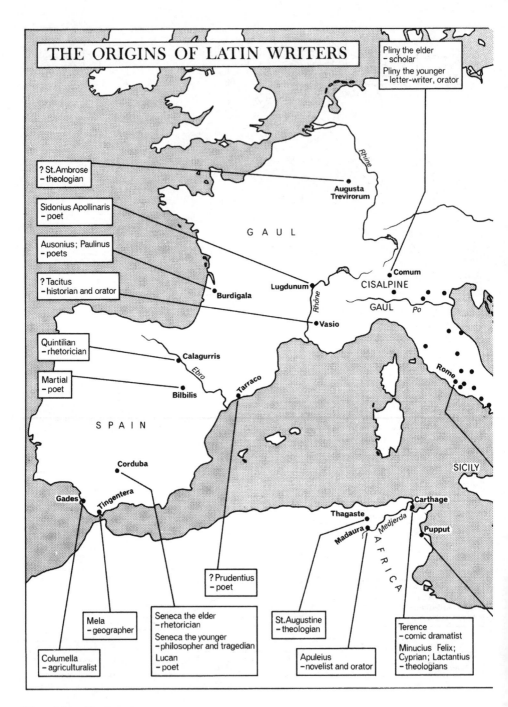

THE ORIGINS OF LATIN WRITERS

Pliny the elder
– scholar
Pliny the younger
– letter-writer, orator

? St. Ambrose
– theologian

Sidonius Apollinaris
– poet

Ausonius; Paulinus
– poets

? Tacitus
– historian and orator

Quintilian
– rhetorician

Martial
– poet

Augusta
Trevirorum

Rhine

G A U L

Comum

Lugdunum   CISALPINE

Rhône

Burdigala

Po

GAUL

Vasio

Calagurris

Ebro

Tarraco

Bilbilis

S P A I N

Rome

Corduba

SICILY

Gades   Tingentera

Carthage

Thagaste

Madaura   **Medjerda**

Pupput

A F R I C A

? Prudentius
– poet

Mela
– geographer

Seneca the elder
– rhetorician
Seneca the younger
– philosopher and tragedian

St. Augustine
– theologian

Terence
– comic dramatist

Columella
– agriculturalist

Lucan
– poet

Apuleius
– novelist and orator

Minucius Felix;
Cyprian; Lactantius
– theologians

The origins of Latin writers

Source: Grant, M. *The Routledge Atlas of Classical History* (London, 1971), pp. 78–9.

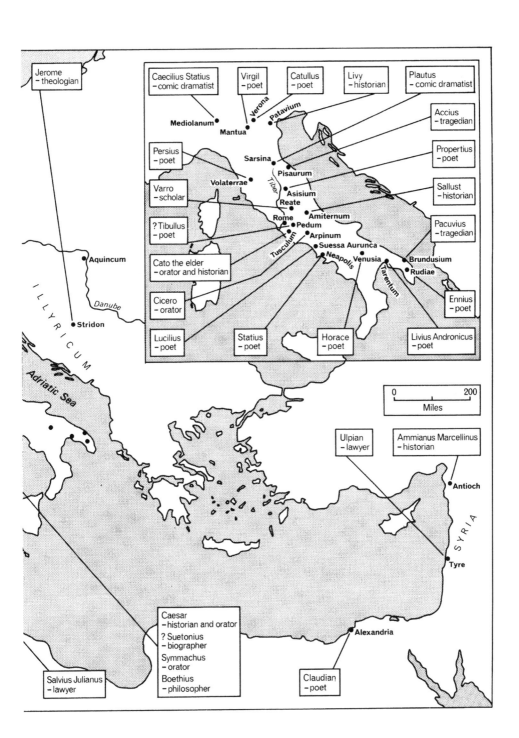

Chronology

	Date	Literary events	Date	Political and cultural events
800–700	c. 750–700	*Iliad*, followed by *Odyssey*	c. 776	First Olympic Games
	c. 700	Hesiod active	c. 753	Traditional date for the founding of Rome
700–600	c. 650	Archilochus active		
	c. 600	Sappho and Alcaeus active		
600–500	c. 540	Anacreon and Ibycus active	590s	Solon's reforms in Athens
	c. 525	Birth of Aeschylus	c. 550–27	Peisistratus tyrant of Athens
	c. 518	Birth of Pindar		
	c. 515–470	Simonides active	c. 509	Expulsion of Tarquinius Superbus by Brutus; Roman republic founded
			508	Cleisthenes' democratic reforms in Athens
500–450	496	Birth of Sophocles	499–4	Ionian Revolt; the Athenians help to sack Sardis
	c. 495–50	Pindar and Bacchylides active	490	The Athenians defeat the Persians at the battle of Marathon
	c. 480s	Birth of Herodotus	480–79	Persian invasion of Greece; 298 Spartans die at Thermopylae; Greek victories at Artemisium, Salamis and Plataea

	Date	Literary events	Date	Political and cultural events
	472	Aeschylus, *Persians*		
	468	Sophocles' first production	469	Birth of Socrates
	c. 460	Birth of Thucydides	c. 462–1	The so-called radical democracy established at Athens (Ephialtes' reforms)
	c. 459	Birth of Lysias	460–46	'First' Peloponnesian War between Athens and Sparta
	458	Aeschylus' *Oresteia*		
	456	Death of Aeschylus		
	455	Euripides' first production		
	c. 450	Birth of Aristophanes		
450–400	c. 440s	Death of Pindar		
	440s–20s	Herodotus active		
	431	Euripides, *Medea*	431–04	'Second' Peloponnesian War between Athens and Sparta
	c. 430	Birth of Xenophon	430s	Protagoras visits Athens
	c. 428	Birth of Plato	430–29	Plague in Athens; death of Pericles
	420s	Death of Herodotus	427	Gorgias visits Athens
	425	Aristophanes, *Acharnians*		
	420s–390s	Thucydides writing		
	415	Euripides, *Trojan Women*	415–13	Athenian expedition against Sicily
	411	Death of Antiphon; Aristophanes, *Lysistrata*	411	Oligarchic coup (of the 400) in Athens
	409	Sophocles, *Philoctetes*		

(Continued)

(Continued)

	Date	Literary events	Date	Political and cultural events
	406	Death of Euripides		
	406–5	Death of Sophocles		
	405	Aristophanes, Frogs	404	Athens defeated in the Peloponnesian War; oligarchic coup of the Thirty
	401	Sophocles, Oedipus at Colonus (posthumous)		
400–360	390s	Death of Thucydides	399	Trial and execution of Socrates
	388	Aristophanes' last extant play, Wealth		
	c. 385	Death of Aristophanes; birth of Demosthenes		
	384	Birth of Aristotle		
	c. 380	Death of Lysias	378–7	Second Athenian Confederacy established
			371	The Thebans defeat the Spartans at Leuctra
360–300	350s	Death of Xenophon	359–36	Reign of Philip of Macedon
	351	Demosthenes, First Philippic		
	347	Death of Plato		
	344	Demosthenes, Second Philippic		
	342–1	Birth of Menander; Demosthenes, Third Philippic	338	Philip defeats the Greeks at Chaeronea
	335	Aristotle founds the Lyceum	336	Alexander succeeds Philip
	330	Demosthenes, On the Crown	334 and following	Alexander's expedition to Persia; defeats Darius
	322	Deaths of Aristotle and Demosthenes	323	Death of Alexander

	Date	Literary events	Date	Political and cultural events
	c. 320–05	Birth of Callimachus		
	317	Menander, *Angry Old Man* (*Dyscolus*)		
	307	Epicurus founds his school		
300–250	300	Zeno founds his stoic school	297–72	Pyrrhus of Epirus campaigns in Italy
	c. 290	Death of Menander	264	First gladiatorial show in Rome
	270s–50s	Callimachus, Theocritus, Apollonius *et al.* active in Alexandria	264–41	First Punic War between Rome and Carthage
250–200	c. 240	Livius Andronicus writes first Latin literature	218–01	Second Punic War
	239	Birth of Ennius	218	Battles of Ticinum and Trebia between Rome and Carthage
	c. 216	Fabius Pictor active	217	Roman naval Victory off the Ebro; battle of Lake Trasimene
	c. 205–184	Plautus active	216	Hannibal defeats the Romans at the battle of Cannae
	200	Birth of Polybius	202	Scipio defeats Hannibal at the battle of Zama
200–150	191	Plautus, *Pseudolus*		
	185	Birth of Terence	186	Senatorial decree against Bacchic rites
	169	Death of Ennius		
	167	Polybius comes to Rome	168	The Romans defeat the Macedonians at Pydna
	160s	Terence active		
	159	Death of Terence		

(Continued)

(Continued)

	Date	Literary events	Date	Political and cultural events
	150s	Moschus active		
150–100	140s	Panaetius comes to Rome	149–6	Third Punic War; sack of Carthage
			146	Sack of Corinth; Rome subjects Greece
	130s–20s	Lucilius active	133	Tiberius Gracchus, tribune of the plebs, is assassinated
	c. 120s and later	Bion active	123–1	Gaius Gracchus, tribune of the plebs (123–2), is assassinated in 121
	118	Death of Polybius		
			112–05	Jugurthine War
	106	Birth of Cicero	107, 104–100	Marius' consulships
100–50	100	Birth of Caesar; Meleager active	91–89	Social War (war between Rome and its Italian 'allies (socii)')
	90s	Birth of Lucretius; Posidonius active	87–4	Rule of Cinna
	c. 86	Birth of Sallust	86	Death of Marius
	c. 84	Birth of Catullus	84	Death of Cinna
	81	Cicero's first extant speech	82–79	Sulla's dictatorship
	70s and after	C. Nepos active	78	Death of Sulla
	70	Cicero, Verrines; birth of Virgil	73–1	Slave revolt led by Spartacus, eventually defeated by Crassus
	65	Birth of Horace	67–2	Pompey in the east
			63	Catiline's conspiracy during Cicero's consulship
	59	Birth of Livy	60	First triumvirate established

Date	Literary events	Date	Political and cultural events
56	Cicero, *Pro Caelio* (*In Defence of Caelius*)	58–7	Cicero in exile
c. 55–49	Lucretius, *De Rerum Natura*	58–49	Caesar campaigns in Gaul
c. 54	Death of Catullus	53	Crassus killed at Carrhae
52	Cicero, *Pro Milone* (*In Defence of Milo*)		
c. 50	Death of Lucretius		
late 50s	Births of Propertius, Tibullus		
50s and after	Didorus Siculus active		
c. 50	Birth of Seneca the Elder		
50–I BCE		49	Caesar crosses the Rubicon thus starting Civil War
mid-40s	Cicero, in retirement, writes philosophical works	48	Caesar defeats Pompey at Pharsalus
44–3	Cicero, *Philippics*	48–44	Caesar's dictatorship
43	Death of Cicero; birth of Ovid	44	Caesar assassinated
late 40s	Sallust, *Catiline* and *Jugurthine War*; Gallus' love elegies	42	Caesar's assassins defeated at Philippi; Julius Caesar deified
c. 38	Virgil, *Eclogues*	30s	Second triumvirate
35	Death of Sallust		
c. 31	Horace, *Epodes*	31	Octavian defeats Antony and Cleopatra at Actium

(Continued)

(Continued)

	Date	Literary events	Date	Political and cultural events
	20s	Dionysius of Halicarnassus active; Strabo active		
	c. 29	Virgil, Georgics		
	early 20s	Propertius' and Tibullus' elegies appear; Livy begins to appear as well	27	Octavian becomes Augustus; first settlement of the principate
	23	Horace, Odes 1–3	23	Augustus' second settlement
	c. 20	Ovid, Amores 1		
	19	Death of Virgil; death of Tibullus; Horace, Epistles 1		
	17	Horace, Carmen Saeculare (Centennial Hymn)		
	c. 16	Death of Propertius		
	13	Horace, Odes 4		
	8	Deaths of Horace and Maecenas		
1 CE–50	by 8 CE	Ovid, Metamorphoses		
	8	Exile of Ovid		
	9–12	Ovid, Tristia, Letters from Pontus		
			14	Death of Augustus; accession of Tiberius (14–37)
	17	Death of Ovid; death of Livy		
	23	Birth of Pliny the Elder		
	30	Velleius Paterculus' History	31	Downfall of Sejanus
	35	Birth of Quintilian		

	Date	Literary events	Date	Political and cultural events
	c. 38–41	Birth of Martial	37	Death of Tiberius; accession of Caligula (37–41)
	39	Birth of Lucan		
	c. 40	Death of Seneca the Elder		
			41	Death of Caligula; accession of Claudius (41–54)
			43	Invasion of Britain
	late 40s	Birth of Statius		
	c. 50	Birth of Plutarch		
50–100	54	Seneca, Apocolocyntosis	54	Death of Claudius; accession of Nero (54–68)
	mid-50s	Birth of Tacitus; Philip of Thessalonica active; Curtius active (?)	59	Nero has his mother, Agrippina, murdered
	60s	Persius, Lucan, Lucillius, Petronius, Silius Italicus active	60	Boudicca's revolt
	c. 61–2	Birth of Pliny the Younger		
	c. 63	Seneca, Letters		
			64	Fire in Rome; Nero blames Christians
	65	Deaths of Lucan, Petronius, Seneca	65	Piso's conspiracy against Nero
	67	Josephus deserts to Rome	68	Death of Nero; Galba becomes Emperor
			69	Year of the four emperors: Galba, Otho, Vitellius, Vespasian (69–79)
	c. 70	Birth of Suetonius	70	End of the Jewish Revolt when Jerusalem falls

(Continued)

(Continued)

	Date	Literary events	Date	Political and cultural events
			77–84	Agricola as the governor of Britain
	79	Death of Pliny the Elder	79	Eruption of Mount Vesuvius; death of Vespasian; accession of Titus
	80	Martial's *Book of Spectacles* celebrates the opening of the Colosseum	80	Colosseum opened in Rome
	80s and 90s	Dio of Prusa, Martial, Statius, Valerius Flaccus active	81	Death of Titus; accession of Domitian (81–96)
	c. 96	Death of Quintilian; death of Statius	96	Assassination of Domitian; Nerva emperor
	98	Tacitus, *Agricola* and *Germania*	98–117	Trajan's principate
	99–109	Pliny, *Letters*		
100–150	100	Birth of Appian; Pliny, *Panegyricus*		
	c. 100–20	Plutarch active		
	c. 101–2	Tacitus, *Dialogus*	101–2	First Dacian War
	c. 102	Death of Silius Italicus		
	c. 104	Death of Martial	105–6	Second Dacian War; annexation of the province of Arabia Petraea by Trajan
	c. 108	Tacitus, *Histories*	113	Annexation of Armenia as a province by Trajan. Trajan's column is built in Rome
	c. 113	Death of Pliny the Younger		

Date	Literary events	Date	Political and cultural events
c. 115–30	Juvenal, Satires	116	Conquest of much of Parthia by Trajan. The Roman empire reaches its greatest size, 3.5 million square miles, and an estimated 60 million people
c. 116	Tacitus, Annals	117–38	Hadrian's principate
117 or after	Death of Tacitus		
c. 120	Birth of Lucian; Suetonius, Lives of the Caesars; Dionysius Periegetes active		
120 or after	Death of Plutarch; Arrian active		
c. 125	Birth of Apuleius		
c. 130	Death of Suetonius; Xenophon of Ephesus active (?)	138–61	Antoninus Pius' principate
140s	Florus, Fronto, Herodes Atticus, Mesomedes active		
150–200 c. 150	Pausanias, Description of Greece; Aelius Aristides active		
c. 150–80	Lucian active	160s	First incursions into the empire by northern tribes and Parthians
160s and after	Galen active	161–80	Marcus Aurelius' principate
165	Death of Appian		
170s	Death of Apuleius; Aulus Gellius active		
170–80	Marcus Aurelius, Meditations	180–92	Commodus' principate

(Continued)

(Continued)

	Date	Literary events	Date	Political and cultural events
200–250	c. 200	Longus, *Daphnis and Chloe*; Aelian, Athenaeus, Nestor of Laranda, Oppian, Philostratus active	193–211	Septimius Severus' principate
	third century	Achilles Tatius, Pisander of Laranda, Quintus Smyrnaeus active	211–17	Caracalla's principate
			217–18	Macrinus' principate
	c. 224	Cassius Dio, *Roman History*	218–22	Elagabalus' principate
	c. 229	Death of Cassius Dio	222–35	Alexander Severus' principate
	c. 249	Origen, *Against Celsus*	230s–40s	Sasanian Persians invade eastern provinces
250–300	269/70	Death of Plotinus	235–84	Anarchy in the empire; conflict with Persians, Franks, Gauls and Goths
			284	Diocletian divides the empire
300–350	c. 300	Triphiodorus active	303–5	Persecution of Christians
			312	Battle of Milvian Bridge; 'conversion' of Constantine to Christianity
	c. 317	Lactantius, *On the Deaths of the Persecutors*	324	Foundation of Constantinople
			325	Council of Nicaea
350–400	350s	Libanius active; publication of *Historia Augusta* (?)		
	360s–70s	Aurelius Victor, Ausonius, Eutropius, Festus active	361–3	Pagan revival under Julian
			362–3	Julian invades Parthia
			374	Ambrose becomes Bishop of Milan

	Date	Literary events	Date	Political and cultural events
	c. 380–91	Ammianus composes his History	386	Conversion of Augustine
	382–c. 405	Jerome starts his translation of the Bible (the Vulgate)	391	Closure of pagan temples
	397–400	Augustine, Confessions	395	Augustine becomes Bishop of Hippo
400–450	c. 400	Avianus, Avienus, Claudian, Jerome active		
	410s	Rutilius Namatianus active	410	Alaric sacks Rome
	413–29	Augustine composes City of God	410–50	Conflict with Visigoths, Vandals, Huns
	420s	Macrobius active	430	Death of Augustine
450–500			455	The Vandal Gaiseric sacks Rome
			476	Last western emperor deposed
	480s	Martianus Capella active	480s–90s	Conflict between the eastern empire and the west
500			500	Theoderic enters Rome as emperor
			526	Death of Theoderic
			529	Closure of the Academy in Athens by Justinian I; codification of Roman law

Bibliography

Ackrill, J. (1981) *Aristotle the Philosopher*. Oxford

Adams, C. (1919) *The Speeches of Aeschines*. Cambridge, MA

Ahl, F. (1976) *Lucan: An Introduction*. Ithaca, NY

Alston, R. (1998) *Aspects of Roman History AD 14–117*. London

Anderson, G. (1993) *The Second Sophistic*. London

Anderson, J. (1974) *Xenophon*. London

Anderson, W. (1982) *Essays on Roman Satire*. Princeton, NJ
    ed. (1999) *Why Horace?* Wauconda

Andrewes, A. (1956) *The Greek Tyrants*. London

Annas, J. (2000) *Ancient Philosophy: A Very Short Introduction*. Oxford
    (2003) *Plato: A Very Short Introduction*. Oxford

Armitage, S. (2006) *The Odyssey (A Radio Play)*. London

Armstrong, A. (1967) *Later Greek and Medieval Philosophy*. Cambridge

Armstrong, R. (2005) *Ovid and his Love Poetry*. London

Ash, R. (1999) *Ordering Anarchy: Armies and Leaders in Tacitus' Histories*. London
    (2006) *Tacitus*. London
    and Sharrock, A. (2002) *Fifty Key Classical Authors*. London

Atwood, M. (2005) *The Penelopiad*. Edinburgh

Augoustakis, A. (2010) *Motherhood and the Other: Fashioning Female Power in Flavian Epic*. Oxford

Austin, N. (1975) *Archery at the Dark of the Moon*. Berkeley, CA

Bailey, C. (1947) *Titi Lucreti De Rerum Natura*. Oxford

Baldwin, B. (1983) *Suetonius*. Amsterdam

Barchiesi, A. (1997) *The Poet and the Prince: Ovid and Augustan Discourse*. Berkeley, CA
    (2001) *Speaking Volumes: Narrative and Intertext in Ovid and Other Latin Poets*. London

Barnes, J. (1982) *The Presocratic Philosophers*. London
    ed. (1984) *The Revised Oxford Translation of Aristotle*. Princeton, NJ
    ed. (1995) *The Cambridge Companion to Aristotle*. Cambridge
    (2000) *Aristotle: A Very Short Introduction*. Oxford
    (2002) *Early Greek Philosophy*. Harmondsworth

Barsby, J. (1986) *Terence, The Eunuch, Phormio, The Brothers: A Companion to the Penguin Translation*. London
    (1991) *Plautus: Bacchides*. Warminster
    (2001) *Terence*. 2 vols. Cambridge, MA

Bartsch, S. (1994) *Actors in the Audience: Theatricality and Doublespeak from Nero to Hadrian.* Cambridge, MA

(1997) *Ideology in Cold Blood: A Reading of Lucan's Civil War.* Cambridge, MA

Beacham, R. (1991) *The Roman Theatre and its Audience.* London

Beard, M. and Crawford, M. (1985) *Rome in the Late Republic.* London

Beard, M. and Henderson, J. (2000) *Classics: A Very Short Introduction.* Oxford

Beard, M., North, J. and Price, S. (1998) *Religions of Rome.* 2 vols. Cambridge

Beare, W. (1964) *The Roman Stage.* London

Bernstein, N. (2008) *In the Image of the Ancestors: Narratives of Kinship in Flavian Epic.* Toronto

Beye, C. (1982) *Epic and Romance in the Argonautica of Apollonius.* Carbondale, IL

Bilde, P. (1988) *Flavius Josephus between Jerusalem and Rome.* Sheffield

Bing, P. (1988) *The Well-Read Muse: Present and Past in Callimachus and the Hellenistic Poets.* Gottingen

Bird, H. (1994) *Aurelius Victor: De Caesaribus.* Liverpool

Blundell, M. Whitlock (1989) *Helping Friends and Harming Enemies: A Study in Sophocles and Greek Ethics.* Cambridge

Blundell, S. (1998) *Women in Classical Athens.* London

Boardman, J., Griffin, J. and Murray, O. eds (1986) *The Oxford History of the Classical World.* Oxford

Booth, J. (2007) *Cicero on the Attack: Invective and Subversion in the Orations and Beyond.* Oxford

and Lee, G. (1999) *Catullus to Ovid: Reading Latin Love Elegy.* London

Bowersock, G. (1969) *Greek Sophists in the Roman Empire.* Oxford

et al. eds (1999) *Late Antiquity.* Cambridge, MA

et al. eds (2001) *Interpreting Late Antiquity.* Cambridge, MA

Bowie, A. (1993) *Aristophanes: Myth, Ritual and Comedy.* Cambridge

(1997) 'Thinking with Drinking: Wine and the Symposium in Aristophanes', *Journal of Hellenic Studies* 117: 1–21

Bowie, E. (1990) 'Greek Poetry in the Antonine Age', in D. A. Russell ed. *Antonine Literature*: 53–90. Oxford

Bowman, A. and Woolf, G. eds (1994) *Literacy and Power in the Ancient World.* Cambridge

Boyd, B. (1997) *Ovid's Literary Loves.* Michigan

Boyle, A. ed. (1993) *Roman Epic.* London

(1997) *Tragic Seneca.* London

(2006) *An Introduction to Roman Tragedy.* London

Bracht, B. (1989) *Unruly Eloquence: Lucian and the Comedy of Traditions.* Cambridge, MA

Bradley, K. (1994) *Slavery and Society at Rome.* Cambridge

Bramble, J. (1974) *Persius and the Programmatic Satire.* Cambridge

Braund, S. (1988) *Beyond Anger: A Study of Juvenal's Third Book of Satires.* Cambridge

(1992) *Roman Verse Satire.* Oxford

(1996) *The Roman Satirists and their Masks.* Bristol

(2002) *Latin Literature.* London

Bremmer, J. (2004) *Greek Religion.* Oxford

Brink, C. (1963–82) *Horace: Epistles.* 3 vols. Cambridge

Brown, P. (1989) *The World of Late Antiquity.* London

(1990) *The Body and Society.* New York

Brown, P. (trans.) (2008) *Terence: The Comedies.* Oxford

Bruit Zaidman, L. and Schmitt Pantel, O. (1992) *Religion in the Ancient Greek City.* Cambridge (trans. P. Cartledge)

Brunt, P. (1971) *Italian Manpower 225 BC–AD 14*. Oxford

Buck, C. (1998) *Greek Dialects*. London

  (2009) *Introduction to the Study of Greek Dialects*. Charleston, SC

Buckley, T. (1996) *Aspects of Greek History 750–323 BC*. London

Budelmann, F. ed. (2009) *The Cambridge Companion to Greek Lyric Poetry*. Cambridge

Burkert, W. (1985) *Greek Religion*. Oxford (trans. J. Raffan)

Burnett, A. (1998) *Three Archaic Poets: Archilochus, Alcaeus, Sappho*. Bristol

  (2008) *Pindar*. London

Burnyeat, M. ed. (1994) *Socratic Studies*. Cambridge

Burton, J. (1995) *Theocritus' Urban Mimes*. Berkeley, CA

Buxton, R. (1982) *Persuasion in Greek Tragedy*. Cambridge

  (1994) *Imaginary Greece: The Contexts of Mythology*. Cambridge

  ed. (2001) *From Myth to Reason? Studies in the Development of Greek Thought*. Oxford

  (2004) *The Complete World of Greek Mythology*. London

Cairns, D. ed. (2002) *Oxford Readings in Homer's Iliad*. Oxford

Cairns, F. (1979) *Tibullus: A Hellenistic Poet at Rome*. Cambridge

  (2006) *Virgil's Augustan Epic*. Cambridge

  (2009) *Sextus Propertius: The Augustan Elegist*. Cambridge

Cameron, Alan (1995) *Callimachus and his Critics*. Princeton, NJ

  (2004) 'Poetry and literary culture in Late Antiquity' in S. Swain and M. Edwards eds *Approaching Late Antiquity: The Transformation from Early to Late Empire*: 327–54. Oxford

Cameron, Averil (1993a) *The Later Roman Empire AD 284–430*. London

  (1993b) *The Mediterranean World in Late Antiquity*. London

Campbell, B. (2002) *War and Society in Imperial Rome 31 BC–AD 284*. London

Campbell, D. (1982–93) *Greek Lyric*. 5 vols. Cambridge, MA

Carey, C. ed. (2007) *Lysiae Orationes Cum Fragmentis*. Oxford

Carter, D. (2007) *The Politics of Greek Tragedy*. Exeter

Cartledge, P. (1990) *Aristophanes and his Theatre of the Absurd*. Bristol

  (2002a) *The Greeks: A Portrait of Self and Others*. Oxford

  ed. (2002b) *The Cambridge Illustrated History of Ancient Greece*. Cambridge

  (2003) *The Spartans: An Epic History*. London

  (2009) *Ancient Greek Political Thought in Practice*. Cambridge

Cartwright, D. (1997) *A Historical Commentary on Thucydides*. Michigan

Cawkwell, G. (1997) *Thucydides and the Peloponnesian War*. London

Clausen, W. (1994) *A Commentary on Virgil's Eclogues*. Oxford

Coffey, M. (1976) *Roman Satire*. London

Coleman, R. (1977) *Vergil Eclogues*. Cambridge

Collins, R. (1999) *Early Medieval Europe 300–1000*. London

Colonna, A. (1938) *Heliodorus*. Rome

Connor, W. (1984) *Thucydides*. Princeton, NJ

Connors, C. (1998) *Petronius the Poet: Verse and Literary Tradition in the Satyricon*. Cambridge

Conte, G. B. (1994) *Latin Literature: A History*. Baltimore, MD (trans. J. B. Solodow, rev. D. Fowler and G. W. Most)

  (1996) *The Hidden Author: An Interpretation of Petronius' Satyricon*. Berkeley, CA

Cornell, T. (1995) *The Beginning of Rome: Italy and Rome from the Bronze Age to the Punic Wars*. London

Cornford, F. (1932) *Before and after Socrates*. Cambridge

Costa, C. ed. (1973) *Horace*. London

  ed. (1974) *Seneca*. London

Courtney, E. (2001) *A Companion to Petronius*. Oxford

Croally, N. (1994) *Euripidean Polemic: The Trojan Women and the Function of Tragedy*. Cambridge
(2005) 'Tragedy's Teaching', in Gregory (2005): 55–70

Crotty, K. (1982) *Song and Action: The Victory Odes of Pindar*. Baltimore, MD

Csapo, E. and Slater, W. eds (1994) *The Context of Ancient Greek Drama*. Michigan

Dalmeyde, G. (1962) *Xenophon of Ephesus*. Paris

D'Ambra, E. (2006) *Roman Women*. Cambridge

Davidson, J. (2008) *The Greeks and Greek Love: A Radical Reappraisal of Homosexuality in Ancient Greece*. London

Davies, J. (1993) *Democracy and Classical Greece*. London

Davies, M. and Swain, H. (2010) *Aspects of Roman History: 82 BC–AD 14*. London

Davis, P. (2005) *Ovid and Augustus*. London

DeForest, M. (1994) *Apollonius' Argonautica: A Callimachean Epic*. Leiden

Dennison, W. (2009) *The Epigraphic Sources of the Writings of Gaius Suetonius Tranquillus*. Michigan

Detienne, M. (1996) *The Masters of Truth in Archaic Greece*. New York (trans. J. Lloyd)

Dewald, C. and Marincola, J. eds (2006) *The Cambridge Companion to Herodotus*. Cambridge

Dihle, A. (1994) *Greek and Latin Literature of the Roman Empire*. London

Dillery, J. (1995) *Xenophon and the History of his Times*. London

Dilts, M. (2002–09) *Demosthenis Orationes*. 4 vols. Oxford

Dominik, W. (1993) 'From Greece to Rome: Ennius' *Annales*', in Boyle (1993)
and Hall, J. (2006) *A Companion to Roman Rhetoric*. Oxford

Dorey, T. ed. (1971) *Livy*. London

Douglas, A. E. (1968) *Cicero*. Oxford

Dover, K. J. (1968) *Lysias and the Corpus Lysiacum*. Berkeley, CA
(1972) *Aristophanic Comedy*. Berkeley, CA
(1973) *Thucydides*. Oxford
(1980) *Greek Homosexuality*. London

Dowden, K. (1992) *Religion and the Romans*. London

DuBois, P. (1995) *Sappho is Burning*. Chicago

Duckworth, G. E. (1994) *The Nature of Roman Comedy*. London

Dyck, A. ed. (2008) *Cicero: Catilinarians*. Cambridge

Earl, D. (1961) *The Political Thought of Sallust*. Cambridge

Easterling, P. (1985) 'Anachronism in Greek Tragedy', *Journal of Hellenistic Studies* 105: 1–10
ed. (1989) *The Hellenistic Period and the Empire*. Cambridge
ed. (1997) *The Cambridge Companion to Greek Tragedy*. Cambridge

Easterling, P. and Knox, B. eds (1985) *The Cambridge History of Classical Literature*. Vol. 1. Cambridge

Easterling, P. and Muir, J. eds (1985) *Greek Religion and Society*. Cambridge

Eck, W. (2007) *The Age of Augustus*. Oxford

Edmunds, L. ed. (1989) *Approaches to Greek Myth*. Baltimore, MD

Edwards, M. (1987) *The Poet of the Iliad*. Baltimore, MD

Erasmo, M. (2004) *Roman Tragedy*. Austin, TX

Fagles, R. (2007) *The Aeneid*. London

Fairweather, J. (1981) *The Elder Seneca*. Cambridge

Fantham, E. (1996) *Roman Literary Culture: From Cicero to Apuleius*. Baltimore, MD
(2004) *Ovid's Metamorphoses*. Oxford

Fantuzzi, M. and Hunter, R. (2004) *Tradition and Innovation in Hellenistic Poetry*. Cambridge

Farrell, J. (1991) *Virgil's Georgics and the Traditions of Ancient Epic*. Oxford

Feeney, D. (1992) '*Si licet et fas est*: Ovid's *Fasti* and the problem of free speech under the principate', in Powell (1992)

(1998) *Literature and Religion at Rome*. Cambridge

(2007) *The Gods in Epic: Poets and Critics of the Classical Tradition*. Berkeley, CA

Feldherr, A. (1998) *Spectacle and Society in Livy's History*. Berkeley, CA

ed. (2009) *The Cambridge Companion to Roman Historians*. Cambridge

Ferguson, J. (1988) *Catullus*. Oxford

Figueira, T. and Nagy, G. eds (1985) *Theognis of Megara: Poetry and the Polis*. Baltimore, MD

Finkelpearl, E. (1998) *Metamorphosis of Language in Apuleius*. Ann Arbor, MI

Finley, M. ed. (1960) *Slavery in Classical Antiquity*. Cambridge

(1973) *The Ancient Economy*. Berkeley, CA

(1980) *Ancient Slavery and Modern Ideology*. London

(1981) *Economy and Society in Ancient Greece*. London

(1983) *Politics in the Ancient World*. Cambridge

ed. (1987) *Classical Slavery*. London

and Pleket, H. (1976) *The Olympic Games*. London

Fisher, N. (1998) *Slavery in Classical Greece*. London

Fitzgerald, W. (1995) *Catullan Provocations*. Berkeley, CA

(2000) *Slavery and the Roman Imagination*. Cambridge

Flower, H. ed. (2004) *The Cambridge Companion to the Roman Republic*. Cambridge

Foley, H. (1985) *Ritual Irony: Poetry and Sacrifice in Euripides*. Ithaca, NY

Foley, J. ed. (2005) *A Companion to Ancient Epic*. Oxford

Forrest, W. G. (1980) *A History of Sparta*. London

Fowler, R. ed. (2004) *The Cambridge Companion to Homer*. Cambridge

Fraenkel, E. (1957) *Horace*. Oxford

(2007) *Plautine Elements in Plautus*. Oxford (trans. F. Muecke and T. Drevikovsky)

Fraser, P. (1972) *Ptolemaic Alexandria*. 3 vols. Oxford

Freudenburg, K. (1993) *The Walking Muse: Horace on the Theory of Satire*. Princeton, NJ

(2001) *Satires of Rome*. Cambridge

ed. (2005) *The Cambridge Companion to Roman Satire*. Cambridge

Futrell, A. (1997) *Blood in the Arena*. Austin, TX

Gagarin, M. (2005) *The Cambridge Companion to Ancient Greek Law*. Cambridge

Gagarin, M. and Woodruff, P. eds (1995) *Early Greek Political Thought from Homer to the Sophists*. Cambridge

Gale, M. (1994) *Myth and Poetry in Lucretius*. Cambridge

(2000) *Virgil on the Nature of Things*. Cambridge

(2001) *Lucretius and the Didactic Epic*. London

Galinsky, K. (1975) *Ovid's Metamorphoses: An Introduction to the Basic Aspects*. Oxford

ed. (2005) *The Cambridge Companion to the Age of Augustus*. Cambridge

Gamberini, F. (1983) *Stylistic Theory and Practice in the Younger Pliny*. Hildesheim

Gardner, J. (1987) *Women in Roman Law and Society*. London

Garlan, Y. (1975) *War in the Ancient World*. London (trans. J. Lloyd)

(1988) *Slavery in the Ancient World*. Ithaca, NY (trans. J. Lloyd)

Garnsey, P. (1996) *Ideas of Slavery from Aristotle to Augustine*. Cambridge

Gelzer, M. (1968) *Caesar: Politician and Statesman*. Oxford

Gildenhard, I. (2010) *Creative Eloquence: The Construction of Reality in Cicero's Speeches*. Oxford

Gill, C. (1995) *Greek Thought*. Oxford

Gill, M. L. and Pellegrin, P. eds (2006) *A Companion to Ancient Philosophy*. Oxford

Ginsburg, J. (1981) *Tradition and Theme in the Annals of Tacitus*. New Hampshire

Godwin, J. (1996) *Catullus: Poems 61–8*. Warminster

(1999) *Catullus: The Shorter Poems*. Warminster

(2004) *Lucretius*. London

(2008) *Reading Catullus*. Bristol

Gold, B. (2009) *Literary Patronage in Greece and Rome*. North Carolina

Goldberg, S. (1980) *The Making of Menander's Comedy*. London

(1986) *Understanding Terence*. Princeton, NJ

(1995) *Epic in Republican Rome*. Oxford

Goldhill, S. (1984) 'Two Notes on τελος and Related Words in the *Oresteia*', *Journal of Hellenistic Studies* 104: 169–76

(1986) *Reading Greek Tragedy*. Cambridge

(1990) 'The Great Dionysia and civic ideology', in Winkler and Zeitlin (1990)

(1991) *The Poet's Voice*. Cambridge

(1992) *Aeschylus: The Oresteia*. Cambridge

(1995) *Foucault's Virginity: Ancient Erotic Fiction and the History of Sexuality*. Cambridge

(2000) 'Civic ideology and the problem of difference: the politics of Aeschylean tragedy, once again', *Journal of Hellenic Studies* 120: 34–56

ed. (2001) *Being Greek under Rome*. Cambridge

(2002) *The Invention of Prose*. Oxford

(2007) *How to Stage Greek Tragedy Today*. Chicago

and Osborne, R. eds (1999) *Performance Culture and Athenian Democracy*. Cambridge

and Osborne, R. eds (2006) *Rethinking Revolutions through Ancient Greece*. Cambridge

and Hall, E. eds (2009) *Sophocles and the Greek Tragic Tradition*. Cambridge

Goodman, M. (1997) *The Roman World: 44BC–AD180*. London

Gould, J. (1989) *Herodotus*. London

Gould, T. and Herington, J. (2009) *Greek Tragedy*. New Haven, CT

Gransden, K. (1984) *Virgil's Iliad*. Cambridge

(1990) *Virgil: The Aeneid*. Cambridge

and Harrison, S. eds (2003) *Virgil: The Aeneid*. Cambridge

Green, P. (1990) *Alexander to Actium*. Berkeley, CA

(2007) *The Hellenistic Age: A Short History*. New York

Greene, E. ed. (1996) *Reading Sappho: Contemporary Approaches*. Berkeley, CA

(1998) *The Erotics of Domination*. Baltimore, MD

Greenwood, E. (2006) *Thucydides and the Shaping of History*. London

Gregory, J. ed. (2005) *A Companion to Greek Tragedy*. Oxford

Griffin, J. (1980) *Homer on Life and Death*. Oxford

(1985) *Latin Poets and Roman Life*. London

(1986) *Virgil*. Oxford

(1987) *Homer: The Odyssey*. Cambridge

(1999a) 'The social function of Attic tragedy', *Classical Quarterly* 48: 3–61

ed. (1999b) *Sophocles Revisited*. Oxford

Griffin, M. (1976) *Seneca: A Philosopher in Politics*. Oxford

Gunderson, E. ed. (2009) *The Cambridge Companion to Ancient Rhetoric*. Cambridge

Guthrie, W. K. C. (1971a) *Socrates*. Cambridge

(1971b) *The Sophists*. Cambridge

Gutzwiller, K. (1991) *Theocritus' Pastoral Analogies*. Wisconsin
  (2007) *A Guide to Hellenistic Literature*. Oxford
Habinek, T. (2005) *Ancient Rhetoric and Oratory*. Oxford
  and Schiesaro, A. eds (1997) *The Roman Cultural Revolution*. Cambridge
Hagel, S. (2009) *Ancient Greek Music: A New Technical History*. Cambridge
Hagg, T. (1983) *The Novel in Antiquity*. Berkeley, CA
Hall, E. (1989) *Inventing the Barbarian*. Oxford
  (2008) *The Return of Odysseus: A Cultural History of Homer's Odyssey*. London
  (2010) *Greek Tragedy: Suffering under the Sun*. Oxford
Hall, J. (1981) *Lucian's Satire*. New York
Hall, J. (2006) *A History of the Archaic Greek World*. Oxford
Hamilton, N. (2010) *American Caesars: Lives of the US Presidents from Franklin D. Roosevelt to George W. Bush*. London
Hamilton, R. (1989) *The Architecture of Hesiodic Poetry*. Baltimore, MD
Hansen, M. (1976) 'How many Athenians attended the Ekklesia?', *Greek, Roman and Byzantine Studies* 17: 115–34
  (2006) *Polis*. Oxford
Hansen, W. (1996) *Phlegon of Tralles' Book of Marvels*. Exeter
Hanson, V. (1989) *The Western Way of War*. London
  ed. (1991) *Hoplites: The Classical Greek Battle Experience*. London
Hardie, P. (1989) *Virgil's Aeneid: Cosmos and Imperium*. Oxford
  (1993) *The Epic Successors of Virgil*. Cambridge
  (1998) *Virgil*. Oxford
  (1999) *Virgil: Critical Assessments of Classical Authors*. London
  ed. (2002) *The Cambridge Companion to Ovid*. Cambridge
  (2007) *Ovid's Poetics of Illusion*. Cambridge
Hare, R. (1986) *Plato*. Oxford
Harris, E. (1995) *Aeschines and Athenian Politics*. Oxford
Harris, R. (2006) *Imperium*. New York
  (2010) *Lustrum*. London
Harris, W. (1979) *War and Imperialism in Republican Rome 327–70 BC*. Oxford
  (1989) *Ancient Literacy*. Cambridge, MA
Harrison, S. ed. (1990) *Oxford Readings in Vergil's Aeneid*. Oxford
  ed. (1995) *Homage to Horace: A Bimillenary Celebration*. Oxford
  ed. (1999) *Oxford Readings in the Roman Novel*. Oxford
  ed. (2000a) *Seneca in Performance*. London
  (2000b) *Apuleius: A Latin Sophist*. Oxford
  ed. (2005) *A Companion to Latin Literature*. Oxford
  ed. (2007) *The Cambridge Companion to Horace*. Cambridge
Harrison, T. (2000) *Divinity and History: The Religion of Herodotus*. Oxford
Hartog, F. (1988) *The Mirror of Herodotus*. Berkeley, CA (trans. J. Lloyd)
Havelock, E. (1972) 'War as a way of life in classical culture', in E. Gareau ed. *Classical Values and the Modern World*. Ottawa
  (1982) *The Literate Revolution in Greece and its Cultural Consequences*. Princeton, NJ
Hawley, R. and Levick, B. eds (1995) *Women in Antiquity: New Assessments*. London
Haynes, H. (2003) *Tacitus on Imperial Rome*. Berkeley, CA
Heath, M. (1986) *The Poetics of Greek Tragedy*. Stanford, CA
Henderson, J. (1997) *Figuring out Roman Nobility: Juvenal's Eighth Satire*. Exeter

(1998) *Fighting for Rome*. Cambridge

(1999) *Writing Down Rome*. Oxford

(2002) *Pliny's Statue: The Letters, Self-Presentation and Classical Art*. Exeter

(2004) *Morals and Villas in Seneca's Letters*. Cambridge

Herington, J. (1985) *Poetry into Drama: Early Tragedy and the Greek Poetic Tradition*. Berkeley, CA

Herschowitz, D. (1998) *Valerius Flaccus' Argonautica*. Oxford

Hesk, J. (2000) *Deception and Democracy in Classical Athens*. Cambridge

Heslin, P. (2005) *The Transvestite Achilles: Gender and Genre in Statius' Achilleid*. Cambridge

Hills, P. (2005) *Horace*. London

Hinds, S. (1998) *Allusion and Intertext*. Cambridge

Hoffer, S. (1999) *The Anxieties of Pliny the Younger*. Atlanta, GA

Hofmann, H. ed. (1999) *Latin Fiction: The Latin Novel in Context*. London

Holford-Stevens, L. (1988) *Aulus Gellius*. London

Holzberg, N. (1994) *The Ancient Novel: An Introduction*. London

Hooley, H. (2006) *Roman Satire*. Oxford

Hopkins, K. (1978) *Conquerors and Slaves*. Cambridge

(2000) *A World Full of Gods*. London

Hopkinson, N. (1984) *Callimachus: Hymn to Demeter*. Cambridge

(1988) *A Hellenistic Anthology*. Cambridge

ed. (1994) *Greek Poetry of the Imperial Period: An Anthology*. Cambridge

Hornblower, S. (1987) *Thucydides*. London

ed. (1996) *Greek Historiography*. Oxford

(2002) *The Greek World 479–323 BC*. London

and Spawforth, A. eds (2003) *The Oxford Classical Dictionary*. Oxford

Horrocks, G. (1997) *Greek: A History of the Language and its Speakers*. London

Houghton, L. and Wyke, M. (2009) *Perceptions of Horace*. Cambridge

Howatson, M. (1997) *The Oxford Companion to Classical Literature*. Oxford

Hubbard, M. (2001) *Propertius*. London

Hunter, R. L. (1983) *A Study of Daphnis and Chloe*. Cambridge

(1985) *The New Comedy of Greece and Rome*. Cambridge

(1993) *The Argonautica of Apollonius: Literary Studies*. Cambridge

(1996) *Theocritus and the Archaeology of Greek Poetry*. Cambridge

Hurley, A. (2004) *Catullus*. London

Hussey, E. (1972) *The Presocratics*. London

Hutchinson, G. (1988) *Hellenistic Poetry*. Oxford

(1998) *Cicero's Correspondence: A Literary Study*. Oxford

Inwood, B. (1988) *Hellenistic Philosophy: Introductory Readings*. Indianapolis

Irwin, T. ed. (1999) *Classical Philosophy*. Oxford

Jaeger, M. (1997) *Livy's Written Rome*. Michigan

Jaeger, W. (1945) *Paideia*. Vol. 3. Oxford (trans. G. Highet)

James, S. (2003) *Learned Girls and Male Persuasion*. Berkeley, CA

Jenkyns, R. (1998) *Classical Epic: Homer and Virgil*. London

Jocelyn, H. D. ed. (1967) *The Tragedies of Ennius*. Cambridge

Johnson, W. (1987) *Momentary Monsters: Lucan and his Heroes*. Ithaca, NY

(2000) *Lucretius and the Modern World*. London

Johnson, M. and Ryan, T. eds (2004) *Sexuality in Greek and Roman Literature and Society: A Sourcebook*. London

Jones, A. (1967) *A History of Sparta*. New York

(1986) *The Later Roman Empire AD 284–602*. Baltimore, MD

Jones, C. (1986) *Culture and Society in Lucian*. Cambridge, MA

Jones, P. ed. (1984) *The World of Athens*. Cambridge

Jones, P. (1992) *Homer's Odyssey: A Companion*. London
  and Sidwell, K. eds (1997) *The World of Rome*. Cambridge

Joyce, J. (1922) *Ulysses*. Paris (= Oxford World Classics, 2008)

Just, R. (1989) *Women in Athenian Law and Life*. London

Kagan, D. (2009) *Thucydides: The Reinvention of History*. New York

Kahn, C. (1996) *Plato and the Socratic Dialogue*. Cambridge

Keane, C. (2006) *Figuring Genre in Roman Satire*. Oxford

Keil, H. (1857) *Grammataci Latini*. Vol. 1. Leipzig

Keith, A. (2002) *Engendering Rome*. Cambridge

Kelly, G. (2008) *Ammanus Marcellinus: The Allusive Historian*. Cambridge

Kennedy, D. (1993) *The Arts of Love*. Cambridge

Kennedy, G. (1963) *The Art of Persuasion in Greece*. Princeton, NJ
  (1972) *The Art of Rhetoric in the Roman World*. Princeton, NJ
  (1994) *A New History of Classical Rhetoric*. Princeton, NJ

Kenney, E. and Clausen, W. eds (1983) *The Cambridge History of Classical Literature Volume 2: Latin Literature*. Cambridge

Kerferd, G. (1981) *The Sophistic Movement*. Cambridge

Keuls, E. (1985) *The Reign of the Phallus*. New York

Kirk, G. S., Raven, J. E., and Schofield, M. (1983) *The Presocratic Philosophers*. Cambridge

Knox, B. (1952) 'The *Hippolytus* of Euripides', *Yale Classical Studies* 13: 3–31
  (1961) 'The *Ajax* of Sophocles', *Harvard Studies in Classical Philology* 65: 1–39
  (1964) *The Heroic Temper: Studies in Sophoclean Tragedy*. Berkeley, CA

Konstan, D. (1983) *Roman Comedy*. Ithaca, NY

Kraus, C. and Woodman, A. (1997) *Latin Historians*. Oxford

Kraut, R. ed. (1992) *The Cambridge Companion to Plato*. Cambridge

Kurke, L. (1991) *The Traffic of Praise: Pindar and the Poetics of the Social Economy*. Ithaca, NY

Kyle, D. (1987) *Athletics in Ancient Athens*. Leiden
  (1998) *Spectacles of Death in Ancient Rome*. London
  (2007) *Sport and Spectacle in the Ancient World*. Oxford

Lambropoulos, V. (2006) *The Tragic Idea*. London

Lane Fox, R. (1986) *Pagans and Christians*. London
  ed. (2004) *The Long March: Xenophon and the Ten Thousand*. New Haven, CT

Latham, R. and Godwin, J. (1994) *On the Nature of the Universe*. London

Lee, G. (2006) *The Eclogues*. London

Lee-Stecum, P. (1998) *Powerplay in Tibullus: Reading Elegies Book One*. Cambridge

Lefkowitz, M. (1991) *First-Person Fictions: Pindar's Poetic 'I'*. Oxford
  and Fant, M. eds (2005) *Women's Life in Greece and Rome*. London

Leigh, M. (1997) *Lucan: Spectacle and Engagement*. Oxford
  (2004) *Comedy and the Rise of Rome*. Oxford

Lesher, J. H. ed. (1999) *The Greek Philosophers: Selected Texts from the Presocratics, Plato, and Aristotle*. London

Lindheim, S. and Rosenmayer, P. (2003) *Male and Female: Epistolary Narrative and Desire in Ovid's Heroides*. Wisconsin

Lissarague, F. (1990) *The Aesthetics of the Greek Banquet*. Princeton, NJ (trans. A. Szegedy-Maszak)

Lloyd, G. (1979) *Magic, Reason, Experience*. Cambridge
  (1996) *Aristotelian Explorations*. Cambridge

Lloyd, M. ed. (2006) *Oxford Readings in Aeschylus*. Oxford

Logue, C. (1981) *War Music*. London

  (1991) *Kings*. London

  (1994) *The Husbands*. London

  (2003) *All Day Permanent Red*. London

  (2005) *Cold Calls*. London

Long, A. ed. (1999) *The Cambridge Companion to Early Greek Philosophy*. Cambridge

  and Sedley, D. eds (1987) *The Hellenistic Philosophers*. Cambridge

Loraux, N. (1986) *The Invention of Athens*. Chicago (trans. A. Sheridan)

Lovatt, H. (2005) *Statius and Epic Games*. Cambridge

Lowe, N. (2007) *Comedy* (Greece and Rome New Surveys in the Classics). Cambridge

Lowrie, M. (1997) *Horace's Narrative Odes*. Oxford

Luce, T. and Woodman, A. eds (1993) *Tacitus and the Tacitean Tradition*. Princeton, NJ

Lyne, R. (1980) *The Latin Love Poets*. Oxford

  (1987) *Further Voices in Virgil's Aeneid*. Oxford

McCarthy, K. (2000) *Slaves, Masters and the Art of Authority in Plautine Comedy*. Princeton, NJ

Macleod, C. (1983) *Collected Essays*. Oxford

McClure, L. (2002) *Sexuality and Gender in the Classical World: Readings and Documents*. Oxford

McCoy, M. (2008) *Plato on the Rhetoric of Philosophers and Sophists*. Cambridge

MacDowell, D. (1986) *The Law in Classical Athens*. Ithaca, NY

  (1995) *Aristophanes and Athens*. Oxford

  (2009) *Demosthenes the Orator*. Oxford

McKechnie, P. and Kern, S. eds (1988) *Hellenica Oxyrhynchia*. Warminster

MacKendrick, P. (1989) *The Philosophical Works of Cicero*. London

McKeown, N. (2007) *The Invention of Ancient Slavery*. London

McNeill, R. (2001) *Horace: Image, Identity and Audience*. Baltimore, MD

MacQueen, B. (1990) *Myth, Rhetoric and Fiction: A Reading of Longus' Daphnis and Chloe*. Lincoln, NE

Maidment, K. (1941) *Minor Attic Orators*. Vol. 1. Cambridge, MA

Malcolm Errington, R. (2008) *A History of the Hellenistic World 323–30 BC*. Oxford

Manning, J. and Morris, I. (2005) *The Ancient Economy: Evidence and Models*. Stanford, CA

Marchesi, I. (2008) *The Art of Pliny's Letters*. Cambridge

Marincola, J. (1997) *Authority and Tradition in Ancient Historiography*. Cambridge

  (2001) *Greek Historians*. Oxford

  ed. (2007) *A Companion to Greek and Roman Historiography*. Oxford

Marrou, H. (1956) *A History of Education in Antiquity*. London (trans. G. Lamb)

Martin, J. ed. (1996) *Juvenal: A Farrago*. Las Palmas

Martin, R. (1981) *Tacitus*. Berkeley, CA

Martindale, C. ed. (1997) *The Cambridge Companion to Virgil*. Cambridge

Mason, A. (2010) *Plato*. Durham, NC

Masters, J. (1992) *Poetry and Civil War in Lucan's Bellum Civile*. Cambridge

Matthews, J. (1989) *The Roman Empire of Ammianus Marcellinus*. Baltimore, MD

Meier, C. (1993) *The Political Nature of Greek Tragedy*. Baltimore, MD (trans. A. Webber)

Mellor, R. (1994) *Tacitus*. London

Melville, R. (1997) *On the Nature of the Universe*. Oxford

Michelini, A. (1987) *Euripides and the Tragic Tradition*. Madison, WI

Millar, F. (1996) *A Study of Cassius Dio*. Oxford

  and Segal, E. eds (1984) *Caesar Augustus: Seven Aspects*. Oxford

Miller, P. (1994) *Lyric Texts and Lyric Consciousness*. London

  (2002) *Latin Erotic Elegy*. London

Missiou, A. (1992) *The Subversive Oratory of Andocides*. Cambridge
  (2010) *Literacy and Democracy in Fifth-Century Athens*. Cambridge
Mitchell, S. (2006) *The Later Roman Empire AD 284–641*. Oxford
Mitchell, T. (1991) *Cicero: The Senior Statesman*. New Haven, CT
Moore, T. (1998) *The Theatre of Plautus*. Austin, TX
Morales, H. (2004) *Achilles Tatius Leucippe and Clitophon*. Cambridge
Morello, R. and Morrison, A. (2007) *Ancient Letters: Classical and Antique Epistolography*. Oxford
Morford, M. (1996) *The Poet Lucan*. London
  and Lenardon, R. (2000) *Classical Mythology*. Oxford
Morgan, J. and Stoneman, R. eds (1994) *Greek Fiction: The Greek Novel in Context*. London
Morris, I. and Powell, B. eds (1997) *A New Companion to Homer*. Leiden
Morrison, J. (2006) *Reading Thucydides*. Ohio
Morstein-Marx, R. (2008) *Mass Oratory and Political Power in the Late Roman Republic*. Cambridge
Mossman, J. ed. (1997) *Plutarch and his Intellectual World*. London
  ed. (2003) *Oxford Readings in Euripides*. Oxford
Mouritsen, H. (2007) *Plebs and Politics in the Late Roman Republic*. Cambridge
Munn, M. (2002) *The School of History: Athens in the Age of Socrates*. Berkeley, CA
Murray, O. (1993) *Early Greece*. London
  ed. (1990) *Sympotica: A Symposium on the Symposium*. Oxford
Murrell, J. (2008) *Cicero and the Roman Republic*. Cambridge
Mynors, R. (1990) *Virgil Georgics*. Oxford
Nagy, G. (1990) *Pindar's Homer: The Lyric Possession of an Epic Past*. Baltimore, MD
  ed. (2001) *Greek Literature in the Hellenistic Period*. London
Newlands, C. (1995) *Playing with Time: Ovid and the Fasti*. Ithaca, NY
  (2002) *Statius' Silvae and the Poetry of Empire*. Cambridge
Nisbet, R. and Hubbard, M. (1970) *A Commentary on Horace Odes, Book I*. Oxford
  (1978) *A Commentary on Horace Odes, Book II*. Oxford
  and Rudd, N. eds (2004) *A Commentary on Horace Odes, Book III*. Oxford
Nixon, P. (1916) *Plautus*. 5 vols. Cambridge, MA
Norlin, G. (1968) *Isocrates*. 3 vols. Cambridge, MA
North, J. (2000) *Roman Religion*. Oxford
Nussbaum, M. (2002) *The Sleep of Reason: Erotic Experience and Sexual Ethics in Ancient Greece and Rome*. Chicago
Ober, J. (1989) *Mass and Elite in Democratic Athens*. Princeton, NJ
  (1998) *The Athenian Revolution*. Princeton, NJ
  (2001) *Political Dissent in Democratic Athens*. Princeton, NJ
Ogden, D. (2010) *A Companion to Greek Religion*. Oxford
Ogilvie, R. (1980) *Roman Literature and Society*. London
O'Gorman, E. (2000) *Irony and Misreading in the Annals of Tacitus*. Cambridge
O'Hara, J. (2007) *Inconsistency in Roman Epic*. Cambridge
Oliensis, E. (1998) *Horace and the Rhetoric of Authority*. Cambridge
Olson, S. ed. (2007) *Broken Laughter: Select Fragments of Greek Comedy*. Oxford
Ormand, K. (2008) *Controlling Desires: Sexuality in Ancient Greece and Rome*. Santa Barbara, CA
Osborne, C. (2004) *Presocratic Philosophy: A Very Short Introduction*. Oxford
Osborne, R. (2000) *Classical Greece*. Oxford
  (2004) *Greek History*. London
  (2009) *Greece in the Making, 1200–479 BC*. London
  and Hornblower, S. eds (1994) *Ritual, Finance, Politics*. Oxford

Otis, B. (1963) *Virgil: A Study in Civilized Poetry*. Oxford

Page, D. (1962) *Poetae Melici Graecae*. Oxford

   (1974) *Supplementum Lyricis Graecis*. Oxford

Papanikolaou, A. (1973) *Xenophon of Ephesus*. Leipzig

Parker, R. (1996) *Athenian Religion: A History*. Oxford

   (2005) *Polytheism and Society at Athens*. Oxford

Paschalis, M. ed. (2005) *Roman and Greek Imperial Epic*. Herakleion

Pearson, L. (1976) *The Art of Demosthenes*. Meisenheim am Glan

Pelling, C. ed. (1990) *Characterization and Individuality in Greek Literature*. Oxford

   ed. (1997) *Greek Tragedy and the Historian*. Oxford

   (2000) *Literary Texts and the Greek Historian*. London

Pichlmayr, F. and Gruendel, R. (1970) *Sexti Aurelii Victoris Liber de Caesaribus*. Leipzig

Plaza, M. (2007) *The Function of Humour in Roman Verse Satire*. Oxford

Podlecki, A. (1984) *The Early Greek Poets and their Times*. British Columbia

Porter, J. (1997) 'Adultery by the book: Lysias 1 and comic diegesis', *Echos du Monde Classique*
   41: 421–53

Powell, A. ed. (1990) *Euripides, Women and Sexuality*. London

   (1991) *Athens and Sparta*. London

   ed. (1992) *Roman Poetry and Propaganda in the Augustan Age*. London

   ed. (1995) *The Greek World*. London

Powell, B. (2004) *Homer*. Oxford

Powell, J. ed. (1999) *Cicero the Philosopher*. Oxford

   and Patterson, J. eds (2006) *Cicero the Advocate*. Oxford

Price, S. (1984) *Rituals and Power*. Cambridge

   (1999) *Religions of the Ancient Greeks*. Cambridge

   and Kearns, E. eds (2003) *The Oxford Dictionary of Classical Myth and Religion*. Oxford

Pritchett, W. (1971–91) *The Greek State at War*. 5 vols. Berkeley, CA

Rabinowitz, N. (2008) *Greek Tragedy*. Oxford

Raby, F. (1927) *A History of Christian Latin Poetry*. Oxford

   (1934) *A History of Secular Latin Poetry in the Middle Ages*. 2 vols. Oxford

Ramsey, J. (2007) *Sallust's Bellum Catilinae*. Oxford

Rattenbury, R., Lumb, T. and Maillon, J. (1960) *Heliodorus*. Paris

Raven, D. (1965) *Latin Metre*. London (paperback 1998)

Rawson, E. (1975) *Cicero: A Portrait*. London

   (1985) *The Intellectual Life of the Late Republic*. Baltimore, MD

Reardon, B. ed. (1989) *Collected Ancient Greek Novels*. Berkeley, CA

Reckford, K. (1987) *Aristophanes' Old and New Comedy*. Chapel Hill, NC

Redfield, J. (1975) *Nature and Culture in the Iliad: The Tragedy of Hector*. Chicago

Reeve, M. (1994) *Longus: Daphnis and Chloe*. Leipzig

Rehm, R. (2002) *The Play of Space*. Princeton, NJ

Rhodes, P. (2003a) 'Nothing to do with democracy: Athenian drama and the *polis*', *Journal of
   Hellenic Studies* 123: 104–19

   (2003b) *Ancient Democracy and Modern Ideology*. London

   (2004) *Athenian Democracy*. Edinburgh

   (2010) *A History of the Classical Greek World*. Oxford

Rich, J. and Shipley, G. eds (1993a) *War and Society in the Greek World*. London

   (1993b) *War and Society in the Roman World*. London

Robinson, C. (1979) *Lucian and his Influence in Europe*. Chapel Hill, NC

Robinson, E. (2003) *Ancient Greek Democracy: A Sourcebook*. Oxford
Robson, J. (2009) *Aristophanes: An Introduction*. London
Rohrbacher, D. (2002) *The Historians of Late Antiquity*. London
Rood, T. (1998) *Thucydides: Narrative and Explanation*. Oxford
Rosenstein, N. and Morstein-Marx, R. eds (2010) *A Companion to the Roman Republic*. Oxford
Rowe, C. (1995) *Plato*. London
   (2007) *Plato and the Art of Philosophical Writing*. Cambridge
Rudd, N.(1986) *Themes in Roman Satire*. London
   ed. (1993) *Horace 2000: A Celebration. Essays for the Bimillennium*. London
Russell, D. (1972) *Plutarch*. London
   (1983) *Greek Declamation*. Cambridge
Rutherford, R. (1995) *The Art of Plato*. London
   (1996) *Homer*. Cambridge
   (2005) *Classical Literature: A Concise History*. Oxford
Sabin, P., Van Wees, H. and Whitby, M. eds (2007) *The Cambridge History of Greek and Roman Warfare*. 2 vols. Cambridge
Sage, M. (1996) *Warfare in Ancient Greece: A Sourcebook*. London
Said, S. and Trédé, M. (1999) *A Short History of Greek Literature*. London
Ste. Croix, G. de (1972) *The Origins of the Peloponnesian War*. London
   (1981) *The Class Struggle in the Ancient World*. London
Salkever, S. ed. (2009) *The Cambridge Companion to Ancient Greek Political Thought*. Cambridge
Saller, R. (2002) *Personal Patronage under the Early Empire*. Cambridge
Santirocco, M. (1986) *Unity and Design in Horace's Odes*. Chapel Hill, NC
Scanlon, T. (1980) *The Influence of Thucydides on Sallust*. Heidelberg
Schein, S. (1984) *The Mortal Hero: An Introduction to Homer's Iliad*. Berkeley, CA
   (1996) *Reading the Odyssey*. Princeton, NJ
Schlegel, A. and Rosenmayer, P. (2003) *Satire and the Threat of Speech in Horace Satires Book 1*. Wisconsin
Scully, S. (1990) *Homer and the Sacred City*. Ithaca, NY
Seaford, R. (2000) 'The social function of Attic tragedy: a response to Jasper Griffin', *Classical Quarterly* 50: 30–44
Sealey, R. (1993) *Demosthenes and his Time*. Oxford
Sedley, D. (1998) *Lucretius and the Transformation of Greek Wisdom*. Cambridge
   ed. (2003) *The Cambridge Companion to Greek and Roman Philosophy*. Cambridge
Segal, C. (1981) *Tragedy and Civilization: An Interpretation of Sophocles*. Cambridge, MA
   (1982) *Dionysiac Poetics and Euripides' Bacchae*. Princeton, NJ
   (1990) *Lucretius on Death and Anxiety*. Princeton, NJ
   (1995a) *Sophocles' Tragic World*. Cambridge, MA
   (1995b) *Singers, Heroes and Gods in the Odyssey*. Ithaca, NY
Segal, E. (1987) *Roman Laughter*. Oxford
   ed. (1989) *Oxford Readings in Greek Tragedy*. Oxford
   (trans.) (1996a) *Plautus: Four Comedies*. Oxford
   ed. (1996b) *Oxford Readings in Aristophanes*. Oxford
   (2001) *The Death of Comedy*. Cambridge, MA
   ed. (2002) *Oxford Readings in Menander, Plautus and Terence*. Oxford
Sharrock, A. (2009) *Reading Roman Comedy*. Cambridge
Sherwin-White, A. (1966) *The Letters of Pliny the Younger*. Oxford
Shipley, G. (1999) *The Greek World after Alexander 323–30 BC*. London

Shorrock, R. (2001) *The Challenge of Epic: Allusive Engagement in the Dionysiaca of Nonnus*. Leiden

Sidebottom, H. (2004) *Ancient Warfare: A Very Short Introduction*. London

Silk, M. (1987) *Homer: The Iliad*. Cambridge

 ed. (1996) *Tragedy and the Tragic*. Oxford

 (2000) *Aristophanes and the Definition of Comedy*. Oxford

Skinner, M. (2004) *Sexuality in Greek and Roman Culture*. Oxford

Skutsch, O. ed. (1985) *The Annals of Ennius*. Oxford

Slater, N. (1985) *Plautus in Performance*. Princeton, NJ

 (1990) *Reading Petronius*. Baltimore, MD

Slavitt, D. (2008) *De Rerum Natura*. Berkeley, CA

Snodgrass, A. (1980) *Archaid Greece: The Age of Experiment*. Berkeley, CA

Solodow, J. (1988) *The World of Ovid's Metamorphoses*. Chapel Hill, NC

Sommerstein, A. (2002) *Greek Drama and Dramatists*. London

Spivey, N. (2005) *The Ancient Olympics: War Minus the Shooting*. Oxford

Stadter, P. (1980) *Arrian of Nicomedia*. Chapel Hill, NC

 ed. (1992) *Plutarch and the Historical Tradition*. London

Stahl, H. (1985) *Propertius: 'Love' and 'War': Individual and State under Augustus*. Berkeley, CA

Steel, C. (2005) *Reading Cicero: Genre and Performance in Late Republican Rome*. London

 (2006) *Roman Oratory*. Cambridge

Steiner, D. (1986) *The Crown of Song: Metaphor in Pindar*. London

Stockton, D. (1971) *Cicero: A Political Biography*. Oxford

Sullivan, J. (1976) *Propertius: A Critical Introduction*. Cambridge

 ed. (1963) *Critical Essays on Roman Literature: Satire*. London

 (1991) *Martial: The Unexpected Classic*. Cambridge

Swain, S. ed. (1999) *Oxford Readings in the Greek Novel*. Oxford

Syme, R. (1939) *The Roman Revolution*. Oxford

 (1958) *Tacitus*. 2 vols. Oxford

 (1974) *Sallust*. Oxford

 (1987) *The Augustan Aristocracy*. Oxford

Szlezak, T. (1999) *Reading Plato*. London

Taafe, L. (1993) *Aristophanes and Women*. London

Taplin, O. (1978) *Greek Tragedy in Action*. London

 ed. (2000) *Literature in the Greek World*. Oxford

 ed. (2001) *Literature in the Roman World*. Oxford

Tarkow, T. (1983) 'Tyrtaeus 9D: the role of poetry in the new Sparta', *L'Antiquité Classique* 52: 48–69

Tatum, J. (1989) *Xenophon's Imperial Fiction*. Princeton, NJ

 ed. (1994) *The Search for the Ancient Novel*. Baltimore, MD

Taylor, C. (2000) *Socrates: A Very Short Introduction*. Oxford

Thomas, R. (1992) *Literacy and Orality in Ancient Greece*. Cambridge

 (2000) *Herodotus in Context*. Cambridge

Tipping, B. (2010) *Exemplary Epic: Silius Italicus' Punica*. Oxford

Todd, S. (1993) *The Shape of Athenian Law*. Oxford

 (1996) *Athens and Sparta*. London

Too, Y. (1995) *The Rhetoric of Identity in Isocrates*. Cambridge

Townend, G. ed. (2002) *Divus Julius*. Bristol

Treadgold, W. (1997) *A History of Byzantine State and Society*. Stanford, CA

Tredennick, H. and Waterfield R. trans. (1990) *Xenophon: Conversations of Socrates*. Harmondsworth

Usher, S. (2008) *Cicero's Speeches: The Critic in Action*. Warminster

Van Wees, H. (2004) *Greek Warfare: Myth and Realities*. London
  (2009) *War and Violence in Ancient Greece*. Wales

Vasaly, A. (1993) *Representations: Images of the World in Ciceronian Oratory*. California

Verducci, F. (1985) *Ovid's Toyshop of the Heart: Epistulae Heroidum*. Princeton, NJ

Vernant, J.-P. (1980) *Myth and Society in Ancient Greece*. Brighton (trans. J. Lloyd)
  (1983) *Myth and Thought among the Greeks*. London

Vernant, J.-P. and Vidal-Naquet, P. (1988) *Myth and Tragedy in Ancient Greece*. New York (trans. J. Lloyd)

Vessey, D. (1973) *Statius and the Thebaid*. Oxford

Veyne, P. (1988) *Roman Erotic Elegy*. Chicago
  (2003) *Seneca: The Life of a Stoic*. London

Vlastos, G. (1991) *Socrates: Ironist and Moral Philosopher*. Ithaca, NY

Voight, E. (1971) *Sappho et Alcaeus*. Amsterdam

Volk, K. (2002) *The Poetics of Latin Didactic*. Oxford

Walbank, F. (1972) *Polybius*. Berkeley, CA
  (1981) *The Hellenistic World*. London

Walcott, D. (1990) *Omeros*. London
  (1993) *The Odyssey: A Stage Version*. London

Walker, B. (1952) *The Annals of Tacitus*. Manchester

Walker, J. (2000) *Rhetoric and Poetics in Antiquity*. Oxford

Wallace-Hadrill, A. (1983) *Suetonius*. London
  ed. (1990) *Patronage in Ancient Society*. London
  (1993) *Augustan Rome*. London
  (2008) *Rome's Cultural Revolution*. Cambridge

Walsh, P. (1961) *Livy: His Historical Aims and Methods*. Cambridge
  (1970) *The Roman Novel*. Cambridge

Wardy, R. (1998) *The Birth of Rhetoric*. London
  (2005) *Doing Greek Philosophy*. London

Warmington, E. H. ed. and trans. (1935–40) *Remains of Old Latin*. 4 vols. Cambridge, MA

Warren, J. (2007) *Presocratics*. Durham, NC

Waterfield, R. (2000) *The First Philosophers*. Oxford

Watkiss, L. (1984) *Sallust Bellum Jugurthinum*. London

Webster, T. (1974) *An Introduction to Menander*. Manchester

Welch, K. and Powell, A. eds (1998) *Julius Caesar as Artful Reporter*. London

Wells, C. (1984) *The Roman Empire*. London

West, D. (1967) *Reading Horace*. Edinburgh
  (1969) *The Imagery and Poetry of Lucretius*. Edinburgh
  (2003) *The Aeneid*. London
  and Woodman, A. (1975) *Quality and Pleasure in Latin Poetry*. Cambridge
  and Woodman, A. (1979) *Creative Imitation in Latin Literature*. Cambridge

West, M. (1966) *Hesiod: Theogony*. Oxford
  (1974) *Studies in Greek Elegy and Iambus*. Berlin
  (1978) *Hesiod: Works and Days*. Oxford
  (1987) *Introduction to Greek Metre*. Oxford
  (1989) *Iambi et Elegi Graeci*. 2 vols. Oxford
  (1993) *Greek Lyric Poetry*. Oxford
  (1994) *Ancient Greek Music*. Oxford

(1997) *The East Face of Helicon*. Oxford

(2003a) *Greek Epic Fragments*. Cambridge, MA

(2003b) *Homeric Hymns*. Cambridge, MA

Wheeler, S. (1999) *A Discourse of Wonders: Audience and Performance in Ovid's Metamorphoses*. Philadelphia, PA

Whitby, M. (1994) 'From Moschus to Nonnus: the evolution of the Nonnian style', Cambridge Philological Society. Supplementary Vol. 17 (ed. Hopkinson, N. *Studies on the Dionysiaca of Nonnus*). Cambridge

White, P. (1993) *Promised Verse: Poets in the Society of Augustan Rome*. Cambridge, MA

Whitmarsh, T. (2001) *Greek Literature and the Roman Empire: The Politics of Imitation*. Oxford

(2004) *Ancient Greek Literature*. Cambridge

(2005) *The Second Sophistic*. Cambridge

(2007) *The Cambridge Companion to the Greek and Roman Novel*. Cambridge

and Morales, H. (2003) *Achilles Tatius: Leucippe and Clitophon*. Oxford

Wiedemann, T. (1987) *Slavery*. Oxford

(1992) *Emperors and Gladiators*. London

(1998) *Cicero and the End of the Roman Republic*. London

Wiles, D. (1991) *The Masks of Menander*. Cambridge

(1997) *Tragedy in Athens: Performance and Theatrical Meaning*. Cambridge

(2000) *Greek Theatre Performance*. Cambridge

Wilkinson, L. (2005) *The Georgics*. London

Williams, B. (1998) *Plato*. London

Williams, G. (1968) *Tradition and Originality in Roman Poetry*. Oxford

Williams, G. D. (1994) *Banished Voices: Readings in Ovid's Exile Poetry*. Cambridge

Williams, R. (1972–3) *The Aeneid of Virgil*. 2 vols. London

Williamson, M. (1995) *Sappho's Immortal Daughters*. Cambridge, MA

Wilson, L. (1996) *Sappho's Sweetbitter Songs: Configurations of Female and Male in Ancient Greek Lyric*. London

Wilson, N. and Reynolds, L. (1974) *Scribes and Scholars*. Oxford

Winkler, J. (1985) *Auctor and Actor: A Narratological Reading of Apuleius' Golden Ass*. Berkeley, CA

and Williams, G. (1982) *Later Greek Literature*. Cambridge

and Zeitlin, F. eds (1990) *Nothing to Do with Dionysos?* Princeton, NJ

Winnington-Ingram, R. (1980) *Sophocles: An Interpretation*. Cambridge

(1983) *Studies in Aeschylus*. Cambridge

Wiseman, T. ed. (1985) *Roman Political Life 90 BC–AD 69*. Exeter

(1986) *Catullus and his World*. Cambridge

Woodard, R. ed. (2008) *The Cambridge Companion to Greek Mythology*. Cambridge

Woodman, A. (1998a) *Rhetoric in Classical Historiography*. London

(1998b) *Tacitus Reviewed*. Oxford

ed. (2010) *The Cambridge Companion to Tacitus*. Cambridge

and Powell, J. eds (1992) *Author and Audience in Latin Literature*. Cambridge

and Fenney, D. eds (2002) *Traditions and Contexts in the Poetry of Horace*. Cambridge

Woolf, G. ed. (2003) *The Cambridge Illustrated History of the Roman World*. Cambridge

(2006) *Et tu Brute?: Caesar's Murder and Political Assassination*. London

Worthington, I. ed. (1994) *Persuasion: Greek Rhetoric in Action*. London

(2000) *Demosthenes: Statesman and Orator*. London

ed. (2007) *A Companion to Greek Rhetoric*. Oxford

Wright, M. (2009) *Introducing Greek Philosophy*. Durham

Wyke, M. (2002) *The Roman Mistress*. Oxford

Yavetz, Z. (1983) *Caesar and his Public Image*. London

Yunis, H. (1996) *Taming Democracy: Models of Political Rhetoric in Classical Athens*. Ithaca, NY

Zagovin, P. (2008) *Thucydides*. Princeton, NJ

Zanker, P. (1987) *Realism in Alexandrian Poetry*. London

Zeitlin, F. (1986) 'Thebes: theatre of self and society in Athenian drama', in P. Euben ed. *Greek Tragedy and Political Theory*. Berkeley, CA (reprinted in Winkler and Zeitlin, 1990)

(1995) *Playing the Other: Gender and Society in Classical Greek Literature*. Chicago

Index